KOVELS'
BOTTLES
PRICE LIST

13TH EDITION

KOVELS'
BOTTLES
PRICE LIST

Ralph and Terry Kovel

RANDOM HOUSE REFERENCE

NEW YORK TORONTO LONDON SYDNEY AUCKLAND

Visit the Random House Reference Web site: *www.randomwords.com*

Thirteenth Edition

Printed in the United States of America

10 9 8 7 6 5 4 3 2 1

Libary of Congress Catalog Card Number: 92-5192
ISBN-13: 978-1-4000-4730-7
ISBN-10: 1-4000-4730-7

KEEP UP ON PRICES ALL YEAR LONG

Have you kept up with prices? They change! Prices change with discoveries, auction records, even historic events. Every entry and every picture in this book is new and current, thanks to computer technology and a staff that searches for prices all year. It includes prices from auctions, shows, price lists, and sales, as well as Internet auctions, malls, and shops. This book is a handy overall price guide, but you also need news and the very latest stories of bottle sales and discoveries.

Books on your shelf get older each month, and prices do change. Important sales produce new record prices. Rarities are discovered. Fakes appear. You will want to keep up with developments from month to month rather than from year to year. *Kovels on Antiques and Collectibles,* a nationally distributed newsletter, illustrated with over 40 color pictures in each issue, includes up-to-date information on bottles and other collectibles. This monthly newsletter reports current prices, collecting trends, and landmark auction results for all types of antiques and collectibles, including bottles, and also contains tax, estate, security, and other pertinent news for collectors.

Additional information and a free sample newsletter are available from the authors at P.O. Box 22200-B, Beachwood, Ohio 44122. Read excerpts or order from our website: www.kovels.com.

CLUES TO THE CONTENTS OF THIS BOOK

Hundreds of black and white and color photographs have been used to illustrate this all-new, better-than-ever, thirteenth edition of *Kovels' Bottles Price List.* We wrote our first bottle price guide in 1971, thirty-five years ago. That was a different century, and collectors today save many types of bottles that were of no interest then. Milk bottles and applied color label (ACL) soda bottles were not included in our first book. But many of the figural bottles once used by liquor companies have been discontinued and there is little interest in those bottles today. We have included some modern figurals in this edition because they are still bought and sold at flea markets and garage sales. This year the book's format has been updated to reflect the changing interests of the new century. Paragraphs have been expanded. The histories of companies and their products have been updated, and we have tried to note any important changes in ownership of modern brands. A new color-photo section explores the world of bottles and their shapes.

All of the prices in this book are new. They are compiled from sales and offerings of the past two years. You will find that some modern bottles are no longer listed by brand, because collector interest has waned. We still have extensive listings of the more popular modern bottles like Jim Beam and Ezra Brooks.

"Go-withs," the bottle-related items that are bought and sold at all the bottle shows and antiques shows, are listed in their own section at the end of the book. Jar openers, advertisements, corkscrews, bottle caps, and other items that picture or are used with bottles have been classified as bottle go-withs. A bibliography and list of publications are included to aid you in further research. This list was checked and is accurate as of June 2005. The national and state club lists are also accurate as of June 2005. Unfortunately, addresses do change; if you cannot find one of the listed clubs, write to us at P.O. Box 22200-B, Beachwood, Ohio 44122.

Note: Bottles that contained alcoholic beverages must be sold empty to conform with the law in most states. To sell a filled liquor bottle, you must have a liquor license from the state where you live or where you sell the bottle. It is illegal to ship full bottles across state lines. The value is the same for full or empty liquor bottles.

DEFINITIONS

Novice collectors may need a few definitions to understand the terms used in this book. A *pontil mark* is a scar on the bottom of a bottle. It was made by the punty rod that held the glass for the glassblower. If the scar is rough, it is called a *pontil.* If it is smoothed out, it is called a *ground pontil. Free-blown* or *blown* means that the glass was blown by the glassmaker, using a blowpipe; it was not poured into a mold. *Mold-blown* means it was blown into a mold as part of the forming process. A *kick-up* is the deep indentation on the bottom of a bottle. Kick-ups are very often found on wine bottles. Describing glass as *whittled* or having *whittle marks* means there are irregular marks that look like the rough surface of a piece of whittled wood. Such marks are found on bottles that were made before 1900 and were caused by hot glass being blown into a cold mold. *Embossed* lettering is raised lettering. *Etched* lettering was cut into the bottle with acid or a sharp instrument. *Bubbles, teardrops,* or *seeds* describe types of bubbles that form in glass. A *seam* is the line left on the bottle by the mold. A seam may go up the neck of the bottle. If it goes over the lip, the bottle was machine-made. An *applied lip* is handmade and applied to the bottle after the glassmaker has formed the bottle. A *sheared lip* is found on bottles made before 1840. The top of the bottle was cut from the blowpipe with shears and the result is the sheared lip. The *2-piece,* or *BIMAL,* mold was used from about 1860 to 1900. The *3-piece mold* was used from 1820 to 1880. The automatic bottle machine was invented in 1903 and *machine-made* bottles were the norm after that date. Black glass is not really black. It is very dark olive green or olive amber and appears black unless seen in a bright light. *Milk glass* is an opaque glass made by using tin or zinc in the mixture. Although most milk glass is white, it is correct to call colored glass of this type "blue" or "green" milk glass. If glass that was made from 1880 to 1914 is left in strong sunlight, it often changes color. This is because of the chemical content of old glass. Bottles can turn purple, pale lavender, or shades of green or brown. These bottles are called *sun-colored.* Bottles can also be *iridized* and colored by a radiation process similar to that used for preserving vegetables. These bottles turn dark purple, green, or brown. There are a few other terms that relate to only one type of bottle, and these terms have been identified in the proper paragraphs. The word *picnic* has two meanings; it refers to a shape in the flask category and to a large size in the beer category.

Bottle clubs, bottle shows, and bottle auctions have set the vocabulary rules for this edition of *Kovels' Bottles Price List*. We have used the terms preferred by collectors and have tried to organize the thousands of listings in an easy-to-use format. Many abbreviations have been included that are part of the bottle collectors' language. The abbreviations are listed below and appear throughout the book.

ABM means automatic bottle machine.

ACL means applied color label, a pyroglaze or enameled lettering. This type of label became very popular in the 1930s.

BIMAL means blown in mold, applied lip.

DUG means literally dug from the ground.

FB means free blown.

IP means iron pontil.

ISP means inserted slug plate. Special names were sometimes embossed on a bottle, especially a milk bottle, with a special plate inserted in the mold.

OP means open pontil.

Pyro means pyroglaze or enameled lettering often found on milk bottles and soda bottles. Today most collectors prefer the term ACL (applied color label).

SC means sun-colored.

SCA means sun-colored amethyst.

The federal government has given collectors a few clues that might help date a bottle. The clues are linked to federal laws about food and drink.

1906: The Pure Food and Drugs Act required that content information be included on containers for food and bottled drinks. Reuse of unlabeled bottles became illegal.

1911: The use of false therapeutic claims like "cure" were prohibited. A bottle with a paper label or embossing saying "cure" was no longer made. Alcohol products could no longer be labeled "cure."

1913: The volume or weight of the contents had to be listed on food containers, including bottles. So the terms quart, pint, and ounces are printed on labels.

1920: Prohibition restricted beverages to less than one-half percent alcohol. The word "beer" could no longer be used. Some labels used the word "brew." Other labels said "for medicinal purposes only."

1927: Poison bottles must have warning labels and antidotes listed.

1933: Prohibition was repealed.

1938: Packaged food must be labeled with the name of the food, its weight, and the name and address of the manufacturer or distributor.

1970: Bar codes were first used.

1973: Nutrition labeling was required on food with added nutrients.

1975: Congress called for voluntary conversion to the metric system. In 1988 it became the preferred system for commerce. Bottles measured in liters became more common, especially in the wine industry.

1984: Sodium content must be listed on labels.

1994: Metric measures as well as English units must be on food labels.

To make the descriptions of the bottles as complete as possible, an identification number has been added to the description in some categories. The serious collector knows the important books about a specialty, and these books have numbered lists of styles of bottles. Included in this book are identification numbers for flasks from McKearin and Wilson, bitters from Ring and Ham, and fruit jars from *Red Book of Fruit Jars* by Leybourne. The full titles of the books used are included in the bibliography and listed in the introductory paragraph for each category.

Medicine bottles include all medicine bottles except those under more specific headings, such as "Bitters" or "Sarsaparilla" or "Cure." Modern bottles of major interest are listed under the brand name.

If you are not a regular at bottle shows, it may take a few tries to become accustomed to the method of listing used in this book. If you cannot find a bottle, try several related headings. For instance, hair products are found under "Cosmetic" and "Cure."

Many named bottles are found under "Medicine," "Food," "Fruit Jar," etc. If your fruit jar has several names, such as "Ball Mason," look under "Fruit Jar, Ball" or "Fruit Jar, Mason." If no color is listed, the bottle is clear. We edit color descriptions to make the comparisons of bottles easier. It is impossible to explain the difference between olive yellow, light olive yellow, yellow olive, and light greenish yellow—all terms used at sales. Where possible, we used the description selected by the seller. A favored bottle-collector color is puce, which is a deep red to grayish purple. Bottles are described as pink puce, copper puce, strawberry puce, and plum puce. Aqua is a familiar color, but bottle collectors often list it as aqua green or aqua blue. To see examples, go online to www.antiquebottles.com/color.

The prices shown for bottles are the *actual* prices asked for or bid for bottles during the past two years. We know collectors try to get discounts, so some of these bottles may have sold for a little less than the asking price. Prices vary in different parts of the country. The condition of the bottle is a major factor in determining price. We do not list broken or chipped bottles, but sometimes flaws or scratches are noticed after a sale. If more than one price for a bottle has been recorded, a range is given. When selling your bottles, remember that the prices here are retail, not the wholesale price paid by a dealer. You can sell your collection to a dealer at about half the prices listed here. At auction you may get the same prices found in the book, but auctions are unpredictable. Prices may be low or high because of a snowstorm or a very determined pair of bidders. Internet auctions have the added risk of an unknown seller, so the condition may not be accurately reported. Low-priced bottles sell best at flea markets and garage sales.

Because of the idiosyncrasies of the computer, it was impossible to place a range on prices of bottles that are illustrated. The prices listed for the bottles illustrated in the book are for the bottle pictured.

Particular spellings are meant to help the collector. If the original bottle spelled "Catsup" as "Ketchup," that is the spelling that appears. The abbreviation "Dr." for doctor may appear on bottles as "Dr" (no period) or "Dr." (period). However, we have included a period to keep the computer alphabetizing more consistent, except in the case of bottles of Dr Pepper. The period was omitted in Dr Pepper by the company in 1950, and we use whatever appeared on the bottle. Also, if a word is spelled as, for example, "Kennedy's," "Kennedys'," or "Kennedys," we have placed the apostrophe or omitted it as it appeared on the bottle. A few bottles are included that had errors in the original spelling in the bottle mold. In these cases the error is explained. Medicine, bitters, and other bottle types sometimes use the term "Dr." and sometimes use just the last name of the doctor. We usually have used the wording as it appears on the bottle, except for "Whiskey" which is used even if the bottle held scotch or Canadian or was spelled "Whisky."

Every bottle or go-with illustrated in black and white is indicated by the abbreviation "Illus" in the text. Bottles shown in color photographs are priced in the center section where they appear.

We have tried to be accurate, but cannot be responsible for any errors in pricing or information that may appear. Any information or suggestions you give us about clubs, prices, or content will be considered for the next book. Please send it to Kovels, P.O. Box 22200, Dept. BPL, Beachwood, Ohio 44122.

Ralph M. Kovel, Life Member, Federation of Historical Bottle Clubs
Terry H. Kovel, Life Member, Federation of Historical Bottle Clubs
March 2006

ACKNOWLEDGMENTS

Those who sell bottles are the most informed experts in the field. Special thanks to Ed and Kathy Gray of Great Antique Bottles, Jim Hagenbuch of Glass-Works Auctions, Norm Heckler Jr. and Norm Heckler Sr. of Norman C. Heckler & Co., and Jeff Wichman of American Bottle Auctions for their help.

Thank you also to those who provided photographs and additional information, including Bob Alexander; Anderson Auction & Realty; Antique Bottle Trader; Kevin Applegate; *Avon Times;* Vinson Baldiga; BBR Auctions; William Beckett; Bertoia Auctions; Bo R. Black; Bottles & Bygones; *Bottles and More Magazine*; Jan Boyer; Norma Boyles; Brewery Gems; Jeff Buckhardt; Steve Burton; Allen Christel; Cincinnati Art Galleries; Clars Auction Gallery; Collection Liquidations Auction Services & Sales; Conestoga Auction Company; Cowan's Historic Americana Auctions; Robert H. Cronin; F. Cross; Delmarva Acquisitions & Appraisals; Jim & Julie Dennis; Mike Dickman; Perry D. Driver; Early American History Auctions; Curt Faulkenberry; Federation of Historical Bottle Collectors; James Fennelly; Jim Ferrara; Susan Fox; Sam Fuss; Garth's Auctions; Lynn Geyer's Advertising Auction; Rob Goodacre; Don Gosselin; Green Valley Auctions; Marilyn Hannold; Bottle Bill Herbolsheimer; Steve Hesse; Tom Hicks; High Desert Books, Bottles, & Collectibles; Holabird Associates; Jeff Hooper; Nevin Hoy; Ian & Grahame's Bottles; Randy Inman Auctions; Insulator Store; Ivey-Selkirk Auctioneers; James D. Julia, Inc.; Kevin Kelly; C. D. Knibbe; Knotty Pine Antiques; Tim Landry; Mary Legare; Norman Lewis; Elvin Loader; Ken Loakes; Marc Lutsko; Maine Idea; Manion's International Auction House; W. Marquart; MastroNet; Douglas May; David McCalman; Marshall McMasters; McMasters Harris Auction Co.; McMurray Antiques & Auctions; Melissa Milner; Monson & Baer; William Morford Auctions; Morphy Auctions; National Association Breweriana Advertising; National Association of Milk Bottle Collectors; New Orleans Auction Galleries; Jeff & Holly Noordsy Antiques; Old Barn Auction; One Man's Junk Is Another Man's Treasure; Richard Opfer Auctioneering; Jim Parkhurst; John Pastor; Bruno Pavlovski; Jean M. Pouliot; Ron Ridder; John Ronald; Ruby Lane, Inc.; Wendell Sack; Seeck Antique Auction; Ronald Selibovsky; Clarence "Corky" Shore; Showcase Antique Center; Skinner, Inc.; Sold USA; Pat Stambaugh; Bill Stankard; Lucille Stanley; Stufforsale; Robert L. Swartz; Bill Tanner; Danese Theisen; Thomaston Place Auction Galleries; TIAS; Mark Tollis; Noel Tomas; Ralph Van Brocklin; Waddington's; Warners Bottles; John Webster; Jim Withelder; Woody Auctions; Mark Yates; Scott Yeargin; Keith Yunger.

We write the book and collect the prices, but it is the very competent group at Random House Reference that makes sure everything is in order, on time, and accurate. We thank Elizabeth Bennett, publishing director; Beth Levy, associate managing editor; Oriana Leckert, editorial assistant; and Lisa Montebello, production manager. The cover and attractive layout are the work of the talented Fabrizio LaRocca, creative director, and Moon Sun Kim, designer. No book can exist without a concerned editor and we are fortunate to have Mark LaFlaur guiding our book. Thanks, too, to David Naggar, president, Random House Information Group and Sheryl Stebbins, vice president and publisher, Random House Reference, who understand the reasons for a book filled with pictures and prices.

This is the twelfth year that Merri Ann Morrell has done the computer magic that turns all of the information into printed book pages. Extra thanks to her for her work and wisdom. And most of all we want to thank our amazing staff, who spell, punctuate, research, write, solve the mysteries of disappearing screens on our computers, and do the many strange tasks required to finish a book. More thanks to Karen Kneisley, who does magic with the pictures; to Cherrie Smrekar, who is the last word on corrections; to Linda Coulter, who proofread and did research to verify company names and dates; to Grace DeFrancisco, Marcia Goldberg, Katie Karrick, Liz Lillis, Heidi Makela, Tina McBean, Nancy Saada, Julie Seaman, June Smith, and others who recorded prices and helped in many ways. But most of all we want to tell Gay Hunter that without her this book wouldn't be as good. She guides it through the many processes at the office, reads and rereads it for errors, chases the bottle clubs and bottle publications, and even keeps us on schedule. The book is indeed the sum of the parts done by each of these people.

Ralph and Terry Kovel

RESOURCES
MUSEUMS & ARCHIVES

COCA-COLA COMPANY ARCHIVES, Industry & Consumer Affairs, PO Drawer 1734, Atlanta, GA 30301, 800-438-2653, website: www.cocacola.com.

CORNING MUSEUM OF GLASS, Rakow Library, One Museum Way, Corning, NY 14830-2253, 800-732-6845 or 607-974-8649, fax: 607-974-8677, e-mail: rakow @cmog.org, website: www.cmog.org.

DR PEPPER MUSEUM, 300 S. 5th St., Waco, TX 76701, 254-757-1025, e-mail: dp-info@drpeppermuseum.com, website: www.drpeppermuseum.com.

MUSEUM OF AMERICAN GLASS, Wheaton Village, 1501 Glasstown Rd., Millville, NJ 08332-1566, 800-998-4552, e-mail: museum@wheatonvillage.org, website: wheatonvillage.org/museumamericanglass.

NATIONAL BOTTLE MUSEUM, 76 Milton Ave., Ballston Spa, NY 12020, 518-885-7589, e-mail: nbm@crisny.org, website: nationalbottlemuseum.org.

THE SCHMIDT MUSEUM OF COCA-COLA MEMORABILIA, 109 Buffalo Creek Dr., Elizabethtown, KY 42701, 270-234-1100, website: www.schmidtmuseum.com.

WORLD OF COCA-COLA, 55 Martin Luther King Dr., Atlanta, GA 30303-3505, 800-676-COKE or 404-676-5151, website: www.woccatlanta.com.

PUBLICATIONS OF INTEREST TO BOTTLE COLLECTORS

See the club list for other publications

NEWSLETTERS

Avon Times
PO Box 9868
Kansas City, MO 64134
e-mail: avontimes@aol.com

Fruit Jar News
FJN Publishers, Inc.
364 Gregory Ave.
West Orange, NJ 07052-3743
e-mail: tomcaniff@aol.com

Just For Openers
PO Box 64
Chapel Hill, NC 27514
e-mail: jfo@mindspring.com
website: www.just-for-openers.org
(bottle openers and corkscrews)

Kovels on Antiques and Collectibles
PO Box 420347
Palm Coast, FL 32142-0347
website: www.kovels.com

MAGAZINES

Antique Bottle & Glass Collector
PO Box 180
East Greenville, PA 18041
e-mail: glswrk@enter.net
website: www.glswrk-auction.com

BBR: British Bottle Review
Elsecar Heritage Center
Barnsley, South Yorkshire S74 8HJ, UK
e-mail: sales@onlinebbr.com
website: www.onlinebbr.com

Collectors News
PO Box 306
Grundy Center, IA 50638
e-mail: collectors@collectors-news.com
website: collectors-news.com

Miniature Bottle Collector
PO Box 2161
Palos Verdes Peninsula, CA 90274
e-mail: editor@bottlecollecting.com
website: www.bottlecollecting.com

BOTTLE CLUBS

There are hundreds of bottle clubs that welcome new members. The list of local clubs is arranged by state and city so you can find the club nearest your home. If no club is listed nearby, we suggest you contact the national organizations, which follow. Any active bottle club that is not listed and wishes to be included in future editions of *Kovels' Bottles Price List* should send the necessary information to the authors, PO Box 22200, Beachwood, Ohio 44122. The information in this list has been compiled with the help of the Federation of Historical Bottle Collectors and the National Bottle Museum.

NATIONAL CLUBS

Many of these clubs have local chapters and shows.
Write them for more information.

American Breweriana Association, Inc.
American Breweriana Journal (magazine)
PO Box 11157
Pueblo, CO 81001
e-mail: breweriana1 @earthlink.net
website: www.american breweriana.org

American Collectors of Infant Feeders
Keeping Abreast (newsletter)
331 Edenwood N.
Jackson, TN 38301
website: www.acif.org

Antique Advertising Association of America
Past Times (newsletter)
PO Box 76
Petersburg, IL 62675
e-mail: aaaanewsletter @mac.com
website: www.pastimes.org

Antique Poison Bottle Collectors Association
312 Summer Ln.
Huddleston, VA 24104
e-mail: jjcab@b2x online.com
website: poisonbottle club.org

Brewery Collectibles Club of America
Beer Cans & Brewery Collectibles (magazine)
747 Merus Ct.
Fenton, MO 63026-2092
e-mail: bcca@bcca.com
website: www.bcca.com

British Beermat Collectors' Society
British Beermat Collectors' Society Newsletter (newsletter)
69 Dunnington Ave.
Kidderminster
DY10 2YT, UK
e-mail: cosmic@tm mathews.freeserve.co.uk
website: www.british beermats.org.uk

Canadian Corkscrew Collectors Club
The Quarterly Worme (newsletter)
One Madison St.
East Rutherford, NJ 07073
e-mail: clarethous @aol.com
website: www.corkscrew net.com/ CCCC.htm

Candy Container Collectors of America
Candy Gram (newsletter)
115 Macbeth Dr.
Lower Burrell, PA 15068-2628
e-mail: lost_in_candy land2004 @yahoo.com
website: www.candy container.org

Coca-Cola Collectors Club
Coca-Cola Collectors News (newsletter)
PMB 609
4780 Ashford Dunwoody Rd., Suite A
Atlanta, GA 30338
website: www.cocacola club.org

Crowncap Collectors Society International
Crowncappers' Exchange (newsletter)
1130 40th St.
Bellingham, WA 98229-3118
e-mail: BobBurr @comcast.net
website: www.bottle capclub.org
(crown caps from beer and soda bottles)

Dr Pepper 10-2-4 Collectors Club
Lion's Roar (newsletter)
Charles Brizius, Treasurer/Membership Director
4040 North Central Expressway, Suite 600
Dallas, Texas 75204
website: www.drpepper collectorsclub.com

Federation of Historical Bottle Collectors
Bottles and Extras (magazine)
1021 W. Oakland Ave., #109
Johnson City, TN 37604
e-mail: antiquebottles @visto.com
website: www.fohbc.com

Hamm's Club
Bruins Gazette (newsletter)
2300 Central Ave. NE
Minneapolis, MN 55418
e-mail: hammsclub @hammsclub.com
website: www.hamms club.com

International Association of Jim Beam Bottle and Specialties Clubs
Beam Around the World (newsletter)
PO Box 486
Kewanee, IL 61443-0486
e-mail: pbiba@msn.com
website: www.jimbeam clubs.com

International Chinese Snuff Bottle Society
Journal (magazine)
2601 N. Charles St.
Baltimore, MD 21218
e-mail: icsbs @verizon.net
website: www.snuff bottle.org

International Perfume Bottle Association
Perfume Bottle Quarterly (newsletter)
PO Box 1299
Paradise, CA 95967
e-mail: paradise @sunset.net
website: www.perfume bottles.org

International Swizzle Stick Collectors Association
Swizzle Stick News (newsletter)
PO Box 1117
Bellingham, WA 98227-1117
e-mail: veray.issca @attglobal.net
website: www.swizzle sticks-issca.com

Jelly Jammers
Jelly Jammers Journal (newsletter)
6086 W. Boggstown Rd.
Boggstown, IN 46110
e-mail: emshaw @myvine.com
(jelly container collectors)

Lilliputian Bottle Club
Gulliver's Gazette (newsletter)
12732 E. Charlwood St.
Cerritos, CA 90703-6052

Midwest Miniature Bottle Collectors
Midwest Miniature Bottle Collector (newsletter)
PO Box 16912
Raytown, MO 64133
website: www.miniature bottles.com

National Association of Avon Collectors
PO Box 7006
Kansas City, MO 64113
(write for list of Avon clubs in your area)

National Association Breweriana Advertising
Breweriana Collector (newsletter)
PO Box 64
Chapel Hill, NC 27514-0064
website: www.naba brew.org

National Association of Milk Bottle Collectors
The Milk Route (newsletter)
18 Pond Place
Cos Cob, CT 06807
e-mail: milkroute @yahoo.org
website: www.milk route.org

New England Moxie Congress
Nerve Food News (newsletter)
c/o Kurt D. Kabelac
2783 N. Triphammer Rd.
Ithaca, NY 14850-9756
e-mail: njmoxie1@att.net
website: www.moxie world.com

Painted Soda Bottles Collectors Association
Soda Net (newsletter)
414 Molly Springs Rd.
Hot Springs, AR 71913
e-mail: psbca@thesoda fizz.com
website: psbca.thesoda fizz.com

Pepsi-Cola Collectors Club
Pepsi-Cola Collectors Club Newsletter (newsletter)
PO Box 817
Claremont, CA 91711
e-mail: doubledot @earthlink.net
website: pepsigifts.com

Society of Inkwell Collectors
The Stained Finger (newsletter)
PO Box 324
Mossville, IL 61552
e-mail: inkwellsociety @aol.com
website: www.soic.com

Violin Bottle Collectors Association
Fine Tuning (newsletter)
33 E. 35th St.
Hamilton, ON L8V 3X7, Canada
e-mail: fbviobot @mountaincable.net
website: viobot. tripod.com

Watkins Collectors Club
Watkins Collectors Club Newsletter (newsletter)
1623 Poplar Dr.
Red Wing, MN 55066
e-mail: rfanderson @charter.net

STATE CLUBS

ALABAMA
Mobile Bottle Collector Club
c/o Rod Vining
8844 Lee Cr.
IRVINGTON, AL 36544

ARIZONA
The Phoenix Antiques, Bottles, & Collectibles Club
c/o Julie Blake, Treasurer
4702 W. Lavey Rd.
GLENDALE, AZ 85306
website: phoenixantiques club.org

ARKANSAS
Indian Country Antique Bottle & Relic Society
3818 Hilltop Dr.
JONESBORO, AR 72401

Little Rock Antique Bottle Club
c/o Ed Tardy
16201 Hwy. 300
ROLAND, AR 72135

CALIFORNIA
California Mini Bottle Club
1911 Willow St.
ALAMEDA, CA 94501

Fresno Antique Bottle & Collectors Club
c/o David Kennedy, Secretary
4318 Kenmore Dr. South
FRESNO, CA 93703

Mother Load A.B.C.
c/o Bill Ham
4237 Hendricks Rd.
LAKEPORT, CA 95453-9365

Los Angeles Historical Bottle Club
2842 El Sol Dr.
LANCASTER, CA 93535
website: www.lahbc.org

Golden Gate Historical Bottle Society
c/o Gary Antone
752 Murdell Ln.
LIVERMORE, CA 94550-5104

San Luis Obispo Bottle Society
c/o Darrell Heineman
124 21st St.
PASO ROBLES, CA 93446

49er Historical Bottle Association
c/o Pat Patocka
PO Box 561
PENRYN, CA 95663

Superior California Bottle Club
c/o Mel Hammer
3220 Stratford Ave.
REDDING, CA 96001

**Mission Trail Historical
  Bottle Club**
1475 Teton Ave.
SALINAS, CA 93906

**San Diego Antique
  Bottle Club**
PO Box 5137
SAN DIEGO, CA 92165
e-mail: jfwalker
  @electriciti.com

**Northwestern Bottle
  Collectors Association**
c/o PO Box 1121
SANTA ROSA, CA
  95402

**Sequoia Antique Bottle
  & Collectors Society**
c/o Carl Simon, President
PO Box 3695
VISALIA, CA 93278

COLORADO
**Colorado Antique
  Bottle Club**
9545 Oak Tree Ct.
COLORADO SPRINGS,
  CO 80925

**Peaks & Plains Antique
  Bottle & Collectors
  Club, Inc.**
308 Maplewood Dr.
COLORADO SPRINGS,
  CO 80907-4326

**Antique Bottle
  Collectors of Colorado
  (ABCC)**
PO Box 1895
ENGLEWOOD, CO
  80150-1895

**Western Slope Bottle
  Club**
PO Box 354
PALISADE, CO 81526

CONNECTICUT
**Southern Connecticut
  Antique Bottle
  Collectors Assoc., Inc.**
34 Dartmouth Dr.
HUNTINGTON, CT
  06484

DELAWARE
**Delmarva Antique
  Bottle Collectors**
c/o Rick Preston,
  President
50 Syracuse St.
OCEAN VIEW, DE
  19970
website: antique
  bottles.com/delmarva

**Tri-State Bottle
  Collectors & Diggers**
c/o 2510 Cratchett Rd.
WILMINGTON, DE
  19808

FLORIDA
**M-T Bottle Collector
  Association Inc.**
PO Box 1581
DELAND, FL 32721

**Antique Bottle
  Collectors of North
  Florida**
c/o Wayne Harden
3867 Winter Berry Rd.
JACKSONVILLE, FL
  32210-9266
e-mail: ABCNF
  @juno.com
website: www.waynes
  bottles.com/ABC
  NF.html

**Suncoast Antique Bottle
  Club**
c/o Jay Stone
6720 Park St.
SOUTH PASADENA,
  FL 33707

GEORGIA
Rome Bottle Club
c/o Bob Jenkins
285 Oak Grove Rd.
CARROLLTON, GA
  30117

Southeastern A.B.C.
1546 Summerford Ct.
DUNWOODY, GA
  30338

HAWAII
**Hawaii Historical Bottle
  Collector's Club**
PO Box 90456
HONOLULU, HI 96835

ILLINOIS
**Metro-East Bottle &
  Jar Association**
309 Bellevue Dr.
BELLEVILLE, IL 62223

1st Chicago Bottle Club
PO Box 224
DOLTON, IL 60419

**Pekin Bottle Collectors
  Association**
PO Box 372
PEKIN, IL 61554

**Antique Bottle Club of
  Northern Illinois**
c/o Dan Puzzo, President
270 Stanley Ave.
WAUKEGAN, IL 60085

INDIANA
**Wabash Valley Antique
  Glass & Pottery Club**
c/o Ron Glasscock,
  President
PO Box 690
FARMERSBURG, IN
  47868
e-mail: ronsan
  @ccrtc.com

**Midwest Antique Fruit
Jar & Bottle Club**
c/o Norm Barnett,
President
PO Box 38
FLAT ROCK, IN 47234
website: www.fruitjar.org

**Ft. Wayne Historical
Bottle Club**
c/o Jack Potts, Secretary
PO Box 203
HARLAN, IN 46743

IOWA
Iowa Antique Bottleers
c/o Tom Southard,
Treasurer
2815 Druid Hill Dr.
DES MOINES, IA 50315

KANSAS
**Southeast Kansas Bottle
& Relic Club**
c/o Deanne Schoenberger
612 E. 10th St.
CHANUTE, KS 66720

MAINE
**New England Antique
Bottle Club**
c/o Jack Pelletier
211 Main St.
GANHAM, ME 04038

MARYLAND
**Baltimore Antique
Bottle Club, Inc.**
c/o Steve Charing,
President
PO Box 36061
TOWSON, MD 21286-
6061
e-mail: scharing
@comcast.net
website: www.baltimore
bottleclub.org

MASSACHUSETTS
**Merrimac Valley Bottle
Club**
c/o Gary Koltookian
3 Forrest St.
CHELMSFORD, MA
01824

MICHIGAN
**Huron Valley Bottle &
Insulator Club**
4122 Lakeside
BEAVERTON, MI 84612
e-mail: hemingray
@mac.com
website: www.insulators.
com/clubs/hvbic.htm

**Flint Antique Bottle &
Collectibles Club**
c/o Bill Heatley,
President
11353 W. Cook Rd.
GAINES, MI 48436-
9742
e-mail: tbuda
@shianet.org

Grand Rapids A.B.C.
3647 Remembrance Rd.
NW
GRAND RAPIDS, MI
49544-2284

Jelly Jammers
c/o Janet Lee, President
4300 W. Bacon Rd.
HILLSDALE, MI 49242-
8205
e-mail: dequiltbear
@aol.com

**Kalamazoo Antique
Bottle Club**
c/o Charles H. Parker Jr.,
President
607 Crocket Ave.
PORTAGE, MI 49024
e-mail: prostock
@net-link.net
e-mail: crebel1892
@aol.com

**Metropolitan Detroit
Antique Bottle Club**
c/o Bruce Heckman
2725 Creek Bend Rd.
TROY, MI 48098
e-mail: bottlemike
@wowway.com
e-mail: skeetbeer
@aol.com

MINNESOTA
**Minnesota 1st Antique
Bottle Club**
c/o Dave Robetus
5001 Queen Ave. N.
MINNEAPOLIS, MN
55430

**North Star Historical
Bottle Association, Inc.**
c/o Doug Shilson
3308 32nd Ave. S.
MINNEAPOLIS, MN
55406-2015
e-mail: Bittersdug
@aol.com

MISSOURI
**St. Louis Antique Bottle
Collectors Assoc.**
c/o Ron Sterzik
2080 Sterzik Rd.
ARNOLD, MO 63010-
5402

NEBRASKA
**Nebraska Antique Bottle
& Collectible Club**
c/o Stephen J. Spargen
407 N. 13th St.
ASHLAND, NE 68003

NEVADA

Las Vegas Antique Bottle & Collectibles Club
c/o Peter Sidlow, President
3901 E. Stewart Ave., #19
LAS VEGAS, NV 89110
e-mail: gittuslv@aol.com
e-mail: dandlv @earthlink.net
website: www.lasvegas bottleclub.com

Reno & Sparks Antique Bottle Club
c/o Willy Young
PO Box 1061
VERDI, NV 89439

NEW HAMPSHIRE

Yankee Bottle Club
c/o Alene Hall
382 Court St.
KEENE, NH 03431-2534

New England Antique Bottle Club
4 Francour Dr.
SOMERSWORTH, NH 03878-2339

NEW JERSEY

North Jersey ABC Assoc.
c/o Paul Borey
251 Vista View Dr.
MAHWAH, NJ 07430

New Jersey Antique Bottle Club
c/o Joe Butewicz
24 Charles St.
SOUTH RIVER, NJ 08882-1603

Jersey Shore Bottle Club
c/o Dave Trippett
PO Box 995
TOMS RIVER, NJ 08753
e-mail: jtripet @comcast.net
e-mail: jsbc @stufforsale.com
website: geocities.com/ dtripet2000/jsbc/ jsbc.html

NEW MEXICO

Historical Bottle Society of New Mexico
c/o Dr. Jerry Simmons
1463C State Rd. 344
SANDIA PARK, NM 87047

NEW YORK

Greater Buffalo Bottle Club
c/o Peter Jablonski
66 Chassin Ave.
AMHERST, NY 14226
e-mail: psjablon102 @cs.com
website: www.geocities. com/thegbbca

Capital Region Antique Bottle & Insulator Club
c/o Bob Latham
463 Loudon Rd.
LOUDONVILLE, NY 12211
e-mail: blath@capital.net

Finger Lakes Bottle Collectors Association (FLBCA)
c/o Dave Guntren, President
PO Box 3894
ITHACA, NY 14852-3894
e-mail: joinflbca@aol.com
website: members.aol. com/joinflbca/index. html

Genessee Valley Bottle Collectors Association
c/o John DeVolder, President
PO Box 15528
ROCHESTER, NY 14615
e-mail: barthology @aol.com
e-mail: jstecher @rochester.rr.com
website: www.gvbca.org

Long Island Antique Bottle Association
c/o Mark & Laura Smith
10 Holmes Ct.
SAYVILLE, NY 11782

Berkshire Antique Bottle Association
c/o David Buddenhagen
414 West Rd.
STEPHENTOWN, NY 12168

Empire State Bottle Collectors Association
c/o Barb Schwarting
PO Box 3421
SYRACUSE, NY 13220-3421
website: www.esbca.org

Hudson Valley Bottle Club
c/o Art Church
411 Hillside Lake Rd.
WAPPINGERS FALLS, NY 12590

Mohawk Valley Antique Bottle Club
8646 Aitken Ave.
WHITESBORO, NY 13492

NORTH CAROLINA

Western North Carolina Antique Bottle Club
c/o Bill Retskin
PO Box 18481
ASHEVILLE, NC 28814

Southeast Bottle Club
c/o Reggie Lynch,
 President
PO Box 13736
DURHAM, NC 27709
e-mail: rlynch
 @antiquebottles.com
website: www.antique
 bottles.com/southeast

Raleigh Bottle Club
c/o David Tingen, Editor
PO Box 18083
RALEIGH, NC 27619
e-mail: smann2
 @nc.rr.com
website: www.antique
 bottles.com/raleigh

OHIO
Ohio Bottle Club
c/o Alan DeMaison,
 President
PO Box 585
BARBERTON, OH
 44203-0586
e-mail: violinbottle
 @aol.com
website: www.ohio
 bottles.freehome
 page.com

**Findlay Antique Bottle
 Club**
PO Box 243
BOWLING GREEN, OH
 43402
e-mail: theglassapothecary
 @wcnet.org
website: fabclub.free
 yellow.com/home.html

**Southwestern Ohio
 Antique Bottle & Jar
 Club**
PO Box 53
NORTH HAMPTON,
 OH 45349

**Superior Thirteen
 Bottle Club**
22000 Shaker Blvd.
Shaker Heights, OH
 44122

OKLAHOMA
**Oklahoma Territory
 Bottle & Relic Club**
c/o Johnnie Fletcher
1300 S. Blue Haven Dr.
MUSTANG, OK 73064

**Tulsa Antiques & Bottle
 Club**
c/o Bruce Stiles,
 President
PO Box 4278
TULSA, OK 74159

OREGON
Siskiyou A.B.C.
c/o Keith Lunt
2668 Montara Dr.
MEDFORD, OR 97504

**Oregon Bottle
 Collector's Association**
c/o Bill Bogynska
1762 Sunset Ave.
WEST LINN, OR 97068
e-mail: billb
 @easystreet.com
website: www.geocities.
 com/drkilmer69/
 obca1.html

PENNSYLVANIA
**Bedford Co. Antique
 Bottle Club**
c/o Leo McKenzie
115 Seifert St.
BEDFORD, PA 15522

**Washington County
 Antique Bottle &
 Insulator Club**
c/o Bill Cole
588 E. George St.
CARMICHAELS, PA
 15320

**Pittsburgh Antique
 Bottle Club**
c/o Bob DeCroo
694 Fayette City Rd.
FAYETTE CITY, PA
 15438

**Laurel Valley Bottle
 Club**
PO Box 131
LIGONIER, PA 15658

**Forks of the Delaware
 Bottle Collectors
 Association**
164 Farmview Rd.
NAZARETH, PA 18064-
 2500

**Jefferson County
 Antique Bottle Club**
6 Valley View Dr.
WASHINGTON, PA
 15301

**Pennsylvania Bottle
 Collectors Assoc.**
251 Eastland Ave.
YORK, PA 17402

RHODE ISLAND
**Little Rhody Bottle
 Club**
c/o Arthur Pawlowski
PO Box 314
HOPE, RI 02831-0314

SOUTH CAROLINA
**Horse Creek Antique
 Bottle Club**
c/o Mrs. Geneva Green
PO Box 1176
LANGLEY, SC 29834

TENNESSEE
**Memphis Bottle
 Collectors Club**
c/o William C. Smith
6700 Palomino Dr.
ARLINGTON, TN 38002

State of Franklin Antique Bottle & Collectibles Association
c/o Melissa Milner
230 Rockhouse Rd.
JOHNSON CITY, TN
  37601-5201
website: hometown.aol.
  com/sfabca/sfabca.html

Middle Tennessee Bottle Club
c/o Neal Ferguson
2926 Westmoreland Dr.
NASHVILLE, TN 37212

Tennessee Valley Traders and Collectors Club
821 Hiwassee St.
NEWPORT, TN 37821
e-mail: botlfarm@usit.net

East Tennessee Antique Bottle Club
220 Carter School Rd.
STRAWBERRY
  PLAINS, TN 37871

VIRGINIA

Potomac Bottle Collectors
4211 N. 2nd Rd., #1
ARLINGTON, VA 22203
e-mail: searsjim
  @usa.net
website: www.potomac
  bottlecollectors.org

Historical Bottle Diggers of Virginia
2516 Hawksbill Rd.
McGAHEYSVILLE, VA
  22840
e-mail: historyed
  @webtv.net

Richmond Area Bottle Collectors Assoc.
c/o Ed Faulkner,
  President
4718 Kyloe Lane
MOSELEY, VA 23120
e-mail: faulkner
  @antiquebottles.com
website: www.antique
  bottles.com/rabca

Apple Valley Bottle Coll.
c/o Francis J. Kowalski
3015 Northwestern Pike
WINCHESTER, VA
  22603-3825

WASHINGTON

Washington County Antique Bottle Club
c/o Tom Chambers,
  President
905 24th St.
SEATTLE, WA 92144

WEST VIRGINIA
Whimsey Club
c/o Dale Murschell
HC 65 Box 2610
SPRINGFIELD, WV
  26763

WISCONSIN
Milwaukee Antique Bottle Club
c/o Michael R. Reilly
W259 N9116 Hwy. J
HARLAND, WI 53029
website: www.milwaukee
  bottleclub.org

CANADA

Bytown Bottle Seekers
PO Box 375
RICHMOND, ON
  K0A-2Z0, CANADA

AUCTION GALLERIES

Some of the prices and pictures in this book were furnished by these auction houses and dealers and we thank them. If you are interested in buying or selling bottles or related collectibles, you may want to contact these firms.

American Bottle Auctions
(online auctions)
2523 J St., Suite 203
Sacramento, CA 95816
800-806-7722
fax: 916-443-3199
email: info@american
  bottle.com
website: www.american
  bottle.com

Bertoia Auctions
2141 DeMarco Dr.
Vineland, NJ 08360
856-692-1881
fax: 856-692-8697
e-mail: bill@bertoia
  auctions.com
website: www.bertoia
  auctions.com

BBR Auctions
Elsecar Heritage Centre
Barnsley, S. Yorkshire
  S74 8HJ, UK
011-44-1226-745156
fax: 011-44-1226-361561
email: sales@online
  bbr.com
website: www.online
  bbr.com

Bruce and Vicki Waas-dorp Stoneware Auctions
PO Box 434
Clarence, NY 14031
716-759-2361
fax: 716-759-2397
email: waasdorp
  @antiques-stoneware.
  com
website: www.antiques-stoneware.com

Conestoga Auction Company, Inc.
768 Graystone Rd.
PO Box 1
Manheim, PA 17545
717-898-7284
fax: 717-898-6628
email: ca@conestoga
  auction.com
website: www.conestoga
  auction.com

Cowan Auctions, Inc.
673 Wilmer Ave.
Cincinnati, OH 45226
513-871-1670
fax: 513-871-8670
e-mail: info@historic
  americana.com
website: www.historic
  americana.com

Early American History Auctions
PO Box 3507
Rancho Santa Fe, CA
  92067
858-759-3290
fax: 858-759-1439
e-mail: history@early
  american.com
website: www.early
  american.com

Early Auction Co.
123 Main St.
Milford, OH 45150
513-831-4833
fax: 513-831-1441
e-mail: info@early
  auctionco.com
website: www.early
  auctionco.com

Garth's Auctions, Inc.
2690 Stratford Rd.
PO Box 369
Delaware, OH 43015
740-362-4771
fax: 740-363-0164
email: info@garths.com
website: www.garths.com

Glass-Works Auctions
PO Box 180
East Greenville, PA 18041
215-679-5849
fax: 215-679-3068
email: glaswrk@enter.net
website: www.glswrk-
  auction.com

Green Valley Auctions
2259 Green Valley Ln.
Mt. Crawford, VA 22841
540-434-4260
fax: 540-434-4532
e-mail: info@green
  valleyauctions.com
website: www.green
  valleyauctions.com

Ivey-Selkirk Auctioneers
7447 Forsyth Blvd.
St. Louis, MO 63105
314-726-5515
fax: 314-726-9908
website: www.iveysel
  kirk.com

James D. Julia, Inc.
PO Box 830
Skowhegan Rd.
Fairfield, ME 04937
207-453-7125
fax: 207-453-2502
e-mail: julia@julia
  auctions.com
website: www.julia
  auctions.com

John R. Pastor Antique Bottle & Glass Auction
7288 Thorncrest Dr. SE
Ada, MI 49301
616-285-7604

Manion's International Auction
P.O. Box 12214
Kansas City, KS 66112
913-299-6692
fax: 913-299-6792
website:
www.manions.com

McMasters Harris Auction Co.
PO Box 1755
Cambridge, OH 43725
800-842-3526 or 740-432-7400
fax: 740-432-3191
e-mail: info@mcmasters harris.com
website: mcmasters harris.com

McMurray Antiques & Auctions
PO Box 393
Kirkwood, NY 13795
607-775-5972
fax: 607-775-2321

Monsen and Baer
PO Box 529
Vienna, VA 22183
703-938-2129
fax: 703-242-1357
email: monsenbaer @erols.com
(perfume bottles)

Norman C. Heckler & Company
79 Bradford Corner Rd.
Woodstock Valley, CT 06282
860-974-1634
fax: 860-974-2003
email: heckler@neca.com
website: heckler auction.com

NSA Auctions
Newton-Smith Antiques
88 Cedar St.
Cambridge, ON N1S 1V8, Canada
519-623-6302
email: info@nsa auctions.com
website: www.nsa auctions.com

Old Barn Auction
10040 St. Rt. 224 W.
Findlay, OH 45840
419-422-8531
fax: 419-422-5321
e-mail: auction@old barn.com
website: www.old barn.com

Randy Inman Auctions
PO Box 726
Waterville, ME 04903-0726
207-453-6444
fax: 207-453-6663
e-mail: inman@inman auctions.com
website: www.inman auctions.com

Richard Opfer Auctioneering, Inc.
1919 Greenspring Dr.
Timonium, MD 21093
410-252-5035
fax: 410-252-5863
email: info@opfer auction.com
website: www.opfer auction.com

Richard W. Withington, Inc.
590 Center Rd.
Hillsboro, NH 03244
603-464-3232
email: withington@con knet.com
website: www.withington auction.com

Seeck Auctions
PO Box 377
Mason City, IA 50402
641-424-1116
e-mail: JimJan @seeckauction.com
website: seeck auction.com

Skinner, Inc.
357 Main St.
Bolton, MA 01740
978-779-6241
fax: 978-779-5144
website: www.skinner inc.com

Waddington's
111 Bathurst St.
Toronto, ON M5V 2R1, Canada
416-504-9100
toll free: 877-504-5700
fax: 416-504-0033
e-mail: info @waddingtons.ca
website: www.wadding tons.ca

William Morford Auctions
RR #2
Cazenovia, NY 13035
315-662-7625
fax: 315-662-3570
e-mail: morf2bid @aol.com
website: morfauction.com

Woody Auction
PO Box 618
Douglass, KS 67039
316-747-2694
fax: 316-747-2145
e-mail: woodyauction @earthlink.net
website: www.woody auction.com

BIBLIOGRAPHY

We have found these books to be useful. Some of them may be out of print, but your local library should be able to get them for you through interlibrary loan.

GENERAL

Barlow, Raymond E., and Joan E. Kaiser. *A Guide to Sandwich Glass: Cut Ware, A General Assortment and Bottles.* Atglen, PA: Schiffer, 1999.

Brown, William E. *The Auction Price Report,* 2002 edition. Privately printed (12247 NW 49th Dr., Coral Springs, FL 33076).

Ketchum, William C., Jr. *A Treasury of American Bottles.* Indianapolis: Bobbs-Merrill, 1975.

Kovel, Ralph and Terry. *Kovels' American Antiques, 1750-1900.* New York: Random House Reference, 2004.

_____. *Kovels' Advertising Collectibles Price List.* New York: Random House Reference, 2005.

_____. *Kovels' Antiques & Collectibles Price List 2006,* 38th edition. New York: Random House Reference, 2005.

_____. *Kovels' Bottles Price List,* 13th edition. New York: Random House Reference, 2005.

Mario's Price Guide to Modern Bottles, December–June 2004 edition. Privately printed (Anthony Latello, 146 Sheldon Ave., Depew, NY 14043).

McKearin, George L. and Helen. *Two Hundred Years of American Blown Glass.* New York: Crown, 1950.

Polak, Michael. *Antique Trader Bottles Identification and Price Guide,* 4th edition. Iola, WI: Krause, 2002.

_____. *Warman's Bottles Field Guide,* Iola, WI: Krause, 2005.

AVON

Hastin, Bud. *Bud Hastin's Avon Products & California Perfume Co. Collector's Encyclopedia,* 16th edition. Privately printed, 2000 (P.O. Box 11004, Ft. Lauderdale, FL 33339).

BEAM

Higgins, Molly. *Jim Beam Figural Bottles.* Atglen, PA: Schiffer, 2000.

BEER

Bull, Donald, et al. *American Breweries.* Privately printed, 1984 (P.O. Box 106, Trumbull, CT 06611).

Friedrich, Manfred, and Donald Bull. *The Register of United States Breweries, 1876–1976,* 2 vols. Privately printed, 1976 (P.O. Box 106, Trumbull, CT 06611).

Van Wieren, Dale P. *American Breweries II.* Privately printed, 1995 (Eastern Coast Breweriana Association, P.O. Box 1354, North Wales, PA 19454).

Yenne, Bill. *The Field Guide to North America's Breweries and Microbreweries.* New York: Crescent Books, 1994.

BITTERS

Ring, Carlyn, and W.C. Ham. *Bitters Bottles.* Privately printed, 1998 (4237 Henricks Rd., Lakeport, CA 95453).

_____. *Bitters Bottles Supplement.* Privately printed, 2004 (4237 Henricks Rd., Lakeport, CA 95453).

Watson, Richard. *Bitters Bottles.* Fort Davis, TX: Thomas Nelson & Sons, 1965.

_____. *Supplement to Bitters Bottles.* Camden, NJ: Thomas Nelson & Sons, 1968.

CANDY CONTAINERS

Braun, Debra S. *Candy Containers for Collectors.* Atglen, PA: Schiffer, 2002.

Eikelberner, George, Serge Agadjanian, and Adele L. Bowden. *The Compleat American Glass Candy Containers Handbook.* Privately printed, 1986 (6252 Cedarwood Rd., Mentor, OH 44060).

Miller, William, and Jack Brush. *Modern Candy Containers and Novelties.* Paducah, KY: Collector Books, 2001.

COCA-COLA

Goldstein, Shelley and Helen. *Coca-Cola Collectibles with Current Prices and Photographs in Full Color,* 4 vols. and index. Privately printed, 1971–1980 (P.O. Box 301, Woodland Hills, CA 91364).

Henrich, Bob and Debra. *Coca-Cola Commemorative Bottles,* 2nd edition. Paducah, KY: Collector Books, 2001.

Mix, Richard. *Commemorative Bottle Checklist and Cross-Reference Guide*: Featuring Coca-Cola Bottles, 5th edition. Privately printed, 1999 (P.O. Box 558, Marietta, GA 30061).

Petretti, Allan. *Petretti's Coca-Cola Collectibles Price Guide,* 11th edition. Iola, WI: Krause, 2001.

Schaeffer, Randy, and Bill Bateman. *Coca-Cola: A Collector's Guide to New and Vintage Coca-Cola Memorabilia.* London: Courage Books, 1995.

Summers, B.J. *B.J. Summers' Guide to Coca-Cola,* 4th edition. Paducah, KY: Collector Books, 2003.

COLOGNE, SEE PERFUME

CURES, SEE MEDICINE

DRUG, SEE MEDICINE

FIGURAL, SEE ALSO BITTERS

Revi, Albert Christian. *American Pressed Glass and Figure Bottles.* New York: Thomas Nelson & Sons, 1964.

FLASKS

McKearin, Helen, and Kenneth M. Wilson. *American Bottles & Flasks and Their Ancestry.* New York: Crown, 1978.

FRUIT JARS

Leybourne, Douglas M., Jr. *The Collector's Guide to Old Fruit Jars: Red Book 9.* Privately printed, 2001 (P.O. Box 5417, North Muskegon, MI 49445).

McCann, Jerry. *The Guide to Collecting Fruit Jars: Fruit Jar Annual,* Vol. 10. Privately printed, 2005 (5003 W. Berwyn Ave., Chicago, IL 60630-1501).

Roller, Dick. *Fruit Jar Patents,* 3 vols. Privately printed, 1996–1998 (Jerry McCann, 5003 W. Berwyn Ave., Chicago, IL 60630-0443).

Toulouse, Julian Harrison. *Fruit Jars: A Collector's Manual.* Camden, NJ: Thomas Nelson & Sons; and Hanover, PA: Everybody's Press, 1969.

GINGER BEER

Yates, Donald and Elizabeth. *Ginger Beer & Root Beer Heritage, 1790-1930.* Privately printed, 2003 (8300 River Corners Rd., Homerville, OH 44235).

INK

Cattaneo, Giovanni. *Pump Inkwells: A History and a Short Guide for Collectors.* Privately printed, 2004 (The Pen & Pencil Gallery, Church House, Skelton, Penrith, Cumbria CA11 9TE, UK).

Covill, William E., Jr. *Ink Bottles and Inkwells.* Taunton, MA: William S. Sullwold, 1971.

Jaegers, Ray and Bevy. *The Write Stuff: Collector's Guide to Inkwells, Fountain Pens, and Desk Accessories.* Iola, WI: Krause, 2000.

Rivera, Betty and Ted. *Inkstands and Inkwells.* New York: Crown, 1973.

JARS, SEE FRUIT JARS

MEDICINE

Baldwin, Joseph K. *A Collector's Guide to Patent and Proprietary Medicine Bottles of the Nineteenth Century.* Nashville, TN: Thomas Nelson, 1973.

MILK

Giarde, Jeffrey L. *Glass Milk Bottles: Their Makers and Marks.* Bryn Mawr, CA: The Time Travelers Press, 1980.

MILK GLASS, SEE ALSO FIGURAL

Belknap, E.M. *Milk Glass.* New York: Crown, 1959.

Ferson, Regis F. and Mary F. *Yesterday's Milk Glass Today.* Privately printed, 1981 (122 Arden Rd., Pittsburgh, PA 15216).

MINERAL WATER, SEE SODA

NURSING

Ostrander, Diane Rouse. *A Guide to American Nursing Bottles.* Privately printed, 1992 (Will-o-Graf, P.O. Box 24, Willoughby, OH 44094).

PEPSI-COLA

Ayers, James C. *Pepsi-Cola Bottles Collectors Guide.* Privately printed, 1995; price update, 2001 (RJM Enterprises, P.O. Box 1377, Mount Airy, NC 27030).

_____. *Pepsi-Cola Bottles & More Collectors Guide,* Vol. 2. Privately printed, 2001 (RJM Enterprises, 5186 Claudville Hwy., Claudville, VA 24076).

Stoddard, Bob. *The Encyclopedia of Pepsi-Cola Collectibles.* Iola, WI: Krause, 2002.

Vehling, Bill, and Michael Hunt. *Pepsi-Cola Collectibles with Prices*, 3 vols. Gas City, IN: L-W Book Sales, 1988–1993.

PERFUME, COLOGNE, AND SCENT

Baccarat: The Perfume Bottles. Privately printed, 1986 (Addor Associates, P.O. Box 2128, Westport, CT 06880).

Breton, Anne. *Collectible Miniature Perfume Bottles.* Paris: Flammarion, 2001, distributed by Rizzoli through St. Martin's Press, New York.

Diamond I Perfume Bottles Price Guide and Other Drugstore Ware. Gas City, IN: L-W Book Sales, 2000.

Hastin, Bud. *Bud Hastin's Avon Products & California Perfume Co. Collector's Encyclopedia,* 16th edition. Privately printed, 2000 (P.O. Box 11004, Ft. Lauderdale, FL 33339).

Magic of Perfume: Perfumes of Caron. Monsen and Baer auction catalog, 2001 (Box 529, Vienna, VA 22183).

Prescott-Walker, Robert. *Collecting Lalique: Perfume Bottles and Glass.* London: Francis Joseph, 2001.

PICKLE

Zumwalt, Betty. *Ketchup Pickles Sauces.* Privately printed, 1980 (P.O. Box 413, Fulton, CA 95439).

POISON

Antique Bottle Collectors Association. *The American Poison Bottle Work Book and Price Guide.* Privately printed, 2005 (312 Summer Lane, Huddleston, VA 24104).

ROYAL DOULTON

Dale, Jean. *Royal Doulton Jugs: A Charlton Standard Catalogue,* 8th edition. Toronto: Charlton Press, 2004.

Lukins, Jocelyn. *Doulton Kingsware Whisky Flasks.* Yelverton, Devon, UK: M.P.E., 1981.

SCENT, SEE PERFUME

SODA, SEE ALSO COCA-COLA; PEPSI-COLA

Bowers, Q. David. *The Moxie Encyclopedia.* Vestal, NY: The Vestal Press, 1984.

Ellis, Harry E. *Dr Pepper, King of Beverages.* Dallas: Dr Pepper Company, 1979.

Ferguson, Joel. *New Orleans Soda Water Manufacturers History.* Privately printed, 1995 (106 Dixie Circle, Slidell, LA 70458).

Fowler, Ron. *Washington Sodas: The Illustrated History of Washington's Soft Drink Industry.* Privately printed, 1986 (Dolphin Point Writing Works, P.O. Box 45251, Seattle, WA 98145).

Mix, Richard. *Commemorative Bottle Checklist and Cross-Reference Guide: Featuring Dr Pepper, Pepsi, 7Up, NSDA and Other Soda Brands.* Privately printed, 1999 (P.O. Box 558, Marietta, GA 30061).

Petretti, Allan. *Petretti's Soda Pop Collectibles Price Guide,* 3rd edition. Iola, WI: Krause, 2003.

Summers, B.J. *Collectible Soda Pop Memorabilia Identification & Value Guide,* Paducah, KY: Collector Books, 2004.

Sweeney, Rick. *Collecting Applied Color Label Soda Bottles,* 3rd edition. Privately printed, 2002 (9418 Hilmer Dr., La Mesa, CA 91942).

TONIC, SEE MEDICINE

WHEATON

Clark, Lois. *Wheaton's: My Favorite Collectibles.* Privately printed, 1998 (Classic Wheaton Club, P.O. Box 59, Downingtown, PA 19335).

WHISKEY

Neese, Chuck. *The Whiskey Jug Book.* Privately printed, 2002 (P.O. Box 50667, Nashville, TN 37205).

AESTHETIC SPECIALTIES

In 1979 the first bottle was released by ASI, or Aesthetic Specialties, Inc., of San Mateo, California. It was a ceramic vodka bottle that was made to honor the 1979 Crosby 38th National Pro-Am Golf Tournament. According to the company president, Charles Wittwer, 400 cases of the bottle were made. The company continued making bottles: the 1979 Kentucky Derby bottle (600 cases); 1909 Stanley Steamer (5,000 cases in three different colors made in 1979); 1903 Cadillac (2 colors made in 1979, gold version, with and without trim, made in 1980); World's Greatest Golfer (400 cases in 1979); World's Greatest Hunter (1979); 38th and 39th Crosby Golf Tournaments (1979 and 1980); 1981 Crosby 40th Golf Tournament (reworked version of World's Greatest Golfer, 100 cases); Crosby Golf Tournaments (1982, 1983, and 1984); Telephone Service Truck (1980); Ice Cream Truck (1980); 1910 Oldsmobile (1980, made in three colors); Packard (1980); 1911 Stanley Steamer (1981, 1,200 cases); 1937 Packard (1981, produced with McCormick); 1914 Chevrolet (1981); and Fire engine (1981).

Cadillac, 1903 Model, Blue, Box, 1979 . . . . 10.00
Chevrolet, 1914 Model, Black, Box, 1979 . . . . 27.00
Ford Model T Ice Cream & Sarsaparilla Truck, Box, 1980, 8 x 12 In. 17.00
Ford Model T Telephone Truck, 4th In Series, 1980, 8 x 11 1/2 x 6 1/2 In. 90.00
Oldsmobile, 1910 Model, Cream, 1980 . . . . .22.00 to 26.00
Stanley Steamer, 1909 Model, Green, Box, 1978 . . . . 31.00
World's Greatest Golfer, 1979, 12 In. 8.00
ALPHA, see Lewis & Clark
AUSTIN NICHOLS, see Wild Turkey

AVON

David H. McConnell started a door-to-door selling company in 1886. He recruited women as independent sales representatives to sell his perfume. The company was named the California Perfume Company even though it was located in New York City. The first product was a set of five perfumes called Little Dot. In 1928 it was decided that CPC was too limiting a name so a new line called Avon was introduced. By 1936, the Avon name was on all of the company's products, including perfumes, toothbrushes, and baking items. Avon became a public company in 1946. Collectors want the bottles, jewelry, figurines, sales awards, early advertising, pamphlets, and other go-withs. For information on national and local clubs, books, and other publications, contact the National Association of Avon Collector Clubs, PO Box 7006, Kansas City, MO 64113. Avon bottles are listed here by shape or by name.

Airplane, Spirit Of St. Louis, Box, 1970-72, 6 Oz. 18.00
Angel, Angel Song, 1978-79, 1 Oz. 13.00
Apothecary, Breath Fresh, 1973, 8 Oz. 20.00
Armoire, Box, 1970-72 . . . . 10.00
Barber Pole, 1974-75, 3 Oz. 7.00
Baseball Mitt, Fielder's Choice, Brown, 1971, 5 Oz. 10.00
Bell, Crystal Song, 1975-76, 4 Oz. 8.00
Bell, Fragrance, Gold Handle, 1968-69, 1 Oz. 12.00
Bell, Joyous, Box, 1978, 1 Oz. . . . . .5.00 to 10.00
Bell, Liberty, 1971, 5 Oz. . . . . .5.00 to 12.00
Bell, Moonlightglow, 1981, 3 Oz. 5.00
Bell, Rosepoint, 1978, 4 Oz. 8.00
Benjamin Franklin, 1974-76, 6 Oz. . . . . .10.00 to 16.00
Betsy Ross, 1976, 4 Oz. 10.00
Betsy Ross, Box, 1976, 4 Oz. 20.00
Bird, American Eagle, Dark Amber, 1971, 5 Oz. 13.00
Bird, Bird Of Paradise, Gold Head, 1970-72, 5 Oz. . . . . .7.00 to 15.00
Bird, Bold Eagle, Box, 1976-78, 3 Oz. 10.00
Bird, Canada Goose, Brown, Black Head, 1973-74, 5 Oz. 15.00
Bird, Flamingo, 1971-72, 5 Oz. 8.00
Bird, Goose, Mrs. Quackles, 1979-80, 2 Oz. 2.50
Bird, Island Parakeet, 1977-78, 1 1/2 Oz. . . . . .8.00 to 10.00
Bird, Mallard-In-Flight, Box, 1974-76, 5 Oz. 10.00
Bird, Owl, Dr. Hoot, 1975-76, 4 Oz. 4.50
Bird, Owl, Precious Owl, Contents, Box, 1972-74, 1 1/2 Oz. . . . . .7.00 to 10.00

Bird, Owl, Snow, Box, 1976-77, 1 1/4 Oz. 7.00
Bird, Owl, Wise Choice, 1969-70, 4 Oz. 5.00
Bird, Pheasant, 1972-74, 5 Oz. ....5.00 to 11.00
Bird, Pheasant, Contents, Box, 1972-74, 5 Oz. 15.00
Bird, Quail, Box, 1973-75, 5 1/2 Oz. 14.00
Bird, Regal Peacock, Blue, 1973-74, 4 Oz. 7.00
Bird, Rooster, Country Kitchen, Milk Glass, 1973-75, 6 Oz. 7.00
Bird, Royal Swan, 1971, 1 Oz. 8.00
Bird, Wild Turkey, Amber, 1974-76, 6 Oz. ....15.00 to 20.00
Blacksmith's Anvil, Black, 1972-73, 4 Oz. 6.00
Boat, American Schooner, Contents, Box, 1972, 4 1/2 Oz. 25.00
Boat, Side Wheeler, Box, 1971-72, 5 Oz. 6.00
Boy, Fly-A-Balloon, Box, 1975-77, 3 Oz. 9.00
Boy, Tug-A-Brella, Box, 1979-80, 2 1/2 Oz. ....8.00 to 18.00
Burro, Little Burro, Box, 1978-79, 1 Oz. 12.00
Butterfly, 1972-73, 1 1/2 Oz. 6.00
Cable Car, Box, 1974-75, 4 Oz. ....17.00 to 20.00
California Perfume Co., 90th Anniversary, 1976, 1 3/4 Oz. 16.00
California Perfume Co., 90th Anniversary, Box, 1976, 1 3/4 Oz. .. 20.00
California Perfume Co., Anniversary Keepsake, Men's, 1981-82, 3 Oz. .. 10.00
Cannon, Revolutionary, 1975-76, 2 Oz. 8.00
Capitol Building, 1970-72, 5 Oz. ....9.00 to 12.00
Captain's Pride, Box, 1970, 6 Oz. 12.00
Car, Army Jeep, Box, 1974-75, 4 Oz. 5.00
Car, Checker Cab, 1926 Model, 1977-78, 5 Oz. 7.00
Car, Jaguar, Box, 1973-76, 5 Oz. 6.00
Car, Jeep Renegade, Box, 1981-82, 3 Oz. 10.00
Car, Maxwell, 1923 Model, 1972-74, 6 Oz. 10.00
Car, Maxwell, 1923 Model, Contents, Box, 1972-74, 6 Oz. 25.00
Car, REO Depot Wagon, Contents, Box, 1972-73, 5 Oz. 25.00
Car, Rolls Royce, 1972-75, 6 Oz. ....10.00 to 18.00
Car, Silver Duesenberg, Box, 1970-72, 6 Oz. 7.50
Car, Stanley Steamer, 1971-72, 5 Oz. 5.00
Car, Station Wagon, Box, 1971-73, 6 Oz. 7.00
Car, Sterling Six II, Green, 1973-74, 7 Oz. ....8.50 to 25.00
Car, Sterling Six, Amber, 1968-70, 7 Oz. ....5.00 to 20.00
Car, Straight 8, 1969-71, 5 Oz. 8.00
Car, Stutz Bearcat 1914, Box, 1974-77, 6 Oz. 5.00
Car, Sure Winner, 1972-75, 5 1/2 Oz. ....5.00 to 13.00
Car, Thomas Flyer 1908, 1974-75, 6 Oz. ....5.00 to 18.00
Car, Thunderbird, 1955 Model, 1974-75, 2 Oz. ....5.00 to 20.00
Car, Volkswagen Bus, 1975-76, 5 Oz. 12.00
Car, Volkswagen Rabbit, 1980-82, 3 Oz. 5.00
Car, Volkswagen, Black, 1970-72, 4 Oz. ....4.00 to 15.00
Cat, Felina Fluffles, 1977-78, 2 Oz. 14.00
Cat, Kitten Little, 1975-76, 1 1/2 Oz. 23.00
Cat, Kitten Petite, White Plastic, Amber Ball, 1973-74, 1 1/2 Oz. .. 14.00
Cat, Kitten's Hideaway, 1974-76, 1 Oz. 6.00
Cat, Purrfect Cat, 1987, 1 1/2 Oz. 23.00
Cat, Royal Siamese Cat, 1978, 4 1/2 Oz. 6.00
Champagne Bottle, Vintage Year, Contents, Box, 1979, 2 Oz. 6.00
Charlie Brown, Shampoo, Plastic, 1968-72, 4 Oz. 3.00
Chess Piece, Bishop II, 1975-78, 3 Oz. ....13.00 to 15.00
Chess Piece, Bishop, Box, 1974-78, 3 Oz. ....6.00 to 13.00
Chess Piece, King II, 1975-78, 3 Oz. ....9.00 to 13.00
Chess Piece, King, 1972-78, 3 Oz. ....4.00 to 13.00
Chess Piece, Pawn II, 1975-78, 3 Oz. 9.00
Chess Piece, Pawn, Box, 1974-78, 3 Oz. ....6.00 to 13.00
Chess Piece, Queen II, 1975-78, 3 Oz. ....13.00 to 15.00
Chess Piece, Rook II, 1975-78, 3 Oz. 14.00
Chess Piece, Rook, Box, 1974-78, 3 Oz. ....6.00 to 14.00
Christmas Bells, 1979-80, 1 Oz. 5.00
Christmas Ornament, Red, 1967, 4 Oz. 5.00

Christmas Ornament, Silver, 1967, 4 Oz. . . . . .5.00 to 8.00
Christmas Soldier, 1980, 3/4 Oz. 5.00
Christmas Sparkler, Green, 1968-69, 4 Oz. 6.00
Christmas Sparkler, Red, 1968-69, 4 Oz. 5.00
Clock, Cuckoo, 5 1/2 x 3 1/4 In. 5.00
Clock, Daylight Shaving Time, 1968-70, 6 Oz. 12.00
Clock, Enchanted Hours, Box, 1972-73, 5 Oz. 10.00
Clock, Fragrance Hours, 1971-73, 6 Oz. 12.00
Clock, Leisure Hours, 1970-72, 5 Oz. . . . . .10.00 to 14.00
Coach, Royal, 1972-73, 5 Oz. 6.00
Coffee Mill, Country Store, 1972-76, 5 Oz. 10.00
Coffeepot, Koffee Klatch, 1971-74, 5 Oz. . . . . .5.00 to 10.00
Compote, 1972-75, 5 Oz. 10.00
Cornucopia, 1971, 6 Oz. 12.00
Deer, Precious Doe, 1976-78, 1/2 Oz. 10.00
Deer, Silver Fawn, Box, 1978-79, 5 Oz. 5.00
Dog, At Point, Brown, 1973-74, 5 Oz. 8.00
Dog, Baby Bassett, 1978-79, 1 1/4 Oz. . . . . .3.00 to 8.00
Dog, Dachshund, 1973-74, 1 1/2 Oz. 12.00
Dog, Faithful Laddie, Amber, 1977-79, 4 Oz. . . . . .7.00 to 20.00
Dog, Princess Of Yorkshire, Yorkshire Terrier, 1976-78, 1 Oz. 8.00
Dog, Queen Of Scots, Scottish Terrier, 1973-76, 1 Oz. 6.00
Dog, Royal Pekinese, 1974-75, 1 1/2 Oz. 8.00
Dollars 'n Scents Bill, Partial Contents, 1966-67, 8 Oz., 4 1/2 In. 6.00
Dolphin, 1968-69, 8 Oz. . . . . .6.00 to 10.00
Eiffel Tower, 1970, 3 Oz. 7.00
Elephant, Good Luck, 1975-76, 1 1/2 Oz. 6.00
Elephant, Good Luck, Box, 1975-76, 1 1/2 Oz. 15.00
Faucet, Just A Twist, 1977-78, 2 Oz. 12.00
Fire Alarm Box, 1975-76, 6 Oz. 6.00
Fish, Sea Trophy, Sailfish, 1972, 5 1/2 Oz. 10.00
Fishing Reel, Angler, 1970, 5 Oz. . . . . .8.00 to 10.00
Frog, Emerald Prince, Green Over Clear, 1977-79, 1 Oz. 20.00
Frog, Enchanted Frog Cream Sachet, 1973-76, 1 1/4 Oz. 15.00
Gas Pump, Remember When, 1976, 4 Oz. 6.00
Gas Pump, Remember When, Contents, Box, 1976, 4 Oz. 20.00
Giraffe, Graceful, 1976, 1 1/2 Oz. . . . . .5.00 to 9.00
Girl, Dear Friends, 1974, 4 Oz. 8.00
Girl, First Prayer, 1981-82, 1 1/2 Oz. 15.00
Girl, Garden Girl, Box, 1978-79, 4 Oz. . . . . .6.00 to 13.00
Girl, Little Bo Peep, 1976-78, 2 Oz. . . . . .5.00 to 12.00
Girl, Little Dream Girl, Box, 1980-81, 1 1/4 Oz. 20.00
Girl, Little Girl Blue, 1972-73, 3 Oz. . . . . .7.00 to 12.00
Girl, Little Miss Muffett, 1978-80, 2 Oz. 5.00
Girl, Mary Mary, 1977-79, 2 Oz. 6.00
Girl, Mary Mary, Box, 1977-79, 2 Oz. 15.00
Girl, Roll-A-Hoop, Contents, Box, 1977, 3 3/4 Oz. 10.00
Girl, Skip-A-Rope, 1977, 4 Oz. 9.00
Girl, Wedding Flower Maiden, Box, 1979-80, 1 3/4 Oz. 5.00
Golf Ball, Tee Off, Box, 1973, 3 Oz. 8.00
Guitar, Electric, Box, 1974-75, 6 Oz. 13.00
Hammer On The Mark, Contents, Box, 1978, 2 1/2 Oz. 8.00
Hard Hat, Box, 1977-78, 4 Oz. 7.00
Horn, Viking, 1966, 7 Oz. 8.00
Horns, Steer, Western Choice, Box, 1967 . . . . 25.00
Horse, Bucking Bronco, 1971-72, 6 Oz. . . . . .6.00 to 15.00
Horse, Pony Express, 1971-72, 5 Oz. 15.00
Horse, Pony Post, 1968-69, 4 Oz. 7.00
Horse, Sport Of Kings, Amber, 1975, 5 Oz. 10.00
Horseshoe, Triple Crown, 1974-76, 4 Oz. 7.00
Indian Chieftain, 1972-75, 4 Oz. . . . . .4.00 to 7.50
Indian Head Penny, 1970-72, 4 Oz. 5.00
Juke Box, 1977-78, 4 1/2 Oz. 5.00

Keg, After-Shave On Tap, Amber, 1974-75, 5 Oz. ....4.00 to 12.00
Lamb, Little Lamb, 1977-78, 3/4 Oz. ....5.00 to 7.00
Lamp, Aladdin, 1971, 6 Oz. ....8.00 to 12.00
Lamp, Country Charm, Box, 1976-77, 4 3/4 Oz. 20.00
Lamp, Courting, 1970-71, 5 Oz. 9.00
Lamp, Courting, Box, 1970-71, 5 Oz. 20.00
Lamp, Hearth, Box, 1973-76, 8 Oz. 25.00
Lamp, Library, 1976-77, 4 Oz. 8.00
Lamp, Mansion, Box, 1975-76, 6 Oz. 25.00
Lamp, Parlor, Box, 1971-72, 3 Oz. 20.00
Lamp, Tiffany, Box, 1972-74, 5 Oz. 17.00
Lantern, Casey's, Contents, 1966-67, 10 Oz. 7.00
Lantern, Coleman, 1977-79, 5 Oz. 17.00
Lantern, Whale Oil, 1974-75, 5 Oz. 6.00
Log Cabin, Homestead, 1973-74, 4 Oz. ....7.00 to 10.00
Longhorn Steer, 1975-76, 5 Oz. 10.00
Looking Glass, Box, 1970, 1 1/2 Oz. 13.00
Lotion Lovely, Clear, Gold Letters, Cork Top, 1964, 5 3/4 x 3 In. 6.00
Meadow Blossoms, Box, 1987, 1 3/4 Oz. 8.00
Monkey Shines, Contents, Box, c.1979-80, 1 Oz. 6.00
Motorcycle, Road Runner, Box, 1973-74, 5 1/2 Oz. 30.00
Mouse, Church Mouse Bride, Box, 1978-79, 2 Oz. 14.00
NAAC, 11th Annual Club, 1956 Avon Lady, 1982, 7 1/2 In. 45.00
Ornament, see Avon, Christmas Ornament; Avon, Christmas Sparkler
Paid Stamp, 1970-71, 5 Oz. 6.00
Pear Lumiere, 1975-76, 2 Oz. 10.00
Piano, Perfume Glace, 1972, 4 Oz. 40.00
Pig, Petite Piglet, 1972, 1/4 Oz. 12.00
Pipe, American Eagle, Box, 1974-75, 5 Oz. 12.00
Pipe, Bloodhound, 1976, 5 Oz. 12.00
Pipe, Bulldog, 1972-73, 6 Oz. ....6.00 to 17.00
Pipe, Bulldog, Box, 1972-73, 6 Oz. ....16.00 to 23.00
Pipe, Collector's, 1973-74, 3 Oz. 14.00
Pipe, Corncob, 1974-75, 3 Oz. ....10.00 to 12.00
Pipe, Dutch, 1973-74, 2 Oz. ....11.00 to 16.00
Pipe, Pipe Full, 1972-74, 2 Oz. ....9.00 to 12.00
Pipe, Pony Express Rider, 1975, 3 Oz. 11.00
Pipe, Pony Express Rider, Box, 1975, 3 Oz. 13.00
Pipe, Uncle Sam, 1975-76, 3 Oz. 10.00
Pipe, Uncle Sam, Box, 1975-76, 3 Oz. 13.00
Pipe, Wild Mustang, 1976-77, 3 Oz. 5.00
Pipe, Wild Mustang, Box, 1976-77, 3 Oz. ....10.00 to 13.00
Pistol, 1760 Dueling, 1973-74, 4 Oz. 10.00
Pistol, 1760 Dueling, Box, 1973-74, 4 Oz. 29.00
Pistol, Derringer, 1977, 2 Oz. 10.00
Pistol, Pepperbox Pistol 1850, 1979, 3 Oz. ....6.00 to 8.50
Pistol, Philadelphia Derringer, 1980-82, 2 Oz. 10.00
Pistol, Thomas Jefferson Hand Gun, 1978-79, 10 In. 8.50
Pitcher, Grecian, Woman's Head, 1972-76, 5 Oz. 8.00
Pitcher & Bowl, Victoriana, 1971-72, 6 Oz. 8.00
President Lincoln, 1973, 6 Oz. 12.00
President Lincoln, Bronze, 1979, 6 Oz. 5.00
President Washington, 1974, 6 Oz. ....13.00 to 16.00
Radio, Remember When, Amber, Box, 1972-73, 5 Oz. ....7.00 to 14.00
Rhino, Big Game, 1972-73, 4 Oz. ....8.00 to 10.00
Saddle, Western, Plastic Fence, Box, 1971-72, 5 Oz. ....10.00 to 12.00
Santa, Jolly, 1978-79, 1 Oz. 5.00
Schroeder, 1970-72, 6 Oz. 9.50
Sea Horse, 1973-76, Miniature, 1/4 Oz. ....5.00 to 10.00
Seashell, Sea Treasure, 1971-72, 5 Oz. 25.00
Sewing Notions, Box, 1975, 1 Oz. 10.00
Skater's Waltz, Box, 1977-78, 4 Oz. 6.00
Snail, Perfume, Contents, 2 1/2 In. 12.00

Snoopy Surprise, 1969-71, 5 Oz. ....10.00 to 35.00
Stagecoach, 1970-77, 5 Oz. ....5.00 to 8.00
Stein, Age Of The Iron Horse, 1982, 8 1/2 In. ....40.00 to 55.00
Stein, Age Of The Iron Horse, 1985, Miniature, 5 1/4 In. ....7.50 to 25.00
Stein, America The Beautiful, 2002, 11 In. 50.00
Stein, American Armed Forces, 1990, 9 1/4 In. 23.00
Stein, Bald Eagle, 1990, 5 1/4 In. ....14.50 to 30.00
Stein, Basketball, 1993, 9 1/2 In. ....23.00 to 60.00
Stein, Blacksmith, 1985, 8 1/2 In. ....21.00 to 50.00
Stein, Car Classics, 1979, 9 In. ....15.00 to 21.00
Stein, Car Classics, Box, 1979, 9 In. ....35.00 to 55.00
Stein, Casey At The Bat, 1980, 6 In. 11.00
Stein, Christmas Carol, 1996, 9 1/2 In. 23.00
Stein, Christopher Columbus, 1992, 12 In. ....28.00 to 60.00
Stein, Conquest Of Space, 1991, 9 3/4 In. ....25.00 to 60.00
Stein, Country & Western Music, 1994, 9 1/4 In. ....25.00 to 60.00
Stein, Ducks Of American Wilderness, 1988, 8 3/4 In. ....23.00 to 55.00
Stein, Father Christmas, 1994, 9 1/2 In. ....22.00 to 60.00
Stein, Firefighters, 1989, 9 In. ....30.00 to 60.00
Stein, Fishing, 1990, 8 1/2 In. ....35.00 to 60.00
Stein, Flying Classics, 1981, 9 1/2 In. ....20.00 to 50.00
Stein, Giant Panda, 1991, 5 1/2 In. 30.00
Stein, Gold Rush, 1987, 8 1/2 In. ....12.00 to 24.00
Stein, Great American Baseball, 1984, 8 3/4 In. ....40.00 to 55.00
Stein, Great American Football, 1982-83, 9 In. ....35.00 to 55.00
Stein, Great Dogs Of Outdoors, 1991, 9 In. ....25.00 to 50.00
Stein, Great Kings Of Africa, 1997, 5 3/4 In. 14.50
Stein, Hunters, 1972, 8 Oz. ....8.00 to 20.00
Stein, Indians Of The American Frontier, 1988, 9 In. ....23.00 to 50.00
Stein, Jaguar, 1991, 5 1/2 In. ....13.00 to 30.00
Stein, Knight Of The Realm, 1995, 9 1/2 In. ....28.00 to 40.00
Stein, Mountain Zebra, 1992, 5 1/2 In. ....14.50 to 30.00
Stein, Racing Car, 1989, 9 1/4 In. ....23.00 to 55.00
Stein, Salute To Postal Service, 1996, 9 1/2 In. 30.00
Stein, Shipbuilder, Box, 1986, 8 1/2 In. 55.00
Stein, Silver, 1968, 6 Oz. 6.00
Stein, Sperm Whale, 1992, 5 1/2 In. ....14.50 to 30.00
Stein, Sporting Stein, 1978, 9 In. ....19.00 to 60.00
Stein, Sporting Stein, 1983-84, 5 In. ....6.50 to 20.00
Stein, Tall Ships, 1977, 8 1/2 In. ....19.00 to 45.00
Stein, Tribute To North American Wolf, 1997, 9 1/2 In. ....28.00 to 70.00
Stein, Tribute To Rescue Workers, 1997, 9 1/2 In. 23.00
Stein, Western Round-Up, 1983, Miniature, 5 In. ....20.00 to 25.00
Stein, Western Round-Up, Box, 1980, 8 1/2 In. ....20.00 to 33.00
Stein, Wild West, 1993, 8 1/2 In. ....28.00 to 60.00
Stein, Wildlife, 1995, 9 1/2 In. 23.00
Stein, Winners Circle, 1992, 10 In. ....20.00 to 50.00
Stove, Potbelly, 1970, 5 Oz. 13.00
Teddy Bear, 1976-78, 3/4 Oz. 4.00
Teepee, Indian, 1974-75, 4 Oz. 6.00
Telephone, Avon Calling '1905, 1973, 7 Oz. 8.00
Thermos, 1978-79, 3 Oz. ....7.00 to 12.00
Totem Pole, 1975, 6 Oz. 5.00
Town Pump, 1968-69, 6 Oz. 5.00
Tractor, Harvester, 1973-75, 5 1/2 Oz. 14.00
Train, 1876 Centennial Express, 1978-86, 5 1/2 Oz. ....5.00 to 12.00
Train, Atlantic 4-4-2, Contents, Box, 1973, 5 Oz. 25.00
Train, General 4-4-0, Contents, Box, 4 x 7 In. 25.00
Train, Golden Rocket 022, Contents, Box, 1974, 6 Oz. 25.00
Train, Lionel, Blue Comet, 1991, 9 3/4 x 3 3/4 In. 12.00
Train, Lionel, No. 381E, 1992, 9 3/4 x 3 3/4 In. 14.00
Truck, Big Rig, 1975-76, 3 1/2 Oz. 16.00
Truck, Country Vendor, Box, 1973, 5 Oz. 6.00

Balantine, Golf
Bag, Box, 1969

Balantine, Zebra,
1969

Truck, Extra Special Male, Contents, Box, 1977-79, 3 Oz.	6.00 to 20.00
Truck, Ford Ranger Pickup, 1973 Model, Blue, 1978-79, 5 Oz.	16.00
Truck, Highway King, Box, 1977-79, 4 Oz.	7.00
Turtle, Treasure Turtle, 1971-73, 1 Oz.	5.00 to 16.00
Unicorn, 1974-75, 2 Oz.	6.00 to 8.00
Unicorn, Box, 1974-75, 2 Oz.	9.00
Urn, Athena Bath Urn, 1975-76, 6 Oz.	18.00
Urn, Bath Urn, Milk Glass, 1971-73, 5 Oz.	14.00
Vase, Emerald Bud, Green, 1971, 3 Oz.	20.00
Vase, Floral Bud, Milk Glass, 1973-75, 5 Oz.	11.00
Vase, Garnet Bud, Box, 1973, 3 Oz.	25.00
Vase, Grape Bud, Frosted, 1973, 6 Oz., 9 In.	10.00
Vase, Sea Fantasy Bud, 1978-79, 6 Oz.	8.00
Warrior, Tribute, Ribbed, Clear, 1971-73, 6 Oz.	6.00
Warrior, Tribute, Silver, 1967, 6 Oz.	7.00
Winnebago Motor Home, Box, 1978-79, 5 Oz.	5.00 to 20.00
Woman, Bridal Moments, Contents, Box, 1976-79, 5 Oz.	10.00
Woman, Elizabethan, Pink, 1972, 4 Oz.	18.00
Woman, Gay Nineties, 1974, 3 Oz.	7.00 to 18.00
Woman, Roaring Twenties, Box, 1972-74, 3 Oz.	25.00
Woman, Victorian, 1973-74, 4 Oz.	9.00
Woman, Victorian Lady, 1972-73, 5 Oz.	9.00 to 14.00

BALLANTINE

Ballantine's Scotch was sold in figural bottles in 1969. The five bottles were shaped like a golf bag, knight, mallard, zebra, or fisherman. Ballantine also made some flasks and jugs with special designs.

Fisherman, 1969		5.00
Fisherman, Box, 1969		10.00 to 36.00
Golf Bag, Box, 1969	*Illus*	19.00
Jug, Blue Rim, 3 1/2 In.		10.00
Jug, Brown Top, 8 In.		1.80
Knight, Box, 1969		22.50
Mallard Duck, 1969		.75
Mallard Duck, Box, 1969		15.00
Zebra, 1969	*Illus*	10.00
Zebra, Box, 1969		26.00 to 39.00

BARBER

The nineteenth-century barber either made his own hair tonic or purchased it in large containers. Barber bottles were used at the barbershop or in the home. The barber filled the bottles each day with hair oil, bay rum, tonic, shampoo, witch hazel, rosewater, or some other cosmetic. He knew what was inside each bottle because of its distinctive shape and color. Most of the important types of art glass were used for barber bottles. Spatter glass, milk glass, cranberry, cobalt, cut, hobnail, vaseline, and opalescent glass were used alone or in attractive combinations. Some were made with enamel-painted decorations. Most of the bottles were blown. A pontil mark can be found on the bottom of many bottles. These special fancy bottles were popular during the last half of the nineteenth-century. In 1906 the Pure Food and Drugs Act made it illegal to use refillable, nonlabeled bottles in a barbershop, and the bottles were no longer used.

Amethyst, Bell, Ribs, White Enamel, Sheared, Tooled Lip, Pontil, 7 1/2 In. 123.00
Amethyst, Bulbous, Polished Band, Orange Enamel Design, Flowers, 6 3/4 x 3 3/4 In. . . . 125.00
Amethyst, Cylindrical, Vertical Ribs, Enamel Dancing Girl, 8 3/4 In. 392.00
Amethyst, Ribs, Enamel Stag, Tooled Lip, 8 In. 308.00
Amethyst, White Enamel Art Nouveau Woman's Head, 8 In. 476.00
Amethyst, White Enamel Boy Playing, 8 1/2 In. . . . .*Illus* 179.00
Amethyst, White Enamel Daisies, Hand Blown, Polished Pontil, 7 x 3 1/2 In. 110.00
Amethyst, White Enamel Girl, Sitting, Lady's Leg, 7 3/4 In. 202.00
Amethyst, White, Enamel Girl, Rolled Lip, Pontil, 7 7/8 In. . . . . .224.00 to 235.00
Amethyst, Yellow Enamel, Gold Paint, Art Nouveau, Tooled Rolled Lip, Pontil, 8 1/8 In. . 245.00
Antiseptic, Milk Glass, Blue Clover & Bow, Stripes, Rolled Lip, 9 In. 213.00
Bay Rum, Blue Milk Glass, Multicolored Enamel Bird, Metal Screw Stopper, 9 1/2 In. . . . 213.00
Bay Rum, Michelsen St. Thomas, Black Glass, Embossed, Qt. 19.00
Bay Rum, Milk Glass, A.J. Davis, Enamel Bird, Pink Ground, Ground Lip, 9 1/2 In. 532.00
Bay Rum, Milk Glass, Bird, Cattail, Applied Lip, Pontil, 8 3/4 In. 213.00
Bay Rum, Milk Glass, Fiery Opalescent, Enamel Roses, Rolled Lip, 8 5/8 In. 235.00
Bay Rum, Milk Glass, Powder Blue Opalescent, Enamel Flowers, Pontil, 11 1/4 In. 1344.00
Bay Rum, Milk Glass, Swallow & Flower, Applied Lip, Pontil, 9 In. 190.00
Bay Rum, W.T. & Co., Milk Glass, Multicolored Roses, 9 5/8 In. 616.00
Black, Tooled Lip, Label, Pour Stopper, 8 1/8 In. 202.00
Blue, Enamel Flowers, Pontil, 8 In. 77.00
Blue, Roller Lip, Pontil, 9 1/2 In. 330.00
Brilliantine, Purple Amethyst, Ribs, Multicolored, Flowers, Tooled Lip, 8 1/4 In. 179.00
Brilliantine, Purple Amethyst, Ribs, Multicolored, Polished Lip, 3 7/8 In. . . 308.00
Brilliantine, Turquoise Blue, Ribs, White, Orange Enamel Flowers, Metal Cap, 2 7/8 In. . . 123.00
Brilliantine, Turquoise Blue, Ribs, White, Orange Enamel Flowers, Metal Collar, 3 1/8 In. 112.00
Brilliantine, Turquoise Blue, White, Orange Enamel, Metal Neck Ring, Screw Cap, 3 In. . 100.00
Brilliantine, Turquoise, White, Orange & Gold Enamel Flowers, Rose Stopper, 2 3/4 In. . 43.00
Brilliantine, Yellow Amber, 8-Panel Neck, Tooled Lip, 1910-25, 4 In. 78.00
Brilliantine, Yellow Green, Bulbous, Lady's Leg Neck, Pewter Stopper, 4 3/4 In. 59.00
Bristol Glass, Blue, Gold & Multicolored Enamel, Clear Stopper, 8 In. . . . . *Illus* 75.00
Bristol Glass, Enamel, Gold Trim, No Stopper, c.1900, 7 In. 58.00
Buerger Bros. Supply Co., Denver, Colorado, Turquoise, Fluted Sides, 10 In. 112.00
Chas. C. Dissel, Tonic, Milk Glass, Enamel, 11 1/4 In. 230.00
Clambroth, Shaving Paper Vase, 12-Sided, 7 1/2 In. 29.00
Clear, Blue Green, Cranberry Red, Polished Lip, 1885-1915, 7 In. 840.00
Clear, Cranberry Flashing, Coin Spot, Smooth Base, Tooled Lip, 1900s, 7 1/4 In. 56.00
Clear, Frosted, Overall Stars In Diamonds, Twisted Neck, 8 1/8 In. 403.00
Clear, Horizontal Ribs, Scalp Tonic, 9 In. 364.00
Clear, Opalescent Cobalt Blue, White, Tooled Lip, 1885-1925, 12 1/4 In. 146.00
Clear Opalescent, White Stars & Stripes, Tooled Lip, 7 In. 358.00
Clear Over Cranberry, Overall Hobnail, Pontil, 7 In. 123.00
Clear Over Cranberry, White Enamel Boy Playing Tennis, 8 In. 364.00
Clear Over Pink, White & Black, Swirls, Lady's Leg Neck, Sheared Mouth, Pontil, 10 In. 253.00
Cobalt Blue, 3-Colors Flower, Enamel, 8 x 3 1/2 In. 148.00
Cobalt Blue, Bird, Flowers, Leaves, Gold Paint, Silver Tone Metal Top, 8 3/4 In. 195.00
Cobalt Blue, Bulbous, Pontil, Pewter Top, 7 In. 149.00
Cobalt Blue, Flowers, Multicolored Enamel, Rolled Lip, Pontil, 7 7/8 In. 100.00
Cobalt Blue, Gray & Orange Enamel, Bulbous, Open Pontil 140.00
Cobalt Blue, Lady's Leg, Ribs, Art Nouveau Decoration, Rolled Lip, 8 1/2 In. 392.00
Cobalt Blue, Multicolored Dotted Flowers, Barrel Shape, 7 5/8 In. 520.00
Cobalt Blue, Ribs, Dotted Flowers, Barrel Shape, Long Neck, Pontil, 7 5/8 In. 420.00
Cobalt Blue, Ribs, Enamel Stag, Tooled Lip, 8 In. 392.00
Cobalt Blue, Ribs, Red Band, White & Gold Enamel Flowers, Tooled Lip, 7 3/4 In. 90.00
Cobalt Blue, Ribs, White, Yellow, Orange Enamel, Rolled Lip, Pontil, 7 1/2 In. 157.00
Cobalt Blue, Ribs, Yellow, Gold, Rolled Lip, Pontil, 7 1/2 In. 179.00
Cobalt Blue, White Enamel Girl Playing Tennis, Rolled Lip, Pontil, 8 1/8 In. 179.00
Cobalt Blue, White Enamel, Girl Smelling Flower, 6 x 3 In. 210.00
Cobalt Blue, Yellow Enamel, Gold Paint, Art Nouveau, Rolled Lip, Pontil, 8 1/8 In. 255.00
Cobalt Blue, Yellow, Gold, Art Nouveau, Rolled Lip, Pontil, 8 1/4 In. 246.00
Coin Spot, Blue Opalescent, Shaker Top, 7 1/8 In. 110.00

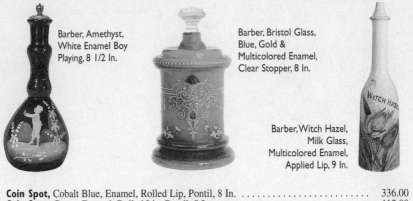

Barber, Amethyst, White Enamel Boy Playing, 8 1/2 In.

Barber, Bristol Glass, Blue, Gold & Multicolored Enamel, Clear Stopper, 8 In.

Barber, Witch Hazel, Milk Glass, Multicolored Enamel, Applied Lip, 9 In.

Coin Spot, Cobalt Blue, Enamel, Rolled Lip, Pontil, 8 In.	336.00
Coin Spot, Green, Enamel, Rolled Lip, Pontil, 8 In.	112.00
Coin Spot, Multicolored Enamel Flowers, Rolled Lip, Pontil, 8 In.	308.00
Coin Spot, Teal Blue, Melon, Rolled Lip, 1900-30, 8 1/2 In.	90.00
Coin Spot, Yellow Green, White Enamel, Rolled Lip, 8 1/8 In.	224.00
Cranberry, Hobnail, Opalescent, Rolled Lip, Ground Pontil, Stopper, 7 x 4 1/2 In.	237.00
Cranberry Flash, Vertical Ribs, White Enamel, 10 1/2 In.	672.00
Cranberry Opalescent, Coin Spot, Melon Sides, Rolled Lip, 8 3/8 In.	120.00
Cranberry Opalescent, Coral, Rolled Lip, Pontil, 8 1/8 In.	532.00
Cranberry Opalescent, Flowers, Rolled Lip, Pontil, 7 1/4 In.	504.00
Cranberry Opalescent, Melon Sides, 8 1/2 x 4 In.	187.00
Cranberry Opalescent, Stars & Stripes, Rolled Lip, Pontil, 7 3/8 In.	168.00
Cranberry Opalescent, Stripe, Rolled Lip, 7 3/8 In.	420.00
Cranberry Opalescent, Swirl To Left, Rolled Lip, Pontil, 6 7/8 In.	123.00
Cranberry Opalescent, Swirl, 7 In.	248.00
Cranberry Opalescent, White Herringbone, Pinched Waist, Tooled Lip, 7 1/4 In.	3360.00
Cranberry Opalescent, White Stars & Stripes, Tooled Lip, Pontil, 7 In.	385.00
Cranberry Shaded To Yellow, Coin Spot, Tooled Lip, Pontil, 7 In.	1232.00
Emerald Green, Pontil, White Enamel, Red Band	75.00
Emerald Green, Ribs, White Enamel, Rolled Lip, Pontil, 7 1/8 In.	168.00
Emerald Green, Yellow, Gold Gilt, Art Nouveau, Rolled Lip, Pontil, 8 1/8 In.	280.00
Enamel Flower Decoration, Marigold	50.00
Enamel Flowers, Cobalt Blue, Gold Trim, Pontil, Victorian, 6 7/8 In.	145.00
Enamel Woman, Light Marigold	50.00
Fenton, Cranberry, Ruby Overlay, Polka Dot Pattern, No Stopper, c.1958, 8 1/2 x 4 In.	250.00
Florida Water, Christiena Noeckel, Milk Glass, Painted, Woodpecker, Dispenser, 10 In.	1064.00
Frosted Flashed, Ruby Red, Ribs, Multicolored Enamel Flowers, Pontil, 7 1/4 In.	364.00
Frosted Lavender To Clear, Flowers, Multicolored Enamel, Flat, Polished Lip, 7 In.	330.00
Frosted Pink, Flowers, White Enamel, Sheared & Polished Lip, 8 1/8 In.	190.00
Frosted Topaz, Flowers, White Enamel, Sheared & Polished Lip, 8 1/8 In.	180.00
Frosted Turquoise, Flowers, White Enamel, Sheared & Polished Lip, 8 1/8 In.	180.00
Grape Amethyst, Yellow, Gold Enamel, Flowers, Rolled Lip, Art Nouveau, 7 7/8 In.	224.00
Grass Green, Enamel Girl, Butterfly Net, Tooled Lip, Pontil, 8 1/8 In.	213.00
Grass Green, Ribs, Yellow, Gold Paint, Art Nouveau, Tooled Rolled Lip, Pontil, 8 In.	265.00
Green, Ribs, Enamel Stag, 7 3/4 In.	476.00
Green, White, Enamel Crane, Leaves, c.1870, 8 x 3 In.	178.00
Hair Oil, Clear, Frosted, Ruby Overlay, Gold Letters, Double Collar, 11 1/2 In.	560.00
Hair Oil, Milk Glass, Opalescent, Enameled Thistle, E. Berlinghaus, Cincinnati, 8 3/4 In.	179.00
Hobnail, Amber, 7 In.	95.00
Hobnail, Blue Opalescent, 7 In.	100.00
Hobnail, Cranberry Opalescent, Rolled Lip, Polished Pontil, 6 7/8 In.	90.00
Hobnail, Cranberry Red Flashing, Clear, Rolled Lip, Polished Pontil, 7 1/8 In.	45.00
Hobnail, Turquoise Opalescent, Rolled Lip, Pontil, 7 1/8 In.	56.00
Hyki Tonic, World's Greatest Dandruff Remedy, Cleveland, Label Under Glass, 8 In.	308.00
Jade, Enamel, Stopper, Pontil, 7 3/4 In.	242.00
Kennedy's Dandruff Cure Hair Restorer, Clear, Label Under Glass, 7 In.	1120.00

Keystone Ware, A.M. & R. & Co., 7 3/4 x 5 In. 230.00
Koken Barbers' Supply Co., Milk Glass, Cobalt Blue Band, Flowers, 7 5/8 In., Pair 168.00
LeVarn's Golden Wash Shampoo, Mettowee, Granville, N.Y., Label Under Glass, 8 In. .. 70.00
Light Amber, Enamel Flowers, Pontil, 8 In. 88.00
Light Blue, Hobnail, Rolled Lip, Porcelain Stopper, 7 1/8 x 4 1/4 In. 242.00
Liquid Head Rest, Clear, Label Under Glass, 7 3/4 In. 304.00
Mauve, Gold Dots, Fluted, Stretch Neck, 9 x 4 1/2 In. 296.00
Milk Glass, 3 Cherubs, Dog Head, Pontil, Sheared, Tooled Lip, 7 1/2 In. 202.00
Milk Glass, Cherub On Dog's Head Cloud, Yellow & Blue Ground, 7 5/8 In. 146.00
Milk Glass, Cherub With Grapes, Yellow & Blue Ground, 7 3/4 In. 123.00
Milk Glass, Cherubs On Dog's Head Cloud, Colored Enamel, Tooled Lip, Pontil, 8 In. ... 200.00
Milk Glass, Cherubs With Dove, Multicolored Enamel, Tooled Lip, Pontil, 8 In. 200.00
Milk Glass, Cherubs With Grapes, Multicolored Enamel, Tooled Lip, Pontil, 8 In. 200.00
Milk Glass, Enameled Fox Hunt Scene, Tooled Lip, Pontil, 7 1/2 In. 179.00
Milk Glass, Fiery Opalescent, Enamel Flowers, Bulbous Neck, Sheared Mouth, 8 In. 112.00
Milk Glass, Frosted, Multicolored Enamel Flowers, Ground Lip, 1890-1925, 7 In. 100.00
Milk Glass, Multicolored Enamel, Cherub Reading, Blue, Yellow Ground, Pontil, 7 5/8 In. 190.00
Milk Glass, Multicolored Enamel, Cherub, Sheaf Of Grain, Blue, Yellow Ground, 7 5/8 In. 190.00
Milk Glass, Multicolored, Flower, Leaf, Flared Mouth, Cone Shape, 8 1/4 In. 392.00
Milk Glass, Multicolored, Flowers, 1885-1925, 7 7/8 In. 140.00
Milk Glass, Powder Blue, Bead & Flute, Tooled Lip, c.1900, 6 1/4 In. 210.00
Moser, Portrait, Gold Stenciling, c.1885, 7 1/4 In. 575.00
Olive Green, White Enamel Girl, 8 In. 364.00
Pink Amethyst, Yellow, Gold, Rolled Lip, Art Nouveau, 1885-1925, 7 3/4 In. 123.00
Pompeian Hair Massage, Cleveland, Label Under Glass, Lady's Leg Neck, 8 In. 258.00
Purple Amethyst, Blue, Orange, Yellow Enamel, Rolled Lip, Pontil, 1890-1925, 8 In. ... 78.00
Purple Amethyst, Multicolored Enamel Cherubs, Shaker Spout, Pontil, 8 In. 1792.00
Purple Amethyst, Ribs, Yellow, Orange & White Flowers, Rolled Lip, Pontil, 7 3/4 In. .. 123.00
Purple Amethyst, Yellow, Gold Gilt, Flowers, Rolled Lip, Pontil, 8 1/8 In. 280.00
R.R. Hean, Tonic, Flowers, Milk Glass, Ground Lip, Screw Cap, 8 7/8 In. 360.00
Ruby Cut To Clear, Bohemian Flowers, Polished Lip, 8 3/4 In. 112.00
Ruby Red, Short Lady's Leg, Sheared Mouth, Laid On Neck Ring, 7 In. 139.00
Sapphire Blue, Frosted, Ribs, Art Nouveau Decoration, 8 3/8 In. 308.00
Satin Glass, Blue & White Vertical Venetian Stripes, Tooled Lip, Pontil, 8 5/8 In. 112.00
Shampoo, Amethyst, Lady's Leg Neck, White Enamel Mill, 8 In. 392.00
Shampoo, Clear, Label Under Glass, 7 5/8 In. 420.00
Spanish Lace, Clear Opalescent, Pinched Waist, Rolled Lip, 7 5/8 In. 1430.00
Sterling Pure Coconut Oil Shampoo, Indian, Clear, Label Under Glass, 8 1/4 In. 1064.00
Tarentum, Harvard Yard, Original Stopper, 1890s, 7 1/4 In. 160.00
Teal Green, White Enamel Decoration, Rolled Lip, Pontil, 7 3/4 In. 280.00
Teal Green, White Enamel, Polished Lip, 7 3/4 In. 1568.00
Topaz, Opaque, Frosted, Multicolored Enamel Roses, Tooled Lip, 8 In. 112.00
Topaz, Ribs, Pink, Yellow, White Flowers, Sheared, Tooled Lip, Pontil, 7 1/2 In. 101.00
Turquoise Blue, Ribs, Red, White & Yellow Enamel, Outward Rolled Lip, Pontil, 8 In. .. 67.00
Turquoise Blue Opalescent, White Stars & Stripes, Tooled Lip, Pontil, 7 In. 300.00
Turquoise Opalescent, Coral, Rolled Lip, Pontil, 8 1/4 In. 840.00
Turquoise Opalescent, Stars & Stripes, Rolled Lip, Pontil, 7 3/8 In. 168.00
Turquoise Opalescent, Swirl To Left, Rolled Lip, Pontil, 6 1/4 In. 157.00
Vaseline, Opalescent & Flower Design, Silver Tone Metal Top, 8 1/2 In. 195.00
Vegederma, Apple Green, White Enamel Art Nouveau Bust, Lady's Leg Neck, 8 In. 336.00
Vegederma, Purple Amethyst, White Enamel Girl, Rolled Lip, Pontil, 8 1/8 In. 392.00
Wild Root, For The Hair, Buffalo, N.Y., Label Under Glass, Lady's Leg Neck, 8 3/8 In. .. 168.00
Witch Hazel, Milk Glass, Multicolored Enamel, Applied Lip, 9 In. .... *Illus* 235.00
Witch Hazel, Milk Glass, Red & Green Enamel Clover, Tooled Lip, 9 1/4 In. 213.00
Witch Hazel, Milk Glass, Red & Olive Green Clover, Smooth Base, Tooled Lip, 9 1/4 In. 112.00
Witch Hazel, Purple Amethyst, Rib, White Enamel House, Rolled Lip, Pontil, 7 7/8 In. .. 235.00
Yellow Green, Red, Yellow, White Enamel, Ribs, Rolled Lip, Pontil, 1890-1925, 8 In. 67.00
Yellow Green, Ribs, Lady's Leg, White Enamel Woman With Flowers, 8 In. 269.00
Yellow Green, Ribs, White, Orange Enamel, Tooled Lip, Pontil, 7 3/4 In. 112.00
Yellow Green, Ribs, Yellow, White, Orange Flowers, Rolled Lip, Pontil, 7 1/2 In. 90.00
Yellow Green, White & Orange Enamel, Bell Shape, Vertical Ribs, Open Pontil, 7 3/4 In. . 119.00
Yellow Orange Opalescent, White Splotches, Tooled Lip, Pontil, 8 In. 157.00
BATTERY JAR, see Oil

———————————————————— **BEAM** ————————————————————

The history of the Jim Beam company is confusing because the progeny of the founder, Jacob Beam, favored the names David and James. Jacob Beam had been a whiskey distiller in Virginia and Maryland before moving to Kentucky in 1788. He was selling Kentucky Straight Bourbon in bottles labeled *Beam* by 1795. His son David continued to market Beam bourbon. His grandson, David M. Beam, was the next to inherit the business. One of David M.'s brands was Old Tub, started in 1882 at Beam's Clear Springs Distillery No. 230. The company was called David M. Beam. The next Beam family member in the business was Col. James B. Beam, son of David M., who started working at the distillery in 1880 at the age of 16. By 1914 he owned the Early Times Distillery No. 7 in Louisville, Kentucky. J.B. Beam and B.H. Hurt were partners in the distillery from 1892 to 1899. In 1915, when the colonel died, the distillery was acquired by S.L. Guthrie and some partners. Then T. Jeremiah Beam, son of James B. Beam, inherited the James Beam Company, and with his cousin, Carl Beam, continued to make the famous bourbon. Booker Noe, Baker Beam, and David Beam, sixth-generation descendants of Jacob Beam, continued in the business. Today, Jim Beam Brands is a wholly-owned subsidiary of Fortune Brands.

Beam bottles favored by today's collectors were made as containers for Kentucky Straight Bourbon. In 1953, the company began selling some Christmas season whiskey in special decanters shaped like cocktail shakers instead of the usual whiskey bottles. The decanters were so popular that by 1955 the company was making Regal China bottles in special shapes. Executive series bottles started in 1955 and political figures in 1956. Customer specialties were first made in 1956, decanters (called *trophy series* by collectors) in 1957, and the state series in 1958. Other bottles are classed by collectors as Regal China or Glass Specialty bottles. A small number of special bottles were made by The Royal Doulton Company in England from 1983 to 1985. The rarest Beam bottle is the First National Bank of Chicago bottle; 117 were issued in 1964. The Salute to Spiro Agnew bottle made in 1970 was limited to 196. Six men making counterfeits of the very rare Beam bottles were arrested in 1970. Jim Beam stopped making decanters for the commercial trade in 1992.

The Foss Company made a limited number of decanters exclusively for the International Association of Jim Beam Bottle and Specialties Club (IJBBSC). Cinnamon Teal was issued in 1994 and Harlequin Duck in 1995 with the Ducks Unlimited label.

The Jim Beam company has also made many other advertising items or *go-withs* such as ashtrays and openers. The International Association of Jim Beam Bottle & Specialties Clubs (PO Box 486, Kewanee, IL 61433) has regional and sectional meetings. There is a pictorial index on the club's website. www.jimbeamclubs.com.

Bottles are listed here alphabetically by name or under Convention, Executive, Political, or other general headings. This is because beginning collectors find it difficult to locate bottles by type. Miniature bottles are listed here also. Go-withs are in the special section at the end of the book.

101st Airborne Division, Armed Forces, 1977	....	13.00
AC Spark Plug, 1977	....*Illus*	15.50
Alaska Purchase, 1966	....	15.00
Alaska Star, 1958	....	15.50
Ambulance, Emergency, White, 1985	....	38.00 to 44.00
American Cowboy, 1981	....	58.00
AMVETS, 25th Anniversary Of American Wars, 1970	....	6.00 to 15.50
Antioch, Indian Head Nickel, 1967	....	8.00 to 9.00
Antique Trader, 11th Anniversary, 1968	....	5.00 to 10.00
Arizona, State, 1968	....	5.00 to 12.00
Armadillo, 1981	....*Illus*	45.00
Army Jeep, Box, 1986	....	5.50
Ashtray, Coaster, Matchbook Holder, White, 1955	....	18.50
Barney's Slot Machine, 1978	....	30.00 to 60.00
Baseball, 100th Anniversary, 1969	....	6.00 to 20.00
Bass Boat, Box, 1987	....	28.00 to 41.00
Beam Pot, 1980	....	2.00
Bell Scotch, 1969, Miniature	...............................*Illus*	5.00
Bing Crosby, 29th National Pro-AM, 1970	....	2.00 to 26.00
Bing Crosby, 30th, 1971	....	5.00 to 7.00

Beam, AC Spark Plug, 1977

Beam, Bell Scotch, 1969, Miniature

Beam, Armadillo, 1981

Bing Crosby, 31st, 1972	20.00
Bing Crosby, 32nd, 1973	30.00
Bing Crosby, 33rd, 1974	28.00
Bing Crosby, 34th, 1975	51.00
Bing Crosby, 35th, 1976	30.00
Bing Crosby, 36th, 1977	25.00
Bing Crosby, 37th, 1978	23.00
Blue Hen, 1982	5.00 to 7.00
Blue Jay, 1969	10.00 to 20.00
Bluegill, 1974, 9 3/4 In.	55.00
Bob Hope Desert Classic, 14th, Box, 1973	38.00
Bob Hope Desert Classic, 15th, Box, 1974	40.00
Boothill, Dodge City, 1972	2.00
Bowling Pin, Clear, Gold Top, 1980	5.50 to 9.00
Bowling Pin, White, 1980	4.00 to 15.00
BPAA, National Convention, Bowling Ball & Pin, 1974	10.00 to 15.00
BPO Does, 1971	6.50
Broadmoor Hotel, 1968	5.00 to 15.00
Buffalo Bill, 1971	5.00 to 7.00
Cable Car, 1968	10.00 to 20.00
Cadillac, Convertible, 1959 Model, Pink, Box, 1992	44.00 to 50.00
Canteen, 1979	2.00
Captain & Mate, 1980	2.00 to 15.00
Cardinal, Male, 1968	10.00
Cat, Burmese, 1967	5.00 to 25.00
Cat, Siamese, 1967	10.00 to 26.00
Catfish, 1981	41.00 to 51.00
Cherry Hills Country Club, 1973	10.00
Chevrolet, Bel Air Convertible, 1957 Model, Black, Box, 1990	50.00
Chevrolet, Bel Air Convertible, 1957 Model, Red, 1990	32.00
Chevrolet, Bel Air Convertible, 1957 Model, Turquoise, 1991	31.00
Chevrolet, Bel Air, 1957 Model, Red, 1987	45.00 to 51.00
Chevrolet, Bel Air, 1957 Model, Red, Box, 1987	61.00
Chevrolet, Bel Air, 1957 Model, Turquoise, Box, 1987	66.00
Chevrolet, Camaro, 1969 Model, Blue, 1989	33.00
Chevrolet, Camaro, 1969 Model, Blue, Box, 1989	83.00 to 124.00
Chevrolet, Camaro, 1969 Model, Orange Hugger	72.00
Chevrolet, Camaro, 1969 Model, Pace Car, 1989	52.00
Chevrolet, Camaro, 1969 Model, Pace Car, Box, 1989	128.00
Chevrolet, Camaro, 1969 Model, Red Hugger, 1988	51.00 to 66.00
Chevrolet, Camaro, 1969 Model, Yellow, 1989	41.00 to 50.00
Chevrolet, Corvette Stingray, 1963 Model, White, 1987	61.00
Chevrolet, Corvette, 1953 Model, White, 1989	94.00
Chevrolet, Corvette, 1953 Model, White, Box, 1989	66.00
Chevrolet, Corvette, 1954 Model, Blue, 1989	81.00
Chevrolet, Corvette, 1957 Model, Black, 1990	32.00

Chevrolet, Corvette, 1957 Model, Black, Box, 1990 .... .50.00 to 100.00
Chevrolet, Corvette, 1968 Model, Blue, Box, 1992 .... .32.00 to 50.00
Chevrolet, Corvette, 1968 Model, Maroon, Box, 1992 .... 43.00
Chevrolet, Corvette, 1978 Model, Black, 1984 .... 22.00
Chevrolet, Corvette, 1978 Model, Pace Car, Box, 1987 .... .100.00 to 178.00
Chevrolet, Corvette, 1978 Model, Red, 1988 .... 20.00
Chevrolet, Corvette, 1978 Model, Red, Box, 1988 .... .29.00 to 50.00
Chevrolet, Corvette, 1978 Model, White, Box, 1985 .... .26.00 to 76.00
Chevrolet, Corvette, 1978 Model, Yellow, 1985 .... .40.00 to 77.00
Chevrolet, Corvette, 1984 Model, White, 1988 .... 39.00
Chevrolet, Corvette, 1984 Model, White, Box, 1988 .... .33.00 to 61.00
Chevrolet, Corvette, 1986 Model, Pace Car, Yellow, Box, 1990 .... 81.00
Cheyenne, 1967 .... .2.00 to 5.00
Chicago Art Museum, 1972 .... 15.00
Chicago Club Loving Cup, 1977 .... 13.00
Chicago Fire, 1971 .... 8.00
Churchill Downs, Kentucky Derby, 95th, Pink Roses, 1969 .... 35.00
Churchill Downs, Kentucky Derby, 95th, Red Roses, 1969 .... .8.00 to 10.50
Churchill Downs, Kentucky Derby, 97th, Horse & Rider, 1971 .... .5.00 to 16.00
Churchill Downs, Kentucky Derby, 98th, Horse & Rider In Wreath, 1972 ....20.00 to 25.00
Churchill Downs, Kentucky Derby, 100th, 1974 .... .10.00 to 13.50
Circus Circus, Clown, 1987 .... 26.00
Circus Wagon, 1979 .... .10.00 to 24.00
Civil War, North, 1961 .... 45.00
Civil War, South, 1961 .... 30.00
Cleopatra, Rust, 1962 .... 2.00
Coach Devaney, Nebraska, National Champions, Football, 1972 .... .23.00 to 61.00
Coho Salmon, 1976 .... .5.00 to 10.00
Collectors Edition, Vol. 1, Famous Paintings, Series Of 6, Each, 1966 .... .2.00 to 5.00
Collectors Edition, Vol. 2, Renaissance Period Paintings, Series Of 6, Each, 1967 ..... .2.00 to 5.00
Collectors Edition, Vol. 3, American Paintings, Series Of 8, Each, 1968 .... .4.00 to 8.00
Collectors Edition, Vol. 4, Famous French Paintings, Series Of 8, Each, 1969 .... .2.00 to 5.00
Collectors Edition, Vol. 4, The Judge, 1969 .... 8.00
Collectors Edition, Vol. 5, French Paintings, Series Of 6, Each, 1970 .... .1.00 to 5.00
Collectors Edition, Vol. 6, Series Of 3, Each, 1971 .... .1.00 to 5.00
Collectors Edition, Vol. 7, Bag Piper, 1972 .... 7.50
Collectors Edition, Vol. 7, Series Of 3, Each, 1972 .... .2.00 to 5.00
Collectors Edition, Vol. 8, Edward H. Weiss, Composers, Series Of 3, Each, 1973 ..... .4.00 to 7.00
Collectors Edition, Vol. 9, James Lockhart, Bird Paintings, Series Of 3, Each, 1974 ..... 10.00
Collectors Edition, Vol. 10, James Lockhart, Fish Paintings, Series Of 3, Each, 1975 ...5.00 to 8.00
Collectors Edition, Vol. 10, Sailfish, 1975 .... .5.00 to 29.00
Collectors Edition, Vol. 11, James Lockhart, Wildlife Paintings, Series Of 3, Each, 1976 .. 6.00
Collectors Edition, Vol. 11, Pronghorn Antelope, Box, 1976 .... 18.00
Collectors Edition, Vol. 12, German Shorthaired Pointer, 1977 .... 17.00
Collectors Edition, Vol. 12, James Lockhart, Dog Paintings, Series Of 4, Each, 1977 . .5.00 to 12.00
Collectors Edition, Vol. 14, Cottontail Rabbit, 1978 .... 18.50
Collectors Edition, Vol. 14, James Lockhart, Wildlife Paintings, Series Of 4, Each, 1978 . 5.00
Collectors Edition, Vol. 15, Frederic Remington Paintings, Series Of 3, Each, 1979 ...5.00 to 10.00
Collectors Edition, Vol. 16, James Lockhart, Duck Paintings, Series Of 3, Each, 1980 ..3.00 to 6.00
Collectors Edition, Vol. 16, Redhead, 1980 .... 10.00
Collectors Edition, Vol. 17, Wildlife Portraits, Series Of 3, Each, 1981 .... .3.00 to 5.00
Collectors Edition, Vol. 18, Wildlife, Series Of 3, Each, 1982 .... .2.00 to 3.00
Collectors Edition, Vol. 19, Wildlife, Series Of 3, Each, 1983 .... .6.00 to 9.00
Collectors Edition, Vol. 20, First Duck Stamp Series, 1984 .... .2.00 to 4.00
Collectors Edition, Vol. 21, Second Duck Stamp Series, 1985 .... .2.00 to 4.00
Collectors Edition, Vol. 22, Third Duck Stamp Series, 1986 .... .2.00 to 4.00
Colorado, State, 1959 .... 26.00
Convention, No. 1, Denver, 1971 .... 5.50
Convention, No. 2, Anaheim, June 19-25, 1972 .... 5.00
Convention, No. 3, Detroit, 1973 .... 25.00
Convention, No. 4, Lancaster, 1974 .... .10.00 to 14.50
Convention, No. 5, Sacramento, 1975 .... 6.00
Convention, No. 6, Hartford, 1976 .... .1.50 to 5.00

Convention, No. 7, Louisville, 1977 .... 5.00
Convention, No. 8, Chicago, 1978 .... 12.00
Convention, No. 9, Houston, Tiffany On Rocket, 1979 .... 38.00
Convention, No. 10, Norfolk, Ship & Wheel, 1980 .... 16.00
Convention, No. 11, Las Vegas, Dealer Fox, 1981 .... 20.00
Convention, No. 11, Las Vegas, Showgirl, Blond, 1981 .... 20.00
Convention, No. 11, Las Vegas, Showgirl, Brunette, 1981 .... 41.00
Convention, No. 12, New Orleans, King Rex, 1982 ....5.00 to 20.00
Convention, No. 13, St. Louis, 1983 .... 50.00
Convention, No. 14, Mermaid, Blond, 1984 .... 5.50
Convention, No. 15, Las Vegas, Roullette Wheel, 1985 ....6.25 to 20.00
Convention, No. 16, Boston, 1986 ....20.00 to 35.00
Convention, No. 17, Kentucky, 1987 .... 55.00
Convention, No. 18, Portland, Portland Rose, Yellow, 1988 ....5.00 to 10.00
Convention, No. 19, Kansas City, 1989 .... 20.00
Convention, No. 20, Florida, 1990 .... 5.00
Convention, No. 21, Reno, Sheriff With Guns, Dice & Money, 1991 .... 6.50
Convention, No. 22, St. Louis, 1992 .... 20.00
Convention, No. 23, Charlotte, John Paul Jones, Box, 1993 .... 11.00
Convention, No. 24, Dallas, 1994 .... 24.00
Convention, No. 25, Louisville, Steamboat, 1995 .... 25.00
Convention, No. 26, Seattle, 1996 .... 30.00
Convention, No. 27, Oconomowoc, 1997 .... 30.00
Convention, No. 28, Buffalo, 1998 .... 30.00
Crappie, 1979 ....5.00 to 22.00
Crystal Glass Series, Genie, Olive Green, Milk Glass Stopper, 1964 .... 18.00
Crystal Glass Series, Genie, Red, 1980 .... 11.00
Crystal Glass Series, Genie, Smoky Green, 1964 ....22.00 to 39.00
Crystal Glass Series, Genie, Teal Blue, 1973 .... 10.00
Crystal Glass Series, Pressed Glass, Amber, 1966-74 .... 4.00
Crystal Glass Series, Pressed Glass, Blue, 1966-74 .... 5.00
Crystal Glass Series, Pressed Glass, Brown, 1966-74 .... 10.00
D-Day, 1984 .... 5.45
Delaware, State, 1972 .... 6.00
Delco Battery, 1978 ....15.00 to 35.00
Dodge Challenger Hotrod, 1970 Model, Green, Box, 1992 .... 86.00
Dodge Challenger Hotrod, 1970 Model, Yellow, 1992 .... 50.00
Doe, 1963 .... 30.00
Duck, Mallard, 1957 .... 6.00
Ducks & Geese, Etched, Pyrex, 1955 .... 10.00
Ducks Unlimited, American Widgeons, Box, 1983 ....20.00 to 48.00
Ducks Unlimited, Black Duck Family, 1989 ....35.00 to 43.00
Ducks Unlimited, Blue-Winged Teal, 1980 ....*Illus* 19.00
Ducks Unlimited, Bluebill, 1987 ....10.00 to 15.50

Beam, Ducks Unlimited,
Blue-Winged Teal, 1980

Beam, Ducks Unlimited,
Mallard, 1974

Beam, Ducks Unlimited,
Redhead, 1986

Ducks Unlimited, Canada Goose, 1990 .... 41.00
Ducks Unlimited, Canvasback Drake, 1979 ....5.00 to 20.00
Ducks Unlimited, Cinnamon Teal, 1993 .... 25.00
Ducks Unlimited, Gadwall Family, Box, 1988 .... 20.00
Ducks Unlimited, Green-Winged Teal, 1981 ....10.00 to 38.00
Ducks Unlimited, Harlequin Ducks, 1995 .... 50.00
Ducks Unlimited, Harlequin Ducks, Box, 1995 .... 109.00
Ducks Unlimited, Mallard Head, 1978 .... 9.00
Ducks Unlimited, Mallard, 1974 ....*Illus* 10.00
Ducks Unlimited, Mallard, 1984 ....13.00 to 19.00
Ducks Unlimited, Mallard, Hen, 40th Anniversary, 1977 ....16.00 to 20.00
Ducks Unlimited, Pintail, Pair, 1985 ....10.00 to 19.00
Ducks Unlimited, Redhead, 1986 ....*Illus* 35.00
Ducks Unlimited, Ringneck, 1992 .... 20.00
Ducks Unlimited, Tundra Swan, Box, 1991 .... 15.50
Ducks Unlimited, Wood Duck Family, 1982 ....20.00 to 30.00
Ducks Unlimited, Wood Duck, 1975 .... 20.00
Duesenberg, 1934 Model J, Dark Blue, 1981 .... 75.00
Duesenberg, 1934 Model J, Dark Blue, Box, 1981 .... 40.00
Duesenberg, 1934 Model J, Light Blue, 1981 ....11.00 to 31.00
Duesenberg, 1934 Model J, Light Blue, Box, 1981 .... 63.00
Duesenberg, 1935 Convertible, Coupe, Cream, 1983 ....36.00 to 46.00
Duesenberg, Light Blue, 1982 ....11.00 to 12.00
Eagle, 1966 ....6.50 to 8.00
Elks Club, 1968 ....10.00 to 32.00
Elks National Foundation, 1977 ....7.00 to 21.00
Emmett Kelly, Willie The Clown, 1973 ....*Illus* 10.00
Executive, 1955, Royal Porcelain 76.00
Executive, 1956, Royal Gold Round 21.00
Executive, 1957, Royal Del Monte 33.00
Executive, 1958, Gray Cherub 34.00
Executive, 1959, Tavern Scene ....10.00 to 18.50
Executive, 1960, Blue Cherub ....5.50 to 15.00
Executive, 1961, Golden Chalice 15.00
Executive, 1962, Flower Basket ....3.00 to 10.00
Executive, 1963, Royal Rose ....15.50 to 25.00
Executive, 1964, Royal Gold Diamond 15.00
Executive, 1965, Marbled Fantasy 28.00
Executive, 1966, Majestic, Box 11.00
Executive, 1967, Prestige ....5.50 to 27.00
Executive, 1968, Presidential ....*Illus* 6.00
Executive, 1968, Presidential, Box 10.00
Executive, 1969, Sovereign, Box ....14.00 to 20.00
Executive, 1970, Charisma ....6.50 to 18.50
Executive, 1971, Fantasia, Box 3.00
Executive, 1972, Regency, Box ....5.00 to 12.50

Beam, Emmett Kelly, Willie The Clown, 1973

Beam, Executive, 1968, Presidential

Beam, Executive, 1975, Reflections In Gold

Executive, 1973, Phoenician, Box . . . . .8.00 to 13.00
Executive, 1974, Twin Cherubs 20.00
Executive, 1974, Twin Cherubs, Box 6.75
Executive, 1975, Reflections In Gold . . . .*Illus*   5.00
Executive, 1976, Floro De Oro 10.00
Executive, 1977, Golden Jubilee 10.00
Executive, 1978, Yellow Rose Of Texas 1.00
Executive, 1979, Vase, Mother Of Pearl, Box 10.00
Executive, 1980, Titian 36.00
Executive, 1980, Titian, Box 10.00
Executive, 1981, Cobalt Deluxe, Royal Filagree 6.00
Executive, 1982, Antique Pitcher 20.00
Executive, 1983, Bell, Embossed Partridge, Musical, 29th Executive 35.00
Executive, 1984, Bell, Noel, Carolers, 30th Executive, District 11, Blue, Box . . . . . . .10.00 to 15.00
Executive, 1985, Italian Marble Urn 20.00
Executive, 1986, Executive Blue Font 25.00
Executive, 1987, Twin Doves 15.00
Expo '74, World's Fair, Spokane, 1974 . . . .   10.00
Father's Day Card, 1988 . . . .   10.00
Fighting Bull, 1981 . . . .   10.00
Fiji Islands, 1971 . . . .   10.00
Fire Chief Helmet, Black, 1990 . . . .   34.00
Fire Chief Helmet, Black, Box, 1990 . . . .   35.00
Fire Chief Helmet, White, 1991 . . . .*Illus*   43.00
Fire Chief Helmet, White, Box, 1991 . . . .   61.00
Fire Engine, 1867 Model, Mississippi, 1978 . . . . .20.00 to 45.00
Fire Engine, Ford, 1930 Model A, 1983 . . . .*Illus*   54.00
Fire Engine, Ford, 1930 Model A, Box, 1983 . . . .   79.00
Fire Pumper, Ford, 1934 Model, 1988 . . . .   4.00
Fire Truck, Mack Bulldog, 1917 Model, 1982 . . . . .22.00 to 31.00
Florida Shell, 1968 . . . . .1.00 to 19.00
Football Hall Of Fame, 1972 . . . . .5.00 to 16.50
Ford, 1903 Model A, Black, 1978 . . . . .13.50 to 20.00
Ford, 1903 Model A, Red, 1978 . . . . .15.50 to 25.00
Ford, 1913 Model T, Black, 1974 . . . . .10.00 to 21.00
Ford, 1913 Model T, Green, 1974 . . . . .10.00 to 24.00
Ford, 1928 Model A, 1980 . . . . .15.50 to 30.00
Ford, 1928 Model A, Green, Box, 1980 . . . . .21.00 to 34.00
Ford, 1930 Model A, Black, 1978 . . . .   13.50
Ford, Delivery Wagon, International, Woodie, 1929 Model, Green, 1984 . . . .   42.00
Ford, Delivery Wagon, International, Woodie, 1929 Model, Tan, 1984 . . . .   35.00
Ford, Fire Chief, 1928 Model A, Box, 1981 . . . . .43.00 to 50.00
Ford, Fire Chief, 1934 Model, 1988 . . . .   100.00
Ford, Mustang, 1964 Model, Red, 1986 . . . .   40.00
Ford, Mustang, 1964 Model, White, 1986 . . . . .31.00 to 50.00
Ford, Mustang, 1964 Model, White, Box, 1986 . . . .   42.00
Ford, Phaeton, 1929 Model, Box, 1982 . . . .   26.00
Ford, Pickup Truck, 1928 Model A, Palumbo, 1984 . . . .   500.00
Ford, Pickup Truck, 1928 Model A, Parkwood Supply, 1984 . . . .   120.00
Ford, Pickup Truck, 1928 Model A, Western/Davis, 1984 . . . .   600.00
Ford, Pickup Truck, 1935 Model, Clermont Supply, Box, 1988 . . . . .29.00 to 37.00
Ford, Police Car, 1929 Model A, Blue, 1982 . . . . .10.00 to 45.00
Ford, Police Car, 1929 Model A, Blue, Box, 1982 . . . .   61.00
Ford, Police Car, 1934 Model, Black & White, 1989 . . . . .77.00 to 79.00
Ford, Police Tow Truck, 1935 Model, 1988 . . . .   10.00
Ford, Police Tow Truck, 1935 Model, Box, 1988 . . . .   39.00
Ford, Roadster, 1934 Model, Cream, Box, 1990 . . . .   77.00
Ford, Salesman's Award, 1928 Model, Black, Box, 1981 . . . .   50.00
Ford, Thunderbird, 1956 Model, Blue, Box, 1986 . . . .   76.00
Ford, Thunderbird, 1956 Model, Yellow, 1986 . . . .   44.00
Ford, Woodie Delivery Wagon, 1929 Model A, 1983 . . . .   40.00
Foremost, Black & Gold, 1956 . . . .   90.00
Foremost, Gray & Gold, 1956 . . . .   90.00

Beam, Giant
Panda, 1980

Beam, Fire Chief Helmet,
White, 1991

Beam, Fire Engine, Ford,
1930 Model A, 1983

Foremost, Pink Speckled Beauty, 1956	96.00
Fox, Blue Coat, 1967	15.00
Fox, Gold Coat, 1969	10.00
Fox, Gold Coat, Queen Mary, 1969	7.00
Fox, Green Coat, Trophy Series, 1965-67	15.50 to 30.00
Fox, On Dolphin, 1980	35.00
Fox, Red Coat, 1973	5.00
Fox, Renee, 1974	9.00 to 15.00
Fox, Runner, 1974	2.00
Fox, Surfer, 1975	60.00
Fox, Uncle Sam, 1971	1.00 to 5.00
Fox, White Coat, 1969	12.50
Franklin Mint, 1970	10.00 to 12.00
Galah Bird, Australia, 1979	7.00 to 22.00
General Stark, 1972	1.00
George Washington, 1976	6.00
Giant Panda, 1980	*Illus* 51.00
Glad Festival, Momence, Illinois, 1974	10.00
Glen Campbell, 1976	5.00 to 10.00
Golden Gate Casino, 1969	43.00
Golf Cart, 1986	*Illus* 23.00
Goose, Blue, 1979	10.00
Great Dane, 1976	4.00 to 8.00
Grecian, 1961	20.00
Green China Jug, Pussy Willow, 1965	2.00 to 4.25
Hannah Dustin, 1973	26.00 to 46.00
Harolds Club, Covered Wagon, 1969	3.00 to 9.00
Harolds Club, Covered Wagon, 1974	35.00
Harolds Club, Man In Barrel, No. 1, 1957	128.00
Harolds Club, Man In Barrel, No. 2, 1958	75.00
Harolds Club, Pinwheel, 1965	30.00
Harolds Club, Slot Machine, Blue, 1967	20.00 to 58.00
Harolds Club, Slot Machine, Gray, 1968	5.00 to 15.00
Harolds Club, VIP, 1967	20.00
Harolds Club, VIP, 1968	15.00 to 41.00
Harolds Club, VIP, 1969	50.00
Harolds Club, VIP, 1970	25.00
Harolds Club, VIP, 1971	25.00
Harolds Club, VIP, 1972	10.00
Harolds Club, VIP, 1973	6.00 to 8.00
Harolds Club, VIP, 1974	10.00
Harolds Club, VIP, 1975	6.00
Harolds Club, VIP, 1976	10.00
Harolds Club, VIP, 1977	20.00
Harolds Club, VIP, 1978	10.00
Harolds Club, VIP, 1979	10.00
Harolds Club, VIP, 1980	20.00

Harolds Club, VIP, 1981 .... 45.00
Harolds Club, VIP, 1982 .... 25.00
Harrah's Club, Nevada, Gray, 1963 .... 103.00
Hawaii, State, 1959 ....15.50 to 22.00
Hawaiian Open, 7th, Pineapple, 1972 .... 9.00
Hawaiian Open, 8th, Golf Ball, 1973 .... 10.50
Hawaiian Open, 9th, Tiki God, 1974 .... 22.00
Hawaiian Open, 10th, Menehune, 1974 .... 39.00
Hawaiian Open, 11th, Outrigger, 1975 .... 10.00
Hemisfair, San Antonio, Tower Of Americas, 1968 .... 10.00
Home Builders, 1978 .... 5.00
Horse, Appaloosa, 1974 ....15.00 to 44.00
Horse, Black, 1962 ....10.50 to 21.00
Horse, Brown, 1962 ....9.00 to 15.50
Hula Bowl, 1975 .... 9.00
Illinois, State, 1968 .... 4.00
Indianapolis Sesquicentennial, 1971 .... 2.25
Indianapolis Speed Race, 1970 .... 21.00
International Petroleum Exposition, Tulsa, 1971 ....5.00 to 21.00
Jackelope, 1971 ....5.00 to 12.00
Jewel Tea, 50th Anniversary, 1974 ....20.00 to 51.00
Kentucky, Black Horse Head Stopper, State, 1967 ....10.00 to 15.50
Kentucky Colonel, 1970 .... 10.00
Key West, Florida, 1972 ....9.00 to 13.00
King Kamehameha, 1972 ....*Illus*   10.00
King Kong, 1976 .... 5.00
Kiwi Bird, 1974 .... 22.00
Koala Bear, Gray, 1973 ....3.00 to 10.00
Laramie, Centennial Jubilee 1868-1968, 1968 .... 10.50
Largemouth Bass, 1973 ....5.00 to 25.00
Las Vegas, 1969 ....5.00 to 20.00
Liberty Eagle, Attucks, Hamilton, Hancock Coins, Regal China, 1970 .... 12.00
Louisville Downs, 1978 .... 5.00
Maine, State, 1970 .... 25.00
Marine Corps, Devil Dog, 1979 ....10.00 to 31.00
Martha Washington, 1975 .... 2.00
McCoy, 1973 .... 20.00
Mercedes Benz, 1974 Model, Blue, 1987 .... 27.00
Mercedes Benz, 1974 Model, Blue, Box, 1987 .... 20.00
Mercedes Benz, 1974 Model, Green, 1987 .... 25.00
Mercedes Benz, 1974 Model, White, 1986 ....10.00 to 16.00
Michigan, State, 1972 ....*Illus*   6.25
Mint 400, 3rd, Metal Stopper, 1970 .... 3.00
Mint 400, 4th, 1971 ....21.00 to 63.00
Mint 400, 5th, 1972 .... 10.00
Mint 400, 6th, 1973 .... 10.00
Mint 400, 7th, 1975 ....9.50 to 31.00
Mint 400, 8th, 1976 .... 12.00

Beam, Golf Cart, 1986

Beam, King
Kamehameha,
1972

Beam, Michigan,
State, 1972

Monterey Bay Club, 1977 .... 15.25
Mr. Goodwrench, 1978 .... 19.00
Muskie, 1971 ....9.50 to 16.00
Nebraska, State, 1967 .... 1.00
New Hampshire, State, Regal China, 1968, 13 1/2 x 5 1/2 In. 15.00
New Mexico, Bicentennial, 1976 .... 5.00
New Mexico, Taos Pueblo, 1967 .... 9.00
New Mexico, Wedding Vase, 1972 .... 9.00
New York World's Fair, 1964 .... 10.00
Northern Pike, 1978 ....10.00 to 23.00
Ohio, State, 1966 ....1.00 to 5.00
Ohio State Fair, 1973 .... 5.50
Oldsmobile, 1904 Model, 1972 ....10.00 to 30.00
Olsonite Race Car, No. 48, 1975 ....10.00 to 47.00
Olsonite Race Car, No. 48, Box, 1975 ....33.00 to 65.00
Order Of Blue Goose, Green Lakes Wisc., 1971 ....5.00 to 6.00
Oregon, State, Centennial, Beaver, Trees, River, Fisherman, 1959 .... 25.00
Paddy Wagon, 1929 Model A, 1983 .... 10.00
Paul Bunyan, 1970 .... 4.00
Pearl Harbor, Regal China, 1972, 11 1/2 x 7 In. 45.00
Pennsylvania, State, 1967 ....2.25 to 5.00
Permian Basin Oil Show, 1972 ....5.50 to 10.50
PGA, 53rd Golf Tournament, 1971 ....*Illus*   20.00
Pheasant, 1961 .... 30.00
Phi Sigma Kappa, Ohio University, 1973 .... 36.00
Political, Donkey, 1956, Ashtray 10.00
Political, Donkey, 1960, Campaigner 8.00
Political, Donkey, 1964, Boxer 10.00
Political, Donkey, 1968, Clown 25.00
Political, Donkey, 1972, Football ....5.00 to 10.25
Political, Donkey, 1976, Drum 6.00
Political, Donkey, 1980, Superman 10.00
Political, Donkey, Elephant, Regal China, 1972, 8 x 10 x 4 In., Pair 20.00
Political, Elephant, 1956, Ashtray 7.00
Political, Elephant, 1964, Boxer ....5.00 to 15.00
Political, Elephant, 1968, Clown ....12.00 to 15.00
Political, Elephant, 1972, Football, San Diego 5.00
Political, Elephant, 1976, Football ....10.25 to 20.00
Political, Elephant, 1980, Superman 49.00
Ponderosa, 1969 ....5.00 to 10.00
Pony Express, 1968 ....3.50 to 6.50
Poodle, Gray, 1970 .... 10.00
Poodle, White, 1970 .... 8.00
Poulan Chain Saw, 1979 ....10.00 to 25.00
Preakness, 100th Anniversary, Pimlico, 1970 .... 5.00
Preakness, 100th Race, Pimlico, 1975 ....3.00 to 7.00
Rainbow Trout, 1975 ....7.00 to 20.00
Redwood Empire, 1967 .... 5.50
Reno, 100 Years, 1968 .... 15.00
Robin, 1969 .... 5.00
Rocky Marciano, 1973 ....21.00 to 51.00
Rocky Mountain Club, Rush To The Rockies, 1970 ....*Illus*   1.00
Royal Emperor, 1958 .... 4.50
Royal Opal, 1957 .... 12.50
Ruidoso Downs, Pointed Ears, 1968 ....5.00 to 8.00
Sahara Invitational, 1971 .... 25.00
Sailfish, 1957 ....6.50 to 16.00
San Francisco Cable Car, 1983 ....17.50 to 20.00
Sand & Gravel Dump Truck, Box, 1992 .... 39.00
Saturday Evening Post, Benjamin Franklin, 1975 ....1.00 to 10.00
Saturday Evening Post, Elect Casey, 1975 .... 5.00
Saturday Evening Post, Game Called Because Of Rain, 1975 .... 8.75
Saturday Evening Post, Homecoming GI, 1975 .... 5.00

Beam, PGA, 53rd Golf
Tournament, 1971

Beam, Rocky Mountain Club,
Rush To The Rockies, 1970

Beam, South Dakota,
Mt. Rushmore, 1969

Saturday Evening Post, Pioneers, 1975	6.00
Saturday Evening Post, Ye Pipe & Bowl, 1975	5.00
Screech Owl, Gray, 1979	4.00 to 7.50
Screech Owl, Red, 1979	40.00
Seafair, 1972	16.00
Seattle World's Fair, 1962	6.50 to 29.00
Short Timer, Helmet & Boots, 1975	10.00 to 30.00
Shriners, El Kahir Pyramid, 1975	16.50
Shriners, Moila, Sword, 1972	10.50
Shriners, Western Shrine Association, 1980	8.00 to 11.00
Smith's North Shore Club, Box, 1972	15.50
Snow Goose, 1979	5.50 to 8.00
South Carolina, State, 1970	10.00
South Dakota, Mt. Rushmore, 1969	*Illus* 20.00
St. Bernard, 1979	10.00 to 17.00
St. Louis Arch, 1964	7.00 to 13.00
Statue Of Liberty, 1975	3.00
Stone Mountain, 1974	10.00
Sturgeon, 1980	58.00
Stutz Bearcat, 1914 Model, Yellow, 1977	9.00 to 26.00
Submarine Redfin, 1970	10.00 to 15.00
Sunburst Crystal, Amber, 1974	7.00
Superdome, Louisiana, 1975	20.00
Swagman, Australian Hobo, 2nd National Convention, 1979	15.50
Telephone, 1897 Model, 1978	10.00
Telephone, 1904 Model, 100-Digit Dial, 1983	22.00 to 70.00
Telephone, 1907 Model, Wall, 1975	10.00 to 25.00
Telephone, 1919 Dial, 1980	*Illus* 10.00
Telephone, French Cradle, 1979	2.00 to 10.00
Telephone, Pay Phone, 1981	10.00 to 26.00
Texas Rabbit, 1971	2.00 to 10.00
Thomas Flyer, Blue, Box, 1976	22.00
Thomas Flyer, White, 1976	12.50 to 40.00
Tiffany Poodle, 1973	11.00
Tobacco Festival, 1973	5.00
Tombstone, Town Too Tough To Die, 1970	8.00 to 9.00
Train, Boxcar, Yellow, Box, 1983	42.00 to 71.00
Train, Casey Jones Tank Car, 1990	49.00
Train, General Caboose, Gray, 1988	66.00
Train, General Flat Car, Box, 1988	64.00
Train, Grant Baggage Car, Box, 1981	18.00 to 25.00
Train, Grant Caboose, 1980	20.00 to 61.00
Train, Grant Caboose, Box, 1980	10.00 to 40.00
Train, Grant Coal Tender, 1980	36.00 to 51.00

Beam, Telephone, 1919 Dial, 1980

Beam, Zimmerman Liquors, 50th Anniversary, 1983

Beam, Volkswagen, Blue, 1973

Train, Grant Coal Tender, Box, 1980	62.00
Train, Grant Dining Car, Box, 1982	31.00 to 70.00
Train, Grant Locomotive, 1872, 1979	22.00 to 45.00
Train, Grant Observation Car, 1985	42.00
Train, Grant Observation Car, Box, 1985	66.00 to 81.00
Train, Grant Passenger Car, 1981	23.00 to 54.00
Train, Grant Passenger Car, Box, 1981	26.00 to 31.00
Train, Turner Boxcar, Box, 1983	31.00
Train, Turner Locomotive, 1982	18.00 to 26.00
Train, Turner Locomotive, Box, 1982	18.50 to 36.00
Train, Turner Log Car, 1984	81.00
Train, Turner Log Car, Box, 1984	51.00
Train, Turner Lumber Car, Box, 1986	35.00 to 48.00
Train, Turner Tank Car, 1983	16.00 to 20.00
Train, Turner Tank Car, Box, 1983	16.00 to 35.00
Train, Turner Wood Tender, Box, 1988	153.00
TraveLodge, Sleepy Bear, 1972	5.00 to 8.00
Treasure Chest, 1979	10.50
Trout Unlimited, 1977	19.00
Turtle, 1975	39.00
Twin Bridges Club, 1971	10.00
Veterans Of Foreign Wars, 1971	7.50
Viking, 1973	17.00
Volkswagen, Blue, 1973	*Illus* 25.00
Volkswagen, Red, 1973	25.00 to 32.00
Von's 75th Anniversary, 1981	10.60
Walleye Pike, 1977	5.00 to 28.00
Washington, State, 1975	5.00
West Virginia, State, 1963	30.00
WGA, Western Open, 1971	1.00
Wolverine Club, 1975	10.50
Woodpecker, 1969	5.00
Wyoming, State, 1965	45.00
Zimmerman Liquors, 50th Anniversary, 1983	*Illus* 10.00
Zimmerman Liquors, Bell, Dark Blue, 1976	2.00
Zimmerman Liquors, Bell, Light Blue, 1976	2.00
Zimmerman Liquors, Eldorado, Marble Brown, 1978	2.00
Zimmerman Liquors, Eldorado, Marble Green, 1978	2.00
Zimmerman Liquors, Peddler, 1971	10.00

BEER

History says that beer was first made in America in the Roanoke Colony of Virginia in 1587. It is also claimed that the Pilgrims brought some over on the already crowded Mayflower. William Penn started a brewery in 1683. By the time of the Civil War, beer was made and bottled in all parts of the United States. In the early years the beer was poured from kegs or sold in ordinary unmarked black glass bottles. English stoneware bottles were in common use in this country from about 1860 to 1890. Excavations in many inner cities still unearth these sturdy containers. A more or less standard bottle was used by about 1870. It held a quart of liquid and measured about 10 inches high. The early ones were plain and had a cork stopper. Later bottles had embossed lettering on the sides. The lightning stopper was invented in 1875 and many bottles had various types of wire and lever-type seals that were replacements for the corks. In the 1900s Crown corks were used. It wasn't long before plain bottles with paper labels appeared, but cans were soon the containers preferred by many. The standard thick-topped glass beer bottle shape of the 1870s, as well as modern beer bottles, are included in this category. The bottles can be found in clear, brown, aqua, or amber glass. A few cobalt blue, milk glass, or red examples are known. Some bottles have turned slightly amethyst in color from the sun. Picnic is the collector's name for a 64-ounce beer bottle. The Internal Revenue Tax Paid (IRTP) statement was required on labels from 1933 until March 1950. Collectors are often interested in local breweries and books listing the names and addresses of companies have been written. (See Bibliography.) Beer bottle collectors often search for advertising trays, signs, and other *go-withs* collected as *breweriana*. These are listed under Go-Withs at the end of this book.

A. Gettelman Brewing Co., Machine Crown, Private Mold, Wisc., Pt., 9 1/2 In. 5.00
A. Waldron, Stoneware, Cobalt Blue Decoration, 10 3/4 In. 110.00
ABGM Co., Belleville, Ill., Cobalt Blue, Applied Ringed Mouth, 1880-90, 9 3/4 In. 78.00
Acme Brewing Company, Tooled Crown, Private Mold, Embossed, Ga., Pt., 91/2 In. 17.00
Adam Scheidt Brewing Co., Blob Top, Private Mold, Embossed, Pa., Pt., 9 1/4 In. 15.00
Ahrens Bottling Co., Oakland, Ca., Amber, Tooled Lip, Qt. 33.00
Aigeldinger & Butterman Cronk Beer, Scranton, Pa., Aqua, 1/2 Pt. 125.00
Alpen Brau Beer, Columbia Brewing Company, Paper Label, Qt., IRTP . . . . .8.00 to 15.00
American Brewing Ass'n., Machine Crown, Private Mold, Embossed, Texas, 1/2 Pt., 8 In.   27.00
Anchor Brewing, Dobbs Ferry, Anchors, Aqua, Pt. 12.00
Anchor Brewing Co., San Francisco, Special Christmas Ale, 1987 . . . .   10.00
Anderson & Co., Home Brewed Ale, Red Amber, Collared Mouth, Cylindrical, 1860-70 . .   2016.00
Anheuser-Busch, Logo, Eagle, A, Harrisburg Bottling Works, Amber, Crown Top 39.00
Anheuser-Busch Bwg. Ass'n., Baltimore Md. Branch, Eagle, Aqua, Crown Top 29.00
Anheuser-Busch Bwg. Ass'n. F. Agency, Eagle, A Monogram, Qt. 660.00
Arnold Brewing Co., Tooled Crown, Plate Mold, Embossed, Mich., Pt., 9 1/2 In. 5.00
Atlas Brg. Co., Tooled Crown, Plate Mold, Embossed, Ill., Qt., 11 1/2 In. 15.00
Austin Craven Ltd., Manchester, Man In Life Vest, Green, Cork Neck, Embossed 20.00
Barber & Riehe Bottlers, Redding, Cal., Crown Top, Pt.11 1/2 In. 39.00
Bartholomay Brewery, Tooled Crown, Private Mold, Embossed, Md., Pt., 9 1/2 In. 10.00
Bartholomay Brewing Co., Phila. Branch, Fill Or Sell Is Criminal Offense, Aqua, Pt. 35.00
Bartholomay Brewing Co., Rochester, N.Y., Baltimore Branch, Wing Wheel, Amber, Pt. .   35.00
Bay View Brewing Co., Seattle, Wash., Green . . . .   225.00.
Beadleston Woertz Empire Brewing, N.Y., Shield Eagle, Blob Top 12.00
Bellweiser Buffalo Brewing Co., Tooled Crown, Private Mold, Embossed, Pt., 9 1/2 In. . .   15.00
Berkshire Brewing Ass'n., Machine Crown, Private Mold, Embossed, Mass., Pt., 9 1/2 In.   4.00
Berkshire Brewing Association, Pittsfield, Mass., Aqua, Stopper, Pt. 13.00
Birk Bros. Brewing Co., Trophy Beer, Chicago, Ill., Paper Label, IRTP 20.00
Blatz, Machine Crown, Private Mold, Embossed, Wisc., 1/2 Pt., 8 3/4 In. 2.00
Blatz Private Stock Beer, Blatz Brewing Co., Milwaukee, Wisc., Paper Label, IRTP 15.00
Bohemian Bock Beer, Spokane, Wash., IRTP, c.1938 . . . .   30.00
Bohemian Lager Beer, Katz Brothers BB Co., Aqua, Pt. 20.00
Bosch, Lake Linden, Mich., Red Amber, Tooled Lip, 1890-1900, 12 In. 11.00
Boston Premium Lager, Roessle Brewery, Clear, Stopper, Pt. 12.00
Brainerd Brewing, Brainerd, Minn., Crown Top, Embossed 40.00
Buckingham Brand Ale, Bloomer Brewery, Bloomer, Wisc., Paper Label, IRTP 7.00
Buffalo Brewing Co., Amber, Applied Lip, Baltimore Loop Finish, 4-Piece Mold, 1/2 Pt. .   40.00
Buffalo Brewing Co., S.F. Agency, Green, Applied Lip, Pint . . . .*Illus*   300.00
Buffalo Brewing Co., Sacramento, Calif., Aqua, Crown Style Top, Qt. 44.00
Buffalo Brewing Co., Sacramento, Calif., Red, Applied Lip, Qt.   88.00
Bunker Hill Lager, JC Joseph, Charlestown, Mass., Aqua, Stopper, Blob Top, Pt. 75.00
C. Berry, 84 Leverett St., Boston, Not Artificially Radiated, Amethyst, Pt. 40.00
C. Cunningham, Warrington, BC, Green, Embossed, Stopper, England, Early 1900s, 8 In. .   40.00
C.B. Seeley's Son, Bartender Pouring Beer, N.Y., Slant Shoulder, Blob Top, Qt. 120.00
C.D. Postel T.M. S.F. Cal., Sheaf Of Wheat, Applied Lip, c.1884 . . . .   2860.00
California Bottling Works, Sacramento, Amber, 4-Piece Mold, Pre-Prohibition, Qt. 50.00
Camden Lager Beer, Crown Top, Amber, Label 100.00
Canada Malt Beer, Monte Christo Bottling, 543 & 545 10th Ave., N.Y., Amber, Pt. 50.00

Chas Graf Berliner Weiss, Amber, Blob Top, 1/2 Pt. 34.00
Chas Grove, Brown Stout, Green, Double Tapered Collar, Squat, Pontil 145.00
Chas Joly No 9, Philadelphia, Yellow Olive, Blob Top 89.00
Chesapeake Brewing Co., Tooled Crown, Private Mold, Md., Pt., 9 1/2 In. 12.00
Chr. Heurich Brewing Co., Tooled Crown, Private Mold, Embossed, Va., Pt., 9 1/2 In. . . .   15.00
Christian Moerlein Brewing, Old Jug Lager, Krug Beer, Stoneware, Pre-Prohibition, Pt., 9 In.   65.00
Christian Moerlein Brewing, Old Jug Lager, Stoneware, Pre-Prohibition, Qt., 10 1/2 In. 85.00
City Brewing Company, Hops Picture, Titusville, Pa., Aqua, Qt. 20.00
Clausen Flanagan Champagne Beer, Phoenix Bottling Co., N.Y., Label, Pre-Prohibition . .   25.00
Columbia Weiss, St. Louis, Amber, Stopper, Tepee Shape, Pt. 55.00
Consumers Br'g. Co., Tooled Crown, Private Mold, Embossed, Ohio, Pt., 9 1/2 In. 9.00
Cornbrook Brewery, Manchester, Relief Logo, Amber, Early 1900s, 8 1/4 In. 30.00
Crosby & Bradley, 231-243 Nutfield Lane, Manchester, N.Y., Aqua, Stopper, Pt. 8.00
Daeufer's Bock Beer, Daeufer Lieberman Brewery, Allentown, Pa., Paper Label, IRTP 25.00
Dallas Brewery, Malt Wein, Dallas, Tex., Amber, Tooled Lip, 1890-1900, 8 1/4 In. 78.00
Danville Brew. & Ice Co., Baltimore Loop, Plate Mold, S B & G Co, Ill., Pt., 10 In. 22.00
Des Moines Brewing Co., Amber, Porcelain Stopper, Pre-Prohibition, 1/2 Gal. 50.00
Donora Brewing Co., Tooled Crown, Plate Mold, Embossed, Pa., Pt., 9 1/2 In. 12.00
Dubuque Star Beer, Dubuque Star Brewing Company, Dubuque, Ia., Paper Label 1.00
Dubuque Star Premium Beer, Dubuque Star Brewing Company, Dubuque, Ia., Label 1.00
Dukehart & Co., Maryland Brewery, Baltimore, Orange Amber, Squat, Double Collar . . .   39.00
Duluth Brewing & Malting, Moose & Angel 500.00
E. Raab & Co., Ale, L & W Base, Amber, Double Collar Top, Qt. 85.00
E. Wagnet, Maltese Cross, Manchester, N.H., Amber, Blob Top 20.00
Edelweiss, Machine Crown, Private Mold, Embossed, Schoenhofen, Chicago, Pt., 9 1/2 In.   4.00
El Paso Brewery, Tooled Crown, Private Mold, Embossed, 1/2 Pt., 7 1/2 In. 35.00
Eldorado Brewing, Stockton, Calif., Amber, Blob Top, Pre-Prohibition, Pt. 25.00
Elk Brewing Co., Kittanning, Penn., Aqua, Tooled Crown Top, Pt. 18.00
Elk Run Br'g. Co., Tooled Crown, Private Mold, Pa., Pt., 9 3/4 In. 5.00
Empress Brewery Co. Ltd., Manchester, Queen Victoria, Green, Internal Screw 30.00
Enterprise Brewing Co., S.F., Cal., Amber, Pre-Prohibition, 1/2 Pt. 30.00
Erie Br'g. Co., Baltimore Loop, Plate Mold, Embossed, Pa., Pt., 9 1/2 In. 10.00
F. Robinson Unicorn Brewery, Stockport, Unicorn, Rearing, Green, Cork Neck, Embossed   15.00
F.&I. Schaum, Baltimore Glass Works, Forest Green, Applied Lip, Iron Pontil, 7 1/4 In. . . .   2640.00
Falls City Premium Beer, Falls City Brewing Co., Louisville, Ky., Gold, Anniversary . . .   10.00
Falstaff Beer, Falstaff Brewing Corp., Paper Label, IRTP 15.00
Farmer's Brewing Company, Shawano Club Beer, Shawano, Wisc., Paper Label, IRTP . . .   15.00
Finlay's Superior Lager, Aqua, Blob Top, Qt. 18.00
Fondersmith's, Amber, 12-Sided, Applied Sloping Collar, 9 7/8 In. 672.00
Fondersmith's, Amber, 12-Sided, Red Iron Pontil, Applied Sloping Collar, 10 In. 952.00
Fred Bauernschmidt American Brewery, Crown, Private Mold, Embossed, Md., Pt., 9 In.   5.00
Fred K Hollender, 115 & 117 Elm Street, New York, Aqua, 3-Part Mold, Pt. 25.00
Fred York, Somersworth, N.H., Aqua, Pt. 12.00
Fredericksburg Brewing Co., Ventura, Ca., Golden Amber, Tooled Lip 198.00
Frey & Co., San Rafael, Amber, Stopper 55.00
Frontier Bottling, Rous's Point, N.Y., Aqua, Stopper, Pt. 30.00
G. Heileman Brg. Co., LaCrosse, Wis., Old Style Lager, Aqua, Machine Molded 5.00
G.B. Seely's Son, New York, Bartender, Filling Glasses, Bottles, Blob Top, Qt. 29.00
G.H. Hausburg, Blue Island, Ill., Olive Green, Yellow, 1885-1900, 8 3/8 In. 56.00
Gambrinus Bottling Co., San Francisco, Amber, Pt. . . . . .Illus   50.00
Geo. Gunther Jr. Brg. Co., Machine Crown, Private Mold, Embossed, Md., Pt., 9 3/4 In. . . .   5.00
Geo. Norris & Co. City Bottling Works, Detroit, Mich., Slant Shoulder, Blob Top, Qt. . . .   40.00
Geo. Ringler & Co., Brewers, New York, Registered, Embossed, BIMAL, Crown Top 10.00
Geo. W. Hoxsie's Premium, Black Olive Amber, Applied Lip, 1860-70, 7 1/4 In. 202.00
Geo. Weber Trademark, Star, Weiss, Albany, Amber, Lightning Closure, c.1900, 7 3/8 In.   34.00
George Bohlen, Excelsior Bottled Lager, 358 & 360 Hart St., Brooklyn, Aqua, Stopper, Pt.   80.00
George Kernwein, Washington, D.C., Yellow Cream, Glaze, Stoneware, 1855-75, 7 5/8 In.   145.00
George Weber's Weiss, Albany, N.Y., Amber, Squat, Stopper, Pt.   85.00
German Brewing Co., Cumberland, Md., Embossed Indian Queen, Amber, Crown Top . . .   14.00
Globe, San Francisco, Amber, Barrel Shape, Handle, IRTP, 1933-38, 1/2 Gal. 60.00
Goetz Country Club, Wooden Arrow Through Bottle, Novelty, 9 1/4 In. 35.00
Goetz Country Club Pilsener Beer, M.K. Goetz Brewing Co., St. Joseph, Mo., Label, IRTP   3.00
Gold Edge Bottling Works, J.F. Deininger, Vallejo, Amber, Tooled Lip, Qt. 33.00

Beer, Buffalo Brewing Co., S.F. Agency, Green, Applied Lip, Pint

Beer, Gambrinus Bottling Co., San Francisco, Amber, Pint

Beer, Union Brewing & Malting Co., S.F., Cal., Amber, Stopper, Pint

Golden Gate Bottling Works, Bear Drinking Beer, Stopper, 1/2 Pt. 121.00
Gowdy's Medicated Beer, Qt. 24.00
Grace Bros. Brewing Co., Santa Rosa, Calif., Amber, Blob Top, Applied Lip, 1/2 Pt. 25.00
Grace Bros. Brewing Co., Santa Rosa, Calif., Amber, Stopper 55.00
Grand Prize Lager Beer, Gulf Brewing Company, Houston, Texas, Paper Label, IRTP . . . 25.00
Green & Clark, Stoneware, Paneled, Cobalt Blue Top Ring, 10 In. 110.00
Groveton Bottling Works, Groveton, N.H., Aqua, Pt. 22.00
Guinness, Bi-Centenary, Souvenir, 3 Paper Labels, 1959, 2/5 Oz., 3 1/2 In. 16.00
H. Sproatt, Cobalt Blue, Fire Polished Pontil, Applied Lip, 1850-60, 10 In. 400.00
Haley's California, Yellow Amber, Applied Lip, Closure Wire, 10 3/4 In. 224.00
Hamm's Preferred Stock Beer, Theo. Hamm Brewing Co., St. Paul, Label, IRTP . . . .8.00 to 20.00
Henry Rusch, Rye Neck N.Y., Aqua, Squat, 1/2 Pt. 18.00
Hinckel Brewing Co., Albany, Boston, Manchester, Amber, BIMAL, Crown Top . . . .10.00 to 16.00
Hoster, Col., O., Embossed, Amber, Blob Top 16.00
Hoster's Wiener Beer, Baltimore Loop, Private Mold, Embossed, Ohio, Pt., 9 3/4 In. 15.00
Houston Ice & Brewing Co., Tooled Crown, Private Mold, 1/2 Pt., 7 3/4 In. 22.00
Hubner Toledo Brewing Co., Machine Crown, Private Mold, Embossed, Ohio, Pt., 9 In. . . 5.00
Huntington Brewing Co., Tooled Crown, Plate Mold, Embossed, Indiana, Pt., 9 3/4 In. . . 15.00
Independent Milwaukee Brewery, Tooled Crown, Private Mold, Pt., 9 In. 10.00
Indianapolis Brewing Co., Tooled Crown, Private Mold, Embossed, 1/2 Pt., 7 1/4 In. 9.00
Isengart Brewing Co., Baltimore Loop, Plate Mold, Embossed, N.Y., Pt., 9 1/4 In. 15.00
J. F. Wiessner & Sons Brewing Co., Machine Crown, Private Mold, Embossed, Pt., 9 3/4 In. 5.00
J. Gahm, Boston, Jos. Schlitz Milwaukee Lager, Golden Yellow, Porcelain Stopper, 10 In. . 66.00
J. Straubmiller's Brewery, York & Adams Street, Philada, Aqua, Stopper, Squat, 1/2 Pt. . . 76.00
J. Walker Brewing Co., Cincinnati, O., Qt. 18.00
J.A. Lomax, Ale, 14 & 16 Charles Place, Chicago, Amber, Qt. 98.00
J.H. Wright, Keene, N.H., Aqua, Stopper, Pt. 14.00
James Reedy Brewer, Blob Top, Tall 8.00
John Cullity, Manchester, N.H., Clear, Lady's Leg Shape, Pt. 8.00
John Eichler Brewing Co., New York, Registered, Embossed, Aqua, Blob Top 10.00
John Eichler Extra Beer, John Eichler Brewing Company, N.Y., Label, Pre-Prohibition . . 25.00
John Heldt, Long Branch, N.J., Green, Crown Top 19.00
John Lyon, Manchester, Fluted Neck, Dark Green, Early 1900s, 9 1/4 In. 30.00
John Rainvelle, Suncook, N.H., Clear, Pt. 10.00
John Stanton Brewing Co., Troy, N.Y., Emerald Green, Porcelain Stopper, Pt. 85.00
John Stanton Brewing Co., Yellow Green, Tooled Lip, 9 1/2 In. 179.00
Jung Br'g. Co., Machine Crown, Private Mold, Embossed, Wisc., Pt., 9 1/4 In. 10.00
Keller Candy Company Distributors, Celery Beer, Oakland, Amber, Tooled Lip, Qt. 88.00
L. House Weiss, Syracuse, Amber, Squat, Blob Top, 1/2 Pt. 65.00
Labor Brewing Co., Tooled Crown, Private Mold, Embossed, Pa., Pt., 10 In. 12.00
Latrobe Brewing Company, Rolling Rock, ACL 95.00
Leisy Brewing Co., Tooled Crown, Plate Mold, Embossed, Ill., Pt., 9 1/2 In. 15.00
Leisy Brewing Co., Tooled Crown, Plate Mold, Ill., Qt., 11 1/2 In. 20.00
Los Angeles Brew. Co., Blob Top, Plate Mold, Embossed, Qt., 11 1/4 In. 22.00
Lucky Lager, Cap, 1936, Qt. 12.00
M. Richardson, 12-Sided, Applied Lip, 1850-60 . . . . 3850.00
Magnus Brewing Co., Tooled Crown, Plate Mold, S B & G Co, Embossed, Iowa, Qt., 11 In. 40.00

Maryland Brewing Co., Tooled Crown, Private Mold, Embossed, Pt., 9 In. 6.00
Michael Valaro, Silver Lake Park, White Plains, N.Y., Aqua, Pt. 32.00
Mills & O'Brian, Waverly, N.Y., Amber Yellow, Blob Top, Lightning Closure, c.1885, 11 In. 67.00
Milwaukee Waukesha Brew. Co., Tooled Crown, Private Mold, Pt., 9 1/4 In. 9.00
Minneapolis Brewing Co., Grain Belt Beer, Minneapolis, Minn., Paper Label, IRTP 15.00
Moerlein-Gerst Brewing Co., Old Jug Lager, Stoneware, Pre-Prohibition, Pt., 8 3/4 In. ... 145.00
National Bottling Works, Fulton St., Amber 44.00
National Lager Beer, HR, Stockton, Cal., Amber, Blob Top, Applied Lip, 4-Piece Mold .. 35.00
North Pacific Brewery, Tooled Crown, Private Mold, Embossed, Ore., 1/2 Pt., 8 In. 35.00
North Star Bottling Works, S.F. Cal., Yellow Amber, Tooled Lip 33.00
Obermeyer & Liebmann's Bot'g. Dept., New York City, Sun, Aqua, Porcelain Stopper, Pt. 35.00
Oertel's Special Cream Ale, 12 Oz. 25.00
P. Connor Weiss, PC Philada, Aqua, 1/2 Pt. 17.00
P. Ebner Bottler, Wil., Del., Aqua, Stopper, Pt. 14.00
P. Stumpf & Co., This Bottle Is Never Sold, Golden Yellow Amber, Applied Lip, 8 1/4 In. 258.00
P.E. Cumaer Trademark, Port Jervis, N.Y., Blob Top, Aqua, Qt. 19.00
Pabst Brewing Company, Pabst Blue Ribbon Beer, Peoria Heights, Il., Paper Label, IRTP 10.00
Peerless Beer, Gnome, 12 Oz., 9 5/8 In. 14.99
Perkiomen Valley Brewery, Green Lane, Pa., Aqua, Blob Top, 1/2 Pt. 36.00
Peter Stumpf, Orange Amber, Blob Style Lightening Closure, 1893-97, 8 3/4 In., Pt. 187.00
Phillip Best Brewing Co., Milwaukee Lager, Olive Amber, Tooled Lip, 9/3/4 In. 67.00
Phipps Brewers, Northampton, Moss Green, Screw Cap, Early 1900s, 9 In. 30.00
Pittsburg Brewing Co., Honey Amber, Blob Top, Applied Lip, Baltimore Loop Finish, Pt. 45.00
Pittsburgh Brewing Co., Iron City Beer, Pittsburgh, 100 Year Anniversary, Label, IRTP .. 20.00
Potosi Brewing Co., Potosi Export Beer, Potosi, Wisc., Paper Label, IRTP 10.00
Premier-Pabst Corp., Pabst Old Tankard Ale, Milwaukee, Peoria Heights, Label, IRTP .. 50.00
Prospect Brewing Co., Philadelphia, Amber, Blob Top, Bent Neck, 1/2 Pt. 20.00
R.G. & Old Bristol Porter Co., Deep Olive Amber, Clover Leaf Pontil, England, 10 In. .. 650.00
R.H. Inman XI, Huddersfield, Aqua, Cobalt Blue Lip, 8 In. 69.00
R.H. Ripperger, Hackensack, N.H., Red Amber, Blob Top, Lightning, Qt., 11 In. 45.00
R.W. & S. White Ltd., Screw Top, Riley's Patent W, Dark Green, 9 x 2 1/2 In. 30.00
Rainier, Seattle Brewing & Malting Company, Amber, Blob Top, Applied Lip, 1/2 Pt. 45.00
Rainier, Seattle Brewing & Malting Company, Amber, Tooled Crown, 1/2 Pt. 20.00
Rainier, Seattle Brewing & Malting Company, Clear, Blob Top, 1/2 Pt. 25.00
Raspiller Brewing Co., Berkley, Amber, Embossed 55.00
Red Top Beer, Ferd. Westheimer & Sons, Cincinnati, Ohio, St. Joseph, Mo., 4 1/4 In. 83.00
Red Top Brewing Company, Red Top Ale, Cincinnati, Ohio, Paper Label, IRTP 20.00
Rich Pennistan, 439 Chestnut St., Philada, Amber, Double Collar Top, Blob Top, 1/2 Pt. . 26.00
Richter Brewing Co., Escannabe, Mich., Amber, Tooled Lip, Pt. 12.00
Ridley Cutter & Firth Manor Brewery, Stout, Stoneware, Scotland, c.1910, 8 1/4 In. 22.00
Robet H. Glaupner Brewer, Harrisburg, Pa., Amber, Lady's Leg, Neck, 6 1/2 In. 25.00
Rochester Brewery, Tooled Crown, Plate Mold, Embossed, Mo., 1/2 Pt., 7 3/4 In. 15.00
S. Fulford Manchester, Green, Blob Top, Lion, Embossed 15.00
S.A. Cottwalt, 70 S. 8th St., Newark, N.J., Embossed, Amber, Blob Top, Wire, Stopper .. 20.00
Salt Lake City Brewing Co., Blob Top, Plate Mold, Embossed, 1/2 Pt., 7 3/4 In. 350.00
Saltzmann Bros. Palace Hill Brewery, Oil City, Pa., Amber, Blob Top 8.50
San Jose Bottling Co., C. Maurer, Amber, Tooled Lip, Stopper, Label 110.00
Scarborough Brewery Co., Green Hamilton Glass, Embossed, Dolphin Fountain, 9 In. ... 348.00
Scheuermann Brewery, Hancock, Mich., Amber, Blob Top, Pt. 15.00
Scheyer Bros., Allentown, Pa., Aqua, Stopper, Squat, 1/2 Pt. 18.00
Schlitz, Jos. Schlitz Brewing Co., Milwaukee, Crown Cap, Paper Label, IRTP, c.1939 ... 16.00
Schlitz, Royal Ruby, Red, Paper Label 35.00
Schmidt's City Club Beer, Jacob Schmidt Brewing Co., St. Paul, Paper Label, IRTP ..6.00 to 10.00
Schmulbach Brewing Co., Orange Amber, Blob Top, Pt., 11 1/2 In. 39.00
Schmulback Brewing Co., Bird Type Monogram, Amber, Tall 5.00
Seattle Brewing & Malting, Green, Stopper, Blob Top, 1/2 Pt. 400.00
Seely & Bro., XXX Porter, New York, Philadelphia, Squat, Applied Top 66.00
Simmonds 1854, Stoneware, Cobalt Blue Highlights 250.00
Skilton Foote & Co., Bunker Hill, Olive Yellow, Applied Sloping Collar, 9 3/8 In. 420.00
South Bethlehem Brewing Co., Supreme Bock Beer, Bethlehem, Pa., Paper Label, IRTP . 25.00
St. Joseph Brewing Co., St. Joseph, Mo., Phoenix Blob Top, Plate Mold, Embossed, Pt. .. 40.00
St. Joseph Brewing Co., St. Joseph, Mo., Phoenix Blob Top, Plate Mold, Embossed, Qt. .. 50.00
Stoll Brewing Co., Eagle On Barrel, Troy, N.Y., Ice Blue, Blob Top, Pre-Prohibition, Pt. .. 40.00

T. Monroe Herkimer, N.Y., Aqua, Stopper, Pt. 16.00
T. Robinson & Sons, Stout, 2-Tone, Black Transfer, 8 In. 81.00
Take & Veile, Lager Beer, Easton, Pa., Blue Green, Sloping Double Collar, 7 1/4 In. 728.00
Terre Haute Brewing Co., Machine Crown, Private Mold, Embossed, Pt., 9 1/2 In. 5.00
Texas Three Rivers Glass Company, Clear, Cap, 1922-37 .... 40.00
Tiffany & Allen Spruce Beer, Washington Market, Cobalt Blue, 7 3/4 In. 1200.00
Toledo Brewing & Malting Co. Bottling Works, Yellow Amber, Stopper, 1881 Slug, Qt. . 65.00
Tuscarawas Valley Brewing, Cover Canal, Ohio, Chocolate Amber, Pt. 44.00
U.S. Bottling Co., John Fauser & Co., S.F., Amber, Blob Top, Pre-Prohibition, Qt. 65.00
Union Brewing & Malting Co., S.F., Cal., Amber, Stopper, Pint ....*Illus* 30.00
United States Brewing Co., Chicago, Ill., Amber, Crown Top, Pt. 8.00
Virginia Brewing Co., Aquamarine, Baltimore Seal Type Closure, 1890-1900, 9 In. 77.00
Virginia Brewing Co., Tooled Crown, Private Mold, Embossed, Pt., 10 In. 5.00
W. Simpson Ltd., Newcastle-On-Tyne, Embossed Logo, Stopper, Moss Green, 9 1/2 In. ... 30.00
W. Wagner, Manchester, N.H., Yellow Green, Stopper Cap, 9 1/4 In. 44.00
Wallabout Pottery Co., Brooklyn, Stoneware, Red Brown, 6 In. 90.00
Walter Bros. Gem Pilsener Beer, Walter Bros. Brewing Co., Menasha, Wisc., Label, IRTP 3.00
Warsaw Brewing Corp., Old Tavern Lager Beer, Warsaw, Ill., Paper Label, IRTP, 7 Oz. .. 20.00
Weber's Weiss, Garnick Bros., Troy N.Y., Squat, Blob Top, 1/2 Pt. 24.00
Weiss, Baltimore Berliner Weiss Beer Brewing Co., Aqua, Squat, Blob Top, 6 3/4 In. 48.00
Weiss Beer, A Koch's Sons, Aqua, Stopper, Squat, 1/2 Pt. 23.00
Weiss Beer, F. Sandkuhler's, Baltimore, Stoneware, Pre-Prohibition, c.1895, 10 Oz., 7 In. 95.00
Weiss Beer, Hohrlacher Bottling Co., Allenstown, Pa., Aqua, 1/2 Pt. 32.00
Weiss Beer, M.J. Ryan, Mahanoy City, Pa., Squat, Blob Top, 1/2 Pt. 90.00
Weiss Beer, Max Stadelhofer, Newark, N.J., Aqua, Squat, 1/2 Pt. 45.00
Weiss Beer, P.J. Cleary, Shenandoah, Pa., Aqua, Squat, Stopper, Pt. 50.00
Weiss Beer, Park Bottling, L. Goodwin Agt., Conn., Amber, Blob Top, c.1875, 1/2 Pt. ... 175.00
Westmacott Manchester, 3 Masted Ship, Embossed 20.00
Whittakers Ardwick, Queen Victoria, Embossed, Green, Internal Screw Neck 30.00
William Penn & Wm. Penn Brewery, South Chester, Clear, Blob Top 59.00
Wun Der Bottling Works, Oakland, Calif., Amber, Pony, Single Collar, Lightning Stopper 39.00
Z.L. Pierce & Co., Stoneware, Blue Blob Top, Cobalt Blue Embossing, 1852 .... 90.00
BENNINGTON, see Figural

--- **BININGER** ---

Bininger and Company of New York City was a family-owned grocery and dry goods store. It was founded by the 1820s and remained in business into the 1880s. The store sold whiskey, wine, and other liquors. After a while they began bottling their products in their own specially designed bottles. The first bottles were ordered from England but it wasn't long before the local glass factories made the Bininger's special figural containers. Barrels, clocks, cannons, jugs, and flasks were made. Colors were usually shades of amber, green, or puce.

A.M. & Co., 19 Broad St., N.Y., Applied Lip, Handle, 8 1/4 In. 468.00
A.M. & Co., 19 Broad St., N.Y., Barrel, Yellow Amber, Double Collar, 1840-60, 9 1/2 In. . 420.00
A.M. & Co., 19 Broad St., N.Y., Golden Amber, Applied Double Collar, Handles, 7 7/8 In. . 364.00
A.M. & Co., 19 Broad St., N.Y., Jug, Golden Amber, Applied Handle, Double Collar, 8 In. . 420.00
A.M. & Co., 19 Broad St., N.Y., Old Kentucky Bourbon, Barrel, Yellow Amber, 9 1/2 In. .. 280.00
A.M. & Co., 19 Broad St., N.Y., Urn, Amber, 8 5/8 In. 125.00
A.M. & Co., 19 Broadway, Old London Dock Gin, Yellow Amber, 10 In. 246.00
A.M. & Co., 338 Broadway, N.Y., Barrel, Amber, Pontil, Double Collar, 8 In. .....258.00 to 336.00
A.M. & Co., 338 Broadway, N.Y., Clock, Amber, Pontil, Applied Double Collar, 6 In. 336.00
A.M. & Co., 338 Broadway, N.Y., Old Kentucky Bourbon, Barrel, Golden Amber, 8 In. 336.00
A.M. & Co., 375 Broadway, N.Y., Pink Topaz Puce, Sloping Collar, 1855-70, 9 7/8 In. 1008.00
A.M. & Co., 375 Broadway, N.Y., Yellow, Amber Tone, Sloping Collar, 9 7/8 In. 728.00
A.M. & Co., 375 Broadway, Yellow, Square, Beveled, Sloping Collar, c.1865, 10 In. 875.00
A.M. & Co., Barrel, Yellow Amber, Applied Double Collar, Pontil, 8 In. 308.00
A.M. & Co., Blue, Green, Applied Flared Mouth, Iron Pontil, 9 3/8 In. 2352.00
A.M. & Co., Cannon, Amber, Sheared Mouth, 12 1/2 In. 1320.00
A.M. & Co., Old Kentucky Bourbon, 1849 Reserve, Barrel, Amber, OP, 8 In. .....336.00 to 350.00
A.M. & Co., Old Kentucky Bourbon, 1849 Reserve, Barrel, Amber, Open Pontil, 9 1/2 In. . 392.00
A.M. & Co., Old Kentucky Bourbon, 1849 Reserve, Barrel, Chocolate Amber, 8 In. 420.00
A.M. & Co., Old Kentucky Bourbon, 1849 Reserve, Barrel, Light Amber, OP, 8 In. 440.00
A.M. & Co., Old Kentucky Bourbon, 1849 Reserve, Double Roll Collar, Open Pontil, 8 In. . 330.00

A.M. & Co., Old Kentucky Bourbon, Distilled In 1848, Medium Amber, 8 In. 358.00
A.M. & Co., Yellow Green, Tapered Collar Mouth, 9 3/4 In. 224.00
Barrel, Amber, Applied Double Collar, Open Pontil, 8 In. 345.00
Cannon, Golden Amber, Burst Top 880.00
Cannon, Medium Amber, Tooled Lip, 12 1/2 In. 834.00
Clock, Amber, Double Collar, Pontil, c.1870, Pt. 840.00
Clock, Regulator, Amber, Applied Lip, Pontil, 6 In. 468.00
Clock, Regulator, Medium To Dark Amber, Applied Lip, Open Pontil, Pt. 546.00
Cylindrical, Amber, Applied Handle, Lip, 8 In. 431.00
Old Kentucky Bourbon, Blown Molded, Raised Rings, Amber, 1848, 8 1/8 In. 235.00

BISCHOFF

Bischoff Company, founded in 1777 in Trieste, Italy, made fancy decanters. The modern collectible Bischoff bottles were imported into the United States from about 1950. Glass, porcelain, and stoneware decanters and figurals were made.

Clown, On Drum, 1963 . . . . 70.00
Deer, 1969 . . . . .7.00 to 8.00
Grecian Vase, Box 10.00
Venetian Glass, Hand Blown, Flowers, Gold 27.00

BITTERS

Bitters seems to have been an idea that started in Germany during the seventeenth century. A tax was levied against gin in the mid-1700s and the clever salesmen simply added some herbs to the gin and sold the mixture as medicine. Later, the medicine was made in Italy and England. Bitters is the name of this mixture. By the nineteenth century, bitters became a popular local product in America. It was usually of such a high alcoholic content that the claim that one using the product felt healthier with each sip was almost true. One brand had over 59% alcohol (about 118 proof). Although alcoholism had become a problem and social drinking was frowned upon by most proper Victorians, the soothing bitters medicine found wide acceptance. At that time there was no tax on the medicine and no laws concerning ingredients or advertising claims.

The word *bitters* must be embossed on the glass or a paper label must be affixed to the bottle for the collector to call the bottle a bitters bottle. Most date from 1862, the year of the Revenue Act tax on liquor, until 1906, the year the Food and Drugs Act placed restrictions on the sale of bitters as a medicinal cure. Over 1,000 types are known. Bitters were sometimes packaged in figural bottles shaped like cabins, human figures, fish, pigs, barrels, ears of corn, drums, clocks, horses, or cannons. The bottles came in a variety of colors. They ranged from clear to milk glass, pale to deep amethyst, light aqua to cobalt blue, pale yellow to amber, and pale to dark green. A bottle found in an unusual color commands a much higher price than a clear bottle of the same shape. The numbers used in the entries in the form R-00 refer to the book *Bitters Bottles* by Carlyn Ring and W.C. Ham. Each bottle is pictured and described in detail in the book.

A.M.S.2, 1864, Constitution, Seward & Bentley, Buffalo, Pink Topaz, 9 3/8 In., R-C222 . . 2750.00
A.T. & Co., Yellow Amber, Sloping Double Collar, 10 1/4 In. 935.00
Amazon, Amber, Applied Sloping Collar, 9 In., R-A44 . . . . 308.00
American Flag & New York Hop, Semi-Cabin, Blue Aqua, Embossed 119.00
Apple, J.W. Brant Co., Clear, Tapered Collar, 2 Shoulder Ridges, 1885-95, 6 1/8 In. 40.00
Aromatic Orange Stomach, Square, Panel Shoulders, 10 In., R-A90 . . . . 1904.00
Aromatic Stomach & Appetizer, Amber, Tooled Lip, Label, 8 In., R-A94 . . . . 280.00
Atwood's Jaundice, Moses Atwood, Georgetown, Mass., Aqua, 12-Sided, OP, R-A115 . . . 67.00
Atwood's Quinine Tonic, Gilman Bros., Boston, Mass, Aqua, Sample, 4 1/2 In. 94.00
Augauer Bitters Co, Medium Emerald Green, Tooled Lip, Label, 4 1/8 In., R-A134.5 . . . . 300.00
Augauer Bitters Co, Medium Grass Green, Tooled Lip, Label, 8 In., R-A134 . . . . *Illus* 180.00
Ayala Mexican, M. Rothenberg & Co., San Francisco, Amber, Square, 9 3/8 In., R-A142 . 400.00
Baker's Orange Grove, Amber Puce, Applied Collar, Roped Corners, 9 1/2 In., R-B9 . . . . 523.00
Baker's Orange Grove, Medium Amber, Applied Collar, Roped Corners, 9 1/2 In., R-B9 . 330.00
Baker's Orange Grove, Orange, Applied Collar, Roped Corners, 9 1/2 In., R-B9 . . . . 413.00
Baker's Orange Grove, Pink Puce, Applied Collar, Roped Corners, 9 1/2 In., R-B9 . . . . . . 2200.00
Baker's Orange Grove, Topaz Puce, Applied Collar, Roped Corners, 9 1/2 In., R-B9 . . . . . 2000.00
Baker's Orange Grove, Yellow Amber, Roped Corners, 9 1/2 In., R-B9 . . . . .336.00 to 896.00
Bakers Orange Grove, Medium Amber, Applied Collar, Roped Corners, 9 1/2 In., R-B9 . . 625.00
Barnett & Lion's, New Orleans, La., Amber, Embossed Soldier, Arched Panels, R-B26 . . 3520.00

Barrel, Cobalt Blue, Applied Lip, 9 3/4 In. 1680.00
Bavarian, Hoffheimer Bros., Amber, 9 5/8 In., R-B34.5 . . . .   242.00
Beck's Herb, York, Pa., Amber, 9 1/2 In., R-B46 . . . .   425.00
Bell's Cocktail, Lady's Leg, Medium Amber, Applied Lip, 10 1/2 In., R-B58 . . . .   1045.00
Ben Franklin, Blue Green, Labels, c.1850, 10 In., R-F80L 8960.00
Ben Franklin, Blue Green, Tapered Barrel, Applied Double Collar, Pontil, 10 In., R-F80L   880.00
Berkshire, Amann & Co., Cincinnati, O., Pig, 9 1/2 In., R-B81 . . . .   1210.00
Berkshire, Amann & Co., Cincinnati, O., Pig, Medium Amber, 10 1/2 In., R-B81.4 . . . . .   457.00
Big Bill Best, Medium Amber, Tooled Lip, 12 1/8 In., R-B95 . . . . .100.00 to 300.00
Big Bill Best, Red Amber, Square, Tapered, 12 1/8 In., R-B95 . . . .   99.00
Big Bill Best, Red Amber, Tooled Lip, Label, 12 1/8 In., R-B95 . . . .*Illus*   470.00
Bissell's Tonic, Patented Jany 21 1868, Peoria, Ill., Amber, 9 In., R-B109 . . . .   134.00
Boerhaves Holland, Blue Aqua, Applied Double Collar, Label, 7 5/8 In., R-B134 . . . .   408.00
Boggs Cottman & Co., German Tonic, Aqua, Applied Top 2200.00
Botanic, Sphinx, Medium Yellow Amber, Sloping Double Collar, 10 In., R-B165 . . . .   2016.00
Bourbon Whiskey, Barrel, Copper Puce, Applied Lip, 9 1/4 In., R-B171 . . . .   308.00
Bourbon Whiskey, Barrel, Pink Puce, Applied Lip, 9 1/4 In., R-B171 . . . .   308.00
Bourbon Whiskey, Barrel, Purple Puce, Applied Lip, 9 1/4 In., R-B171 . . . .   1650.00
Bourbon Whiskey, Barrel, Smoky Pink Puce, Applied Lip, 9 1/4 In., R-B171 . . . .   880.00
Bourbon Whiskey, Barrel, Strawberry Puce, Applied Lip, 9 1/4 In., R-B171 . . . . .320.00 to 504.00
Bourbon Whiskey, Barrel, Topaz Puce, Applied Lip, 9 1/4 In., R-B171 . . . .   1100.00
Boykin Carmer & Co., Granger, Baltimore, Amber, Tooled Lip, 8 3/8 In. 378.00
Brown's Celebrated Indian Herb, H. Pharazyn, Phila, Yellow Amber, Rolled Lip, 12 In. .   2750.00
Brown's Celebrated Indian Herb, Patented 1867, Amber, Rolled Lip, 12 In., R-B223 . . . .   840.00
Brown's Celebrated Indian Herb, Patented 1867, Chocolate, 12 In., R-B223 . . . .825.00 to 1400.00
Brown's Celebrated Indian Herb, Patented 1867, Medium Amber, 12 In., R-B223 . .*Illus*   630.00
Brown's Celebrated Indian Herb, Patented 1867, Medium Golden Amber, 12 In., R-B223   825.00
Brown's Celebrated Indian Herb, Patented 1867, Tobacco Amber, 12 1/4 In., R-B223 . . .   680.00
Brown's Celebrated Indian Herb, Patented 1868, Golden Amber, 12 1/4 In., R-B225 . . . .   880.00
Brown's Celebrated Indian Herb, Patented 1868, Yellow Amber, 12 1/4 In., R-B225 . . . .   575.00
Brown's Celebrated Indian Herb, Patented Feb. 11 1868, Amber, 12 In., R-B226 . . .*Illus*   672.00
Brown's Celebrated Indian Herb, Patented Feb. 11 1868, Yellow, 12 1/4 In., R-B226 . . . .   2600.00
Brown's Celebrated Indian Herb, Patented Feb. 11, 1868, Clear, 12 1/8 In., R-B222 . . . . .   7900.00
Brown's Iron, Amber, Square, 8 1/2 In., R-B231 . . . .   39.00
Brown's Iron, Yellow Amber, Square, 8 1/2 In., R-B231 . . . .   29.00
Bryant's Stomach, 8-Sided Lady's Leg, Olive, Double Collar, 12 In., R-B243 . .2500.00 to 2800.00
Bryant's Stomach, 8-Sided, Lady's Leg, Olive Green, Pontil, 12 1/2 In., R-B243 . . . .   4840.00
Buhrer's Gentian, Yellow Amber, Applied Sloping Collar, 9 In., R-B252 . . . .   67.00
Byrne, see Bitters, Professor Geo. J. Byrne
C. Gates & Cos, Life Of Man, Aqua, Tooled Lip, 1890-1900, Canada, 8 1/8 In., R-G7 . . . .   70.00
C. Gautiers, Native Wine, Washington, D.C., Patented 1867, Yellow Amber, Seal, R-G8 . .   385.00
C. Lediard St. Louis, Amber, Applied Lip, 6-Sided, 11 In. 1210.00

Bitters, Augauer Bitters
Co, Medium Grass
Green, Tooled Lip, Label,
8 In., R-A134

Bitters, Big Bill Best,
Red Amber,
Tooled Lip, Label,
12 1/8 In., R-B95

Bitters, Brown's
Celebrated Indian Herb,
Patented 1867, Medium
Amber, 12 In., R-B223

Bitters, Brown's
Celebrated Indian Herb,
Patented Feb. 11 1868,
Amber, 12 In., R-B226

Bitters, California Fig,
California Fig Co.,
Red Amber, Label,
10 In., R-C15

Bitters, Carmeliter
Stomach, Medium
Amber, Tooled Lip, Label,
4 3/4 In., R-C55

Bitters, Coca, Best
Tonic, Medium Amber,
Applied Lip,
9 1/4 In., R-C180

Bitters, Dr. Flint's Quaker,
Providence, R.I.,
Blue Aqua, Label,
9 1/2 In., R-F58

C.A. Richards, 99 Washington St., Boston, Square Case, Paneled, Amber, 9 1/2 In., R-R53 ... 45.00
C.W. Roback's, see Bitters, Dr. C.W. Roback's
Cabin, see Bitters, Drake's Plantation; Bitters, Golden; Bitters, Kelly's Old Cabin; Bitters,
Old Homestead Wild Cherry
Caldwell's Wine & Iron, Medina, N.Y., Medium Amber, Applied Lip, 9 3/4 In., R-C10 ... 267.00
Caldwells Herb, Great Tonic, Amber, Applied Lip, Iron Pontil, 12 3/8 In., R-C8 ...269.00 to 330.00
Caldwells Herb, Great Tonic, Deep Amber, Applied Lip, Iron Pontil, 12 3/8 In., R-C8 .... 385.00
California Fig, California Fig Co., Red Amber, Label, 10 In., R-C15 ....*Illus* 300.00
California Fig & Herb, California Fig Products Co., Amber, Square, 9 7/8 In., R-C16 .... 60.00
California Fig & Herb, California Fig Products Co., Yellow Amber, 4 1/2 In., R-C17 ..... 770.00
California Fig & Herb, California Fig Products Co., Yellow Amber, 9 7/8 In., R-C16 ..... 100.00
California Fig Syrup, Sterling Products, Embossed, Stopper, 1920-30, 7 In. 12.00
Cannon's Dyspeptic, Golden Amber, Cannon Barrels, Square, 9 5/8 In., R-C33 .... 5040.00
Canteen, Disorders Of Stomach, John Hart & Co., Blue Green, 9 7/8 In., R-C34 .... 3300.00
Canton, 5-Pointed Stars, Lady's Leg, R-C35 .... 413.00
Carl Mampe, Elephant, Amber, Tooled Lip, 2 1/4 In., R-M25 .... 56.00
Carl Mampe, Elephant, Olive Green, Tooled Lip, 8 1/4 In., R-M23 .... 78.00
Carmeliter Stomach, Medium Amber, Tooled Lip, 9 7/8 In., R-C54 .... 190.00
Carmeliter Stomach, Medium Amber, Tooled Lip, Label, 4 3/4 In., R-C55 ....*Illus* 935.00
Carmeliter Stomach, Olive Green, Tooled Lip, 10 In., R-C54 .... 448.00
Carnhart & Kelly, St. Louis, Amber, Square, Arched Panels, Applied Lip, 9 In. 2200.00
Carpathian Herb, Hollander Bros. Drug Co., Braddock, Pa., Amber, 8 1/4 In., R-C61.5 .. 280.00
Carter's Liver, C.M. Co., New York, Amber, 8 1/4 In., R-C67 .... 400.00
Cassin's Grape Brandy, Green, Applied Lip, 10 In., R-C79 .... 3960.00
Castilian, Golden Yellow Amber, Applied Lip, 10 In., R-C80 .... 240.00
Castilian, Yellow Amber, Double Collar, 10 In., R-C80 .... 224.00
Celebrated Club House, G.M. Smith, 1864, Semi-Cabin, Amber, 10 In., R-C177.5 ...... 3850.00
Celebrated Crown, Amber, Applied Lip, 8 7/8 In., R-C93 .... 364.00
Clark's Stomach, Dark Olive Green, Applied Lip, 9 1/2 In., R-C167.5 .... 880.00
Clarke's Sherry Wine, Only 25C, Aqua, Applied Lip, 8 In., R-C164 .... 168.00
Clarke's Sherry Wine, Sharon, Mass., Aqua, 9 In., R-C163 .... 150.00
Clarke's Vegetable Sherry Wine, Sharon, Mass, Blue Aqua, 11 3/4 In., R-C159 .... 600.00
Clarke's Vegetable Sherry Wine, Sharon, Mass, Blue Aqua, 11 3/4 In., R-C160 .... 350.00
Clarke's Vegetable Sherry Wine, Sharon, Mass, Blue Aqua, 14 In., R-C155 .... 425.00
Clotworthy's Oriental Tonic, Amber, Square, Sloping Collar, c.1885, 9 3/4 In., R-C176 .. 265.00
Coca, Best Tonic, Medium Amber, Applied Lip, 9 1/4 In., R-C180 ....*Illus* 1430.00
Cole Bros. Vegetable, Aqua, Rectangular, 7 7/8 In., R-C189 .... 68.00
Columbo Peptic, L.E. Jung, New Orleans, Red Amber, Square, 9 In., R-C200 .... 69.00
Congress, Blue Aqua, Semi-Cabin, Sloping Collar, 10 3/8 In., R-C217 .... 224.00
Connell's Brahminical Moon Plant East Indian Remedies, Amber, Feet & Stars 550.00
Constitution, Seward & Bentley, Gold Amber Red, Sloping Collar, 9 3/8 In., R-C222 ... 1600.00
Corwitz Stomach, Aqua, 7 1/4 In., R-C236 .... 123.00

Crookes's Stomach, Olive Green, Cream Top Neck, Sloping Collar, 10 1/2 In., R-C253 .. 2016.00
Dallimores Celebrated Brandy, Olive Green, Arched Panels, Pontil, 8 5/8 In. 4675.00
Damiana, Manuf'r Lewis Hess, Aqua, 11 3/4 In., R-D5 .... 100.00
Dandelion & Wild Cherry, Aqua, Applied Lip, 8 3/4 In., R-D14.7 .... 515.00
David Andrews Vegetable Jaundice, Providence, R.I., Aqua, Open Pontil, 8 In., A-A57 ... 2700.00
David Andrews Vegetable Jaundice, Providence, R.I., Blue Aqua, Pontil, 8 In., R-A57 ... 1980.00
De Witt's Stomach, Chicago, Amber, Contents, 7 1/2 In., R-D66 .... 358.00
Depose, Olive Green, Applied Lip, 12 1/2 In. 56.00
Digestine, P.J. Bowlin Liquor Co., St. Paul, Minn., Amber, Tooled Lip, 8 1/4 In., R-D73 .. 275.00
Digestine, Yellow Amber, Tooled Lip, 3 1/2 In., R-D74 .... 1430.00
Doyles Hop, 1872, Semi-Cabin, Amber, Labels, 9 1/2 In., R-D93 .... 303.00
Doyles Hop, 1872, Semi-Cabin, Yellow Amber, 9 1/2 In., R-D93 .... 90.00
Doyles Hop, 1872, Semi-Cabin, Yellow Green, Tapered Mouth, 9 1/2 In., R-D93 ... 728.00
Dr. A.S. Hopkins, Lady's Leg, Yellow Amber, Applied Lip, 12 1/4 In., R-H177 .... 5500.00
Dr. A.S. Hopkins Union Stomach, Green, Applied Lip, 9 3/4 In., R-H180 .... 3300.00
Dr. Ball's Vegetable Stomachic, Northboro, Mass., Open Pontil, 6 7/8 In., R-B14 .... 270.00
Dr. Barnard's Wild Cherry, Label, 8 In. 176.00
Dr. Baxter's Mandrake, Burlington, Vt., Aqua, R-B36 ....20.00 to 45.00
Dr. Bell's Liver & Kidney, Blue Aqua, Single Collar, Domed Base, 9 In., R-B61 ...179.00 to 279.00
Dr. Birmingham's Anti Bilious Blood Purifying, Blue Green, c.1865, 9 In., R-B101 .. 4400.00
Dr. Bishop's Wa-Hoo, Semi-Cabin, Yellow Amber, Applied Lip, 10 1/2 In., R-B103 ..... 700.00
Dr. C.W. Roback's Stomach, Cincinnati, Barrel, Amber, IP, 9 7/8 In., R-R73 .....425.00 to 625.00
Dr. C.W. Roback's Stomach, Cincinnati, O, Barrel, Golden Amber, 9 1/2 In., R-R74 ..... 224.00
Dr. C.W. Roback's Stomach, Cincinnati, O, Barrel, Tobacco Amber, 9 3/8 In., R-R74 ..... 179.00
Dr. C.W. Roback's Stomach, Cincinnati, O, Barrel, Yellow Amber, 10 In., R-R73 ..672.00 to 735.00
Dr. C.W. Roback's Stomach, Cincinnati, O, Barrel, Yellow Amber, 9 1/2 In., R-R74 ..... 123.00
Dr. C.W. Roback's Stomach, Cincinnati, O, Yellow Amber, Applied Lip, 9 1/2 In., R-R74 . 715.00
Dr. Caldwell's Herb, Great Tonic, Amber, 12 3/4 In., R-C9 .... 253.00
Dr. Caldwell's Herb, Great Tonic, Yellow Amber, Sloping Collar, Iron Pontil, 13 In., R-C9 112.00
Dr. Campbells Scotch, Tooled Lip, 1/2 Pt., 6 1/8 In., R-C31 .... 240.00
Dr. Corbett's Renovating Shaker, Aquamarine, Double Collar, c.1850, 9 5/8 In., R-C234 . 2240.00
Dr. Dunlap's, Embossed Anchors, Semi-Cabin, Yellow Amber, 10 1/2 In., R-D122L 532.00
Dr. Elmore's Rhumatine Coutaline, Amber, Square, Embossed, 7 1/2 In. 45.00
Dr. Fischs, W.H. Ware, Patented 1866, Fish, Golden Amber, 12 In., R-F44 ......303.00 to 336.00
Dr. Fischs, W.H. Ware, Patented 1866, Fish, Lemon Yellow, c.1875, 12 In., R-F44 ...... 825.00
Dr. Flint's Quaker, Providence, R.I., Applied Square Lip, 9 1/2 In., R-F58 .... 110.00
Dr. Flint's Quaker, Providence, R.I., Blue Aqua, Label, 9 1/2 In., R-F58 ....*Illus* 935.00
Dr. Geo Pierce's Indian Restorative, Lowell, Mass., Aqua, Iron Pontil, 8 In., R-P96 ..... 190.00
Dr. Geo Pierce's Indian Restorative, Lowell, Mass., Blue Aqua, Pontil, 7 7/8 In., R-P96 . 425.00
Dr. Geo. Pierce's Indian Restorative, Lowell, Mass., Clear, Pontil, 9 In., R-P95 .... 143.00
Dr. Geo. Pierce's Indian Restorative, Lowell, Mass., Aqua, OP, 7 3/4 In., R-P96 ..125.00 to 275.00
Dr. Green's Poleish, Yellow Amber, Applied Lip, Iron Pontil, 11 In., R-G107 .... 532.00
Dr. H.S. Flint's Quaker, Man Holding Bottle, Aqua, Contents, 1872, 9 1/2 In. 121.00
Dr. Harter's Wild Cherry, Dayton, O., Embossed, 8 In., R-H46 .... 245.00
Dr. Harter's Wild Cherry, St. Louis, Amber, Rectangular, 7 3/4 In., R-H50 .... 48.00
Dr. Henley's Wild Grape Root IXL, Light Green Aqua, Applied Lip, R-H84 .... 2200.00
Dr. Herbert John's, Great Indian Discoveries, Medium Amber, 8 5/8 In., R-J43 .... 235.00
Dr. Hoofland's German, Ice Blue, 8 In., R-H168 .... 28.00
Dr. Hoofland's German, Liver Complaint, Dyspepsia, Aqua, OP, 6 3/4 In., R-H168 ...... 59.00
Dr. Iman's Compound Blood Purifier, Label, Box, 9 1/4 In. 154.00
Dr. J. Boveedods Imperial Wine, Aqua, Rectangular, Panels, 10 In., R-D80 .... 420.00
Dr. J. Hostetter's Stomach, Dark Olive Amber, Applied Lip, 9 In., R-H194 .... 440.00
Dr. J. Hostetter's Stomach, Dark Olive Green, Applied Lip, 9 1/2 In., R-H194 .... 495.00
Dr. J. Hostetter's Stomach, L & W, Yellow Amber Olive, Applied Lip, 8 3/4 In., R-H195 . 1210.00
Dr. J. Hostetter's Stomach, Olive Amber, Applied Lip, 8 3/4 In., R-H194 .... 300.00
Dr. J. Hostetter's Stomach, Olive Green, Sloping Collar, Label, 9 1/2 In., R-H194 ...... 336.00
Dr. J. Hostetter's Stomach, Orange Amber, 9 In., R-H195 .... 40.00
Dr. J. Hostetter's Stomach, W. MCG & Co., Olive Yellow, Applied Lip, 9 In., R-H195 .. 180.00
Dr. J. Sweet's Strengthening, Aqua, Square, 8 1/4 In., R-S234 .... 55.00
Dr. Langley's Root & Herb, 99 Union St., Boston, Green, Square Collar, 8 1/2 In., R-L21 . 100.00
Dr. Loew's Celebrated Stomach & Nerve Tonic, Apple Green, 9 5/8 In., R-L111 .... 550.00
Dr. Loew's Celebrated Stomach & Nerve Tonic, Green, R-L112.5, 9 1/4 In. ....*Illus* 495.00
Dr. Loew's Celebrated Stomach & Nerve Tonic, Pale Aqua, 3 7/8 In., R-L112.5 ...... 180.00

Dr. Loew's Celebrated Stomach & Nerve Tonic, Yellow Amber, 3 1/2 In., R-L113 ...... 275.00
Dr. Loew's Celebrated Stomach & Nerve Tonic, Yellow Green, 3 7/8 In., R-L112 ...... 360.00
Dr. Loew's Celebrated Stomach & Nerve Tonic, Yellow Green, 9 1/4 In., R-L111 ...... 235.00
Dr. Lovegood's Family, Golden Amber, Building, 1860-80, 10 1/4 In., R-L124 .... 5040.00
Dr. Mackenzie's Wild Cherry, Chicago, Tooled Lip, 8 3/8 In., R-M5 .... 130.00
Dr. Manly Hardy's Jaundice, Aqua, 7 3/8 In., R-H36 .... 85.00
Dr. Mowe's Vegetable, Lowell Mass, Aqua, Embossing 440.00
Dr. Petzold's Genuine German, Incept. 1862, Orange Amber, Tooled Lip, 7 7/8 In., R-P76 90.00
Dr. Petzolds Genuine German, Incept. 1862, Amber To Yellow Amber, 10 1/4 In., R-P74 . 213.00
Dr. Petzolds Genuine German, Incept. 1862, Amber, Double Collar, 10 1/8 In., R-P75 ... 110.00
Dr. Petzolds Genuine German, Incept. 1862, Orange Amber, 10 1/4 In., R-P74 .... 145.00
Dr. Petzolds Genuine German, Incept. 1862, Red Amber, Tooled Lip, 10 1/4 In., R-P74 .. 200.00
Dr. Porter, New York, Medicated Stomach, Aqua, Embossed, Label, 7 1/2 In., R-P127 ... 83.00
Dr. Rattinger's Herb & Root, St. Louis, Mo., Amber, 9 1/4 In., R-R11 .... 180.00
Dr. Renz's Herb, Olive Green, Applied Lip, Square Collar, R-R38 .... 1900.00
Dr. Sawen's Life Invigorating, Utica, N.Y., Golden Amber, 9 1/8 In., R-S41 .... 200.00
Dr. Saylor's Rheuma Stomachic Herb, Red Amber, Square, Panels, 8 7/8 In., R-S45 ..... 1100.00
Dr. Skinner's Celebrated 25 Cent, Blue Aqua, Double Lip, Pontil, 8 5/8 In., R-S115 .... 235.00
Dr. Skinner's Sherry Wine, Aqua, Olive, Applied Lip, Open Pontil, 8 5/8 In., R-S116 .... 336.00
Dr. Soule Hop, 1872, Semi-Cabin, Apricot Puce, England, 9 7/8 In., R-S145 .... 100.00
Dr. Soule Hop, 1872, Semi-Cabin, Copper Puce, Sloping Double Collar, 9 5/8 In., R-S145 60.00
Dr. Soule Hop, 1872, Semi-Cabin, Olive Yellow, Double Collar, 9 3/4 In., R-S145 .180.00 to 450.00
Dr. Soule Hop, 1872, Semi-Cabin, Yellow Amber Olive, Double Collar, 9 7/8 In., R-S145 160.00
Dr. Soule Hop, 1872, Semi-Cabin, Yellow Amber, Double Collar, 8 In., R-S147 .... 100.00
Dr. Soule Hop, 1872, Semi-Cabin, Yellow Amber, Double Collar, 9 1/2 In., R-S145 .60.00 to 150.00
Dr. Soule Hop, 1872, Semi-Cabin, Yellow Topaz, Double Collar, 9 7/8 In., R-S145 ..... 110.00
Dr. Soule's Hop Bitterine, 1872, Semi-Cabin, Topaz, Applied Lip, 9 1/2 In., R-S144.5 ... 850.00
Dr. Sperry's Female Strengthening, Clear, Tooled Lip, 9 1/4 In., R-S161 .... 330.00
Dr. Stephen Jewett's Celebrated Health, Olive Green, Pontil, 7 3/8 In., R-J37 .... 5500.00
Dr. Stewart's Tonic, Columbus, O., Amber, Contents, Labels, 8 In., R-S194 .... 240.00
Dr. Stoughten's National, Loaf Of Bread, Amber, 10 In., R-S208 .... 1792.00
Dr. Thornton Compound Syrup Wild Cherry, Cobalt Blue, Blob Top, Pontil, 6 7/8 In. ... 5225.00
Dr. Van Dyke's Holland, Headless Man Running, Embossed Base, 9 3/4 In., R-V7 ...... 330.00
Dr. Von Hopf's, Curacoa, Chamberlain & Co., Des Moines, Amber, Label, Pt., 8 In., R-V28 59.00
Dr. Von Hopf's, Curacoa, Chamberlain & Co., Des Moines, Iowa, Amber, 8 In., R-V28 ... 125.00
Dr. Wheeler's Tonic Sherry Wine, Green Aqua, 4-Sided, Roped Corners, 9 1/2 In., R-W87 3920.00
Dr. XX Lovegood's Family, Cabin, Medium Amber, Applied Sloping Lip, 10 In., R-L124 . 3015.00
Dr. Hostetter's, see Bitters, Dr. J. Hostetter's
Drake's Plantation, 4 Log, Amber, Applied Lip, 10 1/8 In., R-D110 .... *Illus* 134.00
Drake's Plantation, 4 Log, Golden Amber, 10 1/4 In., R-D110 ....110.00 to 165.00
Drake's Plantation, 4 Log, Medium Amber, Applied Lip, 10 1/4 In., R-D110 .....100.00 to 550.00
Drake's Plantation, 4 Log, Yellow Amber, 10 1/4 In., R-D110 ....121.00 to 239.00
Drake's Plantation, 4 Log, Yellow Gold, 10 1/2 In., R-D110 .... 825.00
Drake's Plantation, 4 Log, Yellow Green, Applied Lip, 10 1/4 In., R-D110 ....2576.00 to 4200.00
Drake's Plantation, 5 Log, Golden Yellow Amber, Applied Lip, 10 In., R-D109 .... 705.00
Drake's Plantation, 5 Log, Medium Lime Green, Applied Lip, 9 7/8 In., R-D109 .... 9350.00
Drake's Plantation, 5 Log, Orange Amber, Rolled Lip, 9 1/4 In., R-D109 .... 616.00
Drake's Plantation, 5 Log, Yellow Amber, Applied Lip, 9 7/8 In., R-D109 .....364.00 to 715.00
Drake's Plantation, 6 Log, Amber, Applied Tapered Lip, 10 In., R-D105 .... 364.00
Drake's Plantation, 6 Log, Apricot Puce, Sloping Collar, 10 In., R-D102 .... 840.00
Drake's Plantation, 6 Log, Apricot Puce, Square, Sloping Collar, 10 In., R-D105 .... 1344.00
Drake's Plantation, 6 Log, Cherry Puce, Sloping Collar, 10 In., R-D102 .... 616.00
Drake's Plantation, 6 Log, Cherry Puce, Sloping Collar, 10 In., R-D106 .... 364.00
Drake's Plantation, 6 Log, Cherry Puce, Sloping Collar, 9 3/4 In., R-D102 .... 952.00
Drake's Plantation, 6 Log, Copper Puce, 10 1/8 In., R-D105 .... 350.00
Drake's Plantation, 6 Log, Copper Puce, Sloping Collar, 10 1/8 In., R-D103 .... 476.00
Drake's Plantation, 6 Log, Copper Puce, Sloping Collar, 10 In., R-D108 .... 420.00
Drake's Plantation, 6 Log, Deep Strawberry Puce, Applied Lip, 9 7/8 In., R-D103 ...... 360.00
Drake's Plantation, 6 Log, Gasoline Puce, Applied Tapered Lip, 10 In., R-D105 1456.00 to 2576.00
Drake's Plantation, 6 Log, Golden Yellow Amber, 1862, 10 In., R-D102 .... 900.00
Drake's Plantation, 6 Log, Medium Strawberry Puce, Sloping Lip, 10 In., R-D106 ..... 1870.00
Drake's Plantation, 6 Log, Olive Yellow Amber, 9 7/8 In., R-D108 .... 790.00

Bitters, Dr. Loew's
Celebrated Stomach &
Nerve Tonic, Green,
R-L112.5, 9 1/4 In.

Bitters, Drake's
Plantation, 4 Log,
Amber, Applied Lip,
10 1/8 In., R-D110

Bitters, Fish, W.H. Ware,
Patented 1866, Yellow
Amber, Applied Lip,
11 1/2 In., R-F45

Drake's Plantation, 6 Log, Olive Yellow Amber, Applied Lip, 1862, R-D103 . . . . 2240.00
Drake's Plantation, 6 Log, Pink Strawberry Puce, Sloping Collar, 10 In., R-D108 . . . . . . 616.00
Drake's Plantation, 6 Log, Purple Amethyst, Sloping Collar, 1862, 10 In., R-D105 . . . . . 3080.00
Drake's Plantation, 6 Log, Red Amber, Applied Sloping Lip, 10 In., R-D105 . . . . 120.00
Drake's Plantation, 6 Log, Red Amber, Applied Tapered Lip, 10 In., R-D105 . . . . 112.00
Drake's Plantation, 6 Log, Strawberry Puce, 9 3/4 In., R-D105 . . . . 952.00
Drake's Plantation, 6 Log, Strawberry Puce, Applied Lip, 9 3/4 In., R-D105 . . . . 392.00
Drake's Plantation, 6 Log, Topaz Puce, 9 7/8 In., R-D105 . . . . 395.00
Drake's Plantation, 6 Log, Yellow Amber, 10 1/8 In., R-D105 . . . . .160.00 to 168.00
Drake's Plantation, 6 Log, Yellow Amber, Applied Lip, 9 7/8 In., R-D108 . . . . . . .123.00 to 300.00
Drake's Plantation, 6 Log, Yellow Amber, Sloping Collar, 9 7/8 In., R-D103 . . . . 336.00
Drake's Plantation, 6 Log, Yellow Topaz, 10 In., R-D105 . . . . .725.00 to 1064.00
Drake's Plantation, 6 Log, Yellow, Applied Sloping Lip, 9 7/8 In., R-D108 . . . . 1700.00
E. Dexter Loveridge Wahoo, DWD, Semi-Cabin, Yellow Amber, 10 In., R-L126 . .896.00 to 990.00
E.C. Allen Concentrated Electric Past, Green, Pontil, Rolled Lip, 1845-55, 3 In. 1320.00
Eagle Angostura Bark, Medium Amber, Tooled Lip, 3 7/8 In., R-E3 . . . . 470.00
Eagle Angostura Bark, Medium Amber, Tooled Lip, 7 In., R-E2 . . . . 665.00
Ear Of Corn, see Bitters, National, Ear of Corn
Edw Wilder's Stomach, Louisville, Ky., House, Clear, 10 1/4 In., R-W116 . . . . . .145.00 to 186.00
Edw Wilder's Stomach, Louisville, Ky., House, Clear, Tooled Lip, 10 3/4 In., R-W116.2 . 448.00
Electric, H.E. Bucklen & Co., Chicago., Ill., Amber, Labels, 8 3/4 In., R-E30 . . . . 220.00
Excelsior, Medium Amber, Applied Lip, 9 1/8 In., R-E63 . . . . 165.00
Eye Opener, Apricot Amber, Applied Lip 330.00
F. Brown Sarsaparilla & Tomato, Blue Aqua, Applied Double Lip, Pontil, 9 1/4 In., R-S36 495.00
F. Ditmar's Stomach, Olive Green, Applied Lip, Bubbles, 9 7/8 In., R-D78 . . . . 1650.00
Faith Whitcomb's, Aqua, Applied Double Lip, Label, Box, 9 1/2 In., R-W90 . . . . 150.00
Ferro Quina, D.P. Rossi, 1400 Dupont, S.F. Cal., Yellow Amber, 3 7/8 In., R-F36.5 . . . . . 385.00
Ferro Quina, Dogliani Italia, D.P. Rossi, Yellow Amber, Tooled Lip, 3 3/4 In., R-F33 . . . . 135.00
Ferro Quina, Kidney & Liver, D.P. Rossi, Orange Amber, Tooled Lip, 9 1/8 In., R-F38 . . . 715.00
Ferro Quina, Stomach, Blood Maker, D.P. Rossi, Medium Amber, 9 1/4 In., R-F39 . . . . . . 155.00
Ferro Quina, Stomach, Blood Maker, Dogliani Italia, Yellow Amber, 9 In., R-F40 . . . . . . 165.00
Fish, W.H. Ware, Patented 1866, Amber, Applied Lip, 11 1/2 In., R-F46 . . . . .200.00 to 308.00
Fish, W.H. Ware, Patented 1866, Amber, Applied Lip, 11 5/8 In., R-F45 . . . . .235.00 to 275.00
Fish, W.H. Ware, Patented 1866, Orange Amber, Applied Lip, 10 1/2 In., R-F45 . . . . 200.00
Fish, W.H. Ware, Patented 1866, Yellow Amber, Applied Lip, 11 1/2 In., R-F45 . . . . .*Illus* 530.00
Forestine Blood Remedies, A. Bloomingdale Co., Gloversville, N.Y., Light Aqua, 7 In. . . 165.00
Fostoria American Bitters, Original Top, 5 5/8 x 2 1/4 In. 60.00
Fulton M. McRae, Yazoo Valley, Amber, Applied Sloping Lip, 8 3/4 In., R-Y2 . . . . 213.00
Geo. Benz & Sons Appetine, St. Paul, Minn., Amber, Tooled Lip, 3 1/2 In., R-A79 . . . . . . 470.00
Geo. Benz & Sons Appetine, St. Paul, Minn., Black Amethyst, Tooled Lip, 8 In., R-A78.2 . 880.00
German Balsam, W.M. Watson & Co., Milk Glass, Sloping Collar, 9 In., R-G18 . . . . 672.00
German Hop, Dr. C.D. Warner's, Semi-Cabin, Amber, 9 3/4 In., R-G25.6 . . . . 175.00
German Hop, Dr. C.D. Warner's, Semi-Cabin, Amber, 9 7/8 In., R-G25.6 . . . . 400.00
German Hop, Dr. C.D. Warner's, Semi-Cabin, Amber, Label, 9 3/4 In., R-G25.6 . . . . 672.00
German Hop, Dr. C.D. Warner's, Semi-Cabin, Yellow Amber Olive, 9 1/2 In., R-G25.6 . . 175.00

Gilbert's Sarsaparilla, Amber, 8-Sided, Fluted Neck, Panel, Applied Lip, 8 3/4 In., R-G42   715.00
Gipps Land, Hop, Purity Trade Mark, Semi-Cabin, Aqua, Australia, 9 3/8 In., R-G45 ....   80.00
Globe, Bell, Yellow Amber, Applied Square Lip, 11 1/8 In., R-G47 ....   500.00
Globe Tonic, Amber, 9 5/8 In., R-G49 ....   125.00
Golden, Geo. C. Hubbel & Co., Semi-Cabin, Aqua, Inward Rolled Lip, 3 5/8 In., R-G63.5   300.00
Golden, Geo. C. Hubbel & Co., Semi-Cabin, Aqua, Sloping Lip, 10 1/4 In., R-G63 ......   660.00
Greeley's Bourbon, Barrel, Chartreuse Green, Applied Lip, 9 1/4 In., R-G101 ....   1904.00
Greeley's Bourbon, Barrel, Cherry Puce, 9 1/4 In., R-G101 ....   263.00
Greeley's Bourbon, Barrel, Copper Topaz, Applied Lip, 9 3/8 In., R-G101 ....   2090.00
Greeley's Bourbon, Barrel, Medium Chartreuse, 9 1/4 In., R-G101 ....   3075.00
Greeley's Bourbon, Barrel, Medium Olive Green Yellow, Applied Lip, 9 1/4 In., R-G101 .   2200.00
Greeley's Bourbon, Barrel, Medium Topaz Olive, Applied Lip, 9 1/4 In., R-G101 ....   193.00
Greeley's Bourbon, Barrel, Moss Green, 9 3/8 In., R-G101 ....   4180.00
Greeley's Bourbon, Barrel, Olive Green, Applied Lip, 9 3/8 In., R-G101 ......1540.00 to 3750.00
Greeley's Bourbon, Barrel, Olive Topaz, 9 1/4 In., R-G101 ....   3020.00
Greeley's Bourbon, Barrel, Puce, Applied Lip, 9 1/4 In., R-G101 ....616.00 to 952.00
Greeley's Bourbon, Barrel, Red Puce, Applied Lip, 9 3/8 In., R-G101 ....   1120.00
Greeley's Bourbon, Barrel, Smoky Cherry Puce, 9 3/8 In., R-G101 ....   527.00
Greeley's Bourbon, Barrel, Smoky Copper Topaz, 9 1/4 In., R-G101 ....476.00 to 670.00
Greeley's Bourbon, Barrel, Smoky Green, 9 1/4 In., R-G101 ....   2090.00
Greeley's Bourbon, Barrel, Smoky Olive Green, Applied Lip, 9 1/4 In., R-G101 .1456.00 to 2790.00
Greeley's Bourbon, Barrel, Smoky Pink Puce, 9 1/2 In., R-G101 ....   935.00
Greeley's Bourbon, Barrel, Smoky Topaz Puce, Applied Lip, 9 3/8 In., R-G101 ....   750.00
Greeley's Bourbon, Barrel, Smoky Topaz, 9 1/4 In., R-G101 ....   308.00
Greeley's Bourbon, Barrel, Smoky Topaz, Applied Lip, 9 In., R-G101 ....610.00 to 880.00
Greeley's Bourbon, Barrel, Strawberry Puce, Applied Lip, 9 1/4 In., R-G101 ....   784.00
Greeley's Bourbon, Barrel, Topaz Puce, Square Collar, 9 1/4 In., R-G101 ....   280.00
Greeley's Bourbon Whiskey, Barrel, Amethyst, Applied Lip, 9 1/2 In., R-G102 .2688.00 to 5600.00
Greeley's Bourbon Whiskey, Barrel, Aqua, Applied Lip, 9 1/2 In., R-G102 .....3850.00 to 4480.00
Greeley's Bourbon Whiskey, Barrel, Cherry Puce, 9 3/8 In., R-G102 ....1008.00 to 1792.00
Greeley's Bourbon Whiskey, Barrel, Copper Puce, Applied Square Lip, c.1865, R-G102 ..   523.00
Greeley's Bourbon Whiskey, Barrel, Dark Plum Amethyst, Applied Lip, 9 1/4 In., R-G102   1650.00
Greeley's Bourbon Whiskey, Barrel, Pink Puce, Square Collar, 9 1/4 In., R-G102 ....   700.00
Greeley's Bourbon Whiskey, Barrel, Strawberry Puce, 9 1/2 In., R-G102 ....365.00 to 825.00
Greeley's Bourbon Whiskey, Barrel, Topaz, Applied Lip, 9 1/2 In., R-G102 ....   5040.00
H.P. Herb Wild Cherry, Reading, Pa., Cabin, Bright Green, Tooled Lip, 8 3/4 In., R-H94 .   7150.00
H.P. Herb Wild Cherry, Reading, Pa., Cabin, Gold Amber, 1880-90, 9 In., R-H94 ....   775.00
H.P. Herb Wild Cherry, Reading, Pa., Cabin, Medium Amber, 10 In., R-H93 ....*Illus*   448.00
H.P. Herb Wild Cherry, Reading, Pa., Cabin, Olive Yellow, 10 1/8 In., R-H93 ....   6050.00
H.P. Herb Wild Cherry, Reading, Pa., Cabin, Tree, Yellow Amber, 10 In., R-H93 ....   2352.00
Hall's, Barrel, Copper Amber, Applied Lip, 9 5/8 In., R-H9 ....*Illus*   3300.00
Hall's, E.E. Hall, New Haven, Barrel, Amber, Applied Lip, 9 1/4 In., R-H10 ....220.00 to 280.00
Hall's, E.E. Hall, New Haven, Barrel, Medium Amber, Applied Lip, 9 1/8 In., R-H10 .....   400.00
Hall's, E.E. Hall, New Haven, Barrel, Medium Amber, Square Lip, Label, 9 1/8 In., R-H10   616.00
Hall's, E.E. Hall, New Haven, Barrel, Yellow Amber, 9 1/8 In., R-H10 ....224.00 to 364.00
Hartwig Kantorowicz, Posen, Hamburg, Germany, Milk Glass, Case Gin, 9 In., R-L106 ..   90.00
Hartwig Kantorowicz, Posen, Hamburg, Germany, Yellow Green, Case Gin, 9 In., R-L106   550.00
Hartwig Kantorowicz, Posen, Milk Glass, Tooled Lip, 3 3/4 In., R-L107 ....   90.00
Harvard Yard, No Stopper, Tarentum Glass Company, c.1896, 10 1/2 In. 40.00
Harvey's Prairie, Gold Yellow, Square, Indented Panels, c.1865, 9 1/2 In., R-H67 ....   22400.00
Harz Mountain Herb, W. Trommlitz, Cleveland, O., Semi-Cabin, Yellow Amber, 10 In. ..   2200.00
Hellman's Congress, St. Louis, Mo., Amber, Tobacco Tint, Square, 9 1/8 In., R-H79 .....   550.00
Herb's Acme, Lady's Leg Neck, Amber, Square Collar, 1860-80, 9 1/8 In. 5040.00
Herkules, Emerald Green, 2 Flat Panels, Globular, Tooled Lip, Ring, 7 1/4 In., R-H98 ...   1800.00
Hertrich's Gesundheits, Hans Hertrich Hof., Lime Green, Tooled Lip, 11 7/8 In., R-H104   660.00
Hertrich's Gesundheits, Olive Green, Double Collar, Germany, 1880, 12 1/2 In., R-H104   1100.00
Highland, Scotch Tonic, Barrel, Amber, Applied Lip, 9 3/4 In., R-H117 ....   1680.00
Holtzermann's Patent Stomach, Cabin, Amber, 9 3/4 In., R-H154 ....*Illus*   896.00
Holtzermann's Patent Stomach, Cabin, Amber, Applied Lip, 9 In., R-H155 ...1792.00 to 2016.00
Holtzermann's Patent Stomach, Cabin, Amber, Label, 9 3/4 In., R-H154 ....   550.00
Holtzermann's Patent Stomach, Cabin, Amber, Tooled Lip, 9 3/4 In., R-H154 ...135.00 to 308.00
Holtzermann's Patent Stomach, Cabin, Gold Amber Yellow, Partial Label, 9 In., R-H155   2200.00
Holtzermann's Patent Stomach, Cabin, Gold Amber, Applied Sloping Lip, 9 In., R-H155   2128.00

Holtzermann's Patent Stomach, Cabin, Orange Amber, 9 5/8 In., R-H155 . . . . 2200.00
Holtzermann's Patent Stomach, Cabin, Red Amber, 9 7/8 In., R-H154 . . . . .297.00 to 935.00
Holtzermann's Patent Stomach, Cabin, Yellow Amber, Applied Lip, 9 3/8 In., R-H155 . . 2530.00
Holtzermann's Stomach, Cabin, Yellow Amber, Tooled Lip, Label, Sample, 4 In., R-H153   378.00
Home Bitters Co. St. Louis Mo., Light Green, Tooled Lip, 7 1/2 In., R-H160 . . . .   66.00
Home Stomach, St. Louis, Mo., Light Amber, Applied Lip, 8 7/8 In., R-H162 . . . .   88.00
Hop & Iron, Utica, N.Y., Amber, Partial Label, 8 1/2 In., R-H172 . . . .   80.00
Hop & Iron, Utica, N.Y., Amber, Tooled Lip, 8 5/8 In., R-H172 . . . .   375.00
Hop Bitters Co., Semi-Cabin, Green Aqua, Square, Embossed, 10 In. 200.00
Hops & Malt, Semi-Cabin, Sheaf Of Grain, Amber, Applied Sloping Lip, 10 In., R-H186 .   100.00
Hops & Malt, Semi-Cabin, Sheaf Of Grain, Gold Amber, 9 3/4 In., R-H186 . . . .   255.00
Hops & Malt, Semi-Cabin, Sheaf Of Grain, Yellow Amber, Tooled Lip, R-H187 . . . . 1650.00
Horse Shoe, Horse, Horseshoe, Yellow Amber, 8 5/8 In., R-H189 . . . . 3640.00
Howard's Vegetable Syrup, Yellow Amber, Applied Lip, Pontil, 1840-60, 7 1/2 In. 9350.00
Hubbell Co., see Bitters, Golden
Hunkidori, Amber, Applied Sloping Lip, 8 7/8 In., R-H210 . . . .   448.00
Hutchings Dyspepsia, Aqua, Open Pontil, 9 1/2 In., R-H217 . . . .   295.00
Imperator Stomach, Deimel Bros. & Co., N.Y., Milk Glass, Case Gin, 4 1/8 In., R-I2 . . . .   165.00
Imperial, Levee, Hollywood, Miss., Grape Cluster On Tree Stump, Yellow Amber, 10 In. . . 5320.00
Indian Queen, see Bitters, Brown's Celebrated Indian Herb
Iron & Quinine, N.K. Brown, Burlington, Vt., Aqua, 7 1/4 In., R-I29 . . . .   69.00
J. Walker's V.B., Teal, Mushroom Top, 8 3/8 In., R-W11 . . . .   55.00
J.D. Eastman & Co., Deer Lodge, Montana, Amber, Tooled Lip, 8 7/8 In. 1100.00
J.W. Hutchinson's Tonic, Blue, Applied Double Collar, 8 5/8 In., R-H220 . . . .   840.00
J.W. Hutchinson's Tonic, Gold Amber, Sloping Collar, Seed Bubbles, 9 In., R-H220 . . . . . 2576.00
Jackson's Aromatic Life, Olive Green, Sloping Collar, 8 7/8 In., R-J4 . . . . 5500.00
James L. Davis' Sons, Schiedam, Yellow Amber, 4-Sided, Beveled Corners, 10 In., R-D20   420.00
Jno Moffat, New York, Olive Green, Pontil, 5 1/2 In., R-M110 . . . . 1100.00
Jno Moffat, Price $1, Phoenix, New York, Amber Black, Rolled Lip, 5 1/2 In., R-M110 . . 2800.00
John A. Perry, Dr. Warren's Bilious, Boston, Mass., Aqua, Label, 6 1/4 In., R-W43 . . . . . .   154.00
John Moffat, Phoenix, New York, Aqua, Applied Lip, Open Pontil, 5 1/2 In., R-M112 . . . .   78.00
John Root's, 1834, Buffalo, N.Y., Semi-Cabin, Blue Green, Applied Lip, 10 In., R-R90.4 . . 2530.00
John W. Steele's Niagara Star, Semi-Cabin, Amber, Applied Lip, 10 1/4 In., R-S182 . . . .   520.00
John W. Steele's Niagara Star, Semi-Cabin, Amber, Applied Lip, 10 In., R-S184 . .605.00 to 672.00
John W. Steele's Niagara Star, Semi-Cabin, Amber, Label, 10 1/4 In., R-S182 . . . . 1400.00
John W. Steele's Niagara Star, Semi-Cabin, Medium Amber, 10 In., R-S182 . . . .   770.00
Johnson's Calisaya, Burlington, Vt., Amber, Label, Square, 10 In., R-J45 . . . .   220.00
Johnson's Calisaya, Burlington, Vt., Amber, Sloping Double Collar, 10 1/4 In., R-J45 . . . .   123.00
Johnson's Calisaya, Burlington, Vt., Red Amber, Applied Lip, 10 In., R-J45 . . . .   123.00
Johnson's Indian Dyspeptic, Aqua, Applied Lip, Open Pontil, 6 1/2 In., R-J46 . . . .   680.00
Kaiser Wilhelm, Sandusky, O., Lady's Leg, Clear, 10 1/2 In., R-K5 . . . .   69.00
Karlsbader Sprudel, Milk Glass, Tooled Lip, 8 1/8 In. 157.00
Kelly's Old Cabin, Patented 1863, Cabin, Amber, Applied Lip, 9 5/8 In., R-K21 . 2090.00 to 3020.00
Kelly's Old Cabin, Patented 1863, Cabin, Olive Amber, Double Collar, 9 1/2 In., R-K21 . . 1100.00
Kelly's Old Cabin, Patented 1863, Cabin, Red Amber, Sloping Collar, 9 1/8 In., R-K21 . . 2750.00
Kelly's Old Cabin, Patented 1863, Cabin, Yellow Amber, Sloping Collar, 9 In., R-K21 . . . 2352.00

Bitters, H.P. Herb Wild
Cherry, Reading, Pa.,
Cabin, Medium
Amber, 10 In., R-H93

Bitters, Hall's,
Barrel, Copper
Amber, Applied Lip,
9 5/8 In., R-H9

Bitters, Holtzermann's
Patent Stomach,
Cabin, Amber,
9 3/4 In., R-H154

Kennedy's East India, Iler & Co., Omaha, Neb., Clear, Tooled Lip, 4 1/8 In., R-K28 . . . .   110.00
Keystone, Barrel, Amber, Applied Sloping Collar, 10 In., R-K36 . . . . .700.00 to 880.00
Keystone, Barrel, Medium Orange Amber, Applied Lip, 9 3/4 In., R-K36 . . . .   770.00
Keystone, Barrel, Red Amber, Applied Sloping Collar, 9 3/4 In., R-K36 . . . .   700.00
Kimball's Jaundice, Stoddard, N.H., Olive Green To Olive Amber, Applied Lip 963.00
Kimball's Jaundice, Stoddard, N.H., Olive Yellow, Sloping Collar, Iron Pontil, 6 7/8 In. . . .   1545.00
Kimball's Jaundice, Troy, N.H., Amber, Iron Pontil, 7 In., R-K42 . . . .   1400.00
Kimball's Jaundice, Troy, N.H., Olive Amber, Applied Lip, Iron Pontil, 7 In., R-K42 . . . .   1430.00
Kimball's Jaundice, Troy, N.H., Yellow Amber, Sloping Collar, IP, 7 In., R-K42 .1120.00 to 1200.00
King Solomon's, Seattle, Wash., Amber, Tooled Double Collar, 1900-10, 7 1/4 In., R-K50   100.00
Ko-Hi, Koehler & Hinrichs, St. Paul, Amber, Tooled Lip, 9 In., R-K68 . . . .   504.00
L.N. Kreinbrook's, Mt. Pleasant, Pa., Yellow Amber, Coffin Shape, Pt.6 1/4 In., R-K78.3 .   1008.00
Laboratory Of G.W. Merchant Chemist, Blue Green, 5 1/2 In.   413.00
Laboratory Of G.W. Merchant Chemist, Yellow Green, 5 1/2 In. 413.00
Lacour's Sarsapariphere, Lighthouse, Light To Medium Amber, Applied Lip, 9 In., R-L3 .   3740.00
Lacour's Sarsapariphere, Lighthouse, Tobacco Amber, Applied Lip, 1866-69, 9 In., R-L3   2860.00
Lash's, Natural Tonic Laxative, Amber, 4 3/4 In., R-L33 . . . .   46.00
Lash's, Natural Tonic Laxative, Amber, Contents, Label, Square, 9 1/2 In., R-L32 .132.00 to 154.00
Lash's, Natural Tonic Laxative, Amber, Contents, Paper Label, Square, 4 3/4 In., R-L33 . .   440.00
Leak's Kidney & Liver, Best Blood Purifier & Cathartic, Red Amber, 8 7/8 In., R-L54 . . .   145.00
Lediard's Celebrated Stomach, Blue Green, Double Roll Collar, 10 In., R-L60 . . . .   2420.00
Lediard's Celebrated Stomach, Emerald Green, Double Collar, Pontil, 10 1/8 In., R-L60 .   2016.00
Lediard's Celebrated Stomach, Teal Green, Applied Lip, 10 1/8 In., R-L60 . . . .   1680.00
Lediard's Morning Call, Green, Applied Lip, R-L61 . . . .   413.00
Lediard's O.K. Plantation, 1840, Semi-Cabin, Amber, Applied Lip, 9 3/4 In., R-L62 . . . . .   2860.00
Lediard's O.K. Plantation, 1840, Semi-Cabin, Tobacco Amber, 11 In., R-L62 . . . .   3960.00
Leopold Sahl's Aromatic Stomach, Amber, Applied Sloping Collar, 10 1/4 In., R-S7 . . . .   3080.00
Lindsey's Blood, Dark Olive Amber, Panels, Sloping Collar, 9 3/8 In. 3575.00
Lippman's Great German, Amber, Applied Sloping Double Collar, 9 1/2 In., R-L98 . . . . .   275.00
Litthauer Stomach, see also Bitters, Hartwig Kantorowicz
Litthauer Stomach, Milk Glass, Case Gin, Applied Lip, 9 1/2 In., R-L102 . . . .*Illus*   176.00
Lorimer's Juniper Tar, Elmira, N.Y., Blue Green, Applied Lip, 9 1/2 In., R-L121 . . . .   4690.00
Mack's Orange Tonic, Citrus Extracts Co, Amber, Tooled Lip, Label, 9 In., R-M3 . . .*Illus*   515.00
Mandrake, see Bitters, Dr. Baxter's
Marshall's, Best Laxative & Blood Purifier, Red Amber, Square, 8 1/2 In., R-M40 . . . . . .   79.00
McKeever's Army, Drum Base, Cannon Balls, Orange Amber, 1860-80, 10 3/8 In., R-M58   3080.00
Mishler's Herb, Golden Amber, 8 1/2 In., R-M99 . . . .   80.00
Mishler's Herb, Stoeckels Grad Pat Feb. 11 '66, Orange Amber, Square, 9 In., R-M101 . .   45.00
Mishler's Herb, Table Spoon Graduation, Yellow Gold Amber, 9 1/4 In., R-M100 . . . .   250.00
Mist Of The Morning, Barrel, Amber, Sloping Double Collar, 10 In. 728.00
Morning Inceptum 5869, Star, Amber, 3-Sided, Iron Pontil, 12 5/8 In., R-M135 . . . .   280.00
Morning Inceptum 5869, Star, Medium Amber, Applied Lip, IP, 12 5/8 In., R-M135 . . . .   385.00
Morning Inceptum 5869, Star, Medium Yellow Amber, IP, 12 1/2 In., R-M135 . . . .   330.00
Morning Inceptum 5869, Star, Orange Amber, Iron Pontil, 12 3/4 In., R-M135 . . . .   440.00
Morning Inceptum 5869, Star, Yellow Amber, Tooled Lip, 5 1/8 In., R-M136 . . . .   1540.00
Napoleon Cocktail Dingen, Banjo, Lady's Leg, Amber Yellow, IP, 10 1/2 In., R-N3 . . . . .   3500.00
Napoleon Cocktail Dingen, Banjo, Lady's Leg, Olive, IP, 1850-60, 10 1/2 In., R-N3 . . . .   7150.00
Napoleon Cocktail Dingen, Banjo, Lady's Leg, Smoky Clear, IP, 10 1/2 In., R-N3 . . . . .   5500.00
National, Ear Of Corn, Patent 1867, Amber Olive, Applied Lip, 12 1/4 In., R-N8 . . . .   1980.00
National, Ear Of Corn, Patent 1867, Amber, Applied Lip, 12 3/8 In., R-N8 . . . . . . .336.00 to 504.00
National, Ear Of Corn, Patent 1867, Amber, Painted, Applied Lip, 12 1/8 In., R-N8 . . . . .   1430.00
National, Ear Of Corn, Patent 1867, Blue Aqua, Applied Double Collar, 12 3/8 In., R-N8 .   12100.00
National, Ear Of Corn, Patent 1867, Gold Amber, 12 1/2 In., R-N8 . . . . .450.00 to 560.00
National, Ear Of Corn, Patent 1867, Gold Amber, 1860-80, 12 1/2 In., R-N8 . . . .   504.00
National, Ear Of Corn, Patent 1867, Gold Yellow Amber Olive, 12 1/2 In., R-N8 . . . .   1320.00
National, Ear Of Corn, Patent 1867, Medium Pink Puce, Double Collar, 12 1/2 In., R-N8 .   10450.00
National, Ear Of Corn, Patent 1867, Medium Yellow Amber, 1870-80, 12 1/2 In., R-N8 . .   440.00
National, Ear Of Corn, Patent 1867, Olive Yellow, 12 1/2 In., R-N8 . . . .   2688.00
National, Ear Of Corn, Patent 1867, Strawberry Yellow, 12 5/8 In., R-N8 . . . .   2000.00
National, Ear Of Corn, Patent 1867, Yellow Amber, Applied Lip, 12 1/2 In., R-N8 .440.00 to 616.00
Native American Stomach, Samuel Westheimer, Medium Amber, c.1885, 9 3/4 In., R-N14   134.00
Nibol, Kidney & Liver, Tonic, Laxative, Blood Purifier, 9 1/2 In., R-N31 . . . .   132.00

Bitters, Litthauer
Stomach, Milk Glass,
Case Gin, Applied Lip,
9 1/2 In., R-L102

Bitters, Mack's Orange
Tonic, Citrus Extracts Co,
Amber, Tooled Lip, Label,
9 In., R-M3

Bitters, Old
Homestead Wild
Cherry, Cabin, Amber,
Label, 9 1/2 In., R-O37

Nibol, Kidney & Liver, Tonic, Laxative, Blood Purifier, Amber, 9 1/2 In., R-N31	650.00
O' Leary's 20th Century, Amber, Tooled Lip, 8 5/8 In., R-O55	135.00
OK Plantation, 1840, Strawberry Puce, 3-Sided, Sloping Collar, 11 In.	7840.00
Old Continental, Semi-Cabin, Medium Golden Amber, Applied Lip, 10 In., R-O25	440.00
Old Dr. Goodhue's Root & Herb, Salem, Mass., I.H. Russel & Co., Aqua, 9 In., R-G68	85.00
Old Dr. Warren's Quaker, Flign & Co., Prov., R.I., Aqua, 10 In., R-W48	79.00
Old Dr. Warren's Quaker, Flign & Co., Prov., R.I., Aqua, Label, 9 3/4 In., R-W48	28.00
Old Hickory Celebrated Stomach, J. Grossman, Medium Amber, 8 7/8 In., R-O31	190.00
Old Hickory Celebrated Stomach, J. Grossman, Yellow Amber, 4 1/2 In., R-O32	145.00 to 285.00
Old Homestead Wild Cherry, Cabin, Amber, Label, 9 1/2 In., R-O37 *Illus*	4085.00
Old Homestead Wild Cherry, Cabin, Amber, Sloping Collar, 9 1/2 In., R-O37	1792.00 to 4500.00
Old Homestead Wild Cherry, Cabin, Yellow Amber, 9 1/2 In., R-O37	392.00 to 630.00
Old Sachem & Wigwam Tonic, Barrel, Apricot, Applied Lip, 9 1/4 In., R-O46	735.00 to 1456.00
Old Sachem & Wigwam Tonic, Barrel, Blue Aqua, Pontil, 10 1/4 In., R-O45	4500.00
Old Sachem & Wigwam Tonic, Barrel, Bright Gold Yellow Amber, 9 1/2 In., R-O46	1320.00
Old Sachem & Wigwam Tonic, Barrel, Cherry Puce, Applied Lip, 9 1/2 In., R-O46	392.00 to 500.00
Old Sachem & Wigwam Tonic, Barrel, Dark Amber Orange, Applied Lip, 9 1/2 In., R-O46	468.00
Old Sachem & Wigwam Tonic, Barrel, Gold Yellow Amber, 9 1/2 In., R-O46	450.00 to 616.00
Old Sachem & Wigwam Tonic, Barrel, Medium Copper, Applied Lip, 9 1/2 In., R-O46	1650.00
Old Sachem & Wigwam Tonic, Barrel, Medium Pink Puce, Applied Lip, 9 1/2 In., R-O46	5500.00
Old Sachem & Wigwam Tonic, Barrel, Moss Green, 9 1/2 In., R-O46	9500.00
Old Sachem & Wigwam Tonic, Barrel, Orange Amber, Square Collar, 9 1/2 In., R-O46	468.00
Old Sachem & Wigwam Tonic, Barrel, Red Amber, Applied Lip, 9 1/4 In., R-O46	605.00
Old Sachem & Wigwam Tonic, Barrel, Strawberry Puce, 9 3/8 In., R-O46	573.00 to 672.00
Old Sachem & Wigwam Tonic, Barrel, Strawberry Yellow, 9 1/2 In., R-O46	9520.00
Old Sachem & Wigwam Tonic, Barrel, Topaz, Square Collar, 1865-75, 9 3/4 In., R-O64	4200.00
Old Sachem & Wigwam Tonic, Barrel, Yellow Amber, 9 1/4 In., R-O46	336.00 to 560.00
Old Sachem & Wigwam Tonic, Barrel, Yellow Apricot, 9 3/4 In., R-O46	2420.00
Original Pocahontas, Y. Ferguson, Barrel, Blue Aqua, Applied Lip, 9 1/2 In., R-O86	7150.00
Orizaba, J. Maristany Jr., Amber, Applied Lip, 8 1/2 In., R-O88	6050.00
Oxygenated, For Dyspepsia, Asthma, & General Debility, Aqua, OP, 7 5/8 In., R-O99	119.00
Parker's Celebrated Stomach, 9 1/2 In., R-P22	132.00
Pepsin, Green, Square, 8 1/4 In.	80.00
Pepsin, R.W. Davis Drug Co., Chicago, Apple Green, Tooled Lip, 4 1/2 In., R-P45	275.00
Pepsin, R.W. Davis Drug Co., Chicago, Medium Green, Tooled Lip, 8 1/4 In., R-P44	145.00
Pepsin, R.W. Davis Drug Co., Chicago, Yellow Green, Tooled Lip, 8 1/4 In., R-P44	336.00
Pepsin Calisaya, Dr. Russell Med. Co., Apple Green, Tooled Lip, 4 1/8 In., R-P51	155.00
Pepsin Calisaya, Dr. Russell Med. Co., Medium Amber, Tooled Lip, 4 1/4 In., R-P51	180.00
Pepsin Calisaya, Dr. Russell Med. Co., Medium Grass Green, Tooled Lip, 8 1/4 In., R-P50	135.00
Pepsin Calisaya, Dr. Russell Med. Co., Yellow Green, Tooled Lip, 8 1/4 In., R-P50	67.00
Pepsin Calisaya, Dr. Russell Med. Co., Yellow Green, Tooled Lip, Labels, 8 In., R-P50	180.00
Peruvian, W & K, Medium Amber, Tooled Lip, 9 1/4 In., R-P66	90.00
Pig, see Bitters, Berkshire; Bitters, Suffolk	
Pineapple, Golden Amber, Applied Lip, 9 In., R-P100	358.00
Pineapple, J.F.L. Capitol, Amber, Double Collar, Embossed, Iron Pontil, 9 3/8 In., R-C40	2200.00
Pineapple, Medium Amber, Applied Lip, 9 In., R-P100	300.00

Bitters, Poor Man's Family, Aqua, Tooled Lip, Label, 6 3/8 In., R-P122

Bitters, Royal Pepsin Stomach, L & A Scharff, Sole Agents, Amber, 7 3/8 In., R-R114

Bitters, S.B. Rothenberg Sole Agent, Pat., Milk Glass, Seal, Label, Case Gin, 9 In., R-B82

Pineapple, Olive Yellow Amber, Applied Lip, 9 In., R-P100 .... 825.00
Pineapple, W & Co., N.Y., Emerald Green, Double Collar, Iron Pontil, 8 1/2 In., R-P100 . 10640.00
Pineapple, W & Co., N.Y., Gold Amber, Applied Lip, Pontil, 8 7/8 In., R-P100 .... 715.00
Pineapple, W & Co., N.Y., Green, Applied Double Collar, Graphite Pontil, 9 In., R-P100 . 3300.00
Pineapple, W & Co., N.Y., Olive Yellow, Applied Double Lip, Iron Pontil, 9 In., R-P100 . 3750.00
Pineapple, Yellow Amber Olive, Diamond, Double Collar, Pontil, 8 7/8 In., R-P100 .. 728.00
Pond's, Unexcelled Laxative, Yellow Amber, Neck Foil Seal, Labels, 9 3/4 In., R-P120 .. 200.00
Pond's Kidney & Liver, Unexcelled Laxative, Amber, Square, 9 1/2 In., R-P121 .....48.00 to 79.00
Poor Man's Family, Aqua, Tooled Lip, Label, 6 3/8 In., R-P122 ....*Illus* 300.00
Prickly Ash, Amber, ABM Lip, Label, 9 1/4 In., R-P140 .... 230.00
Prickly Ash, Milk Glass, Square, Embossed, 9 In., R-P143 .... 69.00
Professor Geo. J. Byrne, Great Universal Compound Stomach, Amber, 10 In., R-B280 ... 2640.00
Professor Geo. J. Byrne, Great Universal Compound, Yellow Amber, 10 In., R-B280 .... 1340.00
Prune Stomach & Liver, Best Cathartic & Blood Purifier, Amber, 9 In., R-P151 .... 150.00
Purdy's Cottage, Amber, Applied Double Collar, Pontil, 9 1/4 In., R-P156 .... 4400.00
Purdy's Cottage, Tobacco Amber, Green Tint, Applied Double Collar, 9 1/4 In., R-P156 . 3080.00
Red Jacket, Bennett Pieters & Co., Amber, Applied Lip, 9 1/2 In., R-R19 ....143.00 to 358.00
Reed's, Lady's Leg, Amber, Sloping Double Collar, 12 3/4 In., R-R28 .... 392.00
Reed's, Lady's Leg, Applied Lip, Bubbles, 12 1/2 In., R-R28 .... 990.00
Reed's, Lady's Leg, Gold Yellow Amber, Applied Lip, 12 1/2 In., R-R28 .... 364.00
Reed's, Lady's Leg, Yellow Amber, Double Collar, 12 3/8 In., R-R27 .... 784.00
Rising Sun, John C Hurst, Philada, Amber, Sloping Collar, 9 1/2 In., R-R66 ......130.00 to 330.00
Rockingham Bitters, Dog, Hiking Leg, Cork Stopper, Germany, 3 x 5 In. 65.00
Rohrer's Expectoral Wild Cherry Tonic, Amber, Applied Lip, Graphite Pontil 468.00
Romaine's Crimean, Patend 1863, Medium To Light Amber, Applied Lip, 10 In. 990.00
Romany Wine, Aqua, 6 3/4 In., R-R88 .... 75.00
Royal Italian, A.M.F. Gianelli, Grape Amethyst, Square Collar, 13 1/2 In., R-R111 ...... 1568.00
Royal Italian, A.M.F. Gianelli, Pink Amethyst, Applied Lip, 13 3/4 In., R-R111 .... 1008.00
Royal Pepsin Stomach, L & A Scharff, Sole Agents, Amber, 7 3/8 In., R-R114 ......*Illus* 225.00
Royal Pepsin Stomach, L & A Scharff, Sole Agents, Red Amber, 9 In., R-R113 .... 165.00
Royal Pepsin Stomach, L & A Scharff, Sole Agents, Yellow Amber, Stopper, 4 In., R-R116 . 360.00
Rush's, A.H. Flanders M.D., New York, Amber, Square, 8 3/4 In., R-R124 .... 231.00
Rush's, A.H. Flanders M.D., New York, Orange Amber, 8 7/8 In., R-R124 ....79.00 to 89.00
Rush's, A.H. Flanders M.D., New York, Yellow Amber, Paneled Sides, 9 In., R-R124 .... 100.00
Russ' St. Domingo, New York, Amber, 9 7/8 In., R-R125 .... 175.00
Russ' St. Domingo, New York, Yellow, Applied Sloping Collar, 9 7/8 In., R-R125 ..... 672.00
S.B. Rothenberg Sole Agent, Pat., Milk Glass, Seal, Label, Case Gin, 9 In., R-B82 .*Illus* 440.00
S.O. Richardson's, South Reading Mass., Aqua, Flared Lip, OP, 6 In., R-R57 .....100.00 to 378.00
S.S. Smith Jr & Co., Semi-Cabin, Cobalt Blue, Applied Sloping Collar, 9 3/4 In. 4760.00
S.T. Drake's, see Bitters, Drake's Plantation
Saint Jacob's, Amber, Applied Sloping Collar, 8 1/2 In., R-S13 ....155.00 to 185.00
Saint Jacob's, Yellow, Sloping Collar, Embossed, 8 3/4 In., R-S13 .... 700.00
Sanborn's Kidney & Liver Vegetable Laxative, Amber, Tooled Lip, 9 7/8 In., R-S28 .... 100.00
Sanitarium, Rock Island, 3-Sided, Yellow Green, Tooled Lip, 9 5/8 In., R-S31 .... 180.00
Sarasina Stomach, Amber, Tooled Lip, 4 In., R-S33 .... 360.00
Sarasina Stomach, Orange Amber To Yellow Amber, 9 3/8 In., R-S32 .... 110.00

Sazerac Aromatic, PHD & Co., Lady's Leg, Amber, Applied Lip, 10 In., R-S48 .... 440.00
Sazerac Aromatic, PHD & Co., Lady's Leg, Milk Glass, 12 In., R-S47 ....275.00 to 420.00
Schapperts German Stomach, Philadelphia, Amber, 9 7/8 In., R-S51 .... 400.00
Schnapps, Olive Green, Square, Short Neck, Star Of David, Fish, Embossed, 7 1/4 In. ... 41.00
Schroeder's, Louisville & Cincinnati, Lady's Leg, Amber, Tooled Lip, 5 1/4 In., R-S67 .. 300.00
Schroeder's, Louisville & Cincinnati, Lady's Leg, Amber, Tooled Lip, 11 3/4 In., R-S68 .. 360.00
Schroeder's, Louisville, Ky., Lady's Leg, Amber, Label, 8 3/4 In., R-S64 ....Illus 825.00
Schroeder's, Louisville, Ky., Lady's Leg, Amber, Tooled Lip, 11 3/4 In., R-S65 .... 470.00
Sharp's Mountain Herb, Amber, Applied Sloping Collar, 9 1/2 In., R-S95 .... 300.00
Simon's Centennial, Bust Of Washington, Amber, 9 3/4 In., R-S110 .... 3300.00
Simon's Centennial, Bust Of Washington, Aqua, 9 3/4 In., R-S110 .... 660.00
Simon's Centennial, Bust Of Washington, Aqua, Double Collar, 10 7/8 In., R-S110.5 ... 2320.00
Simon's Centennial, Bust Of Washington, Red Amber, 10 In., R-S110 .... 4080.00
Smyrna Stomach, Prolongs Life, Amber, Tooled Lip, Label, Contents, 9 In., R-S134 .... 1040.00
Sol Frank's Panacea, Lighthouse, Yellow Amber, Sloping Collar, 10 In., R-F79 .... 2576.00
Solomon's Strengthening & Invigorating, Cobalt Blue, Sloping Collar, 9 3/4 In., R-S139 1200.00
Solomons' Strengthening & Invigorating, Cobalt Blue, Applied Lip, 9 1/2 In., R-S140 .. 1045.00
Southern Aromatic Cock Tail, J. Grossman, Lady's Leg, Wheat, 13 In., R-HS-149 ...... 2090.00
St Nicholas Stomach, Tapered, Amber, Applied Lip, Pontil, 7 5/8 In., R-S17 .... 616.00
St. Gotthard Herb, Gold Amber, Applied Lip, 9 In., R-S12 .... 200.00
St. Gotthard Herb, Mette & Kanne Pros, St. Louis, Golden Amber, 9 In., R-S12 .... 180.00
Star Kidney & Liver, Amber, Tooled Lip, 8 3/4 In., R-S178 .... 120.00
Steinfeld's French Cognac Bitters, Semi-Cabin, Amber, 9 7/8 In., R-S186 .... 13200.00
Suffolk, Brook & Tucker, Boston, Pig, Yellow Orange, Applied Lip, 10 1/2 In., R-S217 .. 990.00
Suffolk, Philbrook & Tucker, Boston, Pig, Yellow Amber, 10 1/8 In., R-S217 ....Illus 952.00
Thad Waterman Warsaw Stomach, 8-Sided, Gold Amber, Double Collar, 10 In., R-W54.5 3500.00
Tippecanoe, H.H. Warner & Co., Amber, Mushroom Top, 9 1/8 In., R-T30.8 ....123.00 to 140.00
Tippecanoe, H.H. Warner & Co., Honey Amber, Mushroom Top, 9 In., R-T30.8 .... 159.00
Tippecanoe, H.H. Warner & Co., Medium Amber, Mushroom Top, 9 In., R-T30.8 ...... 143.00
Tippecanoe, H.H. Warner & Co., Olive Yellow, Mushroom Top, 9 In., R-T30.8 .... 3920.00
Turner Brothers, New York, Barrel, Yellow, Applied Lip, 10 In., R-T67 .... 1008.00
Turner Brothers, New York, Buffalo, N.Y., San Francisco, Amber, IP, 9 3/4 In., R-T70.5 . 2200.00
Uncle Sam's Wild Cherry, Green, Square, Rope Twist Neck, Tooled Lip, 9 1/4 In., R-U4 . 1980.00
V Squarza, Cobalt Blue, Applied Lip, 8 In., R-S170 .... 8800.00
W.C. Brobst & Rentschler, Reading, Pa., Barrel, Amber, Tooled Lip, 10 3/4 In., R-W57 .. 1320.00
W.C. Brobst & Rentschler, Reading, Pa., Barrel, Orange Amber, 10 1/2 In., R-W57 ..... 649.00
W.L. Richardsons, Short Neck, 7 In., R-R58 .... 150.00
W.M. Ward's Eureka, Tooled Lip, 8 3/4 In., R-W28 .... 198.00
Wait's Kidney & Liver, California's Own True Laxative, Blood Purifier, Amber, 9 In., R-W6 95.00
Wampoo, Blum Siegel & Bro, Medium Amber, Double Roll Collar, 9 3/4 In., R-W23 .... 209.00
Wampoo, Blum Siegel & Bro, N.Y., Yellow Amber, Sloping Double Collar, 10 In., R-W24 275.00
Wampoo, Siegel & Bro., New York, Amber, Square, Applied Lip, 9 1/2 In., R-W25 ..... 143.00
Warner's Safe, Rochester, N.Y., Oval, Gold Amber, Double Collar, 9 1/2 In., R-W34 .... 728.00
Wheeler's Genuine, Aqua, Oval, 9 In., R-W85 ....139.00 to 165.00
Wheeler's Genuine, Blue Aqua, Oval, c.1860-65, 9 1/2 In., R-W85 .... 89.00
William Allen's Congress, Semi-Cabin, Amethyst, Pontil, 7 3/4 In., R-A30 ....Illus 345.00
William Allen's Congress, Semi-Cabin, Medium Blue Green, Applied Lip, 10 In., R-A29 . 2420.00

Bitters, Schroeder's,
Louisville, Ky., Lady's
Leg, Amber, Label,
8 3/4 In., R-S64

Bitters, William Allen's
Congress, Semi-Cabin,
Amethyst, Pontil,
7 3/4 In., R-A30

Bitters, Suffolk, Philbrook & Tucker, Boston,
Pig, Yellow Amber, 10 1/8 In., R-S217

William Allen's Congress, Semi-Cabin, Tobacco Gold Amber, Applied Lip, 10 In., R-A29   2640.00
Winter's Stomach, A.B.Co., Amber, Tooled Lip, 9 5/8 In., R-W141 . . . .   155.00
Witch, Horseshoe, Tobacco Amber, Applied Double Collar, 8 1/8 In. 360.00
Wormser Bros, San Francisco, Barrel, Gold Amber, Applied Lip, 9 3/4 In., R-W162.5 . . .   3300.00
Wormser Bros, San Francisco, Barrel, Honey Amber, Sloping Collar, 9 3/4 In., R-W162.5   2200.00
Yerba Buena, S.F. Cal., Flask, Amber, Applied Lip, 8 In., R-Y4 . . . .   198.00
Yerba Buena, S.F. Cal., Flask, Olive Amber, 8 1/2 In., R-Y4 . . . .   120.00
Yochim Bros. Celebrated Stomach, Amber, Tooled Lip, Label, 8 3/4 In., R-Y5 . . . .   269.00
Zingari, F. Rahter, Lady's Leg, Medium Topaz, Applied Lip, 12 In., R-Z4 . . . .   1430.00
Zingari, F. Rahter, Lady's Leg, Red Amber, Drippy Top, 12 In., R-Z4 . . . .   275.00

----------------------------------- **BLACK GLASS** -----------------------------------

Black glass is not really black. It is dark green or brown. In the seventeenth century, blown black glass demijohns were used to carry liquor overseas from Europe. They were usually heavy glass bottles that were made to withstand shipping. The kick-up bottom also helped deter breakage. Many types of bottles were made of very dark glass that appeared black. This was one of the most common colors for glass wine bottles of the eighteenth and early-nineteenth centuries.

Ale, B.G.W., Olive Green, Clover Pontil, Applied Lip, 1790-1810, 9 In. 728.00
Ale, Olive Amber, Applied String Lip, Open Pontil, Dutch, 1760-90, 11 1/4 In. 100.00
Ale, Olive Amber, Applied String Lip, Pontil, 3 1/4 In. 336.00
Ale, Olive Yellow Green, Applied String Lip, Pontil, 1760-80, 10 In. 235.00
Cylindrical, Olive Amber, Rolled Lip, 8 1/8 x 4 In. 308.00
Cylindrical, Olive, Double Collar, Kick-Up, 11 3/4 In. 95.00
Cylindrical, Tapered Shoulders, c.1850, 8 1/2 In. 48.00
Dutch Kidney, Olive Amber, Brandy, Painted, Gold, Black, Red, OP, 1760, 7 In. 770.00
Dutch Kidney, Olive Amber, Geneva, Painted, Gold, Black, Red, OP, 1760, 7 In. 440.00
Dutch Kidney, Olive Green, Metallic Patina, Applied String Collar, 5 1/8 In. 1120.00
Dutch Kidney, Olive Green, Rum, Painted, Gold, Black, Red, Applied Lip, OP, 1760, 7 In.   275.00
Dutch Onion, Dark Olive Green, Tapered Neck, Applied Rim, c.1700-10, 7 1/4 In. 346.00
Dutch Onion, Emerald Green, Applied String Lip, Open Pontil, 1720-35, 6 5/8 In. 253.00
Dutch Onion, Horsehoof, Medium Olive Amber, Applied String Lip, OP, c.1730, 7 1/2 In.   154.00
Dutch Onion, Horsehoof, Olive Amber, Applied String Lip, Open Pontil, 1720-35, 8 In. . .   135.00
Dutch Onion, Horsehoof, Olive Amber, Applied String Lip, Open Pontil, 8 In. 101.00
Dutch Onion, Horsehoof, Olive Yellow Amber, Applied String Lip, Open Pontil, 8 1/4 In.   190.00
Dutch Onion, Horsehoof, Olive Yellow, Applied String Collar, Kick-Up, Pontil, 7 3/4 In. .   202.00
Dutch Onion, Olive Green, Applied String Lip, Pontil, 1720-35, 7 5/8 In. . . . .*Illus*   112.00
Dutch Onion, Olive Yellow Green, Applied String Lip, Open Pontil, 1720-35, 5 3/4 In. . .   275.00
Dutch Onion, Olive Yellow Green, Applied String Lip, Open Pontil, 1720-35, 6 1/4 In. . .   100.00
Dutch Onion, Olive Yellow Green, Applied String Lip, Open Pontil, 1720-35, 6 5/8 In. . .   110.00
Dutch Onion, Olive Yellow Green, Applied String Lip, Open Pontil, 1720-35, 7 3/4 In. . .   80.00
Dutch Onion, Olive Yellow Green, Applied String Lip, Open Pontil, 1720-35, 7 In. 145.00
Dutch Onion, Wine, Dark Olive Green, Tapered Neck, Applied Rim, Kick-Up, 8 In. 653.00
Dutch Onion, Yellow Green, Applied String Lip, Kick-Up, Open Pontil, c.1730, 7 1/2 In. .   120.00
Dutch Onion, Yellow Green, Applied String Lip, Open Pontil, 1720-35, 7 1/2 In. 330.00
English Mallet, Olive Amber, Applied String Lip, Pontil, 1740-50, 8 3/8 In. 202.00
English Mallet, Olive Amber, Applied String Lip, Pontil, 1740-55, 7 7/8 In. 157.00
English Mallet, Olive Amber, Applied String Lip, Pontil, 1740-60, 8 In. 190.00
English Mallet, Olive Amber, Applied String Lip, Pontil, 1745-60, 7 3/4 In. 253.00
English Mallet, Olive Amber, Applied String Lip, Pontil, 1745-60, 8 In. 275.00
English Mallet, Olive Amber, Applied String Lip, Pontil, 1750-70, 8 1/2 In. . . . . . .213.00 to 246.00
English Mallet, Olive Amber, Applied String Lip, Pontil, 1835-50, 7 7/8 In. 200.00
English Mallet, Olive Yellow Green, Applied String Lip, Pontil, 1725-40, 7 In. 448.00
English Onion, Deep Olive Amber, Metallic Iridescence, Applied Lip, 4 3/4 x 3 5/8 In. . . .   730.00
English Onion, Wine, Olive Green, Patina, c.1690-1700, 5 1/2 In. 631.00
Globular, Deep Olive Amber, Sloping Double Collar, Pontil, 11 3/4 In. 280.00
Globular, Deep Olive Green, Sloping Double Collar, Pontil, 12 1/4 In. 672.00
Globular, Olive Amber, Painted Number 4, Applied Sloping Double Collar, 12 In. 560.00
Globular, Olive Amber, Pontil, Sheared Mouth, Applied String Lip, Continental, 11 1/2 In.   672.00
Green, Open Pontil, Long Neck, Sheared Mouth, Applied String Lip, 12 3/4 In. 65.00
Mallet, Dip Mold, Olive Amber, Applied String Lip, Open Pontil, Belgium, 8 In. 134.00
Mallet, Dip Mold, Olive Yellow, Applied String Lip, Pontil, Continental, 8 7/8 In. 168.00
Mallet, Medium Olive Amber, Applied String Lip, Pontil, 8 5/8 In. 280.00

Black Glass, Dutch Onion, Olive Green, Applied String Lip, Pontil, 1720-35, 7 5/8 In.

Black Glass, Onion, Pontil, Olive Amber, Applied String Lip, 1680-1710, 6 In.

Black Glass, Onion, Emerald Green, Open Pontil, Applied String Lip, Germany, 6 5/8 In.

Mallet, Olive Yellow Amber, Applied String Lip, Pontil, 1740-50, 7 3/4 In. 390.00
Mallet, Olive Yellow Amber, Applied String Lip, Pontil, 1740-50, 8 7/8 In. 355.00
Mallet, Olive Yellow Green, Applied String Lip, Kick-Up, OP, Belgium, 1735-50, 8 1/8 In. 165.00
Mallet, Olive Yellow Green, Applied String Lip, Open Pontil, 1740-60, 7 1/2 In. 190.00
Mallet, Wine, Dark Olive Green, Long Neck, Applied Rim, Kick-Up, Shield, 9 1/4 In. . . . 133.00
Olive Yellow, Sheared Mouth, String Rim, Double Magnum, Onion Shape, 12 In. 1792.00
Onion, Dark Olive Green, Applied String Lip, Open Pontil, 1720-35, 6 In. 130.00
Onion, Dark Olive Green, Wide Neck, Applied Rim, Kick-Up, Pontil Scar, 7 1/2 In. 1018.00
Onion, Emerald Green, Applied String Lip, Open Pontil, 1720-35, 7 1/4 In. 200.00
Onion, Emerald Green, Applied String Lip, Open Pontil, 1720-50, 6 1/8 In. . . . . . .125.00 to 385.00
Onion, Emerald Green, Applied String Lip, Open Pontil, 1720-50, 6 3/4 In. 155.00
Onion, Emerald Green, Applied String Lip, Open Pontil, 1720-50, 7 3/8 In. 135.00
Onion, Emerald Green, Open Pontil, Applied String Lip, Germany, 6 5/8 In. . . . .*Illus* 140.00
Onion, Horsehoof, Olive Amber, Applied String Lip, Kick-Up, OP, c.1750, 8 3/8 In. 165.00
Onion, Horsehoof, Olive Amber, Applied String Lip, Open Pontil, 1740-60, 7 3/4 In. 125.00
Onion, Horsehoof, Olive Amber, Applied String Lip, Open Pontil, c.1740-60, 8 In. 125.00
Onion, Horsehoof, Olive Amber, Applied String Lip, Open Pontil, c.1750, 7 3/4 In. 125.00 to 225.00
Onion, Horsehoof, Olive Yellow, Applied String Lip, Open Pontil, 1740-60, 8 In. 190.00
Onion, Medium Blue Green, Applied String Lip, Open Pontil, 1720-35, 6 7/8 In. 121.00
Onion, Medium Blue Green, Applied String Lip, Open Pontil, 1720-35, 7 In. 300.00
Onion, Medium Olive Yellow Green, Applied String Lip, Open Pontil, 1720-35, 6 1/4 In. . 130.00
Onion, Medium Olive Yellow Green, Applied String Lip, Open Pontil, 1720-35, 7 3/4 In. . 132.00
Onion, Olive Amber, Applied String Lip, Open Pontil, 1690-1710, 5 5/8 In. 235.00
Onion, Olive Green, Applied String Lip, Open Pontil, 6 3/4 In. . . . . .134.00 to 179.00
Onion, Olive Green, Applied String Lip, Pontil, 1690-1710, 5 1/2 In. 825.00
Onion, Olive Green, Applied String Lip, Pontil, 1690-1710, 5 3/4 In. . . . . .258.00 to 392.00
Onion, Olive Green, Applied String Lip, Pontil, 1690-1710, 6 In. 224.00
Onion, Olive Green, Applied String Lip, Pontil, 1700-10, 6 1/8 In. 532.00
Onion, Olive Yellow Amber, Applied String Lip, Open Pontil, 1720-50, 6 1/4 In. 180.00
Onion, Olive Yellow Amber, Outward Rolled Lip, Open Pontil, 1720-50, 6 7/8 In. 180.00
Onion, Olive Yellow Green, Applied String Lip, Open Pontil, 1720-30, 6 5/8 In. 245.00
Onion, Olive Yellow Green, Applied String Lip, Open Pontil, 1720-40, 6 1/2 In. 300.00
Onion, Olive Yellow Green, Applied String Lip, Open Pontil, 1720-50, 6 1/2 In. . . .110.00 to 235.00
Onion, Olive Yellow Green, Applied String Lip, Open Pontil, 1720-50, 7 5/8 In. 125.00
Onion, Olive Yellow Green, Applied String Lip, Open Pontil, 1720-50, 7 In. . . . . . .100.00 to 215.00
Onion, Olive Yellow Green, Applied String Lip, Pontil, 1720-35, 6 In. 121.00
Onion, Olive Yellow Green, Applied String Lip, Pontil, 1725-35, 7 1/8 In. 300.00
Onion, Olive Yellow Green, Applied String Lip, Pontil, 1730-35, 7 1/8 In. 365.00
Onion, Olive Yellow Green, String Lip, Open Pontil, Continental, 1690-1710, 10 3/4 In. . . . 2016.00
Onion, Olive Yellow, Applied String Lip, Open Pontil, 1720-50, 6 5/8 In. 125.00
Onion, Olive Yellow, Applied String Lip, Open Pontil, 1720-50, 7 1/4 In. 135.00
Onion, Olive Yellow, Applied String Lip, Pontil, 1680-1710, 5 3/8 In. 224.00
Onion, Olive Yellow, String Lip, Pontil, 6 1/4 x 5 1/2 In. 258.00
Onion, Pancake, Olive Yellow Green, Applied String Lip, Pontil, 1690-1705, 5 5/8 In. 825.00
Onion, Pontil, Olive Amber, Applied String Lip, 1680-1710, 6 In. . . . .*Illus* 420.00
Onion, Yellow Amber, Applied String Lip, Open Pontil, 1720-50, 7 1/8 In. 255.00
Onion, Yellow Green, Applied String Lip, Open Pontil, 5 3/4 In. 308.00
Pancake Onion, Olive Yellow Green, Applied String Lip, Pontil, 1700-15, 5 7/8 In. 520.00

Rickett's Glassworks, Briston, 3-Piece Mold, Cylindrical, Open Pontil, Qt., 9 In. 69.00
Storage, Olive Green, Dip Mold, Flared Lip, 5 5/8 In. 420.00
Storage, Olive Yellow Green, Tooled Flared Lip, Open Pontil, 1770-1800, 8 1/2 In. 275.00
T Lawrence Glaston, Olive Amber, 3-Piece Mold, Cylindrical, Pontil, c.1830, 10 1/8 In. .   975.00
Wine, Dip Mold, Long Neck, Olive Yellow Green, Open Pontil, Kick-Up, 10 5/8 In. 146.00
Wine, Olive Green, B.G.W., Clover Pontil, Kick-Up, Applied Lip, 1790-1810, 9 In. 520.00
Wine Deep Olive Green, Double Collar, Pontil, England, 1800-20, 8 3/4 In. 78.00
Wynand Fockink, Amsterdam, Deep Olive Amber, Applied Lip, 9 3/4 In. 135.00
Yellow Olive Green, Rectangular, Beveled Corner Panels, Double Collar, 7 In. 213.00
Yellow Olive Green, Rectangular, Beveled Corner Panels, String Lip, Pontil, 8 In. 308.00
BLACKING, see Household, Blacking

BLOWN

The American glass industry did not flourish until after the Revolution. Glass for windows and blown-glass bottles were the most rewarding products. The bottles were blown in large or small sizes to hold liquor. Many glassworks made blown and pattern-molded bottles. Midwestern factories favored twisted swirl designs. The colors ranged from green and aquamarine to dark olive green or amber. Sometimes blue or dark purple were blown. Some were made of such dark glass they are known as *black glass* bottles.

16 Ribs, Aqua, Club Shape, Tooled Lip, Snap Pontil, Midwestern, 5 x 8 1/2 In. 115.00
22 Ribs, Globular Shape, Aqua, Applied Lip, Snap Pontil, Midwestern, 7 1/2 x 12 In. 633.00
24 Broken Ribs, Swirled To Right, Blue Aqua, Outward Rolled Lip, Open Pontil, 8 1/2 In.   146.00
24 Ribs, Globular, Aquamarine, Swirled To Right, Folded Lip, c.1825, 8 1/2 In. 165.00
24 Ribs, Globular, Vertical, Golden Amber, Outward Rolled Lip, Pontil, 8 In. 2352.00
24 Ribs, Swirled To Right, Blue Aqua, Applied Lip, Pontil, Midwestern, 7 5/8 In. 224.00
24 Ribs, Swirled To Right, Blue Aqua, Tapered Collar, Open Pontil, 8 1/4 In. 112.00
24 Ribs, Swirled To Right, Globular, Golden Amber, Rolled Lip, Pontil, 8 In. 476.00
Amber, Applied Lip, Kick-Up Base, Pontil, 1790-1810, 9 1/4 x 5 In. 250.00
Aqua, Applied & Folded-Over Lip, Pontil, Indented Base, c.1830, 6 1/2 In. 154.00
Bar, 3-Piece Mold, Green Aquamarine, Globular, Pontil, Kent Glassworks, c.1830, 8 7/8 In.   4480.00
Bellows, Yellow Honey Amber, Threading, Pontil, Boston & Sandwich, 11 3/4 In. 308.00
Carboy, Aqua, Applied Lip, Sand Pontil, Oval, 15 x 10 1/2 x 17 1/2 In. 161.00
Case, Cut, Rectangular, Flowers, Applied Lip, Disk Stopper, c.1775, 9 1/4 In. 176.00
Chestnut, 24 Ribs, Yellow Amber, Rolled Lip, Pontil, 1830-60, 5 1/2 In. 420.00
Chestnut, Aqua, Flared Lip, Pontil, 3 1/4 In. 100.00
Chestnut, Keystone, Burgundy, Light Amber, 5 1/4 In. 32.00
Chestnut, Medium Green, Applied Lip, Kick-Up Base, Pontil, c.1800, 9 1/4 In. 1155.00
Chestnut, Olive Amber, Bubbles, Applied Lip, Pontil, 1820-50, 6 1/2 In. 275.00
Chestnut, Olive Green, 5 3/4 In. 450.00
Chestnut, Olive Green, Flat Egg Shape, Tapered Neck, Kick-Up Base, c.1800, 5 1/4 In. . . .   413.00
Chestnut, Olive Green, Unmarked, 5 3/4 In. 450.00
Chestnut, Olive Yellow, Bubbles, Pontil, Applied Lip, 1820-50, 5 3/4 In. 303.00
Chestnut, Olive Yellow, Outward Rolled Collar, FB, New England, 1780-1830, 6 1/2 In. . .   303.00
Chestnut, Olive Yellow, Rolled Lip, Pontil, 5 1/2 In. 420.00
Chestnut, Pale Yellow Green, Applied Lip, Kick-Up Base, Pontil, c.1800, 8 1/2 In. 523.00
Chestnut, Yellow Green, Kick-Up Base, Applied Lip, Pontil, c.1800, 5 1/8 In. 413.00
Cobalt Blue, White Circular Striping, Flared Lip, Pontil, Stopper, c.1850, 11 1/4 In. 358.00
Dutch Onion, Olive Green, 7 In. . . . . .88.00 to 100.00
Dutch Onion, Olive Green, Open Pontil, 8 1/4 In. 193.00
Dutch Onion, Olive Green, Pontil, 7 3/4 In. 110.00
Egg Shape, Swirled Ribs, Aquamarine, 8 1/4 x 4 1/2 In. 55.00
English Onion, Olive Green, Blue Tint, Applied Ring Lip, Pontil, 1720, 6 x 6 In. 242.00
Flytrap, Sapphire Blue, 3 Applied Feet, Crimped, Ground Lip, Tooled Base, 6 3/4 In. 220.00
Gemel, Chestnut Shape, Deep Blue Green, Applied Rolled Collar, 6-Sided, 5 In. 33.00
Globe, Orange Amber, Applied Lip, Open Pontil, 1815-35, 9 1/2 In. 579.00
Globular, Aqua, Applied Sloping Lip, Kick-Up Base, Pontil, 8 7/8 In. 55.00
Globular, Aquamarine, Applied Ring Lip, Open Pontil, c.1815, 8 In. 143.00
Globular, Dark Blue Aqua, Applied Lip, Open Pontil, 1800-20, 9 In. 90.00
Globular, Light Green, Applied Rolled Lip, Pontil, 10 In. 242.00
Globular, Olive Yellow, Amber Tone, Applied Sloping Collar, Pontil, 9 3/4 In. 900.00
Globular, Olive Yellow, Applied Collared Mouth, Pontil, 11 1/4 In. 952.00
Globular, Olive Yellow, Outward Rolled Lip, Pontil, 10 3/8 In. 1232.00

Globular, Olive Yellow, Rolled Collar Mouth, Pontil, 10 1/2 In. 896.00
Globular, Olive Yellow, Sheared Mouth, String Rim, Pontil, 9 3/4 In. 840.00
Globular, Olive Yellow, Sloping Collar, Pontil, 1810-30, 10 3/4 In. 728.00
Globular, Olive Yellow, Tooled Lip, New England, 1780-1830, 11 1/4 In. 1232.00
Globular, Red Amber, Applied Sloping Collar, Solid Handle, Pontil, 6 3/4 In. 66.00
Globular, Teal Blue, Applied Blob Top, Pontil, 1800-20, 7 1/2 In. 330.00
Globular, Yellow Green, Long Neck, Outward Rolled Collar, Horizontal Threads, OP, 7 In. . . 495.00
Globular, Yellow Olive, Applied Lip, Pontil, 1790-1830, 10 1/2 In. 975.00
Jar, Amethyst, Flared Lip, Open Pontil, 8 3/4 x 5 3/8 In. 550.00
Jar, Olive Yellow, Cylindrical, Sheared & Flared Mouth, Pontil, 1820-50, 7 7/8 In. 672.00
Jar, Storage, Sheared Mouth, Light Olive Green, 10 3/4 x 5 In. 165.00
Onion, Olive Yellow, Applied String Lip, Open Pontil, Miniature, 3 3/4 x 2 3/4 In. 952.00
Smelling Salts, 20 Ribs, Swirled Right, Emerald Green, Sheared Mouth, Pontil, 2 3/4 In. . . 179.00
Storage, Aquamarine, Cylindrical, Rolled Rim, Kick-Up, Pontil, c.1825, 9 1/2 In. 110.00
Storage, Dark Amber, Cylindrical, Rolled Rim, Kick-Up Base, Pontil, c.1825, 8 1/2 In. . . 550.00
Storage, Green Tint, Tapered, Folded Lip, Kick-Up Base, Pontil, c.1800, 7 1/2 In. 209.00
Storage, Medium Green, Cylindrical, Flaring Neck, Pontil, c.1825, 6 1/2 In. 825.00
Storage, Olive Yellow, Square, Double Collar Mouth, Pontil, 1810-30, 8 x 3 1/4 In. 952.00
Storage, Teal Blue, Square, Tooled Flared Lip, 8 1/4 In. 1456.00
Storage, Yellow Amber, Pontil, Applied Lip, Dip Mold, 1790-1800, 9 1/2 In. 134.00
Syrup, Cobalt Blue, Pewter Cap, Applied Neck Ring, Pontil, 10 3/4 x 3 1/4 In. 187.00
White Cased Glass, Red & Blue Looping, Pontil, Stopper, 1850-75, 10 3/4 In. 110.00
Witch's Ball, Stand, Cobalt Blue, Tooled & Flared Lip, 1840-70, 10 In. 310.00
BROOKS, see Ezra Brooks
C.P.C., CALIFORNIA PERFUME COMPANY, see Avon
CALABASH, see Flask

———————————————— CANDY CONTAINER ————————————————

The first figural glass candy containers date from the nineteenth century. They were
made to hold candy and to be used later as toys for children. These containers were very
popular after World War I. Small glass figural bottles held dime-store candy. Cars,
trains, airplanes, animals, comic figures, telephones, and many other imaginative containers were made. The fad faded in the Depression years but returned in the 1940s.
Today many of the same shapes hold modern candy in plastic bottles. The paper labels
on the containers help a little with the dating. In the 1940s the words *Contents* or *Ingre-*
dients were included on the labels. Earlier, this information was not necessary. Screw
tops and corks were used. Some of the most popular early shapes have been reproduced
in Taiwan and Hong Kong in recent years. A club with a newsletter is Candy Container
Collectors of America, 115 Macbeth Dr., Lower Burrell, PA 15068-2628.

Acorn, Original Closure 963.00
Airplane, Liberty Motor, Flag, Clear Glass, Tin 1980.00
Airplane, Patent 113053, Paper Label, Original Closure 22.00
Airplane, Spirit Of Goodwill, 80 Percent Paint, Original Prop, Closure . . . .*Illus* 93.50
Airplane, Spirit Of St. Louis, Amber, Original Closure 413.00
Airplane, US P-51 . . . . .33.00 to 39.00
Amos 'n' Andy Car, 80 Percent Paint, Original Closure 275.00
Barney Google & Ball, Green, Original Closure . . . .*Illus* 385.00

Candy Container, Barney
Google & Ball, Green,
Original Closure

Candy Container, Airplane,
Spirit Of Goodwill,
80 Percent Paint,
Original Prop, Closure

Candy Container, Baseball Player
On Base, Painted, Metal Cap,
Original Closure

Candy Container,
Camera on
Tripod, Paint,
Screw Cap
With Legs

Candy Container, Bulldog,   Candy Container, Bus,
Paint, Screw Cap   Jitney, Paint, Tin Roof

Baseball Bank, Plastic Stand, Original Closure 28.00
Baseball Player On Base, Painted, Metal Cap, Original Closure ....*Illus* 605.00
Basket, Wire Handle, Original Closure 28.00
Bear, Flared Lip, Pontil, 4 1/2 In. 44.00
Bell, Fancy School, Original Closure 770.00
Bird Cage, Original Bail, Closure 105.00
Boat, Battleship On Waves, Tin Replacement Closure 83.00
Boat, Miniature Battleship, Red Stacks, Contents, Paper Label, Metal Closure 110.00
Boat, Queen Mary, Original Closure 28.00
Boot, Santa Claus's, Clear, Label, Contents, Paper Closure, 3 1/4 In. 78.00
Buddy Bank, Marx, Tin Figure & Top 385.00
Bulldog, Paint, Screw Cap ....*Illus* 99.00
Bureau, Partial Paint, Original Mirror, No Closure 220.00
Bus, Chicago, Painted, Original Closure 633.00
Bus, Greyhound, 80 Percent Paint, Original Wheels, Closure 523.00
Bus, Jitney, Paint, Tin Roof ....*Illus* 357.00
Bus, New York-San Francisco, Original Closure 825.00
Bus, Victory Lines Special, No Paint, No Closure 11.00
Bus, Victory Lines Special, Painted, Original Closure 121.00
Camel, Reclining, Shriners, No Closure 11.00
Camera On Tripod, Paint, Screw Cap With Legs ....*Illus* 330.00
Candlestick, Handles, Souvenir, St. John's, N.F., Ruby Flashed, Original Closure 413.00
Candlestick, Little Sunshine, Contents, Original Closure, Box 578.00
Cannon, 2-Wheel Mount, No. 1, Original Tin, Original Closure 193.00
Cannon, 2-Wheel Mount, No. 2, Original Tin, Original Closure ....*Illus* 330.00
Cannon, Rapid Fire Gun, Instructions, Original Embossed Tin Top 385.00
Cannon, U.S. Defense Field Gun No. 17, Contents, Original Closure 413.00
Car, Flat Top, Tassels, Maroon Paint, Original Closure 193.00
Car, Green Taxi, Original Closure 825.00
Car, Limousine, Pat Ap'ld For, Green Paint, Original Closure 132.00
Car, Limousine, Rear Trunk, Tire, Partial Red Paint, Original Closure, 1/2 Oz. 61.00
Car, Limousine, West Spec. Co., Green Wheels, Original Closure 138.00
Car, Sedan, 6 Vents, Radiator Cap, Orange & Black Paint, Original Closure 132.00
Car, Streamlined, Red Paint, No Closure 88.00
Car, Streamlined, Yellow Paint, No Closure 83.00
Car, V.G. Co. Coupe, Metal Wheels, Contents, Original Closure 715.00
Car, V.G. Co. Sedan, Yellow Paint, Original Wheels, Closure 193.00
Car, Yellow Taxi, Original Closure 908.00
Careful Chubby Cop, Box, Contents 303.00
Carpet Sweeper, Baby Sweeper, Original Tin, Wheels, Closure 523.00
Cash Register, Original Closure 413.00
Charlie Chaplin, Borgfeldt, Painted, Contents, Original Closure 100.00
Charlie Chaplin, Smith, Painted, Original Closure 715.00
Chick In Basket, Hatching, Milk Glass, Cover, 1900-25, 3 1/4 In. 56.00
Chicken, Round Base, No Paint, Original Closure 413.00

Candy Container, Cannon,
2-Wheel Mount, No. 2, Original
Tin, Original Closure

Candy Container, Chicken, Sagging
Basket, No Paint, Original Closure

Candy Container, Clock, Milk
White, Souvenir, Emery, S.D.,
Painted, Original Closure

Chicken, Sagging Basket, No Paint, Original Closure . . . .*Illus* 1100.00
Chimney Sweep, Ladder, Painted, Germany, 6 1/2 In. 44.00
Clock, Alarm, Original Closure 275.00
Clock, Lynne Clock Bank, Contents, Original Closure . . . . .770.00 to 798.00
Clock, Mantel, Bank Slot Not Knocked Out, Painted, Original Closure . . . . .83.00 to 105.00
Clock, Milk White, Souvenir, Emery, S.D., Painted, Original Closure . . . .*Illus* 193.00
Coach, Parlor Car, New York Central RR, Purple Tint, Original Closure 358.00
Coal Car, Overland Limited, Original Wheels, Closure 385.00
Condiment Set, Rainbow Candy, Original Closure 50.00
Condiment Set, Vanstyle, Original Closure 44.00
Dagger, Original Closure 100.00
Dirigible, Los Angeles, Painted, Original Closure 165.00
Display Case, Painted, Original Paper Sticker, Original Closure 308.00
Dog, Amber, Oblong Base, No Closure 110.00
Don't Park Here, No Paint, Original Closure 110.00
Don't Park Here, No. 2, No Paint, Original Closure 187.00
Don't Park Here, No. 2, Paint Traces, Original Closure 253.00
Don't Park Here, Partial Paint, Original Closure 132.00
Drum, Candy Filled Bank, Painted, Original Closure 688.00
Duck, Large Bill, Paint Traces, Original Closure 94.00
Elephant, G.O.P., Partial Paint, Original Closure 330.00
Fat Boy On Drum, Painted, Original Closure 303.00
Fearless Frankie Fireman, Box, Contents 11.00
Felix, Mitten Hands, Partial Paint, Original Closure . . . .*Illus* 468.00
Felix, On Pedestal, No Paint, Original Closure 2310.00
Fire Engine, 1914 Stough, Original Wheels, Original Closure 50.00
Fire Engine, Fire Dept. No. 99, Paint Traces, No Closure . . . . .28.00 to 33.00
Fire Engine, Ladder Truck, Painted, Contents, Original Wheels, Closure, Sticker 303.00
Fire Engine, Little Boiler No. 2, Original Closure 61.00
Flossie Fisher's Bed, Painted Tin, Original Closure 1430.00
Flossie Fisher's Chair, Cat & Rabbit On Seat, Painted Tin, Original Closure . . . . . .495.00 to 688.00

Candy Container, Felix,
Mitten Hands, Partial
Paint, Original Closure

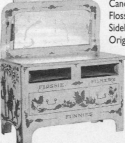

Candy Container,
Flossie Fisher's
Sideboard, Painted Tin,
Original Closure

Flossie Fisher's Dresser, Painted Tin, Original Closure 1980.00
Flossie Fisher's Sideboard, Painted Tin, Original Closure ....*Illus* 660.00
Foxy Doctor Play Kit, 5 Bottles, Contents, Original Closure 303.00
Gas Pump, Gas 23 Cents Today, Paint Traces, Original Closure 209.00
Girl With 2 Geese, No Closure 5.50
Goblin Head, Partial Paint, Original Closure 385.00
Gun, Amber, Sunken Panel, No Closure 28.00
Gun, Cambridge Automatic, Small Opening, Original Closure 110.00
Gun, Kolt, Type 1, Paint, Original Closure 44.00
Hat, Uncle Sam, Milk Glass, Paint ....*Illus* 50.00
Helicopter, 2 Blades, Contents, Sticker, Original Closure 110.00
Horn, Clarinet, Paper Label, Original Closure 39.00
Horn, Musical Clarinet No. 515A, Contents, Original Closure 495.00
Horn, Trumpet, Milk Glass, Bear Decal, Germania Souvenir, Original Closure 88.00
Horn, Trumpet, Milk Glass, Original Closure 44.00
Horn, Trumpet, No Closure 33.00
Hot Doggie, Blue, Original Closure 963.00
Hot Doggie, Partial Brown Paint, Original Closure 825.00
House, All Glass, Paint Traces, Replacement Closure 49.50
Independence Hall, Original Closure 248.00
Irishman With Hat, Original Slotted Closure 4400.00
Iron, Electric, Original Cord, Paper Plug, Closure 50.00
Iron, Flat, Paint, Contents, Original Closure 880.00
Jack-O'-Lantern, Painted, Metal Rim ....220.00 to 440.00
Jack-O'-Lantern, Pop-Eyed, Painted, Bail, Original Closure 385.00
jack-O'-Lantern, Pop-Eyed, Painted, No Bail, Original Closure 523.00
Kewpie By Barrel, Partial Paint, Replacement Closure 50.00
Kiddie Kar, Paint Traces, Replacement Closure 61.00
Kiddies Pencils Box, 11 Pencils 50.00
Lamp, Chamber Stick Type, Original Shade, Closure 3410.00
Lamp, Christmas, Partial Label, Replaced Shade, Original Closure 495.00
Lamp, Easter, Yellow Chick, Replaced Shade, Wire Frame, Original Closure 3960.00
Lamp, George Washington, Contents, Blue Painted Tin, Original Shade, Closure 770.00
Lamp, Hobnail, Contents, Basket Weave Shade, Original Closure 688.00
Lamp, Inside Ribbed Base, Original Shade 275.00
Lamp, Inside Ribbed Base, Souvenir Of Springfield, Mass., Contents, Original Shade 94.00
Lamp, Library, Contents, Original Closure 633.00
Lamp, Miniature Hurricane, Screw-On Plain Chimney, Replacement Closure 248.00
Lamp, Monkey, Original Closure 248.00
Lamp, Ringed Candlestick Base, Red Cap, Contents, Original Shade, Closure 605.00
Lamp, Ringed Candlestick Base, White Cap, Contents, Original Shade 550.00
Lamp, Tin Shade, Paper Sticker, Contents, Original Closure 28.00
Lantern, Barn Type, No. 1, Philadelphia, Ruby Flashed, No Bail, Original Closure 110.00
Lantern, Dec 20 1904, Bail 33.00
Lantern, Magnifying Lens, Chain, Original Closure 44.00
Lawn Swing, Porch, Green Tin Swing Seat, Red Stand, Contents 468.00
Lawn Swing, Porch, Red Tin Swing Seat, Red Stand, Contents 220.00
Lawn Swing, Purple Tint, Original Tin, Original Closure 715.00
Liberty Bell, Crown Straps, Partial Label, Contents, Original Closure 253.00
Liberty Bell, With Hanger, Amber, Original Closure 28.00
Liberty Bell, With Hanger, Contents, Original Closure 55.00
Locomotive, 999, Man In Window, Original Closure ....22.00 to 39.00
Locomotive, Jent. Glass Co., Small 888, Original Wheels, Original Closure 77.00
Locomotive, Little No. 23, Original Closure 66.00
Locomotive, Small, Plain Screw Cap No. 2, No Friction Cap 50.00
Locomotive, Small, Plain Screw Cap, Original Friction Closure 61.00
Mail Box, Green Paint, Original Closure 286.00
Mail Box, Milk Glass, Silver Paint, Original Closure 358.00
Mail Box, Silver Paint, Souvenir Dubua, Ia., Original Closure 193.00
Man On Motorcycle, Side Car, No Paint, Original Closure 220.00
Midget Washer, Washboard, 8 3/4 x 6 x 5/8 In. 11.00
Milk Bottle Carrier, Anco Candy, 4 Original Caps, Original Closure ....110.00 to 330.00
Milk Bottle Carrier, Betty Lou Toy Town Dairy, No. 10, No Closure 385.00

Candy Container, Hat, Uncle Sam,
Milk Glass, Paint

Candy Container,
Rabbit, In
Eggshell, No
Paint, Original
Closure

Candy Container, Santa Claus, Square
Chimney, Partial Paint, Replacement Closure

Mug, Child's Tumbler, Original Closure .... .248.00 to 385.00
Mule, Pulling 2-Wheeled Barrel, Driver, Painted, Original Closure 66.00
My Southern Mammy, Decorations, Contents, Original Closure 440.00
Naked Child, Shy, No Closure 11.00
Naked Elfin Child, Original Closure 121.00
Nursing Bottle, Flat Oval, Contents, Original Closure 33.00
Opera Glass, Plain Panels, Original Closure 66.00
Opera Glass, Plain Panels, Painted, Original Closure 55.00
Opera Glass, Swirl Ribs, Original Closure ....77.00 to 121.00
Opera Glass, Victor, Original Closure, Original Box 605.00
Pencil, Baby Jumbo, Original Label, Original Closure 50.00
Phonograph, Glass Record Type, Paint Traces, Original Closure 143.00
Pipe, Fancy Bowl, Turquoise Blue, Metal Screw Lid, 5 1/4 In. 336.00
Pipe, No Closure, Germany 11.00
Planetarium, Original Closure 825.00
Policeman On Pumpkin, Painted, Original Closure 2310.00
Powder Horn, Bubble End, No. 2, Original Closure 27.50
Powder Horn, Contents, Original Closure 33.00
Powder Horn, Hanger, Original Closure 27.50
Pumpkin Head Jr. Policeman, Partial Paint, Replacement Closure 248.00
Pumpkin Head Policeman, No Paint, Original Closure 385.00
Pumpkin Head Witch, No Paint, Original Closure 275.00
Purse, Ruby Flashed Panel, Original Closure 413.00
Purse, Souvenir, Patton, Pa., Original Closure 660.00
Rabbit, Aluminum Ears, Original Closure 1650.00
Rabbit, Crouching, Brown Paint, Original Closure 605.00
Rabbit, Eating Carrot, No Closure 16.50
Rabbit, Emerging From Tree Trunk, West Bros., Original Closure 2860.00
Rabbit, Feet Together, Round Nose, No Paint, Contents, Original Closure 88.00
Rabbit, Feet Together, Round Nose, No Paint, Original Closure 44.00
Rabbit, Feet Together, Round Nose, No. 2, Paint Traces, Original Closure 523.00
Rabbit, Fore Paws Next To Body, Paint, Original Closure 44.00
Rabbit, In Eggshell, No Paint, Original Closure ....*Illus* 39.00
Rabbit, Legs Apart, Paint Traces, Blue Tint, Original Closure 248.00
Rabbit, Legs Apart, Paint Traces, Original Closure 105.00
Rabbit, Mother & Daughter, Original Closure 633.00
Rabbit, Pushing Chick In Shell Cart, Painted, Original Closure 688.00
Rabbit, Pushing Chick In Shell Cart, Partial Paint, Replacement Closure 275.00
Rabbit, Running On Log, Partial Paint, Original Closure 275.00
Rabbit, Wearing Hat, Paint Traces, Original Closure 1017.00
Rabbit, With Basket On Arm, No Paint, Replacement Closure 66.00
Rabbit, With Basket On Arm, Paint Traces, Original Closure 77.00
Rabbit, With Basket On Dome, Painted, Original Closure ....341.00 to 715.00
Rabbit, With Laid Back Ears, Blue Head, Partial Paint, Replacement Closure 209.00
Rabbit, With Laid Back Ears, Paint Traces, No Closure 44.00
Rabbit, With Wheelbarrow, Painted, Original Closure 440.00
Racer, 12, Painted, Contents, Original Closure 550.00

Racer, 12, Partial Paint, Replacement Closure 187.00
Racer, 6, No. 2 On Grill, Replacement Closure 44.00
Racer, 6, No. 4 On Grill, Original Closure 61.00
Racer, By Stough, Original Wheels 22.00
Radio, Tune In, Paint Traces On Horn & Dials, Original Closure 72.00
Radio, Tune In, Paint Traces On Horn, No Dial Pointers, Original Closure 66.00
Radio, Tune In, Repainted Horn, Original Closure 77.00
Rocking Horse, Clown Rider, Paint Traces, Replacement Closure 50.00
Rocking Horse, Original Closure 110.00
Rocking Settee, Painted, Original Closure 688.00
Rolling Pin, Original Closure 198.00
Rooster, Crowing, Painted, Original Closure 94.00
Safe, Original Closure ....110.00 to 165.00
Safety First, Green Tint, No Closure 143.00
Safety First, Partial Paint, Original Closure 165.00
Santa, Sears, Contents, Original Closure 5.50
Santa Claus, Banded Coat, Partial Paint, Original Closure 72.00
Santa Claus, Leaving Chimney, Paint Traces, Original Closure 55.00
Santa Claus, Leaving Chimney, Partial Paint, Original Closure 61.00
Santa Claus, Leaving Chimney, Tin Lid, Marked U.S.A., 5 In. 27.00
Santa Claus, Paneled Coat, Original Closure ....72.00 to 77.00
Santa Claus, Plastic Head, Partial Paint, Contents, Original Closure 44.00
Santa Claus, Plastic Head, Partial Paint, Original Sticker, Original Closure 22.00
Santa Claus, Repaired Aluminum Cap, Original Closure, Germany 358.00
Santa Claus, Square Chimney, Partial Paint, Replacement Closure ....*Illus* 77.00
Skookum, By Tree Stump, Repainted, Replacement Closure 94.00
Soda Fountain, Yellow, Cups, Box 66.00
Soldier, By Tent, Painted Soldier, Partial Tent Paint, Original Closure 2750.00
Soldier, With Sword, Paint Traces, Original Closure 770.00
Soldier, With Sword, Partial Red Paint, No Closure 440.00
Space Doctor Play Set, 4 Bottles, Contents, Original Closure ....275.00 to 303.00
Spark Plug, Horse, Painted, Replacement Closure ....*Illus* 154.00
Statue Of Liberty, Metal Casting Hole, Original Closure 3300.00
Stop & Go, Yellow Flags, Original Closure 660.00
Suffragette, Pink Tone, c.1910, 5 3/4 In. 253.00
Suitcase, Bail, Original Closure ....22.00 to 27.00
Suitcase, Milk Glass, Bear Decal, Souvenir, Fairbanks, Bail, Original Closure 100.00
Suitcase, Milk Glass, Partial Bear Decal, Bail, Souvenir, Alva, Okla., Original Closure ... 88.00
Swan Boat, With Rabbit & Chick, Partial Paint, Original Closure 825.00
Tank, Man In Turret, Green Paint, Contents, Original Closure 33.00
Tank, U.S. Army, No Closure 16.50
Tank, World War I, No Paint, Original Closure 242.00
Tank, World War I, Tin Sliding Closure, 2 3/8 In. 190.00
Telephone, Millstein's ToT, Dial Label ....*Illus* 33.00
Telephone, Pewter Top, Marked R-7, Receiver, Original Closure 33.00
Telephone, Pewter Top, No. 2, Aqua Tint, Replaced Receiver, 5 1/2 x 2 1/2 In. 88.00
Telephone, Redlich's Cork Top, Original Bell, Receiver, Closure ....*Illus* 578.00

Candy Container, Spark Plug, Horse,
Painted, Replacement Closure

Candy Container, Telephone,
Millstein's ToT, Dial Label

Candy Container, Telephone, Redlich's
Cork Top, Original Bell,
Receiver, Closure

Candy Container,
Village, Bank

Candy Container, Village,
Toys & Confectionery

Telephone, Redlich's Screw Top, Bell, Original Closure 308.00
Telephone, Redlich's Small Screw Top, Receiver, Holder, Original Closure 94.00
Telephone, West Bro's. 1907, Wood Receiver, Line's Busy Sticker, Original Closure 39.00
Telephone, With Bell & Crank, Replaced Receiver, Original Bell, Crank, Closure 300.00
Telephone, Wood Transmitter, No. 3, Sticker, Receiver, Contents, Original Closure 110.00
Toonerville Depot Line, Partial Paint, Original Closure 688.00
Top, Glass, Spinning, Original Winder, Original Closure 100.00
Top, Glass, Spinning, Original Wood Winder, Original Closure 83.00
Top, Glass, Spinning, Replaced Tin Winder, Original Closure 50.00
Truck, Ice, Jitney Bus Body, Replaced Seats, Original Tin Canopy 176.00
Trunk, Round Top, Milk Glass, Gold Paint, Souvenir Of Rock Island, 2 1/4 In. 56.00
Trunk, Round Top, Milk Glass, Partial Paint, Original Closure 83.00
Trunk, Round Top, Milk Glass, Partial Paint, Souvenir, Almena, Kan., Original Closure .. 121.00
Trunk, Round Top, Milk Glass, Partial Paint, Souvenir, Cranville, Original Closure 105.00
Trunk, Round Top, Original Closure 72.00
Turkey, Gobbler, No Paint, Replacement Closure 66.00
Uncle Sam, By Barrel, Partial Paint, Original Closure 198.00
Village, 5 & 10 Cent Store, Original Insert, Original Clip 1100.00
Village, Bank ....*Illus* 66.00
Village, Bungalow, Original Insert, Clip 440.00
Village, Church, Steeple, Original Insert, No Clip 143.00
Village, Church, Steeple, Original Insert, Replaced Clip 99.00
Village, Log Cabin, Original Insert, Original Clip 303.00
Village, Railroad Station, Original Insert, No Clip 198.00
Village, Toys & Confectionery ....*Illus* 22.00
Village, Tudor House, Green Roof, No Insert 105.00
Village, Tudor House, Red Roof, Original Insert, Clip 495.00
Wagon, U.S. Express, Repainted Red, Original Tin Parts, Original Closure 715.00
Watch, Circle Back, Paper Face, Fancy Embossed Back, No Closure 209.00
Watch, Original Strap, Fob, Box, Closure 495.00
Well, Ye Olde Oaken Bucket, Painted, Original Bail, Closure 61.00
Wheelbarrow, Original Wheel, Replacement Closure 27.50
Whip, Contents, Original Closure 3520.00
Wild Willie Western, Contents 523.00
Windmill, Candy Guaranteed, Solid Base, Original Blades, Original Closure 825.00
Windmill, Dutch Wind Mill, Original Blades, No Closure 27.50
World Globe, On Stand, Your Country, Original Closure 209.00
CANNING JAR, see Fruit Jar
CASE, see Gin

───────────────── **COCA-COLA** ─────────────────

Coca-Cola was first served in 1886 in Atlanta, Georgia. John S. Pemberton, a pharmacist, originated the syrup and sold it to others. He was trying to make a patent medicine to aid those who suffered from nervousness, headaches, or stomach problems. At first the syrup was mixed with water; but in 1887, Willis E. Venable mixed it with carbonated water, and Coca-Cola was made. Pemberton sold his interest in the company to Venable and a local businessman, George S. Lowndes, in 1888. Later that year, Asa Griggs Candler, an owner of a pharmaceutical company, and some business friends became partners in Coca-Cola. A short time later they purchased the rest of the company. After some other transactions, Asa Candler became the sole owner of Coca-Cola for a grand total of $2,300. The first ad for Coca-Cola appeared in the *Atlanta Journal* on May 29, 1886. Since that time the drink has been sold in all parts of the world and in a variety of bottles and cans. The *Hutchinson* bottle, sometimes called a *hutch* by collectors was one of the earliest bottles. It has a wire loop stopper with a rubber gasket.The crown top, ten-ounce straight-sided short bottle was used from about 1900 to 1916. It was reintroduced in 1974 for special bottles like the 75th Anniversary bottle. The *Root* bottle, sometimes called the *hobbleskirt* or *Mae West bottle,* first used in 1916 has a pinched "waist." In 1980 to 1992 a 10-inch tall bottle was used for commemorative bottles. The short throwaway or no return bottle was introduced in 1961. Miniature bottles have been made for many years. Over 1,000 diferent commemorative Coca-Cola bottle designs have been issued since 1949. The company advertised heavily, and bottles, trays, calendars, signs, toys, and lamps, as well as thousands of other items, can be found. See listings under Go-Withs at the back of the book.

Coca-Cola written in script was trademarked in 1893. *Coke* was registered in 1945. The first 16-ounce bottle was introduced in 1960. The brand name Diet Coke was first used in 1982. In 1985 the company introduced a new formula but didn't change the name. Six months later they were forced by popular opinion to bring back the old formula under the name Classic Coke. Cherry Coke was also introduced in 1985. There is a national club with a newsletter, The Coca-Cola Collectors Club, PMB 609, 4780 Ashford Dunwoody Rd., Suite A, Atlanta, GA 30338. You can learn from the national about local meetings. Price guides and books about the history of Coca-Cola are listed in the Bibliography in the front of this book. Museums and archives are also listed.

23rd Olympiad, Los Angeles, Bird Carrying Torch, 1984, 10 x 2 1/4 In.	12.00
50th Coca-Cola Bottling Co. Of Cape Cod, Lakeville, Unopened, 1989, 8 Oz.	4.75
Akron Coca-Cola Bottling Co., Clear, Flagship Of Refreshment, White Design, 10 Oz.	1.00
Alabama Crimson Tide, Paul Bear Bryant, 1981	5.00
Albany, N.Y., Light Aqua, Straight-Sided, c.1905, 6 1/2 Oz., 7 1/2 In.	10.00
Aqua, Hobbleskirt, Embossed, December 25, 1923, 20 1/4 x 6 In.	385.00
Arkansas Razorbacks Champs, 1994, 8 Oz.	3.00
Atlantic City, N.J., December 25, 1923, Embossed	10.00
Birmingham, Ala., Blue Tint, Straight-Sided, Script Coca-Cola	22.00
Blue Ridge Bottling Works, Staunton, Va., c.1910, 7 3/4 In.	65.00
Brown, White Letters, 10 Oz.	12.00
Cabbage Patch Kids, 1988, 10 Oz.	49.00
Centennial, Gold Plated, Drawstring Bag, 1986, 7 3/4 In.	50.00
Chipley, Georgia, Straight-Sided	2211.00
Cincinnati, Ohio, December 25, 1923, Embossed	8.00
Cincinnati & Cleveland, O., December 25, 1923, Embossed	8.00
Coatsville Bottling Works, 1922, 6 Oz., 7 1/2 In.	16.50
Coca-Cola Amatil, CCA, Switzerland, Unopened, 1997	150.00
Coke Syrup, Red Cap, Green & Red Label, Gal.	21.00
Copa Del Mundo USA 94, Crown Cap, Vinyl Cover, Contents, Mexico, 355 Ml., 7 In.	45.00
Couer D'Alene, Idaho, Script Coca-Cola, Embossed, 6 Oz.	12.00
Cowboy Riding Bucking Bronco, Kalispell, Mont., Property Of Flathead	150.00
Dale Jarrett, NASCAR, No. 88, 1998	2.00
Denver Broncos, First Team Logo, 8 Oz.	6.50
Diamond Embossed, 1960s, Pt.	12.50
Disney Animal Kingdom, Coca-Cola Classic, Unopened, 1997, 8 Oz.	3.75
Disneyland Tomorrowland Grand Opening, Coca-Cola Classic, 1998, 8 Oz.	4.75
Double Diamond, Crown Top	5.50
Edwards Sodas, Coca-Cola Bottling Co., Newark, Ohio, Patd. Nov. 1923, 6 1/2 Oz.	22.00
Elizabeth City, N.C., 1915	20.00
Enameled Script, Embossed, Hot Soda, Metal Cap, c.1910-20, 12 In.	358.00
Erie, Pa., Green, Straight Sided, Arrows	60.00
Fall River, Mass., Deer, Antlers, Straight-Sided, 8 Oz., 9 In.	24.00
Florida Aquarium, Inaugural Year, Coca-Cola Classic, Unopened, 1995, 8 Oz.	3.00
Florida Gators, Champion, Contents, 1984	1.50
Florida Panthers, Inaugural Season, Coca-Cola Classic, Unopened, 1994, 8 Oz.	3.00
Foil Label, Ei Panttia Ei Palautusta, Riihimaen Lasi, Finland, 1969, 11 1/2 In.	85.00
Grand Opening Of World Of Coca-Cola, Atlanta, 1990	65.00

Green, Hobbleskirt, Coca-Cola Trademark Registered, Pat'd Nov 16 1915, 6 Oz. 35.00
Hamilton, Ontario, Green, 8 Oz., 7 3/4 In. 10.00
Hoover Dam, 50th Anniversary, Box, 1985 . . . . 41.00
Hot August Nights, Reno, Nevada, Corvette, Enamel Paint, Contents, 1993 . . . . 3.24
Houston, Texas, Nov. 15, 1915, 8 In. 10.00
Howard Hopalong Cassidy, 1955 Heisman Trophy Winner, OSU, Contents, 1995, 8 Oz. . . . 3.00
Jackson, Tenn, Bottling Wks., Amber, Tooled Lip, c.1900, 8 In. 190.00
Jar, Pepsin Gum, Franklin Caro Co., Paper Label, 1912-14, 12 x 5 In. 649.00
Jeff Gordon, 1995 . . . . 1.25
Jimmy Carter, Grand Opening Of The Plains Inn, May 11, 2002 . . . . 8.50
John Smoltz, Cy Young Award, Coke Coca-Cola Classic, Unopened, 1996, 8 Oz. 4.27
Jug, Soda Fountain Syrup, Paper Label, Duraglass, Gal. 34.00
Kalamazoo, Mich., 6 Oz. 6.00
Keokuk, Iowa, Green, 6 Oz., 7 3/4 In. 5.00
Kroger, 100th Anniversary, Clear, Painted Label, 1883-1983 . . . . .20.00 to 25.00
Laredo, Texas, 9 Oz. 5.00
Logansport, Indiana, 6 1/2 Oz 1.00
LSU Tigers, National Baseball Champions, 1993 . . . . 2.00
Lynchburg, Va., Light Aqua Green, Straight-Sided, Concave Bottom 46.00
Macon, Ga., Property Of Coca-Cola Bottling Co., Straight-Sided 33.00
Macon, Ga., Reversed N, Second Line Trade Mark Registered, Third Line 10.50
Macon, Georgia, Straight-Sided, Script Coca-Cola, Pre-1915 . . . . 12.00
Madisonville, Ky., Amber 15.50
Memphis, Tenn., Amber, Brown Arrow, 1911, 7 1/2 In. 24.00
Memphis, Tenn., Amber, Brown Arrow, 1912, 7 1/2 In. 19.00
Milledgeville, Ga., Hobbleskirt, Blue Green, 1-In. Thick Base, Nov. 16, 1915 . . . . 175.00
Muskegon, Mich, Pat'd Dec 25, 1923, 6 Oz. 28.00
Muskegon, Mich., Greenish, Straight-Sided, Block Lettering, 7 Oz. 20.00
New Castle, Pa., 1953 . . . . 7.00
New Orleans Jazz & Heritage Festival, 25th Anniversary 2.00
Norton, Kansas, Green, 1967, 6 1/2 Fl. Oz. 10.00
Nov. 16, 1915, Williamsport, Pa., Hobbleskirt, X, Cap 35.00
Olympics, Barcelona, 1992, 8 Oz. 3.00
Orangeburg, S.C., Aqua, Crown Top 39.00
Outback Steakhouse, Cheers Mate, Tube, Bag, Contents, 1988-2000, 8 Oz. 10.00
Peachtree Road Race, 25th, Unopened, 1994, 8 Oz. 3.00
Petersburg, Va., Aqua Green, Straight-Sided, 8 1/2 Oz. 31.00
Phoenix Coyotes, Inaugural, 1997, 8 Oz. 3.00
Piggly Wiggly, Celebrating A New Millennium, 1949-99 . . . . 10.00
Plant City, Fla., Script, BIMAL, Straight-Sided, Clear, Slug Plate 275.00
Poplar Bluff, Mo., 1915-20 . . . . 46.00
Portland, Me., Clear, Slug, 7 Oz., 7 1/2 In. 21.00
Property Of The Salt Lake Coca-Cola Bottling Co. 77.00
Qingdao Coca-Cola Bottling Co., Grand Opening, Stand, Box, China, 1997 . . . . 305.00
Raleigh, N.C., Smoke Color 20.00
Re/Max, Atlanta, No. 1 In Georgia!, 10th Year Atlanta's Most Honored, Box, 1991 . . . . . . 51.00
Reno Rodeo, Decal, Wildest Richest Rodeo In West, 8 Oz., 7 3/4 In. 10.00
Rhinelander Wisconsin Bottling Works, Ribs, Embossed, Clear, 7 Oz., 8 3/4 In. 13.00
Rome, Ca., Straight-Sided, Embossed Script 28.00
Royal Wedding, Lady Diana Spencer, Prince Of Wales, July 29, 1981 . . . . 45.00
Royals, World Champions, Contents, 1985 . . . . 9.50
Sacramento, Big Chief, 7 Oz. 20.50
San Antonio, Tex., December 25, 1923, Embossed 6.00
San Diego Padres Baseball Club, 25 Years, 1969-93, 8 Oz. 4.00
Seltzer, Acid Etched, Berlin, Pa. 330.00
Seltzer, Green, Fluted, Logansport, In. 330.00
Seltzer, Hoover Dam, Red Pyro Glaze, Broken Stem, Las Vegas, Nevada, Qt., 1936 . . . . . 1208.00
Seltzer, Red ACL, Billings, Montana, 26 Oz. 288.00
Seymour, Texas, Longhorn 37.00
Smoke Color, Thick Bottom, Hobbleskirt, Patd Nov 16 1915, 6 Oz. 111.00
Soda Water, Centerville, Iowa, c.1926, 6 Oz. 35.00
Soda Water, Squared Center, Star Banner, Green, 7 3/4 In. 15.00
South Dakota Centennial, Mt. Rushmore, Contents, 1989, 10 Oz. 10.00

Southwest Airlines 20th, Contents, 1991 .... 10.00
Special Olympics, Texas, 1998, 8 Oz 3.00
St. Louis Cardinals Champs, 1996, 8 Oz. 3.00
Starkville, Mississippi, 1948 .... 4.50
Super Bowl VI, Dallas Cowboys Vs Miami Dolphins, 1972 .... 4.00
Super Bowl XVIII, Coke Is It!, Tampa, Fla., Contents, January 22, 1984, 10 Oz. 3.00
Swire, Hefei Ltd., Grand Opening, Tree, Mountains, Unopened, China, 1998 .... 385.00
Sylacauga, Ala., Dark Green, Straight-Sided, Script, Root 1915, 6 1/2 Oz. 500.00
Syrup, Delicious & Refreshing, 5 Cents Per Glass, Cap, Enameled, c.1900 .... 2310.00
Syrup, Drink Coca-Cola, Foil Label, 1920s, 12 In. 523.00
Syrup, Gold Label, Bulbous Metal Lid, 13 1/2 In. 550.00
Tallahassee, Fla., Green, Patented November 6, 1923, 6 1/2 Oz., 8 In. 5.00
Texas Tech University, 75 Years, Unopened, 1998, 8 Oz. 4.25
University Of Kentucky Basketball, 1996, 8 Oz. 3.00
University Of Mississippi, 1848-1998, 8 Oz 3.00
World Cup, New York & New Jersey, 1994, 8 Oz. 3.00
Xian, Grand Opening, Stand, China, 1995. .... 310.00
Yankees, 100th Anniversary, Contents 12.00
Yazoo Coca-Cola Bottling Co., 75th Anniversary, 1978 .... 11.00
Zephyrs, Inaugural Season, 1997, 8 Oz 4.25

-------------------------- **COLLECTORS ART** --------------------------

Collectors Art bottles are made of hand-painted porcelain. The bird series was made in the 1970s. The first issued was the bluebird, then the meadowlark, canary, hummingbird, parakeet, and cardinal. Only 12 birds were issued each year and each was limited to 1,200 pieces. The later editions included bulls (1975), dogs, other animals, and a 1971 Corvette Stingray.

Brahma Bull, 1973, Miniature 25.00
Hummingbird, 1971, Miniature 50.00
Meadowlark, 1971, Miniature 40.00
Poodle, Black, 1976, Miniature 16.50
Schnauzer, 1976, Miniature 6.50

-------------------------------- **COLOGNE** --------------------------------

Our ancestors did not bathe very often and probably did not smell very good. It is no wonder that the perfume and cologne business thrived in earlier centuries. Perfume is a liquid mixture with alcohol. Cologne is a similar mixture but with more alcohol, so the odor is not as strong or as lasting. Scent was also popular. It was a perfume with some ammonia in the mixture so it could be used to revive someone who felt faint. The mixture dictated the type and size of bottle. Scent bottles usually had screw tops to keep the ammonia smell from escaping. Because its odor did not last as long as that of perfume, cologne was used more often and was sold in larger bottles. Cologne became popular in the United States about 1830; the Boston and Sandwich Glass Company of Sandwich, Massachusetts, was making cologne bottles at that time. Since cologne bottles were usually put on display, they were made with fancy shapes, brightly colored glass, or elaborate labels. Blown figural and scroll bottles were favored. The best-known cologne bottle is the 1880 Charlie Ross bottle. It has the embossed face of Charlie, a famous kidnap victim—a strange shape to choose for a cologne bottle! Today the name *perfume* is sometimes used incorrectly as a generic term meaning both cologne and perfume. Old and new bottles for cologne, perfume, and scents are collected. Related bottles may be found in the Perfume and Scent categories.

2 Plumes, Aqua, N.S.P., Flared Lip, Open Pontil, 5 3/8 In. 255.00
3-Sided, Urn With Vines, Aqua, Outward Rolled Lip, Open Pontil, 6 1/2 In. 235.00
4-Sided, Amethyst, Recessed Panels, Rolled & Flared Lip, Open Pontil, 5 In. 1232.00
4-Sided, Chamfered, Blue, Embossed Flowers, Tooled Flared Lip, Pontil, 6 1/2 In. 202.00
6-Sided, Waisted Loop, Purple Blue, Stopper, Boston & Sandwich, c.1850, 7 3/4 In. 2310.00
8 Ribs, Swirled To Right, Cobalt Blue, Cylindrical, Molded Ribs, Tooled Lip, 11 3/8 In. ... 1008.00
8-Sided, Teal Blue, Hourglass Shape, Tooled Lip, 4 5/8 In. ....*Illus* 812.00
8-Sided Bottom, Lavender, Pinched Neck, 6 1/2 In. 400.00
12 Panels, Purple Amethyst, Sandwich Glass, 11 1/2 In. 297.00
12 Ribs, Swirled To Left, Purple Amethyst, Flared Lip, Pontil, 4 1/2 In. 476.00
12-Sided, Amethyst, Sloped Shoulders, Rolled Lip, Pontil, 4 1/2 In. 224.00
12-Sided, Blue Amethyst, Alternate Panels, Ribbing, Tooled Lip, 1860-80, 5 5/8 In. 450.00

12-Sided, Blue, Opalescent, Tooled Lip, Boston & Sandwich Glass Works, 5 1/2 In. 308.00
12-Sided, Cobalt Blue, Pontil, Rolled Lip, Label, 6 3/8 In. 208.00
12-Sided, Cobalt Blue, Rolled Lip, 5 In. 90.00
12-Sided, Cobalt Blue, Sloped Shoulders, Rolled Lip, Pontil, 1850-80, 6 In. 360.00
12-Sided, Cobalt Blue, Tooled Lip, 1860-88, 4 1/4 In. 365.00
12-Sided, Grape Amethyst, Sloped Shoulder, Rolled Lip, 1860-80, 4 1/8 In. 155.00
12-Sided, Lavender Blue, Boston & Sandwich Glass Works, 11 1/4 In. 224.00
12-Sided, Light Teal Blue, Rolled Lip, 1860-80, 5 In. 175.00
12-Sided, Long Neck, Amethyst, Tooled Flange Lip, 6 1/2 In. 176.00
12-Sided, Medium Pink Amethyst, Rolled Lip, 1860-80, 6 1/2 In. 120.00
12-Sided, Medium Purple Amethyst, Rolled Lip, 1860-80, 4 7/8 In. 110.00
12-Sided, Purple Amethyst, Sloped Shoulders, Rolled Lip, 1860-80, 4 3/4 In. 175.00
12-Sided, Sapphire Blue, Flower Label, Hand Tooled Lip, c.1875, 9 7/8 In. 1175.00
12-Sided, Sapphire Blue, Tooled Lip, Pontil, Boston & Sandwich Glass Works, 6 1/4 In. . .   269.00
12-Sided, Teal Blue, Sloped Shoulders, Tooled Lip, 4 3/4 In. 112.00
12-Sided, Teal Green, Tooled Lip, Boston & Sandwich Glass Works, 5 1/2 In. 90.00
16 Ribs, Swirled To Left, Amethyst, Bulbous, Flared Mouth, Pontil, 6 In. 1904.00
16 Ribs, Swirled To Left, Amethyst, Bulbous, Pattern Molded, Pontil, 5 3/8 In. 1344.00
16 Ribs, Swirled To Left, Amethyst, Bulbous, Tooled Flared Mouth, Pontil, 1820-50, 6 In.   784.00
Amber Stained, Vintage Grape, Etched, Tapered, Stopper, c.1885, 7 3/8 In. 110.00
Barrel, Aqua, Thin Flared Lip, Open Pontil, 4 5/8 In. 80.00
Basket Weave, Sheared Mouth, Pontil, 3 1/2 In. 33.00
Basket Weave, Slug Plate, Ring, Pontil, 2 7/8 In. 65.00
Bellows, Aqua, Outward Rolled Lip, Open Pontil, 6 3/8 In. . . . .*Illus*   242.00
Bevel-Sided Neck, Emerald Green, Polished Pontil, 6 1/2 In. 40.00
Blanchard, Jealousy, Partial Contents, N.Y., 1 1/4 Oz. 15.00
Blue Aqua, Embossed Indians, Rolled Lip, Open Pontil, 4 7/8 In.   123.00
Bourjois, Evening In Paris, Cobalt Blue, Screw Cap, Partial Contents, N.Y., 2 Oz. 19.00
Building, Aqua, Pontil, Stopper, 4 3/4 In. 138.00
Bulbous, Amethyst, Tooled Flared Mouth, Pontil, 5 1/8 In. 1008.00
Bunker Hill Monument, Opaque Clambroth, Tooled Mouth, 6 5/8 In. 224.00
Bust, James Garfield, Clear, Label, Clear, Ground Lip, 7 1/4 In. 364.00
Cathedral Arches, Knight In Armor, Aqua, Inward Rolled Lip, Open Pontil, 3 7/8 In. 100.00
Cathedral Arches, Madonna & Child, Aqua, Thin Flared Lip, Open Pontil, 5 1/2 In. 145.00
Cathedral Arches, Victorian, Aqua, Flared Mouth, Open Pontil, 5 3/4 In. 132.00
Christian Dior, Miss Dior, Eau De Toilette, Box, 2 Oz. 20.00
Cobalt Blue, Enameled Swans, 9 5/8 In. 336.00
Cobalt Blue, Stopper, Sandwich, 6 1/2 In. 275.00
Corset Shape, Amethyst, Tooled Lip, Boston & Sandwich Glass Works, 4 1/4 In. 476.00
Corset Shape, Amethyst, Tooled Lip, Panels, 4 1/8 In. 202.00
Corset Shape, Cobalt Blue, Tooled & Flared Mouth, Boston & Sandwich, 1860-80, 7 In. . . 1456.00
Corset Shape, Opalescent Milk Glass, Tooled Lip, 5 5/8 In. 56.00
Corset Shape, Sapphire Blue, Scrolled Acanthus, Rolled Lip, Pontil, 5 5/8 In. . . . . . .*Illus* 2128.00
Coty, L'Aimant, Greeting Card Style Package, 3/8 Oz. 18.00
Cut Glass, Handle, Crystal, Czechoslovakia, 3 7/8 x 2 5/8 In. 90.00
Cut Glass, Hobstar, File, Star & Fan, Ball Shape, Faceted Cut Stopper, 6 In. 175.00

Cologne, 8-Sided,
Teal Blue, Hourglass
Shape, Tooled Lip,
4 5/8 In.

Cologne, Bellows, Aqua,
Outward Rolled Lip,
Open Pontil, 6 3/8 In.

Cologne, Corset
Shape, Sapphire
Blue, Scrolled
Acanthus, Rolled Lip,
Pontil, 5 5/8 In.

Cylindrical, Green, Tooled Lip, Flutes, Boston & Sandwich Glass Works, 10 1/8 In.	3360.00
Czechoslovakian Lady, Pink, Ruffles, Flowered Dress, Head Stopper, 8 x 4 1/2 In.	600.00
Eagdi Cologne Paris, Plume & Vines, 3 Panels, Thin Flared Lip, OP, 1840-60, 6 3/8 In.	45.00
Elephant, Clear, Rolled Lip, Pontil, 4 7/8 In.	392.00
Esscent, Danger, Poodle Dog, 2 Oz.	35.00
Fireplug, Star, Hawley & Co., Philada., Clear	29.00
Flared Rim, Ribbed Sides, Round Finial Stopper, Sandwich Glass, 6 1/4 x 2 3/4 In.	28.00
Gothic Arched Shoulders, Woman, Holding Child, Aqua, Open Pontil, 1840-60, 5 1/2 In.	150.00
Grape & Cable, Carnival Glass, Purple	325.00
Green Cut To Clear, Tulip Stopper, Gold Highlights, 9 In.	275.00
Heart With Plume, Aqua, Flared Lip, Open Pontil, 5 7/8 In.	100.00
Horizontal Oval Paneled Frames, Canary Yellow, Teardrop Stopper, c.1850, 7 1/2 In.	231.00
Hourglass, Ribbons, White Looping, Sapphire Rimmed Mouth, 6 1/8 In.	1344.00
House Of Westmore, For EverMore, Cap, 2 Oz.	20.00
Hoyt's Genuine, Front & Neck Label, Cork Top, 1 Oz., 4 1/4 In.	15.00
Indian, Aqua, Rolled Lip, Open Pontil	55.00
Jester, In Chair, France, 1880-1910, 4 1/8 In.	105.00
Jovan Musk Aftershave, Coty, 1973, 4 Oz.	10.00
LeGalion, Jasmin, Partial Contents, 2 1/2 In.	15.00
Lenel, Bellezza, Gold Leaves, Plastic Cap, 6 In.	33.00
Lion Walking, Embossed, Aqua, Inward Rolled Lip, Open Pontil, 4 3/8 In.	175.00
Lyre, Aqua, Inward Rolled Lip, Pontil, 1840-60, 5 1/2 In.	84.00
Lyre, Aqua, Thin Flared Lip, Open Pontil, 5 3/8 In.	220.00
Lyre, Aquamarine, Outward Rolled Lip, Tubular Pontil, 5 1/2 In.	308.00
Milk Glass, Bead & Flute, Rolled Lip, 5 7/8 In.	78.00
Milk Glass, Fiery Opalescent, Enamel Swallow & Flowers, Rolled Lip, 8 3/4 In.	364.00
Milk Glass, Hobnail, Fenton, 1960s, 6 In.	40.00
Milk Glass, Hobnail, Fenton, Stopper, Early 1940s, 6 1/2 x 4 In.	40.00
Monument, 4-Sided, Teal Green, Tooled Flared Lip, 12 In.	1680.00
Monument, Fiery Opalescent Milk Glass, Rolled Lip, Pontil, 4 1/2 In.	2688.00
Monument, Medium Blue Milk Glass, Tooled Lip, Pontil, c.1870-80, 8 5/8 In. *Illus*	224.00
Monument, Milk Glass, Tooled Lip, 1875-85, 9 1/4 In.	110.00
Monument, Milk Glass, Tooled Lip, 1875-85, 12 In.	110.00
Monument, Small Water Fountains, Embossed, Aqua, Flared Lip, Open Pontil, 4 1/2 In.	190.00
Moser, Enameled Zinnias, Signed, 3 1/2 In.	115.00
Obelisk Shape, Herringbone Corners, Ice Blue, Tooled Lip, 1860-88, 7 1/2 In.	175.00
Opalescent Milk Glass, Bead & Flute, Rolled Lip, 8 1/8 In.	78.00
Opalescent Milk Glass, Stars & Bars, Rolled Lip, 6 5/8 In.	78.00
Opaque Blue & Clambroth, Gold Design, Mushroom Stopper, 7 In.	110.00
Oval Hobnail, Canary Yellow, 6-Lobe Stopper, Boston & Sandwich, c.1860, 7 1/4 In.	248.00
Oval Paneled Frames, Bright Canary, Pointed Stopper, c.1860, 6 1/2 In.	303.00
Overlay, White Over Clear, Multiple Faceting, Enamel Flowers, Gold Highlights, 8 1/2 In.	288.00
Palmer, Green, Oval, BIMAL, Embossed, Slanted Script, 5 1/8 In.	36.00
Palmer, Green, Round, BIMAL, Kick-Up, Embossed, W T & CO, 5 3/4 In.	32.00
Paneled, Teal Green, Sandwich, 4 3/4 In.	105.00
Paneled Cane, Canary Yellow, Short Neck, No Stopper, New England Glass, c.1865, 4 In.	132.00
Phalon Perfumer, N.Y., Light Green, Applied Lip, Open Pontil, 7 1/2 In.	88.00
Plume, Bulbous Neck, Rolled Lip, Tubular Pontil, 6 7/8 In.	134.00
Plumes, 3 Panels, Clear, Flared Rolled Lip, Pontil, 7 3/4 In.	100.00
Plumes, 3 Panels, Clear, Flared Lip, Pontil, 6 3/8 In. *Illus*	90.00
Pocahontas, Aqua, Indian Woman, Sheared Mouth, Open Pontil, 5 In.	165.00
Rectangular, Bulbous Neck Protrusion, Purple Amethyst, 1840-60, 5 x 2 x 1 In.	1456.00
Rectangular, Chamfered Corners, Olive Yellow, Sloping Collar, Pontil, 1840-60, 6 1/4 In.	1064.00
Rectangular, Recessed Panels, Olive Green, Outward Rolled Lip, Open Pontil, 6 3/8 In.	896.00
Ruby Stained, Punty Cut, Footed, Stopper, Spill Holder, 1875-87, 7 In.	176.00
Ruby Stained, Vintage Grape, Etched, Stopper, Boston & Sandwich, 1880-97, 9 In.	275.00
Sandwich Glass, Amethyst, Stopper, 6 In.	408.00
Sandwich Glass, Cobalt Blue Cut To Clear, Stopper, 5 1/2 In.	358.00
Sandwich Glass, White Cutout Cranberry, Stopper, 7 1/2 In.	495.00
Scroll, Aqua, Inward Rolled Lip, Open Pontil, 5 3/4 In.	155.00
Ship, Sailing, Clear, Flared Lip, Pontil, 4 7/8 In.	280.00
Square, Herringbone Corners, Purple, Tooled Flared Mouth, 1860-88, 7 5/8 In.	784.00
Stopper, Northwood Co., Carnival Glass, Grape & Cable Pattern, Amethyst Base, 9 In.	675.00

Cologne, Monument,
Medium Blue Milk
Glass, Tooled Lip, Pontil,
c.1870-80, 8 5/8 In.

Cologne, Plumes,
3 Panels, Clear, Flared
Lip, Pontil, 6 3/8 In.

Cologne, Toilet
Water, Obelisk,
Herringbone
Corners, Stars, Label,
5 5/8 In.

Studio Girl, Que Sera Essense, Gold Color, 2/5 Oz.	20.00
Superior Cologne Water, L.W. Glenn & Son, Philada., Clear, Label, 5 7/8 In.	78.00
Swan, Green Aqua, Flared Lip, Open Pontil, 6 5/8 In.	448.00
Teal Green, Gold, Pontil, Flared Lip, Glass Stopper, 4 3/8 In.	90.00
Tiffin Glass, Enameled, Stopper, 7 x 1 7/8 In.	90.00
Toilet Water, 8 Ribs, Swirled To Right, Canary, Pontil, 12 1/4 In.	840.00
Toilet Water, 20 Ribs, Swirled Left, Cobalt Blue, 3-Piece Mold, Flared Lip, Pontil, 5 3/4 In.	385.00
Toilet Water, 48 Ribs, Swirled Left, Cobalt Blue, 3-Piece Mold, Tooled Lip, Pontil, 5 5/8 In.	145.00
Toilet Water, Clambroth, Gold Vintage, Stopper, Sandwich Glass, 12 1/2 In.	55.00
Toilet Water, Cobalt Blue, Paneled, Sandwich, 4 3/4 In.	220.00
Toilet Water, Cobalt Blue, Swirled Ribs, Stopper, Sandwich Glass, 7 In.	550.00
Toilet Water, Cobalt Blue, Swirled, Stopper, Sandwich, 7 In.	275.00
Toilet Water, Corset Shape, Milk Glass, Fiery Opalescent, Enameled Clover, 9 1/4 In.	168.00
Toilet Water, Milk Glass, Fiery Opalescent, Blue & Green Flowers, 8 3/4 In.	269.00
Toilet Water, Milk Glass, Fiery Opalescent, Enameled Flowers, 8 5/8 In.	213.00
Toilet Water, Obelisk, Herringbone Corners, Stars, Label, 5 5/8 In. . . . .*Illus*	132.00
Toilet Water, Purple Amethyst, Ribs, Windmill, Rolled Lip, Pontil, 7 3/4 In.	448.00
Toilet Water, Purple Lavender, Vertical Ribs, Neck Ring, Folded Lip, Pontil, 5 5/8 In.	308.00
Toilet Water, Ribbed, Cobalt Blue, Sandwich Glass, Stopper, 6 1/2 In.	425.00
Toilet Water, Sandwich Glass, Cobalt Blue, Swirl Pattern, Stopper	550.00
Toilet Water, Sapphire Blue, Midwestern, 6 In.	425.00
Ulysses S. Grant, Inside Wreath, Clear, Tooled Lip, 1868-75, 4 7/8 In.	330.00
Urn, Clear, Tooled Lip, Pontil, 4 5/8 In.	55.00
Valois Kasimir, Stopper, 2 Oz.	55.00
Vine & Flowers, Aqua, Thin Flared Lip, Open Pontil, 6 7/8 In.	187.00
Violin Shape, Aqua, Scrolls, Rolled Lip, Open Pontil, 6 In.	78.00
Violin Shape, Scrolls, Sapphire Blue, Flared Lip, Open Pontil, 5 7/8 In.	2128.00
White To Cranberry Overlay, Window Facets, Stopper, 6 3/4 In.	86.00
Woman Holding Child, Gothic Arched Shoulders, Aqua, Flared Lip, OP, c.1850, 5 1/2 In.	154.00
Woman's Hand, Clear, Tooled Lip, Corning & Tappan, 1890-1915, 5 1/4 In.	50.00
Woman's Torso, Santa Clara, Clear, Metal Screw Cap, Label, 6 1/2 In.	90.00
Yves Rocher, Millennium Nature Eau De Toillette, Amber, Unopened, Box, 16 Oz.	10.00

CORDIAL

Cordials are liqueurs that are usually drunk at the end of the meal. They consist of pure alcohol or cognac, plus flavors from fruits, herbs, flowers, or roots. A cordial may also be a medicinal drink. Curacao is a cordial containing orange peel, Creme de Menthe contains mint, Triple Sec has orange and cognac, and Kummel has coriander and caraway seeds.

Bernard's Old Tom Cordial Genuine, Applied Top, Fifth	33.00
Booth & Sedgwick's, Blue Green, Iron Pontil, Applied Sloping Collar, 8 In.	504.00
Booth & Sedgwick's, London, Case, Emerald Green, Applied Top, Iron Pontil, 8 In.	330.00
Charles London, Case, Olive Green, Applied Sloping Collar, 9 3/4 In.	275.00
Charles London, Olive Green, Pontil, Sloping Collar, 7 3/4 In.	202.00
Clouds, Olive Yellow, Applied Lip, 1870-85, 10 1/2 In.	750.00
Dr. B. Bates, Pineapple, Aqua, Applied Lip, 9 1/4 In.	392.00

Cordial, J.N. Kline &
Co., Aromatic
Digestive, Cobalt Blue,
Teardrop, 5 1/2 In.

Cordial, Wishart's Pine
Tree Tar, Patent 1859,
Embossed Tree, Yellow
Green, 9 1/2 In.

**Do not keep wine and
spirits in lead crystal
decanters. The lead will
leak out and go into
the wine.**

Dr. Harris' Summer, Contents, Label, Box, 6 In. 33.00
Dr. Jacob Webber's Invigorating, Aqua, Applied Double Collar, 1855-65, 9 3/4 In. 168.00
Dr. Keeler's Infant, Aqua, Thin Flared Lip, Open Pontil, 4 5/8 In. 504.00
Dr. Keeler's Infant, Philada., Blue Aqua, Flared Lip, Open Pontil, 1840-60, 4 5/8 In. 308.00
Dr. McLean's Strengthening, Purifier, Aqua, Label, Contents, Box, 8 1/4 In. 688.00
Dr. Warren's Tonic, Aqua, Square, Contents, 9 In. 220.00
J.N. Kline & Co., Aromatic Digestive, Cobalt Blue, Teardrop, 5 1/2 In. . . . .*Illus*   392.00
J.N. Kline & Co., Aromatic Digestive, Wreath, Yellow Amber, Flask, Teardrop, 5 5/8 In. . .   392.00
Jacob's Cholera & Dysentery, Aqua, Applied Mouth, Open Pontil, 6 3/4 In. 134.00
Jacob's Cholera & Dysentery, Aqua, Square, Open Pontil, Cork, Box, 6 1/2 In. 132.00
Mrs. E. Kidder Dysentery, Boston, Green Aqua, Open Pontil, 7 3/4 In. 135.00
Mrs. E. Kidder Dysentery Balsam, Green, Applied Top, Pontil, 8 1/4 In. 2090.00
Peychaud's American Aromatic Bitter, Contents, Label, 6 In. 250.00
Reeds London, Gin, Blue Aqua, Applied Slope Collar, Iron Pontil, 10 In. 350.00
Scheetz Celebrated Bitter, Philada, Blue Aqua, Square, 9 1/2 In.   98.00
Wishart's Pine Tree Tar, Embossed Tree, Amber, Rear Label, 9 3/4 In. 358.00
Wishart's Pine Tree Tar, Emerald Green, Sloping Collar, 1859, 9 1/2 In. 280.00
Wishart's Pine Tree Tar, Patent 1859, Embossed Tree, Aqua, Applied Lip, 8 In. 165.00
Wishart's Pine Tree Tar, Patent 1859, Embossed Tree, Aqua, Applied Lip, 9 3/4 In. 275.00
Wishart's Pine Tree Tar, Patent 1859, Embossed Tree, Blue Green, 7 3/4 In. 168.00
Wishart's Pine Tree Tar, Patent 1859, Embossed Tree, Blue Green, 8 In. . . . . .145.00 to 210.00
Wishart's Pine Tree Tar, Patent 1859, Embossed Tree, Blue Green, 9 1/2 In. . . . . . .90.00 to 275.00
Wishart's Pine Tree Tar, Patent 1859, Embossed Tree, Emerald Green, Applied Lip, 8 In. . .   190.00
Wishart's Pine Tree Tar, Patent 1859, Embossed Tree, Olive Yellow, 7 5/8 In. 200.00
Wishart's Pine Tree Tar, Patent 1859, Embossed Tree, Yellow Green, 7 7/8 In. . . . .145.00 to 880.00
Wishart's Pine Tree Tar, Patent 1859, Embossed Tree, Yellow Green, 8 1/8 In. 300.00
Wishart's Pine Tree Tar, Patent 1859, Embossed Tree, Yellow Green, 9 1/2 In. . . . . . .*Illus*   300.00
Wishart's Pine Tree Tar, Phila, Blue Aqua, Tooled Lip, c.1885, 3 3/8 In. 1540.00
Wishart's Pine Tree Tar, Phila, Embossed Tree, Amber, Tooled Lip, Label, c.1885, 10 In. . .   330.00
Wishart's Pine Tree Tar, Phila, Embossed Tree, Blue Aqua, Applied Lip, c.1885, 10 In. . .   410.00
Wishart's Pine Tree Tar, Phila, Embossed Tree, Blue Green, 10 1/8 In. 728.00
Wishart's Pine Tree Tar, Phila, Embossed Tree, Blue Green, Tooled Lip, 10 1/4 In. 155.00
Wishart's Pine Tree Tar, Phila, Embossed Tree, Blue Green, Tooled Lip, Label, 10 1/4 In.   200.00
Wishart's Pine Tree Tar, Phila, Embossed Tree, Olive Green, Applied Lip, 7 1/2 In. 990.00
Wishart's Pine Tree Tar, Phila, Embossed Tree, Olive Yellow, Applied Lip, 7 1/2 In. 3300.00
Wishart's Pine Tree Tar, Phila, Embossed Tree, Sapphire, Tooled Lip, c.1885, 9 3/4 In. . .   1540.00
Wishart's Pine Tree Tar, Phila, Embossed Tree, Teal Blue Green, Applied Lip, 10 1/8 In. .   200.00

COSMETIC

Cosmetics of all kinds have been packaged in bottles. Hair restorer, hair dye, creams,
rosewater, and many other product bottles can be found. Paper labels on early bottles
add to their value.

Acme Hair Vigor, Label Under Glass, Phil Eismann, Cork, Metal Stopper, 8 In. 230.00
Ambercrude For Hair & Scalp, Phila., U.S.A., BIMAL, Contents, Labels, 8 1/4 In. 45.00

Ayer's Hair Vigor, Cobalt Blue, Stopper, 8 In. 21.00
Ayer's Hair Vigor, Peacock Blue, Embossed, 6 1/2 In. 45.00
Ayer's Hair Vigor, Teal Blue, 6 1/2 In. 21.00
B.F. Fish's Hair Restorative, San Francisco, Blue Aqua, Applied Double Collar, 7 In. 880.00
Barrow Evans, Hair Restorer, Paper Package, 6 1/4 In. 20.00
Barry's New York, Tricopherous For The Skin & Hair, Directions, Aqua 18.00
Barry's Tricopherous For Skin & Hair, Aqua, Open Pontil, 6 In. 35.00
Boswell & Warner's Colorific, Cobalt Blue, Tooled Lip, 5 5/8 In. 470.00
C. Heimstreet & Co., Troy, N.Y., Cobalt Blue, 8-Sided, Double Roll Collar, 6 3/4 In. 187.00
C.A.P. Mason, Hair Balm, Providence, R.I., Olive Yellow, Label, 1860-75, 6 7/8 In. 3025.00
C.F. Collins, Kallocrine For Skin & Hair, Middletown, Conn., Open Pontil 250.00
C.S. Emerson's American Hair Restorative, Cleveland, Pontil, Label, 6 3/8 In. 1045.00
Church's Circassian Hair Restorer, Medium Amber, Applied Lip, 7 5/8 In. 165.00
Circassian Hair Oil, Blue Aqua, Applied Lip, Open Pontil, 5 1/2 In. 476.00
Circassian Hair Restorative, Cincinnati, Yellow Amber, 7 3/8 In. 269.00
Circassian Hair Restorative, Cincinnati, Yellow Amber, Applied Lip, 7 3/8 In. 220.00
Clark's Hair Gloria, Philadelphia, Orange Amber, 8 In. 69.00
Cram's Veg. Compound Hair Preservative, Aqua, Label, Open Pontil 44.00
Cremex Shampooing Vase, Cobalt Blue, Offset Neck, Finger Indents, 7 3/4 In. 41.00
Dental, Ideal Tooth Powder, Eye On Neck, 25 Cents, Vail Bros, Philadelphia, c.1885, 4 In. . 550.00
Dodge Brothers Hair Tonic, Amethyst, Tombstone Shoulders, Double Collar, 7 1/2 In. 896.00
Dodge Brothers Melanine Hair Tonic, Amethyst, Double Ring Top, 7 1/2 In. 935.00
Dodge Brothers Melanine Hair Tonic, Pink Amethyst, Double Collar, 7 1/2 In. 1000.00
Dr. D. Jayne's Hair Tonic, Philada, Tonico Del Dr. D. Jayne, Glass Stopper, 6 In. 10.00
Dr. Graves Tooth Powder, Paper Label, Contents, c.1900, 4 In. 210.00
Dr. Leon's Electric Hair Renewer, Ziegler & Smith, Philada, Amethyst, 7 3/8 In. 1045.00
Dr. Tebbetts' Physiological Hair Regenerator, Amethyst, Double Collar, 7 1/2 In. 224.00 to 364.00
Dr. Tebbetts' Physiological Hair Regenerator, Amethyst, Double Collar, 7 5/8 In. 336.00 to 616.00
Dr. Tebbetts' Physiological Hair Regenerator, Purple, Oversized Top, 7 1/2 In. 300.00
Dr. Tebbetts' Physiological Hair Regenerator, Strawberry Puce, Double Collar, 7 3/8 In. . 235.00
Empire Quinine Hair Tonic, Gal., 12 x 6 1/2 In. 25.00
Farr's Gray Hair Restorer, Boston, Mass., Amber, Tooled Lip, c.1890, 5 1/2 In. 6.00
Fitch's Dandruff Remover, Orange Label, Black Cap, Des Moines, Iowa, 4 Oz. 10.00
Friendship Garden Hand & Body Lotion, Shulton, Blue, Contents, 2 Oz. 15.00
G.S. Emerson's American Hair Restorative, Cleveland, Blue Aqua, Oval, IP, 6 1/2 In. 495.00
Genuine Florida Water, Prof. Geo. J. Byrne, New York, Embossed, 9 In. 15.00
Glycerine & Rosewater Bath Bubbles, Dog Shape, Red Screw Cap, 3 3/4 In. 5.00
Hair Restorer, Amber, Shaker, Double Collar, 7 3/4 In. 143.00
Hall's Hair Renewer, Cobalt Blue, Tooled Lip, ABM Lip, 1885-95, 6 3/8 In. 213.00
Hall's Hair Renewer, Teal Blue, Stopper, Label, 7 3/8 In. 336.00
Hall's Hair Renewer, Teal Blue, Tooled Lip, Stopper, 7 3/8 In. 300.00
Harrison's Columbian Hair Dye, Clear, Beveled Edge, Open Pontil, 3 1/2 In. 145.00
Harry D. Haber's Magic Hair Coloring, Deep Cobalt Blue, Tooled Lip, 1890-1910, 6 In. . 112.00
Heberlings Cream Lotion, Narrow Neck & Mouth, Cover, Label, 5 1/2 In. 15.00
Hood's Tooth Powder, C.I. Hood & Co., Lowell, Mass., Rubber Stopper, 3 1/2 In. . . .10.00 to 12.75
Hood's Tooth Powder, C.I. Hood & Co., Lowell, Mass., Stopper, 4 1/2 In. 28.00
Indian Hair Restorer, A.A. Snyder, Cobalt Blue, Square Collar, 8 3/4 In. 2750.00
Jerome's Hair Color & Restorer, Sapphire Blue, Flared Mouth, Panels, 6 1/8 In. 616.00
Kickapoo Sage Hair Tonic, Cobalt Blue, Label, Stopper, Cylindrical, c.1905, 5 1/2 In. ... 355.00
Kickapoo Sage Hair Tonic, Cobalt Blue, Tooled Lip, Round, Cylindrical Neck, 4 1/2 In. .. 157.00
Kickapoo Sage Hair Tonic, Cobalt Blue, Tooled Lip, Stopper, 7 3/8 In. 235.00
Lavona Hair Tonic, Original Lid, Box, 1906, 4 1/2 In. 18.00
Lentheric Man's After Shave Powder, Brass Top, Label, Partial Contents, 2 Oz., 4 In. ... 15.00
London Hair Color Restorer, Swayne's Philada., Cathedral Shoulders, Clear, 7 1/2 In. ... 45.00
Lorrimer's Excelsior Hair Tonic, Orange Amber, Oval, 8 1/4 In. 100.00
Lucky Tiger Hair Tonic, Contents, 14 Oz. 9.50
Lyon's Kozothium, For Gray Hair, Amethyst, Square Collar, c.1890, 7 3/4 In. 840.00
Mrs. Allen's Hair Restorative, Dark Purple Amethyst 415.00
Mrs. Allen's World's Hair Balsam, Aqua, Double Collar, Open Pontil, 6 7/8 In. 134.00
Mrs. S.A. Allen's World's Hair Restorer, N.Y., Medium Amethyst, Double Collar, 7 3/8 In 495.00
Mrs. S.A. Allen's World's Hair Restorer, N.Y., Strawberry Puce, Double Collar, 7 1/2 In. . 190.00
Mrs. S.A. Allen's World's Hair Restorer, N.Y., Yellow Amber, Double Collar, 7 1/4 In. ... 90.00

Mrs. S.A. Allen's World's Hair Restorer, New York, Amethyst, 7 In. 112.00
Mrs. S.A. Allen's World's Hair Restorer, New York, Amethyst, Double Collar, 7 1/8 In. . . 364.00
Mrs. S.A. Allen's World's Hair Restorer, New York, Amethyst, Flared Lip, 7 In. . . .145.00 to 330.00
Mrs. S.A. Allen's World's Hair Restorer, New York, Dark Purple, 7 In. 214.00
Mrs. S.A. Allen's World's Hair Restorer, New York, London, Olive Yellow, 7 1/2 In. 132.00
Mrs. Wilson's Hair Regenerator, Aqua, Rectangular, 8 In. 138.00
Nattan's Crystal Discovery For Hair, Embossed Star, Blue, Tooled Flared Top, 7 1/2 In. . 825.00
Northrop & Lyman, Co., Hair Dye, Buffalo, N.Y., Aqua, Contents, Label, 3 1/2 In. 84.00
Oldridge's Balm Of Columbia, For Restoring Hair, Aqua, Flared Lip, Pontil, Label, 6 In. . 1430.00
Parker's Hair Balsam, New York, Olive Green, Rectangular, ABM, 1900-15, 7 1/2 In. . . . 29.00
Parker's Hair Balsam, New York, Yellow, 7 In. 39.00
Pearson & Co. Circassian Hair Rejuvenator, Brooklyn N.Y., Amber, 6 3/4 In. 672.00
Phalon & Sons Chemical Hair Invigorator, New York, Light Aqua, 5 1/2 In. 25.00
Pond's Extract, Aqua, Wraparound Label, Wrapper, 5 1/4 In. 66.00
Prevost A Paris, Clear, Sheared Mouth, Open Pontil, Square, 1840-50, 6 In. 39.00
Professor Mott's Magic Hair Invigorator, A.J. Green, Highgate, Vt., Aqua, 6 1/4 In. 246.00
Professor Mott's Magic Hair Invigorator, A.J. Green, Highgate, Vt., Aqua, 7 3/4 In. 364.00
Professor Wood's Hair Restorative, Depots St. Louis & New York, Open Pontil, Aqua . . 60.00
Professor Wood's Hair Restorative Depo, St. Louis, Missouri, Aqua, 4-Sided, 9 1/8 In. . . 364.00
Rathgebers Bijouempyreal For The Hair, New Haven, Ct., Milk Glass, 6 3/4 In. 341.00
Reading Hair Restorer, Brown Glass, Rectangular, Embossed, 6 1/4 In. 102.00
Real Man After Shave Lotion, Paper Label, 4 3/4 x 2 3/4 In. 35.00
Red Cross Toothache Drops, Cork, 2 1/2 In. 4.25
Rexall Ammoniated Tooth Powder, Paper Labels, Contents, 4 3/8 x 2 1/2 x 1 5/8 In. 46.00
Rich's Hair Wash, Aqua, Oval, Rolled Lip, Pontil, 1840-60, 6 3/8 In. 112.00
Shaker Hair Restorer, Golden Amber, Tooled Double Ring Mouth, 1875-90, 7 3/4 In. . . . 143.00
Speicher Dandruff Cure, Philadelphia, BIMAL, 7 3/4 In. 10.00
St. Clair's Hair Lotion, Blue, Tooled Lip, 7 1/4 In. 100.00
T. Jones Coral Hair Restorative, Aquamarine, Open Pontil, Applied Lip, 5 1/8 In. 336.00
Vaseline Hair Tonic, Box, Brochure, Contents, 1943, 2 Oz. 8.00
Velvetina Skin Beautifier, Milk Glass, Contents, Label, 5 1/4 In. 154.00
W.C. Montgomery's Hair Restorer, Amber, Embossed, 7 1/2 In. 16.00
W.C. Montgomery's Hair Restorer, Amethyst, Embossed, 7 1/2 In. 416.00
W.C. Montgomery's Hair Restorer, Philada, Copper Puce, Double Collar, 7 1/2 In. 825.00
W.C. Montgomery's Hair Restorer, Philada, Dark Amethyst, Double Collar, 7 3/4 In. 880.00
W.C. Montgomery's Hair Restorer, Philada, Orange Amber, 7 1/2 In. 29.00
Wildroot Cream Oil Hair Tonic, Partial Contents, Box, Canada, 4 1/4 In. 5.00
Wildroot Hair Tonic, Dandruff Remedy, Clear, Black & Gold Label, Buffalo, New York . 3.00
Wood's Tooth Powder, Nathan Wood & Son, Portland, Me., Cork, 3 1/4 In. 13.25
Yucca For The Hair, Indian, Headdress, Aqua, Label, Box, Vermont, 7 1/2 In. 33.00

─────────────────────── CURE ───────────────────────

Collectors have their own interests and a large group of bottle collectors seek medicine bottles with the word *cure* embossed on the glass or printed on the label. A cure bottle is not a *remedy bottle*. The word cure was originally used for a medicine that treated many diseases. A *specific* was made for only one disease. The Pure Food and Drugs Act of 1906 made label changes mandatory and the use of the word *cure* was no longer permitted. Related bottles may be found in the Medicine and Bitters categories.

Alexander's Sure Cure, Amber, Rectangular, 4 In. 46.00
Ayer's Ague Cure, Aqua, Partial Contents, 7 In. 33.00
Babyhood Cough & Croup, Langham Med. Co., Le Roy, N.Y., Clear, Label, 6 1/2 In. 385.00
Bennett's Hussop Cure, Stockport, Cornflower Blue, 4 7/8 In. 27.00
Buxton's Rheumatic, Aqua, Rectangular, 8 1/4 In. 43.00
Chase's Dyspepsia Cure, Aqua, Rectangular, 4 In. 15.00
Cherokee Kidney & Liver, Square, 5 1/2 In. 56.00
Clem's Summer Cure, Howes & Co., Aqua, Applied Lip, 1860-70, 9 1/4 In. 235.00
Craig's Kidney & Liver Cure Co., Amber, Kidneys On Label, 9 1/2 In. 3850.00
Cramer's Cough Cure, Aqua, BIMAL, Embossed, 6 1/4 In. 20.00
Dr. B.W. Hair's Asthma Cure, Cincinnati, Ohio, Aqua, Label, 5 7/8 In. 165.00
Dr. C.C. Roc's Liver, Rheumatic & Neuralgic Cure, Embossed, Contents, 7 1/2 In. 72.00
Dr. H.S. Edwardes, Gout & Rheumatism, Ice Blue, Square, Embossed, 6 In. 559.00
Dr. J.B. Henion's Sure Cure For Malaria, Cobalt Blue, Applied Disc Type Mouth, 6 3/8 In. 9520.00
Dr. Kilmer's Cough-Cure Consumption Oil Specific, Aqua, Embossed Lungs, 8 3/4 In. . . 99.00

Dr. Kilmer's Indian Cough Consumption Oil, Aqua, Indian On Paper Label, 5 3/4 In. ... 99.00
Dr. Kilmer's Swamp Root Kidney Liver & Bladder Cure, Aqua, Embossed, 5 3/4 In. 77.00
Dr. Kilmer's Swamp Root Kidney Cure, Embossed, Cylindrical, 4 1/4 In. 165.00
Dr. Kilmer's Swamp Root Kidney Cure, London, Sample 15.00
Dr. M.M. Fenner's People's Remedies, Kidney & Backache, Amber, Tooled Lip, c.1880, 10 In. 66.00
Dr. Miles' New Heart, Aqua, BIMAL, 8 1/8 In. 16.00
Dr. S.I. Johnston's Compound, Great For Blood Impurities, Lion, Aqua, 5 5/8 In. 1120.00
Dr. Shoop's Cough, Racine, Wis., Aqua, Contents, Labels, Box, 5 1/4 In. 143.00
Dr. W. Eaton Boynton's Blood Cure & Human Destroyer, Aqua, Pontil, Label, 7 1/2 In. . 470.00
Duffy's Tower Mint, Tower, Windows, Doors, Amber, 1875-90, 9 In. 550.00
E.C. Dewitt & Co., One Minute Cough Cure, Aqua, BIMAL, 6 7/8 In. 18.00
Elepizone & Certain Cure For Fits & Epilepsy, N.Y., Aqua, 8 In. 90.00
Emerson's Rheumatic, Emerson Pharmacal Co., Baltimore, Md., Amber, Round, 5 In. ... 39.00
Great Blood & Rheumatism, No. 6088, J. Johnson, Aqua, Double Collar, c.1895, 9 In. .. 45.00
Great Dr. Kilmer's Swamp Root Kidney Liver & Bladder, Aqua, Tooled Lip, 8 1/4 In. ... 20.00
Great Dr. Kilmer's Swamp Root Kidney Liver & Bladder Cure Specific, Aqua, 8 1/2 In. . 120.00
H.K.B., Safe Cure, Clear, Contents, Label, 9 In. 825.00
Handyside's Consumption, Olive Green, 6-Sided Neck, Double Collar, 11 In. 2250.00
Hires Cough Cure, Phila, Pa., Aquamarine, Label, Contents, 1880-1900, 4 1/2 In. 209.00
Kendall's Spavin, Enosburgh Falls, Vt., Amber, BIMAL, 5 3/4 In. 12.00
Langenbach's Dysentery, San Francisco, Ca., Amber, Label, Contents, 5 3/4 In. 105.00
Liqufruta Cough, Aqua, Rectangular, Embossed, BIMAL, 5 1/4 In. 19.00
Miner's Damiana & Celery Compound, H.C. Miner, N.Y., Amber, 8 3/4 In. .... *Illus* 7280.00
Munyon's Inhaler, Cures Cold Catarrh, All Throat & Lung Diseases, Green, 4 In. 29.00
Munyon's Inhaler, Cures Colds, Green, Cylindrical, Cork, Dropper, Tablets, Box, 4 In. ... 413.00
Piso's Cure For Consumption, Hazeltine & Co., Blue Aqua, 5 1/4 In. 45.00
Piso's Cure For Consumption, Hazeltine & Co., Olive Green, 4 Indented Panels, 5 1/4 In. 15.00
Polar Star Cough, Aqua, BIMAL, Embossed, 6 3/4 In. 15.00
Porter's Cure Of Pain, Bundysburg, Oh., Aqua, Applied Double Collar, Open Pontil, 5 In. 300.00
Porter's Cure Of Pain, Bundysburg, Oh., Blue Aqua, Iron Pontil, 6 1/4 In. 600.00
River Swamp Chill & Fever, Augusta, Ga., Yellow Amber, Alligator, Tooled Lip, 6 1/4 In. 1430.00
Royal Cough Cure, Cold Expeller, Dill Medicine Co., Contents, Label, Box, 6 1/2 In. 220.00
S.B. Catarrh, Smith Bros, Aqua, Tooled Single Collar, c.1900, 8 In. 40.00
Sabine, Liniment, For Rheumatism, Neuralgia, Nervousness, Aqua, 6 In. 33.00
Sanford's Radical, Cobalt Blue, Rectangular, 7 1/2 In. ....41.00 to 70.00
Sanford's Radical, Sapphire Blue, Square Collar, Panels, Rectangular, 7 3/8 In. 157.00
Spark's Kidney & Liver, Camden, N.H., Amber, Sample Size, 4 In. 29.00
Stewart D. Howe's Arabian Milk, Aqua, Label, Contents, 7 3/4 In. 72.00
Warner's Log Cabin Extract, Multi-Cures, Amber, Label, Contents, 6 3/8 In. 688.00
Warner's Safe Cure, 3 City, Orange Amber, Double Collar Lip, Pt., 9 1/2 In. 225.00
Warner's Safe Cure, Amber, 6 In. 75.00
Warner's Safe Cure, Amber, 9 1/2 In. 165.00
Warner's Safe Cure, Amber, Applied Double Collar, 1880-95, 9 5/8 In. 101.00
Warner's Safe Cure, Frankfurt, A/M, Emerald Green, Applied Lip, Label, 9 1/2 In. 896.00
Warner's Safe Cure, Frankfurt, A/M, Olive Green, Applied Lip, 9 In. 280.00
Warner's Safe Cure, Frankfurt, Blood Red Amber, Applied Blob Mouth, 9 1/2 In. 180.00
Warner's Safe Cure, Frankfurt, Olive Green, Applied Blob Mouth, 9 1/8 In. 245.00

Rubber cement solvent, available at art supply and office supply stores, has many uses. Put a few drops on a paper towel and rub off ink smudges, adhesive tape glue, and label glue from glass.

Cure, Miner's Damiana &
Celery Compound, H.C.
Miner, N.Y., Amber, 8 3/4 In.

Warner's Safe Cure, Frankfurt, Yellow, Green Tint, Applied Blob Top, 9 1/4 In.	120.00
Warner's Safe Cure, Honey Amber, Embossed, Label, 9 1/4 In.	176.00
Warner's Safe Cure, London, Amber, Embossed, 7 1/2 In. .37.00 to 52.00
Warner's Safe Cure, London, Amber, Embossed, 9 1/4 In.	23.00
Warner's Safe Cure, London, Golden Amber, Embossed, 2 Pt., 11 In.	1262.00
Warner's Safe Cure, London, Golden Yellow, 9 1/2 In.	7.70
Warner's Safe Cure, London, Green Yellow, 1/2 Pt.	75.00
Warner's Safe Cure, London, Olive Green, Applied Lip, 9 1/4 In.	180.00
Warner's Safe Cure, London, Olive Green, Applied Lip, 9 7/8 In.	112.00
Warner's Safe Cure, London, Olive Green, Embossed, 7 1/4 In. . . . . .69.00 to 126.00
Warner's Safe Cure, London, Olive Green, Embossed, 9 1/4 In.	92.00
Warner's Safe Cure, London, Red Amber, Embossed, 9 1/2 In.	20.00
Warner's Safe Cure, London, Yellow, 1/2 Pt.	40.00
Warner's Safe Cure, Melbourne, Amber, Embossed, 9 1/2 In.	24.00
Warner's Safe Cure, Melbourne, Australia, Amber, 5 3/8 In.	231.00
Warner's Safe Cure, Melbourne, London, Toronto, Rochester, Amber, Double Collar, 9 In. .	100.00
Warner's Safe Cure, Melbourne, London, Toronto, Rochester, Yellow, 9 1/2 In.	300.00
Warner's Safe Cure, Melbourne, Orange To Red Amber, Applied Blob Top, 9 1/4 In.	85.00
Warner's Safe Cure, Pressburg, Red Amber, Applied Lip, Austria, 1890-1900, 9 3/8 In. . .	336.00
Warner's Safe Cure, Pressburg, Red Amber, Applied Lip, Germany, 1885-1900, 9 1/2 In. .	504.00
Warner's Safe Cure, Red, Amber, Embossed, 2 Pt., 11 1/4 In.	1329.00
Warner's Safe Cure, Rochester, 1/2 Pt.	25.00
Warner's Safe Cure, Rochester, N.Y., Amber, 10 In.	41.00
Warner's Safe Diabetes, Rochester, N.Y., Safe, Amber, Applied Lip, 9 1/2 In.	213.00
Warner's Safe Diabetes Cure, London, Olive Green, Embossed, 9 1/4 In.	862.00
Warner's Safe Diabetes Cure, London, Yellow Amber, Applied Lip, 9 3/8 In.	224.00
Warner's Safe Diabetes Cure, London, Yellow Shaded To Yellow Amber, 9 1/2 In.	220.00
Warner's Safe Diabetes Cure, Melbourne, London, Toronto, Rochester, Amber, 9 1/2 In. .	300.00
Warner's Safe Diabetes Cure, Rochester, N.Y., Amber, Tooled Lip, 9 5/8 In.	210.00
Warner's Safe Diabetes Cure, Yellow Amber, Contents, Box, 9 1/2 In.	770.00
Warner's Safe Kidney & Liver, Rochester, Amber, Double Collar, 9 1/2 In.	30.00
Warner's Safe Kidney & Liver, Rochester, Blob Top, Pt.	20.00
Warner's Safe Rheumatic Cure, Embossed, Amber, London, 9 1/2 In.	69.00
Warner's Safe Rheumatic Cure, Rochester, Amber, Applied Lip, 9 1/2 In.	110.00
Warner's Safe Tonic, Rochester, N.Y., Amber, Applied Double Collar, 1880-95, 9 3/4 In. .	476.00
Wilbur's Spavin Cure, Man, Horse, Paper Label, Contents, Cork, 7 1/8 In.	77.00
Wooldridge Wonderful Cure Co., Columbus, Ga., Golden Amber, 1875-85, 8 1/4 In.	154.00

CYRUS NOBLE

This complicated story requires a cast of characters and names: Cyrus Noble, a master distiller; Ernest R. Lilienthal, owner of Bernheim Distillery; Crown Distillers, trade name of Lilienthal & Company; Haas Brothers, successor to Lilienthal & Co.; and another Ernest R. Lilienthal and grandson of the original Ernest Lilienthal, president of Haas Brothers Distributing. Cyrus Noble was in charge of the quality of the whiskey made at the Bernheim Distillery in Kentucky. He was said to be a large man, over 300 pounds, and liked to taste his own product. According to the stories, he tasted to excess one day, fell into a whiskey vat, and drowned. The company, as a tribute, named the brand for him in 1871 and so Cyrus Noble Bourbon came into being.

Ernest R. Lilienthal, the original owner of Bernheim Distillery, moved to San Francisco and opened Lilienthal & Company with the trade name of Crown Distillers. Their best-selling brand was Cyrus Noble. It was made in three grades and sold by the barrel. The company later became Haas Brothers Distributing Company.

In 1901 John Coleman, a miner in Searchlight, Nevada, was so discouraged with the results of his digging that he offered to trade his mine to Tobe Weaver, a bartender, for a quart of Cyrus Noble whiskey. The mine was named Cyrus Noble and eventually produced over $250,000 worth of gold.

One of the early bottles used for Cyrus Noble whiskey was amber with an inside screw top; it was made from the 1860s to 1921. Haas Brothers of San Francisco marketed special Cyrus Noble bottles from 1971 to 1980. The first, made to commemorate the company's 100th anniversary, pictured the miner, the unfortunate John Coleman. Six thousand bottles were made and sold, filled, for $16.95 each. Tobe Weaver, the fortunate bartender, was pictured in the next bottle. A mine series was made from 1971 to

Cyrus Noble,
Landlady, Box, 1977

Cyrus Noble, Middle
Of Piano, Trumpeter,
1979

Cyrus Noble, Penguins, 1978

1978, the full size about 14 inches high and the miniatures about 6 inches; a wild animal series from 1977 to 1978; and a carousel series in 1979 and 1980. Other series are birds of the forest, Olympic bottles, horned animals, and sea animals. W.A. Lacey, a brand of 86 proof blended whiskey distributed by Haas Brothers, was also packed in a variety of figural bottles. They are listed separately under Lacey. Production of decanters for both brands ended in 1981.

Assayer, 1972	5.50
Assayer, 1974	20.00
Assayer, Box, 1972	10.00
Bartender, 1971	21.00
Bartender, 1974, Miniature	5.00
Buffalo Cow & Calf, Box, 1976	13.00
Burro, 1973 ....10.00 to 20.00	
Carousel, Horse, White Charger, 1979	5.00
Gambler, 1974	10.50
Gambler's Lady, 1977, 14 1/4 In.	10.00
Gambler's Lady, Box, 1977, 14 1/4 In.	55.00
Gold Miner, 1974, Miniature	20.00
Landlady, Box, 1977 ....*Illus*	10.00
Man Shaving, 1977	10.50
Middle Of Piano, Trumpeter, 1979 ....*Illus*	20.00
Miner's Daughter, 1975	12.50
Mountain Lion & Cubs, Box, 1977, 1st Edition	11.00
Mountain Lion & Cubs, Box, 1979	15.50
Mountain Sheep, 1978, Box	16.00
Music Man, Box, 1977	10.50
Penguins, 1978 ....*Illus*	20.00
Ship, Carson City, West Indies, 1974	19.00
Snowshoe Thompson, 1972 ....6.00 to 7.50	
Violinist, Box, 1976	10.00
Walrus Family, 1978	20.00
Whiskey Drummer, 1975 ....6.00 to 10.50	

DANT

Dant figural bottles were first released in 1968 to hold J.W. Dant alcoholic products. The figurals were discontinued after a few years. The company made an Americana series, field birds, special bottlings, and ceramic bottles. Several bottles were made with *errors*. Collectors seem to have discounted this in determining value.

Alamo, 1969	14.50
American Legion, 1969, 10 3/4 x 4 1/2 In. ....*Illus*	14.00
Boston Tea Party, Reverse Eagle, 1968 ....*Illus*	14.00
Constitution & Guerriere, Box, 1969	14.00
Field Bird Series, No. 1, Ring-Necked Pheasant, 1969 ....*Illus*	18.00
Field Bird Series, No. 2, Chukar Partridge, 1969	4.00
Field Bird Series, No. 6, California Quail, 1969	4.00

Dant, American Legion, 1969,
10 3/4 x 4 1/2 In.

Dant, Boston Tea Party,
Reverse Eagle, 1968

Dant, Field Bird Series, No. 1,
Ring-Necked Pheasant, 1969

Indy 500, 1969 . . . . .5.00 to 28.00
Mt. Rushmore, 1969 . . . .*Illus*   14.00
Patrick Henry, 1969 . . . .   14.00
Paul Bunyan, 1969 . . . .   2.00
Washington At Delaware, 1969, 8 x 2 3/4 In. . . . . .3.00 to 14.00

DAVIESS COUNTY

Daviess County ceramic bottles were made from 1978 to 1981. The best-known were
the American Legion Convention bottles. About 14 figural bottles were made, including a series of large tractor trailers and Greensboro Golf Tournament souvenirs.

American Legion, Hawaii, 1981 . . . .   25.00
Iowa Hog, 1978 . . . . .9.00 to 11.50
Pontiac Trans Am, 1980 . . . .   52.00
Porsche, Box, 15 In. . . . . .20.00 to 60.00

DECANTER

Decanters were first used to hold the alcoholic beverages that had been stored in kegs.
The undesirable sediment that formed at the bottom of old wine kegs was removed by
carefully pouring off the top liquid, or decanting it. At first a necessity, the decanter
later became merely an attractive serving vessel. A decanter usually has a bulbous bottom, a long neck, and a small mouth for easy pouring. Most have a cork or glass stopper. They were popular in England from the beginning of the eighteenth century. By
about 1775 the decanter was elaborate, with cut, applied, or enameled decorations. Various early American glassworks made decanters. Mold-blown decanters were the most
popular style and many were made in the East and the Midwest from 1820 to the 1860s.
Pressed glass was a less expensive process introduced in about 1850, and many
decanters were made by this method. Colored Bohemian glass consisting of two or
three cased layers became popular in the late-nineteenth century. Many decanters are
now made for home or restaurant use or with special logos to promote products. Bar
bottles, decanter-like bottles with brand names in the glass, were used from about 1890
to 1920 in saloons. The law no longer permits the use of bar bottles because no bottle
may be refilled from another container. Other decanters may be found in the Beam,
Bischoff, Kord, and other modern bottle categories.

3 Applied Neck Rings, Diamond Base, 8 1/2 x 6 3/4 In., Pt. 121.00
8 Pillars, Sapphire Blue, Applied Bar Lip, c.1850, 10 In. 2200.00
8 Pillars, Vertical Ribs, Sapphire Blue, Applied Lip, Pontil, 10 1/4 In., Pair 1680.00
8 Ribs, Swirled, Green, Applied Double Collar, Pontil, Cylindrical, 11 1/2 In., Pair 672.00
10-Sided, Waisted, Forest Green, Applied Neck Ring, Pontil, c.1850, 10 1/2 In. 1210.00
15 Ribs, Lavender, Applied Lip, Pontil, c.1850, 6 In. 952.00
Aqua, Applied Lip, Pontil, Bulbous, 1820, 8 1/2 x 5 1/4 In. 4200.00
Backbar, Loma Grande Pure Brandy, Enamel Lettering, Qt., 9 In. 39.00
Bar, Robin's-Egg Blue, Applied Neck Ring & Bar Lip, Pontil, c.1850, 10 1/2 In. 1320.00
Baroque, 3-Piece Mold, Cobalt Blue, Hollow Ball Stopper, 7 3/8 In. . . . .*Illus* 5500.00
Barrel Shape, Olive Yellow, Keene Marlboro Street, c.1830, Pt.   672.00
Big Bill Best Bitters, Fat Man, In Suit, Golden Amber, Tooled Lip, 1880, 11 1/2 In. 275.00

Bulldog, Spike Collar, Pottery, Detachable Head, Huffman Liqueur, 12 In. 232.00
Chestnut, Deep Teal Green, Polished Pontil, Handle, Silver Pour Spout, 7 3/8 In. 210.00
Cobalt Blue, Cathedral Arches, Applied Lip, 9 3/8 In. 145.00
Cobalt Blue, Teardrop Stopper, Gilt Decoration, Holland Shield Label, 9 1/2 x 3 1/2 In. . . 28.00
Cobalt Blue, Thread Decoration, Plain Lip, Pontil, c.1800, Qt., 9 In. 523.00
Cranberry Glass, White Cut To Cranberry, Stopper, 16 1/2 In. 110.00
Cruciform, Clear, Smoky Amethystine, Pontil, Tooled Lip, Neck Ring, 8 7/8 In. 728.00
Cut & Pressed, 8-Panels, Peacock Green, 6-Panel Stopper, c.1850, 12 1/4 In. 1870.00
Cut Glass, Comet Tails, Rays, Diamond Points, 3 Neck Rings, Stopper, c.1835, 10 1/2 In. . 468.00
Cut Glass, Drape, Stopper, Mid 19th Century Style, England, 10 3/4 In. 173.00
Cut Glass, Eagle, Green, Pewter Head, 9 1/4 In. 50.00
Cut Glass, Fluted Panels On Shoulder & Base, Amethyst, Sandwich Type, 11 1/2 In. 110.00
Cut Glass, Strawberry, Fans, Rays, 3 Applied Neck Rings, Stopper, c.1835, Qt., 11 In. . . . 413.00
Cut Panels At Base & Shoulder, Teal Green, Tooled Lip, Polished Pontil, Stopper, 10 In. . 190.00
Diamond Diaper, Olive Green, Amber Tone, Sunburst, Sheared Mouth, Pontil, 7 In. 660.00
Diamond Diaper, Sunburst, Clear, Bulbous, Stopper, Pontil, Boston & Sandwich, Pt. 308.00
Diamond Diaper Band, Rounded Ribs, Blue Green, Flared Pour Spout Lip, Pontil, 7 In. . . 2240.00
Diamond Diaper Band, Sunburst, Olive Green, Tooled Lip, Pontil, 7 1/8 In. . . . .*Illus* 840.00
Double Chain Band, 2 Applied Neck Rings, Pontil, c.1815, Qt., 10 1/4 In. 1155.00
Fern, Moonstone, Tooled Flared Lip, Stopper, Pontil, Qt 672.00
Flint EAPG, Tulip & Sawtooth, Footed, Stopper, Handle, c.1865, Qt., 9 In. 176.00
Forest Green, Keene Marlboro Street Glassworks, c.1830, Pt. 1064.00
Medium Olive Green, Applied Double Collar, Pontil, New England, 9 1/8 In. 6600.00
Milk Glass, 3 Rings, Enameled Victorian Designs, Pontil, 1850-70, 1/2 Gal. 119.00
Neck Rings, Ribbed Base, Pontil, Stopper, c.1830, Qt., 11 In. 303.00
Olive Amber, Pontil, Sheared Mark, Keene, Pt., 7 In. 805.00
Olive Green, Barrel, Pontil, Applied Sloping Double Collar, 8 3/8 In. 2688.00
Olive Green, Plain Lip, Rayed Base, Rough Pontil, 7 1/4 x 3 In., Pt. 770.00
Olive Green, Plain Lip, Rayed Base, Rough Pontil, 9 1/8 x 4 In., Qt. 2310.00
Olive Green, Rayed Base, Pontil, c.1830, Qt., 9 1/8 In. 1980.00
Olive Yellow, Flared Lip, Blown, Keene Marlboro Street Glassworks, Pt. 1064.00
Pillar Molded, 8 Ribs, Applied Neck Ring, Pontil, c.1850, 3 Pt., 11 1/2 In. 77.00
Pillar Molded, Clear, 8 Pillars, Amethyst Edges, Neck Ring, Double Collar, 10 1/2 In. . . . 784.00
Pineapple, Blown, 3 Applied Neck Rings, Stopper, c.1830, Pt. 336.00
Pineapple, Blown, Yellow Green, Sloping Collar, Pontil, Pt. 4760.00
Plain Base, Pontil, Ribbed Ball Stopper, c.1830, Qt., 11 1/4 In. 143.00
Plain Base, Ribbed Hollow Ball Stopper, 11 In., Qt. 66.00
Ribbed Base, Hollow Stopper, Pontil, Qt. 99.00
Ribs, Applied Thread, Aqua, Open Pontil, 8 1/2 In. 44.00
Ring Neck, Folded Rim, Tam-O-Shanter Stopper, Pontil, 6 1/2 x 2 1/4 In. 88.00
Silver Overlay, 3-Sided, Red, Rye & Gin, 9 1/2 In., Pair 176.00
Sunray, Applied Lip, Applied Band, c.1860, 11 In. 44.00
Taper, Engraved & Cut, Bowknot, Wreath, Masonic Emblem, c.1800, Qt., 11 1/4 In. 440.00
Taper, Engraved & Cut, Eagle, Scroll, Initials, c.1800, Qt., 12 3/4 In. 715.00
Taper, Engraved & Cut, Feathered Swirls, Stars, Stopper, c.1800, Qt., 12 In. 176.00
Taper, Engraved & Cut, Flowers, Bowknots, Laurels, Stopper, c.1800, 1/2 Pt., 7 In. 605.00
Taper, Engraved & Cut, Flowers, Laurels, Stopper, c.1800, Pt., 10 In. 413.00

Dant, Mt. Rushmore, 1969

Decanter, Baroque, 3-Piece
Mold, Cobalt Blue, Hollow
Ball Stopper, 7 3/8 In.

Decanter, Diamond
Diaper Band,
Sunburst, Olive
Green, Tooled Lip,
Pontil, 7 1/8 In.

Taper, Engraved & Cut, Garland, Ovals, Stars, Stopper, c.1800, Qt., 11 1/2 In. 220.00
Taper, Engraved & Cut, Leaves, Daisies, Heart Stopper, c.1800, Qt., 11 1/2 In. 440.00
Taper, Engraved & Cut, R, Sunrays, Clouds, Leaves, c.1800, Pt., 11 In. 660.00
Taper, Engraved & Cut, Rope, Lily Of The Valley, Grapes, Stopper, c.1800, Qt., 11 1/4 In. 253.00
Taper, Engraved & Cut, Sprigs, Ovals, Daisies, Swags, Stopper, c.1800, Pt., 9 1/2 In. 358.00
Taper, Engraved & Cut, Sprigs, Ovals, Flowers, Tassels, Stopper, c.1800, Qt., 11 In. 220.00
Taper, Engraved & Cut, Sprigs, Ovals, Stars, Stopper, c.1800, Qt., 10 1/4 In. 176.00
Taper, Engraved & Cut, Sprigs, Ovals, Swags, Tassels, Stopper, c.1800, Pt., 9 1/2 In. 253.00
Taper, Engraved & Cut, Stars, Roundels, Stopper, c.1800, Qt., 8 3/4 In. 143.00
Taper, Engraved & Cut, Swags, Tassels, Stars, Stopper, Qt., 11 1/4 In. 523.00
Taper, Plain Lip, Crosshatch Disk Stopper, Pontil, c.1800, 1/2 Pt., 8 1/2 In. 275.00
Taper, Plain Lip, Disk Stopper, Pontil, c.1800, Pt., 9 In. 187.00
Teal Blue Green, Flared Lip, Pontil, Keene Marlboro Street Glassworks, Pt. 1568.00
Tuthill Silver Overlay, Flowers, Leaves, Faceted Stopper, 13 1/2 In. 604.00
Westminster Abbey, Circle Of Stars, Aqua, 5 Ribs, Stopper, Italy, 11 x 6 In. 13.00
Windmill, Turquoise Blue, Metal Hangers, Ground Lip, 1890-1920, 8 In. 207.00
World's Fair, New York, Globe Shaped Base, Banner, White, 1939, 9 In. 45.00

―――――――――――――――――――――― **DEMIJOHN** ――――――――――――――――――――――

A demijohn is a very large bottle that is usually blown. Many held alcoholic beverages, molasses, or other liquids. It was usually bulbous with a long neck and a high kick-up. Early examples have open pontils. A carboy is a bottle that was covered with wicker to avoid breakage when the bottles were shipped. A demijohn could hold from one to ten gallons. Most early demijohns were made of dark green, amber, or black glass. By the 1850s the glass colors were often aqua, light green, or clear.

Amber, Applied Lip, 15 In. 55.00
Amber, Pontil, Stoddard, Blown, 16 3/4 In. 77.00
Amber, Tapered Collar Blob, 5 Gal. 48.00
Aqua, Basket, Mold Blown, Applied Lip, 13 In. 40.00
Aqua, Cylindrical, Open Pontil, Gallon, 15 1/2 In. 45.00
Blown, Globular, Olive Green, Applied Lip, Kick-Up Base, c.1800, 10 1/4 In. 880.00
Blue Green, Bulbous, Dip Mold, 1 1/2 Gal., 14 1/2 In. 69.00
Blue Green, Iron Pontil, Cylindrical, 1/2 Gal., 12 In. 49.00
Bullet Head, Medium Olive Amber, Dip Mold, Pontil, Bubbles, c.1810, 12 3/4 In. 605.00
Cobalt Blue, Pontil, Applied Flat Collar, 9 3/4 In. 1792.00
Dark Red Amber, Applied Sloping Collar, 3-Piece Mold, c.1870, 11 1/2 x 4 1/4 In. 165.00
Forest Green, Pontil, 16 1/2 In. 175.00
Golden Amber, Aquamarine, Sloping Collar, Pontil, Kidney Shape, 2 7/8 In. 504.00
Green, Flared Lip, Open Pontil, 14 3/4 In. 150.00
Green, Free-Blown, Gal., 13 1/2 In. 200.00
Green, Pear Shape, 19 1/2 In. 61.00
Green, Round, Open Pontil, 17 In. 85.00
Kidney Shape, Aquamarine, Applied Taper Top, c.1870, 20 x 17 In. 110.00
Kidney Shape, Yellow Olive Green, 18 In. 165.00
Lemon Yellow Citron, Cylindrical, Applied Lip, 16 1/4 In. 69.00
Lime Yellow Citron, Cylindrical, Applied Lip, 1/2 Gal., 13 In. 45.00
Medium Blue Green, Kick-Up, Applied String Lip, Pontil, Bubbles, c.1820, 19 1/4 In. 660.00
Medium Olive Green, Applied Aqua Sloping Collar Mouth, Pontil, 3 7/8 In. 135.00
Medium Olive Yellow Green, Applied Lip, 3-Piece Mold, Pontil, Bubbles, 20 1/2 In. 180.00
Medium Olive Yellow Green, Applied Sloping Collar, Pontil, Bubbles, Swirls, 13 3/4 In. . 115.00
Medium Pink Puce, Pointed Kick-Up, Pontil, Bubbles, 1780-1840, 12 5/8 In. 440.00
Medium Yellow Amber, Applied Sloping Collar Mouth, Pontil, Bubbles, 12 3/4 In. 160.00
Medium Yellow Green, Loaf Of Bread Form, Applied Sloping Collar, 8 1/2 x 10 1/4 In. .. 350.00
Melon, Ribbed, Sapphire Blue, Applied Lip, Pontil, 16 In. 83.00
Mold Blown, 25, Olive Green, Snap Pontil, Hand Tooled Lip, c.1815, 13 1/2 x 22 In. 374.00
Olive, Applied Lip, Rough Pontil, 15 In. 132.00
Olive Amber, Blown, Applied Tapered Collared Mouth, Pontil, 10 5/8 In. 100.00
Olive Amber, Sloping Collar Mouth, Pontil, 13 5/8 In. 168.00
Olive Amber, Yellow, Applied Collar Mouth, 1780-1810, 19 1/4 In. 58.00
Olive Green, Applied Aqua Sloping Collar Mouth, Pontil, 1865-75, 3 7/8 In. 131.00
Olive Green, Deep Kick-Up Pontil, Bubbles, 10 In. 343.00
Olive Yellow, Applied Sloping Collar, 17 1/2 In. 157.00
Olive Yellow, Applied Sloping Collar, Pontil, 11 3/4 In. 392.00

Olive Yellow, Bulbous, 1/2 Pt., 7 In.	45.00
Olive Yellow, Cylindrical, 3-Piece Mold, Open Pontil, 2 Gal., 18 In.	100.00
Olive Yellow, Open Pontil, Kidney Shape, Seed Bubbles, 1830-50, 3 In.	139.00
Olive Yellow, Pontil, Applied Sterling Silver Hinged Cap, Continental, 14 1/2 In.	140.00
Olive Yellow, Pontil, Sheared Mouth, Applied String Lip, 1780-1810, 11 1/4 In.	672.00
Olive Yellow Amber, Bubbles, Swirls, Sloping Collar, 18 3/4 In.	190.00
Olive Yellow Amber, Dutch Kidney Shape, Applied String Lip, Pontil, Stopper, 17 3/4 In. .	950.00
Olive Yellow Green, Applied Collar Mouth, Open Pontil, 1770-1810, 19 3/8 In.	246.00
Olive Yellow Green, Applied Sloping Collar Mouth, Pontil, c.1800-20, 13 3/4 In.	112.00
Sapphire Blue, Applied Sloping Collar, Handle, Wicker, 12 1/2 In.	168.00
Tobacco, Amber, Wicker Cover, 15 In.	66.00
Yellow Amber, Applied Sloping Collar Mouth, Pontil, 1800-20, 12 3/4 In.	158.00
Yellow Citron, Cylindrical, Handled Wicker, Qt., 12 1/2 In.	35.00
Yellow Green, 3-Piece Mold, Applied Lip, Pontil, 18 1/4 In.	112.00
Yellow Green, Rectangular, Applied Sloping Collar Mouth, 8 1/2 x 10 1/4 x 6 1/4 In.	350.00

―――――――――― **DICKEL** ――――――――――

George Dickel Tennessee sour mash whiskey was sold in figural bottles in about 1967. The golf club, powder horn, and ceramic jug were widely advertised then but are of limited interest to today's collectors.

Golf Club, 1967	13.00
Jug, Ceramic, 1988	10.00
Jug, Merle Haggard, Black, 1987, 7 1/2 In.	10.50
Jug, No. 1 In Series, Ceramic, 1976	12.50
Jug, No. 12 Brand, Ceramic	5.00
Old No. 8 Brand, 1930s, 4 1/4 In.	10.00
Powder Horn, 1963, 12 1/2 In.	25.00
Powder Horn, Miniature	7.50
Powder Horn, Qt.	6.00 to 15.00

―――――――――― **DOUBLE SPRINGS** ――――――――――

Double Springs of Louisville, Kentucky, made ceramic figural bottles from 1968 to 1978. They had a classic car series made by the Century Porcelain Company, a Bicentennial series, and other figural bottles.

Bull, Red, Box, 1969, 6 x 10 In.	10.00
Cord, 1937 Model, 1978	10.00
Georgia Bulldog, 1971	15.50
Owl, Brown, 1968	1.25
Peasant Boy, 1968	5.00
Peasant Girl, 1968	5.00

DRUG, see Bitters; Cure; Medicine; Tonic

―――――――――― **EZRA BROOKS** ――――――――――

Ezra Brooks fancy bottles were first made in 1964. The Ezra Brooks brand was purchased by Glenmore Distilleries Company of Louisville, Kentucky, in 1988, three years after Ezra Brooks had discontinued making decanters. About 300 different ceramic figurals were made between 1964 and 1985. The dates listed here are within a year of the time they appeared on the market. Bottles were often announced and then not produced for many months. Glenmore sold the Ezra Brooks label to Heaven Hill Distillery in Bardstown, Kentucky, who sold it to David Sherman Corporation of St. Louis, Missouri, in 1994.

American Legion, Chicago, Salute, 1972	9.00 to 13.00
American Legion, Hawaii, 1973	23.00
American Legion, Houston, 1971	9.00 to 10.00
American Legion, Miami Beach, 1974	5.00 to 15.00
AMVET, Dolphin, 1974	*Illus* 32.00
Arizona, Desert Scene, 1969	5.00 to 8.00
Bordertown Nevada, 1970	2.75 to 13.00
Bowler, 1973	10.00 to 15.50
Brahma Bull, 1971	5.00 to 8.50
Bronco Buster, 1973	14.00
Buffalo Hunt, 1971	10.00
C.B. Convoy Radio, 1976	*Illus* 5.00

Ezra Brooks, AMVET, Dolphin, 1974

Ezra Brooks, C.B. Convoy Radio, 1976

Ezra Brooks, Cannon, 1969

Cannon, 1969	*Illus*	32.00
Card, Jack Of Diamonds, 1969		13.00
Card, King Of Clubs, 1969		13.00
Card, Queen Of Hearts, Box, 1969		5.00
Casey At Bat, 1973		20.00
Charolais Bull, 1972		20.00
Chicago Fire Team, 1974		17.00
Chicago Water Tower, 1969	13.00 to	39.00
Christmas Tree, 1979		7.00
Cigar Store Indian, 1968	3.00 to	10.00
Clown, Head, 1980		12.50
Clown, No. 1, Smiley, 1979	*Illus*	18.00
Clown, With Balloons, 1973	*Illus*	10.00
Clydesdale, 1974	*Illus*	22.00
Dakota Cowboy, 1975		20.00
Deadwagon, Nevada, 1970	*Illus*	15.00
Delta Belle, Riverboat, 1969		1.00
Dog, Setter, 1974		28.00
Drum & Bugle, Conquistador, 1971	5.00 to	8.00
Duesenberg, 1971	10.00 to	11.00
Eagle, Gold, 1971		11.50
Elephant, Big Bertha, 1970	10.00 to	20.00
English Setter With Bird In Mouth, 1971	4.00 to	5.00
Equestrian, 1974		13.00
Fire Engine, 1971		6.00
Fire Engine, Box, 1971		10.00
Fireman, 1975		18.00
Fisherman, 1974	10.00 to	19.00
Ford Thunderbird, 1956 Model, Blue, Box, 1976		10.00

Ezra Brooks, Clown, No. 1, Smiley, 1979

Ezra Brooks, Clown, With Balloons, 1973

Ezra Brooks, Clydesdale, 1974

Ezra Brooks, Deadwagon, Nevada, 1970

Ezra Brooks, Hardy,
Oliver, 1976

Foremost Astronaut, 1970	13.00 to 17.00
Foremost Dancing Man, Box, 1969	46.00
Fox, Redtail, 1979	37.00
Fresno Grape, 1970	1.50
Gamecock, 1970	9.00
Gator, Florida, No. 1, Passing, 1972	60.00
Gator, Florida, No. 2, Running, 1973	68.00
Georgia Bulldog, 1971	13.00
Go Big Red, No. 3, Football, 1972	31.00
Goose, Happy, 1974	4.00 to 20.00
Gopher, Minnesota Hockey Player, 1975	23.00
Grandfather Clock, 1970	5.00
Hambletonian, Gold, 1970	11.00
Happy Goose, 1974	20.00
Hardy, Oliver, 1976	*Illus* 37.00
Historical Flask, Old Ironsides, Green, 1970	17.00
Horseshoe Casino, Box, 1970	10.00
Hunter & Dog, 1973	7.50
Indian, Ceremonial, Box, 1970	6.00
Indy Pace Car, Corvette, Box, 1978	15.50 to 50.00
Indy Pace Car, Ford Mustang, Box, 1979	10.00
Indy Race Car, No. 21, 1970	8.50 to 10.00
Indy STP No. 40, Mario Andretti, 1983	33.00
Jayhawk, Kansas, 1969	24.00
Kachina, No. 2, Hummingbird, 1973	10.00
Kachina, No. 5, Longhair, 1976	18.50
Kachina, No. 6, Buffalo Dancer, 1977	11.00
Kachina, No. 8, Drummer, 1979	15.00 to 25.00
Kachina, No. 9, Watermelon, 1980	*Illus* 25.00
Laurel, Stan, 1976	*Illus* 37.00
Lion On Rock, 1971	5.00 to 20.00
Motorcycle, 1971	5.00 to 8.00

Ezra Brooks,
Kachina, No. 9,
Watermelon,
1980

Ezra Brooks,
Laurel, Stan, 1976

Ezra Brooks, San Francisco Cable Car,
Gray, Green, Brown, 1968

Mule, Missouri, Gold, 1971	35.00
New Hampshire, State House, 1969	15.00
Nugget Gold Rooster, No. 1, 1969	15.00
Old Capital, Iowa, 1971	5.00
Ontario Racer No. 10, 1970	36.00
Owl, Great Gray, 1982	15.00
Panda, 1972	5.00
Pirate, 1971	5.00 to 10.00
Pistol, Dueling, Flintlock, 1968	6.50 to 9.00
Political, Republican Convention, Elephant, 1976	17.00 to 21.00
Quail, California, 1970	4.00 to 16.00
Ram, 1973	6.00 to 10.00
Reno Arch, 1968	3.00
Sailfish, 1970	3.75 to 13.00
Salmon, Washington, 1971	20.00
San Francisco Cable Car, Gray, Green, Brown, 1968 *Illus*	34.00
Sea Captain, 1971	2.00
Shriner, Fez, 1976	4.00 to 6.00
Silver Spur Boot, 1971	24.00
Ski Boot, 1972	15.00 to 17.00
Snowmobile, 1972	9.00 to 13.00
Strongman, 1974	20.00
Telephone, Box, 1971	10.00
Tennis Player, 1973	15.00
Terrapin, Maryland, 1974	56.00 to 76.00
Texas Longhorn Steer, Box, 1971	15.00
Ticker Tape, 1970	10.00
Totem Pole, No. 2, 1973	10.00 to 50.00
Train, Casey Jones Locomotive, Box, 1980	20.00
Train, Iron Horse, Engine, 1969	1.00 to 5.50
Trojan, USC, 1973	62.00
Trojan Horse, 1974	36.00
VFW, Blue, 75th Anniversary, 1973	5.00 to 15.00
Wheat Shocker, Kansas, 1971	13.00 to 26.00
Winston Churchill, 1969	12.50

FAMOUS FIRSTS

Famous Firsts Ltd. of Port Chester, New York, was owned by Richard E. Magid. The first figural bottles, issued in 1968, were a series of race cars. The last figurals were made in 1985.

Bell, Alpine, 1970	6.00
Bennie Bow Wow, 1973	20.00
Butterfly, 1971	4.50
Cable Car, 1973	26.00
Duesenberg, 1933 Model, Limited Edition	124.00
Indy Racer, No. 11, 1971	23.00 to 25.00

Famous Firsts, Telephone,
French, Blue, 1969

Famous Firsts, Tiger,
1975

Famous Firsts, Winnie Mae,
Airplane, 1972, 16 In.

Leopard, 1975 .... 20.00
Lombardy Scale, 1970 .... 15.00
Lotus, Racer, No. 2, 1971 .... 60.00
Marmon Wasp No. 32, 1968 ....20.00 to 50.00
Marmon Wasp No. 32, Gold, 1/2 Pt., 1971 ....25.00 to 26.00
Minnie Meow, 1973 .... 20.00
Panther, 1975 .... 20.00
Phonograph, 1973, Miniature 24.00
Porsche Targa, 1979 .... 64.00
Renault Racer, No. 3, 1969 .... 50.00
Riverboat, Natchez, Mail Packet, 1975 .... 25.00
Riverboat, Robert E. Lee, 1971 .... 25.00
Scale, Lombardy, 1970 .... 15.00
Sewing Machine, 1979, 200 Milliliter ....16.00 to 21.00
Telephone, French, Blue, 1969 ....*Illus* 15.00
Tiger, 1975 ....*Illus* 23.00
Winnie Mae, Airplane, 1972, 16 In. ....*Illus* 51.00
Yacht America, 1970, 14 In. 25.00

FIGURAL

Figural bottles are specially named by the collectors of bottles. Any bottle that is of a recognizable shape, such as a human head, a pretzel, or a clock, is considered to be a figural. There are no restrictions as to date or material. A *Soaky* is a special plastic bottle that holds shampoo, bubble bath, or another type of bath product. They were first made by Colgate-Palmolive in the late 1950s. Figurals are also listed by brand name or type in other sections of this book, such as the Bitters, Cologne, Perfume, Pottery, and Whiskey categories.

Admiral Nelson, Aqua, Applied Ring Flared Top, Open Pontil, 7 1/2 In. 264.00
Airplane, Spirit Of St. Louis, Cobalt Blue Body, Metal Wings & Propeller, 13 In. 392.00
Apple, Green, Frosted, Brown Handle & Spout, Open Pontil, France, 1880-1910, 5 In. ... 72.00
Artillery Shell, Souviens Toi Siege De Paris, 1870-71, Olive Green, Label, 10 In. 285.00
Baby, In Basket Of Grapes, Clear, Tooled Lip, Depose, France, 1890-1910, 13 In. 90.00
Baby Face, Feed The Baby, Marble Game, Frosted, Tooled Lip, Pontil, Rand Bros., 4 In. .. 175.00
Baseball, Cobalt Blue, Ground Lip, 1885-90, 2 3/4 In. 395.00
Baseball, Man's Head On Top, League Bouquet, Milk Glass, Metal Screw Cap, 3 In. 840.00
Baseball Glove, Ground Lip, Screw Cap, 1885-1910, 5 1/4 In. 240.00
Bather, Woman, Clear, Frosted, Tooled Lip, Pineapple Stopper, Depose, France, c.1900, 17 In. 90.00
Bear, Black Glass, Removable Head, 3 7/8 In. 134.00
Bear, Kummel, Black Olive Green, Tooled Lip, 11 1/4 In. 50.00
Bear, Kummel, Milk Glass, Applied Lip, 11 In. 66.00
Bear, Olive Yellow, Medallion, Sheared Mouth, 10 1/4 In. 308.00
Bear, Seated, Black Glass, Applied Face, Tooled Lip, 9 7/8 In. ....*Illus* 365.00
Bear, Seated, Olive Green, Applied Face, Tooled Lip, 8 5/8 In. 350.00
Bear, Seated, Paw In Air, Teddy's Bear, Blue & White Bisque, 1900-20, 7 1/4 In. 240.00
Bear, Seated, Russian Liqueur, Dark Olive Green, Corked, Contents, 11 In. 204.00
Bear, Seated, Russian Liqueur, Dark Olive Green, Medallion, 9 3/4 In. 224.00
Big Bill, Golden Amber, Tooled Lip, 11 3/4 In. 336.00
Big Bill, Medium Yellow Amber, Tooled Lip, 11 5/8 In. ....*Illus* 408.00
Billy Club, Ground Lip, Tin Screw Top, 1890-1925, 9 3/4 In. 22.00
Black Boy, Sitting On Barrel, Black, Tooled Lip, Pontil, Deponirt, Germany, 9 1/8 In. 680.00
Black Boy, Sitting On Barrel, Red Amber Shaded To Yellow Amber, Germany, 9 1/8 In. .. 540.00
Black Waiter, Clear, Frosted, Ground Lip, 1890-1910, 14 3/8 In. 365.00
Black Waitress, Frosted, Glass Head, Ground Top, 14 In. 275.00
Black Woman, Yellow Dress, Hat, Painted Decanter, Pottery, Marked, Robj, Paris, 10 In. . 358.00
Black Woman, Yellow Dress, Stopper, Porcelain, Robj, France, c.1920, 10 1/4 In. 775.00
Blimp, Blue, White, Gold, Whiskey Nipper, 5 1/4 In. 116.00
Book, Battle Of Bennington, Mottled Brown & Olive Glaze, Bennington, 5 1/2 In. 896.00
Book, Battle Of Bennington, Stoneware, Flint Enamel, Bennington, Flask, Pt., 5 1/2 In. .. 805.00
Book, Battle Of Bennington, Stoneware, Flint Enamel, Flask, 4 Qt., 10 3/4 In. 1265.00
Book, Departed Spirits, Mottled Brown Glaze, Bennington, 5 1/2 In. 672.00
Book, Departed Spirits, Stoneware, Flint Enamel, Bennington, Flask, Pt., 5 1/2 In. .460.00 to 480.00
Book, Kossuth, Mottled Brown & Olive Glaze, Bennington, 5 1/2 In. 952.00
Book, Ladies' Companion, Mottled Brown Glaze, Bennington, 5 1/2 In. 1008.00

Figural, Bear, Seated, Black Glass, Applied Face, Tooled Lip, 9 7/8 In.

Figural, Big Bill, Medium Yellow Amber, Tooled Lip, 11 5/8 In.

Figural, Boot, Bennington Glaze, 7 1/4 In.

Figural, Children, Climbing Tree, Clear, Frosted, Tooled Lip, France, 11 3/4 In.

Book, Man Sleeping On Barrel, 2 Men Fighting, Brown Glaze, Bennington, 7 In. 258.00
Book, Suffering Spirits, Mottled Brown & Olive Glaze, Bennington, 5 1/2 In. 1176.00
Boot, Bennington Glaze, 7 1/4 In. ....*Illus* 38.00
Boot, On Hassock, Frosted, Painted, Open Pontil, 1870-1900, 14 3/4 In. 66.00
Boot, On Hassock, Woman's Leg, Frosted, Open Pontil, 1870-1900, 14 3/4 In. 66.00
Boozeville Town Pump, Whiskey Nipper, 6 1/2 In. 55.00
Bouquet, Stemmed Roses, Tooled Lip, Pontil, Rosebud Stopper, 12 3/8 In. 240.00
Boy, Hat, Crossed Arms, Legs, Amethyst, By Jingo Trademark, Tooled Lip, 5 1/2 In. 45.00
Bugle, Ground Lip, Screw Cap, 1885-1910, 8 1/4 In. 220.00
Bulldog, Spike Collar, Ceramic, Huffman Liqueur, 12 x 17 In. 231.00
Bulldog, Tin Base, Screw Cap, England, 5 3/4 In. 22.00
Bulldog Head, Amber, Stippled, France, 1900-25, 4 In. 28.00
Bust, Benjamin Harrison, Clear, Frosted, Cherry Puce Pedestal Base, c.1890, 16 3/8 In. .. 448.00
Bust, Cat, Tooled Lip, 3 3/8 In. 157.00
Bust, Kate Klaxton, Tooled Lip, France, 1880-1910, 6 3/4 In. 83.00
Bust, Lord Nelson, Tan, Salt Glaze, Handle, Eagle's Head, 3 In. 154.00
Bust, Poincare, Milk Glass, France, 1890-1910, 13 In. 495.00
Bust, Queen Victoria, Reform, Pottery, Brown Glaze, 8 1/2 In. 123.00
Bust, Sardi Carnot, Tooled Lip, Open Pontil, France, 1870-90, 11 1/2 In. 50.00
Bust, Woman, Glass Urn On Head, Frosted, Clear, Tooled Lip, France, 1890-1910, 10 In. .. 90.00
Bust, Woman, Urn On Head, Frosted, Tooled Lip, c.1900, 10 In. 88.00
Cannon, JT Gayen, Altona, Red Amber, Round Collared Mouth, 1860-70, 1/2 Pt. 896.00
Car, Blue Aqua, Tooled Lip, Continental, 1900-20, 2 7/8 In. 308.00
Car, Mirabel, Aqua, Embossed, Tooled Lip, 1900-20, 2 7/8 In. 60.00
Cat, Frosted, Clear, Rolled Lip, France, 1890-1920, 1 3/4 In. 45.00
Cat, In Shoe, Tooled Lip, 3 7/8 In. 134.00
Champagne Girl, Whiskey Nipper, 4 1/2 In. 209.00
Cherub, Holding Clock, Pink Puce, Pontil, 10 In. ....60.00 to 100.00
Cherub, Playing Stringed Instrument, Tooled Lip, 1890-1920, 14 In. 115.00
Cherubs, 3 Holding Ball, Aqua, Tooled Lip, Pontil, France, c.1900, 8 1/2 In. 138.00
Cherubs, 3 Holding Globe, Clear, Frosted, Tooled Lip, Open Pontil, Depose, c.1895, 8 In. .. 55.00
Child, Arms At Sides, Tooled Lip, Britain, 1885-1910, 9 In. 97.00
Child, In Rocking Chair, Amethyst Tint, 5 1/4 In. 33.00
Child, Kneeling, White Rose Label, Clear, Smooth Base, Ground Lip, 1890-1915, 3 5/8 In. 90.00
Child, Sitting On Barrel, Ground Lip, G. & T., 1885-1910, 4 7/8 In. 98.00
Child, Sitting On Chamber Pot, Tooled Lip, C.F. Knapp, 4 1/2 In. ....165.00 to 280.00
Child, Wearing Dress, Tooled Lip, 7 In. 28.00
Children, Climbing Tree, Clear, Frosted, Tooled Lip, France, 11 3/4 In. ....*Illus* 75.00
Children, Climbing Tree, Clear, Frosted, Tooled Lip, Open Pontil, Depose, c.1880, 9 3/4 In. 45.00
Children, Climbing Tree, Frosted Figures, Tooled Lip, Open Pontil, 1870-90, 7 1/4 In. ... 55.00
Children, Climbing Tree, Tooled Lip, OP, Bird's Nest Stopper, Depose, 1890-1915, 13 In. 155.00
Christmas Tree, Olive Green, Embossed, Tooled Lip, Continental, 1900-20, 9 1/2 In. 67.00
Church, Medium Blue Green, Applied Lip, Pontil, 1885-1915, 6 7/8 In. 900.00
Cigar, Yellow Amber, Isaac W. Keim, Label, 5 1/4 In. ....*Illus* 80.00
Cigar Bundle, Amber, Ground Lip, Metal Screw Cap, 1/2 Pt. 45.00

Clam, Cobalt Blue, Ground Lip, 1870-90, 5 In. 1008.00
Clam, Cobalt Blue, Metal Screw Cap, 5 1/4 In. 392.00
Clam, Medium Amber, Metal Screw Cap, 5 1/4 In. 78.00
Clown, Milk Glass, Painted, Tooled Lip, Pontil, Removable Head, c.1880, 13 In. . . . . *Illus* 265.00
Clown, Milk Glass, Tooled Lip, Pontil, Continental, 1870-90, 13 1/4 In. 264.00
Clown, With Drum, 9 1/8 In. 56.00
Coachman, Brown Glaze, Pottery, 1870-90, 8 3/4 In. 308.00
Coachman, Pipe, Shot Glass, Medium Amber, Applied Lip, J.H. Carter, 10 7/8 In. 1820.00
Coachman, Pipe, Shot Glass, Teal Blue, Ground Lip, 1885-95, 10 1/4 In. 3680.00
Coachman, Pipe, Van Dunck's Genever, Amber, Qt. 79.00
Coachman, Tan, Brown Mottled Glaze, Pottery, 1849, 10 1/2 In. . . . . *Illus* 784.00
Coachman, Tassels, Holding Flask, Stoneware, Rockingham Glaze, Bennington, 11 In. . . . 403.00
Coachman, Tassels, Holding Mug, Stoneware, Rockingham Glaze, Bennington, 9 3/4 In. . 173.00
Coachman, Van Dunck's Genever, Ware & Schmitz, Amber, Applied Lip, 8 3/4 In. 100.00
Coachman, Van Dunck's Genever, Ware & Schmitz, Dark Chocolate Amber, 8 3/4 In. . . . 112.00
Cobbler, Tooled Lip, Open Pontil, France, 1870-90, 13 3/4 In. 55.00
Cockatoo, Black Amethyst, Ground Lip, c.1885-1910, 13 1/2 In. 197.00
Coffin, Milk Glass, Enamel Flowers, Ground Lip, Lid, Pocket Flask, 1/2 Pt., 6 In. 89.00
Cornucopia, Girl Sitting, Whiskey Nipper, 4 3/4 In. 187.00
Cottage, ABM Lip, Screw Cap, Ges. Gesch 2568, c.1920-30, 3 1/4 In. 38.00
Country Woman, Bare Feet, Apron, Hands On Hips, Ground Stopper, c.1910, 12 1/2 In. . 66.00
Couple Dancing, Turkey Trot, Whiskey Nipper, 5 1/2 In. 176.00
Cucumber, Light Blue Green, Ground Lip, 1885-1910, 4 1/2 In. 78.00
Dinner Pail, Full, Tin Cup Cover, Wood & Wire Handle, Albert Pick & Co., c.1890, 4 In. . 448.00
Dog, Begging, Merry Christmas, Whiskey Nipper, 4 1/2 In. 77.00
Drunken Man, On Way Home, Whiskey Nipper, 4 In. 55.00
Eagle, Cut Glass, Green, Hinged Metal Head, 9 1/4 In. 50.00
Eagle's Claw, Holding Ball, Clear, 3-Piece Mold, 1880-1900, Qt., 14 In. 39.00
Ear Of Corn, Amber, Gold Paint, Applied Lip, 1870-80, 9 3/4 In. 98.00
Ear Of Corn, Cobalt Blue, Traces Of Gold & White Paint, 1885-1915, 8 3/4 In. 500.00
Ear Of Corn, Olive Yellow, Applied Lip, 1865-75, 9 7/8 In. 1420.00
Ear Of Corn, Turquoise Blue, Footed, Sheared, Ground Lip, c.1900, 9 In. . . . . *Illus* 252.00
Egret, Straight Neck, Clear, Frosted, Tooled Lip, Pontil, 1885-1910, 12 3/4 In. 115.00
Egyptian Pharaoh, On Throne, Black Milk Glass, Embossed, France, 13 In. . . . . . . *Illus* 896.00
Eiffel Tower, Embossed, Tooled Lip, Pontil, Stopper, Depose, France, 10 In. 235.00
Eiffel Tower, Tooled Lip, France, 1880-1900, 13 1/4 In. 72.00
Elephant, Frosted, Sultan Stopper, 7 1/2 In. 100.00
Elephant, Trunk Straight Up, Federal Law Forbids Sale Or Reuse, BIMAL, 8 In. 29.00
Elephant, Trunk Up, Frosted, Applied Ring Top, 18 In. 149.00
Elephant, Trunk Up, Tooled Lip, Glass Stopper, 1890-1910, 8 1/4 In. 77.00
Elephant, Trunk Up, Tooled Lip, Stopper, 9 1/2 In. 77.00
Elk, Handle, Whiskey Nipper, 5 3/4 In. 132.00
English Guard, Metal Base, Screw Cap, 8 In. 22.00

Figural, Cigar,
Yellow Amber,
Isaac W. Keim, Label,
5 1/4 In.

Figural, Clown, Milk
Glass, Painted, Tooled
Lip, Pontil, Removable
Head, c.1880, 13 In.

Figural, Coachman, Tan,
Brown Mottled Glaze,
Pottery, 1849, 10 1/2 In.

Figural, Ear Of Corn,
Turquoise Blue, Footed,
Sheared, Ground Lip,
c.1900, 9 In.

Figural, Egyptian Pharaoh, On Throne, Black Milk Glass, Embossed, France, 13 In.

Figural, Grandfather Clock, Clear, Ground Lip, Screw Cap, 1885-1910, 7 7/8 In.

Figural, Hand Holding Bottle, Yellow Green, Tooled Lip, Depose, France, c.1900, 9 In.

Eye, Eye Opener, Milk Glass, Blue, Pink, Black Paint, Screw Cap, Whiskey Nipper, 5 In. .	532.00
Fish, Amber, 10 In.	22.00
Fish, Amber, Pontil, 14 In.	13.00
Fish, Blue & Gray Paint, Ground Lip, Screw Top, 8 3/4 In.	246.00
Fish, Bremer Anker, Black Paint, Cap, ABM Lip, 20th Century, 11 1/4 In.	65.00
Fish, Green, 13 x 4 In.	15.00
Fish, Magenta Glaze, Pottery, 6 1/8 In.	56.00
Fish, Yellow To Topaz, Tooled Collared Mouth, 1870-90, 2 7/8 In.	476.00
Fountain, Clear, Ruby Red Upper Half, Tooled Lip, Pontil, Depose, 11 In.	115.00
Fox, Reading Book, Ground Lip, Screw Cap, 1885-1910, 4 5/8 In.	40.00
Frog, Aqua, Red Paint, Sheared & Polished Lip, c.1890-1920, 7 In.	153.00
Fruit Basket, Multicolored Paint, Tooled Lip, c.1900-25, 7 In.	60.00
General De Brigade, Porcelain, Robj, France, 10 In.	1410.00
George Washington, Cobalt Blue, Chas. Jacquin Inc., Philadelphia, Pa., 9 1/2 In.	20.00
Girl, Dog, Just A Little Nip, Whiskey Nipper, 4 In.	55.00
Girl, Lifting Dress, Applied Tooled Lip, c.1880, 4 3/4 In.	121.00
Girl, On Basket, Ground Stopper, 1890-1920, 9 3/4 In.	155.00
Girl, Reading Book, Embossed ABC, Ground Lip, 1890-1910, 4 3/8 In.	78.00
Girl, Sitting On Basket, Clear, Frosted, Tooled Lip, Pontil, 1885-1910, 8 1/2 In.	87.00
Grandfather Clock, Clear, Frosted, Star, Pendulum, Tooled Lip, Pontil, c.1870, 12 1/2 In. .	66.00
Grandfather Clock, Clear, Ground Lip, Screw Cap, 1885-1910, 7 7/8 In. . . . .*Illus*	60.00
Grandfather Clock, Clear, Tooled Lip, 5 1/4 In.	123.00
Grandfather Clock, Labels, 1885-1910, 5 1/4 In.	85.00
Grandfather Clock, Merry Christmas & Happy New Year, A.B. Houser, Label, 5 5/8 In. . . .	197.00
Grandfather Clock, Opalescent Milk Glass, Open Pontil, 12 1/4 In.	200.00
Grant's Tomb, Milk Glass, Ground Lip, Metal Cap, c.1893, 10 In.	784.00
Grape Cluster, On Tree Stump, Deep Amber, Applied Lip, Iron Pontil, 9 1/2 In.	2240.00
Grape Cluster, Straw Yellow, Frosted, Metal Collar, Screw Cap, 6 7/8 In.	112.00
Greek Courtesan, Aspasia, Milk Glass, Green, 9 3/4 x 8 In.	260.00
Gun, Derringer, Frosted, Ground Lip, 9 1/2 In.	28.00
Gun, Gold Painted Highlights, LPW, Vienna, Austria, 9 1/2 In.	61.00
Gun, Stick 'Em Up, Amber, Whiskey Nipper, 5 In.	77.00
Ham, Amber, Metal Screw Cap, Whiskey Nipper, 6 In.	78.00
Hand, Admiral Dewey At Mouth, Yellowware, 1880-1900, 10 7/8 In.	410.00
Hand, Lend Someone A Drink Or Hand, Whiskey Nipper, 6 In.	55.00
Hand Holding Bottle, Cobalt Blue, Frosted Hand, Tooled Lip, Pontil, 9 5/8 In.	695.00
Hand Holding Bottle, Milk Glass, 1885-1910, 6 5/8 In.	224.00
Hand Holding Bottle, Turquoise, Tooled Lip, Pontil, Depose, France, 9 1/2 In.	100.00
Hand Holding Bottle, Yellow Green, Flared Lip, OP, Stopper, 1925-40, 16 1/2 In.	50.00
Hand Holding Bottle, Yellow Green, Tooled Lip, Depose, France, c.1900, 9 In. . . . . .*Illus*	175.00
Hand Holding Mirror, Frosted, Tooled Lip, Pontil, Depose, France, 1885-1910, 8 In.	120.00
Hand Holding Mirror, Tooled Lip, France, 1890-1910, 11 3/4 In.	55.00
Hand Holding Woman, A Present For You, Whiskey Nipper, 5 1/4 In.	66.00
Handbag, Blue, Brown, Stopper, Bourne Denby, England, 9 1/2 In.	198.00
Helmet, Dark Reddish Purple, Pontil, Stopper, Germany, 3 3/8 In.	98.00
Helmet, Haselhorst, Dresden, Ground Lip, Germany, 1890-1915, 3 1/2 In.	45.00

Hillbilly, Stitzel Weller, 1969, 11 1/2 x 4 In. 18.50
Hobo, Monkey Head, Bennington Glaze, 5 In. 71.00
Horse Head, Gaylord After Shave, Pottery, 2-Piece Metal Top, Cork, 5 7/8 x 3 5/8 In. . . . 40.00
Horsehoof, Gordon's Hoof Ointment, Pat. July 20, 1880, Ground Lip, Screw Cap, 5 1/2 In. 650.00
Horsehoof, Mackay's Hoof Ointment, Aquamarine, Embossed, Tooled Lip, 5 1/4 In. 800.00
Horseshoe, Whiskey Nipper, 5 1/2 In. 55.00
Hot Air Balloon, Ballon Captif 1878, Cobalt Blue, c.1878, 9 1/8 In. 7840.00
Hot Air Balloon, Ballon Captif 1878, Embossed, Tooled Lip, Pontil, France, c.1878, 9 In. 268.00
Hot Tamale, Whiskey Nipper, 6 In. 55.00
House, KLM Airline Giveaway, Whiskey Nipper, 1950s, 3 3/4 In. 55.00
House, Medium Amber, Ground Lip, Screw Cap, 1885-1910, 3 3/8 In. 275.00
House, Paneled Roof, Chimney, Tooled Lip, 4 7/8 In. 235.00
Hunter, Dog, Tooled Lip, 6 1/2 In. 33.00
Hunter, Dog, Yellow, Tooled Lip, 1880-1910, 14 In. 121.00
Independence Hall, Bank, 1876 . . . . 159.00
Indian Queen, see Bitters, Brown's Celebrated
Japanese Mikado, Primicerio & Co., Amber, 1880-1900, 6 3/4 In. 440.00
Jester & Clown, Frosted Figures, Pontil, France, 1870-90, 8 5/8 In. 44.00
Jesus, Sacre Coeur, John Tavernier, Milk Glass, c.1895, 16 1/2 In. 275.00
Joan Of Arc, John Tavernier, Detachable Head, France, c.1900, 17 In. 110.00
Joan Of Arc, John Tavernier, Milk Glass, Brown Paint, Stopper, Label, France, 14 In. . . . 364.00
Joan Of Arc, Milk Glass, Open Pontil, France, 1870-1900, 16 1/2 In. 116.00
Joan Of Arc, Opening On Base, Tooled Rim, France, 1890-1920, 10 In. 65.00
Joan Of Arc, Praying At The Stake, Painted, Tooled Lip, Pontil, 14 In. 123.00
Joan Of Arc, Praying, Frosted Figure, France, 1880-1900, 14 1/2 In. 66.00
Joan Of Arc, Praying, Frosted, Clear, Embossed, Open Pontil, France, c.1895, 14 1/2 In. . . 66.00
Knight, In Armor, Sword, Ground Lip, France, 1880-1900, 12 1/2 In. 28.00
La Cantinere, Porcelain, Robj, 12 1/2 In. 2585.00
Lady's Leg, Victorian Shoe, Frosted, Silver, Black, Red Paint, Tooled Lip, Pontil, 14 3/4 In. 80.00
Le Muscadin Ou L'Incroyable, Porcelain, Robj, 12 1/2 In. 4406.00
Legionnaire, Porcelain, Robj, 9 3/4 In. 3055.00
Lemon, Paul Mangiet Will Hand You One, Aqua, Ground Lip, c.1900, 4 1/4 In. 90.00
Liberty Bell, Proclaim Liberty, Amethyst, Embossed, Wheaton, 7 1/2 x 4 7/8 In. 12.95
Liberty Bell, Proclaim Liberty, Cobalt Blue, Ground Lip, Pewter Cap, 1876, 3 1/2 In. . . . 330.00
Liberty Bell, Proclaim Liberty, Medium Amber, Screw Cap, c.1900, 5 In. 142.00
Life Preserver, Frosted, Ground Lip, 1880-1920, 7 3/4 In. 198.00
Light Bulb, Audubon Utility Mfg. Co., Santa Ana, Calif., Screw Cap, 4 1/2 In. 175.00
Lighthouse, Frosted, Tooled Lip, Stopper, France, 1880-1915, 9 1/8 In. 240.00
Lob Cabin, Green Milk Glass, Ground Lip, Metal Neck Band, Continental, 10 In. 448.00
Lobster Holding Fish, Gold Paint, Tooled Lip, Pontil, France, 17 In. 165.00
Log Cabin, Logo, Gold Eagles, Screw Top, 9 In. 12.00
Madonna & Child, 6 In. 50.00
Mailbox, U.S. Mail, Eagle, Tooled Lip, 1890s, 5 1/2 In. 88.00
Man, Having Drink, Blue, Ivory, Whiskey Nipper, 6 In. 55.00
Man, Holding Flute, Outward Rolled Lip, Label, Extract, 5 1/2 In. 101.00
Man, Long Hair, Beard, Leaning On Stick, Embossed, Ground Lip, Screw Cap, 7 1/2 In. . 240.00
Man, Paysanne Revolutionnaire, Porcelain, Robj, 10 1/2 In. . . . . .2468.00 to 3290.00
Man, Portly, Standing, Aqua, Embossed, M. Husted, Tooled Lip, 11 3/4 In. 1430.00
Man, Portly, Wearing Top Hat, Medium Amber, 11 5/8 In. 784.00
Man, Seated, Mottled 2-Tone Brown, 1875-1900, 9 In. 308.00
Man, Sitting On Barrel, Cobalt Blue, Yellow Paint, Handle, Patd. 1894, 9 1/2 In. 145.00
Man, Smoking Long Pipe, Amber Shaded To Red Amber, c.1900, 11 3/4 In. 520.00
Man, Tasseled Hat, Robe, Grapes, Tooled Lip, Ground Pontil, France, 1870-90, 13 3/4 In. 55.00
Man, Walking, Heart On Chest, Knapsack, Lantern, Frosted, France, c.1900, 14 In. 77.00
Man, With Pipe, Van Dunck's Genever, Ware & Schmitz, Amber, 8 In. 132.00
Man In The Moon, Milk Glass, Wire Holder, 10 In. 1760.00
Man In The Moon, Yellow Amber, Amethyst Base, 12 In. 770.00
Man On High Stool, Whiskey Nipper, 7 In. 66.00
Mary Bull, Shaker, Diamond Shawl, Milk Glass, 5 1/2 In. 44.00
Mermaid, Rockingham Glaze, 7 3/4 In. 165.00
Milk Bottles In Basket, Milk Glass, Tooled Lip, 1885-1910, 3 7/8 In. 101.00
Milk Pail, Boston, Mass., Embossed, Sapphire Blue, Glass, Tin Lid, 1880-90, 4 1/2 In. . . . 1120.00
Milk Pail, Cover, Sapphire Blue, Sheared Mouth, Tin Collar, Wire Handle, 4 1/2 In. 1232.00

Milk Pail, Straw Yellow, Handle, Tin Collar, Lid, Pat., Boston, June 24, 1884, 3 7/8 In. 565.00
Miss Liberty Coin, United States Of America, Screw Cap, Ground Lip, c.1900, 4 1/2 In. . 408.00
Miss Naval Jelly, Frosted, Ground Base, Tooled Lip, 1880-1900, 11 1/2 In. 50.00
Monk, Praying, Clear, Tooled Lip, 1890-1910, 9 In. 50.00
Monk, Praying, Frosted, Tooled Lip, France, 1880-1910, 13 In. 138.00
Monkey, Amethyst Tint, Tooled Lip, 4 5/8 In. 38.00
Monkey, Sitting On Barrel, Milk Glass, Tooled Lip, Metal, Cork Stopper, 9 3/8 In. 1176.00
Moon & Jester, Mandolin, Mon Ami Pierrot, Au Clair De La Lune, France, c.1880, 10 1/4 In. 132.00
Moon Mullins, Brown Glazed Pottery, Stamped, Dickey Clay, 1923-30, 7 In. 317.00
Napoleon, Detachable Hat, Ground Lip, Open Pontil, France, 1870-90, 12 In. 44.00
Oriental Man, Aqua, Applied Lip, Pontil, 1865-75, 10 1/4 In. 1460.00
Oriental Man, Gold Paint, Tooled Lip, 1890-1910, 5 1/4 In. 112.00
Oriental Man, Holding Sword & Fan, Sheared Mouth, Depose, France, 1880-1910, 13 In. . 55.00
Oriental Man, Poland Spring Water, Yellow Amber, H. Ricker & Sons, c.1870, 11 In. 2560.00
Oriental Man, Sitting On Barrel, Cobalt Blue, Metal Head, Original Paint, c.1900, 6 In. .. 350.00
Oriental Man, Sitting, Ground Lip, 1885-1910, 5 7/8 In. 245.00
Owl, Light Amethyst, Tin Screw Top, c.1930, 9 1/2 In. 39.00
Oyster, Aqua, Ground Lip, 1890-1910, 6 In. 179.00
Pail, Boston, Mass., Embossed, Blue Green, Glass, Tin Lid, 1880-90, 4 3/8 In. 896.00
Pail, Boston, Mass., Embossed, Canary, Milk Glass, Tin Lid, 1880-90, 4 1/4 In. 896.00
Peace Pipe, Clear, Ground Top, 8 1/2 In. 59.00
Penguin, Sherry, Heisey, Pt., 8 1/2 x 4 In. 535.00
Pharaoh, Rolled Lip, Pontil, France, 1880-1910, 6 1/8 In. 157.00
Pickle, Pocket Flask, 6 In. 39.00
Pierrot, Playing Stringed Instrument, Standing Inside Half-Moon, Star Stopper, 12 In. ... 275.00
Pig, Amethyst Tint, Tooled Lip, 1870-90, 9 3/4 In. 44.00
Pig, Applied Head, Eyes, Ears, Feet, Razorback & Lip, 11 1/8 In. 157.00
Pig, Bieler's Ronny Club, Yellowware, Porcelain Stopper, 5 1/4 x 9 1/2 In. ....*Illus* 1232.00
Pig, Drink While It Lasts From This Hog, 6 3/4 In. 90.00
Pig, Good Old Bourbon In A Hog's..., Tooled, Sheared Mouth, 1870-90, 7 In. .....77.00 to 220.00
Pig, Pottery, Tan Glaze, Camark, 9 1/2 In. 44.00
Pig, Something Good In A Hog's..., He Won't Squeal, Tooled Ring Top, 1870-90, 4 In. .. 55.00
Pineapple, Golden Amber, Applied Lip, 8 3/4 In. 210.00
Pistol, Amber, Screw Cap, 7 3/4 In. ....*Illus* 55.00
Pistol, Cobalt Blue, Screw Cap, 8 In. 750.00
Pistol, Gold Highlights, LPW, Made In Austria, 9 1/2 In. 60.00
Pistol, Sapphire Blue, Metal Screw Cap, 1860-90, 7 3/4 In. 672.00
Pistol, Yellow Amber, Ground Lip, Metal Screw Cap, 1890-1910, 9 1/2 In. 55.00
Pocket Watch, Extract Magnolia, Metal Neck Band & Hanger, Cork Stopper, 3 In. 146.00
Pocket Watch, Time To Drink, Ground Lip, Screw Cap, 1885-1910, 5 1/4 In. 175.00
Policeman, Aqua Green, Sheared Mouth, Pontil, 8 3/4 In. 75.00
Policeman, Liqueur Raspail, Cobalt Blue, France, 1890-1920, 18 1/2 In. 253.00
Poodle, Black Olive Amber, Tooled Ground Lip, Removable Head, France, 12 3/4 In. ... 395.00
Poodle, Clear, Frosted, Ground Lip, Removable Head, France, 12 3/4 In. 288.00
Potato, Pocket Flask, 5 1/2 In. 29.00
Potato, Purple, Embossed SCA, Ground Lip, 5 1/2 In. 45.00
Potato, Stoneware, Bennington Glaze, 7 1/2 In. 50.00
Potbelly Stove, Clear, Tooled Lip, 1890-1910, 4 3/4 In. 224.00

Figural, Pig, Bieler's Ronny Club, Yellowware,
Porcelain Stopper, 5 1/4 x 9 1/2 In.

Figural, Pistol, Amber,
Screw Cap, 7 3/4 In.

Figural, Santa
Claus, M.G.
Husted, Embossed,
Label, Tooled Lip,
12 1/4 In.

Figural, Santa Claus,
Sack, Staff, Milk Glass,
Green, 8 In.

Figural, Scholar, Cap &
Gown, Vieux Marc De
Champagne, Robj,
Paris, 1928, 10 In.

Pouch, Drawstring, Yellow Amber, Olive, Sheared Mouth, 1885-1915, 2 3/4 In. 408.00
Pouch, Drawstring, Yellow Green, Sheared Mouth, 2 3/4 In. 101.00
Pretzel, Whiskey Nipper, 5 1/2 In. 33.00
Prussian Soldier, Aqua, Sheared Mouth, Open Pontil, 1870-90, 9 In. 22.00
Purse, Pottery, Glazed, Blue, Brown, Bourne, Denby, England, 9 1/2 In. 198.00
Rabbit, Standing, Ground Lip, 1890-1910, 7 1/2 In. 60.00
Ram, Black, Embossed, Deponirt, Ground Lip, Germany, 1890-1910, 13 3/4 In. 550.00
Rebecca At The Well, Frosted, Clear, Open Pontil, France, 1870-90, 10 In. 28.00
Rebecca At The Well, Frosted, Tooled Lip, France, 1880-1910, 13 1/2 In. . . . . .28.00 to 44.00
Revolver, Deep Turquoise, Ground Lip, Whiskey Nipper, 8 1/4 In. 420.00
Revolver, Pink Amethyst, Ground Lip, Metal Screw Cap, 8 3/8 In. 385.00
Revolver, Standard Perf Wk's, Pat'd Nov 6th 1883, Chocolate Amber, Tooled Lip, 10 In. .   123.00
Roasted Turkey, Amber, Ground Lip, Screw Cap, 1885-1910, 4 3/4 In. . . . . .72.00 to 103.00
Roasted Turkey, Aqua, Ground Lip, Screw Cap, 1885-1910, 4 3/4 In. 67.00
Rooster, J.P. Menard Fils, Gold Painted Highlights, Tooled Lip, France, c.1900, 10 In. . . .   50.00
Sad Iron, Wood Handle, Tin Cap, 5 1/4 x 8 In. 66.00
Santa Claus, Christmas, Original Paint, Tooled Lip, c.1890-1920, 7 1/2 In. 76.00
Santa Claus, Ground Lip, Aluminum Cap, 1900-25, 3 In. 75.00
Santa Claus, M.G. Husted, Embossed, Label, Tooled Lip, 12 1/4 In. . . . .*Illus*   175.00
Santa Claus, Painted Beard & Features, Tooled Lip, 7 1/2 In. 125.00
Santa Claus, Red Frosted, Ground Lip, 1973, 10 3/4 In. 77.00
Santa Claus, Sack, Screw Top, Depose, 1900-20, 12 In. 44.00
Santa Claus, Sack, Staff, Milk Glass, Green, 8 In. . . . .*Illus*   88.00
Scholar, Cap & Gown, Vieux Marc De Champagne, Robj, Paris, 1928, 10 In. . . . .*Illus*   83.00
Senorita, Holding Fan, Milk Glass, M. Quiles Benetuser Valencia, 10 3/4 In. 22.00
Senorita, Holding Jug, Milk Glass, Mexico, 1920-40, 11 1/2 In.   88.00
Serving Maid, Clear, Applied Tooled Lip, J & MG, England, 1860-90, 13 1/2 In. 66.00
Ship, Clear, Frosted, Ground Lip, 1890-1915, 6 1/2 x 9 1/4 In. 140.00
Shoe, N. Antoine & Fils, Sheared & Ground Lip, 1885-1910, 4 In. 242.00
Shoe, Protruding Toe, Black Amethyst, Pewter Screw Top, 1890-1920, 3 1/2 In. . . .100.00 to 258.00
Shore Bird, Milk Glass, Tooled Lip, Pontil, 1890-1910, 12 3/4 In. 535.00
Silver Dollar Shape, Bryan, Sewall, In Silver We Trust, Amber, 1896, 5 1/8 In. 604.00
Skeleton, Pottery, White Glaze, Removable Head, Cork, c.1885-1915, 10 1/2 In. 615.00
Skeleton, Warning Not To Drink, Whiskey Nipper, 7 In. 110.00
Soaky, C-3PO, Star Wars Galactic Shampoo, Unopened, Minnetonka, 1999, 8 1/4 In. 15.00
Soaky, He Man, Mattel, 1983, 9 1/4 In. 2.00
Soaky, Pinnochio, 10 In. 35.00
Soaky Set, Movie Monsters, Plastic, Palmolive, 11 In., 4 Piece . . . .*Illus*   728.00
Soldier, Scottish, Medium Olive Green, Tooled Lip, Pontil, 4 7/8 In. 280.00
Soldier, Standing, Tooled Lip, Pontil, 1890-1930, 9 3/4 In. 34.00
Statue Of Liberty, Milk Glass Pedestal, 17 1/2 In. 420.00
Steamer Trunk, A Merry Christmas & A Happy New Year, J. Christman, Tooled Lip, 5 In.   186.00
Stoneware, Grape Fruit, Sparkling Drink, Shield, Lion, Blue Top, .3 Liter, 7 In. . . . . .53.00 to 69.00
Suffragette, Sad Face, Ground Lip, Screw Cap, England, 1900-10, 4 3/4 In. 233.00
Teapot, Whiskey Nipper, 3 In. 132.00
Truffle, Smoky Puce, Tooled Lip, Pontil, 3 7/8 In. 56.00

Figural, Violin,
Ruby Red,
Collared
Mouth, 6 In.

Figural, Soakie
Set, Movie
Monsters, Plastic,
Palmolive, 11 In.,
4 Piece

Turtle, Horseshoe, Good Luck, Embossed, Ground Lip, Screw Cap, 1885-1910, 5 1/4 In.	120.00
Turtle, Whiskey Nipper, 4 In.	154.00
Turtle, Yellow Amber, Hair Oil, Head Stopper, 4 7/8 In.	420.00
Venus, Creme De Violet, Blue, Frosted, Plastic Cap, 10 1/4 In.	66.00
Venus, Nude, Blue, Frosted, Plastic Base, 10 1/4 In.	66.00
Victoria Duchess Of Kent, Stoneware, Flask, Brown Salt Glaze, 10 1/4 In.	286.00
Violin, Cobalt Blue, 6 On Bottom	15.00
Violin, Green, 10 In.	35.00
Violin, Ruby Red, Collared Mouth, 6 In. *Illus*	116.00
Violin, Straw Yellow, Collared Mouth, 7 3/4 In.	33.00
Violin, Violet Cobalt Blue, 9 3/4 In.	39.00
Violin, Yellow Amber, Pat Apld. For, Sheared Mouth, 1885-1910, 6 1/2 In.	240.00
Violin, Yellow Amber, Tooled Lip, 1885-1910, 18 In.	245.00
Whisk Broom, Clear, Tooled Lip, Embossed Knapp, 5 5/8 In.	90.00
Whisk Broom, Ribbed, Diamond Daisy, 6 In.	35.00
Whisk Broom, Whiskey Nipper, 7 In.	77.00
Woman, Black, Yellow Dress, Porcelain, Robj Paris, 10 In.	358.00
Woman, Country Dress, Hands On Hips, Bare Feet, Light Yellow, 1900-25, 12 1/2 In.	66.00
Woman, Holding Beer Keg, Aqua, Tooled Lip, Continental, 1870-90, 10 5/8 In.	77.00
Woman, In Champagne Glass, Whiskey Nipper, 6 In.	55.00
Woman, Nude, Arms Raised, Crown, Tooled Lip, 7 In.	22.00
Woman, Nude, Arms Raised, Frosted, Tooled Lip, 1890-1910, 13 1/4 In.	28.00
Woman, Nude, Cornucopia, Pontil, France, 1870-90, 16 1/2 In.	28.00
Woman, Nude, Holding Jug Overhead, Tooled Lip, 1880-1900, 16 In.	28.00
Woman, On Ball, Milk Glass, Multicolored Enamel, France, 11 In.	1320.00
Woman, Partially Nude, Holding Draped Cloth, Amber, Tooled Lip, 1885-1910, 9 In.	423.00
Yellow Kid, Say, Ain't I Hot Stuff, Opalescent Milk Glass, Frosted Head Stopper, 5 1/4 In.	1120.00

FIRE GRENADE

Fire grenades were popular from about 1870 to 1910. They were glass containers filled with a fire extinguisher such as carbon tetrachloride. The bottle of liquid was thrown at the base of a fire to shatter and extinguish the flames. A particularly ingenious *automatic* type was hung in a wire rack; theoretically, the heat of the fire would melt the solder of the rack and the glass grenade would drop into the fire. Because they were designed to be broken, not too many have survived for the collector. Some are found today that still have the original contents sealed by cork and wax closures. Handle these with care. Fumes from the contents are dangerous to your health.

Amber, Flat Back, Center Groove, Tooled Lip, 1880-1900, 6 1/2 In.	1760.00
C. & N-W RY, Tube, Sheared & Ground Lip, Contents, 17 3/4 In.	146.00
Carbona Fire Extinguisher, Amber, 12-Sided, Label, Tooled Lip, 11 In.	157.00
Deutsche, Loschgranate Eberhardt, Yellow Amber, 8 In. *Illus*	280.00
Harden's Hand, Blue, Segmented, Footed, 1860-1900, 4 3/4 In. *Illus*	560.00
Harden's Hand, Lavender Blue, Rough Sheared Mouth, Footed, 4 7/8 In.	520.00
Harden's Hand, Light Sapphire, Pat No. 2, Aug 8 1871, Ground Lip, 5 1/4 In.	255.00
Harden's Hand, Smoky Light Green, Pat No. 7, Aug 8 1871, Footed, 6 1/4 In.	990.00
Harden's Hand, Star, Cobalt Blue, Ground Lip, Contents, Pt., 6 1/2 In.	220.00
Harden's Hand, Star, Cobalt Blue, Vertical Ribs, Embossed, Sealed, Contents, 6 1/2 In.	92.00
Harden's Hand, Star, Electric Blue, Embossed, Ground Lip, Qt., 8 In.	300.00
Harden's Hand, Star, Extinguisher, Blue Green, Sealed	103.00

Fire Grenade,
Harden's Hand,
Blue, Segmented,
Footed, 1860-1900,
4 3/4 In.

Fire Grenade,
Deutsche,
Loschgranate
Eberhardt, Yellow
Amber, 8 In.

Fire Grenade,
Harkness Fire
Extinguisher,
Cobalt Blue, Ribs,
Ground Lip,
6 1/8 In.

Harden's Hand, Star, Fire Extinguisher, Cobalt Blue, Ribs, Embossed, Contents, 6 1/2 In.	184.00
Harden's Hand, Star, Ribs, Aqua, Contents, 6 1/2 In.	150.00
Harden's Hand, Star, Turquoise Blue, Ground Lip, Qt., 8 In.	210.00
Harden's Hand, Tubular, Star, Ground Lip, Cast Iron Hangers, Contents, 17 5/8 In.	1456.00
Harden's Hand, Turquoise Blue, Pat No. 2, Aug 8 1871, Ground Lip, Footed, 5 1/8 In.	235.00
Harden's Improved Hand, Clear, Cobalt Blue, Patd. Oct 7 1884, 4 3/4 In., 2 Piece	1760.00
Harden's Sprinkler, Star In Star, Cobalt Blue, Tooled Lip, No. 60064, 17 1/4 In.	1340.00
Harkness Fire Destroyer, Cobalt Blue, Horizontal Ribs, Ground Lip, Air Bubbles, 6 In.	728.00
Harkness Fire Destroyer, Cobalt Blue, Horizontal Ribs, Pat Sept. 19 1874, 6 1/4 In.	440.00
Harkness Fire Extinguisher, Cobalt Blue, Ribs, Ground Lip, 6 1/8 In. ....*Illus*	616.00
Harkness Fire Extinguisher, Prussian Blue, Ribs, Ground Lip, 6 1/8 In.	672.00
Hayward's Hand, Aqua, Foil Seal, Tooled Lip, Contents, 6 In.	220.00
Hayward's Hand, Bright Green, Star, Ground Lip, Contents, Qt., 7 7/8 In.	440.00
Hayward's Hand, Cobalt Blue, Ground Mouth, 6 1/4 In.	300.00
Hayward's Hand, Cobalt Blue, Pleated Panels, Tooled Lip, 6 In.	360.00
Hayward's Hand, Grass Green, Embossed, Pleated Panels, Tooled Lip, 6 In.	1100.00
Hayward's Hand, Light Aqua, Embossed, Tooled Lip, Qt., 7 1/2 In.	470.00
Hayward's Hand, Pale Aqua, Embossed, Tooled Lip, Contents, Pt., 6 In.	210.00
Hayward's Hand, Pat Aug 8 1871, Apple Green, Embossed, Tooled Lip, 6 1/4 In.	360.00
Hayward's Hand, Pat Aug 8 1871, Gold Amber, Embossed, Tooled Lip, Label, 6 In.	360.00
Hayward's Hand, Pat Aug 8 1871, Turquoise Blue, Tooled Lip, 6 1/4 In.	380.00
Hayward's Hand, Pat Aug 8 1871, Yellow Amber, Diamond Panels, Tooled Lip, 6 1/2 In.	358.00
Hayward's Hand, Pat Aug 8 1871, Yellow, Embossed, Tooled Lip, Foil Seal, 6 3/8 In.	550.00
Hayward's Hand, Purple Amethyst, 407 Broadway, New York, Contents, 6 1/4 In.	1680.00
Hazelton's High Pressure Chemical Fire-Keg, Gold Amber, Applied Lip, 1880s, 11 In.	408.00
HNS, Yellow Amber, 2 Diamond Panels, Sheared Mouth, c.1885, 7 In.	220.00
Magic Fire Extinguisher Co., Yellow Amber, Sheared Mouth, 6 1/4 In.	930.00
PSN, Yellow Amber, 2 Diamond Panels, Tooled Lip, Grooved Base, 1880-90, 7 In.	660.00
Rockford Kalamazoo Automatic & Hand, Cobalt, Tooled Lip, c.1885, 10 3/4 In. . .725.00 to	770.00
Systeme Labbe, Orange Amber, Ground Lip, France, 5 3/4 In.	246.00
Vertical Rib, Green, ABM Mouth, 5 1/2 In.	336.00
W.D. Allen, Chicago, Ill., Yellow Green, Crescent Moon, Ground Lip, 8 1/4 In.	1540.00

FITZGERALD, see Old Fitzgerald

FLASK

Flasks have been made in America since the eighteenth century. Hundreds of styles and variations were made. Free-blown, mold-blown, and decorated flasks are all popular with collectors. Prices are determined by rarity, condition, and color. In general, bright colors bring higher prices. The numbers used in the entries in the form McK G I-000 refer to the book *American Bottles and Flasks* by Helen McKearin and Kenneth M. Wilson. Each flask listed in that book is sketched and described and it is important to compare your flask with the book picture to determine value, since many similar flasks were made.

Many reproductions of flasks have been made, most in the last 25 years, but some as early as the nineteenth century. The reproduction flasks that seem to cause the most confusion for the beginner are the Lestoil flasks made in the 1960s. These bottles, sold in grocery stores, were filled with Lestoil, a liquid cleaner, and sold for about 65 cents.

Three designs were made: a Washington Eagle, a Columbia Eagle, and a ship Franklin Eagle. Four colors were used—purple, dark blue, dark green, and amber—and mixes were also produced. Over one million of the flasks were made and they now are seen at the collectible shows. The only mark on the bottles was the name Lestoil on the stopper. Other reproductions that are often found are marked *Nuline* or *Taiwan*. A picture dictionary of flask shapes can be found in the front of this book.

10 Diamond, Aqua, Pontil, Pocket, c.1820, 5 In.	616.00
10 Diamond, Aqua, Sheared Mouth, Pontil, 5 1/8 In.	504.00
10 Diamond, Golden Amber, Sheared Mouth, Pontil, c.1820, 5 1/2 In.	1792.00
10 Diamond, Golden Amber, Sheared Mouth, Pontil, c.1820, 5 In.	616.00
16 Ribs, Swirled To Left, Blue Aqua, Sheared Mouth, Pontil, 5 3/4 In.	246.00
16 Ribs, Swirled To Left, Green Aqua, Sheared Mouth, Tooled Lip, Midwest, Pontil, 6 In.	300.00
16 Ribs, Vertical, Golden Yellow, Tooled Lip, Midwest, Pontil, 5 1/2 In.	6720.00
16 Ribs, Vertical, Pink Amethyst, Tooled Lip, Midwest, Pontil, 7 3/4 In.	336.00
18 Ribs, Swirled To Right, Teardrop, Aqua, Sheared Mouth, Pontil, 1/2 Pt.	213.00
18 Ribs, Vertical, Blue, Sheared Mouth, Refired Lip, Open Pontil, 6 3/4 In.	1980.00
18 Wide Ribs, Aqua, Diamond, Sheared Mouth, Pontil, 4 7/8 In.	952.00
20 Diamond, Flattened, Amethyst, Sheared Mouth, Pontil, 5 5/8 x 4 1/4 In.	550.00
20 Melon Ribs, Olive Yellow, Applied Collar, Pontil, 6 3/4 In.	4760.00
20 Ribs, Olive Yellow, Pumpkinseed, Applied Collar, Pontil, 6 3/4 In.	4760.00
20 Ribs, Swirled To Left, Green, Flared Lip, 1/2 Pt.	300.00
20 Ribs, Vertical, Blue, Sheared Mouth, Iron Pontil, c.1850, 1/2 Pt.	200.00
20 Ribs, Vertical, Grass Green, Applied Lip, Pontil, Pocket	175.00
20 Ribs, Vertical, Swirled To Right, Shaded Amber, Sheared Mouth, Pontil, 6 1/8 In.	257.00
24 Ribs, Cobalt Blue, Tooled Lip, Midwest, Open Pontil, 1/2 Pt.	1165.00
24 Ribs, Golden Amber, Sheared Mouth, Pontil, 5 In.	504.00
24 Ribs, Swirled To Left, Amber Shaded To Yellow Amber, Rolled Lip, Pontil, c.1825, 8 In.	770.00
24 Ribs, Swirled To Left, Apple Green, Rolled Lip, Midwest, Pontil, 7 5/8 In. ......*Illus*	1430.00
24 Ribs, Swirled To Left, Aqua, Rolled Lip, Pontil, c.1830, 8 In.	336.00
24 Ribs, Swirled To Left, Beehive, Aqua, Rolled Lip, Midwest, Open Pontil, 7 1/2 In.	165.00
24 Ribs, Swirled To Left, Dark Amber, Rolled Lip, Midwest, Pontil, c.1820, 8 In. ..175.00 to 770.00
24 Ribs, Swirled To Left, Globular, Yellow Amber, Rolled Lip, Pontil, c.1820, 8 3/4 In. ..	616.00
24 Ribs, Swirled To Left, Golden Amber, Rolled Lip, Pontil, c.1830, 7 1/2 In.	616.00
24 Ribs, Swirled To Left, Golden Amber, Sheared Mouth, Pontil, c.1820, 5 1/8 In.	336.00
24 Ribs, Swirled To Right, Amber, Rolled Lip, Midwest, Pontil, c.1820, 7 1/2 In.	660.00
24 Ribs, Swirled To Right, Aqua, Rolled Lip, Midwest, Pontil, c.1820, 7 7/8 In.	245.00
24 Ribs, Swirled To Right, Beehive, Light Green Aqua, Midwest, 7 In.	132.00
24 Ribs, Swirled To Right, Beehive, Midwest, Star Base, 9 In.	77.00
24 Ribs, Swirled To Right, Blue Aqua, Rolled Lip, Midwest, Pontil, c.1825, 7 3/8 In.	495.00
24 Ribs, Swirled To Right, Cobalt Blue, Tooled Flared Lip, Pontil, 4 In.	364.00
24 Ribs, Swirled To Right, Globular, Amber, Rolled Lip, Midwest, c.1820, 7 In. .....*Illus*	660.00
24 Ribs, Swirled To Right, Globular, Yellow Amber, Rolled Lip, Midwest, 8 3/8 In.	1008.00
24 Ribs, Swirled To Right, Olive Yellow, Folded Lip, Midwest, Pontil, c.1820, 7 1/2 In. ..	1045.00
24 Ribs, Vertical, Aqua, Double Rolled Collar, Midwest, 8 In.	143.00
24 Ribs, Vertical, Globular, Aqua, Rolled Lip, Midwest, Pontil, c.1825, 7 1/8 In.	385.00
24 Ribs, Vertical, Golden Amber, Sheared Mouth, Pontil, c.1820, 4 7/8 In. ....150.00 to 440.00
24 Ribs, Vertical, Light Green, Rolled Collar, Midwest, 7 1/2 In.	198.00
24 Ribs, Vertical, Olive Yellow, Sheared Mouth, Pontil, 6 1/4 In.	420.00
24 Ribs, Vertical, Sapphire Blue, c.1830, 6 7/8 In.	1120.00
24 Ribs, Vertical, Sapphire Blue, Tooled Lip, c.1800, 7 1/2 In.	1232.00
24 Ribs, Vertical, Yellow Amber, Sheared Mouth, Midwest, Pontil, 4 1/2 In.	400.00
25 Ribs, Swirled To Right, Globular, Aqua, Applied Lip, Midwest, Pontil, c.1825, 9 In. ..	200.00
32 Ribs, Swirled To Left, Beehive, Blue Aqua, Rolled Lip, Midwest, Pontil, 8 1/2 In.	176.00
A.W. Hoffman, Strap Side, Clear, 1/2 Pt.	67.00
Amethyst, White Herringbone, Pewter Neck Ring, Germany, 7 1/2 In.	1344.00
Amethyst, White Loopings, Beveled Corner Panels, Pewter Mouth, Pontil, 7 5/8 In.	1456.00
Basket Weave, Map Of Australia, Aqua, Applied Lip, c.1876, 8 In.	92.00
Billy Winters, Portland, Ore., Log Cabin, Pumpkinseed, 1/2 Pt.	900.00
Billy Winters, Portland, Ore., Log Cabin, Pumpkinseed, Pt.	900.00
Blood Ball, Paper Label, Box, 3 In.	248.00
Byron-Scott, Honey Amber, Sheared Mouth, Open Pontil, 1/2 Pt.	408.00
C.C. Goodale, Apple Green, Tooled Lip, Pt.	230.00
C.C. Goodale, Golden Yellow Amber, Tooled Lip, 1/2 Pt.	190.00

Chestnut, 10 Diamond, Amber, Sheared Mouth, Tooled Lip, Pontil, 4 3/4 In. 1600.00
Chestnut, 10 Diamond, Aqua, Tooled Lip, Midwest, Pontil, 5 1/2 In. 1160.00
Chestnut, 16 Ribs, Swirled To Right, Pale Green, Flattened, c.1825, Pt., 7 In. 303.00
Chestnut, 16 Ribs, Vertical, Yellow Green, Flattened, c.1825, Pt., 6 1/2 In. 132.00
Chestnut, 18 Broken Ribs, Swirled To Left, Aqua, Sheared Mouth, Midwest, Pontil, 6 In. 175.00
Chestnut, 20 Ribs, Swirled Right, Cobalt Blue, 1815-1835, 3 5/8 In. . . . .*Illus* 300.00
Chestnut, 22 Ribs, Swirled Right, Aqua, Midwest, Open Pontil, 10 In. 189.00
Chestnut, 24 Ribs, Olive Yellow, Sheared Mouth, Pontil, c.1825, 5 1/4 In. 1232.00
Chestnut, 24 Ribs, Swirled To Right, Golden Amber, Tooled Lip, Midwest, Pontil, 5 In. . . . 515.00
Chestnut, 24 Ribs, Vertical, Amber, Sheared Mouth, Tooled Lip, Midwest, Pontil, 4 1/2 In. 350.00
Chestnut, 24 Ribs, Vertical, Aqua, Flattened, Pt., 6 In. 121.00
Chestnut, 24 Ribs, Vertical, Emerald Green, Sheared Mouth, Midwest, Pontil, 5 3/4 In. . . 290.00
Chestnut, 24 Ribs, Vertical, Yellow Amber, Tooled Lip, Midwest, Pontil, 5 1/4 In. .428.00 to 495.00
Chestnut, 24 Ribs, Yellow Amber, Sheared Mouth, Midwest, Pontil, 4 1/2 In. 672.00
Chestnut, 32 Ribs, Swirled To Left, Aqua, 1/2 Pt. 154.00
Chestnut, Amber, Applied Tapered Collar, Pontil, 11 In. 358.00
Chestnut, Amber, Tooled Lip, Pontil, 5 1/2 In. 242.00
Chestnut, Aqua, Applied Collar, Open Pontil, 3 1/2 In. 660.00
Chestnut, Aqua, Ring Collar, Open Pontil, 10 1/4 In. 138.00
Chestnut, Aqua, Rolled Lip, Pontil, 3 1/4 In. 297.00
Chestnut, Aqua, Tooled Lip, Pontil, 6 In. 715.00
Chestnut, Blue Aqua, Applied Lip, Pontil, 10 3/4 In. 275.00
Chestnut, Blue Gray Aqua, Applied Lip, Pontil, Bubbles, c.1800, 7 In. 275.00
Chestnut, Copper Puce, Applied Lip & Handle, Iron Pontil, 8 1/2 In. 224.00
Chestnut, Expanded Diamonds, 10 Rows, Yellow Green, Flared Neck, 5 In. 3575.00
Chestnut, Forest Green, Applied Collar, Pontil, Bubbles, c.1810, 6 5/8 In. 476.00
Chestnut, Golden Amber, Sheared Mouth, Applied & Handle, Pontil, 8 1/4 In. 1064.00
Chestnut, Green, Applied Collar, Pontil, Bubbles, c.1800, 11 1/2 In. 303.00
Chestnut, Green, Applied Collar, Pontil, c.1810, 9 In. 209.00
Chestnut, Light Amber, Applied Handle, Pontil, 8 1/4 In. 121.00
Chestnut, Light Green, New England, 7 1/4 In. 880.00
Chestnut, Light Green, Open Pontil, 7 1/4 In. 352.00
Chestnut, Moonstone, 3 Rings, Pontil, c.1830, 5 In. 1904.00
Chestnut, Olive Green, Applied Lip, Open Pontil, 8 x 4 1/2 In. 257.00
Chestnut, Olive Green, Applied Lip, Open Pontil, Bubbles, 6 7/8 In. 430.00
Chestnut, Olive Green, Applied Lip, Pontil, c.1810, 5 1/4 In. . . . . .275.00 to 303.00
Chestnut, Olive Green, Applied Ring, Pontil, Bubbles, c.1790, 6 5/8 In. 672.00
Chestnut, Olive Green, Flattened, Applied Lip, Open Pontil, Bubbles, 5 3/4 In. 350.00
Chestnut, Olive Green, Pontil, Rolled Lip, 5 1/2 In. 157.00
Chestnut, Olive Yellow, Applied Collar & Handle, Pontil, 8 1/2 In. 448.00
Chestnut, Olive Yellow, Applied Collar, 7 In. . . . . .258.00 to 280.00
Chestnut, Olive Yellow, Applied Collar, Pontil, 4 1/2 In. 896.00
Chestnut, Olive Yellow, Applied Collar, Pontil, 8 1/2 In. . . . . .280.00 to 364.00
Chestnut, Olive Yellow, Applied Lip, Pontil, c.1800, 5 3/4 In. . . . . .168.00 to 364.00

Flask, 24 Ribs, Swirled To Left,
Apple Green, Rolled Lip,
Midwest, Pontil, 7 5/8 In.

Flask, 24 Ribs, Swirled To Right,
Globular, Amber, Rolled Lip,
Midwest, c.1820, 7 In.

Flask, Chestnut, 20 Ribs,
Swirled Right, Cobalt Blue,
1815-1835, 3 5/8 In.

Chestnut, Olive Yellow, Applied Sloping Collar, Pontil, 7 In. 280.00
Chestnut, Olive Yellow, Applied Sloping Double Collar, Open Pontil, 6 In. 56.00
Chestnut, Olive Yellow, Rolled Lip, Open Pontil, 5 5/8 In. 430.00
Chestnut, Olive, Applied Lip, Pontil, c.1810, 5 3/4 In. 275.00
Chestnut, Pink Puce, Applied Lip, Handle, Iron Pontil, 8 1/2 In. 728.00
Chestnut, Puce Amber, Applied Loop Handle, Metal Neck Band, Stopper, 7 3/4 In. 95.00
Chestnut, Red Amber, Applied Lip & Handle, 8 In. 90.00
Chestnut, Red Amber, Applied Lip & Handle, Open Pontil, 6 1/2 In. 112.00
Chestnut, Teal Green, Applied Lip & Handle, Pontil, 6 3/8 In. 134.00
Chestnut, Topaz, Applied Collar, Pontil, 5 1/4 In. 336.00
Chestnut, Yellow Amber, Applied Collar, Pontil, c.1810, 9 1/2 In. 420.00
Chestnut, Yellow Amber, Applied Sloping Double Collar, Pontil, 9 In. 123.00
Chestnut, Yellow Amber, Flattened, 7 3/4 In. 258.00
Chestnut, Yellow Green, Applied Collar, Pontil, c.1810, 6 3/4 In. 258.00
Chestnut, Yellow Green, Applied Lip, Pontil, Bubbles, c.1810, 6 1/2 In. 303.00
Chestnut, Yellow, Applied Lip, Bent Neck, Pontil, c.1810, 5 1/4 In. 385.00
Chestnut, Yellow, Applied Lip, Pontil, Bubbles, 8 In. 253.00
Chestnut, Yellow, Applied Lip, Pontil, Seed Bubbles, c.1810, 6 3/4 In. 303.00
Clock Face, Diamonds, Pumpkinseed, Pt. 35.00
Cobalt Blue, White & Yellow Enameled Flowers, Words, Beveled Corners, Germany, 7 In. 1344.00
Cobalt Blue, White Loopings, Beveled Corners, Germany, 7 5/8 In. 1064.00
Coffin, Opalescent Milk Glass, Tooled Lip, c.1885, Pt. 157.00
Coffin, Ribbed Embossed, Horseshoe, 1/2 Pt. 49.00
Cut Glass, Sterling Silver Screw Cap, Round, 4 1/4 x 3 1/4 In. 169.00
Cut Glass, Sterling Silver Screw Cap, Zipper Cut, 5 1/2 x 3 x 1 In. 169.00
D.E. Dempsey, Geneva, N.Y., Strap Side, Aqua, Applied Double Collar, 1/2 Pt. 50.00
David Netter & Co., N.E. Cor. 5th St. Philada., Red Amber, Rectangular, Qt., 10 In. 59.00
Diamonds, Amethyst, Clevenger Brothers, 1940s, 5 3/8 In. ....*Illus* 250.00
Dragoon & Hound, Light Yellow Amber, Applied Collar, Qt. 1008.00
E. Lock, Wine & Spirit Merchant, Stoneware, Tan Salt Glaze, Barrel Shape, 5 In. 392.00
E. Wattis Jr, Clear, Leather, Ground Lip, Applied Pewter Collar, Cap, c.1865, Pt. 90.00
Eastern Shore House, G. Randloph Vincenti, Clear, Rectangular, Baltimore, Md., 1/2 Pt. . 39.00
Eugene Martin, Opera House Bar, Strap Side, Clear, Austin, Tex., c.1890, Pt. 896.00
Fleckenstein & Mayer, Amber, Portland, O., 1/2 Pt. 265.00
Fraternal Order Of Eagles, Embossed Eagle, Ceramic, c.1900, 5 3/4 In. 56.00
Fred Dunck, Second Street, Napa City, Pumpkinseed, 1/2 Pt. 500.00
Free-Blown, Apple Green, Globular Form, Applied Lip, Pontil, 8 1/2 In. 840.00
Free-Blown, Light Yellow, High Kick-Up, Sheared Mouth, 6 In. 115.00
George Washington Profile, Eagle, Clear, Maroon Metal Top, c.1932, 8 x 5 1/2 In. 35.00
Granite Glass Co., Olive Yellow, Sheared Mouth, c.1855, Pt. 2016.00
Henry Ahlers, The Delay, Pumpkinseed, 1/2 Pt. 770.00
Honey Amber, White Loopings, Beveled Corners, Pewter Mouth, Germany, 6 In. 1232.00
Hotel Townson, Geo. M. Price, Clear, Rectangular, Townson Md., 1/2 Pt. 59.00
J. Schaufele, The Opera, Pumpkinseed, Amethyst, 1/2 Pt. 110.00
J.J. Morrison, Liquor Dealer, SCA, Tooled, Rounded Collar, Lynchburg, Va., c.1890, Pt. .. 176.00
John Ament, Orange Amber, Baltimore, 1/2 Pt. 89.00
John Bourke Thomaston, Aqua, Conn., Pt. 250.00
Kidney, Elongated, Olive Yellow, Sheared Mouth, Pontil, Netherlands, c.1755, 7 1/4 In. ... 1008.00
Label Under Glass, Eagle, Crossed Flags, Shield, E Pluribus Unum, 5 In. 952.00
Levinson's, Full Measure, Our Name, Our Guarantee, Orange Amber, 1/2 Pt., 6 1/2 In. ... 75.00
Louisville Liquor House, Cripple Creek, Col., Coffin, 1/2 Pt. ....840.00 to 1600.00
McK G I-1, Washington & Eagle, Blue Green, Tooled Lip, Pontil, c.1835, Pt. 504.00
McK G I-2, Washington & Eagle, Green Aqua, Tooled Lip, Pontil, c.1835, Pt. .....246.00 to 475.00
McK G I-3, Washington & Eagle, Aqua, Sheared Mouth, Pontil, c.1820, Pt. 2200.00
McK G I-3, Washington & Eagle, Aqua, Sheared Mouth, Tooled Lip, Pontil, c.1835, Pt. ... 1344.00
McK G I-6, Washington & Eagle, Aqua, Sheared Mouth, Pontil, c.1830, Pt. 2576.00
McK G I-6, Washington & Eagle, Clear, J.R. Laird Sc. Pitt, Pontil, c.1830, Pt. 4480.00
McK G I-7, Washington & Eagle, Green Aqua, Tooled Lip, Pontil, c.1835, Pt. 2800.00
McK G I-7, Washington & Eagle, Green, Sheared, Flared Lip, Pontil, c.1835, Pt. 4200.00
McK G I-9, Washington & Eagle, Blue Green, Pontil, Sheared Mouth, c.1830, Pt. 2352.00
McK G I-10, Washington & Eagle, Blue Aqua, Sheared Mouth, Pontil, Pt. ....202.00 to 330.00
McK G I-10, Washington & Eagle, Green Aqua, Sheared Mouth, Pontil, Pt. 1064.00
McK G I-11, Washington & Eagle, Blue Aqua, Sheared Mouth, Open Pontil, Pt. 728.00

Flask, Diamonds, Amethyst,
Clevenger Brothers, 1940s,
5 3/8 In.

Flask, McK G I-37, Washington
& Taylor Never Surrenders,
Emerald Green, Qt.

Flask, McK G I-108,
Jenny Lind & Lyre, Aqua,
Pontil, Pt.

McK G I-14, Washington & Eagle, Adams, Jefferson, Aqua, Pontil, Pt. . . . . .308.00 to 672.00
McK G I-14, Washington & Eagle, Adams, Jefferson, Blue Green, Pontil, Pt. . . . .2016.00 to 7280.00
McK G I-14, Washington & Eagle, Adams, Jefferson, Emerald, Tooled Lip, Pontil, Pt. 5880.00
McK G I-14, Washington & Eagle, Adams, Jefferson, Green, Pontil, Pt. 6160.00
McK G I-16, Washington & Eagle, Aqua, Sheared Mouth, Pontil, Pt. . . . . .176.00 to 364.00
McK G I-17, Washington & Taylor, Aqua Tint, Sheared Mouth, Open Pontil, Pt. 280.00
McK G I-17, Washington & Taylor, Green Aqua, Sheared Mouth, Open Pontil, Pt. 784.00
McK G I-18, Washington & Monument, Aqua, Sheared Mouth, Open Pontil, Pt. . . .154.00 to 269.00
McK G I-18, Washington & Monument, Emerald Green, Sheared Mouth, Open Pontil, Pt. . 2352.00
McK G I-18, Washington & Monument, Pale Aqua Green, Tooled Lip, Pontil, Pt. 168.00
McK G I-20, Washington & Monument, Aqua, Sheared Mouth, Pontil, Pt. 157.00
McK G I-21, Washington & Monument, Aqua, Tooled Lip, Pontil, Qt. . . . . .112.00 to 157.00
McK G I-21, Washington & Monument, Green Aqua, Tooled Lip, Pontil, Qt. . . . . .157.00 to 179.00
McK G I-21, Washington & Monument, Smoky Aqua, Sheared, Tooled Lip, Pontil, Qt. . . . 448.00
McK G I-24, Washington & Taylor, Aqua, Tooled Lip, Open Pontil, Pt. . . . , . , ...179.00 to 325.00
McK G I-24, Washington & Taylor, Blue Green, Sheared Mouth, Tooled Lip, Pontil, Pt. . . 1456.00
McK G I-24, Washington & Taylor, Olive Amber, Sheared Mouth, Tooled Lip, Pontil, Pt. . 3080.00
McK G I-25, Washington, Classical Bust, Aqua, Tooled Lip, Pontil, Qt. . . . . .225.00 to 322.00
McK G I-25, Washington, Classical Bust, Blue Aqua, Tooled Lip, Pontil, Qt. 157.00
McK G I-26, Washington & Eagle, Aqua, Pontil, Qt. 275.00
McK G I-26, Washington & Eagle, Blue Aqua, Sheared Mouth, Open Pontil, Qt. 364.00
McK G I-26, Washington & Eagle, Yellow & Olive, Sheared Mouth, Pontil, Qt. 3500.00
McK G I-28, Washington & Sailing Ship, Aqua, Applied Sloping Collar, OP, Pt. . . .336.00 to 672.00
McK G I-28, Washington & Sailing Ship, Green, Yellow Striations, Double Collar, Pt. 6720.00
McK G I-28, Washington & Sailing Ship, Yellow Amber, Double Collar, Iron Pontil, Pt. . . . 4760.00
McK G I-30, Washington & Albany, Aqua, Tooled Lip, Open Pontil, 1/2 Pt. 448.00
McK G I-30, Washington & Albany, Green Aqua, Sheared Mouth, Pontil, 1/2 Pt. 336.00
McK G I-31, Washington & Jackson, Olive Green, Sheared Mouth, Open Pontil, Pt. 515.00 to 616.00
McK G I-31, Washington & Jackson, Yellow Amber, Sheared Mouth, OP, Pt. . . . . .250.00 to 448.00
McK G I-32, Washington & Jackson, Olive Amber, Sheared Mouth, Pontil, Pt. 303.00
McK G I-32, Washington & Jackson, Olive Green, Pontil, Sheared Mouth, Tooled Lip, Pt. . . 336.00
McK G I-32, Washington & Jackson, Olive Yellow Green, Open Pontil, Pt. 420.00
McK G I-32, Washington & Jackson, Yellow Amber Olive, Tooled Lip, Pontil, Pt. 520.00
McK G I-33, Washington & Jackson, Yellow Amber, Tooled Lip, Pontil, Pt. 728.00
McK G I-34, Washington & Jackson, Olive Yellow, Tooled Lip, Pontil, 1/2 Pt. 728.00
McK G I-34, Washington & Jackson, Yellow Amber, Sheared Mouth, 1/2 Pt. . . . . . .413.00 to 616.00
McK G I-35, Washington & Tree, Calabash, Aqua Blue, Applied Collar, Open Pontil, Qt. . 157.00
McK G I-36, Washington & Tree, Calabash, Aqua, Applied Double Collar, Pontil, Qt. 420.00
McK G I-37, Washington & Taylor Never Surrenders, Emerald Green, Qt. . . . .*Illus* 728.00
McK G I-37, Washington & Taylor Never Surrenders, Golden Yellow, Double Collar, Qt. . 4200.00
McK G I-37, Washington & Taylor Never Surrenders, Sapphire Blue, Qt. . . . . . .3850.00 to 6160.00
McK G I-37, Washington & Taylor Never Surrenders, Apricot, Applied Double Collar, Qt. 4807.00
McK G I-37, Washington & Taylor Never Surrenders, Aqua, Qt. 110.00

McK G 1-37, Washington & Taylor Never Surrenders, Blue Green, Qt. 336.00
McK G 1-37, Washington & Taylor Never Surrenders, Burgundy, Square Collar, Qt. 2800.00
McK G 1-37, Washington & Taylor Never Surrenders, Copper Puce, Double Collar, Qt. . . . 2800.00
McK G 1-37, Washington & Taylor Never Surrenders, Yellow, Double Collar, Qt. 5000.00
McK G 1-38, Washington & Taylor Never Surrenders, Blue Green, Sheared Mouth, Pt. . . . 364.00
McK G 1-38, Washington & Taylor Never Surrenders, Green Aqua, Pontil, Pt. 100.00
McK G 1-38, Washington & Taylor Never Surrenders, Teal, OP, Pt. . . . . .650.00 to 825.00
McK G 1-38, Washington & Taylor Never Surrenders, Emerald Green, Pontil, Pt. 1905.00
McK G 1-38, Washington & Taylor Never Surrenders, Gray Puce, Sheared Mouth, Pt. 4750.00
McK G 1-38, Washington & Taylor Never Surrenders, Olive Green, Pontil, Pt. 2240.00
McK G 1-38, Washington & Taylor Never Surrenders, Olive Yellow, Pontil, Pt. 1792.00
McK G 1-38, Washington & Taylor Never Surrenders, Pink Amethyst, Tooled Lip, Pt. 2576.00
McK G 1-39, Washington & Taylor Never Surrenders, Blue Green, OP, Qt. . . . . . . .410.00 to 784.00
McK G 1-39, Washington & Taylor Never Surrenders, Teal, Tooled Lip, Pontil, Qt. 728.00
McK G 1-39, Washington & Taylor Never Surrenders, Amethyst, Pontil, Qt. 6720.00
McK G 1-39, Washington & Taylor Never Surrenders, Emerald Green, Open Pontil, Qt. . . . 495.00
McK G 1-39, Washington & Taylor Never Surrenders, Olive Green, Qt. 413.00
McK G 1-40, Washington & Taylor, Cobalt Blue, Sheared Mouth, Pontil, Pt. 7840.00
McK G 1-40a, Washington & Taylor, Cobalt Blue, Sheared Mouth, Pontil, Pt. 5040.00
McK G 1-40a, Washington & Taylor, Olive Yellow, Sheared Mouth, Tooled Lip, Pontil, Pt. 2640.00
McK G 1-40b, Washington & Taylor, Cobalt Blue, Sheared Mouth, c.1850, Pt. . . .4480.00 to 7840.00
McK G 1-41, Washington & Taylor, Blue Aqua, Tooled Lip, c.1855, 1/2 Pt. 78.00
McK G 1-42, Washington & Taylor, Cobalt Blue, c.1850, Qt. 7840.00
McK G 1-42, Washington & Taylor, Emerald Green, Applied Double Collar, Pontil, Qt. . . . 364.00
McK G 1-42, Washington & Taylor, Green Aqua, Applied Lip, Qt. 770.00
McK G 1-42, Washington & Taylor, Green, Applied Double Collar, Pontil, Qt. 532.00
McK G 1-42, Washington & Taylor, Sapphire Blue, Tooled Lip, Pontil, Qt. . . . . .7840.00 to 8960.00
McK G 1-42, Washington & Taylor, Yellow Green, Applied Double Collar, Qt. 1456.00
McK G 1-42, Washington & Taylor, Yellow Green, Sheared Mouth, Pontil, c.1850, Qt. 358.00
McK G 1-43, Washington & Taylor, Olive Yellow, Pontil, Qt. 4200.00
McK G 1-43, Washington & Taylor, Teal Blue, Sheared Mouth, Tooled Lip, Pontil, Qt. . . . 1064.00
McK G 1-44, Washington & Taylor, Yellow Green, Tooled Lip, Pontil, Pt. 220.00
McK G 1-47, Washington, Father Of His Country, Blue Green, Pontil, Qt. . . . . .448.00 to 952.00
McK G 1-48, Washington, Father Of His Country, Teal Blue, OP, Pt. . . . . .660.00 to 715.00
McK G 1-50, Washington & Taylor, Emerald Green, Applied Sloping Collar, Pontil, Pt. . . . 650.00
McK G 1-51, Washington & Taylor, Chocolate Amber, Pontil, c.1850, Pt. 5320.00
McK G 1-51, Washington & Taylor, Cobalt Blue, Applied Lip, Pontil, c.1850, Qt. .840.00 to 1792.00
McK G 1-52, Washington & Taylor, Olive Yellow, Applied Double Collar, Pontil, Pt. 3080.00
McK G 1-53, Washington & Taylor, Green, Sheared Mouth, Pontil, 1/2 Pt. 952.00
McK G 1-53, Washington & Taylor, Teal, 1/2 Pt. 950.00
McK G 1-54, Washington & Taylor, Apple Green, Sloping Double Collar Qt. 202.00
McK G 1-54, Washington & Taylor, Apricot, Applied Lip, Qt. 448.00
McK G 1-54, Washington & Taylor, Blue Green, Sloping Collar, Pontil, Qt. 220.00
McK G 1-54, Washington & Taylor, Cobalt Blue, Applied Lip, Pontil, c.1850, Qt. 3640.00
McK G 1-54, Washington & Taylor, Emerald Green, Slooping Collar, c.1850, Qt. . .728.00 to 990.00
McK G 1-54, Washington & Taylor, Green, Applied Lip, Qt. 560.00
McK G 1-54, Washington & Taylor, Green, Applied Double Collar, Pontil, Qt. 990.00
McK G 1-54, Washington & Taylor, Olive Topaz, Applied Lip, Pontil, Qt. 1344.00
McK G 1-54, Washington & Taylor, Olive Yellow, Applied Lip, c.1850, Qt. . . . . . .1344.00 to 4480.00
McK G 1-54, Washington & Taylor, Sapphire Blue, Sloping Double Collar, OP, Qt. 2600.00
McK G 1-54, Washington & Taylor, Teal Blue, Applied Lip, Pontil, Qt. . . . . .190.00 to 269.00
McK G 1-54, Washington & Taylor, Wine Amethyst, Sheared Mouth, Pontil, Qt. 6160.00
McK G 1-54a, Washington & Taylor, Green, Sheared Mouth, Open Pontil, Pt. . . . .532.00 to 1120.00
McK G 1-55, Washington & Taylor, Amber, Open Pontil, Pt. 3640.00
McK G 1-55, Washington & Taylor, Green, Bubbles, Pt. 715.00
McK G 1-55, Washington & Taylor, Light Green, Open Pontil, Pt. . . . . .650.00 to 1100.00
McK G 1-55, Washington & Taylor, Orange Amber, Pontil, c.1850, Pt. . . . . .840.00 to 1210.00
McK G 1-55, Washington & Taylor, Yellow Amber, c.1850, Pt. 3360.00
McK G 1-56, Washington & Taylor, Blue Green, Sheared Mouth, Pontil, 1/2 Pt. 1680.00
McK G 1-57, Washington & Sheaf, Aqua, Pontil, Qt. 22.00
McK G 1-58, Washington & Sheaf, Blue Aqua, Applied Sloping Collar, Pontil, Pt. 101.00
McK G 1-59, Washington & Sheaf, Apricot, Double Collar, 1/2 Pt. 1344.00
McK G 1-59, Washington & Sheaf, Aqua, Applied Double Collar, 1/2 Pt. 88.00

McK G 1-59, Washington & Sheaf, Aqua, Pontil, 1/2 Pt. 72.00
McK G 1-60, Washington & Lockport, Blue Aqua, Applied Double Collar, Pontil, Qt. 1456.00
McK G 1-61, Washington & Lockport, Aqua, Sheared Mouth, Pontil, Qt. 392.00
McK G 1-61, Washington & Lockport, Blue Green, Pontil, Qt. 2860.00
McK G 1-61, Washington & Lockport, Yellow Green, Qt. 1760.00
McK G 1-65, Jackson & Eagle, Green, Sheared Mouth, Tooled Lip, Pontil, Pt. 1568.00
McK G 1-68, Jackson & Flowers, Aqua, Sheared Mouth, Pontil, Pt. 3000.00
McK G 1-71, Taylor & Ringgold, Aqua, Tooled Lip, Pontil, c.1830, Pt. . . . . .174.00 to 190.00
McK G 1-72, Taylor & Ringgold, Ice Blue, Sheared Mouth, Open Pontil, Pt. 168.00
McK G 1-73, Taylor & Monument, Amethyst, Sheared Mouth, Pontil, Pt. 246.00
McK G 1-73, Taylor & Monument, Aqua, Tooled Lip, Pontil, Pt. . . . . .220.00 to 336.00
McK G 1-73, Taylor & Monument, Green Aqua, Sheared Mouth, Open Pontil, Pt. 146.00
McK G 1-73, Taylor & Monument, Olive Yellow, Sheared Mouth, Tooled Lip, Pontil, Pt. . . 4480.00
McK G 1-74, Taylor & Corn, Aqua, Sheared Mouth, Tooled Lip, Pontil, Pt. 504.00
McK G 1-75, Taylor & Corn, Aqua, Sheared Mouth, Tooled Lip, Pontil, Pt. 672.00
McK G 1-77, Taylor & Masterson, Aqua, Sheared Mouth, Tooled Lip, Pontil, Qt. .1792.00 to 2464.00
McK G 1-80, Lafayette & Clinton, Olive Yellow, Tooled Lip, Pontil, Pt. . . . . .1064.00 to 1456.00
McK G 1-80, Lafayette & Clinton, Yellow Amber, Tooled Lip, Pontil, Pt. 1064.00
McK G 1-81, Lafayette & Clinton, Olive Yellow, Tooled Lip, Pontil, 1/2 Pt. 1232.00
McK G 1-84, Lafayette & Masonic, Olive Yellow, Sheared Mouth, Pontil, 1/2 Pt. 4480.00 to 8400.00
McK G 1-85, Lafayette & Liberty, Olive Yellow, Sheared Mouth, Pontil, Pt. 952.00
McK G 1-85, Lafayette & Liberty, Yellow Amber, Pontil, c.1830, Pt. . . . . .840.00 to 896.00
McK G 1-86, Lafayette & Liberty, Olive Amber, Pontil, c.1830, 1/2 Pt. 672.00
McK G 1-86, Lafayette & Liberty, Olive Green, Pontil, c.1830, 1/2 Pt. 1568.00
McK G 1-86, Lafayette & Liberty, Yellow Amber, Pontil, 1/2 Pt. . . . . .660.00 to 840.00
McK G 1-86, Lafayette & Liberty, Yellow Amber, Sheared Mouth, Pontil, 1/2 Pt. .1650.00 to 2688.00
McK G 1-88, Lafayette & Masonic, Olive Green, Pontil, c.1830, Pt. 1456.00
McK G 1-89, Lafayette & Masonic, Olive Green, 1/2 Pt. 1950.00
McK G 1-90, Lafayette & Eagle, Aqua, Sheared Mouth, Pontil, Pt. . . . . .179.00 to 504.00
McK G 1-91, Lafayette & Eagle, Aqua, Tooled Lip, Pontil, c.1825, Pt. 235.00
McK G 1-93, Lafayette & Eagle, Blue Green, Tooled Lip, Pontil, Pt. . . . . .3584.00 to 4480.00
McK G 1-94, Franklin & Dyott, Aqua, Sheared Mouth, Pontil, Pt. . . . . .202.00 to 476.00
McK G 1-94, Franklin & Dyott, Green Aqua, Tooled Lip, Pontil, Pt. . . . . .224.00 to 300.00
McK G 1-95, Franklin & Dyott, Aqua, Pontil, Pt. 518.00
McK G 1-96, Franklin & Dyott, Aqua, Tooled Lip, Pontil, c.1830, Qt. 336.00
McK G 1-97, Franklin & Franklin, Aqua, Tooled Lip, Pontil, Qt. . . . . .179.00 to 280.00
McK G 1-98, Franklin & Franklin, Blue Aqua, Pontil, Sheared Mouth, Tooled Lip, Pt. 6440.00
McK G 1-99, Jenny Lind & Glasshouse, Calabash, Blue Green, Qt. . . . . .3360.00 to 3640.00
McK G 1-99, Jenny Lind & Glasshouse, Calabash, Olive Yellow, Pontil, Qt. . . . .2015.00 to 2520.00
McK G 1-99, Jenny Lind & Glasshouse, Calabash, Aqua, Collar, Pontil, Qt. . . . . . . .100.00 to 123.00
McK G 1-99, Jenny Lind & Glasshouse, Calabash, Blue Aqua, Tooled Lip, Pontil, Qt. 1120.00
McK G 1-100, Jenny Lind & Kossuth, Calabash, Aqua, Double Collar, Open Pontil, Qt. . .   112.00
McK G 1-101, Jenny Lind & Glasshouse, Calabash, Aqua, Double Collar, Pontil, Qt. 168.00
McK G 1-102, Jenny Lind & Glasshouse, Calabash, Aqua, Double Collar, Pontil, Qt. 146.00
McK G 1-103, Jenny Lind & Glasshouse, Calabash, Aqua, Collar, OP, Qt. . . . . .67.00 to 112.00
McK G 1-104, Jenny Lind & Glasshouse, Calabash, Blue Aqua, Double Collar, IP, Qt. 146.00
McK G 1-104, Jenny Lind & Glasshouse, Calabash, Blue, Double Collar, IP, Qt. 896.00
McK G 1-104, Jenny Lind & Glasshouse, Calabash, Ice Blue, Applied Lip, IP, Qt. . .245.00 to 439.00
McK G 1-104, Jenny Lind & Glasshouse, Calabash, Aqua, Applied Lip, Pontil, Qt. 146.00
McK G 1-105, Jenny Lind & Glasshouse, Calabash, Blue Aqua, Ring Collar, IP, Qt. 1008.00
McK G 1-107, Jenny Lind, Calabash, Aqua, Qt. 22.00
McK G 1-108, Jenny Lind & Lyre, Aqua, Pontil, Pt. . . . .*Illus*   935.00
McK G 1-108, Jenny Lind & Lyre, Green Aqua, Sheared Mouth, Pontil, Pt. . . . . . . .715.00 to 840.00
McK G 1-110, Jenny Lind & Lyre, Blue Aqua, Pontil, Sheared Mouth, c.1850, Qt. 784.00
McK G 1-111, Kossuth & Frigate, Aqua, Tooled Lip, Open Pontil, Pt. . . . . .448.00 to 672.00
McK G 1-112, Kossuth & Frigate, Calabash, Blue Aqua, Sloping Collar, IP, Qt. . . . .308.00 to 450.00
McK G 1-112, Kossuth & Frigate, Calabash, Green Aqua, Embossing, Open Pontil, Qt. . . .   385.00
McK G 1-112a, Kossuth & Frigate, Calabash, Aqua, Double Collar, Pontil, Qt. . .840.00 to 1680.00
McK G 1-113, Kossuth & Tree, Calabash, Apple Green, Sloping Collar, Pontil, Qt. .190.00 to 280.00
McK G 1-113, Kossuth & Tree, Calabash, Aqua, Open Pontil, Qt. 101.00
McK G 1-113, Kossuth & Tree, Calabash, Green Aqua, Sloping Collar, IP, Qt. 120.00
McK G 1-113, Kossuth & Tree, Calabash, Olive Yellow, Double Collar, Pontil, Qt. .550.00 to 840.00
McK G 1-113, Kossuth & Tree, Calabash, Yellow, Sloping Collar, c.1850, Qt. 896.00

McK G I-114, Byron & Scott, Olive Green, Tooled Lip, OP, 1/2 Pt. . . . . .408.00 to 500.00
McK G I-114, Byron & Scott, Olive Yellow, Amber Tone, Tooled Lip, Open Pontil, 1/2 Pt.   364.00
McK G I-114, Byron & Scott, Yellow Amber, Sheared Mouth, Pontil, 1/2 Pt. . . . . .224.00 to 358.00
McK G I-117, Columbia & Eagle, Aqua, Sheared Mouth, Open Pontil, Pt. . . . . . . .825.00 to 1280.00
McK G I-121, Columbia & Eagle, Aqua, Tooled Lip, Pontil, Pt. . . . . .202.00 to 448.00
McK G I-121, Columbia & Eagle, Blue Aqua, Tooled Lip, Pontil, Pt. . . . . .504.00 to 532.00
McK G I-121, Columbia & Eagle, Green Aqua, Sheared Mouth, Pontil, Pt.   413.00
McK G I-121, Columbia & Eagle, Olive Green, Sheared Mouth, Pontil, Pt. 460.00
McK G I-125, McKinley & Bee, Yellow To Gold Amber, Coin Shape, 1/2 Pt. 4760.00
McK G I-126, Bryan & Eagle, Amber, Coin Shape, 1/2 Pt. 1792.00
McK G II-2, Double Eagle, Aqua, Open Pontil, Pt. . . . . .127.00 to 364.00
McK G II-2, Double Eagle, Green Aqua, Open Pontil, Pt. 235.00
McK G II-7, Eagle & Sunburst, Blue Green, Sheared Mouth, Pontil, c.1830, Pt. 2128.00
McK G II-10, Eagle & Agriculture, Apple Green, Sheared Mouth, Pontil, Pt. 1905.00
McK G II-11, Eagle & Cornucopia, Aqua, Sheared Mouth, Pontil, 1/2 Pt. . . . . . .269.00 to 504.00
McK G II-12, Eagle & W.C. & Cornucopia, Aqua, Sheared Mouth, Pontil, 1/2 Pt. . .336.00 to 672.00
McK G II-18, Eagle & Cornucopia, Gold Amber, Sheared Mouth, Pontil, 1/2 Pt. .1008.00 to 2016.00
McK G II-19, Eagle & Morning Glory, Aqua, Applied Double Collar, Pt. . . . . .560.00 to 728.00
McK G II-19, Eagle & Morning Glory, Blue Aqua, Open Pontil, Pt. 336.00
McK G II-19, Eagle & Morning Glory, Mottled Brown, Tan Stoneware, Pt. 476.00
McK G II-19, Eagle & Morning Glory, Yellow Green, Applied Lip, Pt. 269.00
McK G II-20, Double Eagle, Blue Aqua, Tooled Lip, Pontil, Pt. 990.00
McK G II-21, Eagle & Prospector, Aqua, Applied Lip, c.1870, Pt. 112.00
McK G II-22, Eagle & Lyre, Aqua, Sheared Mouth, Tooled Lip, Open Pontil, Pt. 1344.00
McK G II-24, Double Eagle, Aqua, Sheared Mouth, Tooled Lip, Pontil, Pt. . . . . . . .112.00 to 269.00
McK G II-24, Double Eagle, Blue Aqua, Sheared Mouth, Tooled Lip, OP, Pt. . . . . .165.00 to 360.00
McK G II-24, Double Eagle, Green Aqua, Pontil, Pt. 335.00
McK G II-24, Double Eagle, Opalescent Moonstone, Tooled Lip, Pontil, c.1835, Pt. 2128.00
McK G II-24, Double Eagle, Orange Amber, Tooled Lip, Pontil, c.1840, Pt. 5320.00
McK G II-24, Double Eagle, Yellow Green, Tooled Lip, Pontil, c.1840, Pt. . . . . .1904.00 to 2240.00
McK G II-25, Double Eagle, Aqua, Sheared Mouth, Tooled Lip, Pontil, c.1835, Pt. 224.00
McK G II-26, Double Eagle, Aqua, Sheared Mouth, Iron Pontil, Qt. . . . . .146.00 to 265.00
McK G II-26, Double Eagle, Blue Green, Sheared Mouth, Pontil, Qt. 840.00
McK G II-26, Double Eagle, Teal Blue, Sheared Mouth, Tooled Lip, Pontil, c.1835, Qt. 246.00
McK G II-26, Double Eagle, Yellow Green, Sheared Mouth, Pontil, Qt. . . . . .532.00 to 1792.00
McK G II-30, Double Eagle, Aqua, Sheared Mouth, Pontil, 1/2 Pt. 235.00
McK G II-31, Double Eagle, Blue, Sheared Mouth, Pontil, Qt. 190.00
McK G II-31, Double Eagle, Green Aqua, Sheared Mouth, Pontil, Qt. . . . . .179.00 to 275.00
McK G II-32, Double Eagle, Aqua, Sheared Mouth, Tooled Lip, OP, Pt. . . . .*Illus* 770.00
McK G II-33, Eagle & Louisville, Vertical Ribs, Aqua, Pontil, c.1860, 1/2 Pt. 202.00
McK G II-33, Eagle & Louisville, Vertical Ribs, Tobacco Amber, Applied Lip, 1/2 Pt. 1870.00
McK G II-35, Eagle & Louisville, Vertical Ribs, Aqua, Applied Lip, Qt. 157.00
McK G II-35, Eagle & Louisville, Vertical Ribs, Blue Aqua, c.1860, Qt. 179.00
McK G II-36, Eagle & Louisville, Vertical Ribs, Aqua, Pt. 77.00
McK G II-36, Eagle & Louisville, Vertical Ribs, Blue, Applied Lip, Pt. . . . . .140.00 to 176.00
McK G II-37, Eagle & Ravenna, Amber, Applied Lip, Iron Pontil, c.1860, Pt. 784.00
McK G II-37, Eagle & Ravenna, Blue Aqua, Ring Collar, Pt. 157.00
McK G II-37, Eagle & Ravenna, Emerald Green, Sheared Mouth, Tooled Lip, Pontil, Pt. . . . 5600.00
McK G II-37, Eagle & Ravenna, Yellow Amber, Applied Lip, Pt. 1792.00
McK G II-39, Eagle & Shield, Aqua, Applied Lip, Pt. . . . . .90.00 to 280.00
McK G II-39, Eagle & Shield, Puce, Sheared Mouth, Pt. 8960.00
McK G II-40, Double Eagle, Blue Aqua, Pt. 143.00
McK G II-40, Double Eagle, Emerald Green, Sheared Mouth, Pontil, Pt. 2464.00
McK G II-41, Eagle & Tree, Aqua, Open Pontil, Pt. 246.00
McK G II-42, Eagle & Sailing Ship, Aqua, Sheared Mouth, Open Pontil, Pt. 336.00
McK G II-43, Eagle & Cornucopia, Aqua, Tooled Lip, Pontil, 1/2 Pt. . . . . .157.00 to 364.00
McK G II-44, Eagle & Cornucopia, Sheared Mouth, Pontil, 1/2 Pt. 253.00
McK G II-45, Eagle & Cornucopia, Aqua, Tooled Lip, Pontil, 1/2 Pt. . . . . .275.00 to 425.00
McK G II-46, Eagle & Cornucopia, Aqua, Sheared Mouth, Open Pontil, 1/2 Pt. . . . . .143.00 to 336.00
McK G I-47, Eagle & Tree, Blue Aqua, 1825-1835, Qt. 840.00
McK G II-48, Eagle & Flag, Coffin & Hay, Aqua, Sheared Mouth, Pontil, Qt. 330.00
McK G II-48, Eagle & Flag, Coffin & Hay, Blue Aqua, Sheared Mouth, Pontil, Qt. 67.00
McK G II-48, Eagle & Flag, Coffin & Hay, Light Green, Open Pontil, Qt. 672.00

McK G II-49, Eagle & Stag, Coffin & Hay, Aqua, Tooled Lip, Pontil, c.1830, Pt. 560.00
McK G II-50, Eagle & Stag, Coffin & Hay, Aqua, Tooled Lip, Pontil, 1/2 Pt. . . . . . .308.00 to 364.00
McK G II-51, Eagle, Coffin & Hay, Aqua, Tooled Lip, Open Pontil, Pt. 2576.00
McK G II-52, Eagle & Flag, Aqua, Open Pontil, Pt. . . . . .190.00 to 225.00
McK G II-52, Eagle & Flag, Aqua, Tooled Lip, Pontil, Pt. . . . . .134.00 to 185.00
McK G II-53, Eagle & Flag, Aqua, Sheared Mouth, Pontil, Pt. 138.00
McK G II-54, Eagle & Flag, Aqua, Tooled Lip, Pontil, Pt. . . . . .190.00 to 275.00
McK G II-54, Eagle & Flag, Blue Aqua, Tooled Lip, Open Pontil, Pt. . . . . .179.00 to 213.00
McK G II-54, Eagle & Flag, Yellow Tobacco Amber, Sheared Mouth, Pontil, Pt. 7500.00
McK G II-55, Eagle & Grapes, Aqua, Tooled Lip, Pontil, Qt. . . . . .157.00 to 202.00
McK G II-55, Eagle & Grapes, Green Aqua, Tooled Lip, Pontil, Qt. 168.00
McK G II-56, Eagle & Grapes, Aqua, Open Pontil, 1/2 Pt. 392.00
McK G II-56, Eagle & Grapes, Gold Amber, Pontil, 1/2 Pt. 231.00
McK G II-60, Eagle & Oak Tree, Amber, Tooled Lip, Pontil, c.1830, 1/2 Pt. 3080.00
McK G II-60, Eagle & Oak Tree, Aqua, Tooled Lip, Pontil, 1/2 Pt. . . . . .448.00 to 612.00
McK G II-60, Eagle & Oak Tree, Blue Aqua, Sheared Mouth, Open Pontil, c.1830, 1/2 Pt. 1456.00
McK G II-61, Eagle & Willington, Amber, Applied Double Collar, Qt. 896.00
McK G II-61, Eagle & Willington, Gold Amber, Applied Double Collar, Qt. . . . . .448.00 to 1150.00
McK G II-61, Eagle & Willington, Olive Amber, Applied Collar, Qt. 358.00
McK G II-61, Eagle & Willington, Red Amber, Applied Double Collar, Qt. . . . . .1430.00 to 2128.00
McK G II-62, Eagle & Willington, Forest Green, Applied Sloping Collar, Pt. 476.00
McK G II-62, Eagle & Willington, Olive Green, Double Collar, c.1865, Pt. . . . . . .392.00 to 784.00
McK G II-62, Eagle & Willington, Olive Green, Sheared Mouth, c.1870, Pt. 336.00
McK G II-62, Eagle & Willington, Olive Yellow, Sheared Mouth, Pt. . . . . .420.00 to 440.00
McK G II-62, Eagle & Willington, Yellow Amber, Sheared Mouth, Pontil, Pt. 132.00
McK G II-62, Eagle & Willington, Yellow Green, Sheared Mouth, c.1870, Pt. . . . . .242.00 to 308.00
McK G II-63, Eagle & Willington, Emerald Green, Sloping Collar, Pt. 392.00
McK G II-63, Eagle & Willington, Forest Green, Applied Double Collar, 1/2 Pt. . . .504.00 to 616.00
McK G II-63, Eagle & Willington, Moss Green, Double Collar, c.1865, 1/2 Pt. 616.00
McK G II-63, Eagle & Willington, Olive Green, Applied Double Collar, 1/2 Pt. 308.00
McK G II-63, Eagle & Willington, Olive Green, 1/2 Pt. . . . . .165.00 to 330.00
McK G II-63, Eagle & Willington, Olive Yellow, Double Collar, 1/2 Pt. . . . . .215.00 to 560.00
McK G II-63a, Eagle & Willington, Olive Amber, Double Collar, 1/2 Pt. 728.00
McK G II-63a, Eagle & Willington, Yellow Amber, Double Collar, c.1865, 1/2 Pt. 280.00
McK G II-64, Eagle & Willington, Blue Green, Applied Collar, Pt. . . . . .1540.00 to 2400.00
McK G II-64, Eagle & Willington, Emerald Green, Applied Lip, Pt. 3080.00
McK G II-64, Eagle & Willington, Forest Green, Sheared Mouth, Tooled Lip, Pt. . .728.00 to 990.00
McK G II-64, Eagle & Willington, Olive Amber, Double Collar, c.1865, Pt. 364.00
McK G II-64, Eagle & Willington, Olive Green, Sheared Mouth, Open Pontil, Pt. . .476.00 to 560.00
McK G II-64, Eagle & Willington, Yellow Amber, Applied Lip, c.1865, Pt. 364.00
McK G II-65, Eagle & Westford, Amber, 1/2 Pt. . . . . .143.00 to 365.00
McK G II-65, Eagle & Westford, Olive Amber, Applied Double Collar, 1/2 Pt. . . . .101.00 to 275.00
McK G II-65, Eagle & Westford, Olive Green, Applied Lip, c.1870, 1/2 Pt. 280.00

Flask, McK G II-32, Double Eagle, Aqua, Sheared Mouth, Tooled Lip, OP, Pt.

Flask, McK G II-73, Eagle & Cornucopia, Olive Green, Sheared Mouth, Pontil, Pt.

Flask, McK G III-17, Cornucopia & Urn, Emerald Green, Tooled Lip, Pontil, Pt.

McK G II-65, Eagle & Westford, Olive Yellow, Double Collar, 1/2 Pt. 246.00
McK G II-66, Eagle & Anchor, Aqua, Applied Double Collar, Qt. 2000.00
McK G II-67, Eagle & Anchor, Aqua, Double Collar, 1/2 Pt. ....400.00 to 672.00
McK G II-67, Eagle & Anchor, Olive Yellow, Double Collar, 1/2 Pt. 2016.00
McK G II-67, Eagle & Anchor, Orange Amber, Applied Double Collar, 1/2 Pt. 504.00
McK G II-67, Eagle & Anchor, Yellow Green, Applied Double Collar, 1/2 Pt. 1232.00
McK G II-68, Eagle & Anchor, Apricot, Applied Double Collar, c.1863, Pt. 2016.00
McK G II-68, Eagle & Anchor, Olive Yellow, Applied Double Collar, Iron Pontil, Pt. 5600.00
McK G II-70, Double Eagle, Amber, Sheared Mouth, Pontil, Pt 288.00
McK G II-70, Double Eagle, Amber, Sheared Mouth, Pontil, Pt 300.00
McK G II-70, Double Eagle, Olive Yellow, Tooled Lip, Pontil, c.1840, Pt. 448.00
McK G II-70, Double Eagle, Tobacco Amber, Sheared Mouth, Pontil, Pt. 358.00
McK G II-70, Double Eagle, Yellow Amber, Tooled Lip, Pontil, Pt. 392.00
McK G II-71, Double Eagle, Olive Green, Tooled Lip, Pontil, 1/2 Pt. 672.00
McK G II-71, Double Eagle, Olive Yellow, Sheared Mouth, Pontil, 1/2 Pt. ....258.00 to 303.00
McK G II-72, Eagle & Cornucopia, Amber, Sheared Mouth, Pontil, Pt. ....178.00 to 230.00
McK G II-72, Eagle & Cornucopia, Aqua, Pt. 400.00
McK G II-72, Eagle & Cornucopia, Olive Amber, Sheared Mouth, Pontil, Pt. ......77.00 to 210.00
McK G II-72, Eagle & Cornucopia, Olive Green, Pontil, Pt. 28.00
McK G II-72, Eagle & Cornucopia, Olive Yellow, Sheared Mouth, Pontil, Pt. .....308.00 to 364.00
McK G II-72, Eagle & Cornucopia, Yellow Amber, Tooled Lip, Pontil, Pt. 232.00
McK G II-72a, Eagle & Cornucopia, Olive Amber, Tooled Lip, Pontil, Pt. 175.00
McK G II-73, Eagle & Cornucopia, Amber, Sheared Mouth, Pontil, Pt. ....231.00 to 330.00
McK G II-73, Eagle & Cornucopia, Green, Sheared Mouth, Pontil, Pt. 345.00
McK G II-73, Eagle & Cornucopia, Olive Amber, Sheared Mouth, Pontil, Pt. 295.00
McK G II-73, Eagle & Cornucopia, Olive Green, Sheared Mouth, Pontil, Pt. ....*Illus* 550.00
McK G II-73, Eagle & Cornucopia, Olive Yellow, Sheared Mouth, Pontil, c.1840, Pt. 213.00
McK G II-73, Eagle & Cornucopia, Orange Amber, Sheared Mouth, Pontil, Pt. ....201.00 to 288.00
McK G II-74, Eagle & Cornucopia, Blue Green, Bubbles, Sheared Mouth, Pontil, Pt. 364.00
McK G II-75, Eagle & Cornucopia, Olive Amber, Sheared Mouth, Pontil, Pt. 6720.00
McK G II-76, Concentric Ring Eagle, Yellow Green, Tooled Lip, Pontil, Qt. 7700.00
McK G II-78, Double Eagle, Olive Amber, Sheared Mouth, Open Pontil, Qt. ......468.00 to 504.00
McK G II-78, Double Eagle, Olive Yellow, Tooled Lip, Pontil, c.1865, Qt. 420.00
McK G II-79, Double Eagle, Olive Amber, Sheared Mouth, Pontil, c.1850, Qt. 420.00
McK G II-80, Double Eagle, Yellow Amber, Pontil, Qt. 1680.00
McK G II-81, Double Eagle, Amber, Sheared Mouth, Pontil, Pt. 242.00
McK G II-81, Double Eagle, Olive Amber, Tooled Lip, Pontil, Pt. 672.00
McK G II-81, Double Eagle, Yellow Amber, Open Pontil, Pt. 616.00
McK G II-82, Double Eagle, Olive Yellow, Sheared Mouth, Pontil, Pt. 420.00
McK G II-82, Double Eagle, Tobacco Amber, Tooled Lip, Pontil, Pt 190.00
McK G II-82, Double Eagle, Yellow Amber, Tooled Lip, Pontil, Pt. ....187.00 to 280.00
McK G II-83, Double Eagle, Olive Yellow, Amber Tint, Sheared Mouth, c.1855, Pt. 112.00
McK G II-84, Double Eagle, Olive Yellow, Sheared Mouth, Pontil, Pt. 213.00
McK G II-84, Double Eagle, Yellow Amber, Open Pontil, Pt. 146.00
McK G II-85, Double Eagle, Olive Green, Pt. 348.00
McK G II-85, Double Eagle, Olive Yellow, Sheared Mouth, Pontil, Pt. 145.00
McK G II-86, Double Eagle, Amber, Sheared Mouth, Pontil 1/2 Pt. 230.00
McK G II-86, Double Eagle, Olive Amber, Sheared Mouth, Pontil, 1/2 Pt. 186.00
McK G II-86, Double Eagle, Olive Yellow, Tooled Lip, Pontil, 1/2 Pt. 175.00
McK G II-86, Double Eagle, Yellow Amber, Open Pontil, 1/2 Pt. 179.00
McK G II-86a, Double Eagle, Olive Amber, Tooled Lip, Pontil, 1/2 Pt. 190.00
McK G II-87, Double Eagle, Olive Amber, Tooled Lip, 1/2 Pt. 121.00
McK G II-87, Double Eagle, Yellow Amber, Rolled Lip, Pontil, 1/2 Pt. 202.00
McK G II-88, Double Eagle, Olive Amber, Tooled Lip, 1/2 Pt. 165.00
McK G II-88, Double Eagle, Olive Green, Pontil, 1/2 Pt. 138.00
McK G II-88, Double Eagle, Yellow Amber, Open Pontil, 1/2 Pt. 213.00
McK G II-89, Double Eagle, Amber, Iron Pontil, Pt. 308.00
McK G II-89, Double Eagle, Golden Amber, Applied Lip, Iron Pontil, Pt. 358.00
McK G II-91, Double Eagle, Golden Amber, Applied Lip, Qt. 440.00
McK G II-92, Double Eagle, Ice Blue, Applied Lip, Pt. 121.00
McK G II-93, Double Eagle, Olive Green, Applied Lip, Iron Pontil, c.1860, Pt. 840.00
McK G II-98a, Double Eagle, Aqua, Applied Lip, c.1865, Pt. 258.00
McK G II-101, Double Eagle, Olive Green, Applied Lip, Qt. 660.00

McK G II-102, Double Eagle, Aqua, Qt. 44.00
McK G II-102, Double Eagle, Blue, Applied Lip, c.1865, Qt. 2576.00
McK G II-103, Double Eagle, Olive Green, Applied Lip, Qt. 715.00
McK G II-104, Double Eagle, Emerald Green, Qt. 468.00
McK G II-104, Double Eagle, Olive Green, Applied Lip, Qt. 115.00
McK G II-105, Double Eagle, Olive Yellow, Applied Lip, Pt. 476.00
McK G II-106, Double Eagle, Emerald Green, Applied Lip, Pt. ....672.00 to 1905.00
McK G II-106, Double Eagle, Olive Amber, Applied Lip, c.1870, Pt. 476.00
McK G II-106, Double Eagle, Olive Yellow, Applied Lip, Pt. 448.00
McK G II-106, Double Eagle, Yellow Green, Applied Lip, Pt. ....520.00 to 728.00
McK G II-107, Double Eagle, Aqua, Applied Lip, Pt. 45.00
McK G II-108, Double Eagle, Olive Green, Applied Lip, Pt. ....100.00 to 440.00
McK G II-108, Double Eagle, Sapphire Blue, Applied Lip, c.1862, Pt. 4200.00
McK G II-109, Double Eagle, Olive Yellow, Applied Double Collar, 1/2 Pt. 935.00
McK G II-118, Double Eagle, Apple Green, Applied Lip, Pt. 935.00
McK G II-118, Double Eagle, Cobalt Blue, Applied Lip, Pt. ....2640.00 to 3640.00
McK G II-118, Double Eagle, Sapphire Blue, Applied Lip, c.1865, Pt. 3640.00
McK G II-120, Double Eagle, Aqua, Pt. 55.00
McK G II-129, Double Eagle, Blue Aqua, Applied Lip, Pt. 1008.00
McK G II-134, Eagle, Green Aqua, Applied Lip, Pt. 5040.00
McK G II-140a, Eagle & Banner, Ice Blue, Pt. 1540.00
McK G II-141, Eagle & Indian Shooting Bird, Aqua, c.1870, Qt. 235.00
McK G II-142, Eagle & Indian Shooting Bird, Blue Aqua, Qt. ....143.00 to 190.00
McK G II-142, Eagle & Indian Shooting Bird, Ice Blue, Applied Lip, c.1862, Qt. 202.00
McK G II-142, Eagle & Indian Shooting Bird, Olive Yellow, Applied Lip, Qt. 560.00
McK G II-143, Eagle, Calabash, 7-Up Green, Applied Lip, Iron Pontil, Pt. ......358.00 to 495.00
McK G II-143, Eagle, Calabash, Aqua, Double Collar, Qt. 77.00
McK G II-143, Eagle, Calabash, Grass Green, Applied Sloping Collar, Iron Pontil, Qt. 213.00
McK G III-1, Cornucopia & Medallion, Aqua, Rolled Lip, Pontil, c.1840, 1/2 Pt. 5600.00
McK G III-2, Cornucopia & Medallion, Aqua, Tooled Lip, Pontil, 1/2 Pt. 202.00
McK G III-4, Cornucopia & Urn, Emerald Green, Sheared Mouth, Pontil, Pt. 187.00
McK G III-4, Cornucopia & Urn, Green, Sheared Mouth, Open Pontil, Pt. 275.00
McK G III-4, Cornucopia & Urn, Olive Amber, Tooled Lip, Pontil, Pt. 154.00
McK G III-4, Cornucopia & Urn, Olive Green, Sheared Mouth, Open Pontil, Pt. .....77.00 to 146.00
McK G III-4, Cornucopia & Urn, Yellow Amber, Sheared Mouth, Pontil, Pt. 198.00
McK G III-7, Cornucopia & Urn, Emerald Green, Sheared Mouth, Tooled Lip, OP, 1/2 Pt. .. 525.00
McK G III-7, Cornucopia & Urn, Olive Amber, Sheared Mouth, Pontil, 1/2 Pt. 115.00
McK G III-7, Cornucopia & Urn, Olive Green, Applied Lip, 1/2 Pt. 575.00
McK G III-7, Cornucopia & Urn, Olive Green, Sheared Mouth, Pontil, 1/2 Pt. ......77.00 to 154.00
McK G III-7, Cornucopia & Urn, Olive Yellow, Pontil, Sheared Mouth, Tooled Lip, 1/2 Pt. .. 101.00
McK G III-8, Cornucopia & Urn, Amber, Sheared Mouth, Pontil, 1/2 Pt. 115.00
McK G III-8, Cornucopia & Urn, Apple Green, Tooled Lip, Pontil, 1/2 Pt. 232.00
McK G III-10, Cornucopia & Urn, Gold Amber, Tooled Lip, Pontil, 1/2 Pt. 180.00
McK G III-11, Cornucopia & Urn, Light Amber, Sheared Mouth, Pontil, 1/2 Pt. ...138.00 to 220.00
McK G III-11, Cornucopia & Urn, Olive Amber, Plain Lip, Pontil, 1/2 Pt. 77.00
McK G III-14, Cornucopia & Urn, Emerald Green, Inward Rolled Lip, Pontil, 1/2 Pt. 532.00
McK G III-15, Cornucopia & Urn, Aqua, Pontil, 1/2 Pt. 127.00
McK G III-15, Cornucopia & Urn, Emerald Green, Sheared Mouth, Tooled Lip, OP, 1/2 Pt. 575.00
McK G III-16, Cornucopia & Urn, Blue Aqua, Sheared Mouth, Open Pontil, Pt. 532.00
McK G III-16, Cornucopia & Urn, Blue Green, Sheared Mouth, Iron Pontil, Pt. 728.00
McK G III-16, Cornucopia & Urn, Blue Green, Sheared Mouth, Tooled Lip, OP, Pt. 1680.00
McK G III-16, Cornucopia & Urn, Light Green, Iron Pontil, Pt. 413.00
McK G III-16, Cornucopia & Urn, Sapphire Blue, Tooled Lip, Pontil, Pt. 4950.00
McK G III-16, Cornucopia & Urn, Teal Blue, Sheared Mouth, Pontil, Pt. 2975.00
McK G III-17, Cornucopia & Urn, Aqua, Tooled Lip, Open Pontil, Pt. 202.00
McK G III-17, Cornucopia & Urn, Blue Green, Tooled Lip, Open Pontil, Pt. 896.00
McK G III-17, Cornucopia & Urn, Emerald Green, Tooled Lip, Pontil, Pt. ....*Illus* 1064.00
McK G III-17, Cornucopia & Urn, Green, Sheared Mouth, Open Pontil, Pt. 1120.00
McK G III-17, Cornucopia & Urn, Olive Yellow, Tooled Lip, Pontil, Pt. 4085.00
McK G III-17, Cornucopia & Urn, Teal Blue, Applied Lip, Open Pontil, Pt. 870.00
McK G III-17, Cornucopia & Urn, Yellow Green, Sheared, Tooled Lip, Open Pontil, Pt. ... 2576.00
McK G III-54, Eagle & Flag, Golden Amber, Sheared Mouth, Pontil, Pt. 3360.00
McK G III-117, Columbia & Eagle, Blue Aqua, Open Pontil, 1/2 Pt. 336.00

McK G IV-1, Masonic & Eagle, Amethyst, Sheared Mouth, c.1825, Pt. . . . .*Illus* 35840.00
McK G IV-1, Masonic & Eagle, Blue Green, Tooled Lip, Pontil, Pt. . . . . .224.00 to 420.00
McK G IV-1, Masonic & Eagle, Clear, Tooled Lip, Pontil, c.1820, Pt. 560.00
McK G IV-1, Masonic & Eagle, Moonstone, Sheared Mouth, Tooled Lip, Pontil, Pt. 4755.00
McK G IV-1, Masonic & Eagle, Teal, Sheared Mouth, Tooled Lip, Iron Pontil, c.1820, Pt. . . 224.00
McK G IV-1a, Masonic & Eagle, Aqua, Tooled Lip, Pontil, Pt. 532.00
McK G IV-1a, Masonic & Eagle, Blue Green, Tooled Lip, Pontil, Pt. . . . . .364.00 to 728.00
McK G IV-1a, Masonic & Eagle, Sheared Mouth, Tooled Lip, Iron Pontil, c.1820, Pt. 1064.00
McK G IV-1a, Masonic & Eagle, Teal, Sheared Mouth, Tooled Lip, Iron Pontil, c.1820, Pt. . 336.00
McK G IV-2, Masonic & Eagle, Green Aqua, Sheared Mouth, Rolled Lip, Pontil, Pt. 730.00
McK G IV-2, Masonic & Eagle, Olive Green, Applied Lip, Pontil, c.1820, Pt. 235.00
McK G IV-2, Masonic & Eagle, Olive Yellow, c.1825, Pt. 5040.00
McK G IV-3, Masonic & Eagle, Yellow Green, Amber Striation, Flared Lip, Pontil, Pt. . . . 3920.00
McK G IV-4, Masonic & Eagle, Green Aqua, Inward Rolled Lip, Pontil, c.1820, Pt. 1232.00
McK G IV-5, Masonic & Eagle, Green Aqua, Tooled Lip, Pontil, Pt. 440.00
McK G IV-5, Masonic & Eagle, Yellow Green, Sheared Mouth, Tooled Lip, Pontil, Pt. 1120.00
McK G IV-7, Masonic & Eagle, Green Aqua, Sheared Mouth, Tooled Lip, Pontil, Pt. 672.00
McK G IV-9, Masonic & Eagle, Green, Sheared Mouth, Open Pontil, Pt. 1568.00
McK G IV-9, Masonic & Eagle, Yellow Green, Tooled Lip, Pontil, c.1820, Pt. 560.00
McK G IV-10, Masonic & Eagle, Blue Green, Tooled Lip, Pontil, c.1820, Pt. . . . . .560.00 to 1456.00
McK G IV-10a, Masonic & Eagle, Green Aqua, Tooled Lip, Pontil, c.1820, Pt. 560.00
McK G IV-10b, Masonic & Eagle, Blue Green, Tooled Lip, Pontil, c.1820, Pt. 1568.00
McK G IV-11, Masonic & Eagle, Clear, Sheared Mouth, Tooled Lip, Pontil, c.1820, Pt. . . . 784.00
McK G IV-13a, Masonic & Eagle, Blue Aqua, Tooled Lip, Pontil, 1/2 Pt. 2240.00
McK G IV-14, Masonic & Eagle, Blue Green, Sheared Mouth, Tooled Lip, Pontil, 1/2 Pt. . 1792.00
McK G IV-14, Masonic & Eagle, Green Aqua, Tooled Lip, Pontil, 1/2 Pt. 840.00
McK G IV-14, Masonic & Eagle, Yellow Green, Applied Lip, Pontil, 1/2 Pt. . . . . .1120.00 to 2240.00
McK G IV-16, Masonic & Eagle, Blue Aqua, Sheared Mouth, Pontil, Pt. 2420.00
McK G IV-16, Masonic & Eagle, Olive Green, Applied Lip, Pontil, c.1820, Pt. 6720.00
McK G IV-17, Masonic & Eagle, Forest Green, c.1825, Pt. 1064.00
McK G IV-17, Masonic & Eagle, Olive Green, Sheared Mouth, Pontil, Pt. 345.00
McK G IV-17, Masonic & Eagle, Olive Yellow, Sheared Mouth, Pontil, Pt. . . . . . . .308.00 to 336.00
McK G IV-17, Masonic & Eagle, Yellow Amber, Sheared Mouth, Tooled Lip, Pontil, Pt. . . 317.00
McK G IV-18, Masonic & Eagle, Olive Green, Pt. 253.00
McK G IV-18, Masonic & Eagle, Yellow Amber, Sheared Mouth, Open Pontil, Pt. 280.00
McK G IV-18, Masonic & Eagle, Yellow Amber, Sheared Mouth, Pontil, c.1820, Pt. 213.00 to 260.00
McK G IV-19, Masonic & Eagle, Olive Amber, Pontil, Pt. 258.00
McK G IV-19, Masonic & Eagle, Olive Yellow, Sheared Mouth, Pontil, c.1825, Pt. 168.00
McK G IV-20, Masonic & Eagle, Yellow Amber, Open Pontil, Pt. . . . . .112.00 to 258.00
McK G IV-21, Masonic & Eagle, Olive Green, Tooled Lip, Pontil, c.1820, Pt. 258.00
McK G IV-24, Masonic & Eagle, Olive Amber, Sheared Mouth, Pontil, 1/2 Pt. 336.00
McK G IV-24, Masonic & Eagle, Olive Yellow, Sheared Mouth, Tooled Lip, Pontil, 1/2 Pt. 400.00
McK G IV-26, Masonic & Eagle, Olive Amber, Sheared Mouth, Tooled Lip, Pontil, 1/2 Pt. 1456.00
McK G IV-27, Masonic & Eagle, Aqua, Sheared Mouth, Pontil, Pt. . . . . .345.00 to 560.00
McK G IV-27, Masonic & Eagle, Blue Aqua, Tooled Lip, Pontil, Pt. . . . . .336.00 to 784.00
McK G IV-28, Double Masonic, Blue Aqua, Tooled Lip, Pontil, c.1820, 1/2 Pt. 364.00
McK G IV-28, Double Masonic, Blue Green, Tooled Lip, Pontil, 1/2 Pt. 532.00
McK G IV-32, Masonic & Eagle, Aqua, Sheared Mouth, Pontil, c.1825, Pt. . . . . . . .336.00 to 765.00
McK G IV-32, Masonic & Eagle, Blue Aqua, Pontil, Pt. 392.00
McK G IV-32, Masonic & Eagle, Blue Green, Sheared Mouth, Pontil, Pt. 896.00
McK G IV-32, Masonic & Eagle, Blue, Tooled Lip, Pontil, c.1830, Pt. 246.00
McK G IV-32, Masonic & Eagle, Gold Amber, Sheared Mouth, Pontil, Pt. 1792.00
McK G IV-32, Masonic & Eagle, Ice Blue, Tooled Lip, Pontil, Pt. 896.00
McK G IV-32, Masonic & Eagle, Olive Yellow, Sheared Mouth, Pontil, c.1825, Pt. 1008.00
McK G IV-32, Masonic & Eagle, Red Amber, Sheared Mouth, Pontil, Pt. . . . . . . .1456.00 to 1680.00
McK G IV-32, Masonic & Eagle, Yellow Amber, Tooled Lip, Pontil, Pt. . . . . .1344.00 to 1904.00
McK G IV-33, Masonic & Eagle, Blue Green, Sheared Mouth, Pontil, Pt. 952.00
McK G IV-34, Masonic Arch & Frigate, Aqua, Sheared Mouth, Pontil, Pt. . . . . . . .224.00 to 476.00
McK G IV-34, Masonic Arch & Frigate, Aqua, Tooled Lip, Pontil, c.1830, Pt. 336.00
McK G IV-36, Masonic Arch & Frigate, Pale Yellow Green, Pontil, Pt. 440.00
McK G IV-37, Masonic & Eagle, Amethyst, Sheared Mouth, Pontil, c.1825, Pt. . . . . . .*Illus* 2240.00
McK G IV-37, Masonic & Eagle, Aqua, Sheared Mouth, Pontil, c.1825, Pt. . . . . . . .190.00 to 202.00
McK G IV-38, Masonic & Eagle, Yellow Amber, Applied Double Collar, Qt. 2800.00

Flask, McK G IV-1, Masonic &
Eagle, Amethyst, Sheared
Mouth, c.1825, Pt.

Flask, McK G IV-37, Masonic &
Eagle, Amethyst, Sheared
Mouth, Pontil, c.1825, Pt.

Flask, McK G V-5, Success
To The Railroad, Olive Green,
Pontil, c.1830, Pt.

McK G IV-42, Masonic Clasped Hands & Eagle, Calabash, Apple Green, Sloping Collar, Qt.   160.00
McK G IV-42, Masonic Clasped Hands & Eagle, Calabash, Aqua, Sloping Collar, Qt. 83.00
McK G IV-43, Masonic & Seeing Eye, Olive Yellow, Sheared Mouth, Pontil, Pt. . . .385.00 to 616.00
McK G V-1, Success To The Railroad, Blue Aqua, Pontil, Sheared Mouth, Pt. 308.00
McK G V-1a, Success To The Railroad, Aqua, Sheared Mouth, Pontil, Pt. 246.00
McK G V-2, Success To The Railroad, Aqua, Open Pontil, Pt. . . . . .560.00 to 952.00
McK G V-3, Success To The Railroad, Aqua, Open Pontil, Pt. . . . . .1200.00 to 1344.00
McK G V-3, Success To The Railroad, Gold Amber, Sheared Mouth, Pontil, Pt. . . . .413.00 to 448.00
McK G V-3, Success To The Railroad, Olive Green, Pontil, Sheared Mouth, Pt. . . . .190.00 to 728.00
McK G V-3, Success To The Railroad, Olive Yellow, Pontil, c.1830, Pt. . . . . .392.00 to 616.00
McK G V-3, Success To The Railroad, Olive Yellow, Topaz Tint, Sheared Mouth, Pt. 784.00
McK G V-3a, Success To The Railroad, Yellow Amber, Tooled Lip, Pontil, Pt. . . . . .336.00 to 672.00
McK G V-4, Success To The Railroad, Green, Sheared Mouth, Open Pontil, Pt. 1320.00
McK G V-4, Success To The Railroad, Olive Green, Pontil, Sheared Mouth, Tooled Lip, Pt.   728.00
McK G V-4, Success To The Railroad, Olive Yellow, Tooled Lip, Pontil, Pt. 840.00
McK G V-5, Success To The Railroad, Amber, Open Pontil, Pt. 448.00
McK G V-5, Success To The Railroad, Emerald Green, Tooled Lip, Pontil, Pt. 308.00
McK G V-5, Success To The Railroad, Gold Amber, Pontil, c.1840, Pt. 550.00
McK G V-5, Success To The Railroad, Olive Green, Pontil, c.1830, Pt. . . . . *Illus*   440.00
McK G V-5, Success To The Railroad, Yellow Amber, Tooled Lip, Pontil, Pt. 504.00
McK G V-6, Success To The Railroad, Olive Yellow, Pontil, c.1830, Pt. . . . . .392.00 to 784.00
McK G V-6, Success To The Railroad, Yellow Amber, Pontil, c.1830, Pt. . . . . .280.00 to 308.00
McK G V-7, Success To The Railroad, Olive Amber, Pt. 650.00
McK G V-8, Success To The Railroad, Gold Amber, Sheared Mouth, Pontil, Pt. 179.00
McK G V-8, Success To The Railroad, Olive Amber, Sheared Mouth, Pontil, Pt. . . .220.00 to 308.00
McK G V-8, Success To The Railroad, Olive Green, Open Pontil, Pt. . . . . .308.00 to 504.00
McK G V-9, Horse Pulling Cart & Eagle, Amber, Pontil, Bubbles, Pt. 468.00
McK G V-9, Horse Pulling Cart & Eagle, Olive Green, Pontil, Pt. 413.00
McK G V-9, Horse Pulling Cart & Eagle, Yellow Amber, Tooled Lip, Pontil, Pt. 269.00
McK G V-10, Lowell Railroad & Eagle, Amber, Sheared Mouth, Pontil, 1/2 Pt. 403.00
McK G V-10, Lowell Railroad & Eagle, Olive Amber, Sheared Mouth, Pontil, 1/2 Pt. 470.00
McK G V-10, Lowell Railroad & Eagle, Olive Green, Pontil, 1/2 Pt. . . . . .275.00 to 616.00
McK G V-10, Lowell Railroad & Eagle, Yellow Amber, Tooled Lip, Pontil, 1/2 Pt. . .308.00 to 952.00
McK G VI-1, Monument, A Little More Grape, Aqua, Inward Rolled Lip, OP, 1/2 Pt. 155.00
McK G VI-1a, Monument, A Little More Grape, Olive Yellow, c.1830, 1/2 Pt. 6160.00
McK G VI-2, Monument & Fell's Point, Amethyst, Tooled Lip, OP, 1/2 Pt. . . . . . .1100.00 to 5040.00
McK G VI-2, Monument & Fell's Point, Aqua, Open Pontil, 1/2 Pt. 146.00
McK G VI-2, Monument & Fell's Point, Clear, Sheared Mouth, Pontil, 1/2 Pt. 784.00
McK G VI-2, Monument & Fell's Point, Olive Yellow, Tooled Lip, Pontil, 1/2 Pt. 1120.00
McK G VI-2, Monument & Fell's Point, Puce, Striations, Sheared Mouth, Pontil, 1/2 Pt. . .   1904.00
McK G VI-3, Monument, Liberty & Union, Aqua, Sheared Mouth, Pontil, c.1825, Pt. 392.00
McK G VI-4, Corn For The World, Amber Shaded To Brown, Qt. . . . . *Illus*   303.00
McK G VI-4, Corn For The World, Aqua, Tooled Lip, Pontil, c.1825, Pt. 134.00
McK G VI-4, Corn For The World, Gold Amber, Applied Lip, Qt. 605.00

Flask, McK G VI-4, Corn
For The World, Amber
Shaded To Brown, Qt.

Flask, McK G VIII-1, Sunburst,
Emerald Green, Sheared
Mouth, Pontil, c.1820, Pt.

Flask, McK G IX-11a, Scroll,
Blue, Applied Double Collar,
IP, c.1850, Pt.

McK G VI-4, Corn For The World, Ice Blue, Applied Lip, Qt. 605.00
McK G VI-4, Corn For The World, Olive Green, Applied Sloping Collar, 1870, Qt. 7280.00
McK G VI-4, Corn For The World, Orange Amber, Applied Double Collar, c.1870, Qt. 560.00
McK G VI-4, Corn For The World, Teal, Double Collar, Wood Stopper, c.1870, Qt. 6600.00
McK G VI-4, Corn For The World, Topaz Yellow, Double Collar, Qt. 3640.00
McK G VI-4, Corn For The World, Yellow, Applied Double Collar, c.1870, Qt. 5320.00
McK G VI-6, Corn For The World, Aqua, Pt. . . . . .308.00 to 336.00
McK G VI-7, Corn For The World, Aqua, Open Pontil, c.1830, 1/2 Pt. 616.00
McK G VII-4, see Whiskey, E.G. Booz's Old Cabin
McK G VIII-1, Sunburst, Emerald Green, Sheared Mouth, Pontil, c.1820, Pt. . . . .*Illus* 3640.00
McK G VIII-1, Sunburst, Lime Green, Pontil, Pt. 1320.00
McK G VIII-2, Sunburst, Green, Sheared Mouth, Pontil, Pt. . . . . .440.00 to 1120.00
McK G VIII-3, Sunburst, Golden Yellow, Sheared Mouth, Pontil, c.1820, Pt. 1850.00
McK G VIII-3, Sunburst, Olive Yellow, Sheared Mouth, Pontil, Pt. . . . . .1456.00 to 1792.00
McK G VIII-4, Corn For The World, Burnt Orange Puce, Qt. 4400.00
McK G VIII-5, Sunburst, Olive Green, Sheared Mouth, Tooled Lip, Pontil, c.1820, Pt. 2576.00
McK G VIII-5a, Sunburst, Olive Yellow, Sheared Mouth, Tooled Lip, Pontil, c.1820, Pt. . . . 4200.00
McK G VIII-5a, Sunburst, Yellow Amber, Sheared Mouth, Open Pontil, Pt. 4200.00
McK G VIII-7, Sunburst, Olive Yellow, Sheared Mouth, Tooled Lip, Pontil, c.1820, Pt. 3360.00
McK G VIII-8, Sunburst, Medium Olive Green, Flared Lip, Pt. 770.00
McK G VIII-8, Sunburst, Olive Yellow, Sheared Mouth, Tooled Lip, Pontil, c.1820, Pt. 728.00
McK G VIII-8, Sunburst, Yellow Amber, Sheared Mouth, Tooled Lip, Pontil, c.1820, Pt. 896.00
McK G VIII-9, Sunburst, Forest Green, Sheared Mouth, Pontil, 1/2 Pt. 672.00
McK G VIII-9, Sunburst, Olive Yellow, Sheared Mouth, Pontil, 1/2 Pt. . . . . .896.00 to 1680.00
McK G VIII-9, Sunburst, Yellow Amber, Tooled Lip, Pontil, c.1820, 1/2 Pt. . . . . . .728.00 to 1480.00
McK G VIII-10, Sunburst, Olive Yellow, Sheared Mouth, Open Pontil, 1/2 Pt. 1120.00
McK G VIII-14, Sunburst, Blue Green, Sheared Mouth, Tooled Lip, Pontil, c.1820, 1/2 Pt. . . 1904.00
McK G VIII-14, Sunburst, Emerald Green, Sheared Mouth, Tooled Lip, Pontil, 1/2 Pt. 4480.00
McK G VIII-14, Sunburst, Yellow Amber, Sheared Mouth, Tooled Lip, Pontil, 1/2 Pt. 728.00
McK G VIII-14a, Sunburst, Emerald Green, Tooled Lip, Pontil, c.1820, 1/2 Pt. 4760.00
McK G VIII-16, Sunburst, Forest Green, Inward Rolled Lip, c.1820, 1/2 Pt. 2016.00
McK G VIII-16, Sunburst, Green, Pontil, 1/2 Pt. 550.00
McK G VIII-16, Sunburst, Olive Green, Tooled Lip, Pontil, 1/2 Pt. . . . . .896.00 to 1375.00
McK G VIII-16, Sunburst, Yellow Olive, Tooled Lip, Pontil, 1/2 Pt. . . . . .896.00 to 1904.00
McK G VIII-18, Sunburst, Olive Yellow, Sheared Mouth, Pontil, 1/2 Pt. . . . . .1008.00 to 1232.00
McK G VIII-19, Sunburst, Forest Green, Sheared Mouth, Pontil, c.1820, 7 In. 4760.00
McK G VIII-20, Sunburst, Aqua, Open Pontil, Pt. 308.00
McK G VIII-22, Sunburst, Moonstone, Amethyst, Sheared Mouth, Pontil, Pt. 2352.00
McK G VIII-24, Sunburst, Amber, Sheared Mouth, Pontil, 1/2 Pt. 4200.00
McK G VIII-24, Sunburst, Amber, Tooled Lip, Pontil, 1/2 Pt. 2975.00
McK G VIII-25, Sunburst, Aqua, Sheared Mouth, Pontil, 1/2 Pt. . . . . .167.00 to 410.00
McK G VIII-25, Sunburst, Green Aqua, Sheared Mouth, Pontil, 1/2 Pt. 364.00
McK G VIII-25, Sunburst, Puce, Sheared Mouth, Pontil, 1/2 Pt. 4760.00
McK G VIII-25, Sunburst, Strawberry Puce, Tooled Lip, Pontil, 1/2 Pt. 4695.00

McK G VIII-27, Sunburst, Aqua, Sheared Mouth, Pontil, 1/2 Pt. . . . . .258.00 to 308.00
McK G VIII-28, Sunburst, Blue Aqua, Tooled Lip, Pontil, 1/2 Pt. . . . . .255.00 to 364.00
McK G VIII-29, Sunburst, Blue Aqua, Tooled Lip, Pontil, 3/4 Pt. . . . . .240.00 to 364.00
McK G VIII-29, Sunburst, Clear, Sheared Mouth, Tooled Lip, Pontil, c.1825, 3/4 Pt. 840.00
McK G VIII-29, Sunburst, Teal Green, Olive Streaks, Pontil, 3/4 Pt. 330.00
McK G VIII-49, Anchor & Sheaf Of Grain, Olive Yellow, Sheared Mouth, Pontil, 1/2 Pt. . . 3000.00
McK G IX-1, Scroll, Aqua, Sheared Mouth, Iron Pontil, Qt. 104.00
McK G IX-1, Scroll, Blue Green, Pontil, Qt. 176.00
McK G IX-1, Scroll, Yellow Amber, Sheared Mouth, Tooled Lip, Pontil, c.1845, Qt. 1232.00
McK G IX-2, Scroll, Aqua, Sheared Mouth, Iron Pontil, Qt. . . . . .44.00 to 112.00
McK G IX-2, Scroll, Cobalt Blue, Sheared Mouth, Iron Pontil, Qt. . . . . .3080.00 to 6160.00
McK G IX-2, Scroll, Green Aqua, Tooled Lip, Pontil, Qt. 88.00
McK G IX-2, Scroll, Moonstone, Sheared Mouth, c.1850, Qt. 2352.00
McK G IX-2, Scroll, Olive Yellow, Sheared Mouth, Tooled Lip, Pontil, c.1845, Qt. 2464.00
McK G IX-2, Scroll, Root Beer Amber, Sheared Mouth, Open Pontil, c.1850, Qt. 2688.00
McK G IX-2, Scroll, Yellow Green, Sheared Mouth, Pontil, Qt. . . . . .3360.00 to 4200.00
McK G IX-3, Scroll, Olive Yellow, Sheared Mouth, Pontil, Qt. 5600.00
McK G IX-3, Scroll, Sapphire Blue, Sheared Mouth, Pontil, Qt. 4200.00
McK G IX-3, Scroll, Yellow Apple Green, Sheared Mouth, Iron Pontil, Qt. 616.00
McK G IX-4, Scroll, Amber, Sheared Mouth, Pontil, Qt. 728.00
McK G IX-4, Scroll, Aqua, Flattened Ring Under Sheared Mouth, Iron Pontil, Qt. 110.00
McK G IX-7, Scroll, Blue Aqua, Iron Pontil, Qt. 190.00
McK G IX-10, Scroll, Cobalt Blue, Sheared Mouth, Iron Pontil, Pt. 3400.00
McK G IX-10, Scroll, Gold Amber, Applied Lip, Iron Pontil, c.1850, Pt. . . . . .840.00 to 1650.00
McK G IX-10, Scroll, Ice Blue, Applied Lip, Iron Pontil, Pt. 168.00
McK G IX-10, Scroll, Olive Green, Applied Lip, Pontil, Pt. 2128.00
McK G IX-10, Scroll, Olive Yellow, Sheared Mouth, Tooled Lip, Pontil, c.1845, Pt. 1344.00
McK G IX-10, Scroll, Orange Amber, Sheared Mouth, Tooled Lip, Pontil, c.1845, Pt. 840.00
McK G IX-10, Scroll, Yellow Green, Applied Lip, Iron Pontil, Pt. 1210.00
McK G IX-10a, Scroll, Blue, Sheared Mouth, Pontil, c.1850, Pt. 504.00
McK G IX-10a, Scroll, Cobalt Blue, Applied Double Collar, Iron Pontil, Pt. 11000.00
McK G IX-10a, Scroll, Olive Green, Applied Lip, Iron Pontil, Pt. 1540.00
McK G IX-10b, Scroll, Sapphire Shaded To Cobalt Blue, Applied Lip, Pt. 5060.00
McK G IX-11, Scroll, Lavender Tint, Sheared Mouth, Pontil, c.1850, Pt. 1008.00
McK G IX-11, Scroll, Sapphire Blue, Sheared Mouth, Pontil, Pt. 1904.00
McK G IX-11a, Scroll, Blue, Applied Double Collar, IP, c.1850, Pt. 3920.00
McK G IX-12, Scroll, Olive Yellow, Sheared Mouth, c.1850, Pt. 1568.00
McK G IX-12a, Scroll, Aqua, Sheared Mouth, c.1855, Pt. 100.00
McK G IX-13, Scroll, Emerald Green, Tooled Lip, Iron Pontil, c.1850, Pt. 7280.00
McK G IX-14, Scroll, Ice Blue, Sheared Mouth, Tooled Lip, Pontil, c.1850, Pt. 123.00
McK G IX-15, Scroll, Sapphire Blue, Sheared Mouth, Pontil, c.1850, Pt. . . . . .Illus 3920.00
McK G IX-17, Scroll, Aqua, Pontil, Pt. 72.00
McK G IX-20, Scroll, Green Aqua, Sheared Mouth, Pontil, c.1850, Pt. 532.00
McK G IX-25, Scroll, Blue Green, Applied Lip, Pontil, Pt. 990.00
McK G IX-29a, Scroll, Green Aqua, Tooled Lip, Pontil, c.1865, 2 1/4 Qt., 10 In. 1680.00
McK G IX-30a, Scroll, Blue Aqua, Tooled Lip, Pontil, Gal., 12 In. 1680.00
McK G IX-31, Scroll, Aqua, Iron Pontil, 1/2 Pt. 66.00
McK G IX-32, Scroll, Amber Shaded To Yellow, Sheared Mouth, Iron Pontil, 1/2 Pt. 1120.00
McK G IX-33, Scroll, Aqua, Sheared Mouth, Iron Pontil, 1/2 Pt. 110.00
McK G IX-34, Scroll, Aqua, Sheared Mouth, Tooled Lip, Pontil, c.1845, 1/2 Pt. 280.00
McK G IX-34, Scroll, Gold Amber, Sheared Mouth, Pontil, c.1850, 1/2 Pt. 1456.00
McK G IX-34, Scroll, Green, Sheared Mouth, Pontil, 1/2 Pt. . . . . .213.00 to 400.00
McK G IX-34, Scroll, Strawberry Puce, Sheared Mouth, c.1850, 1/2 Pt. 5600.00
McK G IX-34, Scroll, Yellow Amber, Tooled Lip, Pontil, 1/2 Pt. 1344.00
McK G IX-36, Scroll, Citron, Sheared Mouth, Iron Pontil, c.1850, 1/2 Pt. 3640.00
McK G IX-36, Scroll, Olive Yellow, Sheared Mouth, Pontil, 1/2 Pt. 4200.00
McK G IX-37, Scroll, Amber, Sheared Mouth, Pontil, 1/2 Pt. 896.00
McK G IX-38, Scroll & BP & B, Blue Aqua, Open Pontil, 1/2 Pt. 364.00
McK G IX-39, Scroll & BP & B, Aqua, Sheared Mouth, Tooled Lip, Pontil, c.1845, 1/2 Pt. . . 504.00
McK G IX-43, Scroll & JR & Son, Aqua, Sheared, Tooled, Pontil, c.1845, Pt. 1064.00
McK G IX-43, Scroll & JR & Son, Blue Aqua, Sheared Mouth, Tooled Lip, OP, Pt. 955.00
McK G IX-44, Scroll, Aqua, Sheared Mouth, Pontil, Pt. 896.00
McK G IX-44, Scroll, Blue Aqua, Sheared Mouth, Open Pontil, Pt. 784.00

McK G IX-45, Scroll, Aqua, Open Pontil, Pt. . . . . .990.00 to 1120.00
McK G IX-45, Scroll, Blue Green, Sheared Mouth, Pontil, Pt. 168.00
McK G IX-49, Scroll, McCarty & Torreyson, Apple Green, Qt. 5600.00
McK G X-1, Stag & Willow Tree, Aqua, Sheared Mouth, Pontil, Pt. . . . . .235.00 to 258.00
McK G X-1, Stag & Willow Tree, Aqua, Tooled Lip, Pontil, c.1830, Pt. . . . . .123.00 to 173.00
McK G X-2, Stag & Willow Tree, Aqua, Open Pontil, 1/2 Pt. 616.00
McK G X-3, Sheaf Of Rye & Grapes, Aqua, Tooled Lip, Open Pontil, 1/2 Pt. 246.00
McK G X-3, Sheaf Of Rye & Grapes, Ice Blue, Open Pontil, 1/2 Pt. 476.00
McK G X-4, Cannon, A Little More Grape, Aqua, Sheared Mouth, Open Pontil, Pt. 476.00
McK G X-4, Cannon, A Little More Grape, Green Aqua, Sheared Mouth, 1/2 Pt. 154.00
McK G X-4, Cannon, A Little More Grape, Green, Sheared Mouth, Tooled Lip, Pontil, Pt. . 7280.00
McK G X-4, Cannon, A Little More Grape, Olive Yellow, Sheared, Tooled Lip, Pontil, Pt. . 4807.00
McK G X-6, Cannon, A Little More Grape, Aqua, Sheared Mouth, Pontil, 1/2 Pt. . .213.00 to 269.00
McK G X-6, Cannon, A Little More Grape, Strawberry Apricot, c.1850, 1/2 Pt. 4760.00
McK G X-6, Cannon, A Little More Grape, Yellow Green, c.1850, 1/2 Pt. 616.00
McK G X-7, Sloop & Bridgeton, Aqua, Pontil, Tooled Lip, 1/2 Pt. . . . . .364.00 to 420.00
McK G X-8, Sloop & Star, Aqua, Sheared Mouth, Pontil, c.1830, 1/2 Pt. . . . . .179.00 to 190.00
McK G X-8a, Sloop & Star, Aqua, Inward Rolled Lip, Open Pontil, 1/2 Pt. 190.00
McK G X-10, Sheaf Of Rye & Star, Sheared Mouth, Open Pontil, Pt. 880.00
McK G X-14, Murdock & Cassel, Blue Green, Sheared Mouth, Pontil, Pt. 2464.00
McK G X-14, Murdock & Cassel, Green Aqua, Tooled Lip, Pontil, c.1835, Pt. 1904.00
McK G X-15, Summer & Winter, Aqua, Applied Double Collar, Pontil, Pt. . . . . . . .100.00 to 129.00
McK G X-15, Summer & Winter, Yellow Green, Double Collar, c.1865, Pt. . . . . . .616.00 to 728.00
McK G X-16, Summer & Winter, Blue Aqua, Applied Double Collar, 1/2 Pt. . . . . . .190.00 to 200.00
McK G X-16, Summer & Winter, Ice Blue, Applied Double Collar, 1/2 Pt. 179.00
McK G X-17, Summer & Summer, Blue Aqua, Applied Sloping Collar, Pontil, Pt. 77.00
McK G X-18, Summer & Winter, Aqua, Pontil, Qt. 143.00
McK G X-18, Summer & Winter, Blue Green, Applied Sloping Collar, Pontil, Qt. 616.00
McK G X-18, Summer & Winter, Cornflower Blue, Sheared Mouth, Pontil, Qt. 1120.00
McK G X-18, Summer & Winter, Yellow Topaz, Double Collar, c.1850, Qt. 4200.00
McK G X-19, Summer & Winter, Aqua, Pontil, Qt. 116.00
McK G X-19, Summer & Winter, Olive Yellow, Double Collar, Pontil, c.1865, Qt. 3360.00
McK G X-19, Summer & Winter, Red Amber, Double Collar, c.1865, Qt. 2128.00
McK G X-21, Steamboat & Sheaf Of Rye, Blue Aqua, Sheared Mouth, Pontil, Pt. 1540.00
McK G X-22, Log Cabin & Flag, Aqua, Pt. 9000.00
McK G X-27, Flag & Stoddard, Amber, Sheared Mouth, Pt. 7763.00
McK G X-30, Hunter & Stag, Aqua, Applied Collar, Pt. 728.00
McK G XI-2, For Pike's Peak, Prospector, Olive Yellow, Applied Collar, c.1870, Pt. 4480.00
McK G XI-5, For Pike's Peak, Prospector, Blue Aqua, Applied Collar, 1/2 Pt. 88.00
McK G XI-9, For Pike's Peak, Prospector, Eagle, Olive Yellow, Applied Collar, c.1870, Pt. 3640.00
McK G XI-10, For Pike's Peak, Prospector, Eagle, Aqua, Applied Collar, 1/2 Pt. 110.00
McK G XI-11, Prospector & Eagle, Blue Aqua, Applied Collar, Pontil, c.1870, Pt. 190.00
McK G XI-15, Prospector & Eagle, Aqua, Applied Collar, Pt. 364.00
McK G XI-15, Prospector & Eagle, Blue, Applied Collar, c.1870, Pt. 504.00
McK G XI-15, Prospector & Eagle, Yellow Green, Applied Collar, Pt. 3640.00
McK G XI-17, Prospector & Eagle, Aqua, Applied Collar, Pt. 110.00
McK G XI-20, For Pike's Peak, Prospector, Eagle, Light Blue Green, Pontil, 1/2 Pt. 408.00
McK G XI-22, For Pike's Peak, Prospector, Eagle, Amber, Applied Collar, Pt. . . . .*Illus* 3920.00
McK G XI-25, For Pike's Peak, Prospector, Eagle, Blue Aqua, Applied Collar, Pt. 246.00
McK G XI-26, For Pike's Peak, Prospector, Eagle, Aqua, Applied Collar, 1/2 Pt. 90.00
McK G XI-34, For Pike's Peak, Prospector, Eagle, Ceredo, Blue Aqua, Qt. 90.00
McK G XI-34, For Pike's Peak, Prospector, Eagle, Ceredo, Ice Blue, Applied Lip, Qt. 308.00
McK G XI-35, For Pike's Peak, Eagle, Ceredo, Ice Blue, Applied Ring, Pt. 190.00
McK G XI-36, For Pike's Peak, Eagle, Ceredo, Blue Green, Sheared Mouth, Pontil, 1/2 Pt. . 308.00
McK G XI-45, Prospector & Eagle, Blue Aqua, Pt. 1120.00
McK G XI-50, For Pike's Peak, Prospector, Hunter, Olive Yellow, Pt. . . . . .3920.00 to 4695.00
McK G XI-52, For Pike's Peak, Prospector, Hunter, Aqua, Applied Collar, 1/2 Pt. 174.00
McK G XI-53, For Pike's Peak, Prospector, Hunter, Clear, Applied Collar, Pt. 4200.00
McK G XII-1, Union, Clasped Hands & Eagle, Light Yellow Green, Qt. 408.00
McK G XII-2, Waterford, Clasped Hands & Eagle, Aqua, Double Collar, Iron Pontil, Qt. . . 213.00
McK G XII-3, Union, Clasped Hands & Eagle, Olive Yellow, Applied Collar, Qt. .1680.00 to 3024.00
McK G XII-6, Clasped Hands & Eagle, Olive Yellow Amber, Applied Collar, Qt. 990.00

McK G XII-8, Union, Clasped Hands & Eagle, Aqua, c.1875, Qt. 77.00
McK G XII-9, Union, Clasped Hands & Eagle, Yellow Green, Applied Collar, Qt. 690.00
McK G XII-10, Union, Clasped Hands & Eagle, Olive Amber, Qt. 2576.00
McK G XII-13, Union, Clasped Hands & Eagle, Red Amber, Applied Collar, Qt. 605.00
McK G XII-13, Union, Clasped Hands & Eagle, Yellow Amber, Applied Collar, Qt. 605.00
McK G XII-17, Union, Clasped Hands & Eagle, Aqua, Applied Collar, Contents, Pt. 784.00
McK G XII-18, Clasped Hands & Eagle, Aqua, Applied Collar, Pt. 55.00
McK G XII-18, Clasped Hands & Eagle, Yellow Green, Applied Collar, Pt. 358.00
McK G XII-18, Clasped Hands & Eagle, Yellow, c.1865, Pt. 1232.00
McK G XII-19, Union, Clasped Hands & Eagle, Amber, Applied Collar, c.1865, Pt. 364.00
McK G XII-19, Union, Clasped Hands & Eagle, Light Olive Yellow, Applied Collar, Pt. . . 605.00
McK G XII-20, Union, Clasped Hands & Eagle, Lime Green, Pt. 468.00
McK G XII-21, Union, Clasped Hands & Eagle, Amber, Applied Collar, Pt. 358.00
McK G XII-21, Union, Clasped Hands & Eagle, Golden Yellow, Applied Collar, Pt. 110.00
McK G XII-22, Union, Clasped Hands & Eagle, Olive Amber, Applied Collar, Pt. 784.00
McK G XII-24, Union, Clasped Hands & Eagle, Yellow, Applied Collar, Pt. 896.00
McK G XII-25, Union, Clasped Hands & Eagle, Yellow Green, Pt. 1430.00
McK G XII-27, Union, Clasped Hands & Eagle, Yellow Amber, Pt. 990.00
McK G XII-28, Union, Clasped Hands & Eagle, Amber, Applied Collar, Pt. . . . . . . .330.00 to 364.00
McK G XII-28, Union, Clasped Hands & Eagle, Yellow Amber, Applied Collar, Pt. 420.00
McK G XII-29, Union, Clasped Hands & Eagle, Amber, Applied Collar, 1/2 Pt. . . . .202.00 to 308.00
McK G XII-29, Union, Clasped Hands & Eagle, Yellow Amber, Applied Collar, 1/2 Pt. . . . 336.00
McK G XII-29, Union, Clasped Hands & Eagle, Yellow Green, Applied Collar, 1/2 Pt. 2090.00
McK G XII-30, Union, Clasped Hands & Eagle, Amber, Applied Collar, 1/2 Pt. 187.00
McK G XII-30, Union, Clasped Hands & Eagle, Yellow Amber, Applied Collar, 1/2 Pt. . . . 425.00
McK G XII-31, Union, Clasped Hands & Eagle, Amber, Applied Collar, 1/2 Pt. 190.00
McK G XII-31, Union, Clasped Hands & Eagle, Yellow Amber, 1/2 Pt. . . . . .385.00 to 560.00
McK G XII-32, Union, Clasped Hands & Eagle, Aqua, Applied Collar, 1/2 Pt. 190.00
McK G XII-33, Union, Clasped Hands & Eagle, Amber, Applied Collar, 1/2 Pt. . . . .247.00 to 448.00
McK G XII-33, Union, Clasped Hands & Eagle, Yellow Green, Applied Collar, 1/2 Pt. 408.00
McK G XII-37, Union, Clasped Hands, Aqua, Applied Collar, Qt. 179.00
McK G XII-37, Union, Clasped Hands, Cobalt Blue, Applied Collar, Qt. 2352.00
McK G XII-37, Union, Clasped Hands, Cornflower Blue, Applied Collar, Qt. 6720.00
McK G XII-38, Union, Clasped Hands & Cannon, Aqua, Applied Collar, Qt. 187.00
McK G XII-38, Union, Clasped Hands & Cannon, Ice Blue, Applied Collar, Pt. . . . . .90.00 to 213.00
McK G XII-38, Union, Clasped Hands & Cannon, Olive Yellow, c.1865, Qt. 2128.00
McK G XII-39, Union, Clasped Hands & Cannon, Ice Blue, Applied Collar, Pt. 242.00
McK G XII-40, Union, Clasped Hands & Cannon, Amber, Applied Collar, Pt. 660.00
McK G XII-40, Union, Clasped Hands & Cannon, Aqua, Applied Collar, Pt. 190.00
McK G XII-40, Union, Clasped Hands & Cannon, Yellow Amber, c.1865, Pt. 532.00
McK G XII-41, Union, Clasped Hands & Cannon, Amber, c.1865, Pt. . . . . .448.00 to 504.00
McK G XII-41, Union, Clasped Hands & Cannon, Aqua, Applied Collar, c.1865, Pt. 157.00
McK G XII-41, Union, Clasped Hands & Cannon, Citron, Applied Collar, Pt. 2320.00
McK G XII-41, Union, Clasped Hands & Cannon, Yellow Amber, c.1865, Pt. 560.00
McK G XII-42, Union, Clasped Hands & Cannon, Amber, 1/2 Pt. 220.00
McK G XII-42, Union, Clasped Hands & Cannon, Aqua, Applied Collar, 1/2 Pt. 185.00
McK G XII-42, Union, Clasped Hands & Cannon, Aqua, Sheared Mouth, Pontil, 1/2 Pt. . . 392.00
McK G XII-43, Union, Clasped Hands & Eagle, Calabash, Amber, Double Collar, IP, Qt. . . 420.00
McK G XII-43, Union, Clasped Hands & Eagle, Calabash, Amber, IP, Qt. . . . .*Illus* 300.00
McK G XII-43, Union, Clasped Hands & Eagle, Calabash, Amber, Pontil, Qt. 616.00
McK G XII-43, Union, Clasped Hands & Eagle, Calabash, Red Amber, Iron Pontil, Qt. . . . 605.00
McK G XII-43, Union, Clasped Hands & Eagle, Calabash, Red Orange Amber, Pontil, Qt. . 468.00
McK G XII-43, Union, Clasped Hands & Eagle, Calabash, Aqua, Iron Pontil, Qt. 44.00
McK G XIII-2, Girl On Bicycle, Blue Aqua, Pt. 157.00
McK G XIII-3, Girl On Bicycle & Eagle, Aqua, Pt. 235.00
McK G XIII-3, Girl On Bicycle & Eagle, Blue Aqua, Applied Collar, Pt. 442.00
McK G XIII-4, Hunter & Fisherman, Calabash, Amber, Applied Sloping Collar, OP, Qt. . . . 275.00
McK G XIII-4, Hunter & Fisherman, Calabash, Aqua, Iron Pontil, Qt. 88.00
McK G XIII-4, Hunter & Fisherman, Calabash, Gold Amber, Sloping Collar, IP, Qt. 330.00
McK G XIII-4, Hunter & Fisherman, Calabash, Salmon Puce, Iron Pontil, Qt. . . . .420.00 to 1680.00
McK G XIII-4, Hunter & Fisherman, Calabash, Teal Blue, Sloping Collar, Qt. . . . . .490.00 to 560.00
McK G XIII-4, Hunter & Fisherman, Calabash, Yellow Amber, Sloping Collar, IP, Qt. 213.00

McK G XIII-5, Hunter & Fisherman, Calabash, Blue Aqua, Open Pontil, Qt. 129.00
McK G XIII-7, Hunter & Hounds, Light Green, Open Pontil, Pt. 672.00
McK G XIII-8, Sailor & Banjo Player, Copper Amber, Sheared Mouth, Pontil, 1/2 Pt. 3080.00
McK G XIII-8, Sailor & Banjo Player, Olive Yellow, Double Collar, 1/2 Pt. 1456.00
McK G XIII-8, Sailor & Banjo Player, Orange Amber, Applied Lip, 1/2 Pt. 410.00
McK G XIII-8, Sailor & Banjo Player, Yellow Amber, 1/2 Pt. 364.00
McK G XIII-8, Sailor & Banjo Player, Yellow, Double Collar, c.1870, 1/2 Pt. 560.00
McK G XIII-11, Soldier & Dancer, Gray Topaz, Sheared Mouth, Pontil, Pt. 8400.00
McK G XIII-12, Soldier & Dancer, Teal Blue, Applied Collar, Pt. 190.00
McK G XIII-13, Soldier & Dancer, Olive Green, Applied Collar, c.1870, Pt. 3640.00
McK G XIII-15, Soldier & Sunflower, Calabash, Blue Aqua, Sloping Collar, IP, Qt. 540.00
McK G XIII-16, Soldier & Hound, Citron, c.1865, Qt. 770.00
McK G XIII-16, Soldier & Hound, Olive Yellow, Applied Collar, Open Pontil, Qt. 910.00
McK G XIII-16, Soldier & Hound, Orange Amber, Applied Collar, Pontil, c.1865, Qt. 1064.00
McK G XIII-16, Soldier & Hound, Teal, Pontil, c.1850, Qt. 825.00
McK G XIII-16, Soldier & Hound, Yellow, Double Collar, Pontil, c.1850, Qt. ....880.00 to 1344.00
McK G XIII-17, Horseman & Hound, Citron, Applied Double Collar, Pt. 616.00
McK G XIII-17, Horseman & Hound, Olive Amber, Applied Collar, c.1865, Pt. 784.00
McK G XIII-17, Horseman & Hound, Olive Green, Double Collar, Pt. 616.00
McK G XIII-17, Horseman & Hound, Puce, Double Ring, c.1865, Pt. 5500.00
McK G XIII-19, Flora Temple, Apricot Puce, Applied Collar, Handle, Ring, Qt. 532.00
McK G XIII-19, Flora Temple, Copper Puce, Applied Lip & Handle, Qt. 410.00
McK G XIII-20, Flora Temple, Copper Puce, Sloping Double Collar, Qt. 896.00
McK G XIII-21, Flora Temple, Apricot Puce, Applied Collar, Handle, Bubbles, Pt. 385.00
McK G XIII-21, Flora Temple, Strawberry Puce, Applied Collar, Handle, Pt. 110.00
McK G XIII-22, Flora Temple, Amber, Applied Lip, Pt. 303.00
McK G XIII-22, Flora Temple, Apricot Amber, Applied Lip, Pt. 246.00
McK G XIII-23, Flora Temple, Blue Green, Applied Lip, Pt. 850.00
McK G XIII-23, Flora Temple, Teal Blue, Pt. 896.00
McK G XIII-24, Flora Temple, Horse, Red Amber, Applied Lip, Ring, Pt. 325.00
McK G XIII-29, Will You Take A Drink, Duck, Aqua, Applied Sloping Collar, Pt. ..231.00 to 616.00
McK G XIII-29a, Will You Take A Drink, Duck, Aqua, 1/2 Pt. ....358.00 to 448.00
McK G XIII-30, Will You Take A Drink, Duck, Blue Aqua, 1/2 Pt. 532.00
McK G XIII-35, Sheaf Of Grain, Westford Glass Co., Amber, Double Collar, Pt. ...146.00 to 165.00
McK G XIII-35, Sheaf Of Grain, Westford Glass Co., Olive Amber, Double Collar, Pt..... 157.00
McK G XIII-35, Sheaf Of Grain, Westford Glass Co., Olive Green, Double Collar, Pt..... 190.00
McK G XIII-35, Sheaf Of Grain, Westford Glass Co., Yellow Amber, Double Collar, Pt. .. 121.00
McK G XIII-36, Sheaf Of Grain, Westford Glass Co., Olive Green, Double Collar, Pt..... 157.00
McK G XIII-36, Sheaf Of Grain, Westford Glass Co., Red Amber, Double Collar, Pt. 179.00
McK G XIII-37, Sheaf Of Grain, Westford Glass Co., Chocolate Amber, 1/2 Pt. 1102.00
McK G XIII-37, Sheaf Of Grain, Westford Glass Co., Olive Amber, c.1870, 1/2 Pt. 168.00
McK G XIII-37, Sheaf Of Grain, Westford Glass Co., Orange Amber, 1/2 Pt. 190.00
McK G XIII-38, Sheaf Of Grain & Star, Green Aqua, Double Collar, Iron Pontil, Qt. 168.00

Flask, McK G XI-22, For Pike's
Peak, Prospector, Eagle, Amber,
Applied Collar, Pt.

Flask, McK G XII-43, Union,
Clasped Hands & Eagle,
Calabash, Amber, IP, Qt.

Flask, Milk Glass, Octopus
Covering Silver Dollar, Painted,
Gold, Red, 4 1/2 In.

McK G XIII-38, Sheaf Of Grain & Star, Olive Yellow, Applied Lip, Pontil, Qt. 6160.00
McK G XIII-39, Sheaf Of Grain & Star, Emerald Green, Applied Collar, Open Pontil, Pt. . . .   428.00
McK G XIII-39, Sheaf Of Grain & Star, Yellow Green, Applied Double Collar, OP, Pt. 4200.00
McK G XIII-40, Sheaf Of Grain & Star, Gold Amber, Applied Double Collar, 1/2 Pt. 1904.00
McK G XIII-44, Sheaf Of Grain & Star, Calabash, Aqua, Qt. 99.00
McK G XIII-45, Sheaf Of Grain & Star, Calabash, Yellow Amber, Iron Pontil, Qt. 210.00
McK G XIII-46, Sheaf Of Grain & Tree, Calabash, Aqua, Iron Pontil, Qt. 88.00
McK G XIII-46, Sheaf Of Grain & Tree, Calabash, Cherry Puce, Double Collar, Qt. 1102.00
McK G XIII-46, Sheaf Of Grain & Tree, Calabash, Pink Amethyst, Double Collar, Qt. 420.00
McK G XIII-46, Sheaf Of Grain & Tree, Calabash, Strawberry Puce, Open Pontil, Qt. 1064.00
McK G XIII-46, Sheaf Of Grain & Tree, Calabash, Aqua, Open Pontil, Qt. 119.00
McK G XIII-47, Sheaf Of Grain, Calabash, Forest Green, Open Pontil, Qt. 895.00
McK G XIII-48, Anchor & Sheaf Of Grain, Orange Amber, Pontil, c.1870, Qt. 1232.00
McK G XIII-48, Anchor & Sheaf Of Grain, Yellow Orange, Qt. 1904.00
McK G XIII-49, Anchor & Sheaf Of Grain, Olive Yellow, 1/2 Pt. . . . . .2128.00 to 3080.00
McK G XIII-53, Anchor & Phoenix, Resurgam, Apricot Puce, Applied Sloping Collar, Pt. .   4000.00
McK G XIII-53, Anchor & Phoenix, Resurgam, Aqua, Sheared Mouth, Pontil, Pt. . . .77.00 to 134.00
McK G XIII-53, Anchor & Phoenix, Resurgam, Olive Yellow, Sheared Mouth, Pontil, Pt. .   1904.00
McK G XIII-53, Anchor & Phoenix, Resurgam, Strawberry Puce, Double Collar, Pt. 5040.00
McK G XIII-53, Anchor & Phoenix, Resurgam, Yellow Green, Applied Lip, Pt. 3100.00
McK G XIII-54, Anchor & Phoenix, Resurgam, Amber, Applied Lip, Pt. 448.00
McK G XIII-54, Anchor & Phoenix, Resurgam, Yellow Amber, Double Collar, Pt. . .715.00 to 896.00
McK G XIII-55, Isabella, Anchor & Glasshouse, Aqua, Open Pontil, Qt. 308.00
McK G XIII-56, Isabella, Anchor & Sheaf Of Grain, Aqua, Open Pontil, Pt. 246.00
McK G XIII-57, Isabella, Anchor & Glasshouse, Aqua, Open Pontil, 1/2 Pt. 420.00
McK G XIII-58, Spring Garden & Anchor, Copper Puce, Applied Lip, Pt. 1760.00
McK G XIII-58, Spring Garden & Anchor, Olive Yellow, Pt. 1680.00
McK G XIII-58, Spring Garden & Anchor, Orange Amber, Double Collar, Pt. 1064.00
McK G XIII-59, Spring Garden & Anchor, Olive Yellow, c.1870, Pt. . . . . .3080.00 to 5600.00
McK G XIII-59, Spring Garden & Anchor, Red Puce, Applied Lip, c.1870, Pt. 1792.00
McK G XIII-60, Spring Garden & Anchor, Golden Amber, 1/2 Pt. 990.00
McK G XIII-61, Spring Garden & Anchor, Yellow Amber, Double Collar, 1/2 Pt. 1568.00
McK G XIII-75, Key, Coffin Shape, Aqua, Tooled Lip, c.1885, Pt. 123.00
McK G XIII-79, Safe, Embossed, Light Aqua, Strap Side, Tooled Lip, Qt. 110.00
McK G XIII-83, Star & Ravenna, Aqua Blue, Applied Collar, Pt.   280.00
McK G XIII-88, Merry Christmas, Happy New Year, Yellow Amber, Double Collar, 1/2 Pt.   476.00
McK G XIV-1, Traveler's Companion & Sheaf Of Grain, Olive Amber, Sloping Collar, Qt.   286.00
McK G XIV-1, Traveler's Companion & Sheaf Of Grain, Olive Green, Qt. . . . . . . .269.00 to 317.00
McK G XIV-1, Traveler's Companion & Sheaf Of Grain, Olive Yellow, c.1870, Qt. 280.00
McK G XIV-1, Traveler's Companion & Sheaf Of Grain, Amber, Qt. . . . . .240.00 to 300.00
McK G XIV-1, Traveler's Companion & Star, Amber, Pt. 220.00
McK G XIV-3, Traveler's Companion, Ravenna, Amber, Applied Lip, Pt. 952.00
McK G XIV-3, Traveler's Companion, Ravenna, Aqua, Applied Ring Lip, 1/2 Pt. 190.00
McK G XIV-4, Traveler's Companion, Lancaster, Aqua, Double Collar, Pt. 392.00
McK G XIV-6, Traveler's Companion, Lockport, Blue Green, Pt. 3080.00
McK G XIV-7, Traveler's Companion & Star, Amber, Sheared Mouth, IP, 1/2 Pt. 1568.00
McK G XIV-7, Traveler's Companion & Star, Gold Amber, Iron Pontil, c.1850, 1/2 Pt. 672.00
McK G XIV-7, Traveler's Companion & Star, Red Amber, c.1850, 1/2 Pt. 784.00
McK G XIV-9, Traveler's Companion & Railroad Guide, Aqua, Open Pontil, 1/2 Pt. 504.00
McK G XIV-9, Traveler's Companion & Railroad Guide, Blue Aqua, Pontil, 1/2 Pt. 330.00
McK G XV-1, Clyde Glass Works, N.Y., Amber, Double Collar, Qt. 280.00
McK G XV-7, Granite Glass Co., Stoddard, NH, Amber, Double Collar, c.1870, Pt. 728.00
McK G XV-7, Granite Glass Co., Stoddard, NH, Olive Amber, Sheared, Tooled Lip, Pt. . . .   784.00
McK G XV-7, Granite Glass Co., Stoddard, NH, Olive Yellow, Double Collar, c.1870, Pt. .   560.00
McK G XV-7, Granite Glass Co., Stoddard, NH, Yellow Amber, Open Pontil, Pt. 896.00
McK G XV-8, Granite Glass Co., Stoddard, NH, Yellow Amber, Open Pontil, Pt. 1344.00
McK G XV-13, Louisville Ky Glass Works, Aqua, Applied Collar, Pt. 179.00
McK G XV-23, Union Glass Works, Aqua, Applied Double Collar, Pt. 616.00
McK G XV-28, Zanesville City Glass Works, Aqua, Applied Collar, Pt. . . . . .67.00 to 90.00
McK G XV-28, Zanesville City Glass Works, Red Amber, Applied Collar, Pt. 840.00
McK G XV-28, Zanesville City Glass Works, Yellow Amber, Applied Collar, Pt. 616.00
Melon Ribs, Apple Green, Sheared Mouth, Pontil, Keene, Pt. 660.00
Melon Ribs, Aqua, Sheared Mouth, Open Pontil, Keene, 1/2 Pt. 275.00

Merry Christmas, Plum Tree, Clear, Tooled Lip, Pumpkinseed, c.1890, 4 5/8 In. 143.00
Milk Glass, Octopus Covering Silver Dollar, Painted, Gold, Red, 4 1/2 In. . . . .*Illus* 1120.00
Old No. 12, Sheffield, Gray Green, Seal, 7 3/4 In. 117.00
Pan-American Exposition, Threaded Ground Mouth, Metal Jigger Cap, c.1900, 1/2 Pt. . . . 242.00
Park & Tilford, N.Y., Gold Amber, Strap Side, Pt. 48.00
Persian Saddle, Aqua, Vertical Ribs, Neck Band, Sheared, Tooled Lip, Pontil, 5 1/2 In. . . 67.00
Picnic, Amber, Tooled Lip, Pumpkinseed, 5 3/8 In. 67.00
Pitkin Type, 16 Broken Ribs, Swirled To Right, Emerald Green, Pontil, 6 In. 532.00
Pitkin Type, 16 Broken Ribs, Swirled To Right, Yellow Green, Tooled Lip, Pontil, Pt. . . . 448.00
Pitkin Type, 16 Ribs, Swirled To Right, Forest Green, Sheared Mouth, Pontil, 5 1/2 In. . . 504.00
Pitkin Type, 16 Ribs, Swirled To Right, Green, Sheared Mouth, IP, c.1830, 5 7/8 In. 728.00
Pitkin Type, 16 Ribs, Swirled To Right, Green, Sheared Mouth, Open Pontil, Pt. 550.00
Pitkin Type, 16 Ribs, Swirled To Right, Sea Green, Sheared Mouth, Pontil, 6 7/8 In. 672.00
Pitkin Type, 18 Broken Ribs, Swirled To Right, Olive Green, Tooled Lip, Pontil, 6 1/2 In. 545.00
Pitkin Type, 19 Broken Ribs, Swirled To Right, Olive Green, Tooled Lip, OP, 6 1/2 In. . . . 850.00
Pitkin Type, 20 Broken Ribs, Swirled To Right, Emerald Green, Tooled Lip, OP, Pt. 616.00
Pitkin Type, 24 Broken Ribs, Amber, Sheared Mouth, Open Pontil, 1/2 Pt. 770.00
Pitkin Type, 24 Broken Ribs, Swirled To Right, Aqua, Tooled Lip, Open Pontil, 6 5/8 In. . 240.00
Pitkin Type, 24 Ribs, Swirled To Left, Green, Inward Rolled Lip, Pontil, 6 5/8 In. 672.00
Pitkin Type, 24 Ribs, Swirled To Left, Sheared Mouth, Pontil, 6 5/8 In. 3360.00
Pitkin Type, 24 Ribs, Swirled To Right, Amber, 6 1/2 In. 600.00
Pitkin Type, 24 Ribs, Swirled To Right, Forest Green, Sheared Mouth, Pontil, 6 1/4 In. . . 1344.00
Pitkin Type, 24 Ribs, Swirled To Right, Green, Sheared Mouth, Pontil, 6 In. . . . . .476.00 to 616.00
Pitkin Type, 24 Ribs, Swirled To Right, Green, Sheared Mouth, Pontil, c.1815, 5 3/4 In. . . 1008.00
Pitkin Type, 30 Broken Ribs, Swirled To Left, Emerald, Tooled Lip, Pontil, 6 3/8 In. 220.00
Pitkin Type, 30 Broken Ribs, Swirled To Right, Emerald Green, Pontil, 6 5/8 In. 476.00
Pitkin Type, 30 Broken Ribs, Swirled To Right, Green, Sheared Mouth, OP, 6 5/8 In. 636.00
Pitkin Type, 30 Ribs, Swirled To Left, Forest Green, Sheared Mouth, c.1830, 6 1/2 In. . . . 952.00
Pitkin Type, 30 Ribs, Swirled To Right, Aqua, Sheared Mouth, 6 1/8 In. 420.00
Pitkin Type, 31 Broken Ribs, Swirled To Left, Olive Green, Sheared Mouth, OP, 6 1/4 In. 728.00
Pitkin Type, 31 Ribs, Forest Green, Sheared Mouth, Pontil, 6 In. 952.00
Pitkin Type, 31 Ribs, Swirled To Left, Yellow Green, Sheared Mouth, Pontil, 6 5/8 In. . . . 532.00
Pitkin Type, 32 Broken Ribs, Swirled To Left, Green, Pt., 7 1/4 In. 825.00
Pitkin Type, 32 Broken Ribs, Swirled To Left, Olive Yellow, Tooled Lip, OP, 5 1/4 In. . . . 725.00
Pitkin Type, 32 Broken Ribs, Swirled To Right, Aqua, Sheared Mouth, Pontil, Pt. 303.00
Pitkin Type, 32 Broken Ribs, Swirled To Right, Yellow Green, Pontil, 6 1/4 In. 630.00
Pitkin Type, 32 Ribs, Swirled To Left, Green, c.1815, 7 7/8 x 4 1/2 In. 728.00
Pitkin Type, 32 Ribs, Swirled To Left, Olive Yellow, Sheared Mouth, Pontil, 6 3/4 In. . . . 1008.00
Pitkin Type, 32 Ribs, Swirled To Right, Green, Sheared Mouth, Pontil, c.1820, 7 1/4 In. . . 672.00
Pitkin Type, 32 Ribs, Swirled To Right, Olive Yellow, Sheared Mouth, Pontil, 4 5/8 In. . . 2240.00
Pitkin Type, 32 Ribs, Swirled To Right, Sea Green, Sheared Mouth, Pontil, 6 3/4 In. 784.00
Pitkin Type, 36 Broken Ribs, Olive Citron, Sheared Mouth, Half Post, Pontil, 1/2 Pt. 715.00
Pitkin Type, 36 Broken Ribs, Swirled To Left, Gold Amber, Open Pontil, 6 In. 1008.00
Pitkin Type, 36 Broken Ribs, Swirled To Left, Green, Pontil, c.1825, 6 1/2 In. 650.00
Pitkin Type, 36 Broken Ribs, Swirled To Left, Olive Green, Tooled Lip, Pontil, 6 3/8 In. . 756.00
Pitkin Type, 36 Broken Ribs, Swirled To Right, Olive Amber, Flattened Oval, 6 3/4 In. . . 358.00
Pitkin Type, 36 Broken Ribs, Swirled To Right, Olive Yellow, Tooled Lip, OP, 5 3/8 In. . . 860.00
Pitkin Type, 36 Broken Ribs, Swirled, Amber, Sheared Mouth, Pontil, 6 In. 605.00
Pitkin Type, 36 Ribs, Citron, Oblong, Sheared Mouth, Open Pontil, Pt. 770.00
Pitkin Type, 36 Ribs, Swirled To Left, Amber, Sheared Mouth, Pontil, 5 7/8 In. 1232.00
Pitkin Type, 36 Ribs, Swirled To Left, Olive Yellow, Pontil, c.1800, 5 3/4 In. 952.00
Pitkin Type, 36 Ribs, Swirled To Left, Olive Yellow, Sheared Mouth, Pontil, 6 In. 840.00
Pitkin Type, 36 Ribs, Swirled To Left, Yellow Amber, Tooled Lip, OP, 6 In. 728.00
Pitkin Type, 36 Ribs, Swirled To Right, Forest Green, Sheared Mouth, Pontil, 5 In. 1064.00
Pitkin Type, 36 Ribs, Swirled To Right, Olive Yellow, Pontil, 5 1/8 In. . . . . .616.00 to 1064.00
Pitkin Type, 36 Ribs, Swirled To Right, Olive Yellow, Pontil, c.1810, 4 3/4 In. 1456.00
Pitkin Type, 36 Ribs, Swirled To Right, Olive Yellow, Tooled Lip, OP, 5 1/4 In. 840.00
Pitkin Type, 36 Ribs, Turquoise, Flattened Oval, Sheared Mouth, Pontil, Pt. 440.00
Pitkin Type, Olive Yellow, Sheared Mouth, Open Pontil, Pt. 64250.00
Pitkin Type, Swirls, Light Olive Green, Open Pontil, 1/2 Pt. 412.00
Pocket Spirits, Bear, Trees, I.B., Wreath, Rolled Lip, Pontil, 1851, 4 1/8 In. 146.00
Red Amber, Coin Spot, Beveled Corner Panels, Rectangular, 6 1/2 In. 1568.00

Saloon, Dan Donahoe, Marysville, Cal., Pt. 500.00
Sapphire Blue, White Loopings, Cone Shape, Pewter Mouth, Pontil, Germany, 6 1/4 In. ... 2352.00
Soldier, Fanny Essler Portrait, Light Gray Topaz, Maryland Glassworks, c.1850 .... 8400.00
Spirits, Lavender, Hobnail, Flattened Chestnut, Pontil, 3 5/8 In. 308.00
Stiegel Type, Multicolored Enamel Flowers, Pontil, Pewter Screw Collar, 5 5/8 In. 190.00
Stiegel Type, Teal Green, Diamond Diaper, Flattened Globular, Pocket, 5 1/4 In. 440.00
Stoddard, Red Amber, Pt. 29.00
Stoddard Type, Orange Amber, 1/2 Pt. 17.00
Stoddard Type, Orange Amber, Hagerty Glassworks, N.Y., Qt. 79.00
Stoddard Type, Red Amber, Qt. 29.00
Stoddard Type, Yellow Amber, Applied Sloping Collar, Pontil, 1/2 Pt. 784.00
Stoddard Type, Yellow, Pt. 39.00
Strap Side, Amber, Vertical Ribs, 1/2 Pt. 29.00
Strap Side, Aqua, Embossed Safe Inside Circle, 1/2 Pt. 48.00
Strap Side, Aqua, Embossed Safe Inside Circle, Qt. 79.00
Strap Side, Blue Aqua, Embossed Star In Circle, Pt. 24.00
Strap Side, Blue Aqua, Vertical Ribs, Pt. 29.00
Strap Side, Dark Amber, Ground Lip, Screw Cap, Pt. 56.00
Strap Side, Gold Amber, Anchor, 1/2 Pt. 45.00
Strap Side, Gold Amber, Anchor, Pt. 45.00
Strap Side, Gold Amber, Vertical Ribs, 1/2 Pt. 20.00
Strap Side, Olive Yellow, A. & D.H.C., Applied Ring Collar, Qt. 168.00
Strap Side, Orange Amber, Embossed Star In Circle, Pt. .... 24.00 to 39.00
Strap Side, Yellow, Double Collar, 1/2 Pt., 6 In. 12.00
Teardrop, Yellow Amber, Tooled Lip, Bubbles, Pontil, 7 In. 110.00
The Dandy, Clear, Ribbed Shoulder, Pumpkinseed, Pt. 39.00
Travel, Gold Amber, 8-Point Star, Applied Double Collar, Pontil, Pt. 392.00
W.M. Watson & Co., Pumpkinseed, 1/2 Pt. 220.00
Walsh & Beck, Pumpkinseed, 1/2 Pt. 605.00
Warranted, B. Bischoff, Gold Amber, Strap Side, Qt. 90.00
Warranted, Dark Amber, Strap Side, Qt. 20.00
Warranted, Gold Amber, Qt. 25.00
Warranted, R.L. Christian & Co., Clear, Strap Side, 1/2 Pt. 202.00
Wheat Price & Co., Fairview Works, Blue Green, Sheared Mouth, Pontil, Pt. 19040.00
Williams, Yesler Way & Occidental Ave, Seattle, Amethyst Tint, Pumpkinseed, 1/2 Pt. ... 200.00
Wormser Bros., San Francisco, Amber, Double Roll Collar, 8 1/2 In. 1320.00
Yellow Green, Honeycomb Diamond Diaper, 14 Rows, Rolled Lip, Pt., 7 3/4 In. 715.00

--- FOOD ---

Food bottles include all of the many grocery store containers, such as those for catsup, horseradish, jelly, and other foodstuffs. Vinegar bottles and a few other special bottles are listed under their own headings.

Abbey's Effervescent Salt, Shakespeare, Square, Contents, Pamphlet, Box, 3 1/2 In. 248.00
Ann Page Lemon Extract, Brown, Box 15.00
As You Like It Horse-Radish, Ceramic, Crock, Cover, Weir Patent 92, 4 1/4 In. ....75.00 to 125.00
Better Than Kimball's Peanut Creme, Delicious, Trademark, No Lid, 1/2 Pt. 15.00
Bireley's Juice, Color Added, Embossed, Round, 6 3/4 Oz. 3.00
Blueberry Preserve, Jar, Willington Glass Works, Olive Yellow, 1860-72, 11 1/8 In. 2016.00
Borden, Elsie The Cow, Jug, Red, 1954, 1/2 Gal. 20.00
Borden, Malted Milk, Jar, Glass Label, Embossed Lid 660.00
Borden's Malted Milk, Jar, Lid, Label, 9 In. 330.00
California Perfume Co., see Avon, California Perfume Co.
Candy Jar, Cover, Gum Drops, Black & Gold Letters, Bulbous, Pedestal Base, 19 In. 1870.00
Candy Jar, Cover, Horehound, Black & Gold Letters, Bulbous, Pedestal Base, 20 In. 880.00
Candy Jar, Cover, Lemon Drops, Black & Gold Letters, Bulbous, Pedestal Base, 19 In. .. 1320.00
Candy Jar, Cover, Licorice, Black & Gold Letters, Bulbous, Pedestal Base, 19 In. 660.00 to 1760.00
Candy Jar, Cover, Taffy, Black & Gold Letters, Bulbous, Pedestal Base, 20 In. 930.00
Candy Jar, Olive Green, Cylindrical, 13 1/4 In. 330.00
Candy Jar, Olive Green, Stopper, 15 1/2 In. 300.00
Candy Jar, Reed's Patties, Olive Green, Embossed, Lid, 11 1/4 In. 83.00
Chicos Peanut Butter, Metal Base, Lid, c.1900, 11 In. 495.00
Donald Duck Chili Sauce, Paper Labels, Salesman Sample, 7 In. 99.00

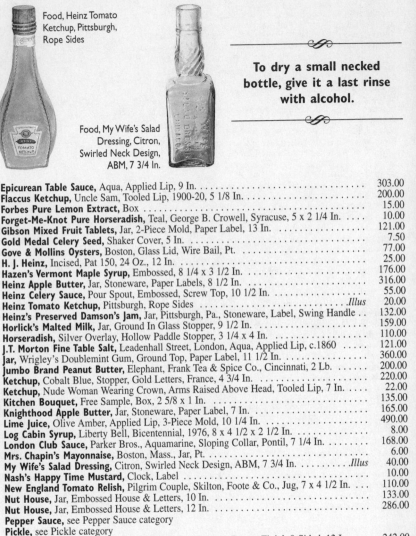

Food, Heinz Tomato
Ketchup, Pittsburgh,
Rope Sides

Food, My Wife's Salad
Dressing, Citron,
Swirled Neck Design,
ABM, 7 3/4 In.

**To dry a small necked
bottle, give it a last rinse
with alcohol.**

Epicurean Table Sauce, Aqua, Applied Lip, 9 In.	303.00
Flaccus Ketchup, Uncle Sam, Tooled Lip, 1900-20, 5 1/8 In.	200.00
Forbes Pure Lemon Extract, Box	15.00
Forget-Me-Knot Pure Horseradish, Teal, George B. Crowell, Syracuse, 5 x 2 1/4 In.	10.00
Gibson Mixed Fruit Tablets, Jar, 2-Piece Mold, Paper Label, 13 In.	121.00
Gold Medal Celery Seed, Shaker Cover, 5 In.	7.50
Gove & Mollins Oysters, Boston, Glass Lid, Wire Bail, Pt.	77.00
H. J. Heinz, Incised, Pat 150, 24 Oz., 12 In.	25.00
Hazen's Vermont Maple Syrup, Embossed, 8 1/4 x 3 1/2 In.	176.00
Heinz Apple Butter, Jar, Stoneware, Paper Labels, 8 1/2 In.	316.00
Heinz Celery Sauce, Pour Spout, Embossed, Screw Top, 10 1/2 In.	55.00
Heinz Tomato Ketchup, Pittsburgh, Rope Sides ....*Illus*	20.00
Heinz's Preserved Damson's Jam, Jar, Pittsburgh, Pa., Stoneware, Label, Swing Handle	132.00
Horlick's Malted Milk, Jar, Ground In Glass Stopper, 9 1/2 In.	159.00
Horseradish, Silver Overlay, Hollow Paddle Stopper, 3 1/4 x 4 In.	110.00
J.T. Morton Fine Table Salt, Leadenhall Street, London, Aqua, Applied Lip, c.1860	121.00
Jar, Wrigley's Doublemint Gum, Ground Top, Paper Label, 11 1/2 In.	360.00
Jumbo Brand Peanut Butter, Elephant, Frank Tea & Spice Co., Cincinnati, 2 Lb.	200.00
Ketchup, Cobalt Blue, Stopper, Gold Letters, France, 4 3/4 In.	220.00
Ketchup, Nude Woman Wearing Crown, Arms Raised Above Head, Tooled Lip, 7 In.	22.00
Kitchen Bouquet, Free Sample, Box, 2 5/8 x 1 In.	135.00
Knighthood Apple Butter, Jar, Stoneware, Paper Label, 7 In.	165.00
Lime Juice, Olive Amber, Applied Lip, 3-Piece Mold, 10 1/4 In.	490.00
Log Cabin Syrup, Liberty Bell, Bicentennial, 1976, 8 x 4 1/2 x 2 1/2 In.	8.00
London Club Sauce, Parker Bros., Aquamarine, Sloping Collar, Pontil, 7 1/4 In.	168.00
Mrs. Chapin's Mayonnaise, Boston, Mass., Jar, Pt.	6.00
My Wife's Salad Dressing, Citron, Swirled Neck Design, ABM, 7 3/4 In. ....*Illus*	40.00
Nash's Happy Time Mustard, Clock, Label	10.00
New England Tomato Relish, Pilgrim Couple, Skilton, Foote & Co., Jug, 7 x 4 1/2 In.	110.00
Nut House, Jar, Embossed House & Letters, 10 In.	133.00
Nut House, Jar, Embossed House & Letters, 12 In.	286.00
Pepper Sauce, see Pepper Sauce category	
Pickle, see Pickle category	
Planters Peanuts, 5 Cent, Embossed Images & Letters, Peanut Finial, 8-Sided, 12 In.	242.00
Planters Peanuts, Barrel, Embossed Mr. Peanut, Letters, Peanut Finial, 12 In. ....385.00 to 440.00	
Planters Peanuts, Blown-Out Peanut Corners, Embossed Letters, 14 In.	165.00
Planters Peanuts, Decal, Peanut Finial, 12 In.	143.00
Planters Peanuts, Embossed Letters, Peanut Finial, Square, 10 In.	60.00
Planters Peanuts, Yellow Letters & Mr. Peanut Figures, 6-Sided, 10 In.	77.00
Roses Lime Juice, Cylindrical, Embossed, Leaves, Fruit, Vines, Brown, England, 13 In.	59.00
Roy Rogers Molasses Barbecue Sauce, Montana Beef Council, Amber, Paper Label, 8 In.	150.00
Sea Gull Baking Powder, Green, Sea Gull Specialty Co., 4 1/2 In.	10.00
Shriver's Oyster Ketchup, Baltimore, Lime Green, 7 1/2 In.	1430.00
Shriver's Oyster Ketchup, Baltimore, Olive Yellow, Applied Lip, Iron Pontil, c.1860, 7 In.	1073.00
Sleggs Toboggan Ginger, Lime, Cylindrical, 4 1/2 In.	25.00
Storage, Blue Aqua, Green Tone, Wide Mouth, Flared Lip, Pontil, 8 3/4 x 6 In.	364.00

Storage, Green, Amber, Applied, Folded Top, Pontil, 8 1/4 In.	55.00
Storage, Olive Amber, Tooled Lip, Pontil, 1790-1830, 7 1/8 In.	2576.00
Storage, Olive Green, Applied Lip, Pontil, 1730-50, 8 1/4 x 4 3/4 In.	88.00
Storage, Olive Green, Applied Top, Pontil, Stoddard, 8 1/2 In.	33.00
Storage, Olive Green, High Shoulder, Flared Lip, Open Pontil, 1820-50, 12 1/2 x 6 3/4 In.	182.00
Storage, Olive Green, Yellow Tone, Wide Mouth, Tooled Rim, Pontil, 8 1/4 In.	785.00
Storage, Olive Yellow Amber, Wide Mouth, Outward Rolled Lip, Stoddard, 8 5/8 In.	3080.00
Storage, Olive Yellow Amber, Wide Mouth, Tooled Flattened Lip, Pontil, 5 7/8 In.	3360.00
Storage, Olive Yellow Green, Tooled Lip, Pontil, 13 3/4 x 5 1/2 In.	168.00
Storage, Olive Yellow, Applied Ring Mouth, Pontil Scar, Square, 4 7/8 x 2 1/8 In.	1568.00
Storage, Red Amber, Wide Mouth, Tooled Rim, Bubbles, Swirls, Pontil, 8 1/4 In.	1905.00
Storage, Ruby Red, Wide Mouth, Flattened Flared-Out Lip, 9 3/4 In.	364.00
Storage, Tobacco Amber, Wide Mouth, Tooled Flared Rim, Pontil, Stoddard, 8 5/8 In.	5310.00
Storage, Yellow Amber, Bubbles, Tooled Flared Wide Mouth, Pontil, 8 3/8 In.	392.00
Storage, Yellow Green, Tooled Flared Wide Mouth, Pontil, Continental, 11 In.	202.00
Su Su Salted Nuts, Jar, Hinged Aluminum Hatch Door, 12 In.	121.00
Sunsweet Prune Juice, Green, c.1925, Qt., 7 In.	27.50
Towle Maple Products Co., Blue, Cover, 22 Oz.	150.00
Virginia Fruit Juice Company, Pear Shape, ABM, 7 1/4 In.	10.00
W.J. Taylor & Co. Sauce, Manchester, Brittania Picture, Aqua, Sheared Mouth, 5 In.	42.00
Wells Miller & Provost, 8 Rounded Panels, Cobalt Blue, Open Pontil, 8 1/8 In.	728.00
Wells Miller & Provost, Squat, 8-Sided, Scalloped, Applied Lip, 8 1/4 In.	88.00
White House Vinegar, Crackled, Cabbage Rose Pattern, Handles, Cork Stopper, 9 1/2 In. .	30.00
Wm. Underwood & Co., Boston, Blue Aqua, 3-Piece Mold, Sloping Collar, IP, 11 In.	213.00
Zetril Lime Fruit Squash, L. Rose & Co., Limes, Vines, Aqua, England, c.1900, 9 3/4 In.	25.00

───────────── **FRUIT JAR** ─────────────

Fruit jars made of glass have been used in the United States since the 1850s. More than 1,000 different jars have been found with varieties of closures, embossing, and colors. The date 1858 on many jars refers to a patent and not the age of the bottle. Be sure to look in this listing under any name or initial that appears on your jar. If not otherwise indicated, the jar listed is of clear glass and quart size. The numbers used in the entries in the form RB-0 refer to the book *Red Book of Fruit Jars Number 9* by Douglas M. Leybourne Jr. A publication for collectors is *Fruit Jar Newsletter,* 364 Gregory Avenue, West Orange, NJ 07052-3743.

I On Base, Amber, Groove Ring, Wax Sealer, Tin Lid, Qt., RB-3047	112.00
A. & D.H. Chambers Union, Pittsburgh, Olive Yellow, Wax Sealer, Qt., 7 5/8 In., RB-582 .	990.00
A. Kline, Pat'd Oct. 27 1863, Stopper, Aqua, Pt., RB-1423	85.00
A. Stone & Co., Philada, Aqua, Threaded Glass Stopper, Qt., RB-2748	400.00
A. Stone & Co., Philada, Aqua, Wax Sealer, 9 3/4 In., RB-2752	1320.00
A.G. Smalley & Co. Boston, Mass., Patented 1896 & 1986, Amber, Qt., RB-2645 . . . .60.00 to 75.00	
Acme, On Shield With Stars & Stripes, Qt., RB-12	2.00
Acme, On Shield With Stars & Stripes, Smoke, 1/2 Gal., RB-12	25.00
Air-Tight Fruit Jar, Aqua, Barrel Shape, Applied Wax Sealer, Lid, Qt., RB-51-2	750.00
All Right, Patd Jan 25th 1868, Aqua, 1/2 Gal., RB-58	200.00
All Right, Patd Jan 26th 1868, Aqua, Ground Lip, Metal Lid, 7 3/4 In., RB-59	110.00
All Right, Patd Jan 28th 1868, Aqua, Metal Lid, 7 1/4 In., RB-61-3	88.00
All Right, Patd Jan 28th 1868, Aqua, Tin Lid, Clamp, Qt., RB-61-3	425.00
All Right, Patd Jan 28th 1868, Aqua, Wire Closure, Qt., RB-58	90.00
Almy, Aqua, Patented Dec. 25, 1877, Star, Screw Lid, 7 In., RB-63	99.00
Alston, Aqua, No Pulp Disk, Qt., RB-65	500.00
Amazon Swift Seal, In Circle, Blue, 1/2 Gal., RB-69	22.00
Amazon Swift Seal, In Circle, Blue, Pt., RB-69	22.00
American, Nag, Porcelain Lined, Aqua, Registered, Zinc Lid, Midget, RB-75	225.00
Arthur's Patent Jan 2 1855, Pottery, Yellow Ware, Wax Sealer, Qt., RB-97-6	800.00
Atlas E-Z Seal, 1/2 Gal., RB-109	2.00
Atlas E-Z Seal, 1/2 Pt., RB-109	3.00
Atlas E-Z Seal, Amber, Qt., RB-114	65.00
Atlas E-Z Seal, Aqua, 1/2 Gal, RB-109	7.00
Atlas E-Z Seal, Aqua, 1/2 Pt., RB-121	20.00
Atlas E-Z Seal, Aqua, Pt., RB-109	5.50
Atlas E-Z Seal, Aqua, Qt., RB-109	3.00 to 5.50
Atlas E-Z Seal, Blue, 1/2 Gal., RB-109	20.00

Atlas E-Z Seal, Blue, Pt., RB-109 . . . . 15.00
Atlas E-Z Seal, Blue, Qt., RB-109 . . . . 15.00
Atlas E-Z Seal, Green, 1/2 Gal, RB-109 . . . . 23.00
Atlas E-Z Seal, Green, Pt., RB-109 . . . . .15.00 to 18.00
Atlas Good Luck, 1/2 Pt., RB-131 . . . . 18.00
Atlas HA Mason, Qt., RB-135 . . . . 5.00
Atlas HA Mason Miniature, Slotted Bank Lid, 1/2 Pt., RB-133 . . . . .15.00 to 25.00
Atlas Junior Mason, 2/3 Pt., RB-139 . . . . .10.00 to 18.00
Atlas Mason, HA In Stippled Circle, Qt., RB-134 . . . . 2.00
Atlas Mason Patent, Aqua, Pt., RB-151 . . . . 4.00
Atlas Mason Patent Nov 30 1858, Aqua, 1/2 Gal., RB-154-2 . . . . 9.00
Atlas Mason's Patent, Apple Green, Qt., RB-151 . . . . 20.00
Atlas Mason's Patent, Cornflower Blue, Cap, Pt., RB-151 . . . . 25.00
Atlas Strong Shoulder Mason, 2-Piece Lid, 1/4 Pt., RB-162 . . . . 25.00
Atlas Strong Shoulder Mason, Apple Green, Qt., RB-164 . . . . .15.00 to 20.00
Atlas Strong Shoulder Mason, Olive Green, Pt., RB-164 . . . . 45.00
Atlas Strong Shoulder Mason, Olive Green, Qt., RB-164 . . . . 25.00
Atlas Wholefruit, 1/2 Gal., RB-170 . . . . 2.00
Atlas Wholefruit, Pt., RB-170 . . . . .2.00 to 4.00
Atlas Wholefruit, Qt., RB-170 . . . . 2.00
Atlas-Mason's Patent, Apple Green, Pt., RB-150 . . . . 35.00
Atlas-Mason's Patent, Apple Green, Qt., RB-150 . . . . 20.00
Atlas-Mason's Patent, Aqua, Pt., RB-150 . . . . 3.00
Atlas-Mason's Patent, Green, Qt., RB-150 . . . . 20.00
Atlas-Mason's Patent, Olive Green, Pt., RB-150 .16.00 to 35.00
Atlas-Mason's Patent, Olive Green, Qt., RB-150 . . . . 25.00
Atlas-Strong Shoulder Mason, Aqua, Pt., RB-161 . . . . 2.00
Atlas-Strong Shoulder Mason, Cornflower Blue, Pt., RB-161 . . . . 25.00
Atlas-Strong Shoulder Mason, Olive Green, Pt., RB-161 . . . . 35.00
Automatic Sealer, Aqua, Qt., RB-177 . . . . 250.00
Automatic Sealer, Aqua, Reproduction Wires, 1/2 Gal., RB-177 . . . . 300.00
B & B, Amber, Strap Clamp, Label, Qt., RB-181-1 . . . . 75.00
B & B, Fancy Script On Base, Amber, Lid, Clamp, 1/2 Pt., RB-181 . . . . 35.00
B. T. & Co., On Base, Aqua, Qt., RB-1875-7 . . . . .60.00 to 85.00
Ball, Script, Dropped A, Pat. Apl'd For, Aqua, 1/2 Gal., RB-267 . . . . 500.00
Ball, Script, Dropped A, Pat. Apl'd For, Aqua, Reproduction Closure, Qt., RB-267 . . 200.00
Ball 3 Tapered Mason, Pt., RB-321 . . . . 53.00
Ball 4, Made In U.S.A, Tapered, 1/2 Pt., RB-201-8 . . . . 23.00
Ball Eclipse Base Patent 7-14-08, Pt., RB-196-5 . . . . 4.00
Ball Eclipse Base Patent 7-14-08, Qt., RB-196-5 . . . . 4.00
Ball Eclipse Wide Mouth, 1/2 Gal., RB-199 . . . . .6.00 to 15.00
Ball Eclipse Wide Mouth, Pt., RB-199 . . . . 1.00
Ball Eclipse Wide Mouth, Qt., RB-199 . . . . 1.00
Ball Freezer Jar, 10 Oz., RB-201-1 . . . . .2.00 to 4.00
Ball Freezer Jar, 16 Oz., RB-201-1 . . . . .2.00 to 4.00
Ball Ideal, B On Base, 1/3 Pt., RB-204-1 . . . . .4.00 to 8.00
Ball Ideal, B On Base, Made In U.S.A, Dipple Neck, 1/3 Pt., RB-213 . . . . 4.00
Ball Ideal, Bicentennial Medallion, Edmund F. Ball, Sample, Qt., RB-349-5 . . . . 300.00
Ball Ideal, Blue, Round, 1/2 Gal., RB-204 . . . . 12.00
Ball Ideal, Bust Of Fisher, Fisher Years, Script, 1941-1986, Qt., RB-350-5 . . . . 50.00
Ball Ideal, Dimple Neck, 1/2 Gal., RB-204-5 . . . . .3.00 to 5.00
Ball Ideal, Dropped A, 1/2 Pt., RB-202 . . . . 85.00
Ball Ideal, Dropped A, Blue, Pt., RB-203-5-1 . . . . .35.00 to 50.00
Ball Ideal, Dropped A, Blue, Round, 1/2 Gal., RB-202 . . . . 12.00
Ball Ideal, Dropped A, Round, 1/2 Gal., RB-202 . . . . 3.00
Ball Ideal, Round Dipple Neck, 1/2 Pt., RB-215-5 . . . . 4.00
Ball Ideal, Square, Pt., RB-204-5 . . . . .3.00 to 4.00
Ball Ideal Pat'd July 14 1908, 1/2 Pt., RB-203 . . . . 10.00
Ball Ideal Pat'd July 14 1908, Blue, 1/2 Gal., RB-212-5 . . . . 12.00
Ball Ideal Pat'd July 14 1908, Blue, Pt., RB-206 . . . . 5.00
Ball Ideal Pat'd July 14 1908, Blue, Qt., RB-212-5 . . . . 10.00
Ball Ideal Pat'd July 14 1908, Light Green, Qt., RB-206 . . . . 6.00
Ball Ideal Pat'd July 14 1908, Pt., RB-206 . . . . .2.00 to 5.00

Ball Improved, 3-L Dropped A, Blue, 1/2 Gal., RB-219 .... 15.00
Ball Improved, 3-L Loop, Dropped A, Aqua, Pt., RB-219 ....9.00 to 12.00
Ball Improved, Dropped A, Pt., RB-219 ....9.00 to 12.00
Ball Improved, Script, Blue, Pt., RB-220-6 ....7.00 to 12.00
Ball Improved Mason, 3-L Loop, Dropped A, Aqua, Pt., RB-226 .... 7.00
Ball Mason, Dropped A, Blue, Pt., RB-239 ....2.00 to 4.00
Ball Mason, Script, Dropped A, Apple Green, 1/2 Gal., RB-239 .... 30.00
Ball Mason, Script, Dropped A, Apple Green, Qt., RB-239 .... 25.00
Ball Mason, Script, Dropped A, Aqua, 1/2 Gal., RB-239 ....4.00 to 10.00
Ball Mason's Patent 1858, Aqua, Pt., RB-253 ....8.00 to 15.00
Ball Perfect Mason, 8 Ribs, Blue, Pt., RB-278 .... 9.00
Ball Perfect Mason, 9 Ribs, Blue, 1/2 Gal., RB-288 .... 15.00
Ball Perfect Mason, Amber, 6 Gripper Ribs, 1/2 Gal., RB-293-5 .... 45.00
Ball Perfect Mason, Blue, Square, Qt., RB-277-5 .... 10.00
Ball Perfect Mason, Dropped A, Amber, Qt., RB-274 .... 500.00
Ball Perfect Mason, Dropped A, Blue, 40 Oz., RB-274 .... 23.00
Ball Perfect Mason, Dropped A, Blue, 64 Oz., RB-274 .... 8.00
Ball Perfect Mason, Dropped A, Blue, 1/2 Pt., RB-274 .... 150.00
Ball Perfect Mason, Dropped A, Olive Amber, Qt., RB-274 .... 250.00
Ball Perfect Mason, Offset Right, Emerald, Qt., RB-272 .... 75.00
Ball Perfect Mason, Over Boyd, Aqua, Pt., RB-270-5 .... 12.00
Ball Perfect Mason, Over Boyd, Aqua, Qt., RB-270-5 .... 12.00
Ball Perfect Mason, Over Boyd, Green, Pt., RB-270-5 .... 18.00
Ball Perfect Mason, Straight Ls, No Italics, Blue, Qt., RB-270-5 .... 10.00
Ball Perfect Mason Distinct, Dual Embossing, Qt., RB-280-5 .... 60.00
Ball R Ideal, Medallion With Eagle & Star, Blue, 1/2 Pt., RB-349 .... 20.00
Ball R Mason, Fruit Medallion, Sculptured, No Threads, Pt., RB-368-5 ...... 8.00
Ball R Mason, John Ketchem, 40 Yrs & Counting, Threadless, Pt., RB-363-1 .. 30.00
Ball R Mason, Sailboat, Happy Sailing, Addison B. Scholes, 1963-1984, Pt., RB-364-1 ... 28.00
Ball R Script Over 12 Stippled Panels, Juice, 26 Oz., RB-191-5 .... 5.00
Ball Refrigerator & Freezer Jar, 13 Oz., RB-297-2 .... 200.00
Ball Sanitary Sure Seal, Blue, Qt., RB-298 .... 5.00
Ball Special, 8 Ribs, Square, Pt., RB-308 .... 5.00
Ball Sure Seal, 3-L Loop, Aqua, Regular Mouth, 1/2 Gal., RB9, No. 315-5 .... 50.00
Ball Sure Seal, Blue, 1/2 Gal., RB-317 .... 12.00
Ball Sure Seal, Blue, Pt., RB-317 .... 2.00
Ball Sure Seal, Blue, Qt., RB-317 .... 2.00
Ball Sure Seal, Blue, Wide Mouth, 1/2 Pt., RB-317 .... 125.00
Banner, Patd Feby 9th 1864, Press Down Glass Lid, Qt., RB-403 .... 132.00
Banner Encircled By Patent Dated, Aqua, 1/2 Gal., RB-403 .... 175.00
Banner Encircled By Patent Dated, Aqua, Qt., RB-403 .... 175.00
Banner In Stippled Banner, 1/2 Pt., RB-404 .... 150.00
BBGM Co, Amber, Qt., RB-340 .... 33.00
Beaver, Below Beaver Chewing Log, Citron, Amber Lid, Qt., RB-425 .... 2200.00
Beaver, Facing Right, Aqua, Glass Lid, Zinc Band, 1/2 Gal., RB-424 .... 162.00
Bernardin Mason, Excellent For Jelly, 1/2 Pt., RB-452 .... 50.00
Bernardin Underlined Mason, Pt., RB-451 .... 10.00
Bloeser Jar, Aqua, Glass Lid, Wire & Metal Clamp, Neck Wire, Qt., RB-468 .. 88.00
Bloeser Jar, Aqua, Qt. 365.00
Bosco Double Seal, Pt., RB-485 .... 40.00
Boston Trade Mark Dagger Brand, Australia, Green, Qt., RB-486 .... 250.00
Brockway Clear Vu Mason, Glass Insert, Qt., RB-514 .... 1.00
C F Spencer's Patent, Rochester, N.Y., Aqua, 1/2 Gal., RB-2682 .... 100.00
Canadian Jewel, Made In Canada, 1/2 Gal., RB-1331 ....8.00 to 15.00
Canadian Jewel, Made In Canada, Pt., RB-1331 .... 8.00
Canadian Jewel, Made In Canada, Qt., RB-1331 .... 4.00
Canadian Mason Jar, Made In Canada, Fabriquee Au Canada, 1/2 Gal., RB-556-1 ...... 6.00
Canadian Mason Jar, Made In Canada, Fabriquee Au Canada, Qt., RB-556-1 .. 1.00
Canadian Mason Jar, Made In Canada, Pt., RB-556 .... 2.00
Canton Domestic, Cobalt Blue, Swirls, Clear Lid, Original Wire, Qt., RB-565 .. 7000.00
Canton Fruit Jar, 1/2 Gal., RB-561 .... 135.00
CFJCo., see Fruit Jar, Mason's CFJCo.
Champion Pat. Aug. 31, 1869, Aqua, Reproduction Clamp, Qt., RB-583 ..... 200.00

Chef's Trademark, Stipple Frame, 1/2 Pt., RB-589-1 .... *Illus*   125.00
Chicago, Aqua Lid, Qt., RB-592-1 .... 225.00
Clyde, Cover, RB-619, Pt. 15.00
Cohansey, Arched, Aqua, 1/2 Gal., RB-628 .... 50.00
Cohansey, Arched, Aqua, 1/2 Pt., RB-628 .... 300.00
Cohansey, Arched, Aqua, Qt., RB-628 .... 40.00
Cohansey Glass Mf'g Co., Pat. Mch 20 77, Barrel Shape, Tin Lid, Aqua, Qt., RB-633 .... 175.00
Cohansey Glass Mfg. Co., Pat. Feb. 12 1867, Cover, Aqua, Pt., RB-630 ... 90.00
Commonwealth Fruit Jar, 1/2 Gal., RB-650 .... 98.00
Corona Jar, Made In Canada, Pt., RB-655 .... 3.00
Coronet, Crown Emblem, Erased Crown Clear, 1/2 Gal., RB-658 .... 165.00
Coronet, Crown Emblem, Sun Colored Amethyst, Pt., RB-657 .... 200.00
Crown, Crown Emblem, Apple Green, Clear Insert, Qt., RB-686 .... 25.00
Crown, Crown Emblem, Aqua, 1/2 Gal., RB-686 .... 7.00
Crown, Crown Emblem, Aqua, Aqua Insert, Qt., RB-684-1 ....12.00 to 15.00
Crown, Crown Emblem, Aqua, Pt., RB-686 ....4.00 to 6.00
Crown, Crown Emblem, Ring Crown, Aqua, 1/2 Gal., RB-680 ....17.00 to 20.00
Crown, Crown Emblem, The T. Eaton Co. Limited, Toronto & Winnipeg, Qt., RB-691 ... 20.00
Crown, Made In Canada, Crown Emblem, Half Imperial Pt., RB-696-1 .... 15.00
Crown, T. Eaton Co. Limited, Toronto & Winnipeg, Midget, RB-691 .... 125.00
Crown Cordial & Extract Co., New York, 1/2 Gal., RB-671 .... 12.00
Crown Cordial & Extract Co., New York, Aqua, 1/2 Gal., RB-671 ....18.00 to 25.00
Crown Imperial, Crown Emblem, Aqua, Qt., RB-694 .... 5.00
Crown Imperial, Crown Emblem, Blue, Qt., RB-694 .... 15.00
Crown Imperial, Crown Emblem, Green, Clear Lid, 1/2 Gal., RB-694 .... 25.00
Crown Mason, Pt., RB-704 .... 2.00
Crown Mason, Qt., RB-704 .... 2.00
Crown Mason, Slant, 1/2 Pt., RB-704-1 .... 3.00
Crystal Jar, Glass Lid, 1/2 Gal., RB-706 ....65.00 to 79.00
Crystal Jar, Glass Lid, Qt., RB-706 .... 25.00
Cunningham & Co., Pittsburg, Aqua, Iron Pontil, 1/2 Gal., RB-721 ....132.00 to 500.00
Cutting, Packing Co., San Francisco In Lid, Screw Band, Glass Lid, RB-736, 1/2 Pt. 125.00
Cutting & Co., San Francisco, Aqua, Wax Seal, Qt., RB-735 .... 1760.00
Dandy Trademark, Amber, Qt., RB-751 ....225.00 to 250.00
Darling Imperial, Adm, Aqua, Midget, RB-754 .... 298.00
Dexter, Circled By Fruit & Vegetables, Aqua, Qt., RB-773 ....235.00 to 250.00
Dexter, Circled By Fruit & Vegetables, Aqua, Qt., RB-774 .... 150.00
Dexter, In Straight Line, Aqua, Qt., RB-772 .... 200.00
Diamond Fruit Jar Improved Trademark Base & Lid, Pt., RB-778 .... 3.00
Diamond Fruit Jar Improved Trademark Base & Lid, Qt., RB-778 .... 3.00
Dictator C, Patented D. I. Holcolmb Dec. 14 1869, Aqua, Wax Sealer, Tin Lid, Qt., RB-785 ... 100.00
Doane's Great Airtight, Aqua, Bulbous, Applied Lip, 1865-70, Qt., RB-794 .... 3248.00
Doolittle, Qt., RB-809-1 .... 50.00
Double Safety, Narrow Mouth, 1/2 Pt., RB-817 ....7.00 to 12.00
Double Safety, Narrow Mouth, Pt., RB-817 .... 2.00

Fruit Jar, Chef's Trademark,
Stipple Frame, 1/2 Pt., RB-589-1

Fruit Jar, Electric Fruit Jar, World
Globe, Aqua, Qt., RB-922

Fruit Jar, Lafayette, Script,
Aqua, 1/2 Gal., RB-1452

Double Safety, Narrow Mouth, Qt., RB-817 .... 2.00
Double Seal, Pt., RB-826 .... 28.00
Double Seal, Qt., RB-826 .... 15.00
Double Seal, Qt., RB-827 .... 20.00
Drey Perfect Mason, 1/2 Gal., RB-843 .... 4.00
Drey Perfect Mason, Pt., RB-843 .... 1.00
Drey Perfect Mason, Qt., RB-843 .... 1.00
Drey Square Mason, Carpenter's Square, Qt., RB-847 .... 6.00
Drey Square Mason Clear Pt., RB-848 .... 6.00
E.C. Flaccus Co., Stag Head, Straw Yellow, Wide Mouth, 6 In., RB-1016 .... 840.00
E.C. Flaccus Co., Steers Head, Flower Band, Milk Glass, Insert, Pt., RB-1013 .....450.00 to 500.00
Eagle, Aqua, Clamp, Qt., RB-872 .... 200.00
Eagle, Aqua, Iron Yoke Clamp, 1/2 Gal., 9 3/4 In., RB-872 .... 110.00
Eclipse Jar, Green, Cover, Qt., RB-885 .... 550.00
Economy, Portland Ore., Qt., RB-892 .... 4.00
Economy Pat. Applied For, Aqua, Qt., RB-903 .... 1000.00
Economy Sealer Patd Sept 15th 1885, Aqua, Qt., RB-908 .... 250.00
Economy Sealer Patd Sept 15th 1885, Aqua, Wax Sealer, Tin Lid, Qt., RB-906 .... 25.00
Egco. Imperial, Aqua, Qt., RB-870-4 .... 55.00
Electric Fruit Jar, World Globe, Aqua, 1/2 Gal., RB-922 .... 150.00
Electric Fruit Jar, World Globe, Aqua, Pt., RB-922 .... 350.00
Electric Fruit Jar, World Globe, Aqua, Qt., RB-922 ....*Illus* 125.00
Empire, Aqua, Reproduction Clamp, 1/2 Gal., RB-927 .... 98.00
Empire, Incomplete Final E, Aqua, Qt., RB-924-3 .... 400.00
Empire, Stippled Cross, Pt., RB-925 .... 5.00
Empire, Stippled Cross, Qt., RB-925 .... 5.00
Empire, Stippled Frame, 1/2 Pt., RB-925-1 .... 50.00
Empire, Stippled Frame, Sun Colored Amethyst, 1/2 Pt., RB-925-1 .... 80.00
Erie, E In Hexagon, Unembossed Lid, Aqua, 1/2 Gal., RB-941 .... 325.00
Eureka, Script, Eureka Jar Co., Boston Mass., 1/2 Pt., RB-945 .... 40.00
Eureka, Script, Eureka Jar Co., Patent Pending, Dunbar, W.V., Green, 1/2 Pt., RB-947 ... 75.00
Eureka, Script, Original Closure, 1/2 Pt., RB-947-2 .... 75.00
Eureka 1 Pat'd Dec. 27th 1864, Aqua, Tin Lid, Qt., RB-948 ....80.00 to 190.00
Eureka Jar Co., Patent Pending, Lid, Clamp, 1/2 Pt., RB-947-1 .... 85.00
F. & J. Bodine Manufacturers Philadelphia Pa., Lid, Aqua, Qt., RB-473 .... 400.00
F. & J. Bodine Philada, Lid, Aqua, Qt., RB-474 .... 300.00
F. A. & Co, On Base, Iron Pontil, Aqua, 1/2 Gal., RB-968-2 .... 290.00
F. A. & Co, On Base, Iron Pontil, Aqua, Qt., RB-968-2 .... 200.00
F. B. Co. 2, Amber, Wax Sealer, Tin Lid, Qt., RB-987 .... 200.00
Fahnestock Albree & Co., Dark Aqua, Qt., 8 1/2 In., RB-970 .... 358.00
Federal Fruit Jar, Draped Flags, Aqua, Qt., RB-996 .... 125.00
Foster Sealfast, 1/2 Pt., RB-2581 ....12.00 to 15.00
Franklin Fruit Jar, Aqua, 1/2 Gal., RB-1033 .... 75.00
French's Medford Brand Prepared Mustard, 14 Oz., RB-1037 ....2.00 to 6.00
Friedley & Cornman's, Aqua, Ground Mouth, Iron Rim, 1/2 Gal. 1400.00
Fruit-Keeper, GCCo, Aqua, 1/2 Gal., RB-1042 .... 100.00
Fruit-Keeper, GCCo, Aqua, Pt., RB-1042 .... 75.00
Full Measure 1/2 Gal. Eng-Skell Co. San Francisco, 1/2 Gal., RB-935 .... 60.00
Gem, 2 Lines, Ghosted The Hero, Aqua, Qt., RB-1061-2 .... 45.00
Gem, Base Pat. Nov. 26 67, Aqua, Midget, RB-1053 .... 50.00
Gem, Base Pat. Nov. 26 67, Aqua, Qt., RB-1053 .... 8.00
Gem, CFJCo, Aqua, 1/2 Gal., RB-1078 .... 25.00
Gem, CFJCo, Aqua, Midget, RB-1078 .... 150.00
Gem, Cross, Aqua, Midget, RB-1059 .... 60.00
Gem, Cross, Aqua, Qt., RB-1059 ....10.00 to 20.00
Gem, H. Brooke, Mould Maker, N.Y., Aqua, Glass Insert, Zinc Band, Gal., RB-1071 .... 880.00
Gem, Hero Glass Works, Aqua, Glass Insert, Screw Band, 3 Gal., 17 5/8 In., RB-1058 ... 3575.00
Gem, Patd Dec 17 61, Aqua, 24 Oz., RB-1068 .... 75.00
Genuine Mason, Mason In Flag, Aqua, 1/2 Gal., RB-1101 ....10.00 to 18.00
Genuine Mason, Mason In Flag, Aqua, Pt., RB-1101 ....10.00 to 18.00
Genuine Mason, Mason In Flag, Aqua, Qt., RB-1101 ....8.00 to 12.00
Gilberds Improved, Star, Aqua, Qt., RB-1108 .... 300.00
Gilberds Jar, Star, Aqua, Glass Lid, Wire Clamp, Pt., RB-1107 .... 1456.00

Gilberds Jar, Star, Aqua, Qt., RB-1107 .... 350.00
Gimbal Brothers Pure Food Store Philadelphia, Qt., RB-1113 .... 75.00
Globe, Amber, 1/2 Gal., RB-1123 .... 150.00
Globe, Amber, Pt., RB-1123 .... 235.00
Globe, Amber, Qt., RB-1123 ....90.00 to 125.00
Globe, Golden Amber, Striations, Glass Lid, Iron Clamp, Qt., RB-1123 .... 90.00
Globe, Red Amber, Glass Lid, Iron Clamp, Qt., 8 In., RB-1123 .... 132.00
Globe, Yellow, 1/2 Gal., RB-1123 .... 250.00
Good House Keepers R, Zinc Lid, 1/2 Pt., RB-1145 .... 35.00
Greek Key Design, Patented July 27th 1886, Emerald Green, No Closure, RB-2308 ..... 400.00
Green Mountain Co., Stippled Frame, 1/2 Pt., RB-1153-1 .... 225.00
Griffen's Patent Oct 7 1862, Aqua, Glass Lid, Cage-Like Clamp, Qt., RB-1154 ...66.00 to 100.00
H Over Anchor, Lighting, Pt., RB-80 .... 1.00
H Over Anchor, Lighting, Qt., RB-80 .... 1.00
H.K. Mulford Chemists, Philadelphia, Amber, No Cork, 1/2 Pt., RB-2215 .... 35.00
H.W. Pettit, Westville, N.J., Aqua, Pt., RB-2362 ....8.00 to 15.00
Hahne Co. Newark N. J., Star, Mason's Patent Nov 30th 1858, Aqua, Qt., RB-1166-1 .... 100.00
Haines's Patent March 1st 1870, Aqua, Qt., RB-1170 .... 125.00
Hansee's Palace Home Jar, PH Monogram, Glass Lid, Wire Clamp, Qt., RB-1206 .. 144.00
Hansee's Palace Home Jar, PH, Original Wire, Qt., RB-1206 .... 125.00
Hansee's Palace Home Jar, PH, Pt., RB-1206 .... 200.00
Hazel HA Preserve Jar, Pt., RB-1231 .... 8.00
Hazel HA Preserve Jar, Qt., RB-1231 .... 8.00
Hazel Preserve Jar, 1/2 Pt., RB-1230-1 .... 40.00
Hazel-Atlas EZ Seal, Aqua, Pt., RB-1227 .... 15.00
Hero, Aqua, Tin Insert, Screw Band, Qt., 7 1/2 In., RB-1242 ....22.00 to 50.00
Hero, Honey Amber, Ground Lip, Metal Lid, Qt., 7 1/2 In., RB-1242 .... 6600.00
Home-Pak, Qt., RB-1262 .... 2.00
IGCo Mason's Patent Nov 30th 1858, Aqua, Pt., RB-1952 ....15.00 to 45.00
Imperial Pat. April 20th 1886, Lid, Aqua, Qt., RB-1294 .... 75.00
Imperial Pat. April 20th 1886, Lid, Pt., RB-1294 .... 150.00
Improved Corona, Made In Canada, 1/2 Gal, RB-656 .... 10.00
Improved Corona Jar, Made In Canada, Pt., RB-656 .... 3.00
Improved Corona Jar, Made In Canada, Qt., RB-656 .... 3.00
Improved Crown, Crown Emblem, Aqua, 1/2 Gal., RB-697 .... 20.00
Improved Crown, Crown Emblem, Aqua, Qt., RB-697 .... 12.00
Improved Crown, Crown Emblem, Green, Qt., RB-697 .... 15.00
Improved Crown, Script Letters, Green, Clear Lid, Qt., RB-700-1 .... 18.00
Improved Gem, Made In Canada, 1/2 Gal., RB-1094 .... 10.00
Improved Gem, Made In Canada, Green, Qt., RB-1094 .... 35.00
Improved Gem, Made In Canada, Pt., RB-1094 .... 5.00
Improved Gem, Made In Canada, Qt., RB-1094 .... 3.00
Improved Mason Jar, Cap, Pt., RB-1305 .... 16.00
Independent Jar, Embossed, Midget, RB-1308 .... 150.00
Ivanhoe Base, Pt., RB-1318 .... 4.00
J & B, Pat'd June 14th 1898, Octagon, Lid, Aqua, Qt., RB-1321 .... 100.00
J & B, Pat'd June 14th 1898, Octagon, Reproduction Lid, Aqua, Pt., RB-1321 .... 70.00
Jeannette J Mason Home Packer, Square J, Qt., RB-1324 ....2.00 to 4.00
Jewel Jar, Block Letters In Frame, Pt., RB-1327 .... 15.00
Jewel Jar, Made In Canada, 1/2 Gal., RB-1328 .... 10.00
Jewel Jar, Made In Canada, Pt., RB-1328 .... 10.00
Jewel Jar, Made In Canada, Qt., RB-1328 .... 5.00
Johnson & Johnson, New York, Cobalt Blue, Glass Lid, Screw Band, Qt., 7 In., RB-1344 .. 358.00
Johnson & Johnson N Y Depp, Cobalt Blue, Qt., RB-1344 .... 500.00
Joshua Wright, Philad, Barrel, Aqua, Rolled Lip, IP, 1/2 Gal., 10 5/8 In., RB-3035 ...... 532.00
Jumbo Peanut Butter, Ribbed, 1/2 Pt., RB-1347 ....45.00 to 65.00
Jumbo Peanut Butter, Ribbed, Tapered, 5 Oz., RB-1347 ....50.00 to 90.00
Jumbo Peanut Butter, Ribbed, Tapered, No Lid, 5 Oz., RB-1347 .... 50.00
K, Star Jar, Patented, In Star, Qt., RB-2730 .... 125.00
Kerr Self Sealing, Trademark Reg Mason, Unembossed, Round, 1/2 Pt., RB-1374 ...... 2.00
Kerr Self Sealing Mason, 65th Anniversary, 1903-1963, Blue Streak, Qt., RB-1387 ...... 75.00
Kerr Self Sealing Mason, 65th Anniversary, 1903-1963, Gold, Qt., RB-1387 .... 75.00
Kerr Self Sealing Mason, Amber, Qt., RB-1386 .... 40.00

Kerr Self Sealing Mason, Bicentennial, Cobalt Bell, Pontil, RB-1389 . . . . 190.00
Kerr Self Sealing Mason, Ralph S. Brown, Years Of Loyal Service, Pt., 1977, RB-1388-2 . 40.00
Keystone, Blue Aqua, Iron Pontil, Applied Lip, 1860-70, 1/2 Gal., RB-8, 1390-3 . . . . 123.00
Keystone Mason Jar, Patent Nov 30th 1858, Aqua, 1/2 Gal., RB-1684 . . . . .25.00 to 90.00
King, King's Head Above King In Banner, 1/2 Gal., RB-1416 . . . . 125.00
King, On Banner, Below Crown, Pt., RB-1414 . . . . 8.00
King, On Banner, Below Crown, Qt., RB-1414 . . . . 8.00
King, Pat. Nov 2 1869, Aqua, Glass Lid, Iron Yoke Clamp, Qt., RB-1418 . . . . .121.00 to 532.00
Kline's Patent Oct 27 63, Aqua, 1/2 Gal., RB-1422 . . . . 175.00
Knowlton Vacuum Fruit Jar, Star, Aqua, ABM Lip, Glass Lid, c.1903, Pt., RB-1432 .45.00 to 75.00
Knox K Mason, In Keystone, 1/2 Pt., RB-1436 . . . . 40.00
Knox K Mason, In Keystone, Carrying Bail, 1/2 Gal., RB9, No. 1435-5 . . . . 50.00
Lafayette, Script, Aqua, 1/2 Gal., RB-1452 . . . .*Illus* 225.00
Lafayette, Script, Aqua, 3-Piece Glass & Metal Stopper, Qt., 8 1/2 In., RB-1452 . . . . 110.00
Le Parfait Super, 1/2 Pt., RB-1480-4 . . . . 10.00
Leader, Amber, Domed Lid, Wire Clamp, Pt., 6 In., RB-1465 . . . . 560.00
Leader, Yellow Amber, Domed Lid, Wire Clamp, Qt., RB-1466 . . . . .275.00 to 448.00
Legrand, Ideal Trade Mark Pat'd 7-5-98 Vacuum Jar, Repro Lid, Aqua, Qt., RB-1472 . . . . . 200.00
Leotric, In Circle, Aqua, 1/2 Gal., RB-1476 . . . . 25.00
Leotric, In Circle, Aqua, Pt., RB-1476 . . . . 5.00
Leotric, In Circle, Aqua, Qt., RB-1476 . . . . 5.00
Leotric, In Circle, Pt., RB-1476 . . . . 3.00
Leotric, In Circle, Qt., RB-1476 . . . . 3.00
Lindell Glass Co. Base, Amber, Wax Sealer, Tin Lid, Qt., RB-1509 . . . . 250.00
Lockport Mason, 1/2 Gal., RB-1512 . . . . 15.00
Ludlow's Patent June 28th 1859, Aqua, Domed Lid, Iron Clamp, Pt., RB-1546 . . . .*Illus* 532.00
Lustre R E Tongue & Bros Phila, Aqua, Pt., RB-1560-1 . . . . 5.00
Lustre R E Tongue & Bros Phila, Aqua, Qt., RB-1560-1 . . . . 5.00
Lustre R E Tongue Bros Inc., Phila., Aqua, Pt., RB-1557 . . . . 7.00
M C Co, On Base, Amber, Wax Sealer, Tin Lid, Qt., RB-2143 . . . . 200.00
Made In Canada Crown, Crown Emblem, Pt., RB-695 . . . . 3.00
Made In Canada Crown, Crown Emblem, Qt., RB-695 . . . . 3.00
Made In Canada Perfect Seal, Wide Mouth, Adjustable, Cornflower Blue, Qt., RB-2344 . 12.00
Made In Canada Perfect Seal, Wide Mouth, Adjustable, Qt., RB-2344 . . . . 10.00
Magic Fruit Jar, Star, Amber, Glass Lid, Metal, Wire Clamp, 1/2 Gal., RB-1606 . . . . ,. 1100.00
Magic Fruit Jar, Star, Aqua, Qt., RB-1606 . . . . 400.00
Magic Fruit Jar, Star, Green, Qt., RB-1606 . . . . 575.00
Magic TM, Mason Jar, Qt., RB-1610 . . . . 1.00
Mansfield Knowlton, May '03 Patent, Aqua, Glass Lid, Metal Screw Cap, Qt., RB-1619 . 77.00
Marston's Restaurant Boston, Qt., RB-1627 . . . . 75.00
Mason, Beaded Neck Seal, Smooth Lip, Amber, Pt., RB-1641 . . . . 100.00
Mason, Cattails, Aqua, 1/2 Gal, RB-1652 . . . . 200.00
Mason, Gilberd's Base, Aqua, Qt., RB-1645-1 . . . . 35.00
Mason, Underlined Squared Shepherd's Crook, Aqua, 1/2 Gal., RB-1633 . . . . .14.00 to 16.00
Mason, Underlined With Squared Shepherd's Crook, Aqua 1/2 Gal., RB-1632 . . . . 20.00
Mason, Underlined, Reverse 1776 Liberty Bell 1976, Qt., RB-1654 . . . . 1.00
Mason Arched Letters, Blue, Qt., RB-1644-1 . . . . 50.00
Mason Jar Of 1872, Aqua, Qt., RB-1749 . . . . 55.00
Mason Patent Nov 30th 1858, Hourglass Emblem, Aqua, Midget, RB-1869 . . . . 200.00
Mason Patent Nov 30th 1858, Hourglass Emblem, Aqua, Qt., RB-1869 . . . . 15.00
Mason Porcelain Lined, Aqua, Qt., RB-2132 . . . . 175.00
Mason Star Jar, Qt., RB-1746 . . . . 1.00
Mason Vacuum Knowlton Patent June 9th 1908, Cornflower, Pt., RB-2134 . . . . 180.00
Mason's I Patent Nov 30th 1858, Aqua, 1/2 Gal., RB-2027 . . . . 15.00
Mason's I Patent Nov 30th 1858, Aqua, Midget, RB-2027 . . . . 40.00
Mason's I Patent Nov 30th 1858, Small 1, Aqua, Smooth Lip, Qt., RB-2026 . . . . 10.00
Mason's 2 Patent Nov 30th 1858, Base L & W, Aqua, 1/2 Gal., RB-2030-2 . . . . 38.00
Mason's 2 Patent Nov. 30th 1858, Aqua, 1/2 Gal., RB-2030 . . . . 20.00
Mason's 2 Patent Nov. 30th 1858, Large 2, H.C. Nt., Qt., RB-2030-1 . . . . 40.00
Mason's 2 Patent Nov. 30th 1858, Small 2, Aqua, Qt., RB-2029 . . . . 12.00
Mason's 2 Patent Nov. 30th 1858, Small 2, Aqua, Smooth Lip, 1/2 Gal., RB-2029 . . . . . . 12.00
Mason's 3 Patent Nov 30th 1858, 1/2 Gal., RB-2038 . . . . 15.00
Mason's 3 Patent Nov 30th 1858, Base H.C. & T., Aqua, 1/2 Gal., RB-2040 . . . . 75.00

Mason's 3 Patent Nov 30th 1858, Large 3, Ground Lip, 1/2 Gal., RB-2038 .... 35.00
Mason's 3 Patent Nov 30th 1858, Qt., RB-2037 .... 15.00
Mason's 3 Patent Nov 30th 1858, Small 3, Aqua, Qt., RB-2037 .... 8.00
Mason's 4 Patent Nov 30th 1858, Ground Top, Lid, Midget, Pt., RB-2044-1 .... 69.00
Mason's 5 Patent Nov 30th 1858, Base WFM., Aqua, 1/2 Gal., RB-2050-3 .... 50.00
Mason's 6 Patent Nov 30th 1858, Aqua, Qt., RB-2056-1 .... 35.00
Mason's 6 Patent Nov 30th 1858, Base H C & T, Aqua, Qt., RB-2055-5 .... 50.00
Mason's 6 Patent Nov 30th 1858, Green, Smooth Lip, Qt., RB-2053 .... 15.00
Mason's 6 Patent Nov. 30th 1858, Aqua, Qt., RB-2053 .... 10.00
Mason's 6 Patent Nov. 30th 1858, Reversed 6, Aqua, Qt., RB-2056 .... 35.00
Mason's 8 Patent Nov. 30th 1858, Aqua, Qt., RB-2060 .... 12.00
Mason's 8 Patent Nov. 30th 1858, Large 8, Aqua, Qt., RB-2061 .... 25.00
Mason's 9 Patent Nov 30th 1858, Aqua, Smooth Lip, Qt., RB-2065 .... 12.00
Mason's 9 Patent Nov 30th 1858, Aqua, Smooth Lip, Qt., RB-2067 .... 12.00
Mason's 12 Patent Nov 30th 1858, Aqua, Ground Lip, Qt., RB-2073 .... 30.00
Mason's 17 Patent Nov 30th 1858, Underlined, Aqua, Qt., RB-2083 .... 35.00
Mason's 18 Patent Nov 30th 1858, Underlined, Aqua, Qt., RB-2086 .... 25.00
Mason's 20 Underlined Patent Nov 30th 1858, 1/2 Gal., RB-2090 .... 35.00
Mason's 21 Underlined Patent Nov 30th 1858, Aqua, Qt., RB-2092 .... 30.00
Mason's 23 Underlined Patent Nov 30th 1858, Aqua, Qt., RB-2096 .... 30.00
Mason's 24 Underlined Patent Nov 30th 1858, Aqua, Qt., RB-2098 .... 40.00
Mason's -C- Patent Nov 30th 1858, Base G, Mold Number, Aqua, Qt., RB-1989 ..... 20.00
Mason's 400 Patent Nov 30th 1858, Underlined, Aqua, Qt., RB-2123 .... 350.00
Mason's 404 Patent Nov 30th 1858, Aqua, Midget, RB-2125 .... 400.00
Mason's CFJCo Butter Jar, 1/2 Gal., RB-1688 .... 250.00
Mason's CFJCo Butter Jar, Aqua, 1/2 Gal., RB-1688 .... 250.00
Mason's CFJCo Butter Jar, Aqua, 3 Qt., RB-1688 .... 650.00
Mason's CFJCo Improved, Amber, Glass Insert, 1/2 Gal., 9 In., RB-1711 .... 187.00
Mason's CFJCo Improved, Aqua, Midget, RB-1711 .... 25.00
Mason's CFJCo Improved, Aqua, Reproduction Band, Midget, RB-1711 .... 20.00
Mason's CFJCo Improved, Butter, Aqua, Sheared Mouth, 1/2 Gal., RB-1688 .... 134.00
Mason's CFJCo Improved, Clyde, N.Y., Aqua, Midget, RB-1712 .... 60.00
Mason's CFJCo Improved Butter Jar, Aqua, Tall, 3 Qt., RB-1688 .... 600.00
Mason's CFJCo Patent Nov 30th 1858, Apple Green, Qt., RB-1920 .... 48.00 to 55.00
Mason's CFJCo Patent Nov 30th 1858, Aqua, 1/2 Gal., RB-1920 .... 12.00
Mason's CFJCo Patent Nov 30th 1858, Aqua, CFJ Zinc Lid, Midget, RB-1920 .... 35.00
Mason's CFJCo Patent Nov 30th 1858, Ball, Blue, 1/2 Gal., RB-1920 .... 100.00
Mason's CFJCo Patent Nov 30th 1858, Color In Base, Midget, RB-1920 .... 100.00
Mason's CFJCo Patent Nov 30th 185, Date Error, Green, Qt., RB-1924 .... 50.00 to 75.00
Mason's CFJCo Patent Nov 30th 1858, Olive Green, 1/2 Gal., RB-1920 .... 200.00
Mason's CFJCo Patent Nov 30th 1858, Olive Green, Qt., RB-1920 .... 100.00 to 325.00
Mason's IGCo Patent Nov 30th 1858, Aqua, Midget, RB-1955 .... 250.00
Mason's II Patent Nov. 30th 1858, Aqua, Ground Lip, Qt., RB-2036 .... 33.00 to 40.00
Mason's Improved, Butter Jar, Wide Mouth, Aqua, 1/2 Gal., RB-1685 .... 250.00
Mason's Improved, Cross, Aqua, Midget, RB-1728 .... 50.00
Mason's Improved, Cross, Erased Trademark, Apple Green, Qt., RB-1733 .... 48.00
Mason's Improved, Fancy M, Amber, 1/2 Gal., RB-1694-1 .... 250.00
Mason's Improved, Hourglass, Aqua, Midget, RB-1707-1 .... 50.00
Mason's Improved, Keystone, Aqua, Midget, RB-1736 .... 60.00
Mason's IV Patent Nov 30th 1858, Aqua, Qt., RB-2049 .... 60.00
Mason's KBGCo Patent Nov. 30th 1858, Pt., RB-1957 .... 45.00
Mason's Patent Nov 30 1858, Olive Yellow, Ground Lip, Zinc Screw Lid, Pt., RB-1787 . 364.00
Mason's Patent Nov 30 1858, Sky Blue, Ground Lip, Zinc Screw Lid, Qt., RB-1787 .... 213.00
Mason's Patent Nov 30 1858, Yellow Green, Ground Lip, Zinc Screw Lid, Pt, RB-1787 . 123.00
Mason's Patent Nov 30th 1858, Apple Green, Ground Lip, Qt., RB-1787 .... 35.00 to 73.00
Mason's Patent Nov 30th 1858, Apple Green, Midget, RB-1784 .... 200.00
Mason's Patent Nov 30th 1858, Aqua, Ground Lip, Qt., RB-1787 .... 3.00
Mason's Patent Nov 30th 1858, Aqua, Smooth Lip, 1/2 Gal., RB-1787 .... 5.00
Mason's Patent Nov 30th 1858, Aqua, Smooth Lip, Pt., RB-1787 .... 5.00
Mason's Patent Nov 30th 1858, Blue, Midget, RB-1784 .... 120.00
Mason's Patent Nov 30th 1858, Blue, Milk Glass Ball Insert, Midget, RB-1784 .... 250.00
Mason's Patent Nov 30th 1858, CFJ, Aqua, Midget, RB-1927 .... 50.00 to 60.00
Mason's Patent Nov 30th 1858, Cross, Amber, Qt., RB-1938 .... 500.00

Mason's Patent Nov 30th 1858, Cross, Circle, Aqua, Qt., RB-1938-2 . . . . 45.00
Mason's Patent Nov 30th 1858, Cross, Olive Green, Qt., RB-1938 . . . . 125.00
Mason's Patent Nov 30th 1858, Green, Ground Lip, 1/2 Gal., RB-1787 . . . . 15.00
Mason's Patent Nov 30th 1858, Green, Ground Lip, Pt., RB-1787 . . . . .15.00 to 30.00
Mason's Patent Nov 30th 1858, Green, Midget, RB-1836 . . . . 75.00
Mason's Patent Nov 30th 1858, Green, Swirls, Milk Glass Insert, 1/2 Gal., RB-1787 . . . 358.00
Mason's Patent Nov 30th 1858, Ground Lip, Green, Qt., RB-1787 . . . . 75.00
Mason's Patent Nov 30th 1858, Keystone, Aqua, Qt., RB-1965 . . . . 12.00
Mason's Patent Nov 30th 1858, Keystone, Green, Pt., RB-1965 . . . . 375.00
Mason's Patent Nov 30th 1858, Keystone, In Circle, Aqua, Midget, RB-1964 . . . . 50.00
Mason's Patent Nov 30th 1858, Tudor Rose, Ball Blue, Qt., 7 1/4 In., RB-1875 . . . . 121.00
Mason's Patent Nov 30th 1858, Tudor Rose, Citron, Zinc Lid, Immerser, Pt., RB-1875 . 2800.00
Mason's Patent Nov 30th 1858, Yellow Amber, Zinc Screw Cap, Qt., RB-1787 . . . . 190.00
Mason's Patent Nov. 30th 1858, Aqua, Midget, RB-1783 . . . . 600.00
Mason's Patent Nov. 30th 1858, Base Port, 1/2 Gal., RB-1894 . . . . 15.00
Mason's Patent Nov. 30th 1858, BCR, Hand Blown, Smooth LIP, Midget, RB-1875-6 . . 150.00
Mason's Patent Nov. 30th 1858, Cross, Amber, Qt., RB-1939 . . . . 500.00
Mason's Patent Nov. 30th 1858, Cross, Apple Green, Qt., RB-1939 . . . . 69.00
Mason's Patent Nov. 30th 1858, Cross, Aqua, 1/2 Gal., RB-1939 . . . . 8.00
Mason's Patent Nov. 30th 1858, Cross, Aqua, Midget, RB-1939 . . . . 60.00
Mason's Patent Nov. 30th 1858, Cross, Aqua, Pt., RB-1939 . . . . 8.00
Mason's Patent Nov. 30th 1858, Cross, Aqua, Qt., RB-1939 . . . . 3.00
Mason's Patent Nov. 30th 1858, Cross, Aqua, Reproduction Lid, Midget, RB-1941 . . . . . 29.00
Mason's Patent Nov. 30th 1858, Cross, Aqua., RB-1941 . . . . 60.00
Mason's Patent Nov. 30th 1858, Cross, Dark Aqua, Zinc Lid, Gal., 12 In., RB-1943 . . . . 1100.00
Mason's Patent Nov. 30th 1858, Cross, Green, Qt., RB-1939 . . . . 10.00
Mason's Patent Nov. 30th 1858, Cross, Reproduction Lid, Midget, RB-1941 . . . . 100.00
Mason's Patent Nov. 30th 1858, E. S. & Co., Aqua, Midget, RB-1880 . . . . 120.00
Mason's Patent Nov. 30th 1858, Green In Base, Midget, RB-1909 . . . . 100.00
Mason's Patent Nov. 30th 1858, Keystone In Circle, Aqua, 1/2 Gal., RB-1959 . . . . 15.00
Mason's Patent Nov. 30th 1858, M Over 2, Aqua, Bee Hive, Midget, RB-1887-5 . . . . . 200.00
Mason's Patent Nov. 30th 1858, P B, Midget, RB-1892 . . . . 120.00
Mason's Patent Nov. 30th 1858, Pat. Nov. 26 67, Aqua, Midget, RB-1890 . . . . 50.00
Mason's Patent Nov. 30th 1858, Reverse Cross, No A Crossbar, Aqua, Midget, RB-1814 125.00
Mason's Patent Nov. 30th 1858, Reversed Apostrophe, Cross, Midget, RB-1941-3 . . . . . 40.00
Mason's Patent Nov. 30th 1858, Reversed N's, Aqua, Qt., RB-1809 . . . . .40.00 to 60.00
Mason's Patent Nov. 30th 1858, Reversed November N, Midget, RB-1810-8 . . . . 150.00
Mason's Patent Nov. 30th 1858, Solid Five Pointed Star, Aqua, Midget, RB-1907 . . . . . . 100.00
Mason's Patent Nov. 30th 1858, Star, Ball Blue, Midget, RB-1909 . . . . 135.00
Mason's Patent Nov. 30th 1858, Star, Midget, RB-1909 . . . . 135.00
Mason's Patent Nov. 30th 1858, W. C. D., Aqua, Midget, RB-1900 . . . . 75.00
Mason's V Patent Nov 30th 1858, L&W, Aqua, Qt., RB-2020 . . . . 50.00
Mason's VIII Patent Nov 30th 1858, Aqua, Qt., RB-2064 . . . . .35.00 to 50.00
Masons CFJCo Patent Nov 30th 1858, No Apostrophe, Aqua, Midget, RB-1920-5 . . . . . . 50.00
Masons Improved, Amber, RB-1694 . . . . 250.00
Masons Patent Nov 30th 1858, The Ball Jar, Aqua, Zinc Screw Lid, Pt., RB-1782 . . . . 168.00
Masons Patent Nov 30th 58, Aqua, 2 Reversed N's, Midget, RB-1833-1 . . . . 125.00
Masons Patent Nov 30th 58, Christmas, Ball Blue, Pt., RB-1780 . . . . 120.00
Masons Patent Nov. 30th 1858, Aqua, Midget, RB-1786 . . . . 900.00
McDonald Perfect Seal, In Circle, Ball Blue, Pt., RB-2147 . . . . 18.00
Metro Easi-Pak Mason, Zinc Lid, Qt., RB-2165 . . . . .1.00 to 2.00
Mid West Canadian Made, Qt., RB-2177 . . . . 14.00
Millville, Hitall's Paten, Aqua, 1/2 Pt., RB-2185 . . . . 500.00
Millville, Hitall's Paten, Blue Aqua, Glass Lid, 1/2 Pt., 3 3/4 In., RB-2186 . . . . 336.00
Millville Atmospheric Fruit Jar, Aqua, 48 Oz., RB-2181 . . . . 80.00
Millville Atmospheric Fruit Jar, Aqua, 68 Oz., RB-2181 . . . . 125.00
Millville Atmospheric Fruit Jar, Aqua, Glass Lid, Yoke Clamp, 56 Oz., 9 In., RB-2181 . . 55.00
Millville Atmospheric Fruit Jar, Aqua, Pt., RB-2181 . . . . .100.00 to 150.00
Millville Atmospheric Fruit Jar, Aqua, Square Shoulder, 68 Oz., RB-2183 . . . . 400.00
Millville WTCo. Improved, Aqua, Glass Insert, Qt., RB-2187 . . . . 110.00
Mission Trade Mark Mason Jar, Made In California, Bell, Aqua, 1/2 Pt., RB-2190 . . . . . . 125.00
Model Jar Patd Aug. 27 1867, Aqua, Reproduction Cardboard Lid, 1/2 Gal., RB-2194 . . . 310.00
Moore's Patent Dec 3d 1861, Aqua, Glass Lid, Iron Yoke Clamp, Qt., 8 In., RB-2204 . . . 55.00

Fruit Jar, Ludlow's Patent June
28th 1859, Aqua, Domed Lid,
Iron Clamp, Pt., RB-1546

Fruit Jar, Proteotor,
Recessed Panels, Aqua,
Lid, Qt.,

Fruit Jar, Yeomans's Fruit
Bottle, Aqua,
1/2 Gal., RB-3039

Mountain Mason, Square, Qt., RB-2212 . . . . .22.00 to 28.00
Mrs. G.E. Haller Pat'd Feb. 25. 73., Aqua, Aqua Stopper, Qt., RB-1178 . . . .   200.00
Mrs. G.E. Haller Pat'd Feb. 25. 73., Reservoir, Aqua, Glass Stopper, 1/2 Gal., RB-1178 . .   336.00
Myers Test Jar, Aqua, Reproduction, Brass Clamp, Qt., RB-2218 . . . .   175.00
National Preserve Can, Nelson Morris Chicago Ill., Original Closure, 1/2 Pt., RB-2237-8   75.00
Ne Plus Ultra Air Tight, Aquamarine, Cylindrical, Glass Lid, c.1865, Pt., RB-475 . . . . . .   3360.00
New Gem, Pt., RB-1088 . . . .   17.00
New Mason Vacuum Fruit Jar Knowlton Patent June 9th 1908, Blue, Qt., RB-2241 . . .   150.00
New Paragone 5, Aqua, Qt., RB-2291 . . . .   250.00
Newmans Patent Dec 20th 1859, Aqua, Qt., RB-2240 . . . .   1500.00
O Mason's Patent Nov. 30th 1858, Embossed Circle, Aqua, Midget, RB-1872 . . . .   50.00
OC Monogram, Reverse Square, Base Putnam, Aqua, Qt., 9 In., RB-2256 . . . .   100.00
Ohio Quality Mason, Small Hi In Ohio, 1/2 Gal., RB-2263 . . . .   25.00
Packed By Collins Wheaton & Luhrs S. F., Aqua 1/2 Gal., RB-637-1 . . . .   2000.00
Pansy, Erased Best, Amber, 20 Panels, Glass Insert, Screw Band, Qt., RB-2287 . . .220.00 to 300.00
Paragon Valve Jar, Patd. April 19th 1870, Aqua, 2-Piece Closure, Qt., 7 3/4 In., RB-2292 .   448.00
Patd Aug 5th 1862 & Feb 9 1864, W.W. Lyman, Repro Lid, Aqua, Pt., RB-1579 . . . . . .   125.00
Patd Feb 9th 1864 W. W. Lyman, Star, Aqua, Pt., RB-1571 . . . .   125.00
Patented Dl Holcomb Dec 14th 1869, Aqua, Wax Seal, Qt., RB-1257-5 . . . .   123.00
Patented Oct. 19 1858, Aqua, Glass Lid, Lugs On Neck, Qt., 7 In., RB-1212 . . . .   44.00
Peerless, Aqua, 1/2 Gal., RB-2322 . . . .   180.00
Peerless, Aqua, Qt., RB-2322 . . . . .180.00 to 200.00
Perfect Seal Tight On The Neck Front & Back Clear, 1/2 Pt., RB-2335 . . . .   100.00
Perfect Seal Wide Mouth Adjustable, 1/2 Gal., RB-2348 . . . .   25.00
Perfection, IGCo In Diamond, New Metal, Pt., RB-2331 . . . .   115.00
Pet, Aqua, 1/2 Gal., RB-2359 . . . .   150.00
Pet, Aqua, Glass Lid, Spring Wire Clamp, 1/2 Gal., 9 7/8 In., RB-2359 . . . .   198.00
Porcelain Lined, Aqua, Midget, RB-2374 . . . .   250.00
Porcelain Lined, Aqua, Qt., RB-2374 . . . .   25.00
Porcelain Lined, Wide Body, Qt., RB-1863-1 . . . .   35.00
Port Mason's Patent Nov 30th 1858, Aqua, Qt., RB-2380 . . . .   200.00
Potter & Bodine Philadelphia, Aqua, Ground Lip, 1/2 Gal., RB-2381 . . . .   168.00
Potter & Bodine Philadelphia, Aqua, Original Lid, Qt., RB-2381 . . . . .150.00 to 200.00
Potter & Bodine's Air-Tight Fruit Jar, Philada, Aqua, Wax Sealer, 1/2 Gal., 8 In., RB-2383   660.00
Potter & Bodine's Air-Tight Fruit Jar, Philada, Aqua, Barrel, 1/2 Gal., RB-2386 . . . .   1456.00
Premium Coffeyville, KAS, Pt., RB-2395 . . . . .25.00 to 40.00
Presto, 1/2 Pt., RB-2399 . . . .   35.00
Presto Glass Top, Pt., RB-2402 . . . .   2.00
Presto Glass Top, Qt., RB-2402 . . . .   2.00
Presto Glass Top W88X, Mfd. By Illinois Glass Co., 1/2 Pt., RB-2406 . . . .   15.00
Presto Supreme, Qt., RB-2407 . . . .   1.00
Presto Supreme Mason, Pt., RB-2407 . . . .   1.00
Presto Supreme Mason W 87X, Mfd. By Owens-Illinois Glass Co., 1/2 Pt., RB-2411-2 . .   15.00
Presto Wide Mouth, Glass Top, Mfg. By Owens Illinois Glass Co., Pt., RB-2416 . . . .   2.00

Presto Wide Mouth, Glass Top, Mfg. By Owens Illinois Glass Co., Qt., RB-2416 ...... 2.00
Princess, Qt., RB-2418 ....18.00 to 30.00
Protector, Aqua, Recessed Panels, 1/2 Gal., RB-2421 .... 80.00
Protector, Aqua, Recessed Panels, Lid, Pt., RB-2421 .... 475.00
Protector, Arched, Aqua, Qt., RB-2420 .... 50.00
Protector, Panels Not Recessed, Aqua, 1/2 Gal., RB-2423 .... 60.00
Protector, Recessed Panel, Aqua, Reproduction Lid, Qt., RB-2421-1 .... 40.00
Proteotor, Recessed Panels, Aqua, Lid, Qt., RB-2422 ....*Illus* 100.00
Putnam, On Base, Amber, Qt., RB-1492 .... 65.00
Putnam Trademark Lightning, On Base, Aqua, 91/4 In., RB-1493 .... 150.00
QG, Smoke Yellow, Pt., RB-1657 .... 225.00
QG, Sun Colored Amethyst, Pt., RB-1657 .... 225.00
QG, Sun Colored Amethyst, Qt., RB-1657 .... 125.00
Queen, Aqua, 1/2 Gal., RB-2433 .... 40.00
Queensland Fruit Jar, Q In Pineapple, Green, Qt., RB-2450 .... 300.00
Ravenna Glass Works, Air Tight Fruit Jar, Barrel, Rings, IP, Ice Blue, Lid, Qt., RB-2471 . 1792.00
Red Mason, Over A Key, Blue Green, Qt., RB-2474 .... 10.00
Retentive, Vertical, Aqua, Qt., RB-2498 .... 900.00
Root Mason, Aqua, 1/2 Gal., RB-2510 .... 15.00
Root Mason, Aqua, Qt., RB-2510 .... 10.00
Royal, Aqua, Zinc Collar, Qt., RB-2514 .... 350.00
Royal, Green Aqua, Lid, Qt., RB-2514 .... 350.00
Royal Trademark Full Measure Registered, Crown, Qt., RB-2517-1 .... 2.00
Royal Trademark Full Measure Registered Quart, Crown, Qt., RB-2516 .... 3.00
Royal Trademark Full Measure Registered Quart, Crown, Qt., RB-2520 .... 8.00
Royal Trademark Full Measure Registered 1/2 Gallon, Crown, RB-2518-1 .... 25.00
Royal Trade Mark Full Measure Registered Pint, Crown, Aqua, RB-2519 ....4.00 to 8.00
S Mason's Patent 1858, Aqua, 1/2 Gal., RB-1770 .... 15.00
Safe Seal, In Circle, Blue, Pt., RB-2530 .... 5.00
Safe Seal, In Circle, Pat'd July 14, 1908, Blue, Qt., RB-2531 .... 5.00
Safe Seal, In Circle, Pat'd July 14, 1908, Blue, Pt., RB-2531 .... 5.00
Safety, Amber, Qt., RB-2534 .... 250.00
Safety Seal, Qt., RB-2537 .... 6.00
Safety Seal Made In Canada, 1/2 Gal., RB-2536-1 .... 10.00
Safety Seal Made In Canada, Pt., RB-2536-1 .... 2.00
Safety Seal Made In Canada, Qt., RB-2536-1 .... 2.00
Safety Valve Patd May 21 1895 HC, 1/2 Gal., RB-2538 .... 12.00
Safety Valve Patd May 21 1895 HC, 1/2 Pt., RB-2538 .... 40.00
Safety Valve Patd May 21 1895, Emerald, Glass Lid, Wire Clamp, Pt., 5 3/4 In., RB-2538 209.00
Safety Valve Patd May 21 1895, Greek Key, Aqua 1/2 Gal., RB-2539 .... 75.00
Safety Valve Patd May 21 1895, Greek Key, Clear 1/2 Gal., RB-2539 .... 60.00
Safety Valve Patd May 21 1895, Greek Key, Emerald Green, 1/2 Gal., RB-2539 ... 500.00
Safety Valve Patd May 21 1895, Greek Key, Green, 1/2 Gal., RB-2539 .... 200.00
Safety Valve Patd May 21 1895 HC, Pt., RB-2538 .... 6.00
Safety Valve Patd May 21 1895 HC, Qt., RB-2538 .... 6.00
Safety Valve Patd May 21 1895 HC, Triangle, Amber, Pt., RB-2538 .... 750.00
Samco, Genuine Mason, In Circle, 1/2 Gal., RB-2545 .... 10.00
Samco, Genuine Mason, In Circle, Pt., RB-2545 .... 2.00
Samco, Genuine Mason, In Circle, Qt., RB-2545 .... 2.00
Samco Super Mason, Pt., RB-2548 .... 5.00
Samco Super Mason, Qt., RB-2548 .... 5.00
San Francisco Glass Works, Aqua, Groove Ring Wax Seal, Qt., RB-2552 .... 935.00
Sanford's, Qt., RB-2551 .... 28.00
Schram Automatic Sealer B, No Lid, Pt., RB-2569 .... 2.00
Schram Automatic Sealer B, Pt., RB-2569 .... 10.00
Schram Automatic Sealer B, Qt., RB-2569 .... 10.00
Sealtite Trademark, Pa G. Co., Qt., RB-2603-2 .... 18.00
Security Seal FGCo In Triangles, 1/2 Gal., RB-2609 .... 30.00
Security Seal FGCo In Triangles, Pt., RB-2608 .... 6.00
Security Seal FGCo In Triangles, Pt., RB-2609 .... 6.00
Security Seal FGCo In Triangles, Qt., RB-2609 .... 6.00
SKO Queen Trade Mark Improved, Twin Side Clamps, 1/2 Pt., RB-2437-1 .... 25.00
SKO Queen Trademark Wide Mouth Adjustable, Tight, Tall, 1/2 Pt., RB-2445 ..... 60.00

SKO Queen Trademark Wide Mouth Adjustable, Twin Wire Clamps, Pt., RB-2437 . . . . . 2.00
SKO Queen Trademark Wide Mouth Adjustable, Twin Wire Clamps, Qt., RB-2437 . . . . . 2.00
Smalley Full Measure Ags Monogram, Amber, Lid, Qt., RB-2648 . . . . 100.00
Smalley Full Measure AGS Qt., Amber, 7 1/4 In., RB-2648 . . . . 88.00
Smalley Nu-Seal Trademark, Diamonds, 1/2 Pt., RB-2657-1 . . . . 85.00
Smalley Nu-Seal Trademark, Diamonds, Sun Colored Amethyst, 1/2 Pt., RB-2657-1 . . . . 85.00
Smalley's Royal, Safety Knox Cover, 1/2 Pt., RB-2660 . . . . 40.00
Smalley's Royal Trademark Nu Seal, Crown, 1/2 Pt., RB-2661 . . . . 75.00
Smalley's Royal Trademark Nu Seal, Crown, 1/2 Pt., RB-2661-1 . . . . 100.00
Smalley's Royal Trademark Nu Seal, Crown, Pt., RB-2661 . . . . 9.00
Smalley's Royal Trademark Nu Seal, Crown, Qt., RB-2661 . . . . 9.00
Smalley's Royal Trademark Nu Seal, Crown, Sun Colored Amethyst, Pt., RB-2661 . . . . . 12.00
Standard, W. McC & Co., Cobalt, Groove Ring Wax Sealer, Qt., 7 1/2 In., RB 2701-1 . . . 880.00
Star, Above Star Emblem, Original Closure, Aqua, Qt., RB-2721 . . . . 450.00
Star, Circled By Fruit, Aqua, Reproduction Closure, 1/2 Gal., RB-2724 . . . . 150.00
Star Emblem, Circle Of Fruit, Aqua, Zinc Insert & Screw Band, Qt., RB-2724 . . . .143.00 to 200.00
Stephens Fruits & Jams, Gloucester, 2 Geese, Aqua, Embossed, 10 In. 17.00
Sun Trademark, In Circle, Aqua, Glass Lid, Metal Yoke Clamp, Qt., 7 3/4 In., RB-2761 . . 99.00
Superior A G Co., In Circle, Aqua, Pt., RB-2770 . . . . 12.00
Sure, Patd June 21st, 1870, Blue Aqua, Glass Lid, Qt., RB-2771 . . . . 364.00
Sure Seal In Circle, Blue, Pt., RB-2773 . . . . 3.00
Sure Seal In Circle, Blue, Qt., RB-2773 . . . . 3.00
Sure Seal Made For L. Bamberger & Co., Blue, Pt., RB-401-1 . . . . 25.00
Sure Seal Made For L. Bamberger & Co., Blue, Qt., RB-401-1 . . . . 25.00
Swayzee's Improved Mason, Ball Blue, 1/2 Gal., RB-2780 . . . . 15.00
Swayzee's Improved Mason, Ball Blue, Imperial, Qt., RB-2780 . . . . 15.00
Swayzee's Improved Mason, Ball Blue, Qt., RB-2780 . . . . 6.00
Swayzee's Improved Mason, Green, Imperial, Qt., RB-2780 . . . . 33.00
Swayzee's Improved Mason, Green, Qt., RB-2780 . . . . 38.00
TF, Mono Base, 1/2 Gal., RB-2820 . . . . 2.00
The Wears Jar, Stippled Frame, 1/2 Pt., RB-2919 . . . . 100.00
Trade Mark Mason's Improved, Aqua, Qt., RB-1717 . . . . 200.00
Trade Marks Mason's CFJCo Improved, Aqua, Midget Pt., RB-1722 . . . . .22.00 to 25.00
Trademark Banner Registered, Pt., RB-404 . . . . 10.00
Trademark Banner Registered, Qt., RB-404 . . . . 10.00
Trademark Banner Warranted, Ball Blue, Pt., RB-406-1 . . . . 7.00
Trademark Banner Warranted, Small Mouth, Aqua, Qt., RB-407 . . . . 12.00
Trademark Banner Wide Mouth, No Circle, Blue, 1/2 Pt., RB-411 . . . . .200.00 to 400.00
Trademark Banner WM Warranted, In Circle, Aqua, Pt., RB-410-1 . . . . 7.00
Trademark Climax Registered, 1/2 Pt., RB-612-1 . . . . 75.00
Trademark Keystone Registered, Pt., RB-1392 . . . . 6.00
Trademark Keystone Registered, Qt., RB-1391 . . . . 6.00
Trademark Lightning, Amber, Qt., RB-1489 . . . . 68.00
Trademark Lightning, Aqua, Pt., RB-1499 . . . . 4.00
Trademark Lightning, Aqua, Qt., RB-1499 . . . . 4.00
Trademark Lightning, Base Putnam, Amber, 1/2 Gal., RB-1489 . . . . 125.00
Trademark Lightning, Base Putnam, Amber, Pt., RB-1489 . . . . 150.00
Trademark Lightning, Base Putnam, Aqua, 24 Oz., RB-1489 . . . . .50.00 to 65.00
Trademark Lightning, Base Putnam, Golden Amber, 1/2 Gal., RB-1489 . . . . 125.00
Trademark Lightning, H.W.P., Amber, Glass Lid, 1/2 Gal., RB-1498 . . . . .101.00 to 125.00
Trademark Lightning, H.W.P., Amber, Qt., RB-1498 . . . . 250.00
Trademark Lightning, H.W.P., Aqua, 1/2 Gal., RB-1498 . . . . 48.00
Trademark Lightning, H.W.P., Base Putnam, Aqua, Qt., RB-1500 . . . . 325.00
Trademark Lightning, H.W.P., Yellow Amber, 1/2 Gal., RB-1498 . . . . 355.00
Trademark Lightning, Putnam On Base, Amber, Ground Lip, Glass Lid, Pt., RB-1489 . . . 67.00
Trademark Lightning, Putnam On Base, Amber, Ground Lip, Glass Lid, Qt., RB-1489 . . . 45.00
Trademark Lightning, Yellow, Pt., RB-1489 . . . . 350.00
Trademark Lightning Base, Putnam, Aqua, Salesman Sample, 1/2 Pt., RB-1489 . . . . 200.00
Trademark Lightning Putnam, Ground Lip, Aqua, 1/2 Pt., RB-1491 . . . . 35.00
Trademark Lightning Putnam, Registered U.S. Patent Office, Aqua, 1/2 Pt., RB-1495 8.00 to 15.00
Trademark Lightning Putnam On Base, Amber, 24 Oz., RB-1491 . . . . 150.00
Trademark Lightning Putnam On Base, Amber, Ground Lip, Glass Lid, Qt., RB-1489 . . 56.00
Trademark Lightning Reg US Patent Office, Aqua, Qt., RB-1501 . . . . 4.00

Trademark Lightning Reg US Patent Office, Pt., RB-1501 .... 1.00
Trademark Lightning Reg US Patent Office, Qt., RB-1501 .... 1.00
Trademark Lightning Registered U.S. Patent Office, Aqua, 1/2 Gal., RB-1502 .... 15.00
Trademark No I Lightning, Aqua, 1/2 Gal., RB-1507-1 .... 135.00
Trademark No I Lightning, Aqua, Qt., RB-1507-1 .... 135.00
Trademark The Dandy, Pat Oct.13, 1885, Amber, Glass Lid, 1/2 Gal., RB-751 ....213.00 to 250.00
Trademark The Smalley Self Sealer, Pt., RB-2666 .... 6.00
Trademark The Smalley Self Sealer, Qt., RB-2666 .... 6.00 to 8.00
Trademark V R Lightning, Fancy Letters, Aqua, Qt., RB-1507-4 .... 150.00
Trues Imperial Brand, D.W. True & Co. Portland, Me., Pt., RB-2828 .... 15.00
Vacuum Seal Fruit Jar, Patented Nov 1st, 1904, Detroit, Tooled Lip, Qt., RB-2870 ...... 78.00
Valve Jar Co. Philadelphia, Patd Mar 10th 1868, Aqua, Glass Lid, Clamp, Qt., RB-2873 .. 385.00
Van Vliet Jar Of 1881, Aqua, Glass Lid, Metal Yoke Clamp, 1/2 Gal., 7 1/2 In., RB-2878 . 523.00
Veteran Bust In Circle & Frame, 1/2 Pt., RB-2884-1 .... 250.00
Victory, Crown Victory Jar, In Shield On Milk Glass Lid, Pt., RB-2901 .... 8.00
Victory, In Shield On Lid, Pt., RB-2900 .... 5.00
Victory, On Lid, Twin Side Clamps, Pt., RB-2897 .... 6.00
Victory, Patd Feb 9th 1864 Reisd June 22 1867, Aqua, Qt., RB-2889-2 .... 100.00
Victory, Shield On Lid, Twin Side Clamps, 1/2 Pt., RB-2897 .... 20.00
Victory, The Victory Jar, In Shield, On Lid, Twin Side Clamps, Pt., RB-2898 .... 4.00
Victory I, Patd Feby 9th 1864 Reisd June 22d 1867, Aqua, Qt., RB-2891 .... 80.00
Victory Reg'd 1925, On Lid, Twin Wire Clamps, 1/2 Pt., RB-2903 .... 15.00
W. Chrysler Pat. Nov. 21 1865, Aqua, Applied Lip, Qt., 7 3/4 In., RB-597-1 .... 1210.00
Wan-Eta, Aqua, Qt., RB-2909 .... 15.00
Wan-Eta Cocoa Boston, Amber, Lid, 1/2 Pt., RB-2909 .... 35.00
Wears, On Banner, Below Crown, Twin Side Clamps, Pt., RB-2913 .... 9.00
Wears Jar, In Circle, Pt., RB-2916 .... 9.00
Wears Jar, In Stippled Frame, Pt., RB-2918 .... 7.00
Wears Jar, In Stippled Frame, Qt., RB-2915 .... 7.00
Wears Jar, In Stipples Oval, 1/2 Gal., RB-2919 .... 20.00
Wears Jar, In Stipples Oval, Pt., RB-2919 .... 7.00
Western Pride Patented June 22, 1875, Aqua, Aqua Lid, Qt., Original Clamp, RB-2945 . 300.00
Wheeler Fruit Jar, Aqua, Qt., RB-2953 .... 250.00
White King Washes Everything, Aqua, Pt., RB-2963 .... 20.00
Winslow Jar, Glass Lid, Brass Wire, Aqua, Qt., RB-3023 .... 100.00
Wo Hop Company, 759 Clay ST. San Francisco Calif USA, Pt., RB-3026 .... 18.00
Woodbury WGW, Aqua, Pt., RB-3028 .... 90.00
Yeomans's Fruit Bottle, Aqua, 1/2 Gal., RB-3039 ....*Illus* 75.00
Young's Pat. May 27 1902, Stoneware, 1/2 Gal., RB-3043 .... 60.00

GARNIER

The house of Garnier Liqueurs was founded in 1859 in Enghien, France. Figurals have been made through the nineteenth and twentieth centuries, except for the years of Prohibition and World War II. Julius Wile and Brothers, a New York City firm established in 1877, became the exclusive U.S. agents for Garnier in 1885. Many of the bottles were not sold in the United States but were purchased in France or the Caribbean and brought back home. Only miniature bottles were sold in the United States from 1970 to 1973. From 1974 to 1978, Garnier was distributed in the United States by Fleischmann Distilling Company. In 1978 the Garnier trademark was acquired by Standard Brands, Inc., the parent company of Julius Wile Sons and Company and Fleischmann Distilling Co., and a few of the full-sized bottles were again sold in the United States. Standard Brands later merged with Nabisco Brands, Inc. In 1987 Nabisco sold the Garnier Liqueurs trademark to McGuiness Distillers, Ltd., of Canada, which was sold to Corby Distillers. The liquor is no longer made.

Bullfighter, 1963 .... 15.00
Cannon, 1964 .... 8.00
Card, King Of Hearts, 1971, 2 Oz., 4 3/4 In. ....5.00 to 12.50
Card, Queen Of Hearts, 1971, 2 Oz., 4 3/4 In. 12.50
Citroen, 1922 Model, 1970 .... 4.00
Clown's Head, 1931 ....108.00 to 222.00
Cockerel, Black, Gold Highlights 60.00
Collie, 1972, Miniature, 4 1/2 In. 12.60
Creme De Cacao, 1940s, Miniature 4.00

Eiffel Tower, 1950 . . . . .32.00 to 75.00
Fish, 1974, 2 Oz., 5 1/2 In. 11.00
Foo Dog 33.00
Goldfinch, Box, 1971, 5 1/2 In. 13.00
Indy 500, No. 1, 1970 . . . . 30.00
Indy 500, No. 2, 1970 . . . . 27.00
MG, 1913 Model, 1969 . . . . 19.00
Mocking Bird, 1969, 11 1/2 In. 30.00
Mocking Bird, Box, 1971, 5 1/2 In. 4.50
Napoleon, 1969 . . . . .10.00 to 21.00
Pelican, 1935 . . . . 455.00
Policeman, 1970 . . . . 5.24
Roadrunner, 1969 . . . . 25.00
Roadrunner, Box, 5 1/2 In. 4.50
Rolls-Royce, 1904 Model, 1970 . . . . 19.00
Rooster, Black, Gold Trim, 1952 . . . . 6.00
Sailor, Blue, White, Late 1930s, 4 1/2 In. 40.00
Stanley Steamer, 1912 Model, 1970 . . . . 20.00
Telephone, 13 In. 100.00
Violin, 1966 . . . . .18.00 to 26.00
Woman, With Jug, 13 In. 77.00

GIN

The word gin comes from the Dutch word genever, meaning juniper. It is said that gin was invented in the seventeenth century in Holland to be used as a medicine. One of the earliest types of gin was what today is called *Geneva* or *Hollands* gin. It is made from a barley malt grain mash and juniper berries. The alcohol content is low and it is usually not used for cocktails. In some countries it is considered medicine. In England and America, the preferred drink is dry gin, which is made with juniper berries, coriander seeds, angelica root, and other flavors. The best dry gin is distilled, not mixed by the process used during Prohibition to make bathtub gin. Another drink is Tom gin, much like dry gin but with sugar added. Gin bottles have been made since the 1600s. Most of them have straight sides. Gin has always been an inexpensive drink, which is why so many of these bottles were made. Many were of a type called *case bottles* today. The case bottle was made with straight sides so that 4 to 12 bottles would fit tightly into a wooden packing case.

A. Houtman & Co., Schiedam, Pig Snout, Case, Black Glass, Shoulder Seal, Dutch, 11 In. 135.00
A. Van Hoboken & Co., Rotterdam, Case, Green, Rolled Lip, Seal 77.00
A. Van Hoboken & Co., Rotterdam, Case, Olive Green, AH Seal 22.00
A. Van Hoboken & Co., Rotterdam, Case, Olive Green, Tapering Square, Seal, 11 In. 61.00
A. Van Hoboken & Co., Rotterdam, Olive Green, Pig Snout Lip, Tapering Square, 11 In. . . 45.00
A. Van Hoboken & Co., Rotterdam, Olive, Tapered, Blob Lip, Embossed, Seal, 11 1/4 In. . 100.00
Bininger, see the Bininger category
Case, Cobalt Blue, Tooled Mouth, Tapered, 10 1/8 In. 1680.00
Case, Emerald Green, Wide Tool Flared Out Lip, Open Pontil, 1770-80, 1 1/4 In. 1100.00
Case, Juniper Leaf, Amber, Tooled Mouth, 10 5/8 In. 45.00
Case, Medium Emerald Green, Dip Mold, Applied Mouth, Open Pontil, 1770-90, 10 In. . . 275.00
Case, Medium Olive Green, Applied Mouth, Open Pontil, 14 1/8 In. 1045.00
Case, Medium Olive Green, Square Shape, Tapered, Pontil, 11 1/4 In. 327.00
Case, Olive Amber, Applied Lip, Pontil, 1770-1800, 18 x 6 In. 1045.00
Case, Olive Amber, Dip Mold, Applied Lip, Mid 1800s, Pt., 9 1/2 In. 39.00
Case, Olive Amber, Embossed African, Pt. 29.00
Case, Olive Amber, Footed Base, Seedy Bubbles, 10 In. 25.00
Case, Olive Amber, Pontil, Applied Mouth, 9 5/8 In. 100.00
Case, Olive Green, Pig Snout, Free-Blown, Dutch, 9 In. 75.00
Case, Olive Green, String Style Top, Pontil, 10 In. 176.00
Case, Olive Green, Tapered Shape, Pig Snout, Lip, Seal, Embossed, 11 1/4 In. 20.00
Case, Olive Yellow Amber, Dip Mold, Applied Mouth, OP, c.1785, 9 5/8 In. . . . . *Illus* 100.00
Case, Pewter Overlay, Vegetation, 10 1/4 In. 55.00
Case, Prussian Blue, Olive Yellow Swirls, Tooled Lip, 10 1/8 In. 392.00
Case, Square, Olive Green, Applied Top, Open Pontil, 11 x 4 In. 126.00
Case, Tobacco Amber, Olive Tone, Dip Mold, Applied Mouth, 13 3/8 In. 224.00

Gin, Case, Olive Yellow
Amber, Dip Mold,
Applied Mouth, OP,
c.1785, 9 5/8 In.

Gin, Cosmopoliet,
J.J. Melchers, WZ,
Schiedam, Case, Olive
Green, 9 7/8 In.

Corning & Company, Olive Amber, Qt., 9 3/4 In. 69.00
Cosmopoliet, J.J. Melchers, WZ, Schiedam, Case, Olive Green, 9 7/8 In. . . . .*Illus* 224.00
Cosmopoliet, J.J. Melchers, WZ, Schiedam, Man Holding Bottle, Olive Amber, 10 1/8 In. 157.00
Cosmopoliet, J.J. Melchers, WZ, Schiedam, Olive Green, Man, Dutch, c.1880, 10 1/2 In. . 190.00
Cut Glass, Olive Green, Applied Lip, 12 1/2 In. 345.00
Daniel Visser & Zonen, Schiedam, Case, Olive, Blob Top, 3-Barrel Shoulder Seal, 11 In. . 75.00
Daniel Visser & Zonen, Schiedam, Case, Olive, Rolled Blob Top, Shoulder Seal, 11 In. . . 65.00
Daniel Visser & Zonen, Schiedam, Clear, Blue Green Shoulder Seal, 11 1/2 In. 119.00
Daniel Visser & Zonen, Schiedam, Clear, Cobalt Blue Shoulder Seal, 11 1/2 In. 89.00
Devils Island Endurance, Clear, Pt. 15.00
Fleischman's, Square, Label, 8 1/2 In. 8.50
Henry H. Schufeldt & Co., Case, Green 65.00
J. Pfaff, 16 Exchange St., Boston, Case, Amber, 2 Seals, Schiedam, Schnapps, 9 3/4 In. . . . 2128.00
J. Van Der Koop & Sons, Case, Clear, Iron Cross Medal, Tooled Top, 7 In. 30.00
Juniper Leaf, This Bottle Property Of Theodore Netter, Golden Orange, Qt., 10 1/2 In. . . . 69.00
Levert & Schudel Haarlem, Case, Clear, Embossed, 5 5/8 In. 30.00
London Jockey Club House, Yellow Green, Applied Sloping Double Collar, 9 3/4 In. 532.00
London Royal Imperial, Cobalt Blue, Applied Mouth, 9 3/4 In. 735.00
Olive Yellow, Square, Tapered, Applied Collared Mouth, 14 7/8 In. 1456.00
P. Loopuyt & Co. Distillers Schiedam, Case, Olive, Applied Top, Dutch, c.1890, 9 1/2 In. 38.00
Pond's Gin-Ger-Gin, Case, Aqua, Glass Stopper, Lip Foil, 9 7/8 In. 65.00
Royal Imperial, London, Cobalt Blue, Sloping Collar, 1870-80, 9 7/8 In. 2016.00
Sapphire, Neck, Shoulders Turn To Teal, Tooled Mouth, 1870-90, 10 In. 392.00
Square, Olive Amber, Applied Sloping Collared Mouth, Pontil Scar, 17 1/2 In. 2300.00
V. Hoytema Q.C., Case, Black, 11 In. 45.00
Warner's Imported English, Aqua, Square, Applied Top, 9 In. 88.00

GINGER BEER

Ginger beer was originally made from fermented ginger root, cream of tartar, sugar,
yeast, and water. It was a popular drink from the 1850s to the 1920s. Beer made from
grains became more popular and very little alcoholic ginger beer was made. Today it is
an alcohol-free carbonated drink like soda. Pottery bottles have been made since the
1650s. A few products are still bottled in stoneware containers today. Ginger beer, vinegar, and cider were usually put in stoneware holders until the 1930s. The ginger beer
bottle usually held 10 ounces. Blob tops, tapered collars, and crown tops were used.
Some used a cork, others a Lightning stopper or inside screw stopper. The bottles were
of shades of brown and white. Some were salt glazed for a slightly rough, glassy finish. Bottles were stamped or printed with names and usually the words *ginger beer.*

A.F. Lawson, Brewed Largs, Millport, Blue Transfer, Buchan, 8 In. 166.00
A.W. Buchan & Co., Waverley Potteries, Portobello, Scotland, Sample, 7 In. 2937.00
A.W. Mackintosh, 2-Tone, Sloping Shoulder, 8 1/2 In. 35.00
Alexanders, London, Blue Print, 7 1/2 In. 164.00
Andrew A. Watt & Co. Ltd., Londonberry, Prancing Lion, 2-Tone, 8 In. 25.00
Arliss Robinson, Blue Top, 6 3/4 In. 205.00
Arliss Robinson & Co., Home Brewed, Sutton Surrey, 2-Tone, Blue Blob Top, 6 3/4 In. . . 33.00
Arnold & Co., Monks Abbey, Lincoln Limited, 2-Tone, Blob Top, 7 1/4 In. 50.00
Barker's, Cambridge, Stoneware, 2-Tone, 6 1/2 In. 24.00

Barnstaple, C.C. Dornat & Co., Tree, Price Bristol, 6 3/4 In. 23.00
Bass & Alsopps Stout, 2-Tone, Sloping Shoulder, Blob Top, 8 In. 20.00
Bath Brewery Limited, Home Brewed, King Blandud, 6 3/4 In. 33.00
Beaufoy & Co., Stoneware, All White Glaze, 6 3/4 In. 97.00
Beuer Meppel, Crown Cap, Pale Blue Neck, Black Transfer, 7 1/2 In. 81.00
Binnington & Co., Good Old Fashioned, House, 6 3/4 In. 255.00
Binnington & Co., Good Old Fashioned, Star Works, Buchan, 6 3/4 In. 23.00
Bowack Brothers, Brown Top, Crown Cork Stopper, Skittle Shape, 5 3/4 In. 818.00
Brewster & Dodgson, Fermented, Stone, Leeds, 2-Tone, Blob Top, 8 1/2 In. 17.00
British Public House Co., Rampant Lion, 2-Tone, Black Transfer, Blob Top, 8 In. 72.00
Brothwell & Essam, Forncett St., Sheffield, 2-Tone, Blob Top, 7 3/4 In. 50.00
C.C. Dornat, Barnstaple, Oak Tree, Honey Glaze, Shouldered 20.00
Campbell Praed & Co., Home Brewed, Unicorn, Stoneware, 2-Tone, 6 3/4 In. 49.00
Carlisle New Brewery, Coat Of Arms, Stoneware, 2-Tone, 8 In. 45.00
Carlisle Old Brewery, Coat Of Arms, Stoneware, 2-Tone, Champagne Shape, 8 1/4 In. . . . 45.00
Comrie & Co., Special, Old Scotch, Helensburgh, White, Black Transfer, Blob Top, 8 In. . 92.00
Coomb Spring, Mineral Water Co., Ltd., All White Glaze, 7 In. 56.00
Corcoran & Co., Carlow, Castle Ruins, Ireland, 6 3/4 In. 685.00
D. Kelly & Co., Stone Ginger, Limited, Leith, 2-Tone, Blob Top, 8 1/4 In. 284.00
Darlington Bottling, Blue Print, 7 1/2 In. 61.00
Dee Mineral Water Co., Crystal Brewed, Portland Works, Price Bristol, 7 In. 33.00
Doulton Lambeth, Tan, Salt Glaze, Blob Top, England, 2 1/4 In. 24.00
E.E. Bevan, Blue Top, 6 3/4 In. 72.00
E.L. Newsomes Ltd., Blackpool, 8 In. 49.00
Edge Ye Olde Brewed Ginger Beer, Longsight, 2-Tone, Champagne Shape, 1919 . . . . 40.00
Edmondson & Co., Liverpool, Girl On Swing, 8 In. 20.00
Edmondson & Co., Ltd., Girl On Swing, 8 In. 62.00
Emmerson Jnr Newcastle On Tyne, Cyclist, 2-Tone 75.00
F. Sandkuhler, Stoneware, Salt Glazed, Hand Thrown, Baltimore, 7 In. 49.00
F.E. Coverdale & Son, 2-Tone, Blob Top, 8 In. 32.00
Firths Darlington, Brewed Ginger Beer, Train, Blue Transfer, 2-Tone, Blob Top, 7 In. . . . 42.00
Fitzgerald's, Fermented, Newcastle On Tyne, Blue Transfer, 2-Tone, Blob Top, 7 1/2 In. . . 17.00
G&C Moore, Limited, Edinburgh, Green Top, Black Transfer, Buchan, 8 1/2 In. 137.00
G. Bullock & Son, White, Mineral Water, Works, Blackpool, Black Transfer, Blob Top, 8 In. 92.00
G.W. Southern Belper, Black Transfer, 8 In. 112.00
Geo Jeff & Co., White, Black Transfer, Pixie On Toadstool, 8 In. 859.00
Gilbert Rae, Green Top, Black Transfer, 7 In. . . . . .41.00 to 52.00
Gilpin & Coy Newcastle & Gateshead, 2-Tone, Blue Print, 8 1/4 In. 55.00
Gould's, Carisbrooke Brewed, One Penny, 6 3/4 In. 20.00
Grantham, G. Dale, Street Lamp, Pearson Chesterfield, 8 1/2 In. 78.00
Groves & Whitnall Globe Works Salford, Globe, 6-Point Star 20.00
Guiness Extra Stout, Blue Print, 8 In. 76.00
H. Firth, Manningham, Sailing Ship, 7 1/4 In. 33.00
H.C. Baildon & Son, 2-Tone, Mallet Shape, Applied Ring, 8 1/2 In. 32.00
H.C. Baildon & Son, Chemists, Edinburgh, Buchan, 8 1/2 In. 59.00
H.C. Baildon & Son, Edinburgh, Buchan Portabello, Number 08, Stoneware, 2-Tone 15.00
Harston & Co., Leeds, Dove, Leaves In Mouth, 2-Tone, Blob Top, 6 3/4 In. 50.00
Hay & Sons, Large Logo, Trademark, Registered, Elgin, c.1900, 11 In. 35.00
Hay & Sons Inverurie, Stoneware, 2-Tone, Brown Print, Blob Top, 8 1/2 In. 45.00
Henley On Thames, 6 3/4 In. 31.00
Holliday & Co., Estra Stout, North Shields, Buchan Portobello, 8 In. 88.00
Home Brewed, Renton Street, Sheffield, Wheat Sheaf, 7 1/4 In. . . . . .43.00 to 49.00
J Robertson & Co., 38 York Place, Edinburgh, Thistle, 2-Tone, Blob Top, 8 1/2 In. 45.00
J. Macintyre & Co., Number 2, Salt Glaze, 8 1/2 In. 15.00
J. Mills & Sons, London, Coat Of Arms, Beehive Lip, 2-Tone, Blob Top, 7 In. 28.00
J. Swenden & Co. Ltd., Fermented, Darlington, Blue Print, 2-Tone, Blob Top, 7 3/4 In. . . . 58.00
J.S. Eyre & Co., Launceston, Return Established 1830, 2-Tone, Blob Top, 7 In. 25.00
J.W. Hall & Sons, Walkden & Patricroft, Cockerel, 8 In. 43.00
Jack N. Baldry Crown Cap, Brown Glass, Crown Cork Closure, Embossed, 7 1/4 In. 41.00
James Alexander, Blue Print, 8 3/4 In. 41.00
James Bros. Manufacturers, Manly, Olive Green Top, 7 In. 215.00
James Jeffery, The Quencher, Jopps Lane, Aberdeen, Fireman, 8 3/4 In. 104.00
James M. Tod, Seafield Tower, Black Transfer, 8 1/4 In. 328.00

James Wilson, Pulteney Town, 2-Tone, Blob Top, Black Transfer, 9 In. 204.00
Jas Rose & Co., Oatmeal Stout, Caistor Lincoln, 2-Tone, Blob Top, 8 3/4 In. 33.00
Jas. Thatcher & Compy, West Drayton Britannia, Cottage, 2-Tone, Blob Top, 6 1/2 In. . . . 500.00
John Breslins, Blue Top, 2-Tone, 7 3/4 In. 204.00
John Milne, Brewed, Established 1846, Stonehaven, Brown Transfer, 2-Tone, 9 In. 25.00
John Milne, Stonehaven, Brown Print, 9 1/4 In. 20.00
John Thompson, Stout For Invalids, Blyth, 8 In. 29.00
Joseph Dalzells, Arm Holding Barrel, 2-Tone, Black Transfer, 6 3/4 In. 176.00
Julius Peters, Bull, Stoneware, 2-Tone, Champagne Shape, 8 In. 49.00
Leigh & Co. Globe Works Salford, Globe, 6-Point Star 15.00
Licensed Victuallers, Blue Top, Blue Transfer, 7 1/4 In. 450.00
Limonade Gazeuse, Blue Top, Black Transfer, 7 1/4 In. 41.00
London Super Aeration Ltd., Green Top, 6 3/4 In. 86.00
Ludford, Crewe Mineral Water Company, Locomotive, Honey Glaze 45.00
Marsom & Sons Maypole, Northill, Biggleswade, Galtee More, White, Blob Top, 6 3/4 In. 25.00
Martins, Ye Old Style Brewed, East Crinstead, Doulton Lambeth, 2-Tone, 6 1/2 In. 33.00
McCall's, D. McCall & Co., Sorba Park, Oban, 2-Tone, 8 1/2 In. 84.00
Milnes & Son Undercliffe, Pure Brewed, Bradford, Blob Top, 7 In. 33.00
Murtough, Portsea, Knight On Horseback, Doulton Lambeth, 2-Tone, Blob Top, 6 1/2 In. 37.00
Newcastle, Wm. Jackson & Co., Man Holding Flag, Bourne Denby, 7 1/4 In. 20.00
North & Randall, Blue Top, 6 3/4 In. 123.00
North & Randall, Blue Top, Bourne Denby, 7 1/4 In. 274.00
Norton & Co., Stoneware, Blue Lip, Blue Print, Blob Top, 7 In. 45.00
P. Mason, Kitt Hill, Callington, Home Brewed, Tin Mine, White Glaze, 6 3/4 In. 159.00
Padiham Aerated Water Co., Ltd., Blue Transfer, 8 In. 73.00
Patrick Sheridan, Stoneware, Cobalt Decoration, Qt. 39.00
Phillips & Co., Wellington, Goalie, 8 1/4 In. 88.00
Pink's, None Nicer, Stoneware, Chichester, 6 3/4 In. 35.00
Pope Staplehurst, Crown, Doulton Lambeth, 6 3/4 In. 117.00
Price Bristol, Galtee More, Sole Makers, Patent No. 4172, White Glaze, 6 3/4 In. 33.00
R. Ellis & Son, Black Transfer, Goat, Skittle Shape, 8 In. 1392.00
R. Stotherton & Sons, Bearded Man, 8 In. 418.00
Redruth Brewery Co Ltd, Bird, Carrying Man In Basket, Moon, Tan Glaze, 7 In. 112.00
Rhyl Mineral Water Co., All White Glaze, Black Transfer, Cricket Bat, Stumps, 7 In. 184.00
Rimmington & Son, Bradford, Alchemist, White Glaze, 6 3/4 In. 50.00
Robert Henderson, Black Man Drinking Ginger Beer, 8 In. 164.00
S. Fulford Manchester, Lion, Honey Glaze 35.00
S.H. Ward & Co. Ltd., Renton Street, Sheffield, Home Brewed, 2-Tone, Blob Top, 7 In. . . 50.00
Silloth, Blue Transfer, Yacht, 8 In. 655.00
Skene & Company, Celebrated, Dufftown, Highlander, Playing Bagpipe, 2-Tone, 8 1/2 In. 69.00
Skene & Company, Dufftown, 8 3/4 In. 20.00
Sketch's, Purity & Excellence, Green Blob Top, 7 In. 163.00
South West Min Water Co., Bournemouth, Castle, Bristol, 6 3/4 In. 20.00
Stone Ginger Beer, 2-Tone, H.C. Baildon & Son, Edinburgh, Buchan Portabello 15.00
Strachan Aberdeen, Blue Print, 8 3/4 In. 61.00
T W Lawson XX, Manchester, Moon, Star, Water, Honey Glazed, Shouldered 20.00
T. Armstrong & Son, Stout, 8 In. 45.00
T. Cook & Son, Folkestone & Dover, Foaming Glass, 7 3/4 In. . . . . .39.00 to 52.00
T. Hills, 2-Tone, Galloping Horse, 8 In. 81.00
T. Hills, Stone Brewed, 247 Beverley Road, Hull, 2-Tone, Blob Top, 8 1/4 In. 117.00
T. Wright, Red Print, 8 In. 286.00
Taff Aerated Water Co., Blue Top, 8 3/4 In. 471.00
Thacker & Christmas, White Glaze, 7 1/4 In. 65.00
Thos. Wood Colchester, 6 1/2 In. 73.00
Tuddenahm Bros., Black Transfer, 2 In. 328.00
Vancouver B.C. Canadian, Ye Old Country Stone, Tan, Off-White, Crown Top, 7 In., 10 Oz. 50.00
Victoria Wind Company, Queen Victoria Portrait, Established 1865, 6 1/2 In. 49.00
W & J Cruickshank, Ye Olden, Buckie, Blue Transfer, 2-Tone, Blob Top, 8 1/2 In. 167.00
W & J Jenkinson, Sea Monster, Black Transfer, 8 3/4 In. 143.00
W & J Jenkinson, Seahorse, 2-Tone, Sloping Shoulder, Blob Top, 9 In. 73.00
W. Atkinson & Sons, Castle Ruins, 10 In. 409.00
W. Magner, Black Transfer, Blue Top, 8 In. 614.00
W. Underwood, Sloping Shoulder, Factories, Lightening, 2-Tone, 8 1/4 In. 183.00

W.B. Mew Langton & Co., Newport Isle Of Wight, Horse, Powell Bristol, 7 In. 23.00
W.F. Cornforth, Edge Lane, Droylsden, White Glaze, Blob Top, 6 3/4 In. 17.00
W.F. Cornforth Edge Lane Droylsden, Bird On Nest, Early 1890s 18.00
Washington Bottling Co., Washington D.C., Stoneware 37.00
Wigmore & Co., Stoneware, Beaumont St. Brewery, White Glaze, 6 3/4 In. 41.00
William Smith, Milton Bridge, Edinburgh, 8 3/4 In. 32.00
Wm. Hill, Blue Top, 7 1/2 In. 225.00
Wm. Hill, Blue Top, Black Transfer, 7 1/2 In. 184.00
Wrexham's Fermented Stone, Goat, Stoneware, 2-Tone, 6 3/4 In. 59.00
Ye Old Fashioned Brewed, W. Tomlinson, Bradford, Coat Of Arms, 2-Tone, 8 In. 33.00

――――――――――――――――――――――――― **GLUE** ―――――――――――――――――――――――――
Glue and paste have been packaged in bottles since the nineteenth century. Most of these bottles have identifying paper labels. A few have the name embossed in the glass.

Mucilage, 8-Sided, Aqua, Thin Flared Out Lip, Open Pontil, 1840-60, 3 1/8 In. 165.00
Mucilage, 8-Sided, Aqua, Whimsy, Inward Rolled Lip, Open Pontil, 1840-60, 3 In. 1320.00

―――――――――――――――――――――――― **GRENADIER** ――――――――――――――――――――――――
The Grenadier Spirits Company of San Francisco, California, started making figural porcelain bottles in 1970. Twelve soldier-shaped fifths were in Series No. 1. These were followed by Series 2 late in 1970. Only 400 cases were made of each soldier. The company continued to make bottles in series, including the 1976 American Revolutionary Army regiments in fifths and tenths, and many groups of minibottles. They also had series of club bottles, missions, foreign generals, horses, and more. The brothel series was started in 1978 for a special customer, Mr. Dug Picking of Carson City, Nevada. These are usually sold as *Dug's Nevada Brothels* and are listed in this book under Miniature. The Grenadier Spirits Company sold out to Fleishmann Distilling Company and stopped making the bottles about 1980. Jon-Sol purchased the remaining inventory of bottles.

Father's Gift, 1979, 8 x 7 In. . . . . .1.00 to 5.00
Horse, Tennessee Walker, 1978 . . . .*Illus*   24.00
Mission San Francisco De Asis, 1978 . . . .*Illus*   9.00
Mr. Spock, Bust, Box, 1979 . . . . .18.00 to 31.00
Mr. Spock, Full Figure, Gold, 1979 . . . .   217.00
Pancho Villa & Rudolpho, 1978 . . . .   25.00
Santa Claus, 1978 . . . .*Illus*   10.00
Soldier, 1st Officers Guard, 1970 . . . .   10.00
Soldier, 3rd Guard, Miniature 10.00
Soldier, General Custer, 1970 . . . . .10.00 to 34.00
Soldier, General Francisco Pancho Villa, On Horse 15.50
Soldier, General Francisco Pancho Villa, On Horse, Box 25.00
Soldier, John Paul Jones, 1976 . . . .   19.00
Soldier, Kings African Rifle Corps, 1970 . . . .   18.00
Soldier, Lannes, 1970 . . . .   18.00

Grenadier, Horse, Tennessee
Walker, 1978

Grenadier, Mission San Francisco
De Asis, 1978

Grenadier, Santa
Claus, 1978

Soldier, Murat, 1970	18.00
Soldier, Ney, 1969	18.00
Soldier, Officer, 1st Guard Regiment, 1971	11.50
Soldier, Robert E. Lee, 1976	33.00
Soldier, Teddy Roosevelt, 1976	13.00 to 30.00

HAIR PRODUCTS, see Cosmetic; Cure
HAND LOTION, see Cosmetic; Medicine

HOFFMAN

J. Wertheimer had a distillery in Kentucky before the Civil War. Edward Wertheimer and his brother Lee joined the business as young men. When Edward Sr. died at age 92, his son Ed Wertheimer Jr., became president. Edward Jr.'s sons, Ed Wertheimer III and Thomas Wertheimer, also worked in the family company. L. & E. Wertheimer Inc. made the products of the Hoffman Distilling Company and the Old Spring Distilling Company, including Old Spring Bourbon, until 1983 when the company was sold to Commonwealth Distillery, a company still in existence. Hoffman Originals, later called the Hoffman Club, was founded by the Wertheimers in 1971 to make a series of figural bottles. The first was the Mr. Lucky series, started in 1973. These were leprechaun-shaped decanters. Five series of leprechauns were made. Other series include wildlife, decoy ducks (1977-1978), Aesop's fables, C.M. Russell (1978), rodeo (1978), pool-playing dogs (1978), belt buckles (1979), horses (1979), Jack Richardson animals, Bill Ohrmann animals (1980-1981), cheerleaders (1980), framed pistols (1978), political (1980), and college football (1981-1982). The miniature Hoffman bottles include series such as leprechauns (1981), birds (1978), dogs and cats (1978-1981), decoys (1978-1979), pistols on stands (1975), Street Swingers (musicians, 1978-1979), pistols (1975), wildlife (1978), and horses (1978). Hoffman decanters are no longer made.

Alaska Pipeline, 1975	13.75
Convention, Leprechaun On Barrel, 1982	10.00 to 25.00
Horse, Appaloosa Yearling, 1979, Miniature	16.00 to 20.00
Horse, Arabian Stallion, 1979, Miniature	8.50 to 17.00
Horse, Quarter Horse, 1979, Miniature	8.50 to 28.00
Horse, Shetland Pony, 1979, Miniature	6.00 to 14.50
Mr. Lucky, 1973	11.00 to 15.00
Mr. Lucky, 1978, Miniature	10.00 to 18.00
Mr. Lucky, Baker, 1978	10.00
Mr. Lucky, Blacksmith, 1976, Miniature	10.00
Mr. Lucky, Butcher, 1979	9.00 to 15.50
Mr. Lucky, Carolers, 1979	10.00
Mr. Lucky, Carpenter, 1979	9.00
Mr. Lucky, Charmer, 1974	9.00
Mr. Lucky, Cobbler, 1973	9.00
Mr. Lucky, Dancer, 1974, Miniature	10.00
Mr. Lucky, Doctor, Box, 1974	*Illus* 15.00
Mr. Lucky, Farmer, Musical, 1980	15.00
Mr. Lucky, Fiddler, 1974, Miniature	*Illus* 9.50
Mr. Lucky, Fireman, Retired, 1983, Miniature	10.00 to 15.00
Mr. Lucky, Guitarist, 1975, Miniature	9.50

Hoffman, Mr.
Lucky, Doctor,
Box, 1974

Hoffman, Mr. Lucky,
Fiddler, 1974,
Miniature

Hoffman,
Mr. Lucky,
Stockbroker, 1976

Mr. Lucky, Harpist, 1974 .... 9.00
Mr. Lucky, Harpist, Musical, 1975 .... 18.00
Mr. Lucky, Mechanic, 1979, Miniature 9.00
Mr. Lucky, Musical, 1973 ....8.50 to 10.00
Mr. Lucky, Organ Player, 1979, Miniature 10.50
Mr. Lucky, Photographer, 1980, Miniature 10.00
Mr. Lucky, Pilot, 1989, Miniature 13.00
Mr. Lucky, Plumber, 1978, Miniature 9.00
Mr. Lucky, Policeman, 1975 .... 9.00
Mr. Lucky, Policeman, 1986, Miniature 23.00
Mr. Lucky, Policeman, Musical, Box, 1975 ....19.00 to 20.00
Mr. Lucky, Sandman, 1974 .... 9.00
Mr. Lucky, Sandman, Musical, 1974 .... 18.00
Mr. Lucky, Saxophonist, 1975 ....9.50 to 59.00
Mr. Lucky, Stockbroker, 1976 ....*Illus* 11.00
Mr. Lucky, Tailor, 1979 .... 9.00
Mr. Lucky, Teacher, 1976 .... 8.50
Mr. Lucky, White & Gold, 1973 .... 50.00
Mrs. Lucky, Dances, 1974 .... 9.00
Pistol, Civil War Colt, With Stand, 1975, 11 In. 26.00
Russell, Buffalo Man, 1976 .... 12.50
Russell, Flathead Squaw, 1976 .... 20.00
Russell, Flathead Squaw, Box, 1976 .... 21.00
Russell, Prospector, 1976 ....21.00 to 23.00
Russell, Red River Breed, 1976 .... 12.50
Russell, Stage Coach Driver, 1976 .... 12.50
Russell, Trapper, 1976 .... 21.00
Wildlife, Panda, 1978, 5 In. 10.00
Wildlife, Wolf & Raccoon, 1978, Miniature 7.00

---------------------------- HOUSEHOLD ----------------------------

Many household cleaning products have been packaged in glass bottles since the nineteenth century. Shoe polish, ammonia, stove blacking, bluing, and other nonfood products are listed in this section. Most of these bottles have attractive paper labels that interest the collector.

3 In 1 Lubricant, 15 Cents, Cork Stopper, Box, c.1927, 1 Fl. Oz. 30.00
Ammonia, Adams Household, Poisonous, Not To Be Taken, Olive Green, 11 3/4 In. 45.00
Ammonia, Caution, Not To Be Taken, National, Cobalt Blue, Oval, 6 1/2 In. 45.00
Ammonia, Caution, Poisonous, Not To Be Taken, Aqua, Embossed, Oval, 6 In. 20.00
Ammonia, Clarkes Clear Fluid, Aqua, 8-Sided, BIMAL, 8 In. 45.00
Ammonia, Clarkes Clear Fluid, Aqua, Offset Neck, 9 In. 40.00
Ammonia, Greer's, Signature, Amber, Tooled Top, 9 In. 176.00
Ammonia, Little Bo-Peep, Post 1900, 7 3/4 In. 10.00
Ammonia, Plynine & Co., Limited Household, Olive Green, BIMAL, 11 3/4 In. ....40.00 to 45.00
Amster's Stocking Darner, Cobalt Blue, Neck Label, 5 1/4 In. 146.00
Black Cat Stove Polish, Paper Label, Screw Top, 6 In. 40.00
Black Silk Stove Polish, Metal Screw Top, Paper Label, 6 In. 9.95
Blacking, Light Emerald Green, Rolled Lip, Open Pontil 165.00
Blacking, Olive Green, Sheared Top, Open Pontil 104.00
C.M. Lina & Co. Oil Blacking, Blue Aqua, Rolled Lip, Open Pontil, 5 In. 420.00
Clothes Sprinkler, Dutch Boy, 8 1/4 In. 295.00
Clothes Sprinkler, Wonder Cave, San Marcos, Texas, 1950s 295.00
Colorite Dye, Old & New Straw Hats, Carpenter Motorn Co., 4 1/2 In. 18.00
Dazzle Detergent, Amber, ABM, c.1949, 32 Oz., 9 1/4 In. 10.00
Dead Stuck For Bugs, Gottlieb Marshall & Co., Philadelphia, Pa., Bug, Aqua, Oval, 9 In. . 19.00
Dr. Hanna Formaldehyde For Shoes, Loeffler Drug Store, Stevensville, Mich., 6 1/4 In. . 10.00
Dutcher's Dead Shot For Bed Bugs, St. Albans, Vt., Aqua, Open Pontil 468.00
Elastic Waterproof Blacking, Square, Olive Green, Paper Label, Pontil, 4 1/2 In. ... 616.00
Electrical Bicycle Lubricating Oil, Bicycle, Embossed, Aqua, Flask Shape, 4 In. 213.00
George Fosters Jim Dandy Oil, 100 Uses For Home, Farm, Factory, 8 Oz., 8 1/2 In. ... 10.00
Gordon's Chafala Furniture Polish, Aqua, Applied Collar Mouth, Open Pontil, 7 In. ... 213.00
Indestructible Gloss, Figural, Japanese Man In Kimono, Amber, 6 3/4 In. 269.00

Household, Mirror
Blacking, Elisha Water,
Troy, N.Y., Label,
Olive, 5 3/4 In.

Ink, Carter's,
Cathedral, Cobalt
Blue, ABM, 9 3/4 In.

Ink, Cottage, S.F., Cal., Ink Co.,
Amber, Tooled Mouth, 2 3/8 In.

JNT Furniture Polish, Home Charm Co., Chicago, Ill., 6 3/4 In.	8.50
Kinning's Blueing, Rochester, N.Y., Aqua, Round, Sheared Lip, 6 In.	8.00
Marble's Nitro Solvent, Embossed, c.1907, 2 Oz., 4 3/4 x 1 1/2 In.	115.00
Mirror Blacking, Elisha Water, Troy, N.Y., Label, Olive, 5 3/4 In. . . . . *Illus*	2320.00
Mrs. Butterworth, Hand Painted, Cap, 9 3/4 In.	15.00
Mrs. Stewart Liquid Bluing, Partial Contents, Cork	20.00
Old Colony, Glue, Rubber Tip	7.00
Osborn's Liquid Polish, Olive Yellow Amber, Rolled Lip, Open Pontil, 1840-55, 3 7/8 In.	504.00
Pratt's Bed Bug Killer, 7 In.	260.00
Price's Soap Company, Diamond, Cobalt Blue, Tapered, England, c.1895, 7 1/8 In.	308.00
Race & Sheldon Waterproof Boot Polish, Emerald, 8-Sided, Pontil, 5 3/8 In. . .3360.00 to	5040.00
Radium Leather Dye, For Shoes & Other Leather Items, Brown, England, 1920s, 3 1/2 In.	88.00
Red Cap Cleaner, Wind-O-Wash, Black Man, Winking, Paper Label, 5 1/2 In.	314.00
Refrigerator, Water, Roosters, Farmhouse, Amish Couple, Tulips, Red Plastic Lid, 7 In. . .	15.00
Refrigerator, Water, Textured, Squiggly Lines, Lid, Qt., 8 1/2 x 5 In.	22.50
Sawyer's Crystal Bluing, Blue Green, 8 1/2 In.	15.00
Sheldon's Magic Water Proof Boot Polish, Green, 8-Sided, Pontil, Applied Lip, 5 1/2 In.	3080.00
Shoe Blacking, Light Emerald Green, Rolled Lip, Open Pontil	165.00
Sprinkler, Clothespin, Yellow, c.1950, 7 3/4 In.	275.00
Sprinkler, Dutch Boy, Ceramic, Souvenir Of Lake George, N.Y., 8 1/4 x 2 5/8 In.	250.00
Sprinkler, Merry Maid, 6 3/4 In.	85.00
Sprinkler, Poodle, Pink, Pottery Bottle, 8 3/8 x 3 3/8 In.	350.00
Sprinkler, Siamese Cat, Ceramic, 8 1/4 In.	195.00
Stovink, The Only Black That Stays Black, Unused, Box, 1908, 5 In.	77.00
W.M. Child & Co. Oil Polish, Aqua, 12-Sided, Flared Lip, Open Pontil, 1840-55, 5 In.	100.00
Whittemore's Gilt Edge Shoe Dressing, Embossed, Label, Stopper, Box, 6 3/4 In.	15.00

INK

Ink was first used about 2500 B.C. in ancient Egypt and China. It was made of carbon mixed with oils. By the fifteenth century, ink was usually made at home by the housewife who bottled it for later use. In the late eighteenth century, ink was sold by apothecary shops and bookstores. The first patented ink was made in England in 1792. Ink bottles were first used in the United States about 1819. Early ink bottles were of ceramic and were often imported. Small ink bottles were made to be opened and used with a dip pen. Large ink bottles, like the cathedral-shaped Carter's inks, held a quart of ink to be poured into small bottles with dips. Inks can be identified by their shapes. Collectors have nicknamed many and the auctions often refer to *teakettles, cones, igloos,* or *umbrellas.*

Ink bottles were made to be hard to tip over. Some inks, especially English examples, were made with *bust-off* tops. The glass was cracked to open the bottle and the rough edge remained. In general the shape tells the age. Cones and umbrellas were used from the early 1800s to the introduction of the automatic bottle machine in the early 1900s. Hexagonal and octagonal bottles were preferred from about 1835 to 1865. Igloos, or turtles, were introduced in 1865 and were very popular for schools until about 1895.

Barrels were made from 1840 to 1900. Square bottles became popular after 1860. Rectangular was the shape chosen in the 1900s. Figural bottles, especially ceramic types, were also made.

For further research, consult the book *Ink Bottles and Inkwells* by William E. Covill Jr. There is a national club, The Society of Inkwell Collectors, PO Box 324, Mossville, IL 61552.

6-Sided, Cobalt Blue, Flared Lip, Continental, Pontil, 2 5/8 In.	134.00
6-Sided, Cobalt Blue, Flared Lip, Pontil, 2 1/2 In.	133.00
8-Sided, Blue, Applied Top, Pontil, 1840-60, 4 In.	385.00
8-Sided, Purple Amethyst, Rolled Lip, Pontil, 1845-60, 2 1/4 In.	280.00
8-Sided, Tipper, Blue Glass, 1 3/4 In.	82.00
12-Sided, Amber, Outward Rolled Lip, Pontil, 1 5/8 In.	935.00
12-Sided, Amethyst, Squat, Tam-O-Shanter Cover, Pontil, 2 x 2 3/4 In.	468.00
12-Sided, Aqua, Open Pontil, 1/2 Pt., 5 In.	48.00
12-Sided, Blue Green, Inward Rolled Lip, Open Pontil, 2 In.	250.00
12-Sided, Blue Green, Inward Rolled Lip, Pontil, 1 7/8 In.	202.00
12-Sided, Cobalt Blue, Vertical Ribs, Tam-O'-Shanter Finial, Pontil, c.1825, 3 1/4 In.	275.00
12-Sided, Emerald Green, Flared Lip, Open Pontil, 3 1/8 In.	123.00
12-Sided, Olive Amber, Polished Top, Pontil, c.1840, 2 In.	715.00
12-Sided, Olive Yellow, Applied Collar, c.1840, 5 3/4 x 2 3/8 In.	5040.00
32 Ribs, Vertical, Tooled Mouth, Pontil, 2 In.	175.00
36 Ribs, Swirled To Left, Cylindrical, Cone, Olive Yellow, Funnel Mouth, Pontil, 1 1/2 In.	1232.00
Amber, Inward Folded Rim, 2 3/4 In.	264.00
Amber, Tooled Pour Lip, Pat April 13, 1875, 9 In.	60.00
B. Firmin & Sons, Cone, 2 1/2 In.	50.00
Barrel, 5 Rings On Each Side, Stone-Ground Lip, 2 3/4 x 1/4 In.	150.00
Barrel, Blue Aqua, Tooled Mouth, c.1880, 2 1/4 In.	123.00
Barrel, Horizontal, Aqua, Sheared Lip, England, 2 x 3 1/2 In.	29.00 to 49.00
Barrel, Tooled Disk Mouth, 2-Piece Mold, Pontil, 2 In.	280.00
Baumans, Pittsburgh, Cone, Ground Lip, 2 3/4 In.	120.00
Beehive, Aqua, Ground Lip, c.1880, 1 1/8 In.	258.00
Beehive, Sapphire Blue, Ground Lip, 2 3/8 In.	784.00
Bertinguiot, Cylindrical, Olive Yellow, Sheared Mouth, Pontil, c.1835, 2 1/4 x 2 3/8 In.	784.00
Bertinguiot, Teal, 2 1/2 In.	303.00
Bird's Jet Black School, Igloo, Teal Blue, Ground Lip, Label, Bird On Branch, 1 1/2 In.	616.00
Birdcage, Embossed M, Aqua, England, 3 1/4 In.	39.00
Black, 3-Piece Mold, Keene, N.H., 2 1/2 In.	4313.00
Blackwood & Co., Cobalt, Round Shoulder, Facetted Base, Birds Beak Pouring Lip, 5 In.	184.00
Blackwood & Co., Igloo, Aqua, BIMAL, Sheared Lip, London, 2 1/2 In.	40.00
Blackwood & Co., London, Medium Blue, Embossed Offset Neck, Sheared Lip, 2 1/4 In.	113.00
Blue Green, Flared Lip, Open Pontil, 4 3/4 In.	179.00
Bonzo, Seated, 3 1/2 In.	400.00
Carter's, Cathedral, 6-Sided, Cobalt Blue, ABM, 6 1/4 In.	308.00
Carter's, Cathedral, 6-Sided, Cobalt Blue, ABM, Label, 8 In.	112.00
Carter's, Cathedral, Cobalt Blue, 9 3/4 In.	358.00
Carter's, Cathedral, Cobalt Blue, ABM, 9 3/4 In. *Illus*	112.00
Carter's, Cathedral, Cobalt Blue, Gothic Panels, Embossed, Ca-Rt-Er, c.1925, 6 1/4 In.	200.00
Carter's, Cathedral, Cobalt Blue, Gothic Panels, Embossed, Ca-Rt-Er, c.1925, 7 7/8 In.	100.00
Carter's, Cathedral, Cobalt Blue, Original Cap, 3 In.	275.00
Carter's, Cathedral, Cobalt Blue, Original Cap, 6 1/4 In.	550.00
Carter's, Cathedral, Cobalt Blue, Original Cap, 8 In.	109.00 to 523.00
Carter's, Cathedral, Gothic Panels, 6-Sided, Cobalt Blue, ABM, c.1925, 6 1/4 In.	198.00
Carter's, Cathedral, Gothic Panels, 6-Sided, Cobalt Blue, ABM, c.1925, 8 In.	99.00
Carter's, Cathedral, Gothic Panels, 6-Sided, Medium Cobalt Blue, Tooled Top, 10 In.	121.00
Carter's, Cobalt Blue, Embossed, ABM, 8 Fluid Oz., 6 1/8 In.	35.00
Carter's, Cylindrical, Full 1/2 Pt., Pat. Feb. 14, 99, Green, 1/2 Pt., 6 In.	29.00
Carter's, Green, 2-Piece Mold, Pt.	60.00
Carter's, Green, 3-Piece Mold, Pt.	75.00
Carter's, Yellow Green, Applied Sloping Double Collar, Tooled Spout, 9 3/4 In.	67.00
Carter's French Railroad Copying, Stoneware, Cream, Blue Gray Glaze, Label, 7 3/4 In.	840.00
Carter's Koal Black, Paper Labels, 8 3/8 x 3 In.	385.00

Carter's Kongo Black, Silhouette, Exaggerated Black African Native, 2 3/4 In.		73.00
Carter's White Ink, Black Screw Cap, 2 1/4 In.		5.00
Chestnut, Olive Green, Tapered Collar, OP, Free-Blown, New England, 9 In. . . . . .374.00 to 420.00
Chestnut Type, Olive, Sheared Lip, Pontil, 10 x 7 1/2 In.		403.00
Chestnut Type, Swirl, Aqua, Open Pontil, 10 1/2 In.		259.00
Clevenger Bros., Igloo, Honey Amber, 2 1/8 In.		66.00
Cobalt Blue, BIMAL, Pour Spout, 9 1/2 In.		20.00
Cone, Amber, Pontil, Rolled Lip, 1840-60, 2 3/8 In.		550.00
Cone, Blue Green, Pontil, Rolled Lip, 1840-60, 2 3/8 In.		605.00
Cone, Cobalt Blue, Applied Double Collar, Open Pontil, 2 1/2 In.		4480.00
Cone, Cobalt Blue, Tooled Mouth, 1890-1910, 2 1/2 In.		130.00
Cone, Draped, Blue Aqua, Applied Lip, Open Pontil, 2 1/4 In		840.00
Cone, Draped, Green Aqua, Applied Lip, Open Pontil, 2 3/4 In.		1680.00
Cone, Draped, Sapphire Blue, Applied Lip, Open Pontil, 2 1/4 In.		2688.00
Cone, Emerald Green, Inward Rolled Lip, Open Pontil, 2 1/2 In.		728.00
Cone, Forest Green, Pontil, Rolled Lip, Bubbles, 2 1/4 In.		605.00
Cone, Olive Green, Open Pontil, Stoddard, N.H., 2 1/4 In.		220.00
Cone, Olive Green, Tooled Flared Mouth, Tubular Pontil, 2 3/8 In.		1064.00
Cone, Olive Yellow, Pontil, Rolled Lip, 2-Piece Mold, 1845-60, 2 1/4 In.		440.00
Cone, Pink Puce, Pontil, Rolled Lip, 2 3/8 In.		3025.00
Cone, Teal, 2 3/4 In.		37.00
Cone, Yellow Green, Inward Rolled Mouth, Pontil, 2 1/4 x 2 1/8 In.		476.00
Cottage, S.F., Cal., Ink Co., Amber, Tooled Mouth, 2 3/8 In. . . . .*Illus*		2090.00
Cylindrical, 3-Piece Mold, Medium Forest Green, Disk Mouth, 1 1/2 x 2 1/4 In.		840.00
Cylindrical, 5 Rings, Olive Green, Tooled Mouth, Pontil, 1 5/8 x 2 3/4 In.		1904.00
Cylindrical, Blue, Shaped Pouring Lip, 6 1/4 In.		61.00
Cylindrical, Cobalt Blue, Tapered, Pontil, 2 1/4 In.		58.00
Cylindrical, Forest Green, Disk Mouth, Pontil, Coventry, Conn., 1 3/4 x 2 1/4 In.		179.00
Cylindrical, Golden Amber, Open Pontil, Stoddard, N.H., Pt.		100.00
Davids, Turtle, Blue Green, Domed Neck, Tooled Mouth, 1 3/4 x 2 1/4 x 2 1/4 In.		364.00
Davids & Black, Blue Green, Sloping Double Collar, Tooled Spout, 10 1/8 In.		532.00
Davids & Black, New York, Cylindrical, Blue Green, Sloping Collar, OP, 5 3/8 In.		168.00
Davids Electro Chemical Writing Fluid, Cobalt Blue, Original Cap, 32 Oz., 9 In.		198.00
Derby All British, 3-Sided, Cobalt Blue, Embossed, Sheared Lip, 2 1/4 In.		53.00
Dome, Blue, Center Neck, Sheared Lip, Pontil, 3 5/8 x 2 3/4 In.		303.00
Dormay, Red, England, 1920s, 2 In.		10.00
E. Halsey Patent, Olive Green, Pontil, France, 2 3/4 x 3 1/2 In.		330.00
E. Waters, Troy, N.Y., Backward S, Olive Amber, Outward Rolled Lip, Pontil, 5 1/2 In. . .		6720.00
E. Waters, Troy, N.Y., Blue Green, Fluted, Applied Mouth, Pontil, c.1850, 5 1/2 In.		1210.00
E. Waters, Troy, N.Y., Light Green, Fluted Shoulders, 6 3/4 In. . . . .*Illus*		880.00
Farley's, 8-Sided, Flared Lip, Bubbles, Pontil, c.1850, 3 3/4 In.		3025.00
Farley's, 8-Sided, Golden Amber, Sheared Mouth, Pontil, Stoddard, N.H., 1 3/4 In.		560.00
Farley's, 8-Sided, Olive Yellow, Sheared Mouth, Pontil, 1 7/8 In.		750.00
Farley's, 8-Sided, Tobacco Amber, Tooled Lip, Pontil, Label, 1 7/8 In.		1008.00
Farley's, 8-Sided, Yellow Amber, Flared Lip, Pontil, 3 3/8 In.		616.00
Farley's, 8-Sided, Yellow Amber, Tooled Lip, Pontil, c.1850, 1 3/4 In.		1430.00
Figural, Benjamin Franklin, Cobalt Blue, 2 3/4 In. . . . .*Illus*		2200.00
Funnel, Cobalt Blue, Open Pontil, 2 1/2 In.		39.00

Ink, E. Waters, Troy,
N.Y., Light Green,
Fluted Shoulders,
6 3/4 In.

Ink, Figural,
Benjamin
Franklin, Cobalt
Blue, 2 3/4 In.

Ink, Geometric, Olive
Green, Tooled Disc
Mouth, Pontil, 2 In.

Ink, Harrison's
Colombian, 8-Sided,
Aqua, Sheared Lip,
Pontil, 2 In.

Funnel, Cobalt Blue, Tooled, c.1875, 1 3/4 In. 90.00
Gaylord's Superior, Olive Green, Flared Lip, Pontil, 5 7/8 In. 4760.00
Geometric, Black Glass, Tooled Disc Mouth, Pontil, 1 7/8 In. 728.00
Geometric, Deep Olive Amber, Pontil, c.1830, 1 1/2 x 2 1/4 In. 523.00
Geometric, Deep Olive Amber, Tooled Disc Mouth, Pontil, 1 1/2 In. . . . . .157.00 to 200.00
Geometric, Deep Olive Yellow Amber, Tooled Disc Mouth, Pontil, 1 3/4 In. 235.00
Geometric, Diamond Point, Ribbed Bottom, Black Olive Amber, Disc Lip, Pontil, 2 In. . . . 190.00
Geometric, Light Olive Green, Keene, N.H., 1 1/2 x 2 1/4 In. 198.00
Geometric, Medium Olive Amber, Pontil, c.1830, 1 1/2 x 2 1/4 In. 209.00
Geometric, Medium Sapphire Blue, Tooled Mouth, Open Pontil, 1 3/4 In. 13440.00
Geometric, Olive Green, 3-Piece Mold, Tooled Disc Mouth, Pontil, 1 7/8 In. . . . . .168.00 to 190.00
Geometric, Olive Green, Coventry, Conn., 1 3/4 x 2 1/8 In. 252.00
Geometric, Olive Green, Open Pontil, Coventry, Conn., 1 5/8 x 2 3/8 In. 186.00
Geometric, Olive Green, Open Pontil, Coventry, Conn., 2 x 2 3/4 In. 193.00
Geometric, Olive Green, Open Pontil, Keene, N.H., 1 5/8 x 2 1/16 In. 176.00
Geometric, Olive Green, Pontil, Keene, N.H., 1 3/4 x 1 7/8 In. 220.00
Geometric, Olive Green, Pontil, Keene, N.H., 2 x 2 1/2 In. 275.00
Geometric, Olive Green, Tooled Disc Mouth, Pontil, 1 7/8 x 2 1/4 In. 157.00
Geometric, Olive Green, Tooled Disc Mouth, Pontil, 2 In. . . . .*Illus* 235.00
Geometric, Yellow Amber Olive, Applied Tooled, Disc Mouth, Pontil, c.1820, 1 1/2 In. . . 220.00
Geometric, Yellow Amber, Tooled Disc Mouth, Pontil, 1 1/2 x 2 1/4 In. 200.00
Globe, Aqua, Embossed World Map, 3 In. 307.00
H.C. Stephens Scarlet, For Steel Pens, Stoneware, Square Neck, Sealed, Contents, 6 In. . . 37.00
Harrison's Columbian, 8-Sided, Aqua, Sheared Lip, Pontil, 2 In. . . . .*Illus* 110.00
Harrison's Columbian, 8-Sided, Aqua, Applied Mouth, Open Pontil, 3 7/8 In. 105.00
Harrison's Columbian, 8-Sided, Aqua, Applied Mouth, Open Pontil, 4 In. 100.00
Harrison's Columbian, 8-Sided, Aqua, Pontil, 2 x 2 1/2 In. 110.00
Harrison's Columbian, 8-Sided, Aqua, Rolled Lip, Open Pontil, 1 7/8 In. 90.00
Harrison's Columbian, 8-Sided, Aqua, Rolled Lip, Pontil, 1 1/2 In. 100.00
Harrison's Columbian, 8-Sided, Green, Applied Mouth, Open Pontil, 1 1/2 In. 604.00
Harrison's Columbian, 8-Sided, Inward Rolled Mouth, Pontil, 1 3/4 x 1 7/8 In. 336.00
Harrison's Columbian, 8-Sided, Medium Grass Green, Rolled Lip, Pontil, 1 5/8 In. 1232.00
Harrison's Columbian, 8-Sided, Straight-Sided, Blue Aqua, Pontil, c.1850, 2 1/8 x 2 In. . . . 225.00

Ink, Harrison's Columbian,
12-Sided, Blue Aqua,
Applied Mouth,
Pontil, 11 In.

Ink, Harrison's Columbian,
Cobalt Blue, Applied Mouth,
Open Pontil, 5 5/8 In.

Harrison's Columbian, 12-Sided, Aqua, Applied Mouth, Open Pontil, 5 3/4 In. . . . .179.00 to 186.00
Harrison's Columbian, 12-Sided, Aqua, Applied Mouth, Pontil, 11 In. 3600.00
Harrison's Columbian, 12-Sided, Aqua, Applied Top, c.1850, 6 In. 358.00
Harrison's Columbian, 12-Sided, Blue Aqua, Applied Mouth, Open Pontil, 5 3/4 In 112.00
Harrison's Columbian, 12-Sided, Blue Aqua, Applied Mouth, Open Pontil, 7 1/2 In. 213.00
Harrison's Columbian, 12-Sided, Blue Aqua, Applied Mouth, Pontil, 11 In. . . . .*Illus* 4480.00
Harrison's Columbian, 12-Sided, Blue, Applied Mouth, Pontil, c.1850, 7 3/8 In. 880.00
Harrison's Columbian, Aqua, Open Pontil, 3 1/8 In. 77.00
Harrison's Columbian, Cobalt Blue, Applied Mouth, Open Pontil, 5 5/8 In. . . . .*Illus* 395.00
Harrison's Columbian, Cobalt Blue, Hammered, Pontil, c.1850, 7 1/8 In. 7700.00
Harrison's Columbian, Cobalt Blue, Inward Rolled Lip, Open Pontil, 2 In. . . . .*Illus* 505.00
Harrison's Columbian, Cobalt Blue, Rolled Lip, Pontil, 2 In. . . . . .840.00 to 950.00
Harrison's Columbian, Green, Applied Top, c.1860, 6 In. 3575.00
Harrison's Columbian, Yellow Green, Bubbles, c.1850, 1 3/8 In. 1760.00
Hohenthal Brothers & Co., Indelible Writing, N.Y., Applied Pouring Lip, Open Pontil . . . 198.00
House, Amethyst, Flared Sheared Mouth, Pontil, 2 1/2 In. 952.00
House, Aqua, Domed Roof, Rounded-Top Windows, Squared Lip, 2 1/2 x 1 3/4 In. 44.00
House, Aqua, Tiled Roof, Windows, Door, Pen Recess, 2 3/4 In. 266.00
House, Blue Aqua, Sheared Lip, c.1870, 2 5/8 In. 246.00
House, Blue Aqua, Tooled Mouth, c.1885, 2 3/4 In. . . . . .112.00 to 157.00
House, Violet Cobalt, Tooled Lip, c.1880, 4 3/4 In. 935.00
Hover, Blue Green, Applied Sloping Double Collar, Tooled Spout, Open Pontil, 7 1/2 In. . 448.00
Hover, Cylindrical, Cobalt Blue, Applied Flared Lip, 5 In. 1650.00
Hover, Cylindrical, Green, Rolled Lip, Open Pontil, 4 1/2 In. 420.00
Hover, Cylindrical, Olive Green, Flared Lip, Open Pontil, 4 1/2 In. 728.00
Hover, Cylindrical, Olive, Applied Flared Lip, Pontil, c.1850, 4 1/4 In. 605.00
Hover, Cylindrical, Yellow Amber, Sheared, Tooled Lip, Open Pontil, Label, 2 5/8 In. 504.00
Hover, Emerald Green, Applied Sloping Double Collar, Tooled Spout, IP, 9 3/8 In. 504.00
Hover, Green, Flared Lip, Open Pontil, 5 7/8 In. 392.00
Hover, Phila., Blue Green, Applied Mouth, Tooled Spout, Open Pontil, 9 1/4 In. 560.00
Hover, Phila., Blue Green, Sloping Collar, Open Pontil, 9 3/8 In. 896.00
Hyde, London, Cobalt Blue, Tooled Lip, Pour Spout, c.1890, 5 3/4 In. 56.00
Hyde, London, Cylindrical, Cobalt Blue, Pouring Lip, 6 In. 17.00
Igloo, Aquamarine, Embossed Bird, Sheared, Ground Lip, c.1880, 1 1/2 In. 123.00
Igloo, Aquamarine, Ground Mouth, 2 x 1 7/8 In. 308.00
J. & I.E.M., Igloo, Dark Chocolate Amber, Sheared & Ground Lip, 1 3/4 In. 560.00
J. & I.E.M., Igloo, Sapphire Blue, Ground Top, c.1880, 1 3/4 In. 1540.00
J. & I.E.M., Igloo, Yellow, Olive Tone, Tooled Mouth, 1 3/4 In. 896.00
J. & I.E.M., Turtle, Green, Tooled Mouth, 2 1/4 In. . . . .*Illus* 448.00
J. Field, 8-Sided, Aqua, Long Neck, Sheared Lip, 3 In. 20.00
J.D. Parker & Sons, 10-Sided, Aqua, Slug Plate, 3 In. 70.00
J.E. Peterman, 12-Sided, Green Aqua, Pontil, Flared Lip, 3 3/4 In. 840.00
J.K. Palmer, Chemist, Boston, Olive Green, Applied Mouth, Tooled Spout, Pontil, 8 In. . . 560.00
J.M. & S., Moore's Excelsior, Igloo, Aqua, Label, Ground Mouth, 2 x 1 7/8 In. . . . . . .*Illus* 308.00
J.S. Mason, Cylindrical, Blue Green, Flared Lip, Pontil, 4 1/2 In. 728.00
J.W. Seaton, Louisville, Ky., Blue Green, Umbrella, 10-Sided, Rolled Lip, OP, 2 1/8 In. . . 1792.00

Ink, Harrison's Columbian,
Cobalt Blue, Inward Rolled Lip,
Open Pontil, 2 In.

Ink, J. & I.E.M., Turtle,
Green, Tooled Mouth,
2 1/4 In.

Ink, J.M. & S., Igloo, Aqua, Moore's
Excelsior, Label, Ground,
Mouth, 2 x 1 7/8 In.

James P. Scotts, House, Green, 2 3/8 In. 45.00
John Bond's Crystal Palace, Square, Cobalt Blue, Tooled Flared Mouth, Label, 1 1/2 In. . 202.00
John Holland, Square, Aqua, 2 1/4 In. 25.00
Jones' Empire, N.Y., 12-Sided, Olive Green, Applied Top, Pontil, c.1850, 5 3/4 In. 6050.00
Josiah Jonson Japan Writing Fluid, London, Umbrella, 8-Sided, Stoneware, 3 x 2 1/2 In. . 269.00
Light Amber, 3-Piece Mold, Disc Top, Open Pontil, 1 1/2 In. ....155.00 to 168.00
Light Yellow Green, Pen Rest Shoulder Indents, 2 1/8 x 2 x 1 3/4 In. 35.00
Lion's Head, Gaping Mouth, Brown, Quill Holes, Stoneware, Salt Glaze, 1 1/2 In. 1105.00
Locomotive, Aqua, Trademark, Reg'd, 2 1/2 In. ....*Illus* 3575.00
Lord Brougham, Head, Shoulders, Brown, 2 Quill Holes, Stoneware, Salt Glaze, 3 In. 818.00
Lyon's, Cotton Reel, Aqua, BIMAL, Sheared Lip, 3 In. 25.00
M & P, New York, Umbrella, 8-Sided, Medium Green, Inward Rolled Mouth, 2 3/4 In. ... 728.00
M. & C. Ltd., Square, Teal, Flared Lip, Beveled Base, 3 x 2 1/2 In. 50.00
Ma & Pa Carter, Pair 120.00
Masonic, Square, Medallion, Star, Stoneware, Tan Glaze, 1 3/4 x 2 1/2 x 2 1/2 In. 1232.00
Maynard & Noyes, Olive Green, Open Pontil, Label, 2 1/2 In. 83.00
Monkey, Teakettle, Aqua, Olive Amber Striations, Sheared & Ground Lip, 2 1/2 In. 364.00
New York World's Fair, Administration Building, Paneled Glass, Label, 1939, 1 1/2 In. .. 99.00
Olive Amber, Tooled, Flared Lip, Pontil, 4 In. 179.00
Olive Green, 3-Piece Mold, 1 1/2 x 2 1/2 In. 144.00
Olive Green, Pontil, Applied String Type Lip, 4 3/8 In. 213.00
Olive Green, Yellow, Tooled Mouth, Pontil, c.1830, 3 7/8 In. 235.00
Olive Yellow, 7 Annular Rings, 2-Piece Mold, Pontil, c.1815, 1 3/8 x 2 1/2 In. 4950.00
Olive Yellow, Applied Sloping Double Collar, 3-Piece Mold, Iron Pontil, c.1860, 9 1/4 In. . 99.00
P & J Arnold, Pottery, J. Bourne & Son, England, 9 3/4 In. 40.00
P & J Arnold's Combined Fluid, Contents, Embossed, Paper Label, Original Top, 5 In. ... 121.00
P & J Arnold's Ledger Red, Embossed, Paper Label, Original Top, 4 1/2 In. 143.00
P & J Arnold's Writing Fluid, Denby Pottery, Stoneware, Salt Glaze, c.1862, 32 Oz., 7 In. 60.00
P & J Arnold's Writing Fluid, Embossed, Paper Label, Original Top, 4 In. 99.00
P & J Arnold's Writing Fluid, Embossed, Paper Label, Original Top, 5 1/2 In. 1322.00
P & J Arnold's Writing Fluid, Embossed, Paper Label, Original Top, 9 In. 209.00
P & J Arnold's Writing Fluid, Stoneware, 2 Paper Labels, c.1862, 32 Oz., 9 1/2 In. 95.00
P. Garrett & Co., Philada, Milk Glass, Tooled Mouth, Stopper, c.1885, 2 1/8 In. 123.00
Pitkin Type, 36 Ribs, Swirled To Left, Olive Green, Disc Mouth, Pontil, c.1805, 1 3/4 In. . 1350.00
Pitkin Type, 36 Ribs, Swirled To Left, Olive Green, Pontil, 1 5/8 x 2 1/4 In. ....*Illus* 896.00
Pitkin Type, 36 Ribs, Swirled To Right, Olive Amber, Tooled Lip, Pontil, 1 3/4 In. 235.00
Pitkin Type, Olive Green, Beveled Corners, Pontil, c.1805, 1 3/4 In. 1760.00
Pitkin Type, Olive Yellow, Disc Lip, Pontil, c.1810, 1 5/8 In. 2090.00
Pyramid, 5 Openings On Top, Soapstone, Carved, c.1780, 2 1/8 In. 355.00
Richd. Penistan, Phila., Emerald Green, 3-Piece Mold, Kick-Up Base, Dot, Pt. 119.00
Russia Cement Co., Signet, Cobalt Blue, ABM Threaded Mouth, Metal Cap, c.1910, Pt. .. 88.00
Russia Cement Co., Sole Mfrs Of Signet Ink & Lepages Glue, Cobalt, ABM, 7 In., 1/2 Pt. 40.00
S. Fine, Cylindrical, Tobacco Amber, Flared Lip, Pontil, 3 1/16 In. 1320.00
S.I., Comp., House, Milk Glass, Tooled Mouth, 2 3/4 In. 560.00
S.O. Dunbar, 12-Sided, Blue Green, Sheared Lip, Pontil, c.1850, 2 1/8 In. 1760.00
S.O. Dunbar, Taunton, Mass, 8 In. 20.00
S.S. Stafford's, Made In USA, Cylindrical, Cobalt Blue, Tooled Pour Top, 1/2 Pt. 45.00
S.S. Stafford's, Made In USA, Cylindrical, Cobalt Blue, Tooled Pour Top, Qt. 48.00
S.S. Stafford's Inks, Cobalt Blue, Pour Spout, Qt., 9 1/2 x 3 1/4 In. 75.00

Ink, Locomotive,
Aqua, Trademark,
Reg'd, 2 1/2 In.

Ink, Pitkin Type, 36
Ribs, Swirled To Left,
Olive Green, Pontil,
1 5/8 x 2 1/4 In.

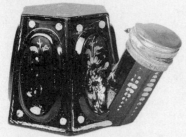 

Ink, Teakettle, 6-Sided, Cobalt Blue, Gold Paint, Tooled Lip, Brass Cap, 3 In.

Ink, Teakettle, 8-Sided, Cobalt Blue, Panels, Gold Design, Hinged Cap, 2 1/8 In.

S.S. Stafford's Inks, Cylindrical, Cobalt Blue, Tooled Pour Lip, Qt., 9 1/8 In.	90.00
Sandal, Light Apple Green, Embossed, Sheared Lip, England, c.1895, 3 1/2 In.	515.00
Sanford's, Cone, Aqua	20.00
Sanford's Fountain Pen, Embossed, Pamphlet, Box, 2 Oz., 2 3/4 In.	198.00
Shaw's Inks Are Best, 8-Sided, Aqua, BIMAL, Sheared Lip, 3 In.	35.00
Sheaffer's Skrip Permanent Blue Black, No. 22, Lid, Label, Built-In Inkwell, 2 Oz.	10.00
Sheaffer's Skrip Washable Blue, No. 42, Lid, Label, Built-In Inkwell, 2 Oz.	10.00
Shoe, Man's, Cobalt Blue, Sheared & Ground Lip, England, c.1900, 4 In.	1010.00
Snail, Ground Lip, c.1885, 1 5/8 In.	215.00
Square, Cobalt Blue, ABM, Cork Top, 2 1/4 In.	15.00
Stafford's, Cylindrical, Teal Blue Green, 2 Rings At Shoulder, Base, 3 1/4 In.	35.00
Stafford's, Emerald Green, Master	83.00
Stafford's, Smoky Puce, Applied Mouth, Tooled Spout, 7 3/4 In.	672.00
Stafford's, Teal Blue, Tooled Mouth, Spout, c.1890, 10 In.	123.00
Stephens, Cotton Reel, Aqua, BIMAL, 2 1/2 In.	29.00
Stephens, Fancy Violet Writing Ink, Square, Stopper, 7 In.	20.00
Stoddard, Cone, Olive Green, Open Pontil	314.00
T & M, Light Blue Green, Inward Rolled Lip, Open Pontil, 2 5/8 In.	345.00
Teakettle, 6-Sided, Brown, Embossed, Pottery, c.1880, 2 1/2 In.	67.00
Teakettle, 6-Sided, Cobalt Blue, Gold Paint, Tooled Lip, Brass Cap, 3 In. ....*Illus*	615.00
Teakettle, 6-Sided, Fiery Opalescent, Raised Painted Flowers, Lobed Panels, 2 1/8 In.	308.00
Teakettle, 6-Sided, Starch Blue, 3-Piece Mold, Double Lobe, Rib Panels, c.1875, 2 3/4 In.	358.00
Teakettle, 6-Sided, Yellow Amber, Ground Lip, c.1885, 2 In.	520.00
Teakettle, 7-Sided, Opaque Lavender, Ground Lip, Hinged Cap, c.1885, 2 3/4 In.	360.00
Teakettle, 8-Sided, Amethyst, Ground Lip, Brass Collar, Hinged Lid, 1875-95, 2 In. ...	780.00
Teakettle, 8-Sided, Amethyst, Vertical Ribs, Concave Panels, Hinged Cap, 2 In.	680.00
Teakettle, 8-Sided, Aqua, Sheared & Ground Lip, 1 1/2 In.	90.00
Teakettle, 8-Sided, Aqua, Upturned Spout, 3 1/2 In.	573.00
Teakettle, 8-Sided, Black Glass, Ground Lip, 1 1/2 In.	672.00
Teakettle, 8-Sided, Cobalt Blue, Ground Lip, Brass Collar, Hinged Lid, c.1885, 2 In.	390.00
Teakettle, 8-Sided, Cobalt Blue, Panels, Gold Design, Hinged Cap, 2 1/8 In. ....*Illus*	350.00
Teakettle, 8-Sided, Cobalt Blue, Polished & Ground Lip, 3 5/8 In.	896.00
Teakettle, 8-Sided, Emerald Green, Double Font, 3 1/2 In.	896.00
Teakettle, 8-Sided, Emerald Green, Ground Lip, Brass Collar, c.1885, 2 1/8 In.	520.00
Teakettle, 8-Sided, Grape Amethyst, Vertical Ribs, Brass Collar, Hinged Lid, c.1885, 2 In.	830.00
Teakettle, 8-Sided, Grass Green, Tooled Lip, 1 7/8 In.	896.00
Teakettle, 8-Sided, Green, 2 1/8 x 2 3/8 In.	330.00
Teakettle, 8-Sided, Milk Glass, Fiery Opalescent, Polished Lip, 2 1/8 In.	476.00
Teakettle, 8-Sided, Milk Glass, Multicolored, Brass Collar, c.1850, 2 1/2 x 3 3/4 In.	235.00
Teakettle, 8-Sided, Milk Glass, Opalescent, Sheared Lip, c.1880, 2 1/8 In.	336.00
Teakettle, 8-Sided, Milk Glass, Powder Blue, Double Font, Tooled Lip, 3 3/8 In.	258.00
Teakettle, 8-Sided, Milk Glass, Red & Blue Flowers, Gold Trim, Pinched Waist, 2 3/16 In.	205.00
Teakettle, 8-Sided, Opaque Lime Green, Ground Lip, Hinged Cap, c.1880, 2 5/8 In.	295.00
Teakettle, 8-Sided, Opaque White, Opalescence At Top, Applied Upper Font, 3 1/4 In.	88.00
Teakettle, 8-Sided, Pink Amethyst, Concave Panels, Ground Lip, 2 In.	364.00
Teakettle, 8-Sided, Purple Amethyst, Concave Panels, Ground Lip, Hinged Lid, 2 1/8 In. .	336.00

Teakettle, 8-Sided, Sapphire Blue, Concave Panels, Brass Ring, 2 In. 515.00
Teakettle, 8-Sided, Smoky Purple, Concave Panels, Hinged Cap, c.1885, 2 In. 575.00
Teakettle, 8-Sided, Turquoise, Opalescent, Flowers, Pinched Waist, Hinged Cap, 2 1/8 In. 350.00
Teakettle, 10-Sided, Cobalt Blue, Raised Flowers, Ground Lip, Brass Ring, 2 1/8 In. 420.00
Teakettle, 10-Sided, Dome, Opalescent, Raised Flowers, Ground Lip, Brass Cap, 3 In. . . . 505.00
Teakettle, 10-Sided, Milk Glass, Multicolored, Raised Flowers, Hinged Cap, 3 In. 460.00
Teakettle, 10-Sided, Milk Glass, Raised Flowers, Brass Ring, 3 1/8 In. 295.00
Teakettle, Barrel, Amethyst, Brass Ring, Ground Lip, c.1880, 2 1/4 In. 920.00
Teakettle, Barrel, Amethyst, Sheared Lip, Brass Top, c.1875, 2 1/4 In. 440.00
Teakettle, Barrel, Cobalt Blue, c.1885, 2 1/4 In. 1430.00
Teakettle, Barrel, Cobalt Blue, Ground Mouth, 2 1/8 In. 700.00
Teakettle, Barrel, Cobalt Blue, Sheared Ground Lip, Brass Ring, c.1875, 2 1/4 In. 330.00
Teakettle, Barrel, Dome, Cobalt Blue, Sheared Lip, Brass Ring, c.1885, 2 1/4 In. 253.00
Teakettle, Barrel, Dome, Green, Sheared Lip, Brass Ring, c.1875, 2 1/4 In. 495.00
Teakettle, Barrel, Green, Sheared Lip, Brass Ring, c.1875, 2 1/4 In. 660.00
Teakettle, Barrel, Ice Blue, Brass Ring, Cap, c.1880, 2 1/8 In. 460.00
Teakettle, Barrel, Teal, Sheared Mouth, Brass Ring, Lid, c.1875, 2 1/4 In. 1980.00
Teakettle, Blue Enamel, Gilt, Ground Lip, c.1885, 2 1/4 In. 112.00
Teakettle, Brown Glaze, Stoneware, Chandler & Co., England, 2 1/2 In. 137.00
Teakettle, Cat, Ground Lip, 2 1/8 In. 336.00
Teakettle, Cobalt Blue, Straight Spout, Gold Top, Cap, Box, 2 In. 418.00
Teakettle, Crown, Cobalt Blue, Sheared Ground Lip, c.1870, 1 1/2 In. 605.00
Teakettle, Dome, Cobalt Blue, Sheared Lip, Brass Ring, c.1875, 2 1/4 In. 253.00
Teakettle, Dome, Yellow Green, Applied Bird, Tooled Mouth, 2 5/8 In. 728.00
Teakettle, Lime Green, Vertical Ribs, Ground Lip, Hinged Brass Lid Neck Ring, 2 3/8 In. 1456.00
Teakettle, Milk Glass, Blue, Ground Lip, Metal Neck Ring, Flower, Leaf Lid, Chain, 2 In. 364.00
Teakettle, Milk Glass, Ground Lip, c.1880, 2 In. 112.00
Teakettle, Milk Glass, Ground Lip, Hinged Cap, c.1885, 2 3/4 In. 295.00
Teakettle, Opaque Clambroth, Hinged Cap, 2 3/8 In. 315.00
Teakettle, Opaque Lime Green, Ground Lip, Hinged Cap, c.1885, 2 7/8 In. 515.00
Teakettle, Opaque Lime Green, Melon Ribbed, Hinged Brass Lid, 2 3/4 In. 476.00
Teakettle, Opaque Powder Blue, Melon Ribbed, Tooled Lip, 2 3/4 In. 476.00
Teakettle, Opaque Turquoise Blue, Ground Lip, Hinged Cap, c.1885, 2 7/8 In. 515.00
Teakettle, Square, Purple, Upturned Spout, 2 Pen Rests, Silver Plated Lift-Up Cap, 2 In. . 655.00
Teakettle, Tan Glaze, Stoneware, Registered, England, 2 1/2 x 3 In. 39.00
Teakettle, Yellow, Sheared Ground Lip, c.1875, 2 In. 385.00
Temple, London, Barrel, Blue, Embossed, Horizontal Ribs, 3 1/2 In. 672.00
Turban, 8-Sided, Blue, Ground Mouth, Copper Hinge Collar, c.1885, 4 1/4 In. 504.00
Turban, 8-Sided, Electric Blue, Lobes, Copper Hinged Collar, Glass Lid, 4 1/4 In. 504.00
Turtle, Amber, Tooled Mouth, 1 3/4 In. 392.00
Turtle, Blue Green, Tooled Lip, 1 5/8 In. 364.00
Turtle, Dome, Blue Green, Tooled Mouth, 1 5/8 x 2 1/4 In. 504.00
Turtle, Sheared & Ground Mouth, c.1885, 1 7/8 In. 245.00
Umbrella, 5-Sided, Olive Green, Rolled Lip, Irregular Label Panel, Open Pontil, 2 1/4 In. 5375.00
Umbrella, 5-Sided, Yellow Amber, Irregular Label Panel, Rolled Lip, OP, 2 1/4 In. 690.00
Umbrella, 8-Sided, Amber Shaded To Yellow, Inward Rolled Lip, Open Pontil, 2 3/8 In. . . 280.00
Umbrella, 8-Sided, Amber, Inward Rolled Lip, 2 5/8 In. 213.00
Umbrella, 8-Sided, Amber, Tooled Lip, Open Pontil, 2 5/8 In. *Illus* 170.00
Umbrella, 8-Sided, Amethyst, Rolled Lip, Pontil, 2 5/8 In. 715.00
Umbrella, 8-Sided, Blue Aqua, Inward Rolled Lip, Open Pontil, 2 5/8 In. 123.00
Umbrella, 8-Sided, Blue Aqua, Rolled Lip, Open Pontil, 2 3/8 In. 202.00
Umbrella, 8-Sided, Blue Green, Inward Rolled Lip, Open Pontil, 2 1/4 In. 134.00
Umbrella, 8-Sided, Blue Green, Inward Rolled Lip, Open Pontil, 3 1/8 In. 616.00
Umbrella, 8-Sided, Blue Green, Rolled Lip, Open Pontil, 5 7/8 In. 269.00
Umbrella, 8-Sided, Blue Green, Rolled Lip, Pontil, 2 5/8 In. 157.00
Umbrella, 8-Sided, Blue Green, Rolled Lip, Pontil, c.1850, 2 1/2 In. . . . . *Illus* 67.00
Umbrella, 8-Sided, Cobalt Blue, Inward Rolled Lip, Pontil, 2 1/4 In. 2998.00
Umbrella, 8-Sided, Cobalt Blue, Inward Rolled Mouth, c.1845, 3 x 3 1/4 In. 5320.00
Umbrella, 8-Sided, Cobalt Blue, Inward Rolled Mouth, c.1870, 2 3/4 x 2 5/8 In. 1150.00
Umbrella, 8-Sided, Cobalt Blue, Inward Rolled Mouth, Pontil, 2 1/2 In x 2 1/2 In. 2200.00
Umbrella, 8-Sided, Emerald Green, Sheared, Tooled Lip, 2 5/8 In. 285.00
Umbrella, 8-Sided, Green Aqua, Rolled Lip, Open Pontil, 2 1/2 In. 90.00

Ink, Umbrella,
8-Sided, Amber,
Tooled Lip, Open
Pontil, 2 5/8 In.

Ink, Umbrella,
8-Sided, Blue Green,
Rolled Lip, Pontil,
c.1850, 2 1/2 In.

Umbrella, 8-Sided, Light Cobalt Blue, Sheared Lip, 2 1/2 In. 365.00
Umbrella, 8-Sided, Light Emerald Green, Open Pontil, 2 1/2 In. 77.00
Umbrella, 8-Sided, Light Green, Inward Rolled Lip, Open Pontil, 2 1/2 In. 140.00
Umbrella, 8-Sided, Light Green, Open Pontil, 2 3/4 In. ....66.00 to 88.00
Umbrella, 8-Sided, Medium Blue Green, Rolled Lip, Open Pontil, 2 1/2 In. 146.00
Umbrella, 8-Sided, Medium Green, Inward Rolled Lip, Open Pontil, 2 1/2 In. 190.00
Umbrella, 8-Sided, Olive Green, Open Pontil Scarred Base, Rolled Lip, c.1850, 2 3/8 In. . . 3680.00
Umbrella, 8-Sided, Olive Green, Open Pontil, Tooled Mouth, 2 1/2 In. 308.00
Umbrella, 8-Sided, Olive Yellow, Sheared Mouth, Pontil, 2 1/2 x 2 3/8 In. 213.00
Umbrella, 8-Sided, Prussian Blue, Tooled Lip, 2 1/4 In. 952.00
Umbrella, 8-Sided, Red Amber, Tooled Lip, Pontil, 2 1/2 In. 258.00
Umbrella, 8-Sided, Red Puce, Tooled Lip, Open Pontil, c.1850, 2 3/8 In. 3950.00
Umbrella, 8-Sided, Root Beer Amber, Neck Ring, Pontil, 2 1/2 In. 246.00
Umbrella, 8-Sided, Sapphire Blue, Tooled Lip, Open Pontil, c.1850, 2 1/2 In. 4200.00
Umbrella, 8-Sided, Sapphire Blue, Tooled Mouth, Label, 2 3/4 In. 1568.00
Umbrella, 8-Sided, Yellow Amber, Inward Rolled Lip, Open Pontil, 2 1/2 In. 285.00
Umbrella, 8-Sided, Yellow Amber, Sheared & Tooled Lip, Open Pontil, 2 3/8 In. 285.00
Umbrella, 8-Sided, Yellow Green, Inward Rolled Lip, Pontil, c.1850, 2 1/2 In. 476.00
Umbrella, 8-Sided, Yellow Green, Olive Tone, Inward Rolled Mouth, Pontil, 2 1/4 In. ... 672.00
Umbrella, 8-Sided, Yellow Green, Sheared & Tooled Lip, Open Pontil, 2 3/8 In. 104.00
Umbrella, 8-Sided, Yellow Olive, Tooled Lip, Open Pontil, 2 3/8 In. 1695.00
Umbrella, 12-Sided, Aqua, Rolled Lip, Open Pontil, 2 In. 336.00
Umbrella, 12-Sided, Blue Green, Rolled Lip, Open Pontil, 1 7/8 In. 1792.00
Umbrella, 12-Sided, Light Green, Open Pontil, 2 1/4 In. 88.00
Umbrella, Amber, Rolled Lip, Open Pontil, 2 1/2 In. 176.00
Umbrella, Amber, Sheared Lip, Open Pontil, Stoddard, N.H., 2 1/2 In. 264.00
Umbrella, Apricot, Label, Rolled Lip, Pontil, 2 3/4 In. 550.00
Umbrella, Citron, Rolled Lip, Open Pontil, 2 1/2 In. 880.00
Umbrella, Cobalt Blue, Rolled Lip, Pontil, c.1850, 2 1/2 In. 1870.00
Umbrella, Cobalt Blue, Sheared Lip, 2 1/2 In. 935.00
Umbrella, Emerald Green, Rolled Lip, Pontil, c.1850, 2 1/2 In. 1540.00
Umbrella, Forest Green, Sheared Lip, Bubbles, Open Pontil, 2 1/2 In. 440.00
Umbrella, Green, Amber, Rolled Lip, Open Pontil, 2 1/2 In. ....264.00 to 440.00
Umbrella, Green, Sheared Lip, Open Pontil, 2 In. 264.00
Umbrella, M & P, 8-Sided, Emerald Green, Inward Rolled Mouth, Pontil, 2 1/2 In. 1120.00
Umbrella, Olive Amber, Sheared Lip, Open Pontil, 2 1/2 In. 253.00
Umbrella, Olive Yellow, Rolled Lip, Pontil, 2 1/2 In. 770.00
Umbrella, Orange, Pontil, Stoddard, N.H., 2 3/8 In. 330.00
Umbrella, Pink, Rolled Lip, Pontil, c.1950, 2 1/2 In. 2090.00
Umbrella, Purple Puce, Rolled Lip, 2 1/2 In. 1100.00
Umbrella, Red Amber, Sheared & Rolled Lip, Open Pontil, 2 1/2 In. 385.00
Umbrella, Root Beer Amber, Pontil, Stoddard, N.H., 2 1/2 x 2 1/4 In. 295.00
Umbrella, Teal, Tooled Lip, 2 1/2 In. 143.00
Umbrella, Violet Cobalt, Rolled Lip, c.1870, 2 1/2 In. 1100.00
Umbrella, Yellow Amber, Rolled Lip, Pontil, c.1880, 2 1/2 In. 2200.00
Uncle Sam Bust, Milk Glass, Ground Lip, c.1890, 3 1/8 In. 520.00
Underwood's, Cobalt Blue, 9 1/2 In. 99.00

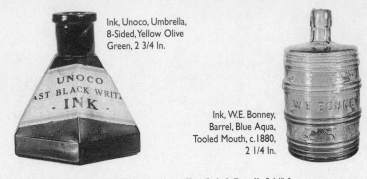

Ink, Unoco, Umbrella,
8-Sided, Yellow Olive
Green, 2 3/4 In.

Ink, W.E. Bonney,
Barrel, Blue Aqua,
Tooled Mouth, c.1880,
2 1/4 In.

United Drug Co., Fountain Pen Ink, Aluminum Top, Label, Rexall, 5 1/8 In.	12.50
Unoco, Umbrella, 8-Sided, Yellow Olive Green, 2 3/4 In. . . . .*Illus*	532.00
W. Thomas & Co., Dark Aqua, Tooled Lip, Indented Panel, Smooth Base, 2 3/8 In.	35.00
W.E. Bonney, Barrel, Blue Aqua, Tooled Mouth, c.1880, 2 1/4 In. . . . .*Illus*	123.00
Walkdens, London, Cylindrical, Embossed, Aqua, Sheared Lip, 2 In.	154.00
Warrens Congress, 8-Sided, Olive Yellow, Rolled Lip, Pontil, c.1850, 2 7/8 In.	3850.00
Warrens Congress, 8-Sided, Yellow Green, Applied Spout, Pontil, c.1850, 7 1/8 In.	7150.00
Waterman's, Paper Label, 15 In.	1650.00
Wilbors, Cylindrical, 8-Sided Shoulder, Tobacco Amber, Sloping Mouth, c.1875, 7 7/8 In.	625.00
Wilbur's, Cylindrical, Black Amber, 8-Sided Base & Shoulder, c.1870, 7 5/8 In.	420.00
Wiltshire's, Aqua, Indented Panel, Tooled Lip, 3 In.	25.00
Wood's Black, Portland, Cone, Green Aquamarine, 1840-60, 2 1/2 In.	504.00
Zieber & Co., Excelsior, 12-Sided, Emerald Green, Pontil, c.1850, 5 7/8 In.	13200.00
Zieber & Co., Excelsior, 12-Sided, Green, Applied Top, Pontil, c.1850, 7 1/2 In.	7150.00

JAR

Jar is the name for a container of a special shape. It has a wide mouth and almost no
neck. Today we see jars of cold cream, but in earlier days jars made of glass or ceramic
were used for storage of home-canned produce and for many commercial products. Jars
are also listed in the Stoneware category in this book.

Adams Pure Chewing Gum, Glass, Acid Etched, 5 x 5 x 11 In.	83.00
Adams Tutti-Frutti Gum, 100 Packages, Pepsin, Paper Label, 11 In.	413.00
Canning, Dallas, Pottery, Brown, 12-Sided, Cogglewheel Inside Lip, Qt.	29.00
Cigar, Belfast Cigars United, Cut Plug, Threaded Machine Lip, Honey Amber, c.1910, 7 In.	198.00
Cigar, Mercantile, Golden Amber, Stamped Tin Lid, Label, 1902-10, 5 1/8 In.	154.00
Compressed Tablets Soda-Mint & Pepsin, John Wyeth & Bro, Amber, c.1885, 2 x 2 In. . .	39.00
Goofus Glass, Light Lime Green, Sheared & Ground Lip, 15 1/8 In.	110.00
Goofus Glass, Lime Green, Embossed Flowers, Rough Sheared & Ground Lip, 15 1/4 In. . .	132.00
Johnson & Johnson, Linton Moist Gauze, Amber, Contents, Label, Metal Clamp, 4 1/2 In.	44.00
Mitchell's Horse Salve, Blue Aqua, Embossed, 2 In.	59.00
P.B. & Co., Philada., Open Pontil, 1840-60, Gal., 8 In.	149.00
Pond's Extract Ointment, Amber, Labels, Tin Cap, Metal Pull Ring, c.1892, 2 3/4 In.	55.00
Refrigerator, White, Black Bakelite Cap, Embossed, Norge Front & Back, 11 1/2 In.	245.00
Star & Crescent Moon, Ground Lip, Pt.	550.00
Storage, Amber, 12-Sided, Smooth Flared Neck, Wide Mouth, Rolled Lip, OP, 5 In.	1568.00
Storage, Citron, Ground Mouth, Oval Panels, Zinc Band, Cylindrical, Glass Lid, Pt.	213.00
Storage, Cylindrical, Olive Green, 2-Piece Mold, Pontil, New England, c.1845, 4 1/4 In. .	325.00
Storage, Cylindrical, Olive Green, Pontil, New England, 1800-30, 5 In.	395.00
Storage, Green, Yellow, Wide Mouth, Cylindrical, Tooled Mouth, Pontil, 8 x 4 1/4 In. . . .	179.00
Storage, Olive Amber, Flared Lip, Pontil, 11 1/2 In.	908.00
Storage, Olive Yellow, Outward Rolled Mouth, Pontil Scar, 6 x 3 1/4 In.	650.00
Storage, Olive Yellow, Tooled Collared Mouth, Pontil, Cylindrical, 3-Piece Mold, 8 1/4 In.	130.00
Storage, Stoddard, Dot, Amber, 7 1/2 In.	77.00
Tobacco, Aristocratic Cigar, 10 Cent Cigar For 5 Cents, Amber, Screw Lid, 5 In.	336.00
Tobacco, Belfast United Cigars, Cut Plug, Golden Amber, ABM, 6 7/8 In.	100.00
Tobacco, G.W. Gable, 9th District Of Pa., 25, Amber, Ground Lip, Screw Lid, 5 3/4 In. . .	308.00
Tobacco, Globe Tobacco Co., Detroit, Windsor, Pat. Oct. 10th 1882, Yellow, Barrel, 7 In. .	224.00
Yellow Amber, Applied Tooled Collared Mouth, Cylindrical, 1860-70, 8 1/2 In.	784.00

Yellow Green, 8-Fluted, Applied Collared Mouth, Pontil, 8 3/8 x 1 7/8 In. 202.00
JIM BEAM, see Beam

--------------------------------- JUG ---------------------------------

A jug is a deep container with a narrow mouth and a handle. It is usually made of pottery. Jugs were often used as containers for liquor. Messages, mottoes, and the name of the distillery or bar are often printed on the jug. Jugs are also listed in the Stoneware category in this book.

Bellarmine Type, Salt Glaze, Applied Handle, Brown, England, 14 1/2 In. 69.00
California W. & L. House, Newark, N.J., Brown, Tan, Cobalt Blue Stencil, 1/2 Gal. 48.00
Chas. Koegel, 9 Hackensack St., Woodbridge, N.J., Brown, Tan, Cobalt Stencil, 1/2 Gal. ... 59.00
Finley Ackers Co., Phila., Pa., Cream, Brown, Pottery, Qt. 125.00
Grotesque Face, Broken Teeth, Goatee, Cork, Handle, 6 1/2 x 3 3/4 In. 275.00
Indian, Cacapaon, GGW On Base, Aqua, 5 Gal. 200.00
Jas. Gioga, Goldfield, Nevada, Blue Ink, Glazed Clay, c.1910-15 .... 6038.00
Jos. Bernard Pure California Wines & Brandies, Cobalt Stencil, Brown, Cream, 1/2 Gal. . 299.00
New Saloon, G.O. Peuse, Square, Cream, Brown, Pottery, Fall Creek, Wis., c.1900, 4 3/8 In. 220.00
Redware, Black Alkaline Glaze, Oval, 1830-60, 8 1/4 In. 123.00
Redware, Oval, 1820-60, 6 3/4 In. 258.00
Stonachie Distillery, Perthshire, Sandy MacDonald Scotch, Royal Doulton, Pub 389.00

------------------------- KENTUCKY GENTLEMAN -------------------------

Kentucky Gentleman bottles were made in 1969. The six bottles in the set were called Frontiersman, Kentucky Gentleman, Pink Lady, Revolutionary Soldier, Union Soldier, and Confederate Soldier.

Confederate Soldier ....6.50 to 20.00
Gentleman, 14 In. 10.50
Gentleman, Fat, 12 3/4 In. 31.00
Pink Lady ....14.50 to 20.00
Revolutionary Soldier, Box 5.00
Union Soldier ....:..............10.50 to 26.00

------------------------- KONTINENTAL CLASSICS -------------------------

Kontinental Spirits Kompanie of Bardstown, Kentucky, made figural bottles from 1976 to 1981 to hold Kontinental Kentucky bourbon. Most of the bottles were full-length figures of people from earlier times, although a bust of John Lennon was added in 1981.

Dentist, 1978 .... 40.00
Editor, 1976, 4/5 Qt., 13 In. 26.00
Gunsmith, 1977, 12 1/2 In. 3.50
Gunsmith, 1977, Miniature ....7.00 to 10.00
Lumberjack, 1978, Full Size 20.00

--------------------------------- LACEY ---------------------------------

Haas Brothers of San Francisco, California, was established in 1851. They made W.A. Lacey and Cyrus Noble bottles in the 1970s. The firm discontinued its ceramic business about 1981 and destroyed all of the molds. Lacey bottles include the log animal series (1978-1980) and the tavern series (1975). Also see the Cyrus Noble category.

Rabbit, Log, Snow, Box, 1980, Miniature, 4 3/4 In. 5.50
Raccoon, Log, 1980, Miniature ....12.00 to 44.00

------------------------------ LAST CHANCE ------------------------------

Last Chance Whiskey was presented in ceramic figural bottles in 1971 and 1972. One series of 8-ounce bottles called Professionals pictured a doctor, dentist, banker, entertainer, politician, and salesman. Another series was a group of six bottles that joined together to form a long bar scene. Two versions of this bar scene were made, one with and one without a frame.

Banker, 1972 .... 10.00
Dentist, 1971, 1/2 Pt., 9 In. 11.50
Doctor, Holding Baby, 1971, 1/2 Pt., 9 1/2 In. 10.50

------------------------------ LEWIS & CLARK ------------------------------

Lewis & Clark bottles were created by Alpha Industries of Helena, Montana. The first bottles, full-length representations of historical figures, were made from 1971 to 1976. The pioneer series of 1977-1978 was released in two-bottle sets. Each bottle was 13 inches high and two placed together created a scene. For example, one was an Indian (bottle) offering to sell some furs to a white man (bottle). A set of six troll bottles was made in 1978-1979.

Indian, 1978	30.00
Major Reno, 1976	25.00
Montana, 1976	6.00 to 10.00
Plaque, Peace Pipe, Indian, 1978	30.00
Trooper, 1976	25.00

LIONSTONE

Lionstone Distilleries Inc. of Lawrenceburg, Kentucky, started making porcelain figural bottles to hold their whiskey for national sale in 1969. The first bottles were Western figures, each with a black label that told the historical facts about the figure. About 15,000 bottles were made for each of the first six subjects, the cowboy, proud Indian, casual Indian, sheriff, gentleman gambler, and cavalry scout. About half of the bottles were never filled with liquor because they leaked. These *leakers* were used by bars as display items on shelves and were clearly labeled with decals stating that they were for display only. More bottles were made for the series, about 4,000 of each. The set had 16 bottles. Lionstone then made a series of race cars (1970-1984), more Western figures (1970-1976), a Western bar scene (1971), birds (1970-1977), circus figures (1973), dogs (1975-1977), European workers (1974), oriental workers (1974), Bicentennial series (1976), clowns (1978-1979), sports series (1974-1983), and others. They also made many miniature bottles. Lionstone was sold to Barton Brands in December 1979. It was sold back to Mark Slepak, the original owner, in December 1983. The whiskey was distilled in Bardstown, Kentucky, but the bottles were made in Chicago. Over 800 styles were made. No decanters were made after 1995.

Bicentennial, Betsy Ross, 1975	2.25
Bicentennial, George Washington, 1975	7.00
Bicentennial, Mecklenberg, 1975	10.50
Bicentennial, Paul Revere, On Horse, 1975	17.00
Bicentennial, Sons Of Freedom, 1975	10.50
Bicentennial, Valley Forge, 1975	5.25
Bird, Emerald Toucanet, 1974	5.00
Bird, Falcon, 1973	5.50
Bird, Flycatcher, 1974	6.00
Bird, Ostriches, 1977, Miniature	16.00
Bird, Owls, 1973	7.50 to 25.00
Bird, Painted Bunting, 1974, Miniature	3.00
Bird, Robin, 1975	50.00
Bird, Yellow Head, 1974, Miniature	5.00
Car, Mercedes, 1978, Miniature	11.00
Car, Stutz Bearcat, 1978, Miniature	13.50
Car, Turbo Car STP, Red, 1972	10.00
Clown, No. 4, Salty Tails, 1978, Miniature	8.50
Dog, British Pointer, 1975, Miniature	8.00 to 9.00

Lionstone, Horse, Secretariat, 1977

Lionstone, Old West, Renegade Trader, 1969

Lionstone, Old West, Belly Robber, 1969

Dog, Cocker Spaniel, 1975, Miniature 35.00
Dog, German Boxer, 1975, Miniature 5.00
Dog, Labrador Retriever, 1977, Miniature 8.50
European Worker, Silversmith, 1974 .... 1.00
Firefighter, Fireman No. 1, Red Hat, 1972 .... 100.00
Firefighter, Fireman No. 2, With Child, 1974 .... 40.00
Firefighter, Fireman No. 3, Down Pole, 1975 ....12.00 to 28.00
Firefighter, Fireman No. 5, International Assoc. Of Firefighters, 60th Anniversary, 1976 .. 20.00
Horse, Secretariat, 1977 ....*Illus* 150.00
Mailman, 1974 ....6.00 to 31.00
Old West, Annie Christmas, 1969 .... 10.50
Old West, Barber, 1976, Miniature 5.00
Old West, Bartender, 1969, Miniature 5.00
Old West, Bath, 1976 ....51.00 to 75.00
Old West, Belly Robber, 1969 ....*Illus* 11.50
Old West, Camp Cook, 1969 .... 27.00
Old West, Cavalry Scout, 1969 ....6.00 to 12.50
Old West, Cavalry Scout, 1970, Miniature 8.50
Old West, Cowboy, 1969 ....10.50 to 13.50
Old West, Cowboy, 1970, Miniature 12.00
Old West, Cowgirl, 1973 .... 31.00
Old West, Dancehall Girl, 1973 .... 25.00
Old West, Frontiersman, 1969 .... 10.00
Old West, Gambler, 1969 ....11.00 to 18.00
Old West, Gambler, 1969, Miniature 6.50
Old West, Gold Panner, 1969 .... 33.00
Old West, Gold Panner, 1975, Miniature ....5.50 to 6.50
Old West, Highway Robber, 1969 ....10.50 to 18.00
Old West, Indian, Casual, 1970, Miniature 8.50
Old West, Indian, Proud, 1969 ....7.50 to 20.00
Old West, Indian, Proud, 1970, Miniature 13.00
Old West, Molly Brown, 1973 .... 13.50
Old West, Mountain Man, 1969 .... 26.00
Old West, Photographer, 1976 ....12.00 to 71.00
Old West, Professor, 1973 .... 41.00
Old West, Renegade Trader, 1969 ....*Illus* 26.00
Old West, Sheepherder, 1969 .... 6.50
Old West, Sheriff, 1969 .... 10.00
Old West, Sheriff, 1970, Miniature 13.00
Old West, Telegrapher, 1969 .... 19.00
Old West, Vigilante, 1969 .... 19.00
Old West, Wells Fargo Man, 1969 .... 24.00
Safari, Hippos, 1977, Miniature 16.00
Safari, Koala Bears, 1977, Miniature 10.00
Safari, Lion & Cub, 1977, Miniature 10.00
Safari, Mona Monkeys, 1977, Miniature 11.50
Safari, Rhinos, 1977, Miniature 16.00
Sport, Backpacker, 1980 .... 1.00
Sport, Baseball Players, 1974 .... 20.00
Sport, Golfer, 1974 .... 41.00
Sport, Hockey Players, 1974 ....15.50 to 17.50

──────────────── **LUXARDO** ────────────────

In 1821 Girolamo Luxardo began making a liqueur from the marasca cherry. The company literature calls this famous drink *the original maraschino.* The business has remained in the family through five generations. Decorative Luxardo bottles were first used in the 1930s at Torreglia near Padua, Italy. Most of the Luxardo bottles found today date after 1943. The date listed here is the first year each bottle was made. The bottles are still being made and some are sold at stores in the United States and Canada. Bottles are of glass or ceramic and come in many sizes, including miniatures. Many of the bottles were pictured in the now-out-of-print book *Luxardo Bottles* by Constance Avery and Al Cembura (1968).

African, Kneeling, Djembe Drum, 12 1/4 In., Pair 19.00

African Head, 1964	100.00
Amphora, Handle, 1956, 8 In.	16.00
Blue Landscape, Antica Este, 1951, 9 1/2 In.	30.00
Cartella Fiori, 1956	35.00
Crema Mandarino, Square, 4 In.	17.50
Eagle, Onyx, 1970	25.00
Fernet, Round, 4 1/2 In.	10.00
Medieval Palace, 1952	32.00
Tower Of Fruit, 1968	15.00
Venus, 1969, Miniature	6.50

MCCORMICK

It is claimed that the first white men to find the limestone spring near Weston, Missouri, were Lewis and Clark on their famous expedition. Over 20,000 gallons of fresh water gush from the spring each day. An Indian trading post was started near the spring by a man named McPhearson about 1830. His friend Joseph Moore decided to establish a town and paid a barrel of whiskey for the land. Bela Hughes and his cousin Ben Holladay came to the new town in 1837. They soon had a dry goods store, a drugstore, a tavern, and a hotel. They even built a Pony Express station. In 1856, Ben Holladay and his brother David started a distillery to make bourbon using the spring water. David's daughter later married a man named Barton and the distillery was renamed Barton and Holladay. It was sold in 1895 to George Shawhan but closed from 1920 to 1936. The property became a cattle and tobacco farm.

In 1936, after the repeal of Prohibition, Isadore Singer and his two brothers purchased the plant and began making Old Weston and Old Holladay bourbon. About 1939 they bought the name *McCormick* from a nearby distillery founded years before by E.R. McCormick. Legend says that Mrs. McCormick would not allow her husband to reopen the distillery because she had "gotten religion." The Singer brothers' new distillery used part of the grain for the mash, and their cattle feed lot used the leftover parts.

During World War II, alcohol was needed by the government and Cloud L. Cray bought the distillery to make industrial alcohol at a company he called Midwest Solvents. After the war, Bud and Dick Cray, sons of Cloud Cray, started making bourbon at the old plant by old-fashioned methods, producing about 25 barrels a day. The bourbon was sold in Missouri, Kansas, Iowa, and Oklahoma. The old plant, listed in the National Register of Historic Sites, is open for tours. In about 1980 the company, under the direction of the new president, Marty Adams, started marketing on a national instead of a local scale, and it is now selling in all of the states. They have a full line, including wine, beer, and many alcoholic beverages such as rum, tequila, vodka, dry gin, blended whiskey, and brandy that are now sold under the McCormick name.

McCormick Distilling Company was bought by Midwest Grain Products in 1950. They created many types of figural bottles for their bourbon, ranging from a bust of Elvis Presley (made in 1979) to a musical apple (1982). The company discontinued making decanters in 1987.

Abe Lincoln, 1976	16.00
Abe Lincoln, Box, 1976	34.00
Air Race, Pylon, Reno, 1970	27.00
Arizona State Sundevils, 1972	76.00
Arizona Wildcat, 1972	31.00
Bat Masterson, 1972	25.00
Bat Masterson, 1977, Miniature	10.50
Baylor Bears, 1972	86.00 to 133.00
Ben Franklin, 1975	15.50
Ben Franklin, 1976	6.00
Betsy Ross, 1975	6.50 to 25.00
Billy The Kid, 1973	25.00
Billy The Kid, 1977, Miniature	10.60
Black Bart, 1974	10.00 to 32.00
Black Bart, 1977, Miniature	14.50
Calamity Jane, 1974	15.00 to 25.00
Calamity Jane, 1977, Miniature	9.00 to 10.00
Capt. John Smith, 1977	25.00

McCormick, Charles Lindbergh, 1977

McCormick, Elvis, No. 2, Yours '55, Box, 1979

McCormick, William Clark, Box, 1978

Charles Lindbergh, 1977 ....*Illus*	22.00
Daniel Boone, 1975	10.00
Davy Crockett, 1975	25.00
Doc Holiday, 1972	22.00
Doc Holiday, 1977, Miniature	14.00
Elvis, Aloha, 1981	50.00
Elvis, Aloha, Box, 1981	69.00
Elvis, Bust, 1978	10.00
Elvis, Designer I, White, Box, 1981	84.00
Elvis, Designer II, White, Box, 1982	76.00
Elvis, Karate, Box, 1982	103.00
Elvis, No. 1, Sincerely '77, 1978 ....10.00 to 45.00	
Elvis, No. 1, Sincerely '77, Box, 1978 ....10.00 to 50.00	
Elvis, No. 2, Yours '55, 1979 ....10.00 to 29.00	
Elvis, No. 2, Yours '55, Box, 1979 ....*Illus*	50.00
Elvis, No. 3, Forever '68, Box, 1980 ....15.00 to 35.00	
Elvis, Sergeant, 1983	91.00
Elvis, Sergeant, Box, 1983	150.00
Elvis, With Teddy Bear, 1985	118.00
Fire Nozzle, 1984, 200 Milliliters	103.00
Garibaldi Warrior, 1969	27.00
George Washington, 1975 ....6.00 to 11.00	
George Washington Carver, Box, 1977 ....16.00 to 20.00	
Hank Williams Jr., Bocephus, 1980	92.00
Houston Cougars, 1972	28.00
Huck Finn, 1980	31.00
Iowa Hawkeye, 1974	69.00
J.E.B. Stuart, 1976 ....11.00 to 24.00	
J.R. Ewing, 1980, 12 In.	12.00
Jefferson Davis, 1976	16.50
Jesse James, 1973	25.00
Jesse James, 1977, Miniature	10.00
Jim Bowie, 1975	10.00
Jimmy Durante, Music Box, 1981 ....35.00 to 64.00	
John Hancock, 1975 ....5.00 to 6.50	
John Paul Jones, 1975 ....5.00 to 13.00	
Mississippi State Bulldogs, 1974 ....40.00 to 61.00	
Missouri, 150th Anniversary, China, 1970 ....5.00 to 6.00	
Missouri University Tigers, 1974	35.00
Packard, 1937 Model, Cream, 1980	20.00
Patrick Henry, Box, 1975	10.00
Paul Revere, 1975 ....15.50 to 24.00	
Pirate, No. 1, Box, 1972, 1/2 Pt.	6.50
Pirate, No. 2, Box, 1972, 1/2 Pt.	7.50
Pirate, No. 3, Box, 1972, 1/2 Pt.	6.00
Pirate, No. 4, Box, 1972, 1/2 Pt.	6.00

Pirate, No. 5, Box, 1972, 1/2 Pt. 14.00
Pirate, No. 6, Box, 1972, 1/2 Pt. 14.00
Pirate, No. 7, Box, 1972, 1/2 Pt. 14.00
Pirate, No. 8, Box, 1972, 1/2 Pt. 6.00
Pony Express, 1978 .... 46.00
Rice Owls, 1972 .... .26.00 to 46.00
Robert E. Lee, 1976 .... 26.00
Robert Peary, 1977 .... 25.00
Samuel Houston, 1977 .... 25.00
Shriner, Mirth King Jester, 1972 .... 30.00
Shriner Circus, Clown & Kids, 1983, 5 1/2 In. 77.00
Shriner Circus, Clown Car, 1983, 5 1/2 In. 50.00
Shriner Circus, Elephant Girl, 1983, 5 1/2 In. 50.00
Shriner Circus, Girl On Horse, 1983, 5 1/2 In. 66.00
Shriner Circus, Seal Act, 1983, 5 1/2 In. 50.00
SMU Mustang, 1972 .... .25.00 to 56.00
Spirit Of '76, 1976 .... 10.00
Stephen F. Austin, 1977 .... 24.00
Stonewall Jackson, 1976 .... 25.00
Texas Long Horns, 1972 .... .15.00 to 77.00
Texas Tech. Raider, 1972 .... 30.00
Thomas Edison, 1977 .... .15.00 to 25.00
Thomas Jefferson, 1975, 12 In. .... .10.00 to 20.00
Train, Jupiter 60 Engine, 1969 .... 8.00
Train, Jupiter 60 Engine, 1969, 4 Piece Set .... .21.00 to 50.00
Train, Passenger Car, 1969 .... 10.00
U.S. Marshall, Box, 1979 .... 38.00
Ulysses S. Grant, 1976 .... .16.00 to 30.00
University Of Alabama Bamma, Elephant, 1974, 10 In. 69.00
University Of Georgia Bulldog, 1974, 11 In. 44.00
University Of Indiana Hoosier, 1974 .... 85.00
Weary Willie, Music Box, 1981, 18 In. 49.00
Wild Bill Hickok, 1973 .... .10.00 to 35.00
Wild Bill Hickok, 1977, Miniature 11.60
William Clark, Box, 1978 .... .Illus 13.00
Wyatt Earp, 1972 .... 34.00
Wyatt Earp, 1977, Miniature .... .10.00 to 13.00

MEDICINE

If you have friends with scrofula or catarrh, they probably can find a medicine from the nineteenth century. The extravagant claims for cures and the strange names for diseases add to the fun of collecting early medicine bottles. Bottles held all of the many types of medications used in past centuries. Most of those collected today date from the 1850-1930 period. An early bottle often had a pontil. Some of the names, like Kickapoo Indian Oil, Lydia Pinkham's Female Compound, or Wahoo Bitters, have become part of the slang of America. Bitters, cures, sarsaparilla, and a few other types of medicine are listed under their own headings in this book. Apothecary and other drug store bottles are listed here. Collectors prefer early bottles with raised lettering. Labeled bottles in original boxes are also sought. For more information, look for *The Bottle Book: A Comprehensive Guide to Historic, Embossed Medicine Bottles* by Richard E. Fike. Related bottles may be found in the Bitters, Cure, Sarsaparilla, and Tonic categories. Sometimes the embossed name on the bottle of a medicine named for a doctor uses the abbreviation Dr. or Dr with no period. We use Dr. with a period.

A. Eaton's Vegetable Universal Restorative, Ice Blue Aqua, 1855-65, 7 1/2 In. 45.00
A.A. Cooley, Hartford, Con, Deep Olive Green, Pebbly, Oval, Sheared Lip, 4 5/8 In. 504.00
A.H. McFarland & Co., Pharmacy, Salida, Colo., 1/2 Round, 4 1/2 In. .... .395.00 to 450.00
A.J. White Ltd., Aqua, Label, Contents, Cork, Box, c.1918, 4 3/4 In. 88.00
Abbey's Effervescent Salt, Shakespeare, Label, 4-Sided, Contents, Unopened, 3 1/2 In. .. 468.00
Abbey's Effervescent Salt, Shakespeare, Square, Contents, Pamphlet, Box, 3 1/2 In. 248.00
ABL Myers AM Rock Rose New Haven, Blue Green, Iron Pontil, 1845-60, 9 1/2 In. 5600.00
Acker Remedy For Throat & Lungs, W.H. Hooker & Co., Cobalt Blue, 4 3/4 In. 45.00
Ackers Elixir, Nervous, Liver, Bladder, Kidney Diseases, Amber, Contents, Label, 7 1/2 In. 73.00
Al S. Lamb Druggists, Aspen, Col., Lamb, 4 1/4 In. 66.00

PICTURE DICTIONARY
of BOTTLES

Gemel, lady's leg, chestnut—these are a few of the names collectors use to describe bottles. Shape-inspired nicknames are often given to bottles. Some names go back to the eighteenth century. Some are names of men and places associated with the making of the bottle. This is a dictionary of these words—words you must understand to be a smart collector.

FLASKS

The calabash flask is shaped like the gourd called a calabash. The hollowed-out vegetable was often used to hold water, just like the flask. This cobalt blue quart flask is embossed with a bust of George Washington on one side and a tree on the other. It is believed to be one of three known examples and sold for $24,640 at auction.

The Pitkin-type flask got its name from the Pitkin Glassworks of East Hartford, Connecticut. The name describes similarly shaped ribbed bottles made by other factories, too. The blowers used the "German" method of putting a second gather of glass halfway up the post, making the glass walls of the flask thicker. The bottle was then blown into a rib mold to impress ribs. The finished bottle could have vertical or swirled ribs. The extra layer is apparent at the shoulder of this yellow green Pitkin. The 6¾-inch flask has 24 broken swirled ribs. Even with a stress crack—a flaw caused while the glass cools—the bottle sold for $400.

The chestnut flask is almost round. It is named for the nut from the chestnut tree that grows in Europe and the United States. Like their namesakes, chestnut flasks are small. This half-pint green aqua version with 32 swirled ribs sold for $140.

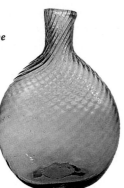

The relatively flat pumpkinseed or punkinseed flask is shaped like the seed of a pumpkin. In the early 1900s, bottle manufacturers called them picnic flasks. The Union Pacific Tea Company clear flask is 4½ inches high. Value at auction, $425.

The coffin flask has a hexagonal base that tapers slightly at the bottom so it resembles a coffin. Many coffin flasks held liquor. This 4½-inch amber example is embossed "C. P. Moorman, Only Manufacturer of J. J. Cutter Old Bourbon." It auctioned for $450.

BLACK GLASS SHAPES

English bottles were made in several shapes in the seventeenth century. One, the **mallet**, was thought to resemble a short-handled hammer. The **onion** was named for the shape of the vegetable. The seal bottle, used about 1630 to 1750, was named for the extra glob of glass or the seal attached to the outside of the bottle. The **seal** was impressed with initials and sometimes a date to identify the owner.

British bottle makers made mallets in glass or stoneware. This 7⅝-inch bottle held My Queen Jubilee Blend whiskey. It is a Scottish example, made between 1890 and 1915. A collector paid $325 for it at auction.

Onion bottles were made with a variety of necks. Collectors nicknamed this 8-inch version "horse hoof" because of the elongated and slightly flattened base. This bottle has an applied string lip. Value at auction, $100.

The seal on this 8³/₄-inch bottle is embossed "Robt. Owen, Aberkin, 1776." The patriotic date sent bidding up to $3,300, even though it is an English bottle.

INKS

Perhaps because so many ink bottles are unmarked, ink bottle collectors have given them descriptive nicknames. All of the names were inspired by the shape of the bottle.

Teakettle inks, like this 2³/₄-inch opalescent lime green example, often have brass neck rings or caps. This ink was made between 1875 and 1890. Auction value, $715.

The namesake of this 1⁷⁄₈-inch Igloo ink is obvious. The yellow amber bottle was made between 1875 and 1890. It sold for $660 at auction.

Umbrella inks usually have eight sides. This medium olive green ink also has an open pontil and an inward-rolled lip. Value at auction, $110.

Collectors need to stretch the imagination a bit to see this ink as a Turtle. It is named that because its upward neck looks like a turtle's head coming out of its shell. This yellow topaz ink, embossed "J & IEM" around the base, sold for $1,400 in an online shop.

OTHERS

A demijohn is a large, narrow-necked bottle.
Demijohns range in size from one to ten gallons
and are often encased in wicker. A carboy is a
larger, heavier-walled version of a demijohn.
This amber example is 15 inches high. It sold for
$50 at auction.

Early soda and mineral water bottlers used blob-top
bottles. The sides and the top of the bottle are
thicker to withstand the pressure of a carbonated
drink. Blob-tops like this aqua Pioneer Soda Works
bottle are fairly common. Value, $20.

A long-necked bottle that only slightly
resembles the leg of a woman has been given
the nickname lady's leg. It was a trademarked
bottle shape first used by Boker's Stomach
Bitters, although other bottlers used it as well.
This yellow olive green example is embossed
"J H Friedewald & Co." It is 11 inches high and
has a tooled mouth. Value at auction, $70.

The unusual bottle that looks like two bottles joined together is called a gemel. It was made to hold two different liquids, like oil and vinegar. Many gemel bottles do not have a flat base and must be kept lying flat on a table or suspended in a stand. Many gemels, like this aqua South Jersey example, are decorative. The 7 ½-inch bottle sold for $300 in an online shop.

Zanesville-type bottles are named for the shape of the bottles made by the Zanesville Manufacturing Company in Zanesville, Ohio, from 1815 to 1838 and from 1842 to 1851. Like the Pitkin-type flask, the name is used for other companies' bottles of the same shape. This 7-inch blue teal example has 24 swirled ribs. It sold for $275 at auction.

A jar is a wide-mouthed cylindrical bottle made of glass or earthenware. Early jars were sealed in a variety of ways. The fruit or canning jar, commonly called a "Mason" jar, is the one most likely to be seen today. Its mouth will usually have a special lip or screw threads for the lid. This yellow olive green French version was probably sealed with fat or a cork. The 12-inch bottle sold for $100 at auction.

A clever glassblower made the first case gin bottles in the seventeenth century. The bottle is more or less rectangular, but slightly smaller at the bottom. It was shaped to fit in a wooden shipping crate. The bottles sat flat against each other in the case. The shape was especially favored by the Dutch, who used it for bottles of exported gin. Dip-molded gin bottles are the same shape, but were molded in boxlike forms. Some case gin bottles are embossed, like this olive green Cosmopoliet Schiedam example. The 9 7/8-inch bottle sold for $225.

TOPS

Before the automatic bottle machine came into use, glassmakers finished the tops of bottles by hand after shaping them in molds. The finishing made slight differences in bottles, and collectors use obvious terms to describe the tops.

This Eagle and Cornucopia flask (McKearin number GII-73) has a tooled lip. A collector paid $100 for the yellow olive green pint bottle.

An applied lip, or ring, makes a smooth opening on this George Washington flask (McKearin number GI-47). The blue green quart bottle has a chipped pontil and sold for $180 at auction.

This emerald green N Richardson mineral water bottle, 7 inches high, has a sloping collar. Value, $70.

BOTTOMS

Bottles get some markings from the glass-blowing process. These marks often reveal the age of a bottle. **Pontil** scars were formed during the shaping process of older, handmade bottles. After a glob (gather) of glass was blown to make it hollow, it was transferred to a pontil rod for shaping by hand or with a mold. To remove the bottle from the rod, the worker had to literally break it free. The area where it was attached usually left a scar, called a **pontil mark** by collectors. Glassmakers sometimes ground and polished the bottom of the bottle to leave a smooth base, also called a **ground pontil**.

The abbreviation IP means iron pontil, indicating that some of the oxidation from the pontil rod was left behind and colored the scar black or rusty red. This blue beer bottle is embossed "Dr Cronk, B & C" on two of its twelve sides. A rare example, it sold for $4,900 in an online shop.

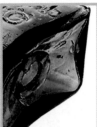

The abbreviation OP means open pontil, indicating that there is a rough indentation where the rod was attached. This rare medicine bottle sold for $4,900 in an online shop. The sapphire bottle is embossed "Dr Robbins', Tecumseh, Rheumatic Drops."

CLOSURES

Soda, mineral water, and beer bottles need closures that keep the gas in the bottle until opened. **Codd** bottles closed with a glass ball that was held in place by the gas, so the bottles had to be filled upside down. Soda pop was nicknamed for the "pop" sound that accompanied the release of the **Hutchinson** rubber stopper. The **lightning closure**, patented in 1875, sealed the bottle with a stopper and a rubber disk held in place by a movable wire. It was used on soda bottles and fruit jars. The **crown top** is the familiar crimped metal cap still being used.

Codd bottles are a distinctly British form. This one is embossed "Whitaker Brushfield & Co Fountain Works." Value, $35 online.

Hutchinson bottles with an intact stopper are hard to find. This one was made by Union Bottling Works in Rochester, New York. Value, $30 online.

Bottles with lightning closures are still valued by home-brewers because they can be resealed. This older version, embossed "Otis S Neale, Boston," sold for $8.50 online.

Beer is still sold in crown cap bottles, and so are some premium sodas. This Coca-Cola bottle was packaged as a convention promotion for Sonny's Bar-B-Q in 1998.

Fruit jar closures used rubber rings to preserve the contents. The earliest jars sealed the rings around the **shoulder**. Later closures, like the **lightning** and **atmospheric**, sealed the ring to the lip.

There are several versions of the lightning closure. These amber Globe (Red Book number 1123) half-gallon, pint, and half-pint jars were made between 1886 and 1890. The set sold for $200 at auction.

There is a slight ledge around the shoulder of this early Mason jar where the cap should seal to the glass. This amber version (Red Book number 1787) of the famous patented jar was made between 1875 and 1895. Value at auction, $616.

DATING CLUES

Legal wording on labels or embossed on the glass can also date bottles.

"Federal Law Prohibits Sale or Re-Use of this Bottle" was used from 1933 to 1964.

Health warnings stating "Women should not drink alcoholic beverages during pregnancy because of the risk of birth defects" and "Drinking impairs the ability to drive a car or operate machinery" have appeared on beer, wine, and liquor labels since 1989.

In 1999, the Bureau of Alcohol, Tobacco, and Firearms allowed winemakers to add a statement to bottles about the possible **health benefits** of wine: "The proud people who made this wine encourage you to consult your family doctor about the health effects of wine consumption."

The word "cure" indicates a date before 1911, when the Sherley Amendment to the Pure Food and Drugs Act prohibited alcohol products from being labeled "cure." This aqua Ayers ague bottle is from Lowell, Massachusetts. The 7-inch bottle sold for $325 online.

Most bottles labeled with the words "For Medicinal Use Only" were used during the Prohibition era (1920–1933), although similar labels were used much earlier to escape liquor taxes and to appease Temperance supporters. This Sunny Brook Rye Whiskey bottle and its box are marked "medicinal," even though the label says the whiskey was distilled before Prohibition. An online bidder paid $110 for the set.

ABBREVIATIONS

There are a few other terms used by bottle manufacturers and collectors that are rarely understood by others.

ISP means inserted slug plate. Names were sometimes embossed on a bottle, especially a milk bottle, with a special plate inserted in the mold. The band around this green Union Glass Works soda bottle could be changed for various bottlers. It's a good thing, too. "Sacramento" is misspelled "Sacrimento" on this early version, making it worth $1,400 to a bidder. Later versions were blue and the spelling error was corrected.

SCA means sun-colored amethyst. When a bottle made before 1914 is put in the sun for a long time, it sometimes turns light purple. The color change is caused by the manganese in the glass. Unfortunately, in recent years some bottles have been exposed to machine-generated radiation that turns the glass dark purple. These purple bottles are decorative, but of no value to serious collectors. This sun-colored amethyst Eye Opener Flask sold for $170 at auction.

Pyro means pyroglaze or enamel lettering, often found on milk bottles and soda bottles. ACL, for applied color label, is another name for the same pyroglaze lettering. This type of label was first used in the 1920s and became very popular in the 1930s. Collectors value multicolored pyroglazes, like this Holly soda bottle. The Betty Boop-like girl makes this bottle worth $20.

Alexander's Silameau, Sapphire Blue, Bell Shape, Lady's-Leg Neck, OP, 6 1/4 In. 1120.00
Allen Druggist, Aspen, Clear, 4 1/4 In. 345.00
Amegin Pyorrhea Liquid, Karlan Laboratories, Paper Label, 4 1/4 x 1 1/2 In. 40.00
American Eagle Liniment, Blue Aqua, 6-Sided, Flared Lip, 1850-60, 5 1/8 In. 90.00
American Oil, Burkesville, Kentucky, Aquamarine, Pontil, 1840-60, 6 3/4 In. 880.00
American Penetrating Salve, Blue Aqua, Embossed, Rolled Lip, Open Pontil, 2 7/8 In. ... 1008.00
Anderson Drug Co., Anderson, Indiana, Clear, 6 1/2 In. 10.00
Apothecary, Alcoolat, D'Aconit, Teal, Recessed Lug, Embossed, Ground Pontil, Label, 10 In. 187.00
Apothecary, Amber, Recessed Lug, Embossed Base, Label, Skull, Crossbones, 10 In. 105.00
Apothecary, Amethyst, Black, Gold Paint, Polished Lip, Glass Stopper, Pontil, c.1860, 11 In. 415.00
Apothecary, Carbonate De Chaux, Teal, Recessed Glass Label, Painted Tin Lid, Pontil, 10 In. 187.00
Apothecary, Cer. Plumbi Subac, Recessed Gold Glass Label, Milk Glass, 6 1/2 In. 242.00
Apothecary, Chlorof., Green, Ribbed, Recessed Red Label Under Glass, Stopper, 6 1/2 In. 94.00
Apothecary, Chlorof., Recessed Label Under Glass, Glass Stopper, 8 In. 50.00
Apothecary, Collyr Adst Lut, Cobalt Blue, Enamel Painted Label, Stopper, 6 1/2 In. 72.00
Apothecary, Dentifrice, Lug, Glass Label, England, 9 In. 100.00
Apothecary, Dentifrice, Lug, Gold Recessed Label, Embossed, Warren Glass, 9 1/2 In. 165.00
Apothecary, Dr. King's New Life Pills Always Satisfy, 4-Sided, Stopper, 13 In. 364.00
Apothecary, E.R. Squibb, Teal Green, Applied Square Color, Clear Stopper, 7 3/4 In. 468.00
Apothecary, E.S. Reed's Sons, Atlantic City, N.J., Milk Glass, Heart Stopper, 4 5/8 In. 157.00
Apothecary, Ferr. Succin., Label Under Glass, Cobalt Blue, 8 In. 358.00
Apothecary, Glycerinum, Etched, Glass Dome Cap, Pouring Spout Stopper, 8 1/2 In. 132.00
Apothecary, Gumm, Arab, Porcelain, 2 Lions, 11 In. 385.00
Apothecary, Hancock's Lozenges, Blown Stopper, Applied Glass Label, 10 1/2 In. 330.00
Apothecary, Hanging, Teardrop Shape, Chains, Cast Iron Crown, 1891, 3 1/2 Gal. 908.00
Apothecary, Hi. Dr. Bichlor. Amm., Cobalt Blue, Stopper, Fluted Shoulders, 3 1/2 In. 132.00
Apothecary, Hyd. Chl. Mit., Gold Label Under Glass, c.1895, 8 1/2 In. 209.00
Apothecary, Hyoscyam, Green, Ribbed, Recessed Red Label, Under Glass, 6 1/2 In. 77.00
Apothecary, Jno. Wyeth & Bro. Philada, Cobalt Blue, Cylindrical, Qt., 10 In. 79.00
Apothecary, Label Under Glass, Cobalt Blue, Label, Flared Mouth, Stopper, 10 1/4 In. 235.00
Apothecary, Label Under Glass, Eau De Rabel, Turquoise, Pontil, France, 6 3/4 In. 125.00
Apothecary, Label Under Glass, Ether Acetio, Turquoise, Pontil, France, 6 3/4 In. 145.00
Apothecary, Label Under Glass, Hancock's Lozenges, Hollow Blown Stopper, 10 1/2 In. .. 578.00
Apothecary, Label Under Glass, Teardrop, Lavender, Olive Yellow, 15 3/4 In. 784.00
Apothecary, Laudanum Rousseau, Recessed Lug, Ground Pontil, Painted Tin Cap, 10 In. .. 220.00
Apothecary, Lin. Bellad, Recessed Lug, Stopper, Cobalt Blue, 8 In. 242.00
Apothecary, Lin. Belladon, Green, Ribbed, Lug, 6 1/2 In. 83.00
Apothecary, Linseed, Recessed Label Under Glass, Tin Cap, Pouring Spout, 8 1/2 In. 176.00
Apothecary, Liq: Morph: Hyd:, Green, Ribs, Recessed Lug, Stopper, 7 In. 165.00
Apothecary, Massa Ziziphi, Glass Top, Ring, Honey Amber, Enamel Label, 4 3/4 x 9 In. . 143.00
Apothecary, Medium Teal Green, Tooled Rim, Tooled Rim, Applied Stem, Lid, 10 In. 180.00
Apothecary, Melin & Badger, Boston, Mass., Cobalt Blue, 6 3/ 8 In. ....*Illus* 242.00
Apothecary, Moschus, Cobalt Blue, Polished Pontil Base, Stopper, 3 1/4 In. 94.00
Apothecary, Ol. Olivae, Recessed Label Under Glass, Pouring Spout, Dome, 10 1/2 In. .. 176.00
Apothecary, Olive Green, Gold Painted Grapevines, Word Cloves, Applied Lip, 12 In. 180.00
Apothecary, Olive Green, Gold Painted Star, Double Collar, Pontil, c.1860, 11 7/8 In. 255.00
Apothecary, P. Ipec. Et Opii, Recessed Lug, Salt Mouth, Stopper, 8 In. 175.00
Apothecary, P. Opii, Roman Recess Style, Gold Label Under Glass, c.1895, 7 In. 275.00
Apothecary, Phosphate Tric, Teal, Recessed Glass Label, Pontil, Painted Tin Lid, 10 1/4 In. 187.00
Apothecary, Piso's Tablet Solution, Label, Cobalt Blue, c.1906, 1/2 Gal., 12 In. 79.00
Apothecary, Porcelain, Alumen, Painted, 10 1/2 In. 275.00
Apothecary, Pot. Bichr. Applied Gold Label Under Glass, Specie Jar, 11 3/4 In. 170.00
Apothecary, Pot. Et Sod. T., Gold Label Under Glass, c.1895, 8 1/2 In. 198.00
Apothecary, Poudre Ac. Borique, Teal, Recessed Glass Label, Pontil, Painted Tin Lid, 10 In. 198.00
Apothecary, Poudre Insecticide, Teal, Recessed Glass Label, Pontil, Tin Lid, 10 1/4 In. .. 198.00
Apothecary, R. Opii Camph., Recessed Label Under Glass, c.1894, 12 In. 198.00
Apothecary, Specie Jar, Applied Gilt Label, Pontil Base, Contents, Tin Lid, 6 x 4 In. 99.00
Apothecary, Strychn. Pulv., Skull, Crossbones, Amber, Enamel, Tooled Lip, Stopper, 5 In. 110.00
Apothecary, Syr Limonis, Cobalt Blue, Enamel Shield, Stopper, Pontil Base, 8 3/4 In. ... 210.00
Apothecary, Syr: Codeinae, Recessed Lug, Stopper, 9 In. 50.00
Apothecary, Tilden & Co.'s Fluid Extract Cinch.C'D, Stopper, 8 1/2 In. 154.00
Apothecary, Tinct. Nucis. Vom, Green, Ribbed, Lug, Glass Label, 6 1/2 In. 83.00
Apothecary, Tr. Bellad., Amber, Veneno, Recessed Lug, Paper Label, Stopper, 10 In. 104.00

Be careful when handling old medicine bottles. The remains of old drugs may still cling to the surface. A broken bit of glass or a sliver could let these toxic materials reach your bloodstream.

Medicine, Apothecary, Melin & Badger, Boston, Mass., Cobalt Blue, 6 3/8 In.

Medicine, Fisher's Seaweed Extract, 3-Sided, Yellow Green, Bulged Neck, England, 5 In

Apothecary, Tr. OpII, Recessed Glass Label, Gold Trim, Blue Corners, 6 7/8 In. 275.00
Apothecary, W.R. Warner & Co., Stopper, Open Pontil, Philadelphia, Sept. 18, 1876 . . . . 55.00
Argent. Nitr., Cobalt Blue, Jar, Recessed Red Label Under Glass, 5 1/4 In. 154.00
Ascatco, Gnu Image On Front, Wrapper, Unopened, 4 In. 28.00
Atwood's Genuine, N. Wood Sole Proprietor, Aqua, Cylindrical, 6 1/2 In. 19.00
Ayer's Cathartic Pills, Contents, Package, Unopened, c.1865 . . . . 339.00
Ayer's Cherry Pectoral, Lowell, Mass., U.S.A., Aqua, BIMAL, 5 1/4 In. 5.00
Ayer's Pills, Lowell, Mass., Aqua, 1840-60, 2 1/8 In. 101.00
B.F. Johnson, Maynard, Cobalt Blue, Round, 3 1/4 In. 35.00
B.R.U. Wilstach Druggist, Lafayette, Indiana, Aqua, 4 3/4 In. 25.00
Bach's American Compound, Auburn, N.Y., Aqua, Open Pontil, 7 1/2 In. 120.00
Ballagh's Drug Store, Nevada, Golden Amber, 3 3/4 In. 65.00
Balsam Copiaba, Standard Drug Co., Elizabeth City, N.C. Ca., Box, 1910-30 . . . . 25.00
Balsam Copiaba, Standard Drug, Elizabeth City, N.C., Box, 1910-30 . . . . 25.00
Barrett's Mandrake Embrocations, Ducks, Green, Rectangular, 4 3/4 In. 45.00
Bartine's Lotion, Green, Applied Lip, Pontil, 6 In. 1430.00
Bartine's Lotion, Yellow Green, Rectangular, Beveled, Pontil, 5 5/8 In. 1456.00
Bayer, Clear, Brown, 2 1/2 In. 4.00
Bear's Oil, Aqua, Flared Lip, Open Pontil, 1840-60, 2 3/4 In. 179.00
Begg's Liver Pills, Jar, Etched, Dakota Globe, Ground Glass Stopper, 11 1/2 In. 220.00
Bendall London, Ice Blue, Rectangular, Embossed, 7 In. 195.00
Bennett & Carroll, 120 Wood St., Pittsburg, Golden Amber, Barrel, 9 1/2 In. 1120.00
Blood Food Prepared By G. Handyside, Olive Green, Rectangular, 5 1/2 In. 53.00
Blue Aqua, Cylindrical, Kick-Up, Dip Mold, Applied Collar, Open Pontil, 1770-90, 6 In. . 48.00
Bonpland's, Fever & Ague Remedy, New York, Aqua, Square, Open Pontil, 5 1/4 In. 165.00
Boots Cash Chemists, Brown, 5 1/2 In. 20.00
Boots Cash Chemists, Brown, Flattened Oval, 4 1/4 In. 15.00
Boots Cash Chemists, Brown, Oval, Flattened Sides, 5 3/4 In. 20.00
Bosaks Horxe Vino Medicinal Bitter Wine, Scranton, Pa., Amber, Box, Label, Qt. 45.00
Boswell & Warner's Colorific, Deep Cobalt Blue, Tooled Lip, 5 5/8 In. 100.00
Boswell & Warner's Colorific, Milk Glass Tool Flared Lip, Pontil, 5 5/8 In. 900.00
Bowman's Vegetable Compound, New Castle, Pa., Blue, Double Collar, IP, 8 In. 784.00
Brandon's Diarrhea Remedy, Box, 5 In. 165.00
Brant's Indian Balsam, Aqua, 8-Sided, Sloping Collar, Pontil, 7 In. 146.00
Brant's Indian Balsam, Blue Aqua, 8-Sided, Applied Sloping Collar, Pontil, 7 3/8 In. 157.00
Brant's Indian Pulmonary Balsam, 8-Sided, Sloping Collar, Open Pontil, 6 3/4 In. 78.00
Brant's Indian Pulmonary Balsam, Blue Aqua, 8-Sided, Sloping Collar Mouth, OP, 7 In. . 112.00
Brant's Indian Purifying Extract, Aqua, Applied Sloping Collar, Open Pontil, 6 3/4 In. . . 145.00
Brant's Indian Purifying Extract, M.T. Wallace Proprietor, Aqua, Open Pontil, 7 In. 165.00
Brant's Purifying Extract, Aqua, Double Collar, Open Pontil, 1840-60, 9 7/8 In. 275.00
Brant's Purifying Extract, Brooklyn, N.Y., Blue Aqua, Double Collar, Open Pontil, 10 In. . 246.00
Brant's Purifying Extract, M.T. Wallace & Co., Brooklyn, Aquamarine, Pontil, 10 In. . . . 358.00
Breinig, Fronefield & Co., Cattle Liniment, Aqua, Open Pontil, 6 1/2 In. 413.00
Bremen Drug Store Waldeck Bros., St. Louis, Mo., Clear, 6 7/8 In. 15.00

Bringhurst's King's Mixture, Wilmington, Aqua, Applied Mouth, OP, 6 1/8 In. . . . .500.00 to 616.00
Bringhurst's Worm Syrup, Wilmington, Rolled Lip, Open Pontil, 4 1/2 In. 504.00
British Oil, Steelman & Archer Wholesale Druggists, Phila., ABM, 5 1/2 In. 12.00
Bromo-Kola For Headaches, Clear, Tooled, Ground Lip, Stopper, 7 1/2 In. 134.00
Brown Pharmacy, Lead, S. Dak., Clear, 5 1/4 In. 20.00
Bucklen's Arnica Salve, Clear, Tooled, Ground Lip, Glass Stopper, 10 1/8 In. 280.00
Bucklen's Arnica Salve, Only Genuine Article, Jar, Ground Stopper, Square, 10 x 5 1/2 In. 110.00
Budd's Wound Nerve & Bone Liniment, Blue Aqua, Applied Sloping Collar, OP, 5 In. . . 672.00
Burgons Limited Manchester, Cobalt Blue, Rectangular, 5 In. 20.00
Burgons Limited Manchester, Cobalt Blue, Rectangular, 6 1/4 In. 20.00
Burnett's Cocoaine, Green, c.1860, 7 In. 120.00
Burns Centenary, Clear, Rectangular, Embossed, Mausoleum, 6 In. 20.00
Burt War's Popular Drug Store, Junction City, Kan., 5 1/4 In. 18.00
C. Brinckerhoffs Health Restorative, Medium Olive Yellow, Pontil, 1840-60, 7 1/4 In. . . . 1430.00
C. Brinckerhoffs Health Restorative, New York, Olive, Applied Top, Ball Pontil, 7 In. . . . 1540.00
C. Brinckerhoffs Health Restorative, Olive Yellow Amber, Sloping Collar, 7 1/4 In. 784.00
C. Brinckerhoffs Health Restorative, Olive Yellow Green, Applied Lip, Pontil, 7 1/4 In. . 800.00
C. Brinckerhoffs Health Restorative, Price $1.00, N.Y., Yellow Olive, Pontil, 7 1/2 In. . . 2464.00
C. Brinckerhoffs Health Restorative, Price $1.00, Olive Yellow, Pontil, 7 1/4 In. 1792.00
C. Goddard Pain Extracting Lotion, Aqua, Applied Mouth, Open Pontil, 7 1/4 In. 660.00
C. Heimstreet & Co., Sapphire Blue, Applied Double Collar, 8-Sided, 6 7/8 In. 392.00
C. Heimstreet & Co., Troy, N.Y., 8-Sided, Sapphire Blue, Double Collar, Pontil, 7 In. 250.00
C. Heimstreet & Co., Troy, N.Y., Blue Green, Sloping Collar, 1840-60, 7 In. 800.00
C. Heimstreet & Co., Troy, N.Y., Cobalt Blue, 8-Sided, Double Collar, Pontil, 7 In. 280.00
C. Heimstreet & Co., Troy, N.Y., Cobalt, 8-Sided, Applied Double Collar, Pontil, 7 1/8 In. 300.00
C. Heimstreet & Co., Troy, N.Y., Medium Sapphire Blue, 8-Sided, Open Pontil, 7 1/8 In. . 275.00
C. Heimstreet & Co., Troy, N.Y., Sapphire Blue, 8-Sided, Double Collar, 7 In. 532.00
C. Heimstreet & Co., Troy, N.Y., Sapphire Blue, 8-Sided, Open Pontil, 7 In. 385.00
C.A. Richards, Amber, Panels, Square Case, 9 1/2 In. 45.00
C.B. Root, Pharmacist, Eagle, Mortar & Pestle, Herkimor, N.Y., 4 1/2 In. 15.00
C.E. Butler Prescription Druggists Lewiston, Idaho, Clear, 4 1/2 In. 25.00
Canfield's One Horse Drug Store, Leadville, Clear, 4 In. 250.00
Canfield's One Horse Drug Store, Leadville, Colo., Clear, 5 1/2 In. 250.00
Carter, Georgetown, Mass., Extract Of Roots, Herbs, Aqua, Cylindrical, 7 In. 275.00
Carter's Spanish Mixture, Forest Green, Applied Mouth, Ring, Pontil, 8 In. 1456.00
Carter's Spanish Mixture, Olive Green, Sloping Double Collar, Iron Pontil, 8 1/4 In. 179.00
Carter's Spanish Mixture, Olive Green, Sloping Double Collar, Label, Pontil, 8 1/4 In. . . 1476.00
Carter's Spanish Mixture, Tobacco Amber, Applied Sloping Double Collar, IP, 8 3/8 In. . 825.00
Carter's Spanish Mixture, Yellow Amber, Applied Sloping Double Collar, IP, 8 In. 1064.00
Cattle Liniment, Breinig, Fronfield & Co., Aqua, Applied Square Collar, Pontil, 6 1/2 In. 476.00
Centaur Liniment, Aqua, Dried Up Contents, Wraparound Label, c.1891, 3 1/2 In. 154.00
Cereal Extract Of Oats & Barley, F.R. Gross & Co., Philadelphia, Amber, 7 1/2 In. 69.00
Chamberlain's Colic, Cholera & Diarrrhoea Remedy, Aqua, Cork, Eye Dropper, 5 In. 25.00
Chamberlain's Diarrhoea Remedy, Aqua, Dry Contents, Wrapper, Canada, 4 1/2 In. 33.00
Chamberlain's Immediate Relief, Clear, Contents, Label, Box, 6 1/4 In. 385.00
Chamberlain's Tablets, Biliousness, Headache, Indigestion, Jar, Stopper, 11 x 5 x 6 In. . . . 187.00
Chamberlain's Tablets, Biliousness, Headache, Indigestion, Jar, Transfer Labels, 12 In. . . . 265.00
Chamberlain's Tablets, They Help Nature, Jar, Ground Stopper, 12 x 6 1/2 x 5 1/2 In. 385.00
Chapman's Cholera Syrup, Geo. Moore, Proprietor, Gt. Falls, N.H., Aqua, Embossed 126.00
Chas. Backman's, Holland, Olive Yellow, Sloping Collar, Ring, 9 3/4 In. 235.00
Chas. J. Getz Druggist & Stationer, Montrose, Colo., Amethyst, 6 7/8 In. 350.00
Chas. J. Getz Druggist & Stationer, Montrose, Colo., Clear, 3 5/8 In. 250.00
Chesbro's Liquid Corn Plaster, Willimatic, Ct., Cobalt Blue, Label, Box, 2 Men, 2 In. . . .   61.00
Chinese Liniment, No 1, Price 50 Ct., Blue Aqua, Rolled Lip, Pontil, 5 1/8 In. 130.00
Church Druggist Colo. Springs, Clear, 2 1/2 In. 40.00
Citrate Of Magnesia, Cobalt Blue, Applied Double Collar, 7 1/4 In. 258.00
Citrate Of Magnesia, H.P. Wakelee & Co., Druggists, Cobalt Blue, 7 3/4 In. 468.00
City Drug Store, Buena Vista, Colo., 4 3/4 In. 95.00
City Drug Store, G.L. Gallinger, Goldfield, Colo., Clear, 5 3/4 In. 750.00
City Drug Store, Telluride, Colo., Henry L. Baisch, Clear, 6 1/8 In. 200.00
Clinton F. Worden & Co., San Francisco, Cal., Amber, 4 1/2 In. 60.00
Cold Pressed Castor Oil, Aqua, Flared Lip, Mortar & Pestles, Open Pontil, 5 7/8 In. 132.00
Comstock & Brother Turkish Balm, Aqua, Applied Double Collar, Open Pontil, 7 1/4 In. 300.00

Connell S. Brahminical, East Indian Remedies, Amber, Double Collar, 8 1/2 In. 168.00
Constitutional Beverage, W. Olmsted & Company, Golden Amber, 10 1/8 In. 308.00
Conver Drug Store Aspen Colo, Clear, 4 1/8 In. 350.00
Corner Drug Store Druggists, Canon City, Amethyst, 7 1/4 In.   125.00
Crane's Penetrating Liniment, Clear, Label, Contents, Instructions, Box, 1906 . . . .   19.00
Cream Of Fresh Lemons, Central Mfg., Co., Iowa City, Ia., 5 In. 15.00
Crisp's Hot Shot Treatment For Running Fits, Clear, ABM, Contents, Label, Box, 7 In. . .   154.00
Curtis & Trall, N.Y., Aquamarine, Applied Collar, Pontil, 9 1/8 In., Pair 476.00
Cuticura Treatment, For Affections Of Skin, Potter Drug, Boston, Aqua, BIMAL, 7 In. . .   20.00
Daffy's Elixir, Rectangular, Beveled Corners, Cross Hinged, Dark Olive Green, 4 1/2 In. . . .   1425.00
Dalby's Carminative, Aqua, Conical, Embossed, 3 1/2 In. 20.00
Dalby's Carminative Prepared By James Dalby, Clear, Tapered, Cylindrical, 4 1/4 In. 17.00
Dam-I-Ana Invigorator, 2 Nymphs, Man, Forest, Amber, Label, 8 3/4 In. 187.00
Damascus, Stoddart Bros., Camel, Palm Trees, Honey Amber, Tooled Lip, 4 1/2 In. 175.00
Dandelion & Tomato Panacea, Aqua, Applied Mouth, Open Pontil, 1840-60, 8 3/4 In. . . .   168.00
Darry's Elixir, Rectangular, Beveled Corners, Cross Hinged, Mid Olive Green, 4 3/4 In. . .   1262.00
Davis & Miller Druggists, Baltimore, Sapphire Blue, IP, Applied Disc Mouth, 7 3/4 In. . .   3920.00
Davis Vegetable Pain Killer, ABM, Labels, Partial Contents, Pamphlet, Box, 6 1/2 In. . . .   209.00
Davis Vegetable Pain Killer, Aqua, Label, Open Pontil, 5 1/4 In.   55.00
Davison & Son, Fleet Street, Yellow Green, Rectangular, Applied Lip, Pontil, 6 In. 1680.00
Dents Desterine, Dog Heads, Contents, Box, Newburgh, N.Y., 4 1/2 In. 232.00
Dexter Liniment, Aqua, Label, Contents, Outside Wrapper, J.W. Brant Co., 4 1/2 In. 825.00
Dickey Pioneer, Creme De Lis, Amber, Embossed, 1850, 5 1/2 In. 143.00
Dispensary, S.C., Palm Tree, Medium Amber, Strap Side, Tooled Lip, 1893-1900, 1/2 Pt. .   955.00
Dispensary, South Carolina, Palm Tree, Blue Aqua, Strap Side, Tooled Lip, Pt. 400.00
Dispensary, South Carolina, Palm Tree, C.G. Co., Tooled Lip, 9 1/4 In. 625.00
Ditchett's Remedy For Piles, Olive Green, Beveled Corners, Double Collar, 9 In. 3750.00
Doct. Girard's Cherry Brandy, Golden Amber, Applied Band, Open Pontil, Handle 1430.00
Doctor McLane's American Worm Specific, Aqua, Rolled Lip, Pontil, 3 3/4 In. 56.00
Doctr. Davis Philada., Aqua, Bimold, 4 1/2 In. 29.00
Dodd's Nervine For Nervous Diseases, Aqua, Label, 6 1/4 In. 94.00
Dr. A. Boschee's German Syrup, L.M. Green Proprietor, Aqua, 6 1/2 In. 35.00
Dr. A.B. Simpson's Vegetable Compound, Reliable Remedy, Label, Box, 7 1/2 In. 550.00
Dr. A.C. Daniels, Pileozion On Wonderworker, 12-Sided, Contents, Box, 5 In. 302.00
Dr. A.C. Daniels' Liniment, Boston, Mass, U.S.A., Embossed, Rectangular, 6 5/8 In. 6.00
Dr. A.P. Sawyer's, Sunrise, Cough Balsam, Embossed, Aqua, Contents, Box, 8 In. 275.00
Dr. Anderson, Cin., O., Blue Aqua, Flared Lip, Pontil, 4 7/8 In. 66.00
Dr. Armstrong's Pure Herb, Aqua, Open Pontil, 6 5/8 In. 390.00
Dr. Baker's Pain Panacea, Blue Aqua, Applied Mouth, Open Pontil, 7 5/8 In. 330.00
Dr. Birmingham's Antibillious Blood Purifier, Teal Blue, Square Collar, 8 5/8 In. 1200.00
Dr. Bull's, Label, Contents, Box, Pamphlet, c.1885, 5 1/4 In. 468.00
Dr. C. Grattan's Diphtheria, 7 In. 165.00
Dr. C.N. Barber's Inflammation Remedy, 3 Labels, Unopened, Dry Contents, 3 1/2 In. . . .   187.00
Dr. C.W. Roback's Scandinavian Blood Purifier, Aqua, Iron Pontil, 7 3/4 In. 300.00
Dr. C.W. Roback's Scandinavian Blood Purifier, Purely Vegetable, Aqua, IP, 8 1/2 In. 605.00
Dr. Carey's Marsh Root, Elmira, N.Y., Aqua, Label, Contents, Box, 7 1/2 In. 77.00
Dr. Carter's Compound Pulmonary Balsam, Aqua, Thin Flared-Out Lip, 5 1/8 In. 308.00
Dr. Cavanaugh's Pile Salve, St. Louis, Mo., Deep Aqua, Inward Rolled Lip, OP, 2 3/8 In. .   245.00
Dr. Copper's Ethereal Oil For Deafness, Aqua, Rolled Lip, Open Pontil, 2 3/4 In. 275.00
Dr. D. Jayne's Ague Mixture, Philadelphia, Aqua, Tapered Mouth, Open Pontil, 8 In. 532.00
Dr. D. Jayne's Carminative Balsam, Aqua, Flared Lip, Open Pontil, Cork, 4 3/4 In. 143.00
Dr. Daniels' Cough Cold & Fever Drops, Boston, Mass., Clear, Label, Contents, 4 1/2 In. .   88.00
Dr. Daniels' Cough Cold & Fever Drops, Distemper Remedy, 50 Cents, Label, Box, 4 In. .   468.00
Dr. Daniels' Eye Wash, For Animals, Eye Dropper, 50 Cents, Amber, Label, Box, 5 In. . . .   413.00
Dr. Daniels' Family Liniment, Sore Cord, Muscle, 35 Cents, Embossed, Label, Box, 6 In. .   358.00
Dr. Daniels' Veterinary Colic Drops, 2 Bottles, Pamphlet, Box, 3 1/4 In. 55.00
Dr. Davis's Depurative, Blue Green, Sloping Collar, Iron Pontil, 1840-60, 9 1/2 In. 1300.00
Dr. Drake's German Croup Remedy, Findlay, Ohio, Aqua, Label, Contents, 6 1/4 In. 176.00
Dr. Duncan's Expectorant Remedy, Light Green, Rectangular, Pontil, 6 1/8 In. 3080.00
Dr. Edward's Tar Wild Cherry & Naptha Cough Syrup, Aqua, Rolled Lip, OP, 5 1/8 In. . . .   110.00
Dr. F. Houck's Panacea, Blue Aqua, Sloping Double Collar, 8 1/2 In. 235.00
Dr. Fahnestock's Vermifuge, Blue Aqua, Open Pontil, Rolled Lip, 4 In. 34.00
Dr. Filkins' Bros., Genuine Healing Balsam, Clear, 8-Sided, Label, Contents, 4 1/4 In. . . .   99.00

Dr. Flower's Nerve Pills, Amber, Embossed Flower, For Brain, Nerves, Muscles, 4 In. . . .   230.00
Dr. Friend's Cough Balsam, Morristown, N.J., Aqua, Sloping Collar Mouth, Pontil, 6 In. .   336.00
Dr. Geo. W. Blocksom, Druggist, Zanesville, Sapphire Blue, 12-Sided, IP, 8 1/4 In. 1064.00
Dr. Geo. W. Clayton Dog Remedies, Clear, Dog, Label, Contents, 4 1/2 In. 99.00
Dr. Gordack, Tubular, Pale Green, Tooled Flared Mouth, Pontil, 6 7/8 In. 476.00
Dr. H. Austin's, Genuine Ague Balsam, Plymouth, O., Aqua, Sloping Collar, IP, 7 3/8 In. .   470.00
Dr. H. Swayne's Vermifuge, Philada, Aqua, Pontil, Flared Lip, 4 3/4 In. 179.00
Dr. H. Van Vleck's Family Medicine, Aqua, Applied Mouth, Open Pontil, 6 7/8 In. 300.00
Dr. H.A. Ingham's Nervine Pain Extract., Aqua, Label, Contents, 5 In. 77.00
Dr. H.M. Purinton's Tiko, Square, Label, Contents, Box, 5 In. 132.00
Dr. H.W. Bergners Stomachic, Reading, Pa., Aqua, Rolled Lip, Open Pontil, 4 3/4 In. 470.00
Dr. H.W. Swartz, Cancer Specialist, New Oxford, Pa., Clear, Tooled Lip, 6 1/2 In. 78.00
Dr. Ham's Aromatic Invigorating Spirit, N.Y., Aqua, Applied Square Collar, 8 1/2 In. . . .   336.00
Dr. Ham's Aromatic Invigorating Spirit, N.Y., Golden Amber, 1875-85, 8 7/8 In. 112.00
Dr. Harpshorns Family, Bull's-Eye, Applied Top, 7 1/2 In. 44.00
Dr. Harter's Elixer Of Wild Cherry, Aqua, Label, Contents, Box, 10 In. 1980.00
Dr. Harter's Liniment, St. Louis, Mo., Aqua, Label, Contents, Box, 4 3/4 In. 232.00
Dr. Harter's Lung Balm, St. Louis, Mo., Aqua, Label, Contents, Box, 5 7/8 In. 110.00
Dr. Harter's Lung Balm, St. Louis, Mo., Aqua, Label, Contents, Box, 7 3/4 In. 853.00
Dr. Harter's Specific, Aqua Green, Label, Contents, Box, 5 7/8 In. 853.00
Dr. Hitzfeld, Denver, Colo., External Use Only, Cobalt Blue, 3 1/2 In. 395.00
Dr. Hobson's Wire Fence Liniment, Pfeiffer Chemical Co., Label, Contents, Box, 10 In. .   297.00
Dr. Hobsons Spavin Remedy, Pfeifer Chemical Co., Aqua, Contents, Box, 8 1/4 In. 176.00
Dr. Hoofland's German Bitters Liver Complaint Dyspepsia & C C.M., Aqua, 8 In. 29.00
Dr. J. Blackman's Genuine Healing Balsam, Aqua, 8-Sided, 4 1/4 In. 11.00
Dr. J.W. Poland's White Pine Compound, Boston, Mass., Aqua, Label, Contents, 7 1/4 In.   1045.00
Dr. JA Burgoon's Renovator System, Pale Aqua, Tooled Mouth, 1885-95, 8 1/8 In. 269.00
Dr. James Cannabis Indica, Craddock & Co., Proprietors, Aqua, Embossed, Oval, 8 In. . .   248.00
Dr. Jayne's Expectorant, Philada., Aqua, Open Pontil, 6 3/4 In.   39.00
Dr. John Bull's, King Of Pain, Louisville, Ky., Aqua, Oval, Rolled Lip, Open Pontil, 5 In. .   420.00
Dr. Jones Sangvin, Blood & Nerve Remedy, Dr. M. Spiegal, Aqua, Rectangular, 9 In. 45.00
Dr. Kennedy's Rheumatic Liniment, Roxbury, Mass., Blue Aqua, 6 1/2 In. 29.00
Dr. Keyser's Pectoral Syrup, Pittsburg, Pa., Blue Aqua, 1860-70, 6 In. 39.00
Dr. Kilmer's, Metal Cap, U & O Binghampton, N.Y., Embossed Base, 2 3/4 In. 154.00
Dr. Kilmer's Autumn Leaf, Ext. For Uterine Injection, Aqua, Paper Label, Box, 4 1/2 In. .   176.00
Dr. Kilmer's Complete Female Remedy, Aqua, Binghampton, N.Y., 8 3/4 In. 99.00
Dr. Kilmer's Cough Medicine, Aqua, Indian On Paper Label, 30 Cents, 5 1/2 In. 110.00
Dr. Kilmer's Dyspeptics Delight For Stomach, Liver & Kidneys, South Bend, 7 3/4 In. . .   132.00
Dr. Kilmer's Female Remedy, Aqua, Contents, Label, $1.00, 8 3/4 In. 385.00
Dr. Kilmer's Herbal Extract For Uterine Injection, Aqua, Paper Label, Cork, 4 1/2 In. . .   99.00
Dr. Kilmer's Swamp Root, Diuretic To The Kidneys, Cylindrical, Label, Cork, 4 1/4 In. . .   110.00
Dr. Kilmer's U & O Anointment, Jar, Shield Label, Metal Top, 50 Cents, 2 7/8 In. 154.00
Dr. Kilmer's U & O Anointment, Jar, Shield Label, Metal Top, Box, 30 Cents, 2 In. 132.00
Dr. Kilmer's U & O Anointment, Stamford, Conn., Amber, Jar, Label, Contents, Box, 2 In.   132.00
Dr. Kilmer's U & O Anointment, Stamford, Conn., Jar, Label, Box, 60 Cents, 2 5/8 In. . . .   198.00
Dr. King's Liver & Kidney Alterative, Goshen, Ind., Aqua, 9 In. 18.00
Dr. King's New Life Pills, Clear, Label Under Glass, Stopper, 13 1/4 In. 448.00
Dr. Kline's Great Nerve Restorer, Aqua, Embossed, $2.00, 8 1/2 In. 154.00
Dr. Laubach's Electric Liniment Allentown Pa., Aqua, 1860-80, 6 In. 29.00
Dr. Lew Arntz Eye Remedy, Greatest Known, Partial Contents, Iowa, 3 1/2 In. 154.00
Dr. Liebig's German Invigorator, Yellow Orange Amber, Rectangular, 8 1/2 In. 85.00
Dr. M.M. Fenner, Fredonia, N.Y., Amber, Oval, 1905, 5 In. 8.00
Dr. M.M. Townsend's Hay Fever, Asthma, Catarrh, Clear, Pamphlet, Label, Box, 7 1/2 In. .   358.00
Dr. Mann's Celebrated Ague Balsam, Galion, Oh, Aqua, Double Collar, Iron Pontil, 7 In. .   350.00
Dr. McLane's American Worm, Blue Aqua, Pontil, Rolled Lip, 1840-60, 3 7/8 In. 146.00
Dr. McMunn's Elixer Of Opium, Aqua, Embossed, Contents, Cylindrical, 4 1/2 In. 61.00
Dr. Miles' Alterative Compound, Aqua, Contents, Label, Box, Pamphlet, 8 1/4 In. 358.00
Dr. Miles' Blood Purifier, Embossed, Contents, Booklet, Box, $1.00, 8 1/4 In. 187.00
Dr. Miles' Cactus Compound, Aqua, Label, Contents, Box, 8 1/4 In. 165.00
Dr. Miles' Heart Treatment, Aqua, Contents, Label, Box, 8 1/4 In. 330.00
Dr. Miles' Medical Co., Contents, Label, Box, Aqua, ABM, 8 1/4 In. 187.00
Dr. Miles' Restorative Blood Purifier, Aqua, Label, Contents, Box, 8 In. 468.00
Dr. Moore's Venereal Antiseptic, Golden Amber, Tooled Lip, 7 7/8 In. 420.00

Dr. Mowe's Cough Balsam, Lowell, Mass., Aqua, Double Collar, Open Pontil, 5 3/4 In. .. 392.00
Dr. Myers' Vegetable Extract, Wild Cherry Dandelion, Aqua, Applied Mouth, Pontil, 8 In. 1320.00
Dr. Nelson's Inhaler, Ceramic, White, Blue Marbling, Bulbous, Black Transfer, 8 In. 138.00
Dr. Oreste Sinanide's Medicinal Preparations, Milk Glass, Tooled Lip, Stopper, 5 In. .. 1210.00
Dr. Pierce's Anuric Tablets For Kidneys & Backache, Blue, Cylindrical, 3 1/8 In. 20.00
Dr. Porter New York, Aqua, Bimold, Rolled Lip, 1855-60, 4 In. 29.00
Dr. Roberts Laxative For Children, Label, Contents, Box, 6 1/2 In. 22.00
Dr. Rose's Antidispeptic Vermifuge, Philada., Aqua Green, Open Pontil, 5 1/2 In. 672.00
Dr. S Pitcher's Castoria, Blue, 5 3/4 In. 12.00
Dr. S.A. Weaver's Canker & Salt Rheum Syrup, Oval, 9 1/2 In. ....45.00 to 65.00
Dr. S.A. Weaver's Cerate, Aqua, Rolled Lip, Open Pontil, 2 3/4 In. 165.00
Dr. Samuel H.P. Lee's Lithontriptic, Cork, Wrapped, c.1940, 2 1/2 x 2 In. 39.00
Dr. Samuel H.P. Lee's Lithontriptic, Jar, Wrap Around Label, Contents, c.1931, 2 1/2 x 2 In. .. 33.00
Dr. Seth Arnold's Cough Killer, Aqua, 5 In. 22.00
Dr. Shoop's Restorative, Great Nerve Tonic, Contents, Wrapper, Box, 8 In. 275.00
Dr. Simmons Squaw Vine Compound, Strictly Vegetable, Indian, 9 In. 121.00
Dr. Slack's Mexican Catarrh Remedy, Clayton, N Mex, Amethyst, Cylindrical, 6 In. 75.00
Dr. Smith's Dentrifice, James J. Ottinger, Metal Cap, Contents, 4 In. 440.00
Dr. Swett's Panacea, Olive Amber, Yellow Tone, Sloping Collared, Pontil, 8 In. 13440.00
Dr. Sykes New England Liver Tonic & Billious Annihilator, Yellow Amber, c.1870, 7 In. . 1008.00
Dr. Thatcher's Liver & Blood Syrup, Yellow Green, Rectangular, 3 1/2 In. 75.00
Dr. Tobia's Venetian Horse Liniment, Light Green, Applied Top, 8 In. 99.00
Dr. Townsend's Sarsparilla, Green, Sloping Collar, Iron Pontil, 1845-60, 9 1/2 In. 123.00
Dr. Venables Vegetable Panokesia, Ice Blue, Open Pontil, Applied Sloping Collar, 8 In. ... 840.00
Dr. Warren's Cough Mixture, Clear, Pontil, Flared Lip, 4 In. 420.00
Dr. Wilson's Horse Ointment, Teal Blue, Rolled Lip, Pontil, 4 1/4 In. 3300.00
Dr. Wistar's Balsam Of Wild Cherry, Aqua, 8-Sided, OP, Rolled Lip, 6 1/4 In. ....157.00 to 190.00
Dr. Wistar's Balsam Of Wild Cherry, Blue Aqua, 8-Sided, Sloping Collar, OP, 6 1/2 In. .. 157.00
Dr. Woods Aromatic Spirit, Bellows Falls, Vt., Aqua, Open Pontil, Oval, 7 In. 295.00
Dr. Yates Asparagus Wine, For The Kidneys, 3-Sided, Aqua, Embossed, Box, 7 1/4 In. ... 165.00
Drake's Palmetto Compound, Palm Tree, Duck, Label, Contents, Box, 9 1/4 In. 77.00
Drink Wm Radam's Microbe Killer, Medium Amber, Tooled Mouth, 10 3/8 In. 1650.00
Duff Gordon Sherry Medical Department U.S.A., Olive Amber, Applied Top, 10 In. 495.00
Dutchers Dead Shot For Bed Bugs, St. Albans, Vt., Partial Label, 1840-60, 5 In. 1232.00
E.A. Buckhout's Dutch Liniment, Blue Aquamarine, Pontil, c.1850, 4 3/4 In. 825.00
E.C. Allen, Concentrated Electric Past, Lancaster, Pa., Blue Green, Rolled Lip, 3 1/4 In. .. 448.00
E.F. Mahardy Hospital Supply Co., Boston, Square, Qt., 10 1/2 In. 40.00
Ed. F. Trunk Druggist, Denver, Colo., Embossed Trunk, Clear, 4 3/4 In. 85.00
Ed. F. Trunk Druggist, Denver, Colo., Embossed Trunk, Clear, 5 7/8 In. 125.00
Elder Flower Eye Lotion, Amber, Embossed Eye & Eyebrow, Labels, 6 1/2 In. 165.00
Emp D Cicuta, Jar, Porcelain, Cobalt Blue, Paris, 11 1/4 x 4 3/4 In. 385.00
Ext Lait V, Jar, Porcelain, Hand Painted, 7 1/4 x 2 3/4 In. 121.00
Ext Trif F, Jar, Porcelain, Hand Painted, 7 1/4 x 2 3/4 In. 121.00
F. Brown's Ess Of Jamaica Ginger Philada, Aqua, Oval, Open Pontil, 5 1/2 In. 32.00
F. Hoyt & Co., Perfumer's Phila., Clear, Label, Corkscrew, 2 1/4 In. 17.00
F.E. Robinson Druggist, Colorado Springs, Monogram, 7 1/8 In. 175.00
Fairchild's Sure, Blue Aqua, Sloping Collar, Pontil, 1840-60, 7 7/8 In. 1100.00
Federation Francaise Droguistes, Yellow Green, 6-Sided, France, 10 3/4 In. 168.00
Fehringer & Black Druggist, Capple Creek Colo, 10 Oz., 7 3/4 In. 275.00
Fellows Syrup Of Hypophosphites, Aqua, Contents, Label, Canada, 5 1/4 In. 50.00
Fentons Pharmacy, Indiana, Clear, 4 1/2 In. 10.00
Fisher's Seaweed Extract, 3-Sided, Bulbous, Embossed, Bright Green, 5 In. 814.00
Fisher's Seaweed Extract, 3-Sided, Yellow Green, Bulged Neck, England, 5 In. .....Illus 550.00
Fitch & Smithers, Druggists, Kalispell, Mont., Square, Clear, 5 1/8 In. 75.00
Flagg's Good Samaritan's Immediate Relief, Cincinnati, Aqua, 5-Sided, OP, 4 In. 275.00
Fleming's Veterinary Eye Lotion, Paper Label, Round, Dry Contents, c.1914, 3 In. 66.00
Fleming's Veterinary Healing Oil, Wraparound Label, Contents, 3 3/4 In. 99.00
Four Fold Liniment, GF Simmons, St. Louis, Mo., 6 1/2 In. 39.00
Frank Crozer Prescription Druggist, Salida, Colo., Clear, 6 In. 295.00
Frank E. Morgan & Sons, Philadelphia, Orange Amber, Glass Stopper, 9 3/4 In. 29.00
Franklin Howes Medical Discovery, Great Blood Purifier, 10 In. 30.00
Frick-Hahn Drug Co, Rexall Store, St.Louis, Mo., Clear, 5 1/8 In. 15.00
Frost's Liniment, Gratis, Blue Aqua, Applied Double Collar, Open Pontil, 5 1/8 In. 245.00

G. Kern, Pharmacist, Leavenworth, Kan., 6 1/8 In. 25.00
G.R. Lewis & Co., Opposite National Hotel, Cripple Creek, Colo., Clear, 4 In. 75.00
G.W. Merchant, Chemist, Lockport, N.Y., Blue Green, Applied Collar, OP, 5 1/8 In. 410.00
G.W. Merchant, Chemist, Lockport, N.Y., Blue Green, Collar, Pontil, 5 1/4 In. ....168.00 to 308.00
G.W. Merchant, Chemist, Lockport, N.Y., Blue Green, Sloping Collar, Iron Pontil, 7 In. ...   450.00
G.W. Merchant, Chemist, Lockport, N.Y., Emerald Green, c.1850, 5 1/2 In. 550.00
G.W. Merchant, Chemist, Lockport, N.Y., Emerald Green, Sloping Collar, Pontil, 5 1/8 In.   258.00
G.W. Merchant, Chemist, Lockport, N.Y., Green, Sloping Collar, Open Pontil, 5 3/4 In. ..   364.00
G.W. Merchant, Lockport, N.Y., Blue Green, Applied Sloping Collar, Iron Pontil, 7 In. ...   532.00
G.W. Merchant, Lockport, N.Y., Emerald Green, Sloping Collar, 1860-75, 5 3/4 In. 308.00
G.W. Merchant, Lockport, N.Y., Green, Sloping Collar, Pontil, c.1850, 5 1/8 In. 246.00
G.W. Merchant, Lockport, N.Y., Teal Blue, Applied Sloping Collar, Open Pontil, 5 1/2 In.   308.00
Gargling Oil, Cobalt Blue, ABM, Label, 5 In. 61.00
Gargling Oil, Cobalt Blue, ABM, Label, Horse On Front, 5 In. 176.00
Gargling Oil, Green, Label, Family Scene, Partial Contents, 5 1/2 In. 440.00
Gargling Oil, Lockport, N.Y., Blue Green, 5 1/2 In. 29.00
Gargling Oil, Lockport, N.Y., Green, BIMAL, 5 3/4 In. 50.00
Gargling Oil, Lockport, N.Y., Yellow Lime Green, Rectangular, 5 3/4 In. 48.00
Gargling Oil, Lockport, Teal, 5 1/2 In. ....35.00 to 45.00
Gargling Oil Liniment, Cobalt Blue, Paper Label, 5 1/4 In. 330.00
Garland's Cough Drops, Light Aqua Green, Applied Square Collar, 1870s, 7 1/4 In. 358.00
Garligant's Balsam Of Health, Prepared Only By John S. Miller, Aqua, OP, 5 5/8 In. 1064.00
Gell's Dalby's Carminative, Aqua, Pontil, Tooled Lip, 3 7/8 In. 179.00
Gell's Dalby's Carminative, Pale Blue Green, Flared Lip, Open Pontil, 3 7/8 In. 520.00
Genuine Swaim's Panacea, Philada, Aqua, Applied Sloping Collar, Open Pontil, 7 7/8 In..   840.00
Geo. W. Laird & Co., Oleo Chyle, Cobalt Blue, Semi-Cabin, Tooled Lip, 10 In. 336.00
Gleet Seven Day Gonorrhoea, Cobalt Blue, Tooled Lip, 1890-1900, 4 7/8 In. 672.00
Glycozone, Ch. Marchand, Contents, Label, Wrapper, 5 1/4 In. 72.00
Goff's No Dope Cough Syrup, Clear, Label, Box, Contents, 5 In. 12.00
Golden Amber, Oval, Applied Double Collar, 1860-70, 7 1/2 x 3 1/4 In. 420.00
Good Samaritan Ointment Pot, White Glaze, Black Transfer, 1 1/2 In. 777.00
Grana Cathecu, Jar, Porcelain, Gold & Black Trim, Rousseau, Paris, 8 x 3 1/2 In. 165.00
Granular Citrate Of Magnesia, Cobalt Blue, Rectangular, 6 1/8 In. 29.00
Granuline, Milk Glass, Eye Dropper, Murine Eye Remedy Co., Chicago, Box, 3 1/2 In. ..   187.00
Great European Cough Remedy, Rev. Walter Clark, Olive Amber, Pontil, Label, 4 5/8 In.   605.00
Green & Bentley Drug Co., Oskaloosa, Ia., 5 3/8 In. 22.00
Griswold's Malarian Antidote, Blue Aqua, Rectangular, Applied Sloping Collar, OP, 7 In.   336.00
Guinn's Pioneer Blood Renewer, Red Amber, Double Collar, 1875-85, 11 1/8 In. 246.00
Gun Wa's Chinese Remedy, Golden Amber, Sloping Double Collar, 8 In. ....616.00 to 840.00
Gun Wa's Chinese Remedy, Golden, Applied Lip, 8 In. 495.00
H. Clay Glover, New York, Imperial Liniment, Amber, Label, 5 In. 50.00
H. Clay Glover Co., New York, Distemper Medicine, Amber, Paper Label, 5 In. 55.00
H. Lake's Indian Specific, Aqua, Attic, Open Pontil, 8 1/4 In. 925.00
H. Lake's Indian Specific, Aqua, Bulbous Neck, Pontil, 1840-60, 8 1/8 In. 1008.00
H. Lake's Indian Specific, Blue Aqua, Applied Mouth, Open Pontil, 8 1/4 In. 560.00
H.G. Hotchkiss, Oil Of Spearmint, Lyons, Blue, Label, 8 1/2 In. 77.00
H.H. Warner & Co., Ltd., Safe Cure, Amber, Contents, Label, Box, Cork Top, 7 In. 522.00
H.H. Warner & Co., Ltd., Safe Cure, Amber, Contents, Label, Box, Cork Top, 9 In. 440.00
H.H. Warner & Co., Melbourne, Light Amber, ABM, Blob Top, 9 1/2 In. 45.00
H.H. Warner & Co., Tippecanoe, Mushroom Top, Amber, Label, Nov. 20, 83, 9 In. 121.00
H.H. Warner & Co., Tippecanoe, Yellow Amber, Doughnut Mouth, 9 1/8 In. 364.00
H.H.H. Horse Medicine, The Celebrated, Aqua, Paper Label, 1868, 7 1/8 In. 580.00
H.K. Mulford, Chemist, Philadelphia, Cover, 9 In. 30.00
Hall's Balsam For The Lungs, Aqua, Rear Label, Sunken Panels, Long Neck, 7 In. 16.50
Hall's Pulmonary Balsam, J.R. Gates & Co., Aqua, Tooled Lip, 6 1/2 In. 45.00
Haskell's Pharmacy, Grand Junction, Colo., Clear, 4 1/2 In. 55.00
Haviland & Co., New York, Charleston & Savannah, Aqua, 5 7/8 In. 235.00
Healy & Bigalow Kickapoo Oil, Aqua, Contents, Label, Pamphlet, Box, 7 In. 88.00
Healy & Bigalow Kickapoo Oil, Contents, Label, Box, 5 In. 72.00
Healy & Bigalow Kickapoo Sagwa, Clear, Label, Contents, C.I. Hood Co., 8 1/2 In. 154.00
Healy & Bigelow Indian Sagwa, Aqua, Embossed Indian, Contents, Label, 8 1/2 In. 1375.00
Hemlock Oil Co., Derry, N.H., Headache, Toothache, Label, Contents, Box, Square, 5 In. .   50.00
Henshaw & Edmands Druggists, Boston, Blue Green, Applied Mouth, 10 5/8 In. 3080.00

Hepatone, Cobalt Blue, Label, Contents, Aluminum Cap, 7 In. 55.00
Herrick's German Horse Liniment, Aqua, Paneled, 9 In. 40.00
Herrick's German Horse Liniment, Embossed Side Panels, Aqua, 8 1/2 In. 55.00
Hirsts Pain Exterminator, Indian, Barrel, Aqua, Label, Contents, Box, 5 3/4 In. 110.00
Homan's Nature's Grand Restorative, Aqua, Open Pontil, 9 In. 1100.00
Hoofland's Genuine Healing Balsam, Rectangular, 8 In. 26.00
Hooper & Compy, 55 Grosvenor St. & At 7 Pall Mall East, Olive Green, 7 1/4 In. 251.00
Hopkins' Chalybeate, Baltimore, Blue Green, Cylindrical, Double Collar Top, 7 1/2 In. . . 145.00
Houck's Patent Panacea, Aqua, Cylindrical, Applied Lip, Open Pontil, 1840-60, 6 3/4 In. . 146.00
Howell Drug Co., Service Store, Silver City, New Mex., 6 In. 132.00
Hoyt's Rubifoam, Liquid Dentrifice For The Teeth, Embossed, Contents, 2 Oz., 4 1/2 In. . 88.00
Hoyt's Rubifoam, Liquid Dentrifice For The Teeth, Embossed, Sample, Box, 2 In. 1870.00
Humphrey's Homeopathic, Horse Head, Clear, Labels, Colic, Sprains, 3 7/8 In., 2 Piece . 121.00
Humphrey's Medicine Co., Embossed Horse Head, Paper Label, 4 1/2 x 2 3/4 In. 385.00
Hunt's Liniment, Prepared By C.E. Stanton, Sing Sing, N.Y., Aqua, OP, 5 In. 69.00
Hunt's Remedy, Clarke Pharmacist, Providence, R.I., Aqua, Rectangular, 7 1/2 In. 18.00
Hunt's Remedy, Wm. E. Clark Pharmacist, Aqua, Contents, Label, 7 In. 143.00
Hunter Drug Co., Excelsior Springs, Mo., 4 1/2 In. 15.00
Hyatt's Infallible Life Balsam, Grass Green, Sloping Double Collar, IP, 9 3/4 In. 1600.00
I. Calvin Shaffer Co., N.Y., Medicinal Blackberry, Clear, Contents, Label, 8 In. 33.00
I. Covert's Balm Of Life, Yellow Olive Green, Applied Mouth, Open Pontil, 6 In. 1568.00
Indian, see also Medicine, Healy & Bigelow
Indian's Panacea, Green Yellow, Domed Label Panel, Pontil, 1835-50, 8 1/2 In. 7150.00
J. Jungmann Apothecary, Cobalt Blue, Tooled Lip, 6 7/8 In. 202.00
J. Lipman, San Francisco, Applied Lip, 6 1/2 In. 88.00
J.A. Limerick's Great Master Of Pain, Rodney, Miss., Aqua, Sloping Collar, IP, 6 1/2 In. . 364.00
J.A. Mirriam Druggist, Pueblo, Colorado, Paper Label, 6 1/8 In. 195.00
J.B. Marchisi M.D., Uterine Catholicon, Aqua, Contents, Rear Label, 8 In. 44.00
J.B. Wheatley Compound Syrup, Dallasburgh, Ky., Aqua, Double Collar, IP, 6 1/8 In. . . . 200.00
J.H. Jackson, Pullman, Wash., Clear, 5 In. 20.00
J.L. Parsons, Durango, Colo., Druggist, 6 1/2 In. 95.00
J.R. Nichols & Co., Chemists, Boston, Cobalt Blue, Tooled Sloping Collar, 9 3/8 In. 336.00
J.W. Bull's Retco, Mistura Baltimore, Aqua, Applied Mouth, 5 7/8 In. 605.00
Jayne's Balsam Of Tar Compound, 1 Cent Internal Revenue Stamp, BIMAL, 5 5/8 In. . . . 12.00
Jelly Of Pomegranate, Preparate By Dr. Gordak Only, Aqua, Flared Lip, Pontil, 6 3/4 In. . 300.00
Jno. E. Smith's Pharmacy, Victor, Monogram, 7 1/8 In. 149.00
Johann Hoff's Extract, Amber, ABM, Contents, Bottle Cap, 7 7/8 In. 14.00
John C. Baker Co. Cod Liver Oil, Philadelphia, Tooled Lip, Neck Seal, Label, 9 In. 385.00
John G. Hazzard & Co. Chemists, New York, Red Amber, Square, 7 1/4 In. 25.00
John J. Smith, Louisville, Ky., Tubular, Blue Green, Sloping Collar, Pontil, 5 3/4 In. 1344.00
Johnson's Anodyne Liniment, Aqua, Round, Label, Partial Contents, 4 1/2 In. 44.00
Jones, J.D. Park, Cincinnati, American Cholagogue, Blue Aqua, Pontil, 6 3/4 In. 275.00
Jones' Drops For Humors Or Anti-Impetigines, Aqua, Flared Lip, Open Pontil, 4 7/8 In. . 265.00
Jos. C. Wirthman & Co., Kansas City, Mo., Amethyst, Tooled Lip, 8 Oz. 200.00
Karnak, Cork, Partial Contents, Box, 8 1/4 In. 15.00
Katz & Besthoff, Pharmacists, New Orleans, Cobalt Blue, 1890-1900, 7 3/4 In. 330.00
Kennedy's Salt Rheum Ointment, Clear, Screw Cap, Contents, Label, Round, 3 1/2 In. . . 22.00
Kennedy's Salt Rheum Ointment, Jar, Contents, Wraparound Label, Wrapper, 3 1/4 In. . . 11.00
Keough's N-F Foul Remedy For Fouls Or Hoof Rot, Rear Of Cow, Aqua, 7 In. 154.00
Kickapoo Oil, see Medicine, Healy & Bigelow
Kitchel's Liniment, Aqua, Qt., 9 1/2 In. 33.00
Knott's Pharmacy, Aspen, Colo., Clear, Embossed Square Knot, 4 3/8 In. 250.00
Kopp's Baby's Friend Co., York, Pa., Clear, Contents, Pamphlet, Label, Box, 4 3/4 In. 88.00
Lapidar, Order At Once, Large Box, 1000 Tablets, Contents, Square, Box, 3 1/2 In. 143.00
Lediard's, Morning Call, Forest Green, Sloping Collar, Cylindrical, 1860-70, 9 3/8 In. . . . 336.00
Leech, Jar, Ceramic, White, c.1800, 8 In. 4680.00
Lilly Tablet, Jar, Amber, 1000 Solvets, No. 23 Boric Acid, 5 Grains, Cork, 9 3/4 In. 132.00
Lindsey's Blood Searcher, Hollidaysburg, Emerald Green, Paneled Sides, 9 3/8 In. 3920.00
Lindsey's Blood Searcher, R.E. Sellers & Co., Pittsburgh, Clear, 8 3/4 In. 120.00
Lindsey's Blood Searcher, R.E. Sellers & Co., Pittsburgh, Pa., Label, Box, 8 1/2 In. 605.00
Lippincott's One Night Roup Remedy, 25 Cents, Chickens, Embossed, Box, 2 Oz., 5 1/2 In. . 99.00
Listerine, Lambert Pharmacal Company, 5 In. 12.00
Livingston's Gilead Balm, Orange Amber, Double Collar, 9 5/8 In. 179.00

Log Cabin Extract, Amber, Flat Panel, 3 Recessed Panels, Embossed, Contents, 6 1/4 In. . 230.00
Log Cabin Extract, Rochester, N.Y., Amber, Patd Sep 6 1887, Tooled Lip, Label, 6 1/2 In. 275.00
Log Cabin Hops & Buchu Remedy, Amber, 10 In. 715.00
Longley's Panacea, Aqua, Applied Lip, Pontil, Rectangular, 6 1/2 In. 77.00
Longley's Panacea, Olive Green, Double Collar, Pontil, 6 3/4 In. 4710.00
Longley's Panacea, Olive Green, Sloping Double Collar, 6 In. 1064.00
Lorrimer Medical Institute, Baltimore, Md., Amber, 6 1/4 In. 59.00
Louden & Co.'s Indian Expectorant, Philada., Aqua, Oval, Applied Mouth, OP, 7 3/8 In. . 280.00
Louis Daudelin Co., Free Sample, Blood Wine, Worcester, Mass., 3 1/2 In. 75.00
Lovins Drug Store, 2002 Champa St. Denver, Clear, 4 5/8 In. 50.00
Lowes Balsam, Prepared By Taylor Gibson & C, Newcastle, Aqua, Square, 4 1/4 In. 20.00
Lucien Pratte Le Renovateur De La Femme, Waterbury Conn., Cobalt, Panels, 9 1/4 In. . 280.00
Lydia E. Pinkam's Vegetable Compound, Aqua, Label, Contents, Box, 8 1/2 In. 358.00
Lyon's Powder, B & P, N.Y., Copper Puce, Open Pontil, Rolled Lip, 4 1/4 In. 235.00
Lyon's Powder, B & P, N.Y., Medium Blue Green, Tooled Lip, 4 1/4 In. 495.00
Lyon's Powder, B & P, N.Y., Olive Green, Open Pontil, Rolled Lip, 4 3/8 In. 336.00
Lyon's Powder, B & P, N.Y., Orange Amber, Cylindrical, 4 1/4 In. 39.00
Lyon's Powder, B & P, N.Y., Pink Amethyst, Inward Rolled Lip, Open Pontil, 4 3/8 In. 300.00
Lyon's Powder, B & P, N.Y., Red Puce, Inward Rolled Lip, Open Pontil, 4 1/8 In. 275.00
Lyon's Powder, B & P, N.Y., Yellow Amber, Inward Rolled Lip, Open Pontil, 4 3/8 In. 275.00
Lyon's Powder, B & P, N.Y., Yellow Green, Tooled Lip, 4 3/8 In. 110.00
M & J.S. Perrine, Orange Amber, Squat, Applied Seal, Qt. 89.00
M.B. Roberts's Vegetable Embrocation, Blue Green, OP, c.1850, 5 In. . . . . .112.00 to 134.00
M.B. Roberts's Vegetable Embrocation, Blue Green, Sloping Collar, Pontil, 5 1/2 In. 364.00
M.B. Roberts's Vegetable Embrocation, Emerald Green, Applied Collar, OP, 5 1/2 In. 280.00
M.B. Roberts's Vegetable Embrocation, Green, Applied Lip, Open Pontil, 5 In. 300.00
Mad. M.J. Goodman's Excelsior Pearl Drops, Milk Glass, Rolled Lip, 4 5/8 In. 112.00
Maguire Druggist, St. Louis, Mo., Apple Green, Pontil, Applied Sloping Collar, 5 3/4 In. . 134.00
Martis Limatura, Jar, Porcelain, Eagle, Verreries Plefebure, Paris, 11 1/4 x 4 3/4 In. 577.00
Masta's Indian Pulmonic Balsam, Lowell, Mass., Aqua, Double Collar, 5 3/4 In. 308.00
Mathewson's Horse Remedy, Price 50 Cts., Aqua, Double Collar, Pontil, 6 3/4 In. 224.00
Mayhew & Wentzell, San Francisco, Cobalt Blue, 6 In. 990.00
McCambridge & McCambridge Co., M.M. Accuracy, Purity, Amber, 4 In. 19.00
McClelland Diphtheria Remedy, Clear, Tooled Top, 8 In. 99.00
McCormick & Co., Man'F'C, Chemists, Baltimore, Aqua, 3-Sided, Red Label, 4 1/2 In. . . 280.00
McDaniel & Hill West End Drug Store, Florance, Colo., Monogram, 4 1/4 In. 65.00
McDonald's Annihilator Bronchitis, Coughs & Colds, Amber, Tooled Lip, 7 3/4 In. 146.00
McDonald's Improved Liver Pills, Milk Glass, Cylindrical, Pontil, Stopper, c.1906, 7 In. . 89.00
Meador's Reliable Eye Remedy Co., Clear, Label, Eye, Box, Flyer, Dropper, 3 3/8 In. . . . 88.00
Meissneirs Pharmacy, 820 Main St., La Porte, Indiana, Clear, 5 1/4 In. 15.00
Mennen Antiseptic Oil, Baby In Sailboat, Paper Label, Tin Top, 2 1/4 x 1 1/8 In. 48.00
Meugge The Druggist, Baker Ore, Green, 5 1/4 In. 55.00
Mexican Mustang Liniment, Embossed, Aqua, Cylindrical, Rolled Lip, 5 1/2 In. 120.00
Miller & Co. Druggists, Leadville, Colo., Clear, 4 In. 50.00
Miller's Antiseptic Oil, Clear, Label, Contents, Box, Herb Juice Medicine Co., 5 7/8 In. . . 120.00
Mitchell & Egbers Drug Col., Canon City, Colo., Palace Drug Store, Amethyst, 6 3/4 In. . 55.00
Mixer's Cancer & Scrofula Syrup, Label, 24 Page Booklet, Box, c.1921, 7 3/4 In. 523.00
Morely Bros Druggists, Golden Amber, Austin, Texas, 1880-1900, 10 1/4 In. 550.00
Morse's Celebrated Syrup, Prov, R.I., Blue Aqua, Sloping Collar, Iron Pontil, 9 1/2 In. . . 190.00
Morse's Celebrated Syrup, Prov. R.I., Aqua, Oval, Collared Mouth, Pontil, 9 1/4 In. 246.00
Morse's Celebrated Syrup, Prov. R.I., Emerald Green, Sloping Collar, 9 3/8 In. 2464.00
Mother Siegel's Digestive Syrup, Clear, Label, Contents, Box, A.J. White Ltd., 4 1/4 In. . 198.00
Mrs. Winslow's Soothing Syrup, Aqua, Open Pontil, 5 1/8 In. 20.00
Mrs. Winslow's Soothing Syrup, Curtis & Perkins, Aqua, Rolled Lip, Open Pontil, 5 In. . . 39.00
Mrs. Winslow's Syrup, Cylindrical, Contents, Wrapper, Sealed, Screw Cap, 5 In. 50.00
Munyon's Germicide Solution, Green, Rectangular, 3 1/2 In. 23.00
Murine Eye Remedy Co., Chicago, Membrane Inflammation, Milk Glass, Labels, 3 3/4 In. 154.00
Murine For Your Eyes, Rubber Tip, Screw Top, Paper Label, Chicago, 4 In. 85.00
Murray Drug Co., Prescription Druggists, Colorado Springs, Amber, 4 3/8 In. 135.00
Myers' Rock Rose, New Haven, Aqua, Sloping Collar, 1840-60 . . . . 532.00
Nerve Food, Moxie, Lowell, Mass., Patented, Cork, Early 1900s, 10 In. 185.00
Nesom's Drug Store, Los Angeles, Ca., Get It At Nesom's, Tooled Top, 7 1/8 In. 165.00
Norwood's Tinct., Clear, Label, Box, 5 1/4 In. 220.00

Norwood's Veratrum Viride, Clear, Label, United Society Of Shakers, 5 1/2 In. 55.00
O.B. Wilkins Druggist, Oxford, Indiana, Clear, 4 1/2 In. 10.00
Ober & McConkeys, Specific For Fever & Ague, Aqua, 6-Sided, Applied Lip, OP, 6 3/4 In.   440.00
Old Sloan's Liniment, S 5 L-76 12 Made In USA, Box, 5 In. 12.50
Olive Amber, Rectangular, Beveled Panels, Pontil, Applied Double Collar, England, 7 In. .   179.00
Olive Green, Pontil, Flared Lip, Continental, 1760-80, 6 5/8 In. 213.00
Olive Green, Pontil, Tooled Lip, Continental, 1760-90, 5 7/8 In. 90.00
Our Drug Store, C.J. Chapman, Louisiana, Mo., 3 1/2 In. 18.00
Owl Drug, McCreery & Widerfelt, City Drug Store, Florence Colo., Amethyst, 6 7/8 In. ...   295.00
Owl Drug Co., San Francisco, Cal, Aqua, Rectangular, 10 1/2 In. 250.00
Owl Drug Store, John T. Ray Osmers Prop., Lewiston, Idaho, Clear, 4 1/4 In. 30.00
Paine's Celery Compound, Golden Amber, Tooled Double Collar, 1890-1905, 9 1/2 In. ..   25.00
Palace Drug Store, Prescriptions, Goldfield, Colo., Clear, 3 5/8 In. 175.00
Palace Pharmacy Drug Co., A.R. Troxell, Manager, Cheyenne, Wyo., Clear, 4 1/2 In. ...   30.00
Palmer's Opera House Pharmacy, Salina, Kan., 4 7/8 In. 20.00
Parke Davis, Aloin Compound, 100 Gelatin Coated Pills, Label, 4 1/2 In. 40.00
Paul G. Schuh, Rattle Snake Oil, Cairo, Ill., Rattlesnake Inside, Tooled Lip, 5 1/2 In. 1430.00
Pepgen, Dayton, Ohio, Clear, Airplane, Label, Contents, Box, 8 1/2 In. 120.00
Perrin's Pile Specific, Rocky Mountain Pile Remedy, Label, Contents, Box, 6 1/4 In. 154.00
Peuser & Kadish Druggists, Chicago, Teal Blue, Round, Tooled Lip, 7 1/2 In. 504.00
Pfeifer Chemical Co., Aqua, Label, Box, 8 1/4 In. 176.00
Phelp's Arcanum, Worcester, Mass., Yellow Olive Green, Pontil, 9 In. 3080.00
Phoenix Pectoral Levi Oberholtzer M.D., Aqua, 5 1/2 In. 29.00
Pineoleum, 2 1/4 x 3/4 In. 15.00
Pioneer Drug Co., In Business For Your Health, Goldfield, Nevada, Amethyst, 5 3/4 In. ..   200.00
Planters Cuban Relief, For Internal & External Pains, 1 Oz., 6 1/4 In. 154.00
Podophyllin, Teal Green, Cork, 3 1/2 In. 100.00
Pond's Extract, Aqua, Label, 4 1/2 In. 33.00
Poor Man's Friend, Ointment Pot, Blue Transfer, White Glaze, 1 1/4 In. 82.00
Poor Man's Friend, Ointment Pot, Brown Transfer, White Glaze, 1/1/4 In. 225.00
Pratt's Abolition Oil, Aqua, Applied Top, Rectangular, Camphor Corners, 6 In. 135.00
Pratt's Abolition Oil For Abolishing Pain, Backwards S, Applied Top, 5 3/4 In. 121.00
Pratt's Veterinary Liniment, Aqua, Label, Contents, Pratt Food Co., Phila., 5 1/2 In. 77.00
Preston's Veg. Purifying Catholicon, Portsm. N.H., Aqua, Oval, Tubular Pontil, 9 1/4 In. .   258.00
Prices Patent Candle Co. Ltd., Cobalt Blue, Double Collar, Stopper, Pontil, 7 1/8 In. 100.00
Prof. I. Hubert's Cobalt Blue, Tooled Lip, Front & Rear Labels, 5 In. 90.00
Prof. Lorman's Indian Oil, Philada, Pa., Clear, Label, Contents, 5 In. 110.00
Prof. Low's Worm Syrup, Philada, Aqua, Rectangular, 5 In. 9.00
Professor Horsford's Acid Phosphate, 8-Sided, Contents, Wrapped, Unopened, 6 In. ...   132.00
Pucell Ladd & Co., Richmond Va., Aqua, Rolled Lip, Open Pontil, 1840-60, 3 7/8 In. 224.00
Pucell Ladd & Co., Richmond, Va., Aqua, Applied Lip, Open Pontil, 1840-55, 9 3/4 In. ...   1120.00
Pulv: Opii, Jar, Porcelain, Black & Gold Trim, Rousseau, Paris, 11 1/4 x 5 In. 286.00
R.E. Gogings, Sacramento, Cal., Amber, Embossed, Applied Lip, 5 3/4 In. 198.00
R.R.R. Radway Co., N.Y., Rheumatic, Neuralgic, Nervous, Aqua, Label, Contents, 6 1/4 In.   165.00
R.W. Davis Drug Co., Chicago, Milk Glass, Tooled Lip, 1890-1910, 11 1/8 In. 100.00
Ransom & Stevens Druggists, Boston, Dandelion & Tomato, Aqua, Open Pontil, 9 In. ...   840.00
Rawleigh's Trade Mark, Colic & Bloat Compound, Label, ABM, Aqua, 8 In. 105.00
Reakirt's Medicated Breast Julap, Aqua, Applied Lip, Open Pontil, 5 In. 550.00
Reese Chem. Co., For External Use Only, Use 4 Times Daily, Cobalt Blue, ABM, 5 1/2 In.   135.00
Remo Crown Pharmacy, Cleveland, Ohio, Amber, Embossed, BIMAL, 6 7/8 In. 55.00
Renne's Pain Killing Magic Oil, Pittsfield, Mass, Aqua, Trial Size 25 Cents, Label, 5 In. ...   130.00
Rheumatic Trademark Syrup, 1882, Wolcott, N.Y., 4-Sided, Golden Amber, 10 In. 179.00
Robbins' Anod. Drops, Balto, Aqua, Applied Mouth, Open Pontil, 4 1/4 In. 440.00
Robinson's Diarrhoea, Ice Blue, Rectangular, 6 In. 91.00
Rogers & Diamond Druggists, Apothecaries, Cor. Clark & Jackson Std., Chicago, 3 1/2 In.   10.00
Royal Alco Cavity Embalming Fluid, Hour Glass Shape, Portland Chemical 59.00
Rumford Chemical Works, Dyspepsia, Teal Green, 8-Sided, Contents, Label, 5 3/4 In. ...   44.00
Rushton & Aspinwall, No. 86 Williams, Green, Open Pontil, 1835-40, 6 1/2 In. 4180.00
Ruston Clark, New York, Chemists, Aqua, Open Pontil, 10 In. 175.00
S & Co., Blood Purifier, Medium Blue, Applied Lip, 8 1/2 In. 1430.00
S&K Italian Cream London, Blue, Tooled Top, 6 In. 44.00
S.B. Goff's Cough Syrup, Camden, N.J., Aqua, Label, Contents, Box, c.1906, 5 3/4 In. ...   29.00
S.M. Kier Petroleum, Pittsburgh, Pa., Blue, Sloping Collar Mouth, OP, 6 3/8 In. 2576.00

S.M. Kier Petroleum, Pittsburgh, Pa., Deep Blue Aqua, Open Pontil, c.1850, 6 3/4 In. 168.00
S.S. Drug Store, Pettit & Welch, Carrolton, Mo., 5 1/2 In. 25.00
S.S. Ryckman, Hamilton, Ont., Amber, Tooled Mouth, Labels, Canada, 10 1/8 In. 78.00
Salida City Drug Co., Salida, Colo., Clear, 6 13/16 In. 295.00
Salvation Trade Oil Mark, A.C. Meyer, Aqua, Label, Contents, Baltimore, 6 1/2 In. 39.00
Samaritan Nervine, Nerve Conquerer, S.A. Richmond M.D., Embossed, Box, 8 1/4 In. . .   770.00
Sanderson's Blood Renovator, Milton, Vt., Aquamarine, Oval, 1840-60, 8 In. 1344.00
Sanford's Extract Of Hamamelis, Witch Hazel, Cobalt Blue, Applied Mouth, 9 1/4 In. . . .   190.00
Scarpa's Oil For Deafness, Aqua, 6-Sided, Flared Out Lip, Open Pontil, 2 1/2 In. 300.00
Schenck's Syrup, Aqua, 8-Sided, Label, Contents, Cork, Sealed, 5 1/4 In. 61.00
Scholtz & Hanu's Pharmacists, Denver, Colo., Purple, 4 7/8 In. 55.00
Scott & Stewart, Syrup, New York, Blue Green, 1845-60, 9 1/2 x 3 1/2 In. 3360.00
Scott's Emulsion Cod Liver Oil With Lime & Soda, Embossed, c.1925, 7 1/2 In. 18.00
Scovill's Blood & Liver Syrup, Cincinnati, Oh., Blue Aqua, 10 In. 11.00
SEN-KO-NA Chemical Co., Columbus, Amber, Rectangular, 8 In.   39.00
Shaker Cherry Pectoral Syrup, Canterbury, N.H., Aqua, Applied Lip, OP, 5 3/8 In. 100.00
Shaker Fluid Extract Valerian, Blue Aqua, Flared Lip, Open Pontil, 3 7/8 In. 78.00
Siphon Kumysgen, Cobalt Blue, Blob Style Collar, Label, c.1890, 9 In. . . . .*Illus*   176.00
Smelling Salts, Bulbous Neck, Cobalt Blue, 1820-40, 2 5/8 In. 1232.00
Smelling Salts, Stopper, Contents, Sterling Silver Top, c.1908, 3 1/2 In. 75.00
Smith's Green Mountain Renovator, East Georgia, Vt., Yellow Amber, 7 In. 2240.00
Sniteman's X-Ray Liniment, Great Horse & Cattle Remedy, Contents, Box, 12 In. .132.00 to 330.00
Sodium Phosphate, Cork, Aluminum Screw Top, United Drug Co., 4 Oz. 30.00
Soule's Eradicator, Contents, Labels, Box, 5 In. 231.00
Spanish Luster Prepared By J.C. Wadleigh, Open Pontil, 6 In. 40.00
Sparks Perfect Health For Kidney & Liver Diseases, Man, Medium Amber, 9 1/4 In. 308.00
Sparks Perfect Health For Kidney & Liver Diseases, Yellow Amber, c.1880, 9 1/4 In. . . .   616.00
Specie, P. Carbo. Lig, Jar, Gold Label Under Glass, Tin Lid, 11 3/4 x 5 1/2 In. 385.00
St. Andrew's Wine Of Life Root, Amber, Tooled Lip, 1890-1900, 9 In. 168.00
St. Antonius Liniment, Aqua, Contents, Labels, 1875, 6 In. 132.00
Standard Colic Remedy, Horse Head, Standard Stock Food Co., Omaha, Neb., 7 3/4 In. . .   252.00
Star Drug Store, West Liberty, Iowa, 3 1/2 In. 10.00
Strong Cobb & Co., Druggists, Cleveland, O., Golden Yellow Amber, 12 1/4 In. 224.00
Swaim's Panacea, Light Green, 8 In. 275.00
Swaim's Panacea, Philada, Apple Green, Sloping Collar, Pontil, 1840-60, 8 1/8 In. 650.00
Swaim's Panacea, Philada, Aquamarine, Sloping Collar, Pontil, 7 3/4 In. 476.00
Swaim's Panacea, Philada, Blue Green, Applied Sloping Double Collar, 7 3/4 In. 110.00
Swaim's Panacea, Philada, Olive Green, Applied Mouth, Pontil, 1840-60, 7 5/8 In. 600.00
Swaim's Panacea, Philada, Olive Green, Applied Sloping Double Collar, 7 3/4 In. 275.00
Swaim's Panacea, Philada, Olive Green, Applied Sloping Double Collar, 8 In. 300.00
Swaim's Panacea, Philada, Olive Green, Applied Sloping Double Collar, Pontil, 7 3/4 In. . .   550.00
Swaim's Panacea, Philada, Olive Green, Applied Sloping Double Collar, Pontil, 8 In. 300.00
Swaim's Panacea, Philada, Olive Green, Double Collar, Pontil, 8 In. 364.00
Swaim's Panacea, Philada, Olive Green, Pontil, Applied Sloping Collar, 8 In. . . . .728.00 to 1064.00
Swaim's Panacea, Philada, Olive Yellow, Applied Sloping Collar, 9 Panels, 7 5/8 In. 202.00
Swaim's Panacea, Philada, Olive Yellow, Sloping Double Collar, Pontil, 8 In. 560.00
Swaim's Panacea, Philadelphia, Aqua, Sloping Collar, Open Pontil, 1840-60, 7 3/4 In. . . .   952.00

Medicine, Siphon
Kumysgen, Cobalt Blue,
Blob Style Collar, Label,
c.1890, 9 In.

Medicine, Sweet
Spirits, N. Wood &
Son, Portland, Me.,
Flared Lip, OP,
Label, 5 In.

Swaim's Panacea, Philadelphia, Yellow, Green, Pontil, Swirls, Bubbles, 8 In. 385.00
Swaim's Panacea, St. Louis, Mo., Aqua, Indented Panels, Round, Labels, 1820, 8 In. 154.00
Sweet Spirits, N. Wood & Son, Portland, Me., Flared Lip, OP, Label, 5 In. ....*Illus* 300.00
Swift's Syphilitic Specific, Cobalt Blue, Applied Lip, 1870-80, 9 In. ....1344.00 to 1456.00
T. H. Taylor, Aqua, Rectangular, Applied Top, Pontil, Brattleboro, Vt., 8 1/2 In. 358.00
T.&M., Aqua, Open Pontil, 2 5/8 In. 25.00
T.W. Carlin, Pharmacist, Salina, Kan., 5 1/2 In. 20.00
Tamm & Archlous, Leadville, Colo., Clear, 3 5/8 In. 50.00
Tangin, Amber, Labels, Gin Shape, 8 1/2 In. 66.00
Tasmanian Eucalyptus Oil Compy., Hobart, Platypus Brand, BIMAL, Embossed, 5 3/8 In. 50.00
Teissier Prevost A Paris, Embossed Bell, Teal Blue, Beveled Corners, 7 5/8 In. 336.00
Theodore Netter, Cobalt Blue, Barrel, Tooled Mouth, 1890-1910, 6 In. 308.00
Thorn's Compound Syrup Of Cod Liver Oil, Deep Aqua, 8-Sided, Open Pontil, 7 3/8 In. . 550.00
Tinct. Opii Comp, Violet Blue, Label, Stopper, 6 In. 88.00
Triena Laxative Syrup, Allied Drug Products, Chattanooga, Tennessee, Box, 4 1/2 In. ... 6.00
True Daffy's Elixir, Aqua, Dicey & Co., Church Yard, London, 4 3/4 In. 666.00
Trunk Bros. Drug Co., Denver, Colo., Embossed Trunk, Amethyst, 8 1/4 In. 250.00
Truth Brand, White Pine Cough Syrup, Clear, Label, Contents, Box, 7 In. 50.00
Twitchell Champlin & Co., Neuralgic Anodyne, Aqua, Labels, 6 In. 39.00
U.S.A. Hosp. Dept., Amber Olive, Applied Double Collar Mouth, Bubbles, 9 1/2 In. 660.00
U.S.A. Hosp. Dept., Amber, Applied Lip, 9 1/4 In. 660.00
U.S.A. Hosp. Dept., Amber, Qt., 9 In. 231.00
U.S.A. Hosp. Dept., Amethyst, Wide Flared Mouth, 4 3/4 In. 392.00
U.S.A. Hosp. Dept., Aqua, Applied Square Collar, 7 3/4 In. 385.00
U.S.A. Hosp. Dept., Aqua, Wide Mouth, Whittle, 7 1/2 In. 413.00
U.S.A. Hosp. Dept., Blue Aqua, Applied Lip, Oval, 6 In. 264.00
U.S.A. Hosp. Dept., Blue Aqua, Wide Mouth, Outward Rolled Lip, 8 In. 200.00
U.S.A. Hosp. Dept., Citron, Applied Double Collar, 9 1/8 In. 3630.00
U.S.A. Hosp. Dept., Citron, Qt., 9 In. 880.00
U.S.A. Hosp. Dept., Clear, Applied Lip, 5 3/4 In. 99.00
U.S.A. Hosp. Dept., Clear, Tooled Flared Lip, Cylindrical, 3 In. 179.00
U.S.A. Hosp. Dept., Cobalt Blue, Applied Lip, 9 1/8 In. 220.00
U.S.A. Hosp. Dept., Cobalt Blue, Applied Lip, Whittle, Round, 6 1/2 In. 1760.00
U.S.A. Hosp. Dept., Cobalt Blue, Applied Square Collar, 6 1/2 In. 1650.00
U.S.A. Hosp. Dept., Cobalt Blue, Applied Square Collar, 9 1/2 In. 4180.00
U.S.A. Hosp. Dept., Cobalt Blue, Applied Square Collar, Qt., 9 In. 3630.00
U.S.A. Hosp. Dept., Cobalt Blue, Flared Lip, Embossed, 2 1/2 In. 413.00
U.S.A. Hosp. Dept., Cobalt Blue, Tooled Lip, Oval, 1865-75, 3 1/4 In. 308.00
U.S.A. Hosp. Dept., Cobalt Blue, Tooled Lip, Oval, 4 7/8 In. 253.00
U.S.A. Hosp. Dept., Copper, Copper Puce Striations, Qt., 9 1/4 In. 2128.00
U.S.A. Hosp. Dept., Emerald Green, Applied Drippy Top, 9 1/2 In. 1980.00
U.S.A. Hosp. Dept., Emerald Green, Round, Double Collar, 6 In. 560.00
U.S.A. Hosp. Dept., Golden Amber, Puce Swirls, Double Collar, 1862-70, 9 3/8 In. 840.00
U.S.A. Hosp. Dept., Golden Yellow, Double Collar, Qt., 9 1/4 In. 952.00
U.S.A. Hosp. Dept., Green Aqua, Square Applied Collar, Applied Lip, Qt. 523.00
U.S.A. Hosp. Dept., Green, Applied Drippy Top, Star On Base, 9 1/2 In. 1045.00
U.S.A. Hosp. Dept., Ice Blue, Applied Square Collar, 6 5/8 In. 235.00
U.S.A. Hosp. Dept., Inside Oval, Cobalt Blue, Applied Square Collar, Oval, 5 3/4 In. 336.00
U.S.A. Hosp. Dept., Inside Oval, Cobalt Blue, Tooled Wide Mouth, Oval, 6 3/4 In. 392.00
U.S.A. Hosp. Dept., Light Lime Green, Flared Tooled Lip, Stopper, 5 In. 1100.00
U.S.A. Hosp. Dept., Light Orange Yellow, Applied Lip, 9 1/4 In., Qt. 1430.00
U.S.A. Hosp. Dept., Lime Green, Deep Kick-Up, 9 1/4 In. 2128.00
U.S.A. Hosp. Dept., Medium Cobalt Blue, 2 In. Circle, Applied Collar, 6 1/4 In. 1870.00
U.S.A. Hosp. Dept., Medium Cobalt Blue, Applied Lip, 7 1/4 In. 1760.00
U.S.A. Hosp. Dept., Medium Emerald Green, Bubbles, Double Collar, Qt., 9 3/8 In. 3630.00
U.S.A. Hosp. Dept., Medium To Deep Puce, Qt., 9 In. 715.00
U.S.A. Hosp. Dept., Mossy Green, 2 1/4 In. Circle, Clear Stopper, 6 In. 1540.00
U.S.A. Hosp. Dept., Olive Amber, Double Collar, Qt., 9 In. 990.00
U.S.A. Hosp. Dept., Olive Green, Amber, Double Collar, Qt., 9 3/8 In. 1008.00
U.S.A. Hosp. Dept., Olive Yellow Green, Applied Double Collar, 1860-70, 9 3/8 In. 840.00
U.S.A. Hosp. Dept., Olive Yellow, Double Collar Mouth, Cylindrical, 9 1/8 In. ....672.00 to 840.00
U.S.A. Hosp. Dept., Red Amber Shaded To Yellow Amber, Double Collar, 9 3/8 In. 1680.00
U.S.A. Hosp. Dept., Yellow, Amber, Double Collar, 1862-70, 9 3/8 In. 1344.00

University, N.Y. Medical, Cobalt Blue, Embossed Lines, Applied Lip, Box, $2, 7 1/4 In. . . 242.00
University Free Medicine, Philadelphia, Aqua, 6-Sided, Open Pontil, 5 7/8 In. 308.00
Urquhart's Cholera Cordial, Aqua, 1860-70, 5 1/2 In. 22.00
Usage Externe, Golden Amber, 6-Sided, Tooled Mouth, Germany, 1890-1930, 9 In. 112.00
Vanderhoof's Sexual Disease/Nerve Pills, ABM, Contents, Box, 3 1/2 In. 22.00
Vaughn's Vegetable Lithontriptic Mixture, Aqua, Applied Lip, Qt. 440.00
Vaughn's Vegetable Lithontriptic Mixture, Blue Green, Sloping Collar, Panels, 6 In. 616.00
Vaughn's Vegetable Lithontriptic Mixture, Buffalo, Aqua, 8 1/4 In. 220.00
Vaughn's Vegetable Lithontriptic Mixture, Buffalo, Blue Green, 1845-60, 7 7/8 In. 2464.00
Vaughn's Vegetable Lithontriptic Mixture, Buffalo, Blue Green, Square, 8 In. 7280.00
Vaughn's Vegetable Lithontriptic Mixture, Buffalo, Blue, Sloping Collar, 8 1/4 In. 336.00
Vaughn's Vegetable Lithontriptic Mixture, Buffalo, Ice Blue, 1855-70, 8 1/8 In. 448.00
Vaughn's Vegetable Lithontriptic Mixture, Teal, Whittles, Bubbles, 8 In. 4125.00
Vetters Dyspepsia Remedy, Contents, Labels, Pamphlet, Tax Stamp, Box, 6 1/2 In. 176.00
W. Brinker & Son Co., Druggist, New York & Brooklyn, Blob, 8 In. 8.00
W. W. Whipple, Portland, Me., Aqua, Applied Top, Open Pontil, 7 3/4 In. 77.00
W.E. Hagan & Co., Light Blue, 8-Sided, Applied Top, 6 3/4 In. 385.00
W.H. Comstock, Morse Indian Root Pills, Dose 2 To 4, Red Gold, Rectangular, 2 1/2 In. . . 25.00
W.S. Merrell & Co., Cincinnati, Sapphire Blue, 1875-85, 8 5/8 In. 100.00
Wake Up, Wake Up, Olive Green, 3-Sided, Applied Sloping Collar, Iron Pontil, 11 7/8 In. 2800.00
Warner's Acute Rheumatic Compound, Amber, Label, Sealed, Corked Top, 9 In. 385.00
Warner's Safe, Kidney, Liver & Brights Disease, Amber, 9 1/2 In. 165.00
Warner's Safe, Kidney, Liver & Brights Disease, Honey Amber, Embossed, Label, 9 In. . . . 176.00
Warner's Safe, Rheumatic Remedy, Sciatica, Lumbago, Gout, 12 1/2 Fl. Oz., 9 In. 132.00
Warner's Safe Compound, Diuretic Stimulant, Amber, Bakelite Top, 2 7/8 In. 165.00
Warner's Safe Compound, Diuretic, Amber, Contents, 9 In. 143.00
Warner's Safe Compound, Golden Amber, Embossed, 5 1/2 In. 117.00
Warner's Safe Diabetes Remedy, Amber, Label, Contents, Flyers, Box, 16 Oz., 9 1/2 In. . . 468.00
Warner's Safe Kidney & Liver Remedy, Amber, Label, Contents, Flyers, Box, 9 1/2 In. . . . 385.00
Warner's Safe Kidney & Liver Remedy, Medium Olive Green, Contents, Box, 9 1/2 In. . . . 2420.00
Warner's Safe Kidney & Liver Remedy, Rochester, N.Y., Amber, Blob Top, 9 1/2 In. 45.00
Warner's Safe Kidney & Liver Remedy, Rochester, N.Y., Orange Amber, 9 3/4 In. 40.00
Warner's Safe Kidney & Liver Remedy, Rochester, N.Y., Tooled Top, 16 Fl. Oz. 143.00
Warner's Safe Medicines, Melbourne, Pt. 90.00
Warner's Safe Nervine, Clear, Contents, 7 In. 385.00
Warner's Safe Nervine, Embossed Safe, Rochester, N.Y., Amber, 7 In. 50.00
Warner's Safe Nervine, Embossed, Amber, London, 7 1/4 In. 33.00
Warner's Safe Nervine, Embossed, Amber, London, 9 1/2 In. 69.00
Warner's Safe Nervine, Embossed, Olive Green, 7 1/4 In. 42.00
Warner's Safe Nervine, Embossed, Red Amber, London, 7 1/4 In. 59.00
Warner's Safe Nervine, Frankfurt, Emerald Green, 1/2 Pt. 2000.00
Warner's Safe Nervine, London, Amber, 1/2 Pt. 10.00
Warner's Safe Nervine, London, Green, 1/2 Pt. 450.00
Warner's Safe Nervine, London, Yellow, Pt. 100.00
Warner's Safe Nervine, Non-Alcoholic, Embossed, Label, Contents, 6 Fl. Oz., 7 1/8 In. . . 187.00
Warner's Safe Nervine, Orange Amber, Applied Blob Top, Pt., 9 5/8 In. 115.00
Warner's Safe Nervine, Rochester, N.Y., Amber, Applied Mouth, 7 1/2 In. 155.00
Warner's Safe Remedies, Compound A Diuretic, Rochester, Paper Label, 1890-1900, 7 In. 134.00
Warner's Safe Remedies, Diuretic, Amber, ABM, Label, Contents, 6 Oz., 7 In. 88.00
Warner's Safe Remedies, Rheumatic Compound, Amber, ABM, Label, 12 1/2 Oz., 9 In. . . 176.00
Warner's Safe Remedies Co., Compound, Diuretic, Amber, Contents, Label, 7 In. 242.00
Warner's Safe Remedies Co., Embossed Safe, Clear, 12 1/2 Oz. 50.00
Warner's Safe Remedies Co., Rochester, Amber, 12 1/2 Oz. 20.00
Warner's Safe Remedies Co., Rochester, N.Y., Amber, ABM, Label, 9 1/8 In., 12 1/2 Oz. . . 180.00
Watkins Cough Syrup, For Coughs From Colds, 6 1/4 In. 10.00
Watkins Trial, Hindu Pain Oil, Paper Label, Aqua, 8 1/2 In. 22.00
Week's Magic Compound St. Johns Bury, Vt., Aquamarine, 1840-60, 7 1/2 In. 1568.00
Wheeler's Nerve Vitalixer, ABM, Label, Pamphlet, Box, 7 1/2 In. 88.00
White & Hill, Dr. Warren's Expectorant, Nashua, N.H., Aqua, Double Collar, OP, 6 3/8 In. 215.00
Wildroot, Amber, Molded Neck, Wildroot Company Inc., Buffalo, N.Y., c.1920 . . . . 13.00
Witch Hazel, 14 Percent Alcohol, Front Label, Lander Of New York, 5 1/2 In. 15.00
Wm. Craemer Med Co., St. Louis, Kidney Stones, Amber, Labels, 7 3/4 In. 688.00
Wm. R. Warner & Co. Pharmaceutical Chemists, Philada., Clear, 7 In. 12.00

Wm. Radam's Microbe Killer, 111 Oxford St., Man Beating Skeleton, Jug, 1889, 11 In. 99.00
Wm. Radam's Microbe Killer, Cream, Jug, Pottery, Dark Brown Glaze, 10 7/8 In. 200.00
Wm. Radam's Microbe Killer, Cures All Disease, Label, Man Beating Skeleton, 10 1/4 In. .   259.00
Wm. Radam's Microbe Killer, Germ Bacteria, Amber, Man Beating Skeleton, 10 3/4 In. . . .   614.00
Wm. Radam's Microbe Killer, No. 2, Cream, Black Transfer, Stoneware, Handle, Gal., 11 In.   90.00
Woodward Chemist Nottingham, Blue, Oval, 6 In. 15.00
Worner's Rattler Oil, $2.50, F.M. Worner, Label, Box, 4 3/4 In. 154.00
Wright's Indian Cough Balsam, BIMAL, Embossed, 5 In. 60.00
Wyeth & Bros., Hypophosphites & Cod Liver Oil, Cornflower Blue, Collar, 8 1/2 In. 179.00
Yellow Amber, Flared Lip, Pontil, 1835-45, 6 In. 78.00

---------------------------- **MICHTER'S** ----------------------------

Michter's claims to be America's oldest distillery, established in Schaefferstown, Pennsylvania, in 1753, before it was even the state of Pennsylvania. The building was named a national historic landmark in 1980. Special ceramic jugs were first made in 1955 and figural decanters were made beginning in 1977. One of the most famous series was King Tut (1978-1980). About 3,000 were made of the large size. Miniature bottles were also made. Production ended in 1989.

Barn, Daniel Boone, 1977 . . . .   4.00
Fireman, Volunteer Statue, 1979 . . . .   8.50
Football On Tee, Pennsylvania, 1979 . . . .   3.00
Goddess Selket, 1980 . . . . .10.00 to 22.00
Ice Wagon, 1979 . . . .   15.00
Indian Kneeling 50.00
Jug, 1976, 1/2 Pt. 15.50
Jug, Pot Still, Box, 1978, 6 In. 15.50
Jug, Pot Still, c.1953, 4/5 Qt. 7.00
Jug, Sour Mash, 1/2 Gal., 7 3/4 In. 21.00
Jug, Sour Mash, 2 1/2 In. 11.00
Jug, Sour Mash, Series C, 1978 . . . .   3.00
King Tut, 1978 . . . . .4.00 to 8.00
King Tut, Miniature . . . . .8.50 to 10.00
Lamp, c.1980 . . . .   129.00
Liberty Bell, 1969 . . . .   7.90
Queen Nefertiti, 1979 . . . . .10.00 to 20.00

---------------------------- **MIKE WAYNE** ----------------------------

Mike Wayne Distilled Products Company was founded in Bardstown, Kentucky, in 1978. The company was formed to sell original ceramic decanters. A John Wayne bust, a portrait, and two full-figure bottles are among the many decanters made until about 1982.

Eagle, Gold, 1981, 9 1/2 In. 8.00
Iowa, Ear Of Corn, 1981, 10 1/2 In. 21.00
John Wayne, Bust, 1980 . . . . .21.00 to 31.00
John Wayne, Bust, Box, 1980 . . . .   100.00
John Wayne, Portrait, 1979 . . . . .5.00 to 10.00
John Wayne, Statue, Black, 1981 . . . .   53.00
John Wayne, Statue, Gold, 1982 . . . . .54.00 to 78.00
Norman Rockwell, Plumber, 1978 . . . .   15.00
Norman Rockwell, Self-Portrait, 1978 . . . .   15.00

---------------------------- **MILK** ----------------------------

The first milk bottle we have heard about was an earthenware jar pictured on a Babylonian temple stone panel. Evidently, milk was being dipped from the jar while cream was being churned into butter.

Milk came straight from the cow on early farms; but when cities started to grow in America, a new delivery system was needed. The farmer put the milk into large containers. These were taken to the city in horse-drawn carts and delivered to the consumer. The milkman took a slightly dirty dipper and put it into the milk, ladling a quantity into the customer's pitcher.

Flies, dirt, horse hairs, and heat obviously changed the quality of the milk. By the 1860s iceboxes were developed. One type of milk can claimed to keep milk from becoming sour in a thunderstorm. In 1895, pasteurization was invented and another source of disease from milk was stopped. The first milk bottle patent was issued in the 1880s to the Warren Glass Works Company. The most famous milk bottle was designed in 1884 by Dr. Harvey D. Thatcher, a physician and druggist from Potsdam, New York. His glass bottle had a *Lightning* closure and a picture on the side of a cow being milked. In 1889 The Thatcher Company brought out the bottle with a cap that is still used.

The characteristic shape and printed or embossed wording identify milk bottles for collectors. The round bottle was the most popular until 1936 when the squat round bottle was invented. In 1940 a square squat bottle became the preferred shape. The paper carton was introduced in 1932. Plastic has been used since 1964. A slug plate was used in the manufacture of a special type of round milk bottle. The manufacturer would change the name embossed on the bottle by changing a metal plate in the glass mold. The letters *ISP* seen in some publications mean *inserted slug plate*. In the following list of bottle prices, the words *slug plate* are used. Amber-colored glass was used for a short time. Makers claimed it resisted spoiling. A green bottle was patented in 1929. Pyro is the shortened form of the word *pyroglaze,* an enameled lettering used on milk bottles after the mid-1930s. Before that, the name had been embossed. Bottle collectors now refer to these as *ACL,* Applied Color Label.

Cop top, baby face, toothache, and *cream top* are some of the terms that refer to the shapes of bottle necks popular in the 1930s. Near the top of the bottle there was an indentation so the cream, which separated from the standing milk, could be poured off with little trouble. Today, with homogenized milk, few children realize that the cream on natural milk will rise to the top. The glass bottle was displaced by cartons by the 1960s. The National Association of Milk Bottle Collectors publishes a newsletter, Milk Route (18 Pond Place, Cos Cob, CT 06807).

5 Cent Monterey Bay Milk Distributors Inc., Embossed, Neck Dots, Round, Qt.	25.00
A Bottle Of Milk Is A Bottle Of Health, Embossed, 1/2 Pt.	10.00
A Bottle Of Milk Is A Bottle Of Health, Embossed, Italic Type, Round, Pt.	8.00
A Bottle Of Milk Is A Bottle Of Health, Embossed, Qt.	16.00
A.B. Ball Dairy, Buffalo, N.Y., Red ACL, Square, Qt.	17.00
Abbott's Dairies Inc, Ribbed, Embossed, Qt.	8.00
Abbotts, Cottage Cheese, Italic Type, Embossed, Round, 1/2 Pt.	4.00
Abbotts Alderney Dairies, Embossed, Round, Short, 1/4 Pt.	40.00
Abbotts Alderney Dairies, Embossed, Round, Tall, 1/4 Pt.	40.00
Abbotts Alderney Dairies, Ribbed, Embossed, Round, Pt., 9 In.	25.00
Absolutely Pure, Man Milking Cow, Embossed, Tooled Lip, Metal Clamp, Pt., 6 7/8 In.	364.00
Absolutely Pure, Milk Protector, Man Milking Cow, Cylindrical, c.1885, Pt.	784.00
Adams Milk, Rawlins, Wy., Bucking Bronco, Red ACL, Qt.	75.00
Adams Pasteurized, Rawlins, Wyo., Cowboy Riding Bucking Bronco, Red ACL, Qt.	100.00
Alba Dairy Boulder Colo., Qt.	27.50
Alderney Dairy Co., Newark, N.J., Embossed, Qt.	8.00
Alderney Dairy Co., Newark, N.J., Embossed, Round, Pt.	6.00
Alexandria Dairy, Bead Grip, Embossed, Qt.	9.00
Alice R Dairy, Franklin, La., ACL, Round, Pt.	125.00
All Star Dairies, Nashua, N.H., Red ACL, Square, Qt.	19.00
Allendale Dairy, Deposit, Red ACL, 1950, Qt.	5.00
Alpha Dairy, Princeton, N.J., Embossed, Round, 1/2 Pt.	12.00
Alta Crest, Cow's Head, Green, Embossed, Round, Qt.	590.00
Alta Crest Farms, Spencer, Mass., Cow's Head, Yellow Green, Cardboard Closure, Qt.	728.00
Alta Crest Farms, Spencer, Mass., Green, Embossed Steer's Head, Cardboard Cap, Qt.	1093.00
Amber, Embossed, Ground Mouth, Zinc Lid, Square, 90 Oz.	42.00
Amityville Dairy Inc., Beads Around Neck, N.Y., Embossed, Round, Qt.	15.00
Anderson Erickson Dairy Co., Des Moines, Iowa, Orange ACL, Square, 1/2 Pt.	8.00 to 15.00
Annie Oakley, Gail Harris Rearing On Horse, Pt.	22.00
Anthony's Dairy, Nashville, Tenn., Round, Embossed, Qt.	15.00
Aristocrat Dairy, Atlanta, Ga., Embossed, Round, Pt.	20.00
Arrowhead Shoemaker Dairies, Cow's Head, N.H., Embossed, Round, Qt.	20.00
Artic Quality, Belt, Embossed, Round, Pt.	5.00
Artz Dairy Inc., Black ACL, Square, 1/2 Pt.	9.00
Ashmeade Farms, Warren, Ohio, Green ACL, Round, Qt.	43.00
Associated Dairies, Los Angeles, Orange Letters, Babyface, Pink, Round, Gallo, 1/2 Pt.	416.00
Athletes Drink Milk, Football Player, Cream Top, Red ACL, Square, Qt.	30.00

Atlanta's Freshest Milk, Atlanta Dairies, Orange ACL, Square, Qt. 27.00
Augusta Dairies, Staunton, Va., 3 Children Playing In Yard, ACL, Qt. 25.00
Aurora Meadows Dairy, Black ACL, Square, Qt. 12.00
Avondale Farms Dairy Farms Inc., Embossed, Round, Qt. 12.00
Ayershire Milk, Glencrest Farm, Concord, N.H., PH Sanborn, Qt. 20.00
Baisch, Hornell, Ribbed, Embossed, Round, Qt. 10.00
Baker & Son Dairy Atlanta, Michigan, Orange ACL, Round, Lid, Qt. 13.50
Baldwin Dairies, Embossed, Round, Tall, Qt. 8.00
Baldwin Registered Dairies, Embossed, Round, Qt. 9.00
Barbados Dairy, Evaporated Milk From Pine Hill, Orange ACL, Round, 500 Milliliters .. 18.00
Bartholomay Co Inc Rochester NY, Raised Print, Cream Top, Pat March 3, 1925, Qt. ... 55.00
Batavia Dairy Co., Milk Builds Great Champions, Ball Players, Black, Orange ACL, Qt. . 40.00
Batchelors, Canon City, Colorado, Children, Eating Ice Cream, Yellow & Red ACL, Pt. .. 250.00
Baxter's Dairy, Watkins Glen, N.Y., Maroon ACL, Square, Qt. 20.00
BCMP Co., Burlington, Vt., Red ACL, Pt. 5.00
Bechtel's, 3-Color ACL, Green, Black, Orange, Square, Qt. 20.00
Beck's Dairy, Marshallfield, Mo., Milky Way, ACL, Round, Qt. 85.00
Beck's Dairy, Marshalltown, Iowa, ACL, Round, Qt. 45.00
Bellevue Dairy Inc., Syracuse, N.Y., Orange ACL, Square, 1/2 Gal. 12.00
Benware Creamery, Farm Scene, N.Y., Orange ACL, Round, Qt 38.00
Big Elm Dairy Co., Amber, ABM Lip, Qt. 78.00
Bill Bros Dairy, Cortland, N.Y., Orange ACL, Round, 1/4 Pt. 40.00
Birdseye Dairy, Green Bay, Wisc., Red ACL, Square, Pt. 9.00
Bisgrove Dairy, Audubon, N.Y., Orange, Black, ACL, Square, Qt. 19.00
Blais Dairy, Lewiston, Babytop, A Child's Vitality, Red ACL, Qt. 250.00
Blue Boy, Sta-Trim, Amber, Blue & Pink ACL, Qt. 19.00
Blue Boy Sparkle Vitamin-Mineral Fortified Milk, Painted Label, Amber, Qt. 28.00
Bonnie Brae Dairy, Eau Clair, Wisc., Orange ACL, 1/2 Pt. 9.00
Boone Dairy, Red ACL, Round, Qt. 30.00
Borden Wieland, Embossed, Round, Qt. 15.00
Borden's, Buy At Cornell Dairy Stores, Red & Yellow ACL, Plastic Lid, Gal., 11 In. 27.00
Borden's, Eagle Type, Ribbed, Embossed, Round, Pt. 8.00
Borden's, Elsie, Red ACL, 1/2 Gal. 18.00
Borden's, Elsie, Red ACL, Square, Gal. 40.00
Borden's, Elsie, Red ACL, Square, Qt. 10.00
Borden's, Phoenix, Ariz., Saguaro Cactus, Red ACL, 1/2 Gal. 60.00
Borden's, Property Of Borden's Farm Products, Quality Service, Qt., 9 3/4 In. 20.00
Borden's, Red ACL, Square, Qt. 15.00
Borden's, Reg. U.S., Qt., 2 1/8 In. 30.00
Borden's, Ribs, Embossed Round, Qt. ....*Illus* 9.00
Borden's, Ribs, Embossed, Round, 1/2 Pt. 6.00
Borden's, Shield, Cow, Embossed, 2 1/8 In. 40.00
Borden's Dacro, Fill To Flange On Top, Round, Embossed, 1/2 Pt. 25.00
Bowman Dairy Company, Chicago, Ill., Embossed, 1/2 Pt. 30.00
Brandt Dairy, Barrington, Ill., Orange ACL, Wide Mouth, 4 1/2 In. 24.00
Brawand's Dairy, Wilcox, Pa., Orange ACL, Square, Qt. 12.00
Breununger's, Embossed, Square, Qt. 5.00

Milk, Borden's,
Ribs, Embossed
Round, Qt.

**Some disciplined collectors have a rule:
Only add a new piece to the collection if
you can get rid of a less desirable old
one. Most of us just keep adding.**

Breyer's Ice Cream Co., Pt. 35.00
Bright Star Dairy Products, Milwaukee, Wisconsin, Brown ACL, Round, 1/2 Pt. 7.50
Brighton Place, Cow's Head, Embossed, Green, Round, Qt. 675.00
Broguiere's Dairy, Ca., Black & Red ACL, Square, Qt. 18.00
Broguiere's Dairy, Salutes 1992 U.S. Olympics Team, Ca., Black & Red ACL, Square ... 25.00
Brook Road Dairy, Mather Dairy, Riverhead, Long Island, N.Y., Red ACL, Square, Qt. .. 18.00
Brook View Dairy, Bourbonnais, Ill., Orange ACL, 1/2 Pt. 6.00
Brookfield, Babyface, Blue, 9 1/4 In. 35.00
Brookfield, Babyface, Embossed, 1/2 Pt. 40.00
Brookfield, Babyface, Qt., 9 1/2 In. 15.00
Brookfield Dairy, Hellertown, Pa., Babyface, Embossed, Pt. 50.00
Brookfield Dairy, Hellertown, Pa., Babyface, Mothers Who Care, 1/2 Pt. 45.00
Brookfield Dairy, Hellertown, Pa., Embossed, Round, 1/2 Pt. 6.00
Brookside Dairy, Cow, Greenfield Center, Ct., Orange ACL, Square, Qt. 17.00
Buffalo Creamery Co., Brooklyn, N.Y., Embossed, Qt. 12.00
Buffalo Hygienic Dairy, Buffalo, N.Y., Embossed, Round, Qt. 19.00
Buffalo Milk Co., Amber, Round, Qt. 88.00
Burroughs Brothers Walnut Grove Farm, Cream Top, Boy, Diaper, Red ACL, Qt. 65.00
Butler Dairy, Willimantic, Conn., Blue ACL, Qt. 35.00
Butler Dairy, Willimantic, Conn., Green ACL, Qt. 35.00
Byrne Dairy, Cap, Anniversary, 60 Years, Maroon & Yellow ACL, Square, Qt. 30.00
C.A. Dorr Dairy, Guard Your Health, Soldiers, Orange ACL, Round, 1/4 Pt. 50.00
C.A. Stewart's Dairy, Bogalusa, La., Orange ACL, Square, Gal. 65.00
C.E. Van Schoick, Point Pleasant, N.J., Embossed, Qt. 9.00
Cacoosing Dairy, Owl, Green, Orange & Black ACL, Square, Qt. 20.00
Cannon's Dairy, Catlow, Nelson, Red ACL, International, 568 Milliliters 25.00
Cantwell Creamery, Clifton, N.Y., Orange ACL, Square, Qt. 18.00
Carnation Milk Company, Red ACL, Square, Gal. 20.00
Carnation Milk Farm, Dairy, Cows, Green & Red ACL, c.1950, Qt. 2000.00
Carver's Milk, 45 Years, Blue & Red ACL, Square, 1964, Qt. 30.00
Casey Dairy, Cortland, New York, Green Spot, Green Circle, 1/2 Pt. 10.50
Casper Hitchner, Salem, N.H., Embossed, Round, Qt. 9.00
Cedar Dairy, Geo. Lodes, 687-689 3rd Ave., Brooklyn, Embossed, Round, Pt. 30.00
Cedar Gate Farm Dairy, F.E. Parks & Son, Mt. Tabor, N.J., Embossed, Round, Qt. 19.00
Cedar Tree Farms, Embossed, Round, Qt. 9.00
Cedarvale Farms, H. Smith, N.Y., Embossed, Round, 1/2 Pt. 6.00
Central Cairy Co., Rockford, Ill., Embossed, Square, Qt. 16.00
Cerstungs Dairy, Lackawanna, Embossed, Round, Qt. 7.00
CFS Dairy, Heuvelton, N.Y., Quality Sealed In Every Bottle, Black ACL, Qt. 65.00
Charmany Farms Milk, Madison, Wisconsin, Round, Embossed, Red ACL, 1/2 Pt. 38.00
Cherry Lane Dairy, Westover, Pa., Red ACL, Square, Qt. 17.50
Chestnut Farms Dairy, Washington, D.C., Safe Milk, Ribbed, Embossed, Round, 1/4 Pt. . 38.00
Chestnut Farms Sealtest Chevy Chase Dairy, Square, Cream Top, Qt. 30.00
Chipola Dairy, Marianna, Fla., ACL, Squat, Qt. 25.00
Cico, Columbus, Miss., Embossed, Round, Qt. 15.00
City Dairy, Kento, Maroon ACL, Round, Qt. 36.00
Clarke's Gallup N.M., Indian, Support Home Industry, Round, Painted, Red Letters, 1/2 Pt. 25.00
Cloister Dairies, Ephrata, Pa., 37 Year Anniversary, Red ACL, Square, Qt. 38.00
Clover Dairy Farms Inc., Cottage Cheese, Parsippany, N.J., Orange ACL, Embossed, Qt. . 15.00
Cloverdale, Dickinson, N.D., Orange ACL, Square, Qt. 35.00
Cloverdale Borden's Dairy, N.J., Embossed, Qt. 10.00
Cloverleaf Blue Ribbon Dairy, Stockton, Ca., Cream Top, Round, Red, Store Bottle, Qt. .. 25.00
Cloverleaf Blue Ribbon Farm, Stockton, Ca., Cream Top, Grocer's Face, Red ACL, Qt. .. 55.00
Cloverleaf Dairy, Springfield, Missouri, Red & Green ACL, Square, Qt. 25.00
Cloverleaf Farm, Seminary, N.Y., Round Embossed, 1/2 Pt. 27.00
Coleman Dairy, Grade A Dairy Products, Belvidere & Merengo, Ill., Pt. 19.00
Coles Diamond Dairy, Port Jervis N.Y., ACL, Cream Top, 9 1/2 In. 15.00
College Creamery, University Of S.D., Orange Blue & Brown ACL, Round, Qt. 1150.00
Colorado State Dairy, Aggie Dairy, Football Players, Orange & Green ACL, Round, Qt. . 200.00
Columbia, Qt., 8 3/4 In. 15.00
Conewago Dairy, Orange & Yellow ACL, Qt. 12.00
Connelly's Milk, 50 Year Anniversary, Gold & Red ACL, Square, Qt. 38.00
Conover's Highstown Guernsey Dairy, N.J., Embossed, Round, Qt. 9.00

Conover's Sanitary Dairy, Ribs, Embossed, Round, 1/2 Pt. 11.00
Copper Country Dairy, Dollar Bay, Michigan, Red ACL, Square, Qt. 10.00
Copper Country Pasteurized, Dollar Bay, Mich., ACL, Round, 1/2 Pt. 35.00
Country Store Countertop, Aqua, ABM Lip, Glass Lid, Wire Handle, 17 1/2 x 12 In. 560.00
Cramling Diary, Cramling, S.C., Embossed, Round, 1/2 Pt. 6.00
Crane Dairy Co., Orange ACL, Square, Qt. 25.00
Crauston, Boston Registered, Embossed, Round, Pt. 6.00
Cream Valley Dairy, Orange ACL, 1875-1966 Anniversary, Qt. 25.00
Creamer, Absolutely Pure Milk & Milk Protector, Cylindrical, Lid, Brass Bail 700.00
Creamer, Billings Dairy, Green ACL, Square 45.00
Creamer, Borden, Red ACL 18.00
Creamer, Crowley's Dairy, Maroon ACL, Square 45.00
Creamer, Freedman's Dairy, Best By Test, Red ACL, Square, 1/2 Oz. 45.00
Creamer, Meadow Gold, Red ACL 30.00
Creamer, Mowrer's, Orange ACL 30.00
Creamer, Raritan Valley Farms, Somerville, N.J., Red ACL, Square 15.00
Creamlike Dairy, Pryor, Oklahoma, Green & Red ACL, Boy, Drinking Milk, Pt. 10.00
Crocker Farms, Orange & Yellow ACL, Square, Qt. 25.00
Curly's Dairy, Amber, White ACL, 1/2 Gal. 17.00
Dairimaid, Creamer, 1/2 Pt. 15.00
Dairy Gold, Cheyenne, Wy., Black ACL, Square, 1/2 Pt. 25.00
Dairylea, Dairymen's League Cooperative Assoc., Round, Embossed, Qt. 15.00
Dairylea, Dairymen's League, Embossed, Round, Pt. 7.00
Dairylea, Hand Holding Glass, Red ACL, Qt. 19.00
Dairylea, Miss Dairylea, Glass Of Milk, Family, Amber, White & Yellow ACL, Qt. 21.00
Dairylea, Miss Dairylea, Glass Of Milk, Family, Red ACL, Qt. 18.00
Dairylea, Red ACL, Square, Qt. 12.00
Dairymen's Association Ltd., Honolulu, Try Gold Guernsey, ACL, Squat, Qt. 125.00
Damascus, Portland, Ore., You'll Like Our Old Fashioned, Red ACL, Handle, 10 3/4 In. .. 115.00
Danzeisen, Listen Pal, Farmer, Cow, Barn, Orange ACL, Qt. 25.00
Dean's, Cleveland Hts., Ohio, Orange ACL, Square, Squat, 1/2 Pt. 5.00
Decker's Farm Dairy, Plastic Handle, Pa., Red ACL, Square, 1/2 Gal. 25.00
Deer Foot Farm, Bowling Pin Shape, Embossed, Round, Qt. 45.00
DeLaval, Embossed, Round, Pt. 20.00
Dennery Ideal Dairy Service, Embossed, Round, Pt. 6.00
Dimick's Dairy, Glenburn, Ca., Donald Duck, Orange ACL, Round, Qt. 160.00
Dolfinger, Philadelphia, Embossed, Round, Pt. 8.00
Driftwood Dairy, El Monte, Orange ACL, Square, Qt. 15.00
Drink Hoffman's Milk, ACL, Pt. 18.00
Drink Pearce Milk, State College, Pa., Orange ACL, Policeman, Child, Round, 1940s, Pt. 61.00
Drink Pearce Milk, State College, Pa., Orange Red ACL, Round, Qt. 54.00
Duncan & Beery, Winfield, Kansas, ACL, Round, Qt. 75.00
Dunsmuir, 8 Cent, Store Bottle, Embossed Slug Plate, 1/2 Pt. 35.00
Dyke's Dairy, Warren, Pa., War Slogan, Red ACL, Qt. 100.00
E.F. Mayer, Hollenbeck St., Amber, ABM Lip, Cardboard Closure, Qt. 78.00
Eagle Nursing Bottle, M.S. Burr & Co., Boston, Tooled Mouth, 5 1/8 In. 56.00
Eagle Valley Farms, Red ACL, Round, 1/2 Pt. 10.00
East Greenwich Dairy Co., Ice Cream Cone, Black & Orange ACL, Round, Qt. 35.00
East Malta Farms, Golden Guernsey Seal, Red ACL, Square, Qt. 20.00
Eaton's Dairy, Balanced Guernsey, Cow, Orange ACL, Round, 1/4 Pt. 45.00
Edgewood, Girl's Head, Ice Cream Cone, 3-Color ACL, Red, Orange, Black, Qt. 19.00
Edgewood, Orange Red & Black ACL, Square, Qt. 25.00
Eisenhart's Purity Milk Co., Buy, Burn & Boost Anthracite, Shamokin, Pa., 9 1/2 In., Qt. 406.00
Elm Point Dairy, St. Charles, Mo., Green ACL, Round, Gal. 35.00
Elm-Co Milk, Blue, Orange, Maroon, Yellow ACL, Square, Qt. 25.00
Elmwood Farms, Hanover, Mass., Farm Scene, Store Bottle, Red ACL, Round, 1/2 Pt. ... 19.00
Emmadine, Key To Success Is Education, Orange ACL, Square, Qt. 15.00
Empire State, Brooklyn, N.Y., 2 People, Sunrise, Embossed, Round, Qt. 13.00
Engel, Embossed, Round, Qt. 8.00
Erikson's, Maynard, Massachusetts, Maroon ACL, Round, 1/2 Pt. 12.50
Estes Park Creamery, Estes Park, Colo., Girl, On Horse, ACL, Squat, Qt. 125.00
Ethan Allen Creamery, Essex Junction, White ACL, Amber, Square, Qt. 25.00
Everett Milk & Ice Cream Co., Everett, Pa., Orange ACL, Pt. 18.00

Excelsior, Chas. F. Rothenhoefer, Frederick, Md., Embossed, Pt. 25.00
Ezell Mackie Dairies, Purity Pasteurized Product, Embossed, 1/2 Pt. 15.00
F A Cobbs Dairy, Best Since 1910, Round, 1914, Pt. 35.00
F.W. Elliott, Twin Dairy Farm, Petersham, Mass., Black & Orange ACL, Round, Qt. 45.00
Fair View Farms Jersey Milk, Waterloo, N.Y., Cow, Blue ACL, Cap, Round, Qt. 35.00
Fairfax Farms Dairy, Embossed, Round, 1/4 Pt. 25.00
Fairfield Western Maryland Dairy, Embossed, Pt. 25.00
Fairfield Western Maryland Dairy, Frederick, Md., Embossed, 1/2 Pt. 25.00
Fairfield's Farms, Williamstown, Mass., Green ACL, Square, Qt. 14.00
Fairlea Farms, Ice Cream, Try It, Red Letters, Square, c.1960, Qt., 9 3/4 In. 18.00
Fanning Bros., West Haven, Ct., Hey Diddle Diddle, Burgundy ACL, Qt. 225.00
Farley's Dairy, Thatcher & Safford, Ariz., Woman Holding Glass Of Milk, Red ACL, Qt. .. 180.00
Farm Dairy, Edwardsville, Pa., Red ACL, Qt. 25.00
Farmer's Creamery Inc., Beloit, Kans., Round, Embossed, 1/2 Pt. 20.00
Farmer's Dairy Products Co. Inc., Cumberland, Md., Embossed, Pt. 16.00
Faughan River Farm, Embossed, Round, 1/2 Pt. 5.00
Fenn's Guernsey Dairy, S.D., Red ACL, Square, Qt. 18.00
Fern's, Coffee Cup, Round, Tapered, Red Letters, Creamer, 3/4 Oz., 1 7/8 In. 40.00
First In Fine Flavor, Blue ACL, Square, Qt. 14.00
Fischl's Dairy, Manitowoc, Wisc., Cream Top, Red ACL, Qt. 24.00
Fisher Dairy, Crystal Falls, Mich., Woman Holding Bottle, Black ACL, Round, 1/2 Pt. ... 25.00
Fisher Dairy, Crystal Falls, Mich., Woman Holding Bottle, Black ACL, Round, Qt. 45.00
Flanders Dairy, Black & Red ACL, Cap, Store, Square, Qt. 22.00
Folker's Dairy, Orange ACL, Square, Qt. 14.00
Force Valley Dairy, Medicine Bottle Shape, Green, Embossed, 4 1/2 In. 15.00
Foremost, Policeman, Children, Contoured, Netting Design, White ACL, c.1940, Pt. 21.00
Fort Bragg Creamery, Pasteurized Milk, Fort Bragg, Cal., Embossed, Round, 1/2 Pt. 40.00
Four Mile Dairy, Canon City, Co., Red ACL, Qt. 55.00
Fraas Dairy, McKeesport, Pa., Embossed, Round, Pt. 25.00
Franzkes, Appleton, Wisc., Green ACL, Round, 1/2 Pt. 7.50
Fred F Field Holstein, Montello, Mass., Cows, Embossed, Round, Qt. 95.00
Fred Harvey, Embossed, Round, 1/2 Pt. 35.00
Freese & Rissler, Health & Wealth, Sedalia, Mo., Red Paint, 1914, Qt., 8 3/4 In. ....18.00 to 23.00
Freeze & Rissler Dairy, Health & Wealth, Our Milk Is Health, Red Paint, Qt. 18.00
Funny Cow, 10 In. 30.00
Gail Borden Eagle Brand, Embossed Eagle, Round, Pt., 9 In. 40.00
Gardenville Farms Dairy, Doylestown, Pa., ACL, Square, 1/2 Pt. 25.00
Gay's Dairy, Pinellas Park, Fla., Red ACL, Qt., 9 1/2 In. 9.00
Gear's Dairy, Menasha, Wisc., Plastic Handle, Orange ACL, Square, Gal. 20.00
Gentle's Dairy, Safe Guards Your Health, Rochester, Soldier, Maroon ACL, Round, Qt. .. 30.00
George's Dairy, Batavia, N.Y., Green ACL, Square, Qt. 3.25
Gitt's Dairy, Stork Carrying Diapered Baby, Listen Pa!, Paper Cap, 9 1/2 In. 40.00
Glen Cliff Dairy, ACL, Round, Qt. 15.00
Glendale Dairy, Lakewood, N.J., Embossed, Round, 1/2 Pt. 5.00
Glendale Woodlawn, Embossed, Qt. 12.00
Glendfield Dairy, Watkins, N.Y., Black ACL, Round, Qt. 45.00
Glenside Dairy, Babyface, Cap, N.J., ACL, Round, Pt. 60.00
Gloucester Milk Co., Embossed, Round, Qt. 8.00
Gold Bloom Registered Pasteurized, Paducah Ky., Chef, Red ACL, Qt. 10.00
Golden Glo, Missoula, Mont., Orange ACL, 1/2 Pt. 15.50
Golden Guernsey, Mounds, Okla., ACL, Squat, Qt. 15.00
Golden State, Red ACL, Round, Qt. 27.00
Goldenrod Pure Cream Products, Tell City, Indiana, Gold ACL, Round, Qt., 9 In. 34.00
Grade HB Pasteurized Dairy Products, Frankfort, Kentucky, Red ACL, Qt. 12.25
Graf's Milk, Baby, Holding Bottle, Verse, Green ACL, Round, Qt. 76.00
Graham Bros. Dairy, Lincoln, Nebraska, 1/2 Pt., 6 3/4 In. 14.00
Grandma Sheeters Dairy, Black ACL, Round, 1/4 Pt. 40.00
Green Spring Dairy, Belmont 4477, Square, Red Painted Label, Qt. 17.00
Green's All Star Dairies, York, Pa., Red & Yellow ACL, Qt. 16.00
Green's Dairy Products, Baby's Best Friend, Ashland Pa., Green & Red ACL, Qt. 45.00
Gridley, Amber, Embossed, Round, Qt. 50.00
Gulf Hill Dairy, Alex Bay, 1000 Islands, N.Y., Orange ACL, Square, Qt. 19.00
H.R. & M.J. Eminson, Higham, Green Stripe ACL, Embossed, Foreign, 568 Milliliters 25.00

H.R. Thompson, Milk & Cream, Winooskie, Vt., Embossed Beads, Round, Qt. 10.00
Haleakala Dairy, Pineapple, Orange & Gray ACL, Square, 1/2 Pt. 43.00
Hancock Co. Creamery, Paraffined Carton In Cone Shape, Qt., 10 In. 28.00
Hansen Dairy, Green Bay, Wisc., Red ACL, Square, Qt. 9.00
Harris Hersey Farms, Salt Lake City, Utah, Cow Head & Ribbon, Red ACL, Qt. 100.00
Harrison's Dairies, Embossed, Qt. 6.00
Hayward Farms, Orange & Maroon ACL, Square, Qt. 20.00
Haywood Farms, Since 1905, Maroon ACL, Square, Qt. 22.00
Heath Dairy Farm, WW II Fighter Plane, America, First, Robinson, Ill., Red, Blue, Qt. .. 312.00
Heisler's Cloverleaf Dairy Inc., Tamaqua, Pa., Baby, Green ACL, Square, 8 Oz. 51.00
Heritage Dairy, Thorofare, N.J., Brown & Orange ACL, Square, 1/2 Pt. 20.00
Heritage Dairy, Thorofare, N.J., Brown & Orange ACL, Square, Qt. 30.00
Hershey Estates Local Farms, Hershey, Pa., Red & Green ACL, Square, Qt. 19.00
Hetzler Dairy, Muscatine, Iowa, Red ACL, Square, Gal. 18.00
Highland Diary, Athol, Mass., Cow, Green ACL, Round, Qt. 35.00
Hillcrest Dairy, Pennington, N.J., Farm, Green ACL, Round, Qt. 35.00
Hillcrest Dairy Farms, Better Milk For Particular People, Orange ACL, Square, Qt. 13.00
Hillside Farm Dairy, Fruit Jar Shape, Aqua, Wide Mouth, Wooden Lid, Gal., 10 In. 2200.00
Hilton Dairy, Madison, Mass., Red ACL, Round, Qt. 50.00
Hirschman's Diary, Florence, N.J., Red ACL, Round, Pt. 38.00
Hoffman's Dairy, Gratz, Pa., Orange ACL, Round, 1/2 Pt. 35.00
Hoffman's Golden Guernsey Milk, Red & Orange ACL, Square, Qt. 20.00
Hoffmans, In Any Season Serve Delicious Hot Or Cold Chocolate Milk, Pt. 19.00
Holly Dairy, Ribbed Top, Mt. Holly, N.J., Embossed, Round, Qt. 10.00
Home Dairy, Jamestown, Pa., Red ACL, Square, 1/2 Gal. 12.00
Home Dairy, Marysville, Calif., Red ACL, Round, Qt. 25.00
Honickers Dairy, St. Clair, Pa., Babyface, Round, Embossed, 1/2 Pt. 180.00
Hoppy's Favorite O'Fallon Milk, O'Fallon Milk Is A Winner, Qt., 9 In. 22.00
Horlick's Malted Milk, Racine, Wis., 11 In. 34.00
Horlick's Malted Milk, Racine, Wis., Embossed, Screw-On Lid, 7 In. 50.00
Horlick's Malted Milk, Racine, Wis., Embossed, Screw-On Tin Lid, 5 In. 39.00
Horn's Dairy, Ringtown Pa., ACL, Qt. 9.00
Howell G.M. & C. Co., Orange Co., Goshen, N.Y., Embossed, Wire Clamp, Qt. 258.00
Hutt Dairies, Embossed, Round, 1/2 Pt. 4.00
Hygienic Dairy, New Brunswick, N.J., Embossed, Round, Pt. 12.00
I.X.L. Creamery Inc., Friedens, Pa., Red & Orange ACL, Square, Qt. 16.00
Ideal Dairy Inc., Established 1927, Amber, White ACL, Square, Qt. 25.00
Ideal Farms, Frederick, Md., Bridge, ACL, Round, Qt. 100.00
Independent Dairies, Kansas City, Mo., Embossed, Cursive, Round, Qt. 16.00
Independent Dairies, Kansas City, Mo., Round, Embossed Around Top Ring, 9 1/2 In. .. 25.00
Indian Hill Dairy, Jobstown, N.J., Orange ACL, Square, Qt. 20.00
Indian Hill Farm Dairy, Greenville, Me, Indian Head, Red ACL, Qt. 55.00
International Milk Co. Inc., Hillside, N.J., ACL, Pt. 25.00
Isaly's Swiss Dairymen, Red ACL, Tall, Round, Qt. 10.00
J. Sterling Dairy, Wrightstown, N.J., Embossed, Round, 1/2 Pt. ....5.00 to 6.00
J. Sterling Davis, Wrightstown, N.J., Embossed, Round, Qt. 12.00
J.F. Deeney, N. 60th Street, 1/2 Pt. 15.00
J.P. Murawski, Southington, Conn., Yellow ACL, Qt. 108.00
J.R. Swing's Dairy, Baby, Red ACL, Qt. 183.00
Jacksonville Producers Dairy, Orange ACL, Round, 1/2 Pt. 5.00
Janeczek's, Green & Orange ACL, Round, Qt. 38.00
Janeczek's Milk, Drums, Cows, Baby, Green & Orange ACL, Square, Qt. 19.00
Jersey Dairy Co., 413 S. Chester St., Embossed, Pt. 12.00
John A. Reehl Dairy, East Greenbush, N.Y., Orange ACL, Round, 1/2 Qt. 30.00
Johnson Farms Dairy, Waterloo, Iowa, Quality You Can Taste, Qt., 9 1/2 In. 28.00
Johnstown Sanitary Dairy, Famous American Firsts, Orange ACL, Round, Qt. 173.00
Johnstown Sanitary Dairy Co., Red ACL, Round, Person Clearing Land, Qt. 325.00
Jones Hill Dairy, Cream Top, Embossed, Qt. 10.00
Kane Dairy, Pa., Orange ACL, Square, Gal. 15.00
Ken Ayr Farms Ayrshire, Brown & Green ACL, Round, Qt. 127.00
Keystone Dairy, Green, Orange & Maroon ACL, Square, Qt. 20.00
Keystone Dairy Co., N.Y. & N.J., Strictly Pure Cream, Embossed, Round, 8 Oz., 1/2 Pt. .. 9.00
Keystone Farms Dairy, Green & Yellow ACL, Square, Qt. 15.00

Kingston Dairy, Red ACL, Square, Qt. 19.00
Kingston Milk Distributors, Canada, Embossed, Qt. 12.00
Krauser's Dairy, New Brunswick, Pa., Embossed XX, Round, 1/2 Pt. 10.00
Kress Farm Dairy, Embossed, Round, 1/4 Pt. 35.00
L.B. Haines, Hurffville, N.J., Embossed, Round, Tall, Qt. ....9.00 to 10.00
Lake County Maid, Woman In Swimsuit, Black ACL, Qt. 65.00
Lake Placid Club Dairy, Arched In Slug Plate, Embossed, Round, 1/2 Pt. 70.00
Lakeville Dairy, Hans Jorgensen, Petaluma, Sleepy Hollow Milk, Brown ACL, Round, Qt. 69.00
Lancaster Creamery, Boy, For Mothers Who Care, Amber, White ACL, Qt. 19.00
Lawrence Dairy Co., Chocolate, Smiling Black Children, Maine Seal, Qt., 9 1/2 In. ..33.00 to 51.00
Lawton Bros. Dairy, Dixon, Ill., For Mothers Who Care, Red Printing, 1/2 Pt. 22.00
Ledge Ever Farms Dairy, Ticonderoga, N.Y., Barn, Yellow ACL, Qt. 70.00
Lester Milk Co., 1537 Broadway, Tin Lid, Embossed, Qt. 22.00
Lewes Dairy, Delaware, ACL, 1/2 Pt. 31.00
Lewes Dairy, Delaware, ACL, Metal Handle, 1/2 Gal. 13.50
Lewes Dairy, Delaware, Cow, Red ACL, Round, Gal. 50.00
Lewes Dairy, Delaware, Cow, Red ACL, Square, Gal. 18.00
Lexington Dairy, Lexington, Ky, Cow's Head, Hand Holding Glass, Red ACL, Qt. 45.00
Liberty Dairy, Shillington, Pa., Raised Letters, Pt., 7 1/2 In. 30.00
Liberty Milk Co. Inc., Buffalo, N.Y., Statue Of Liberty, Embossed, Round, Pt. 30.00
Little's Dairy, Hanover, Pa., Red Painted Square Label, Pt. 22.00
Local Milk, Deposit, Embossed, Round, Qt. 8.00
Locust Lane Farms, Moorestown, Girl Spilling Milk, Blue, Orange ACL, Square, 1/2 Gal. 22.00
Loganbell Farms, Bellwood, Pa., Bell, Indian, ACL, Square, Qt. 10.00
Long Creek Lodge, Devotion, N.C., Cow On Reverse, Blue ACL, Pt. 135.00
M.F. Vossler, Farmingdale, Amatheisist Thatcher, Embossed, Round, Qt. 18.00
Maine Dairy Inc., Portland, Maine, Orange ACL, Cream Top, Tall, Round, 1937, Pt. 77.00
Major Diary, Homogenized Milk, Red ACL, Gal. 9.00
Manasquan & Bayhead Dairies, Manasquan, N.J., Stars, Embossed, Round, 1/2 Pt. 10.00
Manchester Dairy System Inc., Est. 1923, Maroon ACL, Square, Qt. 19.00
Manor View Dairy, Millersville, Pa., Painted Label, Qt. 22.00
Manor View Dairy, Quality Dairy Products, Millersville, Pa., Cow's Head, Qt. ......22.00 to 25.00
Maple Hill Dairy, Waterbury, Est. 1876, Red ACL, Square, Qt. 17.00
Maple Hurst Farms, Bound Brook, N.J., Red ACL, Qt. 25.00
Maple Lawn Dairy, Cow's Head, Red ACL, Square, Qt. 19.00
Maplehurst Farms, Raymond Bros., Red Letters, Square, Creamer, 3/4 Oz. 40.00
March's Deer Park Creamery, Port Jarvis, N.Y., Red ACL, Round, Pt. 25.00
Marshall Dairy Co., Ithaca, N.Y., Cottage Cheese Logo, Creamer, Red ACL, 1/2 Pt. ... 5.00
Mass O Seal, Sam Bookless, Pittsfield, Mass., Embossed, Qt. 20.00
Matuella's, Cop The Cream, Hazelton, Pa., Embossed, Round, 1/2 Pt. 45.00
Maurer's Wayside Dairy, Mt. Carmel, Pa., Red ACL, Round, Qt. 11.00
McCue's Dairy, Long Branch, Embossed, Round, 1/4 Pt. 40.00
McCue's Dairy, Long Branch, Product List, Embossed, Round, Qt. 12.00
McDaniel's Dairy, Williamsport, Pa., Baseball Player, After The Game, Cool Off, 1/2 Pt. ... 45.00
McKean County Creamery, Smethport, Pa., For Charm & Beauty, Woman, Red, Pt. 25.00
Me-La Milk Dealers Ass'n, Big Rapids, Mi., 5 Cent Store Bottle, Registered, Qt. 60.00
Meadow Dairies, Leaksville, N.C., Blue Neck Swirl, Embossed, 1/2 Pt. 25.00
Meadowbrook Dairy, J.L. Long, Centerburg, Ohio, ACL, Round, Qt. 75.00
Meadowdale Farm, Hills Bros., Canton, N.Y., Golden, Jersey, Light Orange ACL, Pt. 50.00
Medosweet, Jack & Jill Nursery Rhyme, Red ACL, Round, Qt. 55.00
Meisner's, Dover Foxcroft, Orange ACL, Square, Qt. 22.00
Melrose Dairy, Ormond, Fl., Cartoon, I Want To Go Home, Qt. 60.00
Meyer, Phone 34-F-04, Red Paint, Round, Qt., 9 1/2 In. 18.00
Meyer, Round, Red Paint, Qt., 9 1/2 In. 25.00
Mid Valley Farm Dairy, Green ACL, Square, Qt. 19.00
Midwest Dairy, Plymouth, Wisc., ACL, Round, Qt. 50.00
Milk Products Co., Inc., Pennsgrove, N.J., Embossed, Round, Pt. 6.00
Miss Georgia Dairy Products, Atlanta, Ga., Red & Blue ACL, Round, Qt. 31.00
Missouri Pacific Lines, Sunnymeade Farm, Bismarck, Red ACL, 1/2 Pt. 32.00
Mo Jonnier Bros. Co., Chicago, Laboratory Test Bottle, Rubber Cap, Round, 1/2 Pt. 10.00
Model Dairy, Ogden, Red ACL, Have No Regrets, Drive Carefully, Round, 1941, Qt .47.00 to 97.00
Model Dairy, Waukon, Iowa, Red ACL, Round, Qt. 60.00
Model Dairy, Waukon, Iowa, Try Our Creamed Cottage Cheese, Red ACL, Qt. 45.00

Modern Dairy, Idaho Falls, Make America Strong, Eagle & Flag, Qt. 325.00
Molen's Dairy Farm, Dayton, Oh., 5 Cents Direct From Farm, Cow's Head, Blue ACL, Qt.   95.00
Molen's Dairy Farm, Dayton, Oh., From Farm, Ribbons, Cow, Elves, Blue, Round, Qt. ..   75.00
Mong's, Oil City, Pa., Dark Red ACL, Pt., 5 1/2 In. 16.00
Monterey Bay Milk Distr., 5 Cents, Ca., Embossed, Round, 1/4 Pt. 45.00
Moon's Dairy, Catskills, N.Y., Black ACL, Square, Qt. 20.00
Moonson Milk Company, Springfield, Mass., Embossed, Round, 1/4 Pt. 40.00
MOPAC, Missouri Pacific Rail Lines, Sunnymeade Farm, Bismarck, 1/2 Pt., 4 1/2 In. 25.00
Moscow Store Bottle, Yellow ACL, Deposit 10 Cents, Round, Qt. 23.00
Muller Dairies, Inc., N.Y., Embossed, Round, 1/2 Pt. 6.00
Mutual McDermott Dairy Corp., New York, Embossed, Pt. 20.00
Nakoma Farms Dairy, N.Y., Embossed, Round, Pt. 9.00
Nelson's Cloverland Creamery, Manistique, Mich., Ice Cream Sundae, Black ACL, Qt. ..   75.00
Netherlands, 2 Dutch Children, Red & Blue ACL, Pt. 21.00
Netherlands, Children, Windmill, Amber, Orange & White ACL, Qt. 21.00
Nevada Creamery & Dairy, Colorado Springs, Co., Family Silhouette, Blue ACL, Qt. 75.00
New Mexico College A&M, ACL, 1/2 Pt. 20.00
Norris Bros. Dairy, New Windsor, Il., Food Fights Too, Use It Wisely, Black ACL, Qt. ...   100.00
North American Creameries, Interlake Creamery, Browns Valley, Minn., ACL, Round, Qt.   85.00
North Shore Dairy Co., Chicago, Embossed, Squat, Round, Qt. 7.00
Northland Farms, Amber & White ACL, 1/2 Gal. 16.00
Northwestern Dairy, Portland, Ore., Embossed, Pt. 25.00
O'Donnell's, Maroon & Orange ACL, Round, Qt. 35.00
Oakhurst Dairy, Red ACL, Square, Qt. 16.00
Old Oak Dairy, Shipley Heights, Md., Round, Embossed, Qt. 15.00
Old Tavern Farm, Inc., Portland, Mi., Shield, Waving Man, Red & Black ACL, Qt. 75.00
Oldfield, 508 Noble St., Pt. 20.00
Orchard Farm, Dallas, Pa., Babyface, Red ACL, Square, Qt. 50.00
Ottawa Dairy, Embossed, Round, Canada, Qt. 12.00
P.M.D. Assn., San Diego, Calif., Amber, 1/2 Pt. 75.00
Park Dairy, Ludington, Mich., 9 x 4 In. 15.00
Parks Farm Dairy, N.Y., Orange ACL, Square, Gal. 15.00
Parry Dairy, Forty Fort Wyoming, Pa., ACL, Cap, Qt., 8 3/4 In. 7.50
Parson's Dairy, Hasleton, Pa., Cream Separator, Embossed, Round, 1/2 Pt. 60.00
Paso Robles, Cal., Crescent Moon, Mountain, Cow, Black, Round, Store Bottle, Qt. 75.00
Paul F. Burkholder, Harrisonburg, Va., Cap, Embossed X, Round, Qt. 15.00
Paulus Dairy, New Brunswick, N.J., ACL, Round, Qt. 25.00
Pearce's, State College, Pa., Orange Red ACL, Round, Qt. 103.00
Peerless Creamery, Clifton Forge & Covington, Va., Black ACL, Square, Qt. 19.00
Peffer Farms, Jersey Creamline, Stockton, Ca., Store, Orange ACL, Round, Qt., 9 1/2 In. ..   77.00
Peoples Milk Co., Amber, Embossed, Round, Qt. 50.00
Peoples Sanitary Dairy, Perth Amboy, N.J., Ribbed, Embossed, Round, Qt. 12.00
Peplau's Dairy, Forestville, Conn., Babyface, Qt. 375.00
Peplau's Dairy, Forestville, Conn., Qt. 600.00
Perry Bros., Sutton, Mass., The Maples, Cow, Green ACL, Round, Qt. 26.00
Perry's Creamery, Buy Defense Bonds, Tuscaloosa, Al., Qt. 45.00
Pet Dairy Products, Red ACL, Rectangular, 1/2 Gal. 6.50
Pet Pasteurized Milk, Red ACL, Square, Qt. 22.00
Pettibon Dairy Co., Rochester, N.Y., Man With Milk, Before Retiring, Green ACL, Qt. ...   75.00
Philadelphia Quaker Maid Milk Company, Embossed, Round, Qt. 12.00
Pinehurst Farms Dairy, Rockford, Ill., Boy Drinking Milk, Girl Pouring Milk, 1/2 Pt. ...   31.00
Plainfield Milk & Cream Co., N.J., Embossed, Round, 1/4 Pt. 40.00
Plains Dairy, Cheyenne, Wyoming, Frontier Days, Black ACL, Round, Qt. 37.00
Pleasant Dairy, Lewiston, Maine, Green & Yellow ACL, Square, Qt. 21.00
Pleasant Farms Dairy, Van Schoick's, N.J., Embossed, Round, 1/2 Pt. 4.00
Poplar Hill Dairy, P.A. Hobbs, Frederick, Md., ACL, Round, Qt. 75.00
Potomac Farms Quality Dairy Products, ACL, Square, 1/2 Pt. 12.50
Preston Dairy, Woman Running, Vitamin & Mineral List, Amber Glass, White ACL, Qt. .   20.00
Price's Sunset Creamery, Rosewell, N.M., Setting Sun, Orange ACL, Qt. 65.00
Producers Dairy, Kirkland Lake, Ontario, Red ACL, Square, Pt. 59.00
Property Of & Filled By McGill Dairy, McGregor, Iowa, Orange ACL, Round, 1947, Qt. ..   49.00
Property Of Sacto Cal. Capital Dairy, Embossed, Round, 1/2 Pt. 15.00

Prudential Milk Company, N.Y., Ribbed, Embossed, Round, 1/2 Pt. 20.00
Puritan Dairy, Perth Amboy, N.J., Embossed, Round, 1/2 Pt. 4.00
Purity Dairy, Mother & Baby, Amber Glass, White ACL, Qt. 20.00
Quaker Maid Dairy Products, Pa., Embossed, Round, 1/2 Pt. 6.00
Queen City Dairy, N.Y., Embossed, Round, Qt. 14.00
Queen City Dairy Company, Embossed, Pt. 25.00
Queens Farms Inc., Ozone Park, Long Island, Embossed Triangle, Round, 1/2 Pt. 6.00
R.J. Gagnon, Waterville, Me., ACL, Round, 1/2 Pt. 25.00
R.J. Smith Dairy, Red Silkscreen Letters, Square, Qt., 8 5/8 x 3 3/8 In. 15.00
Raisin & Levine, New York City, Sour Cream, Embossed, Round, Pt. 5.00
Raisin & Levine Inc., N.Y., Embossed, Round, 1/2 Pt. 4.00
Rankin Farm Dairy, J.C. Allen, Manasquan, N.J., Embossed, Round, Pt. 8.00
Rawleigh Farms, Good Health Milk, Freeport, Ill., 1/2 Pt. 43.00
Red Bank Dairy, Inc., Embossed, Round, Qt. 8.00
Red Gate Farm, Newton, N.J., Embossed, Round, Qt. 210.00
Redman Dairy, Indian, Lincoln, Maroon ACL, Round, Qt. 135.00
Reik Dairy, Embossed, Qt. 8.00
Renna Dairy Co., Hobnails, Embossed, Round, Pt. 10.00
Residence Dairy, Houma, La., ACL, Round, Pt. 150.00
Richmond Farms, Va., State Map, Orange & Maroon ACL, Square, Qt. 25.00
Rigoletti Pure Milk, Mountain View, N.J., Round Embossed, Qt. 25.00
Riley M.I. & C.S. Co, N.J., Ribbed, Embossed, Round, Pt. 6.00
Riley's Pitman, N.J., Embossed, Round, 1/4 Pt. 35.00
Riverside Dairy, Henderson & Son, Belmar, N.J., Embossed, Round, Pt. 8.00
Robert S. Pesson, New Iberia, La., Black ACL, Round, Qt. 400.00
Roof Garden Fish Co., Tucson, White ACL, Round, 1/4 Pt. 45.00
Rosedale Dairy Co., New York City, Sour Cream, Embossed, 1/2 Pt. 12.00
Round Top Farms, Maine, ACL, 1948, 1/2 Pt. 54.00
Royal Creamery, Salinas, Monterey, Castroville, Embossed Slug Plate, Round, 1/2 Pt. ... 12.00
Royal Crest Inc., Denver, Co., Aristocrat Of Milks, Black ACL, Square, Qt. 20.00
Royal Oak Dairy, Taste The Difference, Silk-Screen Label, 10 1/4 In. 15.00
Royal-D, Red ACL, Round, Qt. ....15.00 to 25.00
Royale Dairy, Hanover, Pa., Fit For A King, 9 1/2 x 4 In. 16.00
Rubarts Dairy, Vineland, N.J., Embossed, Qt. 9.00
Ruff's Dairy, Girl, Blocks, Building My Future, Orange ACL, St. Clair, Michigan, Qt., 9 In. 12.50
Ruff's Dairy, St. Clair, Mich., Orange ACL, Round, Qt. 32.00
Rutland Hills Co-Op Inc., Watertown, N.Y., Amber, Blue & Yellow ACL, Qt. 25.00
Rutland Hills Co-Op Inc., Watertown, N.Y., Baseball Player, Orange ACL, Qt. 35.00
S.R. Kitchen Dairy, DuBois, Pa., Yellow ACL, Square, 1/2 Pt. 15.00
Sacramento 5 Cent Store Bottle, Embossed Slug Plate, Round, 1/2 Pt. 15.00
Sanida Dairy, Erie, Pa., Red ACL, Square, 1/2 Pt. 6.00
Sanitary Dairy, Crookston, Minn., Red ACL, Square, Qt. 19.00
Sanitary Dairy, Waynesburg, Pa., ACL, Square, Qt. 8.00
Sanitary Dairy Co., Trenton Jct., N.J., Embossed, Round, Pt. 8.00
Sanitary's Best By Test, Pasteurized, Keep Them Rolling, Tank, Red, White, Blue, Qt. .. 336.00
Saratoga Dairy, N.Y., Embossed, Round, Qt. 14.00
Schmalz Milk, Bottled On Our Farm, For The Smile Of Health, Red ACL, Round, 1/2 Pt. . 22.00
Schneider's Dairy, Lancaster, N.Y., Try Our Ice Cream, Red ACL, Square, Qt. 17.00
Schneider's Dairy, Orange ACL, Round, 1/2 Pt. 5.00
Scott Key Dairy, W.H. Moore Prop., Embossed, Qt. 25.00
Scott-Powell, Aristocrat, Embossed, Round, Tall Neck, Qt. 7.00
Scott-Powell Dairies, Phila., Embossed, Round, 1/2 Pt. 6.00
Shadow Brook, Bowling Alley Ad, Orange, Brown, Green, Red ACL, Square, Qt. 25.00
Shady Side Dairy, Dallas, Pa., Green & Red ACL, Square, Qt. 20.00
Sharp's Dairy, Horse, Fresh From The Farm, N.J., Blue ACL, Square, Qt. 20.00
Shaws Dairy, Brattleboro, Vt., Golden Guernsey Milk, Babyface, 9 1/2 In. 33.00
Sheffield, 4, N.Y., Embossed, Round, Qt. 8.00
Sheffield Farms, Cream Top, Embossed, Round, Qt. 22.00
Sheffield Sealtest Milk, Red ACL, Round, Squat, Qt. 12.00
Sherman Dairy Co., South Haven, Mich., Orange ACL, Square, Qt. 25.00
Shirly Hotel Dairy, Fort Logan, Colorado, Purple, Embossed Hotel Logo, 24-Sided, Qt. .. 250.00
Short Horn Dairy, Portland, Oregon, Embossed, Round, Qt. 155.00

Showalter's Dairies, Orangeade, Grapeade, Chocolate Drink, Phoenixville, Pa., 10 In. . . .	19.00
Shrewsbury Dairy Co., N.J., Embossed, Round, Qt.	8.00
Shrum's Dairy, Try Our Farm Fresh, Red & Brown ACL, 1/2 Pt.	9.00
Signor's Dairy, Keeseville, N.Y., Black ACL, Round, Pt.	20.00
Sill's Farms Inc., Greenport, Guard Your Health, Orange ACL, Round, Qt.	40.00
Silver Springs Farms, Drums, Singing Birds, Orange ACL, Square, Qt.	15.00
Skyline Farms, Grade A Dairy Products, Lincoln, Nebr., Red ACL, Square, Qt.	8.00
Skyline Farms Co., Grade A Dairy Products, Lincoln, Nebr., Red, Round, Qt.	50.00
Smith's Modern Dairy, Palmyra's Only Dairy, Orange ACL, Square, 1/2 Gal.	15.00
Snow White Dairy, Brown, Green, Snow White & 7 Dwarfs	863.00
Snyder-Crogan Dairy, Inc., Kingwood, W.Va., Red ACL, Square, Qt.	15.50
Someret Dairy Co., Johnstown, Pa., Round Embossed, Qt.	20.00
Somerset Farms Dairy, Middlebush, N.J., Red ACL, Square, Pt.	8.00
Southern Dairies, Embossed, Pt.	25.00
Southern Maid Inc., Bristol, Home Office, Embossed, Round, Qt.	18.00
St. Clair Dairy, Ed. Hornicke, Red ACL, Round, Pt.	22.00
St. James Trade School, Springfield, Ill., Embossed, Round, 1/2 Pt.	9.00
St. Lawrence Pasteurized Milk, St. Lawrence Dairy, Raised Letters, 1/2 Pt., 6 In.	25.00
St. Louis Dairy, St. Louis, Mo., Embossed, Qt.	25.00
St. Mary's Dairy, Pa., Brown ACL, Round, Qt.	40.00
St. Thomas Virgin Islands, Orange & Red ACL	25.00
Stafford Spring Dairy, Leicester, Mass, Farm Scene In Circle, Red ACL, Qt.	70.00
Stan The Milk Man, It Whips, Stan's For Quality, Red ACL, Cream Top, Square, Qt.	100.00
State College Creamery, Round, Qt.	210.00
State Seal Dairy, Milk Man, State Picture, N.J., Orange ACL, Square, Qt.	25.00
State University Of N.Y. Agricultural & Technical Institute, Canton, Enamel, Embossed, Qt.	50.00
Steuer's Dairy, Aliquippa, Pa., Red & Green ACL, Square, Qt.	8.00
Steward's Thermopolis, Wy., World's Largest Hot Springs, ACL, Round, Qt.	250.00
Stewart's Dairy, Bogolusa, La., Orange ACL, Round, Gal.	250.00
Stocker's Easton, Pa., Square, Red Painted Label, Have You Tried Our Other, Qt.	22.00
Store Bottle, 3 Cents, Embossed, Round, 1/4 Pt.	45.00
Sun Valley Dairy, Highland Park, Ill., Green, Yellow ACL, Square, 1/2 Gal.	65.00
Sunny Brook, Bradford, Pa., Guard Your Health, Soldier, Red ACL, Square, Qt.	19.00
Sunny Crest Farm, Rocky Hill, Conn., Red ACL, Square, Qt.	5.00
Sunny Slope Dairy, S, 9 3/4 In.	19.00
Sunnydale, Footman Hillman, Bangor, Brewer, Me., Orange & Black ACL, Qt., 9 1/2 In. .	10.00
Sunrise Dairy, Gastonia, N.C., Boy, Carrying Bottle, Red Letters, Square, c.1951, Qt. . . .	18.00
Supplee, 150 Year Anniversary, 1804-1954, Red ACL, Square, Qt.	25.00
Supplee Mills-Jones, Clean Milk, Embossed, Round, Qt.	9.00
Supplee Mills-Jones, Embossed, Round, 1/2 Pt.	4.00
Suprema, Garantiza Su Salud, Happy Cow, Blue ACL, Qt.	29.00
Swiss Dairy, Turtle Creek, Pa., Green ACL, Round, 1/2 Pt.	15.00
Tampa Stock Farm Dairy, Script Letters, Embossed, Duraglas Insignia, Qt.	25.00
Tate Brothers Dairy, Idaho, Orange ACL, 1/2 Pt.	10.00
Te Croney Dairy, Clymer, N.Y., Baby Reaching For Bottle, Maroon ACL, Round, Qt.	45.00
Thackston Dairy, Yankee Doodle Verse, Maroon ACL, Tall, Round, 1940s, Qt.	50.00
Thatcher Farm, Milton, Estab. 1891, Orange ACL, 1/2 Pt.	8.00
Thatcher's Dairy, Man Milking Cow, Absolutely Pure, Porcelain Top, Embossed, Qt.	25.00
Thompson's Dairy, Embossed Chain, Round, 1/4 Pt.	35.00
Tilton Dairy Farms, Asbury Park, N.J., Embossed, Round, Qt.	20.00
Tilton's City Dairy, Asbury Park, N.J., Ribbed, Embossed, Round, Qt.	15.00
To Be Washed & Returned, Heavy, Embossed, Round, Pt.	9.00
Trammater's Dairy, Hart, Mich., Embossed, Round, 1/2 Pt.	6.00
Tri Valley Dairies, Morrisville, Cazenovia, Hamilton, N.Y., Orange ACL, Square, Qt.	18.00
Try Rocky Crock, Dancing Crocodile, England, Multicolored ACL, Round, Pt.	20.00
Tumbling Run Park Dairy, J.H. Brockhoff, Pottsville, Pa., Cream Top, Embossed, Pt.	19.00
Tuscan Farm Products, Union, N.J., Orange ACL, Square, 1/2 Gal.	16.00
Twin Elm Farm Dairy, Springfield, Mo., Orange ACL, Boy Drinking Milk, Round, Qt.	15.00
U.S. Naval Academy, Annapolis, Md., Anchor, Embossed, Round, Pt.	150.00
U.S.V.A., Hospital Bottle, Blue ACL, Square, Qt.	35.00
Union Dairy, Embossed, Chicago, Ill., 1/2 Pt., 5 1/2 In.	10.00
United Farmers Co-Operative, Boston, Mass., Red Letters, Cream Top, Square, Qt.	50.00
United Farmers Co-Operative, Mass., Red ACL, Embossed, Round, Qt.	30.00

Universal 5 Cent Store, Ribbed, Embossed, Qt.	12.00
University Of Georgia, George Washington, Red ACL, Round, Qt.	160.00
University Of Maryland Dairy, College Park, Md., Qt	125.00
University Of Wisconsin, Babcock, Pasteur, Red ACL, Round, Qt.	210.00
Unmarked Bottle, Young's Yankee Dairy On Cardboard Lid, 10 1/2 x 3 In.	15.00
Uservo Inc., 1/2 Pt., 5 1/2 x 2 1/2 In.	7.00
V.K. Barnes, Olean, N.Y., Embossed, Round, 1/4 Pt.	28.00
Valley Creamery, Oakland, Embossed Slug Plate, Round, 1/2 Pt.	30.00
Valley Hoe Dairy, Ed. Schlaepfer & John O'Leary Proprietors, Embossed, Paper Lid, Qt. .	325.00
Van Kampen's Dairy, Milkman, Ca., Red ACL, Square, Qt.	20.00
Van Schoick's Pleasant Farms Dairy, Pt. Pleasant, N.J., Embossed, Round, Qt.	8.00
Van's Dairy, Grand Rapids, Mich., Black ACL, Round, 1/2 Pt.	5.00
Velvet Cream & Dairy Products, Reno, Nev., Red ACL, Tall, Round, 1940s, 1/2 Pt.	11.00
Velvet Ice Cream & Dairy Products, Owensboro, Kentucky, Red ACL, 1/2 Pt., 4 1/2 In. .	8.00
Velvet Ice Cream & Dairy Products, Owensboro, Kentucky, Red ACL, Pt., 7 In.	5.50
Vermont Country Milk, Burlington, Vt., Red Foil Cap, Late 1980s, Qt.	10.00
Victor Dairies, 426 Christian Street, 1/2 Pt.	20.00
Villa Park Dairy, Trenton, N.J., Attend Church, Orange ACL, Square, Qt.	20.00
Virginia Dairy Company, Home Of Better Milk, Embossed, Qt.	9.00
W. Flickert & Son, Middleboro, Orange ACL, Round, 1/2 Pt.	11.00
W.D. Van Schoik City Dairy, Asbury, N.J., Embossed, Round, Tall, 1/2 Pt.	9.00
W.S. Van Schoick, Quality Dairy Products, Lakewood, N.J., Embossed, Round, Qt.	12.00
Walander, Pt., 7 1/4 In.	10.00
Walker Gordon, Black ACL, Embossed, Round, 1/2 Pt.	6.00
Walker-Gordon Nat. Control Cert., Black & Red ACL, Square, Qt.	15.00
War Slogan, Paper Neck Collar, Uncle Sam, Hitler, Hirohito, Orange ACL, Round, Qt.	230.00
Wardell, Embossed, Square, Qt.	5.00
Warefield Dairy Simpson Bros., D.C., Embossed, Round, Qt.	20.00
Warner Bros., Bugs Bunny, Only 10,200 Made, Multicolored ACL, Square, Qt.	28.00
Warner Bros., Cat Woman, Only 6456 Made, Multicolored ACL, Square, Qt.	28.00
Warner Bros., Daffy Duck, Despicable Dairies, Only 6672 Made, Colored ACL, Square, Qt. .	28.00
Warner Bros., Martin Milk, No. 1, Only 7343 Made, Colored ACL, Square, Qt.	25.00
Warner Bros., Martin Milk, No. 2, Only 5952 Made, Colored ACL, Square, Qt.	28.00
Warner Bros., Pepe & Penelope, Only 7128 Made, Colored ACL, Square, Qt.	20.00
Warner Bros., Superman, Only 8016 Made, Colored ACL, Square, Qt.	35.00
Warner Bros., Tweety, Not Just For Puddy Tats, 6480 Made, Colored ACL, Square, Qt.	28.00
Warner's Dairy, Red Lion, 50 Year Anniversary, Since 1903, Maroon ACL, Qt.	40.00
Washington Dairy, North Tarrytown, N.Y., Cow's Head, Embossed, Round, Qt.	18.00
Wason-MacDonald, Haverhill, Massachusetts, Orange ACL, Round, 1/2 Pt.	5.00
Wawa Dairy, Flowers, Embossed Dots, Round, Pt.	20.00
Wawa Dairy Farms Turner Wescott, Square, Handle, Duraglass, Pa., 1962	17.00
Waynesboro Sanitary Milk Plant, Round Embossed, Pt.	27.00
Weckerle, Inspected, Protected Milk, Red ACL, Round, Qt.	25.00
Wehr Dairy, Snow White, Red ACL, Round, Qt.	300.00
Weisglass Gold Seal Dairy, Staten Islands, N.Y., Graduates, Orange ACL, Square, Qt. ...	20.00
Western Dairy & Ice Cream Co., St. Joseph, Mo., Justrite, 1/2 Pt.	20.00
Western Maryland Dairy, Sealtest System, Orange ACL, Fluted Sure Grip Neck, Qt.	12.00
Westover Dairy, Inc., Lynchburg, Va., Taste Tested Ice Cream, Qt.	70.00
Westwood, California Westwood Creamery, Cream, 1930s, 4 1/4 x 2 In.	28.00
Westwood Farm, Aberdeen, Md., Embossed, Qt.	25.00
Whitcomb's Farms, Littleton, Mass., Babyface, Qt.	212.00
White Clover, Embossed Tin Top, Qt.	45.00
White Oak Dairy, Tree, 2 Cows, Orange Printed, Embossed Diamond, 1/2 Pt.	12.00
Will's Dairy, Est. 1870, Red ACL, Square, Qt.	16.00
Winnisimet Dairy, Tiverton, R.I., Amber, White ACL, Indian Head, Square, Qt.	10.00
Winnisquam Farms, Waterbury, Amber, White ACL, Square, 1/2 Gal.	16.00
Winnisquam Farms, Waterbury, Amber, White ACL, Square, Qt.	12.00
Wm. R. Sickles, Asbury Park, N.J., Embossed X, Round, Qt.	22.00
Yingling's Dairy, Titusville, Pa., Milk Is Nature's, Orange ACL, Pt.	5.00
Young's Yankee Dairy, Grade A Pasteurized, Cardboard Lid, Walla Walla, 10 1/2 In.	15.00
Zapp's Dairy, That Good Flavor, ACL, Round, Qt., 9 1/2 In.	11.50
Zenda Farms, Golden Guernsey, Clayton, N.Y., Orange ACL, Round, 1/4 Pt.	45.00

MILK GLASS

It makes perfect sense to think that white milk-colored glass is known as *milk glass* to collectors. But not all milk glass is white, nor is all white glass milk glass, so the name may cause a little confusion. The first true milk glass was produced in England in the 1700s. It is a semi-opaque glass, often with slight blue tones. The glass reached the height of its popularity in the United States about 1870. Many dishes and bottles were made. Both new versions of old styles and new styles have been made continuously since that time, many by the Westmoreland and the Kemple glass companies. These pieces, many very recent, often appear at antiques sales. Westmoreland Glass Company worked from 1890 to 1984. In the early years, they made figural milk glass bottles to hold food products, especially mustard. Later they made reproductions of earlier pieces of tableware. Today it is considered correct to talk about blue milk glass or black milk glass. This is glass made by the same formula but with a color added. It is not correct to call a glass that is white only on the surface *milk glass*. Bottles made of milk glass may also be found in this book in the Cologne, Cosmetic, and Figural categories.

Dresser, Bulbous Base, Long Neck, Gold Trim, Raised Design, Stopper, 11 In.	55.00
E.N. Lightner & Co., Detroit, Mich., Cylindrical, 6 1/4 In	39.00
Upham, Philada., Square, Beveled Corners, 5 In.	99.00
World's Fair, New York, Glove Shape, Lid, 1939, 9 1/4 In.	55.00

MINERAL WATER

Although today it is obvious which is soda water and which is mineral water, the difference was not as clear in the nineteenth and early twentieth centuries. Mineral water bottles held the fresh natural spring waters favored for health or taste. Even though some had a distinct sulfur or iron taste, the therapeutic values made them seem delicious. Some mineral waters had no carbonation, but many were naturally carbonated. Soda water today is made with artificial carbonation and usually has added flavor. Mineral water was mentioned by the ancient Greeks, and the Romans wrote about visiting the famous springs of Europe. Mineral springs were often the center of resorts in nineteenth-century America, when it was fashionable to "take the waters." Often the water from the famous springs was bottled to be sold to visitors. Most of the mineral water bottles collected today date from the 1850-1900 period. Many of these bottles have embossed lettering and blob tops. The standard shape was cylindrical with thick walls to withstand the pressure of carbonation. Most were made in a snap case mold although a few can be found with open or iron pontils. Common colors are clear, pale aqua, and light green. More unusual are dark green, black, and amber bottles, while cobalt blue ones are rare. The bottles were sealed with a cork. A few places, like Poland Springs and Ballston Spa, made figural bottles. Related bottles may be found in the Seltzer and Soda categories.

A. Hain & Son, Emerald Green, Squat, Iron Pontil, c.1850, 7 In.	935.00
A. Schroth, Schill Haven, Cobalt Blue, Squat, Pontil, c.1850, 7 1/2 In.	2090.00
A.R. Cox, Norristown, Blue Green, Applied Double Collar, Iron Pontil, 7 1/8 In.	179.00
A.W. Rapp, New York, Cobalt Blue, Applied Sloping Collar, Iron Pontil, 1/2 Pt.	728.00
Adirondack Spring, Westport, N.Y., Emerald Green, Sloping Double Collar, Qt.	308.00
Adirondack Spring, Whitehall, N.Y., Green, Sloping Double Collar, Pt.	134.00 to 179.00
Akesion Spring, Owned By Sweet Springs Co, Orange Amber, Applied Mouth, Pt.	245.00
Alburgh A Springs, Vt., Tobacco Amber, Applied Double Collar, Qt.	1870.00
Alburgh A Springs, Vt., Yellow Amber, 1865-75, Qt.	896.00
Alleghany Springs, Virginia, Aqua, Applied Mouth, 1/2 Gal.	420.00
Apollinaris, Brunnen, Georg Kreuzbery, 3 Neck Rings, Clay, c.1905, 12 1/2 In.	45.00
Artesian Spring Co., AS, Ballston, N.Y., Blue Green, Sloping Double Collar, Pt.	179.00
Artesian Spring Co., AS, Ballston, N.Y., Emerald Green, Pt.	125.00
Artesian Spring Co., Ballston, N.Y., Blue Green, Applied Collar, Pt., 7 5/8 In.	100.00 to 255.00
Artesian Spring Co., Ballston, N.Y., Olive Yellow, Applied Collar, Pt., 8 In. *Illus*	100.00
Artesian Spring Co., Ballston, N.Y., Teal Green, Applied Double Collar, Pt., 8 In.	80.00
Artesian Spring Co., Ballston, N.Y., Yellow Green, Pt.	149.00
Artesian Water, Louisville, Ky., Chocolate Amber, Mug Base, Iron Pontil, Pt.	935.00
Artesian Water, Louisville, Ky., Chocolate Amber, Sloping Collar, Iron Pontil, 7 3/4 In.	672.00
Avon Spring Water, Aqua Blue, Sloping Double Collar, Qt	504.00
Avon Spring Water, Olive Amber, Applied Sloping Double Collar, Qt.	255.00
B. & G., San Francisco, Sapphire Blue, Blob Top, 7 1/2 In.	476.00
B. & G., San Francisco, Superior, Blue, Iron Pontil, 7 1/2 In.	413.00

Bangor City, Purity Guaranteed, Aqua, Codd, 8-Sided, 8 3/4 In. 69.00
Bartlett, California, Aqua, Wine Shape, Slug Plate, Blob Top, 12 In. 30.00
Bear Lithia, Standing Bear, Elkton, Va., Aqua, 1/2 Gal. ....200.00 to 280.00
Bedford Springs Co., Aqua, Tooled Mouth, 1880-95, Qt. 179.00
Blatz Gold Star Carbonated Water, Green, Label, 1924, 11 1/2 In. 40.00
Blount Springs, Natural Sulphur Water, BS, Cobalt Blue, Cylindrical, Qt. 235.00
Blue Ridge Springs, Virginia, Aqua, Applied Mouth, 1880-1890, 1/2 Gal. 532.00
Bolen Waack & Co., New York, Emerald Green, 1875-85, 1/2 Pt. 224.00
British Public House, Pure Aerated Waters, Edinburgh, Aqua, Blue Lip, Codd, 9 In. 600.00
Buffalo, Mineral Springs, Natures, Materia, Medica, Aqua, ABM, 10 1/2 In. 35.00
Buffalo Lithia, Woman, Sitting, Blue Green, Applied Mouth, 1/2 Gal. 336.00
Buffum, Sarsaparilla & Lemon, Sapphire Blue, 10-Sided, Pontil, 7 7/8 In. 935.00
Buffum & Co., Cobalt Blue, Tenpin Shape, 1860-70, 8 In. 1320.00
C. Cleminshaw, Troy, N.Y., Sapphire Blue, Applied Mouth, Blob Top, IP, 7 In. ....179.00 to 420.00
C. Lomax, Chicago, Cobalt Blue, Applied Mouth, Iron Pontil, 7 1/4 In. 308.00
Caladonia Spring, Wheelock, Vt., Amber, Double Collar, 1860-80, Qt. ....672.00 to 880.00
Campbell Mineral Spring Co., Burlington, Vt., Aqua, 1860-70, Qt. 1232.00
Champion Spouting Spring, Saratoga, N.Y., Aqua, Applied Collar, Pt., 7 1/2 In. ....55.00 to 90.00
Champion Spouting Spring, Saratoga, N.Y., Monogram, Aqua, Pt. ....*Illus* 258.00
Champlain Spring, Alkaline Chalybeate, Highgate, Vt., Emerald Green, Qt. ......280.00 to 470.00
Chase & Co., San Francisco, Stockton & Marysville, Cal., Green, Blob Top, IP 660.00
Chistlehurst Mineral Water Works, Aqua, Codd Hamilton Hybrid, 10 In. 69.00
Clarke & Co., New York, Blue Green, Applied Sloping Collar, Cylindrical, Pt. 209.00
Clarke & Co., New York, Blue Green, Double Collar, Iron Pontil, 1850-60, Pt. .....90.00 to 112.00
Clarke & Co., New York, Emerald Green, Double Collar, IP, Pt. ....*Illus* 220.00
Clarke & Co., New York, Medium Teal Blue, Applied Sloping Double Collar, IP, Pt. 100.00
Clarke & Co., New York, Olive Amber, Applied Mouth, Pontil, Pt., 7 3/8 In. 220.00
Clarke & Co., New York, Olive Green, Applied Sloping Double Collar, Qt. ....112.00 to 123.00
Clarke & Co., New York, Olive Green, High Shoulder, Double Collar, Qt. 168.00
Clarke & Co., New York, Olive Green, Sloping Double Collar, Qt. 190.00
Clarke & White, C, New York, Olive Green, Applied Sloping Double Collar, Pt. 35.00
Clarke & White, C, New York, Olive Green, Double Collar, Qt. ....75.00 to 80.00
Clarke & White, New York, Olive Amber, Double Collar, Pontil, Pt., 7 1/2 In. ....110.00 to 220.00
Clarke & White, New York, Olive Green, Applied Sloping Double Collar, Qt. ....157.00 to 200.00
Clarke & White, New York, Olive Green, High Shoulder, Double Collar, Qt. 112.00
Clarke & White, New York, Olive Yellow, Applied Double Collar, Pontil, Qt. 220.00
Clarke & White, New York, Olive Yellow, Sloping Double Collar, Pontil, Pt. 112.00
Clarke & White, New York, Olive Yellow, Sloping Double Collar, Pontil, Qt. 258.00
Clarke & White, Olive Amber, Pt. 59.00
Clarke & White, Olive Green, Pt., 7 3/4 In. 44.00
Codd, Amber, Dumpy Shape, Embossed, 7 1/4 In. 818.00
Codd, Black, Embossed, 8 1/4 In. 940.00
Codd, Cobalt Blue, Embossed, 7 1/2 In. 4500.00
Codd, Emerald Green, Embossed, Bulb Neck, 6 3/4 In. 1023.00
Codd, Green, Embossed, 9 1/4 In. 123.00
Codd, Olive Green, Embossed, 9 In. 307.00

Mineral Water,
Artesian Spring Co.,
Ballston, N.Y., Olive
Yellow, Applied
Collar, Pt., 8 In.

Mineral Water,
Champion Spouting
Spring, Saratoga, N.Y.,
Monogram, Aqua, Pt.

Mineral Water, Clarke
& Co., New York,
Emerald Green,
Double Collar, IP, Pt.

Codd, Olive Green, Embossed, Rearing Horse, 8 3/4 In. 614.00
Coldbrook Medicinal Spring Water, Yellow Amber, 1860-80, Qt. 560.00
Congress & Empire Spring Co., Blue Green, Sloping Double Collar, Qt. 45.00
Congress & Empire Spring Co., C, Blue Green, Applied Double Collar, Qt. 55.00
Congress & Empire Spring Co., C, Emerald Green, Applied Collar, Pt. 825.00
Congress & Empire Spring Co., C, Olive Green, Double Collar, Pt. 78.00
Congress & Empire Spring Co., C, Olive Green, Double Collar, Qt. ....88.00 to 146.00
Congress & Empire Spring Co., C, Olive Yellow, Double Collar, Qt. ....*Illus* 200.00
Congress & Empire Spring Co., E, Emerald Green, Qt. 66.00
Congress & Empire Spring Co., E, Red Amber, Double Collar, Qt. 364.00
Congress & Empire Spring Co., E, Yellow Amber, Applied Double Collar, Qt. 66.00
Congress & Empire Spring Co., Emerald Green, Applied Top, Pt. 88.00
Congress & Empire Spring Co., Emerald Green, Double Collar, Pt. 1120.00
Congress & Empire Spring Co., Emerald Green, Qt., 9 1/4 In. 11.00
Congress & Empire Spring Co., Emerald Green, Tapered Shoulder, Qt. 69.00
Congress & Empire Spring Co., Green, Qt., 9 1/2 In. 110.00
Congress & Empire Spring Co., Hotchkiss' Sons, C, Emerald Green, Double Collar, Qt. .. 157.00
Congress & Empire Spring Co., Hotchkiss' Sons, C, Emerald, Applied Collar, Pt. . . .90.00 to 110.00
Congress & Empire Spring Co., Hotchkiss' Sons, C, Olive Green, Double Collar, Pt. .56.00 to 80.00
Congress & Empire Spring Co., Hotchkiss' Sons, C, Olive Yellow, Double Collar, Pt. 132.00
Congress & Empire Spring Co., Hotchkiss' Sons, C, Olive Yellow, Applied Collar, Pt. ... 95.00
Congress & Empire Spring Co., Hotchkiss' Sons, E, Emerald Green, Double Collar, Qt. ... 235.00
Congress & Empire Spring Co., Hotchkiss' Sons, E, Olive Yellow, Double Collar, Pt. 410.00
Congress & Empire Spring Co., Hotchkiss' Sons, E, Red Amber, Double Collar, Pt. 476.00
Congress & Empire Spring Co., Hotchkiss' Sons, Emerald Green, Qt. 104.00
Congress & Empire Spring Co., Teal Blue Green, Qt. 79.00
Congress & Empire Spring Co., Yellow Olive, 9 1/2 In. 248.00
Congress Spring Co., C, Emerald Green, Pt. ....22.00 to 44.00
Congress Water, Olive Green, Applied Sloping Double Collar, Qt. ....245.00 to 308.00
Congress Water, Olive Yellow, Sloping Double Collar, Cylindrical, 1850-60, Qt. 448.00
Cooper's Well Water, Miss., B.G. Co., Amber, Double Collar, Qt., 9 3/4 In. 78.00
Cooper's Well Water, Miss., B.G. Co., Medium Orange Amber, Applied Collar, Pt. 70.00
Crystal Springs, Sunderlin & Snook, Yellow Amber, Applied Double Collar, Pt. 2090.00
D.A. Knowlton, Saratoga, N.Y., Olive Green, Sloping Double Collar, Qt. ....179.00 to 202.00
D.A. Knowlton, Saratoga, N.Y., Red Amber, Applied Double Collar, Qt., 9 1/8 In. 880.00
Darien Mineral Springs, Tifft & Perry, Darien Centre, N.Y., Aqua, Pt. 448.00
Dawson, Norwich, Olive Green, Codd, Embossed, 9 In. 133.00
De Snelle Sprong, Aqua, Dumpy, Codd, Embossed, 7 1/4 In. 61.00
De Snelle Sprong, Emerald Green, Dumpy, Codd, Embossed, 7 1/4 In. 164.00
De Snelle Sprong, Green, Dumpy, Codd, Embossed, 7 1/4 In. 143.00
Deep Rock Spring, Oswego, N.Y., Aqua, Applied Sloping Double Collar, Pt. 125.00
Deep Rock Spring, Oswego, N.Y., Blue Aqua, Applied Sloping Double Collar, Qt. .135.00 to 308.00
Deep Rock Spring, Oswego, N.Y., City Bottling Works, Toledo, O., Blue Aqua, Pt. 90.00
Dyottville Glass Works, Philada., Cobalt Blue, Blob Top, 7 1/2 In. 78.00
E. McIntire, Patent, Green, Tapered Top, Iron Pontil, 1840-50, 6 7/8 In. 1430.00
Eagle, Shield, Crossed Flags, Cobalt Blue, Applied Collar, Iron Pontil, 7 1/4 In. 560.00
Eureka Spring, Saratoga, N.Y., Blue Aqua, 1860-70, 9 In. 364.00
Eureka Spring, Saratoga, N.Y., Emerald Green, 9 In. 728.00
Excelsior Spring, Saratoga, N.Y., Amber, Pt. 336.00
Excelsior Spring, Saratoga, N.Y., Blue Green, Applied Double Collar, Pt., 7 7/8 In. . .56.00 to 90.00
Excelsior Spring, Saratoga, N.Y., Emerald Green, Pt. ....120.00 to 135.00
Excelsior Spring, Saratoga, N.Y., Olive Yellow Amber, Pt. 123.00
Excelsior Spring, Saratoga, N.Y., Olive Yellow Green, Applied Collar, Pt., 7 7/8 In. 100.00
Excelsior Spring, Saratoga, N.Y., Teal Blue, Applied Double Collar, Pt., 7 7/8 In. 300.00
Farmville Lithia, Woman Standing At Spring, Aqua, Tooled Mouth, 1/2 Gal. 336.00
Fonticello, Chesterfield Co., Va, Blue Aqua, Tooled Lip, 10 3/8 In. 90.00
Franklin Spring, Ballston Spa, Saratoga, N.Y., Olive Green, Double Collar, Pt. 118.00
G. Hill, Aerated Water, Manufacturer, Wombwell, Codd, Amber, 9 In. 200.00
G. Ludwig, Chambersburg, Blue Green, Slug Plate, Blob Top, Iron Pontil, 7 1/2 In. 308.00
G. Muhlhauser, Cincinnati, Oh., Ice Blue, Blob Top, Iron Pontil, 7 3/8 In. 308.00
G. Sidebotham, Philad A., Blue Green, Iron Pontil 120.00
G.A. Kohl, Blue Green, Blob Top, Pontil, 1850-60, 7 3/8 In. 330.00
G.A. Kohl, Easton, Pa., Green, Squat, Double Taper Top, Iron Pontil, 7 1/2 In. 495.00

Mineral Water,
Congress & Empire
Spring Co., C, Olive
Yellow, Double
Collar, Qt.

Mineral Water, Highrock
Congress Spring, 1767,
C & W, Saratoga, N.Y.,
Red Amber, Qt.

Mineral Water,
J. Esposito, Philada.,
Yellow, Tooled Mouth,
1890-1910, 7 3/4 In.

G.H. Goundie, Allentown, Pa., Yellow Green, Squat, Blob Top, 6 3/4 In.	165.00
G.H. Lyford & Co., Green, Cylindrical, Collared Mouth, Iron Pontil, 1/2 Pt.	448.00
G.S. Cushing, Lowell, Patent, Pentucket, Teal Blue Green, Squat, Blob Top	45.00
G.S. Smart, Alnwick, Redfearn Bros., Emerald Green, Codd, 9 1/4 In.	69.00
G.W. Weston & Co., Saratoga, N.Y., Olive Green, Applied Double Collar, Qt.	210.00
G.W. Weston & Co., Saratoga, N.Y., Olive Green, Sloping Double Collar, Pontil, Pt.	200.00
G.W. Weston & Co., Saratoga, N.Y., Olive Green, Sloping Double Collar, Qt.	112.00 to 123.00
G.W. Weston & Co., Saratoga, N.Y., Olive Yellow, Applied Sloping Collar, Pontil, Pt.	224.00
Gardner & Landon, Sharon, Sulphur Water, Yellow Green, Pontil, c.1865, Qt.	4480.00
Geo. W. Felix's, Cobalt Blue, Squat, c.1855, 7 1/4 In.	2200.00
Gettysburg Katalysine Water, Emerald Green, Applied Sloping Double Collar, Qt.	.78.00 to 135.00
Gettysburg Katalysine Water, Olive Yellow, Sloping Double Collar, Qt.	134.00
Geyser Springs, Aqua, Pt.	45.00
Glaceier Spouting Spring, Saratoga Springs, N.Y., Aqua, Double Collar, Pt.	2800.00 to 3585.00
Gleason & Cole, Pittsbg., Cobalt Blue, 10-Sided, Sloping Collar, Pontil, 7 3/4 In.	952.00
Guilford Mineral Spring Water, Guilford, Vt., Blue Green, Applied Sloping Collar, Qt.	110.00
Guilford Mineral Spring Water, Guilford, Vt., Blue Green, Double Collar, Qt.	146.00
Guilford Mineral Spring Water, Guilford, Vt., Emerald Green, Applied Lip, Qt.	82.00
Guilford Mineral Spring Water, Guilford, Vt., Light Emerald Green, Qt., 9 1/2 In.	66.00
Guilford Mineral Spring Water, Guilford, Vt., Teal Green, Qt.	297.00
Hamilton & Church, Brooklyn, Teal Blue, 8-Sided, Slug Plate, Iron Pontil, 7 1/4 In.	825.00
Hansard Genuine Aerated Waters Merthyr, Aqua, Glass Bullet Stopper	20.00
Hathorn Spring, Saratoga, N.Y., Black Amber, Double Collar, 1875-85, Pt., 7 1/4 In.	45.00
Hathorn Spring, Saratoga, N.Y., Black Glass, Applied Sloping Double Collar, Qt.	95.00
Hathorn Spring, Saratoga, N.Y., Emerald Green, Applied Sloping Double Collar, Pt.	95.00
Hathorn Spring, Saratoga, N.Y., Honey Amber, Pt.	17.00
Hathorn Spring, Saratoga, N.Y., Orange Amber, Double Collar, Qt.	39.00
Hathorn Spring, Saratoga, N.Y., Yellow Amber, Qt., 9 3/8 In.	45.00
Hathorn Spring, Saratoga, N.Y., Yellow Green, Pt.	29.00
Healing Springs, Bath County, Va., Blue Green, Tooled Lip, 1880-1890, 1/2 Gal.	1456.00
Heiss' Superior, Cobalt Blue, 10-Sided, Sloping Collar, Pontil, 7 5/8 In.	308.00
Highrock Congress Spring, 1767, C & W, Saratoga, N.Y., Amber, Double Collar, Qt.	308.00
Highrock Congress Spring, 1767, C & W, Saratoga, N.Y., Olive Yellow Amber, Pt.	200.00
Highrock Congress Spring, 1767, C & W, Saratoga, N.Y., Red Amber, Qt. *Illus*	300.00
Highrock Congress Spring, 1767, C & W, Saratoga, N.Y., Root Beer Amber, Qt.	179.00
Highrock Congress Spring, 1767, C & W, Saratoga, N.Y., Teal Blue, Pt.	190.00
Highrock Congress Spring, 1767, C & W, Saratoga, N.Y., Yellow Green, Pt.	258.00
Highrock Congress Spring, 1767, C & W, Saratoga, N.Y., Yellow Green, Qt.	123.00
Highrock Congress Spring, 1767, C & W, Saratoga, N.Y., Yellow Tobacco Amber, Pt.	200.00
Highrock Congress Spring, C & W, Saratoga, N.Y., Emerald Green, Pt., 8 In.	168.00
Highrock Congress Spring, C & W, Saratoga, N.Y., Olive Yellow, Pt.	155.00
Highrock Congress Spring, C & W, Saratoga, N.Y., Teal Blue, Pt.	157.00
Highrock Congress Spring, C & W, Teal Blue, Sloping Collar, 1860-80, Pt.	1064.00
Hopkins Chalybeate, Baltimore, Blue Green, Applied Sloping Collar, Pt.	80.00
Hopkins Chalybeate, Baltimore, Olive Amber, Applied Collar, Iron Pontil, Pt., 7 1/2 In.	110.00
Hopkins Chalybeate, Baltimore, Olive Yellow Green, Double Collar, Iron Pontil, Pt.	123.00

Hopkins Chalybeate, Baltimore, Olive Yellow, Applied Collar, IP, Pt., 7 3/8 In. 255.00
Hubbell, Philad'a, Olive Yellow, Applied Mouth, Pt., 7 5/8 In. 660.00
Hutchinson & Co., Celebrated, Cobalt Blue, Applied Mouth, Iron Pontil, 7 1/4 In. 448.00
Improved, Cobalt Blue, 8-Sided, Applied Blob Top, Iron Pontil, 7 In. 336.00
Iodine Spring Water, L, South Hero, Vt., Golden Amber, Cylindrical, 1860-70, Qt. 1680.00
Iodine Spring Water, Olive Amber, Sloping Collar, Qt. 2100.00
Iodine Spring Water, Orange Amber, Embossed, Stoddard, c.1860, Qt. 2175.00
Ira Harvey, Prov., R.I., Cobalt Blue, Sloping Collar, Iron Pontil, 7 In. 146.00
J & A Dearborn, New York, Cobalt Blue, 8-Sided, Blob Top, Pontil, 6 7/8 In. 880.00
J & A Dearborn, New York, Cobalt Blue, 8-Sided, Iron Pontil, 7 In. 392.00
J & A Dearborn, New York, Sapphire Blue, 8-Sided, Iron Pontil, 1840-60, 7 In 235.00
J. & T. Percey, Philada, Blue Green, Applied Blob Top, Iron Pontil, 7 1/4 In. 504.00
J. Boardman & Co., Star, Cobalt Blue, 8-Sided, Iron Pontil, 1840-60, 7 1/2 In. 146.00
J. Corwell, Germantown, Yellow Green, Pontil, Double Taper Top, 7 1/4 In. 825.00
J. Dowdall, Union Glass Works, Cobalt Blue, Slug Plate, Blob Top, IP, 7 3/8 In. 2128.00
J. Esposito, Philada., Yellow, Tooled Mouth, 1890-1910, 7 3/4 In. ....Illus 246.00
J. Marbacher, Easton, Pa., Yellow Green, Squat, 6 1/4 In. 660.00
J. Steel, Easton, Pa., Blue Green, Squat, Double Collar, Iron Pontil, 7 In. 336.00
J. Steel, Easton, Pa., Green, Squat, Embossed, Pontil, 1840-60, 7 1/4 In. 275.00
J. Steel, Easton, Pa., Yellow Green, Squat, Embossed, Blob Top, Pontil, 6 7/8 In. 275.00
J. Steel, Premium, Blue Green, 8-Sided, Applied Blob Top, Iron Pontil, 7 5/8 In. 476.00
J. Steel, Premium, Blue Green, 8-Sided, Slug Plate, Iron Pontil, 1840-60, 7 3/4 In. 300.00
J. Wise, Allentown, Pa., Violet Cobalt Blue, Applied Top, 1870-80, 7 1/4 In. 253.00
J.B. Bryant, Wilmington, Green, Applied Sloping Double Collar, Iron Pontil, 7 In. 784.00
J.H. Magee, Philada, Cobalt Blue, Double Collar, Iron Pontil, 7 3/8 In. 896.00
J.T. Shardlow, Aqua, Embossed, Skittle Codd, 7 1/4 In. 286.00
John & G.J. Postel's, Cincinnati, Blue Aqua, Squat, Tapered Top, Iron Pontil 59.00
John & G.J. Postel's, Cincinnati, O., Blue Aqua, Squat, Blob Top, Iron Pontil 89.00
John Clarke, Forest Green, Sloping Collar, 1860-70, Qt. 560.00
John Clarke, New York, Emerald Green, Sloping Double Collar, Iron Pontil, Pt. 448.00
John Clarke, New York, Olive Amber, Sloping Double Collar, Qt. 213.00
John Clarke, New York, Olive Yellow Green, Sloping Double Collar, Pontil, Qt. 213.00
John H. Gardner & Son, Sharon Springs, N.Y., Teal, Pt. ....Illus 308.00
John Ryan, S1852t, Columbus, Ga., Cobalt Blue, Applied Blob Top, 7 3/4 In. 550.00
Jos. Doudall, Avondale, Blue Green, 8-Sided, Blob Top, Iron Pontil, 7 3/8 In. 3920.00
Kissingen Water, Hanbury Smith, Olive Yellow, Applied Mouth, Pt., 7 3/4 In. 100.00
Kissingen Water, Patterson & Brazeau, Yellow Green, Applied Mouth, Pt., 8 In. 155.00
Kissingen Water, T.H.D., Spa Phila, Olive Yellow, Applied Sloping Collar, 1/2 Pt. 210.00
Kissingen Water, T.H.D., Spa Phila, Olive Yellow, Applied Sloping Double Collar, Pt. ... 365.00
Kissingen Water, T.H.D., Spa Phila, Orange Amber, Applied Mouth, Pt., 7 7/8 In. 275.00
Kissingen Water, T.H.D., Spa Phila, Yellow Green, Applied Mouth, 1/2 Pt, 6 3/4 In. 255.00
Knauss & Lichtenwallner, Sapphire, Blob Top, 1870-80, 6 7/8 In. 523.00
Lamoille Spring, Milton, Vt., Golden Amber, Cylindrical, 1860-70, Qt. 2016.00
Lauer & Brand, Louisville, Ky., Blue Aqua, Applied Mouth, Iron Pontil, 7 1/2 In. 240.00
Londonderry Lithia, Aqua, Label Only, 10 5/8 In. 45.00
Lynch & Clarke, New York, Olive Amber, Double Collar, 3-Piece Mold, Qt. 213.00
Lynch & Clarke, New York, Olive Amber, Sloping Double Collar, Pontil, Pt. 504.00
Lynch & Clarke, New York, Olive Green, Applied Double Collar, Pontil, Pt. 190.00
Lynch & Clarke, New York, Olive Yellow, Applied Double Collar, Pontil, Pt. 67.00
Lynch & Clarke, New York, Olive Yellow, Applied Sloping Collar, Ring, Pontil, Pt. 246.00
Lynch & Clarke, New York, Olive Yellow, Applied Sloping Double Collar, Pontil, Pt. 190.00
Lynch & Clarke, New York, Olive Yellow, Cylindrical, 1823-33, Qt. 1456.00
Lynch & Clarke, New York, Olive Yellow, Double Collar, Pontil, c.1835, Pt. 112.00
M.T. Crawford, Cobalt Blue, Applied Collar, Pontil, 1/2 Pt. 420.00
M.T. Crawford, Sapphire Blue, Collar, Iron Pontil, 1/2 Pt. 532.00
M.T. Quinan, 1884, Savannah, Geo., Cobalt Blue, Squat, Blob Top 159.00
Magnetic Spring, Henniker, N.H., Yellow Amber, Applied Sloping Collar, Qt. ...990.00 to 1008.00
Manchester Coffee Tavern Co., Aqua, Glass Bobbin Stopper, Early 1870s 25.00
Massena Spring Water, Teal Blue, Applied Sloping Double Collar, Qt. ....197.00 to 224.00
Meyer & Rottman, New York, Cobalt Blue, Applied Mouth, Iron Pontil, 7 1/4 In. 190.00
Middletown Healing Springs, A.W. Gray & Son, Emerald Green, Qt. 896.00
Middletown Healing Springs, Grays & Clark, Middletown, Vt., Amber, Qt. 56.00
Middletown Healing Springs, Grays & Clark, Middletown, Vt., Yellow Amber, Qt. 100.00

Middletown Mineral Spring Co., Middletown, Vt., Emerald Green, Qt. . . . . .280.00 to 448.00
Middletown Mineral Spring Co., Nature's Remedy, Middletown, Vt., Green, Qt. . . .90.00 to 100.00
Mineral Water Co., West Stanley, Green, Embossed, Codd, England, c.1910, 7 3/4 In. . . .   35.00
Minnequa, Bradford Co., Pa., Aqua, Applied Sloping Double Collar, Pt. . . . . .157.00 to 255.00
Minnequa, Bradford Co., Pa., Blue Aqua, Applied Double Collar, Qt., 9 5/8 In. 235.00
Minnequa, Bradford Co., Pa., Blue Aqua, Double Collar, Pt. 89.00
Minnequa, Bradford Co., Pa., Medium Orange Amber, Applied Double Collar, Qt. 495.00
Minnequa, Bradford Co., Pa., Orange Amber, Applied Double Collar, Pt., 7 5/8 In. .157.00 to 165.00
Missisquoi A Springs, Blue Green, Sloping Double Collar, 1865-75, Qt. 78.00
Missisquoi A Springs, Blue Green, Sloping Double Collar, Qt. 134.00
Missisquoi A Springs, Olive Green, Qt. 123.00
Missisquoi A Springs, Olive Yellow Green, Sloping Double Collar, Qt. 112.00
Missisquoi A Springs, Squaw & Papoose, Yellow Green, Applied Double Collar, Qt. 448.00
Missisquoi A Springs, Squaw & Papoose, Yellow Olive, Qt., 9 3/8 In. . . . . .350.00 to 448.00
Netherwood & Shaws, Aqua, Embossed, 8 1/2 In. 1443.00
Oak Orchard Acid Springs, G.W. Merchant, Lockport N.Y., Blue Green, Qt. . . . . . . .67.00 to 90.00
Oak Orchard Acid Springs, G.W. Merchant, Lockport, N.Y., Green, Qt. 112.00
Oak Orchard Acid Springs, G.W. Merchant, Lockport. N.Y., Green, Qt. 445.00
Oak Orchard Acid Springs, H.W. Bostwick, Tobacco Amber, Qt. . . . . .78.00 to 134.00
Oldham Aerated Water Co. Limited, Aqua, BIM, Codd, 7 1/4 In. 39.00
P H Cort, Manchester, Aqua, Embossed, Vallets Patent Bullet Stopper 20.00
P. Babb, Balto, Emerald Green, Sloping Collar, Iron Pontil, 7 3/4 In. 235.00
P. Conway Bottler, Philada, Cobalt Blue, Applied Blob Top, Iron Pontil, 7 1/4 In. 112.00
Pacific Congress Springs, Cornflower Blue, Applied Top, 8 In.   770.00
Pacific Congress Water, Saratoga, Ca., Lime Green, Applied Top, 1870s, 8 In. 440.00
Pacific Congress Water, Saratoga, Ca., Running Deer, Green, 1870s, 8 In. 1760.00
Pacific Congress Water, Saratoga, Ca., Running Deer, Yellow Green, Pt. 935.00
Pacific Congress Water, Saratoga, Ca., Yellow Green, Double Collar, Pt. . . . .*Illus* 2240.00
Panacea Mineral Spring Water, Littleton, N.C., Red Amber, 1880-95, 1/2 Gal. 112.00
Pavilion & United States Spring Co., P, Saratoga, N.Y., Olive Yellow, Pt. 112.00
Pavilion & United States Spring Co., Saratoga, N.Y., Blue Green, Pt. 78.00
Pavilion & United States Spring Co., Saratoga, N.Y., Emerald Green, Pt. . . . . .112.00 to 180.00
Pavilion & United States Spring Co., Saratoga, N.Y., Light Teal Green, Pt. 71.00
Pavilion & United States Spring Co., Saratoga, N.Y., Olive Amber, Pt. 146.00
Poland Water, H. Ricker & Sons, Moses, Aqua, Applied Top, 11 In. . . . . .110.00 to 123.00
Poland Water, H. Ricker & Sons, Moses, Aqua, Blob Top, 1870-90, 11 In. 88.00
Quaker Springs, I.W. Meader & Co., Saratoga Co., N.Y., Blue Green, Applied Collar, Pt. . . 1650.00
Quaker Springs, I.W. Meader & Co., Saratoga Co., N.Y., Teal Blue, Qt. 728.00
R. White, Camberwell, Aqua, Amber Lip, Codd, 7 1/4 In. 92.00
R. White, Camberwell, Aqua, Amber Lip, Codd, 9 1/4 In. 56.00
R. White, Camberwell, Aqua, Red Amber Lip, Codd, 9 1/4 In. 50.00
Rock Bridge, Virginia, Alum Water, Blue Aqua, Cylindrical, Embossed, 9 1/2 In. 79.00
Rock Bridge, Virginia, Alum Water, Blue Green, 1/2 Gal. 448.00
Roussel's, Manufactured In Silver, Dyottville, Blue Green, Pontil, 7 1/2 In. 146.00
S. Keys, Burlington, N.J., Cobalt Blue, Blob Top, Iron Pontil, 7 1/2 In. 728.00
Saratoga A Spring Co., N.Y., Blue Green, Applied Double Collar, Pt. 125.00
Saratoga A Spring Co., N.Y., Olive Yellow, Applied Double Collar, Pt., 8 In. 715.00

Mineral Water, John
H. Gardner & Son,
Sharon Springs, N.Y.,
Teal, Pt.

Mineral Water, Pacific
Congress Water,
Saratoga, Ca., Yellow
Green, Double Collar, Pt.

Mineral Water, Star
Spring Co., Saratoga,
N.Y., Amber, Applied
Sloping Double
Collar, Pt.

Saratoga A Spring Co., N.Y., Olive Yellow, Sloping Double Collar, Qt. 90.00
Saratoga A Spring Co., N.Y., Yellow Green, Double Collar, Pt. ....168.00 to 258.00
Saratoga High Rock Spring, C & W, Saratoga, N.Y., Teal Blue, Pt., 7 3/4 In. 2420.00
Saratoga Red Spring, Blue Green, Qt. 230.00
Saratoga Red Spring, Emerald Green, 1865-75, Pt. 90.00
Saratoga Red Spring, Emerald Green, Applied Sloping Double Collar, Pt. 56.00
Saratoga Red Spring, Emerald Green, Applied Sloping Double Collar, Qt. 134.00
Saratoga Star Spring, Amber, Applied Sloping Collar, 1862-89, Qt. 88.00
Saratoga Star Spring, Amber, Stoddard, Qt. 100.00
Saratoga Star Spring, Backward S, Olive Green, Double Collar, Qt. 112.00
Saratoga Star Spring, Blue Green, Applied Double Collar, Bail Closure, Qt. 165.00
Saratoga Star Spring, Dark Amber, Pt. 140.00
Saratoga Star Spring, Emerald Green, Applied Sloping Double Collar, Pt. 123.00
Saratoga Star Spring, Emerald Green, Applied Sloping Double Collar, Qt. 179.00
Saratoga Star Spring, Light Amber, Stoddard, 7 1/2 In. 138.00
Saratoga Star Spring, Olive Green, Applied Double Collar, Pt. 550.00
Saratoga Star Spring, Red Amber, Stoddard, Qt. 139.00
Saratoga Star Spring, Tobacco Amber, Applied Sloping Double Collar, Pt. 123.00
Saratoga Vichy Spouting Spring, V, Saratoga, N.Y., Aqua, Collar, 2/3 Pt., 7 5/8 In. ... 2640.00
Saratoga Vichy Spouting Spring, V, Saratoga, N.Y., Aqua, Qt., 9 3/8 In. 245.00
Saratoga Vichy Spouting Spring, V, Saratoga, N.Y., Blue Aqua, Double Collar, Pt. 45.00
Saratoga Vichy Spouting Spring, V, Saratoga, N.Y., Blue Aqua, Double Collar, Qt. 112.00
Saratoga Vichy Spouting Spring, V, Saratoga, N.Y., Yellow Amber, Double Collar, Qt. ... 245.00
Scarborough Whitby, Emerald Green, Embossed, 9 In. 205.00
Seitz & Bro., Easton, Pa., Cobalt Blue, 8-Sided, Blob Top, 7 1/4 In. 235.00
Seitz & Bro., Easton, Pa., Cobalt Blue, Blob Top, Iron Pontil, 7 1/4 In. 179.00
Shasta Water, Orange Amber, Tooled Crown, 9 1/2 In. 20.00
Sheldon A Spring, Vt., Red Amber, Applied Double Collar, Qt., 9 3/4 In. 1870.00
Sheldon A Spring, Vt., Tobacco Amber, Sloping Double Collar, Qt. 1568.00
Silver Spring, Barrett & Elers Patent, Codd, Internal Screw, 9 1/4 In. 470.00
Silver Springs Water Company, Detroit, Triangular Shape, c.1900, 11 x 4 1/2 In. 60.00
Smith Spencer Limited, Prize Medal, Stratford On Avon, Siphon, 13 1/4 In. 53.00
Spencer Connor & Co., Manchester, Aqua, Codd, Pear Shape Marble, 9 In. 25.00
St. Leon Spring Water, Earl W. Johnson, Boston, Teal Green, Wicker Cover, Qt. 672.00
Star Spring Co., Saratoga, N.Y., Amber, 1862-89, Pt. 120.00
Star Spring Co., Saratoga, N.Y., Amber, Applied Sloping Double Collar, Pt. .... *Illus* 90.00
Star Spring Co., Saratoga, N.Y., Amber, Stoddard, Pt. 33.00
Star Spring Co., Saratoga, N.Y., Amber, X, Stoddard, Pt. 156.00
Star Spring Co., Saratoga, N.Y., Blue Green, Applied Double Collar, Pt. 235.00
Star Spring Co., Saratoga, N.Y., Olive Yellow, Stoddard, Pt. 134.00
Star Spring Co., Saratoga, N.Y., Orange Amber, Applied Double Collar, Pt. 145.00
Star Spring Co., Saratoga, N.Y., Red Amber, Pt. 280.00
Star Spring Co., Saratoga, N.Y., Tobacco Amber, Applied Double Collar, Pt. 155.00
Stirlings Magnetic, Eaton Rapids, Mich., Amber, Double Collar, Qt. 896.00
Stirlings Magnetic, Eaton Rapids, Mich., Red Amber, Qt. 605.00
Stretton Hills, Green Aqua, Torpedo, England, 1880-90, 9 1/8 In. 67.00
Syracuse Springs, D, Excelsior, A.J. Delatour, New York, Chocolate Amber, Pt. 935.00
Syracuse Springs, Excelsior, Red Amber, Double Collar, Pt. 134.00
Syracuse Springs, Excelsior, Yellow Amber, Double Collar, Pt. 308.00
Syracuse Springs, Excelsior, Yellow Amber, Double Collar, Qt. 258.00
T.S. Waterman, 11 St. Paul St., N.O., Aqua, Applied Lip, Pontil, 7 1/4 In. 280.00
T.W. Gillett, New Haven, Cobalt Blue, 8-Sided, Applied Blob Top, Pontil, 7 5/8 In. 336.00
T.W. Gillett, New Haven, Teal, 8-Sided, Blob Top, 1840-60, 7 1/4 In. 935.00
Union Glass Works, Phila., Cobalt Blue, Cylindrical, Applied Collar, Pontil, 1/2 Pt. .. 190.00
Union Glass Works, Philada, Teal, Applied Blob Top, Iron Pontil, 7 3/8 In. ......168.00 to 175.00
United Mineral Water Co., Binghampton, N.Y., Crown Top, Qt. 29.00
V. Castner & Co., Changewater, N.J., Apple Green, Sloping Double Collar, 6 3/4 In. ... 179.00
Vermont Spring, Saxe & Co., Sheldon, Vt., Green, Qt. 104.00
Vermont Spring, Saxe & Co., Sheldon, Vt., Olive Yellow, Applied Double Collar, Qt. ... 145.00
Vermont Spring, Saxe & Co., Sheldon, Vt., Yellow Amber, Double Collar, Qt. 784.00
Vermont Spring, Saxe & Co., Sheldon, Vt., Yellow Olive, Applied Collar, Ring, Qt. ... 560.00
Vichy Water, Hanbury Smith, Yellow Amber Olive, Applied Sloping Collar, Pt. 145.00
Virginia Arsenic, Bromine & Lithia, Monogram, WW, Amethyst, 1/2 Gal. 202.00

W. Coughlan, Baltimore, Blue Green, Sloping Collar, Iron Pontil, 6 5/8 In. 784.00
W. Eagle, New York, Superior, Cobalt Blue, Applied Mouth, IP, 1840-60, 7 3/8 In. 168.00
W. Heiss Jr's, Cobalt Blue, Pontil, Blob Top, 1840-60, 7 1/4 In. 4400.00
W.C. Chamberlin, Lancaster, Pa., Blue Green, Iron Pontil, 7 1/2 In. 100.00
Wadsworth, Cambridge, Premier Patent, Aqua, Cobalt Blue Lip, Codd, 7 1/4 In. 360.00
Wadsworth, St. Ives, Hunts, Aqua, Cobalt Blue Lip, Codd, 8 In. 400.00
Wadsworth, St. Ives, Hunts, Aqua, Red Amber Lip, Codd, 8 In. 42.00
Washington Lithia Well, Ballston Spa, N.Y., Blue Aqua, Double Collar, Pt. 308.00
Washington Spring, Saratoga, N.Y., Emerald Green, 1865-75, Pt. 246.00
Washington Spring, Saratoga, N.Y., Emerald Green, Sloping Double Collar, Pt. 157.00
Washington Spring Co., Ballston Spa, N.Y., Bust Of Washington, Blue Green, Pt. 336.00
White Rock Mineral Springs Water, Waukesha, Wis., Amber, Crown Top, Pt. 6.50
White Rock Sparkling, Cobalt Blue, Psyche At Nature's Mirror, Twist Cap, Pt. 8.50
White Sulphur Springs, Greenbrier, W. Va., Aqua Blue, Qt. 560.00
White Sulphur Springs, Greenbrier, W. Va., Yellow Amber, Qt. 1008.00
William Clarke's, Providence, R.I., Aqua, Torpedo, Wire Closure, 8 1/2 In. 616.00
William H. Baxter, Haslingden, Green, England, Early 1900s, 7 1/2 In. 35.00
Willis & Ripley, Portsmouth, Sapphire Blue, Pontil, Sloping Collar, 7 3/8 In. 560.00
Wm. Betz & Co., Pittsbg, Blue Olive, 10-Sided, Sloping Collar, Iron Pontil, 7 3/4 In. ...   213.00
Wm. Heiss Jr., Cobalt Blue, 8-Sided, Sloping Collar, Pontil, 7 3/8 In. 560.00
Wm. P. Davis & Co., Excelsior, Cobalt Blue, 8-Sided, Blob Top, c.1850, 7 1/2 In. 179.00
Wm. W. Lappeus, Premium, Albany, Aqua, 10-Sided, Applied Collar, Pontil, 1/2 Pt. 560.00
Wm. W. Lappeus, Premium, Albany, Cobalt Blue, 10-Sided, Blob Top, 7 1/8 In. 476.00
Wm. W. Lappeus, Premium, Albany, Cobalt Blue, 10-Sided, Iron Pontil, 7 1/4 In. 840.00

──────────────── MINIATURE ────────────────

Most of the major modern liquor companies that make full-sized decanters and bottles
quickly learned that miniature versions sell well too. Some modern miniatures are listed
in this book by brand name. There are also many older miniature bottles that were made
as give-aways. Most interesting of these are the small motto jugs that name a liquor or
bar, and the comic figural bottles. Collectors sometimes specialize in glass animal
miniatures, beer bottles, whiskey bottles, or other types. Interested collectors can join
the Lilliputian Bottle Club, 12732 E. Charlwood St., Cerritos, CA 90703-6052, or sub-
scribe to *Miniature Bottle Collector,* PO Box 2161, Palos Verdes, CA 90274.

1870 Brown Foreman, Flask, Kentucky Straight Bourbon Whiskey, 1937 ....   5.00
Baltimore Pure Rye, Flask, Alaska Tax Stamp 18.00
Buxton Rye, Flask, Maryland Tax Stamp, Oct. 1938 ....   20.00
Champagne, Bottle, Florida, Epernay, Green Opaque, France, 6 3/8 In. 20.00
Crown Royal, Flask, 166 ....   5.00
Detrick Distilling Co., While We Live, Let Us Live, Dayton, O., Off-White, Brown 40.00
Four Roses, Flask, Scotch Whiskey, Blended 10.00
Four Roses American, Blended Whiskey 10.00
Glenmore, Flask, Wisconsin Tax Stamp 10.00
Goold's Fruit Punch, Off-White, Brown, Handles, 5 3/8 In. 75.00
Grand Sire, Flask, Maryland Tax Stamp, Jan. 1937 ....   18.00
John Paul Jones Four Star, Whiskey Blend, Round 4.00
Jug, Fawn, 2-Tone, 1880 ....   100.00
Jug, If You Are Dry, See Sam Yost, 2-Tone, Glass City Pottery 100.00
Lincoln Inn, Flask, Maryland Tax Stamp, 1938 ....   18.00
Old Drum, Flask, Maryland Tax Stamp, 1938 ....   15.00
Old Fiddle, Kentucky Blended Bourbon Whiskey, Fiddle, 5 Year 14.00
Old International Sour Mash, Jug, Brown 75.00
Old Methusalem, Maryland Tax Stamp, 1938 ....   22.00
Old Overholt Rye, Maryland Tax Stamp, 1837 ....   11.00
Old Quaker, Flask, Illinois Tax Stamp, 1937 ....   15.00
Schenley's Red Label, Flask, Illinois Tax Stamp 7.00
Seagram's Ancient Rye, Square, Maryland Tax Stamp 18.00
Seagram's VO Canadian, Flask, 6 Year Old, 1932 ....   12.00
Sunnybrook, Flask, Minnesota Tax Stamp 10.00
Town Tavern, Flask, Illinois Tax Stamp, 1938 ....   15.00
Twin Seal Rye, Flask 5.00
Waterfill & Frazier, Flask 5.00
MR. BOSTON, see Old Mr. Boston

NAILSEA TYPE

The intricate glass called *Nailsea* was made in the Bristol district of England from 1788 to 1873. The glass included loopings of white or colored glass worked in patterns. The characteristic look of Nailsea was copied and what is called Nailsea today is really Nailsea type made in England or even America. Nailsea gemel bottles are of particular interest to collectors.

Backbar, Clear, White Looping, Applied Neck Ring, Stopper, Brandy, 12 1/2 In.	725.00
Bellows, Cranberry, White Looping, Rigaree, Neck Rings, Pedestal Base, 13 3/4 In.	364.00
Flask, 12 Ribs, Swirled To Right, Red, Yellow, Pontil, Tooled Lip, 7 In.	224.00
Flask, Aqua, Dark Puce Looping, Tooled Lip, Pontil, 6 7/8 In.	90.00
Flask, Blue, White Looping, 7 1/4 In.	44.00
Flask, Clear, Cobalt Blue Looping, Tooled Lip, Pontil, 6 3/4 In.	80.00
Flask, Clear, Opalescent Loops, Applied Rigaree On Sides, Tooled Lip, Pontil, 8 1/8 In.	100.00
Flask, Clear, Pink, White Lopping, Tooled Lip, Pontil, 8 3/4 In.	150.00
Flask, Clear, White & Blue Alternating Looping, Shaped Sides, Pontil, 7 1/4 In.	336.00
Flask, Clear, White Opalescent Looping, 6 1/2 In., Pt.	44.00
Flask, Cranberry Opalescent, Alternating With White Looping, Pontil, 6 7/8 In.	160.00
Flask, Cranberry, 11 In.	66.00
Flask, Light Turquoise, Opalescent Looping, Tooled Lip, Pontil, 1870-1900, 7 3/8 In.	190.00
Flask, Pink & White Looping, 8 In.	220.00
Flask, Violet, White Spiral, Tooled Lip, Pontil, 7 In.	168.00
Flask, White, Red Looping, 7 1/4 In.	72.00
Flask, Yellow Amber, White Looping, Tooled Lip, Pontil, 5 3/8 In.	308.00
Jug, Olive Amber, White Splotches, Applied Mouth & Handle, Pontil, 1820-40, 10 1/4 In.	525.00
Teardrop, Cranberry, White & Pink Looping, Screw-On Lid, Pontil, 7 1/8 In.	336.00
Utility, Olive Green, White Splotches, Tooled Lip, Pontil, 1810-40, 5 1/4 In.	510.00

NURSING

Pottery nursing bottles were used by 1500 B.C. If a bottle was needed, one was improvised, and stone, metal, wood, and pottery, as well as glass bottles were made through the centuries. A glass bottle was patented by Charles Windship of Roxbury, Massachusetts, in 1841. Its novel design suggested that the bottle be placed over the breast to try to fool the baby into thinking the milk came from the mother. By 1864 the most common nursing bottle was a nipple attached to a glass tube in a cork that was put into a glass bottle. Unfortunately, it was impossible to clean and was very unsanitary. The nursing bottle in use today was made possible by the development of an early 1900s rubber nipple.

Nursing bottles are easily identified by the unique shape and the measuring units that are often marked on the sides. Some early examples had engraved designs and silver nipples but most are made of clear glass and rubber. There is a collectors club, The American Collectors of Infant Feeders, 331 Edenwood N., Jackson, TN 38301, and a publication called *Keeping Abreast.* A reference book, *A Guide to American Nursing Bottles* by Diane Rouse Ostrander, is out of print.

A1 Hygienic Feeder, Clear, Tablespoon & Ounce Graduations	30.00
Acme, Star, Embossed, Graduations	16.50
Allenbury, Semi-Banana Shape, Graduations On Base, c.1890	50.00
Armstrong's, Horizontal Ribbing, Flattened Side, Ounce & Cubic Centimeter Lines	20.00
Baby Doll Nurser, Scale, Dog Begging, ABM, 2 3/4 In.	10.00
Baby Feeder, Ceramic, Blue, White Flowers, 7 1/2 In.	573.00
Baby Feeder, Ceramic, Blue, White Transfer, Meadow, Cows, Farmhouse, Trees, 6 1/4 In.	737.00
Baby Feeder, Ceramic, Blue, White, Flowers, Birds, Fruit, 7 1/4 In.	512.00
Baby Feeder, Ceramic, White Glaze, Brown Transfer, Oriental Scenes, 6 3/4 In.	737.00
Baby-All Natural Nurser, All For The Baby, Screw-On Nipple Cap, Graduations, 8 Oz.	20.00
Crown, HMB, Aqua, Turtle Shape, 1870-80	45.00
Dr. Doyles, Anti-Colic, Santory Pat. Oct. 14th 08, Physicians Specialties, Pittsburgh, Pa.	350.00
Favorite, Kinona Co., New York, Clear Turtle, BIM, Tooled Lip, Screw Cap	500.00
Gotham Co., N.Y., Pat'd Sep.1, 91, Clear, Turtle Type, Elongated Neck	60.00
Graduated Nursing Bottle, Embossed, Graduations, Late 1800s, 6 1/2 x 3 In.	19.00
Green, Pontil, 6 3/4 In.	33.00
Grip-Tight, Curved, Embossed, Box, Pre-1910, 7 In.	135.00
Hughes Chemist Altrincham, Aqua, Turtle Shape	45.00
Hygienic Feeder, Clear, Banana Or Boat	35.00

Medallion, S Burr & Co. Proprietors, Boston, Embossed, Woman's Head, Aqua, 5 3/4 In. . 6.00
O.K. Nurser, Embossed, Oval, Multisided, Graduations, 1890s, 6 1/2 In. 45.00
Savars, Embossed 45.00
Standard Nurser, Embossed, Ounce Graduations, Late 1800s, 5 3/4 x 3 3/4 In. 21.00
Vita Flo, Wide Mouth, Embossed, Pyramid Rubber Co., Ohio, 1937 Patent, 6 1/2 In. 12.00

--- OBR ---
Old Blue Ribbon, or OBR, bottles were made from 1969 to about 1974.

Football Player, No. 7, Black, Gold, 1972 .... 17.00
Football Player, No. 7, Green, Gold, Box, 1972 .... 61.00
Hot Air Balloon, 1969 .... 10.50

--- OIL ---
Motor oil, battery oil, and sewing machine and lubricating oils were all sold in bottles.
Any bottle that has the word *oil* either embossed in the glass or on the paper label falls
in this category. A battery jar has straight sides and an open top. It was filled with a
chemical solution. The jars were usually made with a zinc plate or a copper plate plus
a suspended carbon plate. With the proper connections the chemicals and metals gen-
erated an electric current. Many companies made batteries that included glass jars, and
the jars are now appearing at bottle shows. In the Edison battery, the solution was covered with a special protective layer of oil which kept it from evaporating. Edison battery oil jars, dating from about 1889, were specially made to hold the protective oil and
can still be found.

Amoco Motor Oil, Spout, Chicago, Qt. 31.00
Brookins, Cincinnati, Ohio, Embossed, Brookins Spout, Cap, 13 3/4 In. 36.00
Cocoanut, Aqua, Hair Tonic, Open Pontil, Marked, 6 In. 90.00
Cocoanut, C. Toppan, Aqua, Figure 8 Shape, Applied Top 27.00
Edison Battery Oil, Made In U.S.A., Thomas A. Edison, Bloomfield, N.J., 4 Oz., 4 In. 10.00
Edison Diamond Oil, T.A. Edison Inc., Orange, N.J., 1920s, 3 In. 12.00
Esso, Embossed, ABM, Cylindrical, 18-Sided, Pt., 12 In. 54.00
Esso, Embossed, ABM, Cylindrical, 22-Sided, Qt., 15 In. 69.00
Esso Extra Motor Oil, ACL, ABM, Cylindrical, 22-Sided, London, Qt., 15 In. 69.00
Esso Extra Motor Oil, ACL, Cylindrical, 18-Sided, London, Pt., 12 In. 54.00
Essolube, Anglo American Oil Co., Clear, ABM, Cylindrical, 22-Sided, Qt., 15 In. 69.00
Fenton, Emerald Crest, No. 7269, 1949-55 .... 200.00
Gargoyle Mobil Filpruf Motor Oil, Metal Dispenser Lid, Square, Qt. 156.00
Howard Products Orange Oil, Spray, Instructions, 16 Oz. 10.00
Huffman Manufacturing, Dayton, Ohio, Blue & Red ACL, Funnel, Master, Qt. 43.00
Master Mfg. Co., Litchfield, Ill., Metal Funnel, 1926 Patent, Qt., 14 In. .... 25.00 to 33.00
Maytag Motor Oil, Paper Label, Aluminum Measuring Cup, Cap, Partial Contents, Qt. 90.00
Penn Drake Motor Oil, Super, Lid, Paper Label, c.1940, Qt. 21.00
Pfaff Sew Machine Oil, Spanish, Italian & Dutch Label, Germany, c.1862, 4 1/2 In. 15.00
Rawleigh's Sewing Machine Oil, Paper Label, Cap, Contents 3.00
Remington, Rem-Oil, UMC, Embossed, 5 x 1 3/4 In. 110.00
Sewing Machine Oil, S.F. Baker & Co., Keokuk, Iowa, Cork, Label, 35 Cents, 6 3/4 In. .. 15.00
Shell Motor Oil, Canada, 1933, Imperial Qt., 15 1/4 In. 87.00
Shields Harper & Company Motor Oil, Plastic Top, 1930s, Qt. 30.00
Singer Manufg. Co., Sun Purple, BIMAL, Pre 1906, 5 In. 32.00
Singer Sewing Machine, Green & Orange Label, Twist Cap, Partial Contents, 3 Oz. 13.50
Sunbeam Olive Oil, Cruet Style, Stopper, Label, Austin Nichols & Co Inc., N.Y., 6 3/4 In. 14.00
Sunoco, Metal Spout, Front Labels, Qt., 13 5/8 x 4 In. 60.00
Vanda Captiva Bath Oil, Gold Color Cap, Orlando, Florida, 2 Oz. 15.00
Western Electric Co., New York, Battery, Aqua, Ground Lip, Pour Spout, 9 1/4 In. 22.00
White Filtered Stainless Sewing Machine, D.Y. McIvor, Newville, Pa., Label, 4 3/4 In. .. 12.00

--- OLD BARDSTOWN ---
Old Bardstown was made and bottled by the Willit Distilling Company in Bardstown,
Kentucky. Figural bottles were made from about 1977 to 1980. One unusual bottle pic-
tured Foster Brooks, the actor who is best known for his portrayal of drunks.

Delta Queen, 1980 .... 11.00
Foster Brooks, 1978 .... 28.00
Keg With Stand, 1977, 1/2 Gal. 16.00
Razorback Hog, 1979 .... 10.50 to 27.00

Old Commonwealth, Fireman, Modern No. 4, Fallen Comrade, 1982

❦

Check the supports on wall-hung shelves once a year. Eventually a heavy load will cause "creep," the metal brackets will bend, and the shelf will fall.

❦

OLD COMMONWEALTH

Old Commonwealth bottles have been made since 1975 by J.P. Van Winkle and Sons, Louisville, Kentucky. They also put out bottles under the Old Rip Van Winkle label. An apothecary series with university names and other designs such as firemen, coal miners, fishermen, Indians, dogs, horses, or leprechauns was made from 1978 to the present. As few as 1,600 were made of some of these designs. Some of the decanters were made with music box inserts.

Ancient Order Of Hibernian, 150th Anniversary, 1986	159.00
Birds Of Ireland, 1993	29.00
Coins Of Ireland, Box, 1979	29.00
Cottontail Rabbit, 1981	10.50
Dogs Of Ireland, 1980	22.00
Dogs Of Ireland, Box, 1980	30.00
Fireman, Modern No. 2, Nozzle Man, 1983	10.00
Fireman, Modern No. 2, Nozzle Man, Gold, 1983	58.00
Fireman, Modern No. 3, On Call, Boots, Red Hat, 1983	23.00
Fireman, Modern No. 4, Fallen Comrade, 1982 ....*Illus*	21.00
Flowers Of Ireland, Box, 1983	30.00
Horses Of Ireland, 1981	45.00
Irish & The Sea, 1989	24.00
Irish Idyll, 1982	15.50
North Carolina, Bicentennial, 1975	2.00
Ring Of Kerry, 1995	30.00
Sons Of Erin, No. 2, Box, 1978	29.00
Sports Of Ireland, 1987	26.00
St. Patrick's Day Parade, Box, 1984	29.00
Symbols Of Ireland, 1985	22.00
Thoroughbreds, Kentucky, Box, 1977	30.00
Waterfowler, No. 2, Here They Come, 1980	85.00

OLD CROW

Dr. James Crow of Kentucky was a surgeon and chemist from Edinburgh, Scotland. He started practicing medicine but decided to improve the quality of life by distilling corn whiskey instead. In those days, about 1835, whiskey was made by a family recipe with a bit of that and a handful of the other. The results were uneven. Dr. Crow was a scientist and used corn and limestone water to make a whiskey that he put into kegs and jugs. He used charred oak kegs, and the liquid became reddish instead of the clear white of corn liquor. More experiments led to his development of the first bourbon, named after northeastern Kentucky's Bourbon County, which had been named for the French royal family.

Old Crow became a popular product in all parts of the country and was sold to saloons. Salesmen for competing brands would sometimes try to ruin the liquor by putting a snake or nail into the barrel. In 1870, for the first time, bourbon was bottled and sealed at the distillery. The distillery was closed during Prohibition, and when it reopened in 1933, Old Crow was purchased by National Distilleries. That Old Crow would be packaged in a crow-shaped decanter was inevitable, and in 1954 National Distillers Products Corporation of Frankfort, Kentucky, put Old Crow bourbon into a ceramic crow. Again in 1974 a crow decanter was used; this time 16,800 Royal Doulton bottles were made. The bourbon was sold in the 1970s in a series of bottles shaped like light or dark green chess pieces. Jim Beam Brands bought National Distillers in 1987. Old Crow is still made, but not in figural bottles.

Chess Set, Castle, Yellow	4.25
Chess Set, King & Queen, Yellow, Pair	10.00
Chess Set, Pawn	2.00 to 14.00
Crow, 10 In.	25.00
Crow, Plastic, 5 1/2 In.	25.00
Crow, Porcelain, 13 1/2 In.	10.00 to 28.00
Label, Amber, Miniature	12.00

OLD FITZGERALD

In 1908, Julian P. Van Winkle, Sr., and another salesman for W.L. Weller & Sons, liquor wholesaler, bought the Weller company. Later they bought A. Ph. Stitzel Distillery, of Louisville, Kentucky, which had supplied sour-mash whiskey to W.L. Weller & Sons. The Stitzel Weller firm became known as The Old Fitzgerald Distillery. President Van Winkle, Sr., created the Old Rip Van Winkle series just before Prohibition. Van Winkle remained an active distiller until his death in 1965. His son, Julian, Jr., had become president of Stitzel-Weller in 1947. In 1968 the Old Fitzgerald decanter, "Leprechaun Bottle" carried the words *plase God.* The use of "God" was ruled objectionable under Federal law and the decanters were changed to read *prase be.* In 1972, the distillery was sold to Somerset Importers, Ltd., a division of Norton Simon Company, Inc. Somerset Importers continued to market the Old Rip Van Winkle series until 1978, when they sold to J.P. Van Winkle & Son, a distillery created by Julian Van Winkle, Jr., with his son, Julian, III, after the sale of Stitzel-Weller.

J.P. Van Winkle & Son sold whiskey under the new label, Old Commonwealth, and also the Old Rip Van Winkle series. The Van Winkle series of bottles for both brands included only 20 different bottles through 1986.

Esmark purchased Norton Simon in 1984, then sold the Old Fitzgerald label to Distillers of England in 1985, who sold it to Guinness Stout of Ireland in 1986. The last Old Fitzgerald decanter was made in 1989. Guinness Stout has since become Guinness Distillers Worldwide in Edinburgh, and its Louisville distillery is called United Distillers Mfg., Inc.

An out-of-print pamphlet, *Decanter Collector's Guide,* pictures Old Fitzgerald decanters offered between 1951 and 1971. Most are glass in classic shapes. Besides Old Fitzgerald, the distillery made Cabin Still, W.L. Weller, and Rebel Yell bourbons.

American Sons Of St. Patrick, 1976	5.50 to 34.00
Blarney, Irish Toast, Box, 1970	33.00
Colonial, 1969	12.00
Colonial, Box, 1969	*Illus* 33.00
Eagle, Box, 1973	45.00
Fleur-De-Lis, 1962	4.50
Irish Charm, 1977	5.00
Irish Charm, Box, 1977	33.00
Irish Counties, 1973	30.00

Old Fitzgerald, Colonial, Box, 1969

Old Fitzgerald, Rip Van Winkle, 1971

Old Fitzgerald, Irish Luck, 1972

Irish Luck, 1972 ....*Illus*   7.50
Irish Luck, Box, 1972 ....   33.00
Irish Wish, 1975 ....6.00 to 8.00
Irish Wish, Box, 1975 ....   34.00
Leprechaun, Wearin' O' The Green, Praise Be, 1968 ....4.00 to 6.00
Man O' War, 1969 ....   9.25
Monticello, Right Handle, 1968 ....4.00 to 10.00
Nebraska, 1971 ....   30.00
Nebraska, 1972 ....25.00 to 36.00
Old Fitz 101, 1978 ....   4.35
Old Ironsides 12.00
Old Ironsides, Box 47.00
Rip Van Winkle, 1971 ....*Illus*   7.00
Songs Of Ireland, 1974 ....20.00 to 40.00
Sons Of Erin, Box, 1969 ....3.00 to 5.00
Tree Of Life, 1964 ....   4.50
Virginia, 1972 ....   10.00

OLD MR. BOSTON

It seems strange that a liquor company began as a candy factory, but that is part of the history of Old Mr. Boston. The Ben Burk Candy Company started in 1927 making non-alcoholic cordials during Prohibition. After Repeal, they became the first Massachusetts company to get a license for distilled spirits. They built a still and started making gin. One of the first brand names used was Old Mr. Boston. There was even a live Mr. Boston, an actor who made appearances for the company. In the early 1940s the company was sold to American Distilleries, but four years later Samuel Burk and Hyman Burkowitz, brothers, bought the company back. They expanded the Old Mr. Boston brand to include other beverages, such as flavored cordials and homogenized eggnog. They claim to be the first to introduce the quarter-pint size. In the mid-1960s the company began putting the liquor in decanters. No decanters were made after the early 1970s. They also made Rocking Chair Whiskey in a bottle that actually rocked. Traditionally, whiskey barrels were rolled back and forth on ships to improve the taste. Ships' captains liked the improved flavor and when they retired they would tie barrels of whiskey to their rocking chairs. A series of liquors in glass cigar-like tubes called *The Thin Man* were made in the mid-1960s. Glenmore Distilleries Company acquired Old Mr. Boston in 1969. The brand name was changed to Mr. Boston about 1975. Barton Brands bought the Mr. Boston name about 1994. Mr. Boston products are still made.

The Mr. Boston trademark was redesigned in the 1950s and again in the 1970s. Each time he became thinner, younger, and more dapper. The slogan *An innkeepers tradition since 1868* was used in the 1980s. It refers to the year the Old Mr. Boston mark was first registered.

Bottle, Blackberry Flavored Brandy, 1937, 4 1/2 In. 4.50
Decanter, Ribbed Sides, 9 1/2 In. ....6.00 to 9.00
Eagle Convention, Atlanta, 1972 ....   32.00
Fire Truck, Spirit Of '76, 1974, 10 In. 25.00
Guitar, 1968 ....   10.00
Guitar, Box, 1968 ....   15.00
Loyal Order Of Moose, 1972 ....   25.00
Molly Pitcher, 1975 ....   15.00
Polish American Legion, 1975 ....   25.00
Prestige Bookend, Old Mr. Boston Bust, Box, 1970 ....   22.00
Shriner, AAONMS, Camel, 1975 ....10.00 to 28.00

OLD RIP VAN WINKLE

Old Rip Van Winkle apothecary jars and figurals shaped like Rip Van Winkle were made from 1968 to 1977. J.P. Van Winkle and Son, Louisville, Kentucky, made these bottles and others under the Old Commonwealth and Old Fitzgerald labels. Old Rip Van Winkle bourbon is still sold.

Cardinal, 1975 ....   8.00
New Jersey Bicentennial, 1975 ....   6.50
No. 2, Reclining, 1975 ....2.25 to 10.50
No. 3, Rip Van Winkle, Standing, 1977 ....10.00 to 11.00

OLD TAYLOR

National Distilleries Product Company made one very well-known figural bottle for its Old Taylor brand Kentucky Straight Bourbon Whiskey. The ceramic container was a replica of the Old Taylor Distillery, although most collectors call it a castle bottle. The limited edition decanter was made in 1967.

Castle, 1967 . . . . .3.00 to 10.00

PACESETTER

Bottles shaped like cars and trucks were made under the Pacesetter label from 1974 to about 1983.

Corvette, 1978, Black, Box, 375 Milliliter 15.00
Corvette, 1978, Silver, Box, 1 3/4 Liter 88.00
Corvette, 1978, White, Box 18.50
Corvette, 1978, White, Box, 1 3/4 Liter, 18 In. 84.00
Corvette, 1978, Yellow, Box 18.50
Fire Truck, Snorkel No. 1, Volunteer Fire Department, Red, Unopened, 1982 . . . .   15.00
Tractor, No. 1, John Deere, Box, Opened, 1982 . . . . .45.00 to 150.00
Tractor, No. 3, International Harvester, Red, Black, Box, 1983 . . . .   325.00
Tractor, No. 4, Ford, Big Blue, Box, 1983 . . . .   35.00
Tractor, No. 5, Allis Chalmers, Box, Unopened, 1984 . . . .   50.00

PEPPER SAUCE

There was little refrigeration and poor storage facilities for fresh meat in the nineteenth century. Slightly spoiled food was often cooked and eaten with the help of strong spices or sauces. Small hot chili peppers were put into a bottle of vinegar. After a few weeks the spicy mixture was called *pepper sauce*. A distinctive bottle, now known as a pepper sauce bottle, was favored for this mixture. It was a small bottle, 6 to 12 inches high, with a long slim neck. The bottle could be square or cylindrical or decorated with arches or rings. Most were made of common bottle glass in shades of aqua or green. A few were made of cobalt or milk glass. Very early examples may have a pontil mark. More information on pepper sauce can be found in the book *Ketchup, Pickles, Sauces* by Betty Zumwalt.

Aqua, 8-Sided, Scallop, 3 Neck Rings, Single Collar, Open Pontil, 8 1/4 In. 79.00
Cathedral, 4-Sided, Blue Aqua, Applied Double Ring, 9 3/4 x 2 3/8 In. 242.00
Cathedral, 4-Sided, Light Green, Round, Open Pontil, 9 1/4 In. 330.00
Cathedral, 6-Sided, Aqua, Applied Collar, Ring, Pontil, 10 3/4 In. 308.00
Cathedral, 6-Sided, Aqua, Applied Double Collar, Open Pontil, 8 3/4 In. 78.00
Cathedral, 6-Sided, Blue Aqua, Ribs, Horizontal, Patented Feb. 74, 8 In. 39.00
Cathedral, 6-Sided, Green Aqua, Applied Double Collar, Open Pontil, 8 1/2 In. 169.00
Cathedral, 6-Sided, Green, Applied Double Collar, Pontil, 8 3/4 In. 672.00
Cathedral, Aqua, Applied Mouth, Open Pontil, 8 1/8 In. 100.00
Cathedral, Aqua, Square, Applied Double Collar, Iron Pontil, 8 3/8 In. 78.00
Cathedral, Aqua, Square, C. Co. Pat. Sept. 28 1874, 8 1/4 In. 32.00
Cathedral, Bright Green, 1840-60, 8 3/4 In. 672.00
Cathedral, Cornflower Blue, Double Collar, 1860-70, 8 3/8 In. 672.00
Cathedral, Emerald Green, Applied Double Collar, 10 1/4 In. 100.00

Pepper Sauce,
Green, 8-Sided,
3 Neck Rings, Double
Collar, 8 3/8 In.

❦

To remove a dried cork that has fallen inside a bottle, try this. Pour some household ammonia in the bottle. Let it sit for a few days. Most of the cork should dissolve and can easily be removed.

❦

Cathedral, Green Aqua, Applied Double Collar, 1855-65, 10 1/8 In.	157.00
Cathedral, Green Aqua, Horizontal, Pat. Sept. 28 1875, 8 In.	48.00
E.R. Durkee & Co., New York, Teal Blue Green, Cone, 11 Stacked Rings	59.00
Erd & Co., Cathedral, 6-Sided, Blue Aqua, Patented Feb. 74, 8 1/4 In.	29.00
GCO & Co., Aqua, BIMAL, 7 1/2 In.	24.00
Green, 8-Sided, 3 Neck Rings, Double Collar, 8 3/8 In. . . . .*Illus*	300.00
Olive Green, 8-Sided, Applied Lip, 1860s, 8 In.	110.00
Ridgy, Aqua, 6-Sided, BIMAL, 8 1/4 In.	16.00
Ridgy 6-Sided, BIMAL, 7 7/8 In.	14.00
S & P, 6-Sided, Yellow Green, 13 Spiral Ribs, Double Collar, BIM, Embossed, 8 In.	85.00
S & P, Pat. Appl. For, Emerald Green, Spiral Ribs, 8 In.	59.00
S & P, Pat. Appl. For, Medium Blue Green, Spiral Ribs, 8 In.	45.00
Teal, 6-Sided, Spiral Ribs, Double Collar, 8 In.	85.00
W.H. Clay's Richmond, Aqua, Indented Serpentine Panels, 10 In.	224.00
W.K. Lewis & Co., Applied Top, Open Pontil	55.00
Wells Miller & Provost, New York, Wax Sealed, Cork Lid, Label	77.00

---------------------- **PEPSI-COLA** ----------------------

Caleb Davis Bradham, a New Bern, North Carolina, druggist, invented and named Pepsi-Cola. Although he registered the trademark, the word *Pepsi-Cola* in calligraphy script, in 1903, he claimed that it had been used since 1898. A simpler version was registered in 1906. The bottle is marked with the name. The name in a hexagonal frame with the words *A Sparkling Beverage* was registered in 1937. This logo was printed on the bottle. The bottle cap colors were changed to red, white, and blue in 1941 as a patriotic gesture. Until 1951, the words Pepsi and Cola were separated by 2 dashes. These bottles are called *double dash* or *double dot* by collectors. In 1951 the modern logo with a single hyphen was introduced. The simulated cap logo was used at the same time. The name *Pepsi* was started in 1911, but it was not until 1966 that the block-lettered logo was registered. Both names are still used. A few very early Pepsi bottles were made of amber glass. Many other Pepsi bottles with local bottlers' names were made in the early 1900s. Modern bottles made for special events are also collected. There is a club, Pepsi-Cola Collectors Club, PO Box 817, Claremont, CA 91711.

70-71 Husker, Sealed, Full, 1975, 16 Oz.	10.00
Alliance, Neb., Refreshing, Healthful, Famous For Over 30 Years, Green, 12 Oz.	44.00
Anderson, S.C., Red & White ACL, 12 Oz.	1.70
Burlington, N.C., Double Dash, Red, White & Blue Label, 12 Oz.	10.50
Butte, Mont., 2 Full Glasses, Red, White & Blue Labels, Metal Cap, Unopened, 12 Oz. . .	28.00
Canada Limited, Montreal, Que., Sparkling Pepsi, Contents, 1953, 10 Oz., 9 1/2 In.	2.00
Casper, Wyoming, Double Dash, Red, White & Blue, Metal Cap, Unopened, 12 Oz.	21.00
Clear, Red & White ACL, Original Cap, No Deposit, No Return, Qt.	65.00
Clemson, Undefeated Home Season, Contents, 1975, 12 Oz.	3.00
Crystal Pepsi, Contents, Unopened, 16 Oz. . . . . .18.00 to 25.00	
Dallas, Tex., Double Dash, Paper Label, Embossed Middle Label, 1941, 12 Oz.	22.00
Dallas, Tex., Paper Label, Pepsi-Cola Around Middle, Original Lid, Contents, 12 Oz.	51.00
Danville, Kentucky, 6 Oz., 8 In.	95.00
Danville, Va., Single Dash, Red & White Painted Label, 1956, 10 Oz., 9 3/4 In.	6.00
Diet Crystal Pepsi, Contents, Aluminum Top, 16 Oz.	12.00
Diet Pepsi, Glass, Canada, 1975, 1 1/2 Liter	3.25
Diet Pepsi Free, Swirled, White Neck Label, Blue & Red Letters, 1/2 Liter	2.25
Dispenser, Syrup, Strengthening, Refreshing, Satisfying, Urn, Avon Co., 19 In. 34300.00	
Durham, N.C., Double Dash, Raised Letters, 12 Oz. . . . . .22.00 to 36.00	
Escambia Bottling Co., Clear, Crown Top	110.00
Escambia Bottling Co., Ice Blue, 8 1/4 In.	127.00
Fargo, N. Dak., Double Dash, Red, White & Blue Labels, Metal Cap, Unopened, 12 Oz. .	21.00
Fountain Syrup, Blytheville, Ark., Double Dash, Red & White Label, 1940s	37.00
Fountain Syrup, North Kansas City, Mo., Double Dash, Painted Label, Embossed, 12 Oz.	36.00
Fountain Syrup, Pittsburgh, Pa., Double Dash, Unopened, 12 Oz.	50.00
Greenville, S.C., Double Dash, Red & White ACL, 2 Full Glasses, 1948, 12 Oz.	22.00
Hutchinson, Escambia Bottling Co., Pensacola, Fla., Clear, 6 5/8 In.	220.00
Kansas City, Missouri, Sparkling Pepsi, Double Dash, Embossed, 12 Oz.	5.75
Los Angeles, Ca., Double Dash, Famous For Over 30 Years, Paper Labels, 12 Oz.	37.00
Louisville, Ky., Raised Letters, 10 Oz., 9 3/4 In.	10.00
Lyons, Kansas, Double Dash, ACL, Embossed Vertical Design, 1940s, 12 0z.	13.00

Marion, S.C., Sparkling Pepsi, Contents, 1956, 12 Oz.	20.00
Merced, California, Double Dash, Red, White & Blue Label, 12 Oz.	10.00
Nebraska Cornhusker Football, 1970s, 16 Oz.	8.00
Norwich, N.Y., Double Dash, 3-Color ACL, 12 Oz.	22.00
Ogden, Utah, Red & White On Front, Metal Cap, Unopened, 12 Oz.	10.00
Old Pepsi Logo, Cap, 1950s, 2 1/2 In.	5.00
Orlando Magic Schedule, Shaquille O'Neal, Longnecks, NBA, 1993, 6-Pack, 12 Oz.	6.00
Pepsi Across Middle, Dispose Of Properly, Screw Top, 1978, Pt.	10.00
Portsmouth, N.H., Single Dash, Red, White & Blue ACL, 12 Oz.	90.00
Red & White Label, Single Dash, 12 Oz.	2.00
Red & White Painted Labels, Etching, 1958, 12 Oz.	3.00
Richmond, Va., Double Dash, Sparkling, Painted Label, Red, White, 1948, 8 Oz., 8 3/4 In.	13.00
Roanoke, Va., Single Dash, Red & White Painted Label, 1959, 10 Oz., 9 3/4 In.	6.00
Russia, Paper Label, Contents, Cap, Early 1980s, 12 Oz.	21.00
San Jose Sharks, Greatest Turn Around In NHL History, Longneck, c.1994, 12 Oz.	2.00
Saxton, Pa., Red & White Printing, 1950s Logo, 12 Oz.	2.25
South Hill Virginia Bottling Company, Double Dash, c.1946, 12 Oz.	10.50
Sparkling, Double Dash, Red, White & Blue Label, Cap, 1950s, 12 Oz.	10.50
Sparkling, Red & White Painted Labels, 1955, 12 Oz.	5.50
Suffolk, Va., 7 Oz.	20.00
Tampa Bay Rowdies, Champions, Unopened, 1975, 16 Oz.	2.00 to 6.50
Tarboro, N.C., Straight-Sided, Light Green, This Bottle Must Not Be Sold	10.50
Tarpon Springs, Fla., Light Green, BIMAL, Straight Sides, Block Letters	800.00
Texarkana, Texas, Single Dash, 1955	10.00
University Of Illinois, 1984 Rose Bowl, 1983 Big Ten Champions	22.00 to 25.00
Williamsport, Pa., Red, White, Blue, 12 Oz.	25.00
World Champions Cincinnati Reds, Red & White ACL, 1975, 16 Oz., 11 In.	6.00 to 8.00

PERFUME

Perfume is a liquid mixture of aromatic spirits and alcohol. Cologne is similar but has more alcohol in the mixture so it is not as strong. Perfume bottles are smaller than colognes and usually more decorative. Most perfume bottles today are from the twentieth century. Some were made by famous glass makers such as Lalique or Webb, and some held expensive perfumes such as Schiaparelli, Nina Ricci's Coeur de Joie, or D'Orsay's Le Lys D'Orsay. DeVilbiss is a manufacturer of the spray tops used on perfume bottles and the name sometimes appears in a description. The word *factice*, which often appears in ads, refers to store display bottles. The International Perfume Bottle Association publishes a newsletter (PO Box 1299, Paradise, CA 95967). Related bottles may be found in the Cologne and Scent categories.

4 Corners, Stylized Flowers, Atomizer, 2 1/2 In.	150.00
Ahmed Soliman, Lilac, Crystal, Lilac, 8 Panels, Gilded, Spherical Stopper, 4 In.	926.00
Alexandrite, Cut Diamond, Metal Mounts, Atomizer, Label, Germany, 3 3/4 In.	66.00
Amber Glass, Metal Collar, Glass & Metal Dauber, DeVilbiss, 6 1/2 In.	240.00
Amethyst, Rayed Pattern, Deco Looking, 5 x 2 1/2 x 4 3/4 In.	40.00
Aqua, BIMAL, Early 19th Century, 4 In.	95.00
Art Deco, Duska, Maroon Red, Stepped Design, Black Glass Stopper, France, 2 x 1 In.	179.00
Arys, Lilas, Rectangular, Flower Shaped Stopper, 3 In.	547.00
Arys, Un Jardin La Nuit, Rectangular, Hobnailed, Star, Label, Stopper, 3 In.	1010.00
Atkinson, Chance, Black Glass, Screw Cap, Dabber, Silk Fringe, Flacon, 2 3/4 In.	630.00
Atomizer, Art Deco, Iridescent Peach, Acid Etched, Black Glass Disc Top, DeVilbiss, 6 In.	180.00
Au Fil De L'Eau, Art Nouveau, Green, Embossed, Paris, c.1924, 2 3/4 In.	200.00
Aureole Parfum Concentre, Pink, Stopper, Art Deco Style, 1/2 Oz., 4 1/2 In.	60.00
Avenel, Thais, Amphora, 3 Egyptian Symbols, Enameled Green, Gold, Stopper, 6 1/2 In.	5893.00
Babani, Ambre De Delhi, Clear, Enamel, Gilt, Depinoix, c.1920, 5 1/4 In.	646.00
Babani, Pao-Pe, Oval, Flowers, Birds, Gilding, Dome Shape Stopper, 3 1/2 In.	2020.00
Baccarat, Atomizer, Cut Diamond, Leather Case, 3 x 1 1/4 x 2 3/4 In.	77.00
Baccarat, Carafe Shape, Wedding Bouquet, Enameled, Disk Shaped Stopper, 8 In.	1684.00
Baccarat, Christian Dior, Diorling, Clear, Gilded Bronze, Stopper, Box, c.1963, 6 7/8 In.	2585.00
Baccarat, Christian Dior, Miss Dior, Clear, Frosted, Enameled Labels, Stand, c.1954, 8 In.	646.00
Baccarat, Ciro, Reflexions Paris, 5 In.	195.00
Baccarat, Guerlain, Shalimar, Blue Glass Stopper, Foil Label, France, c.1930, 1/2 Oz.	55.00
Baccarat, Myon, Green Cased, Stopper, Enameled Cover, Box, c.1928, 3 1/2 In.	1645.00
Baccarat, Peggy Hoyt, Flowers, Clear, Blue Patina, Engraved Label, c.1920, 4 1/8 In.	441.00

Baccarat, Ybry, Desir Du Coeur, Pink Cased, Stopper, Enameled, Box, c.1926, 2 In. 1175.00
Baccarat, Ybry, Femme De Paris, Green Cased, Stopper, Enameled, Box, c.1926, 2 In. ... 1528.00
Baccarat, Ybry, Mon Ame, Purple Cased, Stopper, Enameled Cover, Box, c.1926, 2 In. .. 1645.00
Balenciaga, Quadrille, Clear, Hang Tag, Box, c.1956, 6 In. 588.00
Benoit, Lune De Miel, Black Glass, Moon, Stars, Crescent Moon Stopper, 4 1/2 In. 5050.00
Bertelli, Fiori Di Campo, Frosted, Flowers, Stopper, 5 In. 4209.00
Best & Co., Qui M'Aime, Spherical, Stylized Melon, Glass Stopper, 2 In. 1263.00
Blue Opaline, Brass Neck, Stopper, Intaglio Cameo, Atomizer, France, 6 3/4 In. 110.00
Bob Makie, Makie, Clear, Box, c.1970, 4 3/4 In. 94.00
Bonzo, Cat, Frosted, Painted, Detachable Head, England, 1900-30, 3 In. 77.00
Bourjois, Ashes Of Roses, Rectangular, Plastic Screw Cap, Label, 2 In. 168.00
Bourjois, Beau Belle, Ball Shape, Label, Brass Bells, Screw Cap, Box, 2 In. 673.00
Bourjois, Chicote, Black Glass, Rectangular, Chromed Metal Cover, Label, Stopper, 3 In. . 673.00
Bourjois, Evening In Paris, Cobalt Blue Glass, Teardrop, Metal Stopper, Label, 2 1/2 In. . 673.00
Bourjois, Gardenia, Rectangular, Label, Black Glass Stopper, 3 1/2 In. 758.00
Bourjois, Glamour, Opaque, Oval Shape, Brass Screw Cap, Gilded, Label, 4 In. 673.00
Bourjois, Kobako, Disk Shape, Plastic Screw Cap, Tassel, Flacon, c.1950, 2 In. 463.00
Brass, Beveled Glass Inserts, Stopper, 4 Cherubs, Glass Dabber, 8 In. 173.00
Brilliant Cut, Button & Waffle Cut Facets, Sterling Silver Repousse Hinged Lid, 5 In. ... 480.00
Brilliant Cut, Crystal, Stopper, Mid 19th Century, 9 x 13 In. 630.00
Buche D'Auvergne, Bruyere Des Montagnes, Cylindrical, Label, Stopper, 3 In. 185.00
Buddha Shape, Sitting, Yellow, Blue, Crown Top, Schneider, No. 23853, 3 1/2 In. 219.00
Bust, Naked Lady, White Matte Glaze, 2 3/4 In. 92.00
Butterfly, Figural, Parfum De Qualite, Rolled Lip, France, c.1920, 4 1/2 In. 28.00
Cadolle, Clear, Frosted, Flower Blossom, Leaves, Ocher Patina, c.1920, 2 1/2 In. 940.00
Cameo Glass, Flowers, Leaves, Branches, Blue Glass, Silver Top, England, 4 In. 2013.00
Cameo Glass, Laydown, Flowers, Silver Top, Howell & James Case, 3 3/4 In. 1955.00
Cameo Glass, Laydown, Leaves, Flowers, Silver Cover, 6 In. 2160.00
Cameo Glass, Palms, Butterfly, Silver Cover, 8 In. 1380.00
Cameo Glass, Silver Top, Glass Stopper, Mappin & Webb Case, 9 3/4 In. 4370.00
Canarina, Frosted Cobalt Blue, Rectangular, Translucent, Cobalt Blue Stopper, 2 In. 4630.00
Candlewick, Yellow, Flower Atomizer, Imperial, DeVilbiss, Toledo, c.1953, 3 3/4 In. 195.00
Carnival Glass, Grape & Cable, Purple, 4 1/2 In. 700.00
Caron, L'Infini, Clear Crystal, Circular, Labels, Crystal Stopper, Satin Interior Box, 3 In. . 630.00
Caron, Le Narcisse Noir, Lentil Shape, Narcissus Shape, Frosted Black Stopper, Box, 2 In. 673.00
Carrere, Vent Fou, Green, White, Opaline Crystal, Ribbon Label, c.1945, 4 1/4 In. 294.00
Carved Nut, 18K Gold Trim, Star, Handles, Foot, Round Body, 1 1/2 In. 1100.00
Charles Of The Ritz, Directoire, Clear, Gilt Labels, Box, c.1946, 3 3/4 In. 411.00
Charvai, Odeur, Red Glass, Half Moon Shape, Stopper, Metal Cover, 1 1/2 In. 589.00
Cherigan, Chance, Black Glass, Horseshoe Shaped, Pyramid Stopper, Silk Box, 3 In. 2105.00
Christian Dior, Diorissimo, Amphora Shape, Teardrop Stopper, Box, 5 In. 589.00
Christian Dior, Diorissimo, Amphora, Gilded Bronze, Flower Bouquet Stopper, 8 In. 5472.00
Christian Dior, Diorissimo, Frosted, Rectangular, Hound's Tooth, Ribbon, Stopper, 3 In. . 295.00
Christian Dior, Miss Dior, Stopper, Box, 3 1/2 In. 69.00
Ciro, Maskee, Clear, Opaque Black, White Stopper, 4 Labels, Box, c.1923, 3 5/8 In. 2115.00
City Of Paris, Ah!! Paris, Frosted Crystal, Wheat Stalk, 4 Faces Crystal Stopper, 7 In. ... 2525.00
Clear, Applied Spiral Base, 3 In. 33.00
Clear, Stopper, Dabber, Enameled, Jeweled Hinged Metal Cover, Austria, 1920, 9 In. 940.00
Cobalt Blue, Iridescent, White Swirl Pattern, Clear Teardrop Stopper, 1950s, 6 In. 45.00
Colgate, Egypt, Amphora Shape, Greek Style, Ribs, Glass Stopper, 8 In. 337.00
Corday, Femme Du Jour, Black Crystal, Inro Box Shape, Black Crystal Stopper, 4 In. 1684.00
Corday, Toujours Toi, Gilded, Molded Stylized Flowers, Flacon, 2 In. 168.00
Coty, A Suma, Clear, Frosted, Hang Tag, Box, c.1934, 2 1/2 In. 529.00
Coty, Emeraude, Frosted, 3 Panels, Stylized Flowers, 8-Sided, Stopper, 4 In. 2273.00
Coty, Imprevu, Stopper, Label, 9 1/2 In. 92.00
Coty, Jacinthe, Crystal, Inkwell Shape, Star Shape Wheel, Flowers, 3 1/2 In. 4209.00
Coty, L'Aimant, Clear, Frosted, Label, Box, c.1928, 3 1/4 In. 206.00
Coty, L'Aimant, Cream Skin, Black, Gold Writing, Metal Cap, Contents, 1/2 Oz. 20.00
Coty, L'Aimant, Crystal, 4 Panels, Crystal Stopper, 4 Leaves, 4 In. 1094.00
Coty, L'Origan, Clear, Frosted, Label, Box, R. Lalique, c.1920, 2 1/2 In. 294.00
Crackle Glass, Peach, 3 Leaves, Hummingbird Stopper 13.00
Cranberry Glass, Mary Gregory Type, Enamel, Gold Ring, Stopper, Czech, c.1950, 5 3/4 In. . 95.00
Crown Jewel, Crownette, Matchabelli, Crown Shape, Gold Enamel, Box, 1 1/2 In. 138.00

Crown Perfumery Company, London, Crown Stopper, Green, Embossed, 3 1/4 In. 45.00
Crusellas, Un Amor En Venecia, Stopper, Flowers, Label, Box, 4 In. 420.00
Crystal, Black, Green, Pointed Stopper, 6 1/2 In. 150.00
Crystal, Clear, Octagonal, Steeple Form, Intaglio Cut, Pagoda Stopper, 9 1/4 In. 50.00
Crystal, Dark Green, Inner Glass Stopper, Metal Overcap, 2 1/2 In. 92.00
Crystal, Flower Stoppers, 5 In., Pair 115.00
Crystal, Flowers, 4-Sided, DeVilbiss Atomizer, 7 1/4 In. 69.00
Crystal, Glass, Yellow, Inner Glass Stopper, Silver Overcap, Flowers, 3 1/2 In. 196.00
Crystal, Gold Seal, Dieu Et Les Dames, Stopper, Dabber, 8 In. 46.00
Crystal, Stopper, Metal Neck, Chain, Oval, 3 In. 115.00
Cut Crystal, Intaglio Stopper, Czechoslovakia, 1940s, 7 x 3 In. 295.00
Cut Glass, 8-Footed, Intaglio Cut Roses, Stopper, Signed, Czechoslovakia, 5 In. 138.00
Cut Glass, Blue, Clear Stopper, Intaglio Cut, Nude, Signed, Czechoslovakia, 5 1/2 In. . . . 150.00
Cut Glass, Blue, Filigree, Porcelain Plaque, Czechoslovakia, c.1920, 6 In. 529.00
Cut Glass, Blue, Lady With Flowers, Cutout Stopper, Dabber, Czechoslovakia, 8 3/4 In. . . . 575.00
Cut Glass, Blue, Molded Flower Stopper, Signed, Czechoslovakia, 6 In. 230.00
Cut Glass, Blue, Stopper, Star Pattern Cutting, Signed, Czechoslovakia, 5 In. 173.00
Cut Glass, Clear, Frosted, Polished Lily-Of-The-Valley Stopper, 7 1/4 x 3 7/8 In. 44.00
Cut Glass, Clear, Molded Bluebells Stopper, Dabber, Signed, Czechoslovakia, 10 1/2 In. . . 575.00
Cut Glass, Cranberry, Circles, Ovals, Lines, Atomizer, New Bulb, 2 In. 95.00
Cut Glass, Cut Stopper In Rows, Dabber, Signed, Czechoslovakia, 5 1/2 In. 230.00
Cut Glass, Diamonds, Teardrop Circles, Green, Stopper, 5 In. 65.00
Cut Glass, Emerald Green, Double, Brass Closures, No Stopper, 5 In. 185.00
Cut Glass, Fan Top, 1940s, 4 3/4 x 3 1/2 In. 40.00
Cut Glass, Flared, Paneled Shape, Silver Plate, Over Brass, 6 1/2 x 2 1/2 In. 225.00
Cut Glass, Frosted, Woman Holding Flowers, Cutout Stopper, Dabber, 10 In. 805.00
Cut Glass, Frosted, Wreath Shaped Stopper, Dabber, Signed, Czechoslovakia, 5 1/4 In. . . . 104.00
Cut Glass, Gilt Flip Top, c.1900, 4 In. 95.00
Cut Glass, Green, Double, Brass Closure, Clear Stopper, 5 In. 225.00
Cut Glass, Green, Leaf Shaped Stopper, Signed, Czechoslovakia, 6 1/4 In. 115.00
Cut Glass, Green, Pink, Enameled Bronze Holder, Czechoslovakia, 1920, 4 In. 1763.00
Cut Glass, Hob & Lace, Blue To Clear, Stopper, C. Dorflinger & Sons, 4 1/8 In. 209.00
Cut Glass, Intaglio Cut Stopper, Dancer, Flowers, Signed, Czechoslovakia, 4 3/4 In. 80.00
Cut Glass, Lily-Of-The-Valley Frosted Stopper, 7 In. 95.00
Cut Glass, Opaque Green, Double, Brass Closure, Clear Stopper, 5 1/4 In. 250.00
Cut Glass, Pink, Clear, Basket Cut Stopper, Dabber, Signed, Czechoslovakia, 7 3/4 In. . . . 633.00
Cut Glass, Purple, Clear, Czechoslovakia, c.1920, 5 1/4 In. 94.00
Cut Glass, Red Crystal Stopper, 2 Flowers, Dabber, Signed, Czechoslovakia, 4 1/2 In. . . . 276.00
Cut Glass, Red Glass Stopper, Leaf Shaped, Faceted, Signed, 4 In. 196.00
Cut Glass, Ruby, Double, Brass Closure, Clear Stopper, 5 In. 225.00
Cut Glass, Stopper, Faceted, 5 1/2 In. 58.00
Cut Glass, Strawberry & Fan, Crimped Rose, Petals, Whittemore Stopper, 7 3/4 In. 115.00
Cut Glass, Vaseline, Sterling Silver Top, England, c.1897, 8 In. 345.00
Cut Glass, Yellow, Dabber, Czechoslovakia, 6 1/2 In. 323.00
D'Orsay, Divine, Clear, Hang Tag, Box, c.1947, 3 3/4 In. 176.00
D'Orsay, Divine, Clear, Hang Tag, Box, c.1947, 7 1/4 In. 294.00
D'Orsay, Intoxication, Label, 3 1/2 In. 15.00
D'Orsay, Le Fleurs, Crystal, Rectangular, Brass Cover, Crystal Stopper, 3 In. 4209.00
D'Orsay, Le Porte Bonheur, Clear, Frosted, Baccarat, Box, c.1913, 3 1/4 In. 1528.00
D'Orsay, Toujours Fidele, Pillow Shape, Seated Bulldog Stopper, 2 In. 2525.00
D'Orsay, Trophee, Christmas Tree Shape, Molded, 9 Panels, Screw Cap, 1935, 1 3/4 In. . . 210.00
D'Orsay, Voulez-Vous, Square, Label, Screw Cap, 1 1/2 In. 67.00
De Luzy, Le Frais Jardin, Pear Shape, Leaves, Teardrop Shaped Stopper, 3 1/2 In. 1684.00
De Marcy, L'Orange, 8 Enameled Orange Parts, Ceramic Holder, 1925, 2 1/2 In. 1410.00
De Vigny, Guili-Guili, Crystal, 8 Panels, Mahogany African Mask, Crystal Stopper, 6 In. . . 5893.00
Delettrez, Inalda, Stopper, Indented Rows With Dots, Cone Shape Stopper, 3 1/5 In. 1093.00
Delieuvin, Eau De Cologne, Ship Shape, Tiered Brass Screw Cap, Enameled, 5 In. 337.00
Delyna, Sensation Of Paris, Black, Spherical, 4 Gilded Claws, Arrow Shape Stopper, 2 In. 926.00
Diamond Jim Brady, Figural, Tooled Ring Top, Cork, c.1880, 5 1/2 In. 44.00
Dickey Pioneer, Creme De Lis, Embossed, Amber, 1850, 5 1/2 In. 143.00
Doeuillet-Doucet, Mareva, 8-Sided, Rectangular, Label, Stopper, Box, 2 1/2 In. 337.00
Dorothy Gray, Indigo, Clear, Frosted, Label, c.1948, 3 3/4 In. 440.00
Dorothy Gray, Lady In The Dark, Clear, Gold, Label, c.1941, 3 In. 118.00

Dorothy Gray, Savoir Faire, Bulbous, Enameled Black, Eye Mast, Screw Cap, 2 In. 673.00
Dorothy Gray, Savoir Faire, Clear, Gilt, Enamel, Metallic Screw Cap, c.1947, 4 In. 470.00
Dubarry, Bunch Of Violets, Frosted, 3-Sided, Flowers, Crescent Moon Stopper, 3 In. 5893.00
Dubarry, Frosted, Oblong, Drapery, 2 Butterflies, Frosted Stopper, 6 In. 2946.00
E. Fuchs, Jasmin, Clear, Frosted, Lens Shape, 4 Leaf Clovers, Stopper, Dabber, 1.8 In. . . . 589.00
E. Hoyt & Co., Celebrated Perfumers, Sesqui Centennial, 1776-1926, Liberty Bell, 2 In. . . 90.00
Ecrivez-Moi, Tube, Pen Shape, Bakelite Case, 5 1/2 In. 236.00
Edhia, Tabac Doux, Liberty Bell, Blue, Gold Enamel Crack, Gold Metal Cap, Box, 2 In. . . 58.00
Elizabeth Arden, Blue Grass, Cork Stopper, Label, 12 1/2 In. 104.00
Elizabeth Arden, It's You, Opaque White, Gilt, Enameled, Baccarat, c.1939, 6 1/2 In. 4416.00
Elizabeth Taylor, Passion For Men, Purple Glass, Wood Cap, 11 1/2 In. 12.00
Elizabeth Taylor, White Diamonds, Clear, Egg Shape, Rhinestone Bow, 10 1/2 In. 690.00
English Bulldog, Clear, Painted, Screw Cap, 5 3/4 In. 22.00
Ess-Bouquet, Hand Painted, 2-Tone Violets, Stopper, Round, 3 In. 95.00
F. Millot, Crepe De Chine, Gilded Brass, Stones, Screw Cap, Pouch, c.1935, 1 1/4 In. 337.00
Faberge, Aphrodisia, Clear, Gilded, Label, Holder, Box, c.1936, 3 1/2 In. 176.00
Faberge, Tigress, Atomizer Style Top, Box, c.1960, 4 In. 85.00
Fenton, Rosalene, Limited Edition No. 1630, Stopper, c.1998, 6 In. 145.00
Filigree Brass Pedestal, Blue Rhinestones, Rose, Dabber Top, c.1950, 7 3/4 In. 95.00
Flask, Venetian Art Glass, White, Pink, Blue, 8 5/8 x 4 x 1 3/4 In. 450.00
Fontanis, C'Est Paris, Rectangular, Ribs, Stylized Flowers, 6-Point Stopper, 3 In. 547.00
Fontanis, Fleurs De Bagdad, Frosted, 6-Sided, Stopper, Dabber, 1921, 2 In. 1684.00
Fragonard, Chale Indien, Amber, White, Oval, Egg Shape, Flacon, c.1929, 1 1/2 In. 630.00
French Galle Cameo, Atomizer, 7 5/8 x 2 1/4 In. 1200.00
G.W. Laird's Perfumers New York, Milk Glass, Labels, Battleship Tax Stamp, 5 In. 275.00
Gabilla, Chin Li, Opaque Red Glass, Lens Shape, Stopper, 2 1/2 In. 926.00
Gal, Imperial Toledo, Black Glass, Rectangular, Toledo Coat Of Arms, Stopper, 4 In. 1515.00
Glass, 3-Sided, Frosted, Metal, Geometric, Gold Lining, Atomizer, 7 1/2 In. 160.00
Glass, Blue, Brass Metal Overcap, Inner Stopper, 4 3/4 In. 127.00
Glass, Clear, Brass Filigree Stopper, Jewels, Czechoslovakia, 5 3/4 In. 110.00
Glass, Frosted, Man Caressing Woman's Hand, Lovebirds, Cutout Frosted Stopper, 7 In. . . 184.00
Glass, Inner Glass Stopper, Metal Overcap, Enamel Flowers, Leaves, 2 3/4 In. 173.00
Glass, Inner Stopper, Sterling Silver Neck, Overcap, Enameled, 3 In. 92.00
Glass, Metal, Enameled Black, Gold Pink Ball, Atomizer, Tassel, 9 1/2 In. 219.00
Glass, Nude Cupids, Enameled Internally, Atomizer, Tassel, 6 3/4 In. 92.00
Glass, Nude Sitting On Ball, Ball Shaped Base, Frosted Stopper, 7 1/2 In. 460.00
Glass, Orange, Black, Enameled Flower, Brass, Tasseled Bulb, Czechoslovakia, 7 1/2 In. . . 225.00
Glass, Pale Blue, Hobstar Disk Stopper, Czechoslovakia, 5 5/8 In. 154.00
Glass, Pink, Geometric, Metal Stand, Atomizer, 4 3/4 In. 138.00
Glass, Pink, Gold Enamel, Atomizer, 7 In. 184.00
Glass, Red, Silver Neck, Chain, 1850-60, 3 3/4 In. 575.00
Glass, Sabino, Abstract Geometric, Stopper, Basket Of Flowers, Signed, France, 6 3/4 In. . 104.00
Glass, Yellow, Amber, Inner Glass Stopper, Meal Overcap, 4 In. 115.00
Goldtone Brass, Pedestal, Oval Base, Filigree Overlay, Amber Stone On Dabber 95.00
Grenoville, Byzance, Black Glass, Asymmetrical, Chromed Metal Cap, 2 In. 5051.00
Grenoville, Chaine D'Or, Frosted, Horseshoe Shape, Roses, Rosebud Stopper, 3 1/2 In. . . . 9260.00
Gueldy, Gueldiana, Black Glass, 8 Panels, Flowers, Black Glass Stopper, 1928, 4 In. 1684.00
Gueldy, Nazir, Clear, Frosted, Molded Edges, Stylized Flower, Stopper, 4 In. 2020.00
Gueldy, Stellamare, Frosted, Bulbous, Mermaid Holding Sea Shell, 3 1/2 In. 4630.00
Guerlain, Champs-Elysees, Crystal, Faceted Turtle Shaped, Stopper, 6 In. 5050.00
Guerlain, Djedi, Rectangular, Round Shoulders, Blue Band, Half Moon Stopper, 4 In. 547.00
Guerlain, Eau De Cologne Du Coq, Rectangular, Apothecary, Vertical Ribs, Stopper, 7 In. 1094.00
Guerlain, Eau De Cologne Imperial, Stopper, Apothecary Shape, Label, 6 1/4 In. 46.00
Guerlain, Geranium D'Espagne, 3 Sections, Square Stopper, Box, 4 In. 1347.00
Guerlain, Guerlarose, Crystal, Cylindrical, Ribs, Crystal Stopper, 8-Sided, Box, 3 In. 1684.00
Guerlain, Mitsouko, White Opaline Crystal, Cylindrical, Crystal Stopper, 6 In. 7997.00
Guerlain, Mouchoir De Monsieur, 3 Faces, 3-Sided Section, Stopper, 4 1/2 In. 5050.00
Guerlain, Mouchoir De Monsieur, Stopper, 3-Sided, Label, 5 In. 403.00
Guerlain, Ode, Clear, Plastic Screw Cap, Box, Wrapper, c.1950, 4 1/2 In. 206.00
Guerlain, Ode, Frosted, Amphora Shape, Drapery, Label, Rosebud Shape Stopper, 5 In. . . 630.00
Guerlain, Rita, Square Section, Truncated Shoulders, Stopper, Gilded, 6 In. 7997.00
Guerlain, Shalimar, Glass, Frosted, Rosebud Stopper, 4 1/2 In. 58.00
Guerlain, Shalimar, Vaporizer, Cylindrical, Box, 1966, 2 In. 1575.00

Gyska, Djamila, Frosted Crystal, Bulbous, 8 Panels, Leaves, Flower Shape Stopper, 7 In. . . 1515.00
Hattie Carnegie, Hattie Carnegie, Black Glass, Square, Pyramid Stopper, 3 In. 673.00
Hattie Carnegie, Hypnotic, Woman's Head & Shoulder, Stopper, Gold Enamel, 4 In. 575.00
Helena Rubenstein, Slumber Song, Angel, c.1939, 6 1/2 In. 198.00
Hobnail, Blue, White Plastic Rose, 3 1/2 x 2 1/2 In. 32.00
Houbigant, Chantilly, White Cap, Chair, Cushion, Flowers, Box, 2 In. 58.00
Houbigant, La Rose France, Crystal, Rectangular, Young Man With Rose, Stopper, 4 In. . . 673.00
Houbigant, Le Parfum Ideal, Stopper, Gold Label, Box, 3 1/2 In. 69.00
Indian Figure, Applied, Rolled Lip, 1880-1900, 4 1/2 In. 83.00
Isabey, Le Gardenia, Frosted, 5-Sided, 3 Arts, Flowers, Frosted Stopper, 3 1/2 In. 1684.00
Isabey, Le Mimosa, Clear, Frosted, Cone, 12 Panels, Flowers, Label, Stopper, 6 In. 547.00
J. & E. Atkinson, Wild Honeysuckle, Apothecary Shape, Kid Skin Seal, Stopper, 3 1/2 In. . 1179.00
J. Grossmith, White Fire, Red, Lens Shape, Plastic Stopper, Cone, Ribs, Label, 1 1/2 In. . . 253.00
Jacques Griffe, Mistigri, Clear, Enameled Label, Boxes, c.1950, 6 1/2 In. 529.00
Jacques Heim, J'Aime, Cylindrical, Gilding, Stylized Fox Head, 1945, 2 1/2 In. 420.00
Jade, Green, Shouldered, Twisted Stopper, Steuben, 11 3/4 In. 345.00
Jaspy, Le Petit Chose, Pear Shape, Man's Head In Fedora, Stopper, 4 In. 5893.00
Jay Thorpe & Co., Jaytho, Clear, Frosted, Bud Stopper, Molded Bouquet Of Tulips, 4 In. . 6900.00
Jean D'Albret, Ecusson, Clear, Frosted, Gilt, Velvet Jewel Box, c.1950, 7 1/2 In. 3055.00
Jean Desprez, Votre Main, Porcelain, Applied Roses, Sevres, c.1939, 10 In. 3908.00
Jean Laporte, La Parfum Qui Vous Metamorphose, Clear, Opal, Label, c.1970, 6 3/4 In. . . 176.00
Jean Patou, Le Sien, Crystal, 8 Panels, Gilded Crystal Berry Shaped Stopper, 6 In. 2946.00
Jean Patou, Moment Supreme, Stopper, Label, 6 1/2 In. 69.00
Jeanne Lanvin, Arpege, Gold Encased Stopper, Box, 2 In. 403.00
Kanebo, Ambre, Opaque White Glass, Half Moon Shape, Gilded Peaks, Flacon, 1 1/2 In. . 1852.00
Kewpie, Sitting, Hand On Chin, Germany, 2 1/4 In. 85.00
L. T. Piver, Astris, Crystal, Truncated Edges, Faceted Shoulders, Stopper, 5 In. 2794.00
L. T. Piver, Astris, Opaque Pink Crystal, 8-Sided, 6-Pointed Star, Stopper, 4 In. 8418.00
L. T. Piver, Velivole, Crystal, Cylindrical, Engraved, Gilded, Laurel Leaves, Stopper, 3 In. . 2525.00
L. T. Piver, Violette, Violets, Classic Shape, Sweet Pea Bud Shape Stopper, Box, 5 In. 1010.00
Lalique, Coty, Ambre Antique, Clear, Frosted, Sepia Patina, c.1910, 6 In. 2115.00
Lalique, Coty, Lilas Pourpre, Clear, Frosted, Leather Box, c.1911, 2 5/8 In. 588.00
Lalique, Coty, Styx, Clear, Frosted, Sepia Patina, Stopper, c.1912, 4 3/4 In. 1410.00
Lalique, D'Anjou, Reve D'Amour, Clear, Frosted, Labels, c.1930, 6 1/2 In. 3055.00
Lalique, D'Orsay, Le Lys, Clear, Frosted, Sepia Patina, c.1922, 6 3/4 In. 823.00
Lalique, D'Orsay, Le Lys, Clear, Frosted, Sepia Patina, c.1922, 9 3/4 In. 1293.00
Lalique, Deux Fleurs, Frosted, Stopper, Overlapping Flowers, 3 1/2 In. 104.00
Lalique, Flacon, Lily Of The Valley, 4 x 4 3/4 In. 235.00
Lalique, Frosted Flower Front & Back, Signed, France, 3 1/2 In. 475.00
Lalique, Frosted Glass, Cylindrical, Baccarat, Metal Work, c.1912, 5 1/2 In. 1438.00
Lalique, Gabilla, La Violette, Clear, Frosted, Violet Enamel, c.1925, 3 1/4 In. 3525.00
Lalique, Houbigant, La Belle Saison, Clear, Frosted, Sepia, Box, c.1925, 4 1/4 In. 3055.00
Lalique, Jay Thorpe, Jaytho, Clear, Frosted, Ocher, c.1927, 4 In. 470.00
Lalique, Lubin, Lacdor, Clear, Frosted, Label, c.1920, 5 3/8 In. 705.00
Lalique, Nina Ricci, Apple, 2-Leaf Stopper, Stained Glass, France, 2 1/2 x 2 In. 175.00
Lalique, Nina Ricci, Clear, Swirled Ribs, Frosted Love Birds Stopper, 4 1/4 In. 39.00
Lalique, Nina Ricci, L'Air Du Temps, Doves, 4 x 3 1/2 In. 75.00
Lalique, Nina Ricci, L'Air Du Temps, Swirls, Brass Screw Cap, Signed, 2 1/2 In. 716.00

**A ground-glass perfume bottle stopper should
be turned gently to the right for a snug fit.
To remove the stopper, first turn it to the left
to "unlock it" before pulling it out.**

Perfume, Lantern, Globe, Teal Blue,
Metal Cage, Screw Cap, 3 3/8 In.

Lalique, Roger Et Gallet, Cigalia, Wood, Paper, c.1924, 3 In. 705.00
Lalique, Volnay, Mimeomai, Clear, Frosted, Blue Patina, c.1922, 4 3/4 In. 2115.00
Lalique, Worth, Green, 6-Disc Stopper, Cylindrical, Metal & Wood Base, 5 3/4 In. 690.00
Lalique, Worth, Imprudence, Clear, Label, Box, c.1938, 2 1/2 In. 353.00
Lalique, Worth, Vers Le Jour, Clear, Frosted Amberina, c.1927, 4 1/4 In. 764.00
Lancel, Le Parfum De Lancel, Rectangular, Round Shoulders, Cube, 3 In. 463.00
Lancome, Bocages, Rectangular, Concave Sides, Stopper, Label, Box, 3 1/2 In. 842.00
Lancome, Bocages, Rectangular, Stopper, Box With Rose, 3 In. 337.00
Lancome, Conquete, Brown Frosted, 5-Sided, Stopper, Leaves, 7 In. 1263.00
Lancome, Envol, Rectangular, Cylindrical, Plastic Screw Cap, 5-Sided, Label, 3 1/2 In. . .   420.00
Lancome, Envol, Square, Cartouche, Labels, Screw Cap, Box, 2 1/4 In. 547.00
Lancome, Tresor, Teardrop Shape, Screw Cap, Engraved, 3 In. 337.00
Lander, Jasmin, Woman, Frosted Glass, Cork Tip Stopper, 4 In.   173.00
Lantern, Globe, Teal Blue, Metal Cage, Screw Cap, 3 3/8 In. . . . .*Illus*   90.00
Lanvin, My Sin, Black Crystal, Gold, c.1930, 7 In. 206.00
Lanvin, My Sin, Black Crystal, Gold, Label, Box, c.1920, 2 1/2 In. 235.00
Lanvin, My Sin, Gilded Black Crystal, c.1920, 5 1/4 In. 880.00
Lanvin, Pretexte, Clear, Gold, Label, Box, c.1937, 2 1/4 In. 147.00
Laydown, 14K Gold Top, Engraved, c.1900, 3 In. 750.00
Lead Crystal, Wand Cut, Faceted, Prismatic, Western Germany, 5 1/2 x 1 3/4 In. 60.00
Lentheric, Miracle, Blue Cased, Clear, Stopper, Cover, Val St. Lambert, c.1920, 3 1/2 In. . .   206.00
Lentheric, Miracle, Frosted, Stylized Ionic Column, Glass Stopper, 3 In. 673.00
Lentheric, Shanghai, Frosted, Ginger Jar Shape, Handles, Glass Stopper, 2 In. 673.00
Lentheric, Shanghai, Gold Stopper, Box, 1 1/2 In. 46.00
Lentheric, Tweed, Clear, Gold Ball Cap, Box, 1 3/4 In. 104.00
Lerys, Chypre, Black Glass, Diamond Shape, Panels, Dabber, Stopper, 3 In. 253.00
Les Parfums De Rosine, Coeur En Folie, Red, Heart Shape, Wing Stopper, 1 1/2 In. 4209.00
Lilly Dache, Dachelle, Clear, Labels, Hang Tag, Box, c.1960, 6 3/4 In. 206.00
Lily Dache, Dashing, Poodle Sitting, Sash, Roses, Label, 3 1/4 In. 374.00
Liz Claiborne, Vivid, Stopper, Blue Liquid, 14 In. 12.00
Loulette, Mimosa, Opaque, Blue Crystal, 4 Faces, Square, Cobalt Blue Stopper, 7 In. 505.00
Louvre, Je M'Attache, Frosted, Disk Shape, Ribbons, Rectangular, Frosted Stopper, 3 In. .   1684.00
Lubin, Au Soleil, Frosted, Lighthouse Shape, Molded Lizard, Stopper, 6 In. 4209.00
Lubin, Lilas De Luxe, Frosted, Gazelle Running Through Woods, Oval Stopper, 3 In. 3788.00
Lubin, Monbrosia, Black Enamel Edges, 8-Sided, Clear Stopper, Label, 3 1/2 In. 1179.00
Lucien Lelong, Jabot, Screw Cap, Box, 1 3/4 In. 379.00
Lucien Lelong, Opening Night, Clear, Box, c.1934, 2 1/2 In. 440.00
Lucien Lelong, Taglio, Clear, Label, Plastic Box, c.1945, 1 1/2 In. 94.00
Lucien Lelong, Tailspin, Razzle Dazzle, Screw Cap, Gyroscope, Box, c.1940, 2 3/4 In. . . .   470.00
Lucien Lelong, Tailspin, Stopper, Molded Logo, Label, 2 3/4 In.   69.00
Lucien Lelong, Ting-A-Ling, Circular, 2 Necks, Brass Screw Cap, 2 In. 716.00
Lucretia Vanderbilt, Cobalt Blue Overlay Opaque White Glass, Stopper, Dabber, 4 In. 1094.00
Luxor, Lybis, Blue Glass Stopper, Impressed Violets, Frosted, 5 1/2 In. 374.00
Malachite, Frolicking Nudes Stopper, Art Deco, Czechoslovakia, 8 In. 144.00
Man, Tails, Plastic Top Hat, 3 1/2 x 1 1/2 In. 95.00
Man's Shoe, Crystal, Round Stopper, 4 In. 140.00
Marcel Rochas, Femme, Opaque White Glass, Disk Shape, Screw Cap, 1944, 1 3/4 In. . . .   1178.00
Marcel Rochas, Moustache, Clear, Rectangular, Label, Screw Cap, 1 In. 236.00
Marques De Elorza, Argentina, Cobalt Blue, Bulbous, Flower Shape Stopper, 3 1/2 In. . . .   4209.00
Mary Chess, Souvenir D'Un Soir, Clear, Frosted, Hangtag, Box, c.1956, 3 1/2 In. 2938.00
Maubert, Cime D'Or, Black, Gold, Gilt Stopper, Label, c.1927, 3 1/4 In. 1175.00
Max Factor, Wild Musk, Rabbit Shape, Gold Cap, Chain, 1 1/2 In. 69.00
Milk Glass, Green, Embossed Latticework, Gold Trim, Stopper, 6 1/2 In. 35.00
Molinard, Ambre, Clear Crystal, Bulbous, Label, Bell Shaped Stopper, 4 In. 1684.00
Molinard, Habanita, Cube Shape, 4 Faces, Stopper, Box, 1934, 2 In. 379.00
Molinard, Le Provencale, Nude Women, Oval Frieze, Frosted Glass Atomizer, 5 1/4 In. . .   489.00
Molinard, Tabatchin, Cube Shape, Geometric, Label, Black Crystal Stopper, 3 In. 1852.00
Monument, Chocolate Amber, Flared Lip, Pontil, 5 1/8 In. 3080.00
Moser, Chatelaine, Cobalt Blue, Enameled, Multicolored Flowers, Brass Cap, 2 3/8 In. . . .   450.00
Mury, Le Narcisse Bleu, Frosted, 8-Sided, Stylized Narcissus, Frosted Stopper, 3 In. 630.00
Mury, Le Narcisse Bleu, Teardrop, Frosted Stopper, Dabber, 1923, 3 In. 210.00
Myrurgia, A Moi, Frosted, Rectangular, Stylized Flowers, Stopper, 5 In. 420.00
Myrurgia, Embrujo De Sevilla, Clear, Frosted, Label, Half Moon Shape Stopper, 3 In. 1347.00

Myrurgia, Origanum, Frosted, Stylized Flowers, Label, Stopper, 4 In. 463.00
Neuf, Enchantee, Frosted, 5-Sided, Molded Flowers, Label, Stopper, 4 1/2 In. 758.00
Nice-Flore, Divine Chanson, Clear, Frosted, Circular, Flowers, Stopper, 4 In. 2105.00
Nice-Flore, Tout L'Azur, Frosted, Stylized Petals, 3 Cartouches, Hindu, Stopper, 5 In. 2357.00
Nicerose, Chypre, Frosted Crystal, Arch Shaped Panels, Stylized Flowers, 4 In. 4209.00
Nina Ricci, Coeur Joie, 2 Hearts, Gold Cap, Plastic Case, 2 1/4 In. 374.00
Nina Ricci, Douce, Circular, Molded Scallops, Brass Screw Cap, 1944, 1 1/2 In. 2694.00
Nina Ricci, L'Air Du Temps, Frosted Glass, Metal Cap, Sunburst, 2 In. 207.00
Nina Ricci, L'Air Du Temps, Gilded Brass Screw Cap, Ribbon, Box, 1948, 1 1/4 In. 168.00
Nissery, Cyclamen, Rectangular, Flowers, Button Shape Stopper, 3 1/2 In. 673.00
Odeon, Pour Amour, Frosted, Pine Cone Stopper, Pine Branches, Cones, Patina, 3 1/2 In. .. 1745.00
Oriental Man Sitting, Milk Glass, Detachable Head With Dabber, 5 3/4 In. 66.00
Ota, Chypre, Pearl, Cork Closures, Silk Tassel, Box, c.1920, 4 In. 1293.00
Pairpoint, Clear, Rosaria Stripes, Flower Stopper, 6 3/4 In. 180.00
Palmer, May Bloom, Stopper, Tax Stamp March 1, 1899, Box 161.00
Paquin, Espoir, Black Glass, Circular, Brass Screw Cap, 2 In. 210.00
Paquin, Espoir, Lit Candle Graphic, Flacon, c.1940-45, 1 1/2 In. 168.00
Parfum Les Trois Muses, La Danse, Frosted Crystal, Women Dancers, Stopper, 5 In. 9260.00
Paul Rieger, Esprit De France, Flower Drops, Clear, Cylindrical, Stopper, 2 1/4 In. 80.00
Peach Glass Stopper, Cube, 4 1/4 In. 127.00
Perez Guerra, Muntaj, Glazed Ceramic, Gilt, Cork Closure, Stand, c.1940, 7 In. 235.00
Perthshire, Paperweight, Millefiori, Blue, Purple, Red Center, Ribbon Stopper, 4 3/4 In. . 175.00
Peter Raos, Monet Spring, Millefiori Flowers, Green Leaves, Stopper, c.2004, 5 1/4 In. .. 295.00
Piver, Mascarade, Opaque Red, Gilt, Depinoix, Box, c.1927, 2 In. 1293.00
Porcelain, Duckling Shape, Yellow, Orange Bill, Feet, Crown Stopper, Germany, 2 3/4 In. 138.00
Porcelain, Silver Top, Flowers, 1893, 3 In. 125.00
Porcelain, Stopper, Dabber, Painted Roses, 3 In. 104.00
Pressed Glass, Art Deco Shape, Pink, Brass Top, DeVilbiss, Atomizer, 3 1/2 In. 75.00
Pressed Glass, Frosted, Vaseline, Squat, Flower Blossom Stopper, 1 7/8 x 2 5/8 In. 77.00
Pressed Glass, Vertical Ribs, Bulbous, Frosted Bluebird Stopper, 3 3/4 In. 23.00
Prince Matchabelli, Abano, Crown Shape, Screw Cap, Flacon, Box, c.1936, 3 In. 168.00
Prince Matchabelli, Added Attraction, Gold Screw Cap, Enameled Label, Box, 1 1/2 In. . 127.00
Prince Matchabelli, Beloved, Blue, Golden Cross Stopper, Foil Label, Miniature 70.00
Prince Matchabelli, Duchess Of York, Amber, 5-Sided, Coat Of Arms, Stopper, 3 In. 716.00
Prince Matchabelli, Stradivari, Frosted Glass, Stopper, Crown Shape, Signed, 4 In. 150.00
Prince Matchabelli, Violettes De La Reine, Amber, 5-Sided, Flacon, Stopper, 1924, 2 In. . 1852.00
Prince Matchabelli, Wind Song, Crown Shape, Lacquered, Cross Shaped Stopper, 8 In. .. 1515.00
Raquel, Orange Blossom, Stopper, Cone Shape, 2 In. 295.00
Renaud, Sur Deux Notes, Clear, Frosted, Oval, Spire Stopper, Leaves, Label, 5 1/2 In. 1380.00
Richard Hudnut, Aimee, Light Blue Glaze, New York, Porcelain, 1890-1920, 10 In. 110.00
Richard Hudnut, Chypre, Cone, Stylized Flowers, Crystal Stopper, Silk Box, 3 In. 1768.00
Richard Hudnut, Fadette, Frosted, Cylindrical, Flowers, Figural Stopper, 4 In. 4209.00
Richard Hudnut, Pour Vous, Clear, Frosted, Green Patina, Viard, c.1923, 5 3/8 In. 3819.00
Richard Hudnut, R.S.V.P., Ball Shape, Bakelite Screw Cap, Box, 1 1/2 In. 589.00
Rimmel, Mon Yvonnette, Frosted Crystal, 12 Panels, Bulbous, Stopper, 3 1/2 In. 7576.00
Rimy, L'Heure D'Amour, Frosted, Butterfly Wings, Sunburst Stopper, 4 In. 1684.00
Rochambeau, La Pipe Alsacienne, Pipe Shape, Cork Stopper, 3 In. 589.00
Roger & Gallet, Bridalis, 5-Sided, Frosted Stopper, Flowers, Leaves, Box 716.00
Roger & Gallet, Fleurs D'Amour, Frosted, Rectangular, Geometric, Stopper, 3 In. 505.00
Roger & Gallet, Le Triomphe De France, Semi-Circular, Sunburst, Steel Stopper, 3 In. 4041.00
Rosebud Perfume Co, Woodsboro, Md., Box, 2 7/8 x 1 1/2 In. 16.00
Rosine, Coup De Foudre, Clear, Blue, c.1925, 4 1/4 In. 764.00
Rosine, Nuit De Chine, Clear, Blue, Plastic Ring Handle, Box, c.1913, 3 1/4 In. 1058.00
Royal Copenhagen, Porcelain, Stopper, Nude, Flying Goose, Label, 4 3/4 In. 138.00
Santa Claus & Present Bag, Green Milk Glass, Detachable Head, 8 In. 88.00
Satin Glass, Hand Painted, Green, Enamel, Yellow Rose, Bud, Leaves, 1920s, 6 1/4 In. .. 150.00
Satin Glass, Peacock Eye, Mother Of Pearl, Blue, Silver Cover, 3 1/4 In. 633.00
Saville, Mischief, Black Glass, 8 Panels, Cylindrical, Metal Screw Cap, 2 In. 379.00
Saville, Mischief, Black Glass, 8 Panels, Cylindrical, Screw Cap, Labels, Flacon, 1 3/4 In. 379.00
Schiaparelli, Shocking, Cube Stopper, Label, Presentation Box, Unopened, 3 1/2 In. 155.00
Schiaparelli, Si, Chianti Shaped, Basketwork, Red Enamel Stopper, 5 In. 758.00
Schiaparelli, Sleeping, Amber, Flame, Glass Stopper, 1938, 2 1/2 In. 1347.00
Schiaparelli, Sleeping, Candlestick Shape, Gold Trim, 3 1/8 In. 95.00

Schiaparelli, Zut, Stopper, Woman's Body, 5 1/2 In. 460.00
Seahorse Shape, Clear, Ribbed, Sapphire Blue Trim, 3 In. 250.00
Silver Collar, Edwardian, Star Decoration, Fancy Stopper, c.1902, 6 1/4 x 2 1/2 In. 145.00
Simonetta, Incanto, Black Glass, Lantern Shape, Stopper, Label, Box, 2 In. 337.00
Solon Palmer Perfume Co., Painted Label Under Glass, Store Display, 9 x 3 In. 303.00
Sterling Silver, Cased, Pewter Topped Cork Stopper, Open Work Acanthus, 5 1/4 In. 195.00
Steuben, Blue Aurene, Black & Pink Flower Stopper, 4 3/4 In. 2070.00
Steuben, Emerald Green, Melon Ribbed, Flame Stopper, 3 3/4 In. 345.00
Steuben, Peggy Hoyt, Flowers, Iridescent, Verre De Soir, Blue Stopper, c.1913, 3 1/2 In. . 470.00
Steuben, Verre De Soie, No. 15, Stopper, 7 3/4 In. 450.00
Stevens & Williams, Bristol Yellow Shoulder, Pointed Stopper, 8 In. 518.00
Stork Club, Metal Encased, Metal Cap, 1 3/4 In. 46.00
Suzy, Golden Laughter, Clear, Green Enamel, Stand, c.1941, 4 3/8 In. 1645.00
Swarovsky Silver Crystal Flacon, Heart Shaped Body, Napoleon Hat Stopper, Box 95.00
Tapered Square, Metal Mounts, Intaglio Cut Cameo, Atomizer, 6 7/8 x 2 3/8 In. 66.00
Tokalon, Chateau D'Azur Pres Nice, Frosted, Building Shape, Stopper, 3 In. 6735.00
Vial, Sterling Cap, Crystal, Laydown, Twist, Banded, Diamond & Lattice Pattern, 4 3/4 In. 295.00
Victoria's Secret, Encounter, Ball Stopper, 11 3/4 In. 35.00
Vigny, Golliwogg, Frosted Base, Enameled Head, Fur Hair, 1919-26, 2 3/4 In. 55.00
Vigny, Golliwogg, Frosted Base, Enameled Head, Fur Hair, 1919-26, 3 1/2 In. 55.00
Vigny, Golliwogg, Frosted Base, Enameled Head, Fur Hair, 1919-26, 6 In. 83.00
Violet, Bouquet Farnese, Frosted, 4 Panels, Figures, Stopper, 4 1/2 In. 7745.00
Volnay, Ambre De Siam, Bulbous, Handles, Cobalt Blue Lacquer, Stopper, 3 In. 4630.00
Volnay, Firefly, Cobalt Blue, 8-Sided, Metal Cover, Label, Stopper, Box, 2 In. 1179.00
Volnay, Iris Neige, Frosted, Square, Thorns, Stopper, 3 In. 4630.00
Volnay, Lilas De Lorraine, Spheric, Pear Shape, Label, Stopper, 6 1/2 In. 1094.00
Volnay, Perlinette, Circular, Pearlized, Label, Stopper, 2 In. 547.00
Volnay, Violette, Amphora, Stylized Flower, Label, Stopper, 5 In. 5724.00
Webb, Cameo Glass, Vines, Leaves, Butterfly, Gorham Silver Top, 10 1/2 In. 2185.00
Webb Burmese, Laydown, Leaves, Blossoms, Branches, Silver Cover, 3 1/2 In. 1080.00
Weil, Bambou, Chinese Pagoda Shape, Rectangular, Red Stopper, Box, 1 In. 2189.00
Woodworth, Karess, Frosted Crystal, Cylindrical, Geometric, Flame Shaped Stopper, 6 In. 2946.00
Worth, Dans La Nuit, Frosted, Spheric, Crescent Moon, Stopper, 9 In. 2694.00
Worth, Dans La Nuit, Stopper, Stars, Plastic Tip Stopper, 4 1/2 In. 92.00
Worth, Je Reviens, Translucent Blue, Cylindrical, Turquoise Blue Glass Stopper, 5 In. 2862.00
Worth, Projets, Clear, Frosted, Oval, Frosted Ship, 8 Spokes Stopper, 1935, 1 3/4 In. 800.00
Worth, Sans Adieu, Emerald Green, Circular, Stopper, 6 Graduated Discs, 3 In. 1515.00
Yardley, Enchantress, Clear, Box, c.1912, 4 1/4 In. 382.00
Yardley, Strike A New Note, 3-Sided, Screw Cap, Match Box, 1950, 1 In. 253.00
Ybry, Devinez, Opaque Orange, Cube Shape Stopper, Dabber, Label, 1925, 1 1/2 In. 2020.00
Ysianne, Saturnale, Clear, Frosted, Depinoix, c.1927, 6 1/2 In. 1175.00
Yves Rocher La Gacilly, Le Jour, Amber, Frosted, Blue Stopper, Art Deco, 4 3/4 In. 44.00

------------ **PICKLE** ------------

Pickles were packed in special jars from about 1880 to 1920. The pickle jar was usually large, from one quart to one gallon size. They were made with four to eight sides. The mouth was wide because you had to reach inside to take out the pickle. The top was usually sealed with a cork or tin cover. Many pickle jars were designed with raised gothic arches as panels. These jars are clear examples of the Victorian gothic revival designs, so they are often included in museum exhibitions of the period. Their large size and attractive green to blue coloring make them good accessories in a room. Bottle collectors realize that pickle jars are examples of good bottle design, that they are rare, and that a collection can be formed showing the works of many glasshouses. Elaborate molded clear glass pickle jars were popular after 1900. They were decorated with gold, red, and other colors of cold-painted enamel to make a type known as *goofus glass*. Pickle bottles are so popular that they are being reproduced. For more information on pickle jars, see *Ketchup, Pickles, Sauces* by Betty Zumwalt.

4-Sided, Gold Amber, Neck Ring, Applied Rolled Lip, 11 In. 330.00
4-Sided, Green, Indented, Stylized Ferns, Rolled Lip, 11 In. 242.00
6-Sided, Gothic Panels, Aquamarine, Outwardly Rolled Lip, 1860-75, 13 In. 110.00
6-Sided, Green, Outward Rolled Lip, Pontil, 1850, 13 1/4 In. 532.00
Aqua, Goofus Glass, 12 1/2 In. 66.00
Aquamarine, Square, Arches, Crosshatching, Single Collar, Iron Pontil, c.1850, 7 3/8 In. . 365.00

Pickle, Cathedral,
4-Sided, Medium
Green, Outward Rolled
Lip, c.1870, 11 3/8 In.

Pickle, Cathedral,
Light Apple Green,
Acorn In Arch,
Rolled Lip, 10 7/8 In.

If you discover a cache of very dirty bottles and you are not dressed in work clothes, make temporary coveralls from a plastic garbage bag.

Atmore's, Cathedral, Aqua Blue, Rolled Lip, 11 3/8 In. 336.00
C.P. Sanborn & Son, Boston, Pickles In Shield, Dark Amber, Tooled Lip, 5 In. 88.00
C.P. Sanborn & Son, Boston, Union In Shield, Dark Amber, Tooled Lip, 5 In. 88.00
Cathedral, 4-Sided, Aqua, Applied Lip, 12 In. 825.00
Cathedral, 4-Sided, Blue Aqua, 13 1/2 In. 413.00
Cathedral, 4-Sided, Blue Green, Outward Rolled Lip, 11 3/4 In. 784.00
Cathedral, 4-Sided, Blue Green, Rolled Lip, Square, Iron Pontil, 11 1/2 In. 1008.00
Cathedral, 4-Sided, Green, Arches On Panels, Outward Rolled Lip, 11 3/4 In. 896.00
Cathedral, 4-Sided, Green, Arches, On 3 Panels, Tooled Collared Mouth, Pontil, 8 3/4 In. 420.00
Cathedral, 4-Sided, Green, Willington Glass Works, 1860-70, 11 3/4 In. 1232.00
Cathedral, 4-Sided, Medium Green, Outward Rolled Lip, c.1870, 11 3/8 In. . . . . *Illus* 1120.00
Cathedral, 4-Sided, Olive Amber, Outward Rolled Lip, Pontil, 8 1/8 In. 2464.00
Cathedral, 4-Sided, Teal, Applied Lip, 12 In. 495.00
Cathedral, 5-Point Star, Square Panels, 9 In. 345.00
Cathedral, 6-Sided, Blue Aqua, Rolled Lip, 13 1/4 In. 179.00
Cathedral, 6-Sided, Blue, Rolled Collar Lip, 13 1/2 In. 1568.00
Cathedral, 6-Sided, Emerald Green, Applied Lip, 12 5/8 In. 728.00
Cathedral, 6-Sided, Green, Rolled Collar Lip, 13 In. 616.00
Cathedral, 6-Sided, Rblue Aqua, Rolled Lip, 13 In. 413.00
Cathedral, 6-Sided, Yarnall Bros., Aquamarine, Applied Collar, c.1870, 13 1/4 In. 364.00
Cathedral, 8-Sided, Green, Outward Rolled Lip, Arches, 13 In. 2464.00
Cathedral, Aqua Blue, Rolled Lip, Pontil, 11 5/8 In. 196.00
Cathedral, Aqua, 11 1/2 In. 77.00
Cathedral, Aqua, 13 1/4 In. 110.00
Cathedral, Aqua, Outward Rolled Lip, 1865-75, 11 1/2 In. 165.00
Cathedral, Aqua, Rolled Collar Lip, Pontil, Square, 9 1/2 In. 1232.00
Cathedral, Aqua, Rolled Lip, 1855-70, 7 1/2 In. 80.00
Cathedral, Aqua, Rolled Lip, 1860-70, 11 1/2 In. 110.00
Cathedral, Aqua, Smooth Base, 11 1/2 In. 170.00
Cathedral, Aqua, Square, Arches, Ferns, Single Collar Lip, Iron Pontil, c.1850, 11 1/2 In. 725.00
Cathedral, Aqua, Square, Arches, Single Collar, 1860-70, 13 3/4 In. 595.00
Cathedral, Aqua, Square, Gothic Arches, Clover Leaves, IP, c.1850, 11 7/8 In. . . . .395.00 to 595.00
Cathedral, Aqua, Tooled Rolled Collar Lip, Square, 9 In. 532.00
Cathedral, Blue Aqua, Applied Lip, 13 1/2 In. 413.00
Cathedral, Blue Aqua, Applied Lip, 1860, 11 1/2 In. . . . . .123.00 to 336.00
Cathedral, Blue Aqua, Applied Lip, Smooth Base, 1860, 8 3/4 In. 134.00
Cathedral, Blue Aqua, Clockface, Clamshell, Applied Ring Collar, 11 In. 364.00
Cathedral, Blue Aqua, Green Tint, Applied Lip, 11 5/8 In. 213.00
Cathedral, Blue Aqua, Rolled & Tooled Lip, Iron Pontil, 11 3/4 In. 146.00
Cathedral, Blue Aqua, Rolled Lip, 11 1/2 In. 140.00
Cathedral, Blue Aqua, Rolled Lip, 1870, 11 1/2 In. 140.00
Cathedral, Blue Aquamarine, Rolled Collared Lip, 11 5/8 In. 168.00
Cathedral, Blue Green, Applied Lip, 1865, 8 7/8 In. 420.00
Cathedral, Blue Green, Applied Lip, 1865, 11 7/8 In. 672.00
Cathedral, Blue Green, Applied Lip, 1865, 13 3/8 In. 1008.00
Cathedral, Blue Green, Applied Ring Lip, 1865, 14 1/8 In. 1120.00
Cathedral, Blue Green, Outward Rolled Lip, 8 7/8 In. 364.00
Cathedral, Blue Green, Rolled Collared Lip, Iron Pontil, 1845-60, 8 3/4 In. 2240.00

Cathedral, Blue Green, Rolled Lip, Square, Beveled Corners, Cork, 11 1/4 In. 560.00
Cathedral, Emerald Green, Rolled Lip, 1865, 7 1/8 In. 1450.00
Cathedral, Green Aqua, Fancy Arches, 11 1/4 In. 325.00
Cathedral, Green Aqua, Rolled Lip, 11 5/8 In. 134.00
Cathedral, Green Aqua, Rolled Lip, 1860, 9 In. 125.00
Cathedral, Green, Applied Lip, 12 In. 339.00
Cathedral, Green, Applied Lip, 9 1/8 x 2 7/8 In. 523.00
Cathedral, Green, Applied Lip, Impressed Character, 1860-80, 11 1/2 In. 413.00
Cathedral, Green, Applied Ring, Graphite Pontil, 11 1/2 In. 2090.00
Cathedral, Green, Arches, 3 Panels, Outward Rolled Mouth, 11 3/4 In. 2240.00
Cathedral, Green, Outward Rolled Lip, Pontil, Arches, 11 1/4 In. 1792.00
Cathedral, Green, Yellow, Outward Rolled Lip, Square, 2 Piece, 11 7/8 In. 560.00
Cathedral, Honey Amber, 8-Sided, Outward Rolled Lip, 13 1/8 x 5 3/8 In. 896.00
Cathedral, Light Apple Green, Acorn In Arch, Rolled Lip, 10 7/8 In. . . . . .Illus 275.00
Cathedral, Light Blue Green, Rolled Lip, 1865, 11 5/8 In. 330.00
Cathedral, Light Green, Sticky Ball, Square Lip, 12 In. 209.00
Cathedral, Light To Medium Teal, Outward Rolled Lip, 11 5/8 In. 308.00
Cathedral, Lime Aqua, Applied Lip, 12 In. 825.00
Cathedral, Teal, Applied Lip, 12 In. 495.00
Cathedral, Wellington, Deep Blue Aqua, Square, Outward Folded Lip, Pontil, 13 1/4 In. . . 3080.00
Clover Leaf, Octofoil, Red, Amber, Outward Rolled Lip, 8 1/8 In. 1008.00
Cloverleaf, Olive Amber, Stoddard Glass House, 1865, 8 In. 1064.00
Cloverleaf, Yellow Amber, Red Tone, Outward Rolled Lip, Octofoil, 7 3/4 In. 1568.00
Cylindrical, Aquamarine, Arches, 8 Flattened Panels, Iron Pontil, c.1850, 10 3/4 In. 625.00
Cylindrical, Lime Green, 3-Piece Mold, Kick-Up Base, 1860-80, Qt., 10 1/2 In. 139.00
E.V.H.B., N.Y., Cathedral, 6-Sided, Blue Aqua, Diamond Panels, c.1870, 14 1/4 In. 672.00
Goofus Glass, Aqua, Embossed Flowers, Gold, Green Paint, Sheared, Ground Lip, 13 In. . . 150.00
Goofus Glass, Aqua, Roses, 15 1/4 In. 66.00
Goofus Glass, Milk Glass, Embossed Flowers, Sheared, Ground Lip, 15 1/8 In. 292.00
Goofus Glass, Parrot On Branch, Fruit, Gold, Red, Blue Paint, Ground Lip, c.1900, 12 1/2 In. 378.00
Heinz, Sweet Midget Gherkins, Paper Label, 7 1/2 x 2 1/2 In. 55.00
Heinz Dill Pickles, Jar, Paper Label, 13 x 8 1/2 In. 264.00
Jar, Willington, Green Aqua, Twisted Neck, Iron Pontil, 12 In. 1600.00
Lattice Panels, Aqua, Rolled Lip, Open Pontil, 6 3/8 In. 140.00
Petal Shoulders, Aqua, Iron Pontil, 11 3/4 In. 250.00
S.J.G., Cathedral, Aqua Blue, Rolled Lip, 9 1/8 In. 140.00
Seville Packing Co., N.Y., Yellow Green, Crown Logo, 7 1/4 In. 29.00
Shaker Brand, Citron, Square Collar, Cylindrical, c.1870, 5 1/8 In. 1008.00
Skilton Foote & Co's, Bunker Hill, Lighthouse, Citron, Tooled Lip, 11 In. 3080.00
Skilton Foote & Co's, Bunker Hill, Olive Yellow, Tooled Lip, 1880-95, 7 5/8 In. 45.00
Skilton Foote & Co's, Bunker Hill, Yellow Green, Applied Lip, 7 5/8 In. 125.00
Tapered, Aqua, 13 1/2 In. 28.00
TB & Co., Applied Lip, 9 1/4 In. 253.00
W. K. Lewis, Aqua, Iron Pontil, 10 3/4 In. 300.00
W.D. Smith, N.Y., Aqua, Graphite Pontil, 8 1/2 In. 1100.00
Wells Miller & Provost, Diamond, Green, Aquamarine, Embossed, 11 In. 896.00
Wm. Underwood & Co., Blue, Green, 7 Panels, 16 Flutes, Pontil, 11 1/2 In. 1456.00

POISON

Everyone knows you must be careful about how you store poisonous substances. Our ancestors had the same problem. Nineteenth-century poison bottles were usually made with raised designs so the user could feel the danger. The skull and crossbones symbol was sometimes shown, but usually the bottle had ridges or raised embossing. The most interesting poison bottles were made from the 1870s to the 1930s. Cobalt blue and bright green glass were often used. The bottle was designed to look different from any type of food container. One strange British poison bottle made in 1871 was shaped like a coffin and was often decorated with a death's head. Another bottle was shaped like a skull. Poison collectors search for any bottle that held poison or that is labeled poison. Included are animal and plant poisons as well as dangerous medicines. A helpful reference book is *Poison Bottle Workbook* by Rudy Kuhn. See also Household, Ammonia.

Admiralty, Cobalt Blue, Arrow, N, BIMAL, Square, 1 Oz., 4 1/2 In. 85.00
Ancoats Hospital, Cobalt Blue, 6-Sided, Embossed, 4 1/2 In. 73.00
Apothecary, Pulv. Colocynth, Green, Ribbed, Red Recessed Lug, 6 1/2 In. 120.00

Bed Bug, Skull & Crossbones, Aqua, 12-Sided, Rolled Lip, Pontil, Cork, 1 5/8 In. 168.00
Bed-Bug Poison, H.T. Waldner, Cylindrical, Cobalt Blue, c.1885, 8 3/4 In. 39.00
Boots The Chemist, Green, Sunken Panel, Side Warning Lines, 4 1/2 In. 18.00
Boots The Chemist, Green, Sunken Panel, Side Warning Lines, 7 In. 20.00
Boots The Chemist, Montgomeryshire, Cobalt Blue, 6-Sided, Full Label, ABM, 8 1/4 In. . 40.00
Bowmans Drug Stores, Cobalt Blue, 4 Oz. 250.00
Brecklein, Cobalt Blue, 6-Sided, Tooled Lip, 7 1/2 In. 2975.00
Carbolic Acid Poison, Cobalt Blue, Oval, 6 1/2 In. 25.00
Caulk Phenol, Porcelain Screw-On Top, 6 In. 50.00
Chemist, Amber, Square, 3 Ribbed Sides, Glass Stopper, BIMAL, 16 Oz., 7 x 2 1/2 In. ... 90.00
Chemist, Emerald Green, Square, 3 Ribbed Sides, Glass Stopper, 16 Oz., 7 x 2 3/4 In. 95.00
Cobalt Blue, 2 Hobnail Rows, Triangular Front, Curved Back, 3 1/2 In. 40.00
Cobalt Blue, 6-Sided, BIMAL, 1 1/2 In. 35.00
Cobalt Blue, 6-Sided, Hobnail, Curved Back 2 Panels, 4 1/2 In. 32.00
Cobalt Blue, ABM, Oval, 4 In. 20.00
Cobalt Blue, Rectangular, Curved Sides, Ladder Effect Sides, 7 3/4 In. 35.00
Cobalt Blue, Rectangular, Curved Sides, Ladder Effect Sides, Flared Lip, 6 1/2 In. 30.00
Cobalt Blue, Stopper, 3 1/2 In. 50.00
Cobalt Blue, Triangular, Embossed Mesh Design, U.D.C.O., 3 1/2 x 1 1/2 In. 110.00
Cobalt Blue, Triangular, Warning Ribs, BIMAL, 2 1/2 In. 29.00
Coffin, Amber, Tooled Lip, 1890-1910 ....*Illus* 150.00
Coffin, Cobalt Blue, Coffinoids, Crystal Chen Co., Tooled Lip, 3 1/4 In. 4080.00
Coffin, Cobalt Blue, Embossed Shield, 1871, 6 1/4 In. 2046.00
Coffin, Golden Amber, Tooled Lip, 5 In. 1120.00
Columbian Pharmacy Inc., Perth Amboy, N.J., Yellow Green, 6-Sided, Tooled Lip, 5 In. . 4400.00
Cylindrical, Warning Ribs, Emerald Green, Glass Stopper, BIMAL, 7 In. 59.00
Cyona, Cobalt Blue, Man & Horse, Rectangular Shape, Vertical Ribs, 6 In. 614.00
Eli Lilly & Company, Indianapolis, U.S.A., Amber, Tooled Lip, Label, 10 1/2 In. 135.00
Embossed, Cobalt Blue, Stopper, 4 1/4 In. 93.00
Embossed Not To Be Taken, Blue, Rectangular, 10 Oz., 6 1/2 In. 40.00
Embossed Not To Be Taken, Brown, Coffin, Vertical Warning Lines, 6 1/2 In. 35.00
Embossed Not To Be Taken, Cobalt Blue, 6-Sided, 4 1/8 In. 25.00
Embossed Not To Be Taken, Cobalt Blue, 6-Sided, Sheared Lip, Long Neck, 5 1/2 In. 35.00
Embossed Not To Be Taken, Cobalt Blue, Horizontal Ribs, 6 3/4 In. 261.00
Embossed Not To Be Taken, Cobalt Blue, Oval, 6 3/4 In. 30.00
Embossed Not To Be Taken, Cobalt Blue, Rectangular, 4 Oz., 5 1/4 In. 22.00
Embossed Not To Be Taken, Cobalt Blue, Rectangular, 10 Oz., 7 In. 40.00
Embossed Not To Be Taken, Crosshatching, Green, Irregular 6-Sided, 1 Oz., 3 1/4 In. ... 20.00
Embossed Not To Be Taken, Crosshatching, Green, Irregular 6-Sided, 2 Oz., 4 1/4 In. ... 25.00
Embossed Not To Be Taken, Crosshatching, Green, Irregular 6-Sided, 3 Oz., 5 In. 30.00
Embossed Not To Be Taken, Crosshatching, Green, Irregular 6-Sided, 4 Oz., 5 1/4 In. ... 35.00
Embossed Not To Be Taken, Crosshatching, Green, Irregular 6-Sided, 6 Oz., 6 1/4 In. ... 40.00
Embossed Not To Be Taken, Crosshatching, Green, Irregular 6-Sided, 8 Oz., 6 3/4 In. ... 45.00
Embossed Not To Be Taken, Emerald Green, Triangular Front, Curved Back, 6 1/4 In. ... 35.00
Embossed Not To Be Taken, Green, 6-Sided, Widemouth, 3 In. 25.00
Embossed Not To Be Taken, Green, Irregular 6-Sided, BIMAL, 1 Oz., 3 1/2 In. 35.00
Embossed Not To Be Taken, Green, Rectangular, 7 3/4 In. 65.00
Embossed Not To Be Taken, Green, Rectangular, 10 Oz., 6 1/2 In. 40.00
Embossed Not To Be Taken, Green, Rectangular, 12 Oz., 7 In. 40.00
Embossed Not To Be Taken, Ice Blue, Square, Short Neck, Front Panel, Ribs, 4 3/4 In. ... 133.00
Embossed Not To Be Taken, Moss Green, Rectangular, 16 Oz., 7 In. 60.00
Embossed Not To Be Taken, Poisonous On Shoulder, Cobalt Blue, 6-Sided, 4 1/4 In. .25.00 to 30.00
Embossed Owl & Pestle, Square, 6 1/4 In. 121.00
Embossed Poison, Cobalt Blue, 6-Sided, 2 3/4 In. 20.00
Embossed Poison, Cobalt Blue, 6-Sided, 3 1/2 In. 25.00
Embossed Poison, Cobalt Blue, 6-Sided, Squat, 4 1/2 In. 25.00
Embossed Poison, Cobalt Blue, 6-Sided, Widemouth, 2 3/4 In. 25.00
Embossed Poison, Cobalt Blue, Rectangular, BIMAL, 3 1/2 In. 50.00
Embossed Poison, Cornflower Blue, Cylindrical, 7 In. 25.00
Embossed Poison, Martin, Aqua, 6 3/4 In. 712.00
Embossed Poison, P. D. & Co., Light Amber, Diamonds, Tooled Lip, 4 1/4 In. 55.00
Embossed Poison, Pointed Diamonds, Cobalt Blue, Coffin Shape, 3 7/16 In. 130.00
Embossed Poison, Quines, Ice Blue, Wedge Shape, Flat Bottom, 4 Oz. 427.00

Embossed Poison, Skull & Crossbones, Star, Yellow Amber, 4 5/8 In. 532.00
Embossed Poison, Vertical Lines, Cobalt Blue, Tooled Lip, Stopper, 5 1/4 In. 448.00
Embossed Poison Not To Be Taken, Cobalt Blue, 6-Sided, 4 1/4 In. 25.00
Embossed Poison Not To Be Taken, Cobalt Blue, 6-Sided, 5 1/2 In. 25.00
Embossed Poison Not To Be Taken, Cobalt Blue, 6-Sided, BIMAL, 12 Oz., 7 1/2 In. 85.00
Embossed Poison Not To Be Taken, Cobalt Blue, Horizontal Ribs, 3 3/4 In. 117.00
Embossed Poison Not To Be Taken, Cobalt Blue, Oval, 8 In. 45.00
Embossed Poison Not To Be Taken, Cobalt Blue, Rectangular, 5 1/4 In. 30.00
Embossed Poison Not To Be Taken, Cobalt Blue, Rectangular, 6 In. 38.00
Embossed Poison Not To Be Taken, Cornflower Blue, Oval, ABM, 8 In. 35.00
Embossed Poison Not To Be Taken, Green, 6-Sided, 5 1/2 In. 25.00
Embossed Poison Not To Be Taken, Green, Cylindrical, BIMAL, 3 1/2 In. 38.00
Embossed Poison Not To Be Taken, Green, Rectangular, 6 3/4 In. 45.00
Embossed Poisonous Not To Be Taken, Aqua, 9 3/4 In. 30.00
Embossed Poisonous Not To Be Taken, Aqua, Oval, 8 1/2 In. 30.00
Embossed Poisonous Not To Be Taken, Cobalt Blue, 6-Sided, 6 1/4 In. 25.00
Embossed Poisonous Not To Be Taken, Cobalt Blue, 6-Sided, 6 3/4 In. 25.00
Embossed Poisonous Not To Be Taken, Cobalt Blue, 6-Sided, Ribs, 4 1/4 In. 20.00
Embossed Poisonous Not To Be Taken, Emerald Green, Raised Dots, 10 1/2 In. 532.00
Embossed Poisonous Not To Be Taken, Green, 6-Sided, 6 1/2 In. 25.00
Embossed Poisonous Not To Be Taken, R Gerret & Sons Leven, Sash, Green, ABM, 12 In. 55.00
Embossed Property Of The Poplar Borough Council, Cobalt Blue, 6-Sided, 8 3/4 In. . . . 468.00
Embossed Skull & Crossbones, 1000, Orange Amber, 6-Sided, ABM, Cork, 9 1/4 In. 125.00
Embossed Skull & Crossbones, Grass Green, 6-Sided, 3 Crosses, 5 In. 90.00
Embossed Skull & Crossbones, Grass Green, 6-Sided, Germany, 5 1/8 In. 67.00
Embossed Skull & Crossbones, Olive Green, 6-Sided, Germany, 4 7/8 In. 100.00
Embossed Skull & Crossbones, Yellow Green, Tooled Lip, Germany, 5 In. 67.00
Embossed Use With Caution, Cobalt Blue, Pebbly, 1890-1910, 8 3/4 In. 224.00
Embossed Use With Caution, Poison, Cobalt Blue, 6-Sided, ABM, 1 Oz., 3 3/8 In. 45.00
Embossed W, Warning Ribs, Emerald Green, Cylindrical, Stopper, BIMAL, 5 1/2 In. 49.00
Emerald Green, Chemist, Ribbed Sides, Square, Glass Stopper, BIMAL, 20 Oz., 7 x 3 In. 90.00
F. & E. Bailey & Co., Lowell, Mass., Cobalt Blue, Tooled Lip, 1890-1915, 5 In. 990.00
F.A. Thompson & Co., Detroit, Coffin, Amber, Tooled Lip, c.1900, 3 1/8 In. . . . . . .392.00 to 700.00
Figural, Skull, Cobalt Blue, Tooled Flared Mouth, 1880-1900, 2 7/8 In. 3360.00
Figural, Skull, Cobalt Blue, Tooled Flared Mouth, 1880-1900, 4 In. 3925.00
Figural, Skull, Medium Cobalt Blue, Pat June 26th 1894, Tooled Lip, 2 7/8 In. 2420.00
Figural, Skull, Medium Cobalt Blue, Pat. Appl'D For, Tooled Lip, 4 1/4 In. 1760.00
Flask, Allover Hobnail, Ice Blue, Tooled Lip, Pontil, 4 5/8 In. 180.00
Flask, Chestnut Shape, Swirled Ribs, Outward Rolled Lip, Open Pontil, c.1835, 1/2 Pt., 5 In. 59.00
Fureine Weinflasche, Fureine Literflasche, Vertical Ribs, Olive Green, Germany, 6 In. . . . 78.00
George Bathurst, Cobalt Blue, Tooled Top, 4 1/2 In. 110.00
Giftflasche, Skull & Crossbones, Grass Green, 6-Sided, Tooled Lip, Germany, 6 3/4 In. . . 90.00
Giftflasche, Skull & Crossbones, Medium Grass Green, 3-Sided, Tooled Lip, 6 In. 110.00
Gray & Pearse, Poison, Take Care, Cheyenne, Wyo., Cobalt Blue, Tooled Lip, 3 5/8 In. . . 7700.00
H.K. Mulford Co., Chemist, Philadelphia, Skull & Crossbones, Cobalt Blue, 3 1/4 In. 235.00
Human Skull, Cobalt Blue, American, 1880-1900, 2 7/8 In. 3360.00
Human Skull, Cobalt Blue, American, 1880-1900, 4 In. 3920.00
J.T.M. & Co., Medium Red Puce, 3-Sided, Tooled Lip, Label, 5 1/8 In. 605.00
J.T.M. & Co., Yellow Amber, 3-Sided, Tooled Lip, 3 In. 165.00
Jacob's Bichloride Tablets, Skull & Crossbones, Amber, 8-Sided, Tooled Lip, 2 1/4 In. . . . 1540.00
Jacob's Bichloride Tablets, Skull & Crossbones, Amber, 8-Sided, Tooled Lip, 3 3/8 In. . . . 2530.00
Jacob's Bichloride Tablets, Skull & Crossbones, Orange Amber, 8-Sided, 2 1/4 In. 420.00
Killgerm Disinfectant, Poisonous Not To Be Taken, Aqua, Oval, 6 1/2 In. 20.00
Kilner Bros Makers, Cornflower Blue, 9 Warning Grooves, Cylindrical, 7 3/4 In. 45.00
Lattice & Diamond, Cobalt Blue, ABM, Poison Stopper, 5 5/8 In. 55.00
Lattice & Diamond, Cobalt Blue, Poison Stopper, 1890-1910, 4 3/4 In. 196.00
Lattice & Diamond, Cobalt Blue, Poison Stopper, 1890-1910, 5 5/8 In. 157.00
Lattice & Diamond, Cobalt Blue, Poison Stopper, 1890-1910, 7 In. 258.00
Lattice & Diamond, Cobalt Blue, Tooled Lip, 1890-1910, 11 3/8 In. 476.00
Lattice & Diamond, Cobalt Blue, Tooled Lip, 1890-1910, Gal., 13 1/4 In. 3360.00
Lattice & Diamond, Cobalt Blue, Tooled Lip, Poison Stopper, 3 3/4 In. 210.00
Lattice & Diamond, Cobalt Blue, Tooled Lip, Poison Stopper, 4 7/8 In. 70.00
Lattice & Diamond, Smoky Moss Green, Tooled Lip, 4 1/2 In. . . . .*Illus* 532.00

Leath & Ross Neuraline, Green, 8-Sided, Embossed, 1 1/2 In. 78.00
Liq Arsenicalis P.B., Aqua, Cylindrical, Full Label, 6 3/4 In. 25.00
Lyon's Powder, B & P, N.Y., Grape Amethyst, Rolled Lip, Open Pontil, 1840-60, 4 3/8 In. 235.00
Lyon's Powder, B & P, N.Y., Purple Amethyst, Rolled Lip, Open Pontil, 4 1/2 In. 308.00
Lysol, Green, Latticework, Jug, BIMAL, London, 8 1/2 In. 75.00
Lysol Boots All British, Green, Stars, Embossed, BIMAL, 4 In. 39.00
Manchester & Salford Hospital For Skin Diseases, Cobalt Blue, 6-Sided, 4 Oz., 5 3/4 In. 90.00
Manchester & Salford Hospital For Skin Diseases, Cobalt Blue, 6-Sided, 6 1/2 In. 100.00
Manchester & Salford Hospital For Skin Diseases, Cobalt Blue, 6-Sided, 8 3/4 In. 65.00
Manchester Hospital For Consumption, Not To Be Taken, Cobalt Blue, 5 In. 85.00
Manchester Royal Infirmary, Cobalt Blue, 6-Sided, 4 1/8 In. 30.00
Manchester Royal Infirmary, Cobalt Blue, 6-Sided, 5 1/2 In. 37.00
Manchester Royal Infirmary, Green, 6-Sided, 1 1/2 Oz., 3 3/4 In. 25.00
Manchester Royal Infirmary, Green, 6-Sided, 3 1/8 In. 25.00
Manchester Royal Infirmary, Green, 6-Sided, 4 1/8 In. 30.00
Manchester Royal Infirmary, Green, 6-Sided, 6 In. 35.00
Manchester Royal Infirmary, Green, 6-Sided, 7 1/2 In. 35.00
Martin, Aqua, Embossed, 7 In. 246.00
Martin, Patented & Poison, Aqua, 8 Oz. 966.00
Martins U Bend, Liniment, Dried Contents, 3 Oz., 1 3/4 x 5 1/2 In. 480.00
Mercury Bichloride, Lattice & Diamond, Embossed Poison, Cobalt Blue, Label, 8 1/4 In. 3360.00
Moss Green, 6 Oz. 125.00
My-T-Fine, 3-Sided, Brown, Lucknow Mfg Co., Flemington, 11 1/4 In. 98.00
Neuraline, Green, 8-Sided, Embossed, 1 1/2 In. 450.00
Norwich, Coffin, Amber, Rolled Lip, Label, Mercuric Chloride, 4 7/8 In. 725.00
Norwich Pharmacal Co., Amber, Coffin, Tooled Lip, Label, 3 1/2 In. 330.00
Norwich Pharmacal Co., Cobalt Blue, Coffin, Tooled Lip, Label, 7 1/2 In. 1540.00
Not To Be Taken, Teal, 6-Sided, 3 In. 50.00
Owbridge's Embrocation Hull, Cobalt Blue, 6-Sided, 5 In. 35.00
Owl Drug Co., 1-Wing Owl On Mortar & Pestle, Cobalt Blue, 3-Sided, Tooled Lip, 8 In. . 134.00
Owl Drug Co., 2-Wing Owl On Mortar & Pestle, Blue Green, Blob Top, 1895-1910, 9 In. . 165.00
Owl Drug Co., 2-Wing Owl On Mortar & Pestle, Cobalt Blue, 3-Sided, 4 In. 100.00
Owl Drug Co., 2-Wing Owl On Mortar & Pestle, Cobalt Blue, 3-Sided, 5 In. 101.00
Owl Drug Co., 2-Wing Owl On Mortar & Pestle, Cobalt Blue, 3-Sided, 6 1/2 In. 179.00
Owl Drug Co., Owl On Mortar & Pestle, Cobalt Blue, 3-Sided, 4 3/4 In. 67.00
Owl Drug Co., Owl On Mortar & Pestle, Cobalt Blue, 3-Sided, Denatured Alcohol, 8 In. . 550.00
Owl Drug Co., Owl On Mortar & Pestle, Cobalt Blue, 3-Sided, Label, 7 3/4 In. 392.00
Owl Drug Co., Owl On Mortar & Pestle, Cobalt Blue, 3-Sided, Tooled Lip, 8 In. ..224.00 to 523.00
Owl Drug Co., Owl On Mortar & Pestle, Cobalt Blue, Tooled Flared Collar, 3 1/2 In. 95.00
Owl Drug Co., Owl On Mortar & Pestle, Cobalt Blue, Tooled Lip, 2 3/4 In. 55.00
Patersons Local Anesthetic, Amber, Cylindrical, Full Label, Glass Stopper 35.00
Poison Not To Be Taken, Cobalt Blue, Oval, 6 3/4 In. 25.00
Poison Tinct Lobelia Simp., Aqua, Cylindrical, Full Label, 6 3/4 In. 25.00

Poison, Coffin,
Amber, Tooled Lip,
1890-1910

Poison, Lattice & Diamond,
Smoky Moss Green, Tooled
Lip, 4 1/2 In.

Poison, Skeleton In
Robe, Pointing Finger,
Pottery, Japan, 7 1/4 In.

Poison, Skull, Cobalt
Blue, Tooled Lip, 1890-
1910, 4 1/8 In.

Poisonous Not To Be Taken, Aqua, 7 In. 25.00
Property Of Norris Agencies, Brisbane, Brown, Square, Australia, 7 In. 49.00
Rexall, United Drug Co., Cobalt Blue, Tooled Lip, Pt. 150.00
S.A.R. & H. Sick Fund, Not To Be Taken, Cobalt Blue, 6-Sided, Embossed, 3 3/4 In. 84.00
Skeleton In Robe, Pointing Finger, Pottery, Japan, 7 1/4 In. ....*Illus* 27.00
Skull, Cobalt Blue, 4 1/4 In. 5225.00
Skull, Cobalt Blue, Tooled Lip, 1890-1910, 4 1/8 In. ....*Illus* 1568.00
Skull & Crossbones, 2 Stars, Yellow Amber, Tooled Lip, 4 3/4 In. 520.00
Strother Drug Company Carbolic Acid, ABM, Screw Top, Lynchburg, Va., 7 1/4 In. 20.00
Strychnia, Clear, Tooled Lip, Oval, 2 1/2 In. 56.00
Submarine, Cobalt Blue, Tooled Lip, England, 1890-1915, 2 1/2 In. 1232.00
Submarine, Cobalt Blue, Tooled Lip, Flared Mouth, England, 1880-1900, 4 3/4 In. 2688.00
Submarine, England, 1880-1900, 3 x 4 3/4 In. 2688.00
Sulpholine, Cobalt Blue, Rectangular, 4 1/2 In. 25.00
Sulpholine, Cobalt Blue, Rectangular, 6 In. 30.00
Swift's Arsenate Of Lead, Merrimac Chemical, Boston, Stoneware, Crock, 1/2 Gal. 59.00
Tinct, Iodine, Amber, Skull & Crossbones, ABM, Dabber, Embossed, 3 1/4 In. 17.00
Tippers Animal Medicines, Poison, Cobalt Blue, Cylindrical, 7 1/2 In. 195.00
Tippers Animal Medicines, Tapered Cylindrical, Embossed, Brown, 11 In. 39.00
Toxol, Botts The Chemist, Brown, Lattice, 6 3/4 In. 40.00
Use With Caution Not To Be Taken, Usage Externe, Blue, 6-Sided, BIMAL, 3 Oz., 5 In. 65.00
Use With Caution Not To Be Taken, Usage Externe, Blue, 6-Sided, BIMAL, 4 Oz., 5 1/2 In. 80.00
W.R.W. & Co., Medium Golden Amber, Poison Caution, Tooled Lip, Label, 2 3/4 In. 440.00
Widemouth, Cobalt Blue, 6-Sided, Vertical Warning Lines On 3 Panels, 2 3/4 In. 20.00
Widemouth, Cobalt Blue, Triangular, 2 Ribbed Sides, BIMAL, 6 x 2 1/2 In. 80.00
Widemouth, Emerald Green, Cylindrical, BIMAL, 4 1/4 In. 45.00
Widemouth, Green, 6-Sided, Vertical Warning Lines On 3 Panels, 3 3/4 In. ....15.00 to 20.00
Widemouth, Green, 6-Sided, Vertical Warning Lines On 3 Panels, 4 1/2 In. 20.00
Widemouth, Warning Ribs, Cylindrical, Emerald Green, BIMAL, 6 Oz., 5 1/2 In. 39.00

─────────────────────────── POTTERY ───────────────────────────

Many bottles were made of pottery. In this section we have included those that have no brand name and do not fit into another category. Many figural flasks, such as those made at the Bennington, Vermont, potteries or the Anna pottery, are listed. Another section lists stoneware bottles.

Queen Victoria, Duchess Of Kent, Rockingham, 7 1/2 In. 165.00
Saki, Japanese 39th Infantry Regiment, Brown, Blue, World War II, 6 In. 74.00
Saki, Japanese Navy, Battle Flag, Anchor, Blossom, World War II, 6 In. 109.00

─────────────────────────── PURPLE POWER ───────────────────────────

Purple power is the Kansas State University slogan. A series of bottles was made from 1970 to 1972 picturing the wildcat at a sporting event. They were distributed by Jon-Sol.

Wildcat, On Basketball, 1971 .... 92.00
Wildcat, On Football, 1971 ....85.00 to 151.00
Wildcat, Walking, 1970 ....68.00 to 71.00
SANDWICH GLASS, see Cologne; Scent

─────────────────────────── SARSAPARILLA ───────────────────────────

The most widely distributed syphilis cure used in the nineteenth century was sarsaparilla. The roots of the smilax vine were harvested, cleaned, dried, and sold to apothecaries and drug manufacturers. They added alcohol and other flavorings, such as the roots of yellow dock, dandelion, or burdock or the bark from prickly ash, sassafras, or birch trees. A few makers also added fruit or vegetable juice and clover blossoms. All of this was mixed to make the medicine called *sarsaparilla*. It was claimed to cure many diseases, including skin diseases, boils, pimples, piles, tumors, scrofulous conditions including king's evil (a swelling of the neck), and rheumatism. It could cleanse and purify the blood, a process doctors thought should take place regularly for good health. The first labeled sarsaparilla was made in the early 1800s. Some bottled products called sarsaparilla are still made today. The bottles were usually rectangular with embossed letters, or soda-bottle shaped. Most were light green or aqua but some amber and cobalt bottles were made. Later bottles had paper labels.

Allen's, Aqua, Oval, 8 1/4 In. ....20.00 to 55.00

Ayer's, Lowell, Mass, Aqua, Contents, Label, Envelope For Pills, 8 1/2 In. 28.00
Ayer's Compound Ext., Aqua, 8 1/2 In. 7.00
Bristol's, Aqua, 9 1/4 In. 75.00
Brown's Sarsaparilla For Kidneys Liver & Blood, Aqua, 9 1/4 In. 20.00
Dalton's Sarsaparilla & Nerve Tonic, Aqua, Reverse Label, 9 1/4 In. 35.00
Dalton's Sarsaparilla & Nerve Tonic, Belfast, Maine, Aqua, Label, Cork, c.1895, 9 In. ... 45.00
Dana's Sarsaparilla, Belfast, Maine, Aqua, 9 In. 15.00
DeWitt's, Chicago, Aqua, 8 3/4 In. 40.00
Dr. DeAndries Bitters, Root Beer, Applied Collar Mouth, Rectangular, 9 3/4 In. 1344.00
Dr. Green's, Aqua, 9 In. 25.00
Dr. Guysott's Compound, Aqua, Applied Mouth, Pontil, Square, 9 1/8 In. 1232.00
Dr. Guysott's Compound Extract Of Yellow Dock, Aqua, 1840-55, 9 1/4 In. 1000.00
Dr. Guysott's Compound Extract Of Yellow Dock & Sarsaparilla, Aqua, 9 5/8 In. 360.00
Dr. Guysott's Compound Extract, Blue Aqua, Applied Double Collar, 9 1/2 In. 336.00
Dr. Guysott's Compound Extract, Blue Green, Applied Sloping Collar, IP, 9 1/4 In. 3920.00
Dr. Guysott's Extract, Square, Beveled Corners, Blue, Green, 8 7/8 In. 2016.00
Dr. Guysott's Yellow Dock, Blue Aqua, Open Pontil, 6 7/8 In. 504.00
Dr. Guysott's Yellow Dock, Deep Blue Aqua, Double Collar, 1865-75, 9 7/8 In. 190.00
Dr. Guysott's Yellow Dock, Green Aqua, Sloping Collar, Open Pontil, 6 7/8 In. 134.00
Dr. Guysott's Yellow Dock, John D. Park, Tooled Lip, Label, Contents, Box, 9 3/4 In. 385.00
Dr. Ira Baker's Honduras, 1892-1906, 10 1/2 In. 121.00
Dr. J. Townsend's, Albany, N.Y., Yellow Green, Sloping Collar Mouth, Pontil, 9 1/2 In. ... 952.00
Dr. J.S. Rose's, Teal Blue, Applied Sloping Collar, Iron Pontil, 9 1/4 In. 6500.00
Dr. James, Aqua, Tooled Mouth, 1885-1900, 9 1/4 In. 150.00
Dr. Long's, Jacobs' Pharmacy, Atlanta, Ga., Clear, Tooled Mouth, 1885-1900, 9 In. 224.00
Dr. Mile's, Compound Wine, Aqua, Contents, Label, 9 1/8 In. 440.00
Dr. Myers' Vegetable Extract, Wild Cherry, Dandelion, Blue Aqua, IP, 8 3/8 In. 495.00
Dr. Townsend's, Albany N.Y., Green, Square, Beveled Corners, Pontil, 9 1/2 In. 179.00
Dr. Townsend's, Albany, N.Y., Blue Aqua, Pontil, 9 1/2 In. 308.00
Dr. Townsend's, Albany, N.Y., Blue Aqua, Pontil, 9 7/8 In. 146.00
Dr. Townsend's, Albany, N.Y., Blue Green, Iron Pontil, 9 1/2 In. 504.00
Dr. Townsend's, Albany, N.Y., Blue Green, Iron Pontil, 9 3/4 In. 560.00
Dr. Townsend's, Albany, N.Y., Blue Green, Sloping Double Collar, 9 1/8 In. 140.00
Dr. Townsend's, Albany, N.Y., Blue Green, Square, Beveled Corners, 9 3/8 In. 448.00
Dr. Townsend's, Albany, N.Y., Blue Green, Tubular Pontil, 9 3/4 In. 1456.00
Dr. Townsend's, Albany, N.Y., Blue, Sloping Collared Mouth, Pontil, 9 3/8 In. 420.00
Dr. Townsend's, Albany, N.Y., Emerald Green, Applied Mouth, IP, 1845-60, 9 3/4 In. 392.00
Dr. Townsend's, Albany, N.Y., Emerald Green, Iron Pontil, 9 1/2 In. 840.00
Dr. Townsend's, Albany, N.Y., Emerald Green, Iron Pontil, 10 1/8 In. 616.00
Dr. Townsend's, Albany, N.Y., Green, Applied Mouth, Pontil, Square, 9 3/4 In. 616.00
Dr. Townsend's, Albany, N.Y., Green, Applied Sloping Collar, Pontil, 9 3/4 In. 308.00
Dr. Townsend's, Albany, N.Y., Green, Applied Top, 9 1/4 In. 110.00
Dr. Townsend's, Albany, N.Y., Green, Iron Pontil, 9 1/2 In. 364.00
Dr. Townsend's, Albany, N.Y., Green, Yellow Tone, Iron Pontil, 9 1/4 In. 616.00
Dr. Townsend's, Albany, N.Y., Light Green, Iron Pontil, 9 1/4 In. 560.00
Dr. Townsend's, Albany, N.Y., Medium Yellow Green, Iron Pontil, 9 3/8 In. 532.00
Dr. Townsend's, Albany, N.Y., Olive Amber, Applied Sloping Collar, Pontil, 9 1/4 In. 360.00
Dr. Townsend's, Albany, N.Y., Olive Green, Pontil, 9 1/4 In. 532.00
Dr. Townsend's, Albany, N.Y., Olive Green, Square, Applied Lip, Graphite Pontil, 9 1/4 In. 495.00
Dr. Townsend's, Albany, N.Y., Olive Yellow Green, Applied Mouth, Pontil, 9 5/8 In. .*Illus* 475.00
Dr. Townsend's, Albany, N.Y., Olive Yellow, Applied Mouth, Pontil, 9 1/4 In. 448.00
Dr. Townsend's, Albany, N.Y., Olive Yellow, Applied Sloping Mouth, Pontil, 9 3/8 In. 364.00
Dr. Townsend's, Albany, N.Y., Olive Yellow, Iron Pontil, 9 1/2 In. 308.00
Dr. Townsend's, Albany, N.Y., Olive Yellow, Pontil, 9 1/4 In. 532.00
Dr. Townsend's, Albany, N.Y., Olive Yellow, Pontil, 9 1/2 In. ....308.00 to 476.00
Dr. Townsend's, Albany, N.Y., Olive Yellow, Pontil, 9 3/4 In. 364.00
Dr. Townsend's, Albany, N.Y., Olive Yellow, Sloping Collar, Pontil, 9 3/8 In. 134.00
Dr. Townsend's, Albany, N.Y., Olive Yellow, Sloping Collar, Pontil, Square, 9 1/2 In. 269.00
Dr. Townsend's, Albany, N.Y., Olive Yellow, Square, Pontil, 1840-60, 9 1/2 In. 385.00
Dr. Townsend's, Albany, N.Y., Square, Blue Green, Sloping Collar, Pontil, 9 1/4 In. 448.00
Dr. Townsend's, Albany, N.Y., Teal Blue, Sloping Collar, Iron Pontil, 9 5/8 In. 728.00
Dr. Townsend's, Albany, N.Y., Yellow Green, 9 3/8 In. 728.00
Dr. Townsend's, Albany, N.Y., Yellow Green, Square, 9 1/2 In. 225.00

Sarsaparilla, Dr.
Townsend's, Albany,
N.Y., Olive Yellow
Green, Applied Mouth,
Pontil, 9 5/8 In.

Sarsaparilla, Old
Dr. J. Townsend's,
Blue Green,
Sloping Collar,
Iron Pontil,
c.1850, 9 5/8 In.

Scent, Swirl, Blue,
White Sheared,
Ground Lip,
Screw-On Cap,
1860-90, 2 1/8 In.

Dr. Townsend's, Albany, N.Y., Yellow Olive, Tapered Lip, Pontil, c.1850, 9 3/4 In. 242.00
Dr. Townsend's, Blue Green, Applied Sloping Collar, Open Pontil, 9 1/2 In. 504.00
Dr. Townsend's, Blue Green, Beveled Corners, Applied Mouth, Pontil, 9 3/4 In. ...450.00 to 616.00
Dr. Townsend's, Blue Green, Sloping Collar, Iron Pontil, 9 1/2 In. 308.00
Dr. Townsend's, Blue Green, Sloping Collar, Iron Pontil, 9 In. 476.00
Dr. Townsend's, Olive Green, Sloping Collar, Pontil, 1850, 9 1/4 In. ....275.00 to 375.00
Dr. Townsend's, Olive Yellow, Applied Sloping Collar, Pontil, 9 1/2 In. ....157.00 to 308.00
Dr. Townsend's, Olive Yellow, Collar, Pontil, c.1850, 9 1/8 In. 308.00
Dr. Townsend's, Olive Yellow, Sloping Collar, Iron Pontil, c.1850, 1/2 Pt. 258.00
Dr. Townsend's, Sea Green, Square, Collared Mouth, Iron Pontil, 9 1/4 In. 616.00
Dr. Townsend's, Square, Blue Green, Sloping Collar, Iron Pontil, 9 1/2 In. 100.00
Dr. Townsend's, Yellow Green, Applied Sloping Collar, Ring, 9 1/4 In. 168.00
E.M. Parmelee Sarsaparilla & Iodide Of Potassa, Aqua, Rear Label, 8 1/4 In. 88.00
E.M. Parmelee's, Aqua, Embossed, 8 1/2 In. 55.00
Foley's, Chicago, Amber, 9 1/2 In. 35.00
Foley's Kidney Cure, Chicago, Amber, Contents, Label, 9 1/2 In. 28.00
Gilbert's Sarsaparilla Bitters, 8-Sided, Amber, 1870, 8 5/8 In. 672.00
Gooch's Extract, Cincinnati, O., Aqua, 9 1/4 x 4 In. 60.00
Gooch's Extract, Cornflower Blue, Tooled Mouth, c.1890, 9 3/8 In. 300.00
Hall's, Blue, Tooled Mouth, 1880-95, 9 1/4 In. 56.00
Innistallen, Paper Label, Western Bottling Co., San Francisco, 6 1/2 Oz. 26.00
John Bull Extract, Louisville, Ky., Aqua, 9 x 3 3/4 In. ....60.00 to 125.00
John Bull Extract Of Sarsaparilla Cure, Rochester, N.Y., Aqua, 9 1/2 In. 29.00
Joy's, Edwin W. Joy Co., San Francisco, Blue Aqua, 1890s, 8 1/2 In. 45.00
Kennedy's Sarsparilla & Celery Compound, Amber, Rectangular, 9 1/2 In. 150.00
Log Cabin, N.Y., Amber, 1887-95, 8 1/8 In. 123.00
Log Cabin Extract, Rochester, N.Y., Yellow Amber, Label, Contents, Box, 8 1/4 In. 476.00
Old Dr. J Townsend's, New York, Medium Emerald Green, IP, 1845-60, 9 3/4 In. 213.00
Old Dr. J. Townsend's, Blue Green, Sloping Collar, IP, c.1850, 9 5/8 In. ....*Illus* 700.00
Old Dr. J. Townsend's, N.Y., Cornflower Blue, Applied Sloping Collar, Pontil, 9 1/2 In. 269.00
Old Dr. J. Townsend's, New York, Amber, Applied Top, Graphite Pontil, 9 1/2 In. 3960.00
Old Dr. J. Townsend's, New York, Green, Tooled Sloping Mouth, 1870-90, 9 3/4 In. 143.00
Old Dr. J. Townsend's, New York, Pale Blue Green, Iron Pontil, 9 1/2 In. 532.00
Old Dr. Tounsend's, New York, Sapphire Blue, Applied Mouth, 1845-60, 9 1/4 In. 2128.00
Old Dr. Townsend's, Albany, N.Y., Medium Blue Green, Applied Mouth, IP, 9 1/2 In. 165.00
Old Dr. Townsend's, N.Y., Emerald Green, Pontil, Sloping Double Collar, 8 1/2 In. 1792.00
Old Dr. Townsend's, New York, Emerald Green, Sloping Top, 9 5/8 In. 1540.00
Porter's Cure Of Pain, Blue Aqua, Iron Pontil, 6 3/4 In. 600.00
Radway's Sarsaparillian Resolvent, R.R.R., Blue Aqua, 7 1/2 In. 45.00
Sands', Aqua, 10 In. 75.00
Sands' Genuine, New York, Aqua, Double Collar, Open Pontil, 10 1/4 In. 532.00
W. Johnston, Detroit, Embossed Side Panels, Aqua, 10 In. 60.00
Willoughby's, Pottery, 12-Sided, 10 1/2 x 3 1/2 In. 450.00
Wynkoop's Katharsmic, Honduras, Sapphire Blue, Paneled Sides, OP, 10 1/4 In. 8250.00
Yager's, Aqua, 8 1/2 In. 20.00
Yager's, Clear, 8 1/2 In. 20.00

SCENT

Perfume and cologne are not the same as scent. Scent is smelling salts, a perfume with ammonia salts added for a sharp vapor that could revive a person who was feeling faint. Because our female ancestors wore tightly laced corsets and high starched collars, the problem of feeling faint was common. Scent bottles were sometimes small mold-blown bottles in the full spectrum of glass colors. Sometimes the bottles were free blown and made in elaborate shapes to resemble, perhaps, a sea horse. By the mid-nineteenth century molded scents were made, usually of dark green, cobalt, or yellow glass. These were rather squat bottles, often with unusual stoppers. There is much confusion about the difference between cologne and scent bottles because manufacturers usually made both kinds. Related bottles may be found in the Cologne and Perfume categories.

20 Ribs Swirled To Right, Peacock Green, Egg Shape, Flattened, Pontil, 2 1/4 In.	264.00
24 Vertical Ribs, Teal Blue, Egg Shape, Flattened, Tapered, 2 7/8 In.	176.00
26 Ribs Swirled To Right, Amethyst, Egg Shape, Flattened, Tapered, Pontil, 2 7/8 In.	176.00
26 Vertical Ribs, Yellow Amber, Egg Shape, Flattened, Tapered, 3 In.	165.00
Art Deco, Molded, Frosted Design, Nude, Faceted Waist, Glass Stopper, J. Pesnicgk, 7 In.	300.00
Blue & White Cut Overlay, Milk Glass Base, Stopper, 6 Panel Sides, Enamel, Gold, 5 1/2 In.	46.00
Cameo Glass, Bottle, Morning Glory, White, Amethyst, Blue, Silver Top, England, 2 In.	3450.00
Cameo Glass, Bottle, Teardrop Shape, Flowers, Stems, Leaves, Bee, England, 3 1/2 In.	1380.00
Cameo Glass, Duck Bill, Duck Head, White Over Yellow, Silver Top, England, 8 3/4 In.	4600.00
Cameo Glass, Laydown, Lily Of The Valley, Butterfly, Silver Cover, England, 4 In.	2013.00
Cobalt Blue, Ground Lip, Brass Neck Band, Hinged Lid, Chain, Ring, 2 5/8 In.	34.00
Cobalt Blue, Swirled, Tooled Lip, Glass Stopper, 3 1/4 In.	78.00
Cranberry Glass, Double, Cut Glass, Brass Covers At Each End, 5 In.	115.00
Cranberry Swirl, Clear Pressed Swirl Stopper, 6 In.	173.00
Cut Glass, M. Bros, Stopper, Gold Wash Lid, England, c.1874, 2 3/4 x 1 1/4 In.	150.00
Cut Glass, Square, Star Cut Base, Silver Top, 3 1/2 In.	35.00
Dolphin Shape, Clear, Opaque White Stripes, Cobalt Blue Rigaree, 1 3/4 In.	77.00
Double Overlay Cut, Red Over White, Window Facets, Crosshatch Cut, Stopper, 4 In.	115.00
Edwardian, J & RC, Sterling Silver Top, Cut Glass, Hallmark, Chester 1909, 4 3/4 In.	145.00
Enamel, Egg Shape, Brass, Winged Cherub, Flowers, 1 1/4 x 3/4 In.	805.00
Enamel, Woman In Garden, Hinged Lid, Glass Stopper, 2 1/2 In.	1323.00
Feathers, Fern, Teal Green, Inward Rolled Lip, Pontil, Oval, 2 3/8 In.	2016.00
Flowers, Etched, Original Stopper, Sterling Silver Top, C&A, London, c.1909, 4 1/2 In.	125.00
Free-Blown, Canary Yellow, 8 Ribs, Slender Neck, Blown Stopper, 5 In.	403.00
Lalique, 2 Bottles, Holder, Frosted Art Deco Design, 5 1/4 In.	345.00
Lalique, Stopper, Convex Sides, Flowers, Sepia Stain, 1930s, 2 1/4 In.	1508.00
Lalique, Stopper, Panier De Roses, Tapered Cylindrical, Clear, Frosted, c.1930, 4 In.	1885.00
Molded, Cobalt Blue, Straight Ribbed Pattern Sides, 3 In.	165.00
Opalescent Milk Glass, Screw-On Cap, 2 1/2 In.	112.00
Orrefors, 8-Sided, Engraved Fish, Bubbles, Stopper, 9 1/4 In.	180.00
Porcelain, Figural, European Lady, Flowers, Maroon Trim, Brass Dabber, 4 1/2 In.	403.00
Porcelain, Round, Raised Leaves, Silver Collar Hinged Lid, Worcester, 5 3/4 In.	115.00
Sabino, Pomegranate, Opalescent, Art Deco, France, 5 1/2 In.	345.00
Satin Glass, Pink, Cream Loops, Silver Band, Chain & Cap, 6 1/2 In.	575.00
Sterling Silver, Sterling Silver Rim, Birmingham, 1907, 5 In.	140.00
Steuben, Bristol Yellow Pedestal, Candy Cane Stopper, Grapevine, 12 1/2 In.	2040.00
Sunburst, 12 Rays, Sapphire Blue, Sheared Mouth, Pontil, 3 In.	258.00
Sunburst, Sapphire Blue, Beaded Edge, Pontil, 1820-40, 2 3/4 In.	765.00
Sunburst, Sapphire Shaded To Cobalt Blue, Shield Shape, 2 3/4 In.	495.00
Swirl, Blue, White Sheared, Ground Lip, Screw-On Cap, 1860-90, 2 1/8 In. ....*Illus*	325.00
Webb, Cameo, 3-Color, Blossoms, Leaves, Sterling Silver Cover, 6 1/4 In.	4600.00
Webb, Cameo, Lily Of The Valley, Silver Cover, 5 1/4 In.	3738.00
Webb, Laydown, Cameo, Teardrop Shape, Water Lilies, Dragonfly, Cover, 3 1/2 In.	4140.00

SEAL

Seal or sealed bottles are named for the glass seal that was applied to the body of the bottle. While still hot, this small pad of glass was impressed with an identification mark. Seal bottles are known from the second century but the earliest examples collectors can find today date from the eighteenth century. Because the seal bottle was the most popular container for wine and other liquids shipped to North America, broken bottles, seals alone, or whole bottles are often found in old dumps and excavations. Dutch gin, French wine, and English liquors were all shipped in large seal bottles. Seal bottles also held rum, olive oil, mineral water, and even vinegar. It is possible to date the bottle from the insignia on the seal and from the shape of the bottle.

1825 Below A Cross, Black Glass, Olive Yellow, Applied Lip, 11 3/8 In. 90.00
A Von Niessen, Opalescent Olive Amber, Open Pontil, Rolled Lip, 8 1/8 In. 1232.00
A. Kelly, Black Glass, Olive Amber, Double Collar, Pontil, England, 10 1/2 In. 336.00
A.S.C.R., Black Glass, Olive Amber, Applied String Lip, Pontil, 11 In. 179.00
A.S.C.R., Black Glass, Olive Amber, Clover Type, Applied Lip, Pontil, 9 7/8 In. 146.00
A.S.C.R., Black Glass, Olive Amber, Clover Type, Applied Lip, Pontil, 11 In. 157.00
A.S.C.R., Black Glass, Olive Amber, Double Ring Lip, Pontil, 10 3/8 In. 200.00
A.S.C.R., Black Glass, Olive Green, Applied Lip, 8 5/8 In. 360.00
A.S.C.R., Black Glass, Olive Green, Applied Lip, Pontil, 10 3/4 In. 275.00
Anchor, Black Glass, Olive Amber, Applied Lip, Pontil, 6 5/8 In. 730.00
B. Greive, Black Glass, Olive Green, Mallet, String Lip, Pontil, England, 1727, 6 3/8 In. . . 9100.00
B. Greive 1727, Black Glass, Mallet, Olive Green, Applied String Lip, Pontil, 6 3/8 In. . . . 9100.00
Black Glass, Greyhound, Coronet, Olive Amber, String Lip, Pontil, England, c.1695, 6 5/8 In. 3020.00
Black Glass, Onion, Olive Green, Applied Lip, Pontil, 6 3/4 x 4 1/2 In. 7280.00
Black Glass, Wine, Dark Olive Green, 12 In. 133.00
Black Glass, Wine, Dark Olive Green, Cylindrical, 3-Piece Mold, Double Collar, 11 In. . . 285.00
Black Glass, Wine, Dark Olive Green, Cylindrical, Applied Lip, 9 3/4 In. 20.00
Class Of 1846 W., Dyottville Glass Works, Black Glass, Olive Yellow Amber, 11 1/8 In. . . 336.00
Coat Of Arms 1785, Olive Green, Applied Lip, Pontil, 9 1/2 In. 880.00
Crest & Standing Lion, Black Glass, Yellow Amber, Applied String Lip, Pontil, 7 1/4 In. . 1480.00
Crests, Black Glass, Olive Yellow Amber, Applied Lip, Kick-Up, 11 3/4 In. 110.00
Crown, H, Black Glass, Olive Amber, Applied String Lip, Pontil, 9 1/4 In. . . . . *Illus* 295.00
Crown, N, Black Glass, Olive Amber, Applied String Lip, Pontil, 9 1/4 In. 2190.00
Crown Atop Standing Boar, Black Glass, Green Amber, Applied Lip, Pontil, 11 1/4 In. . . 360.00
D P Brechua 1774, Black Glass, Olive Amber, Applied Lip, Pontil, 9 1/8 In. 1980.00
D. Sears 5, H. Ricketts & Co., Black Glass Bristol, Olive Green, Double Collar, 10 1/2 In. . 190.00
Doneraile House, Star, Black Glass, Olive Amber, Double Collar, Pontil, 8 3/8 In. 336.00
Doneraile House, Star, Black Glass, Olive Amber, Double Collar, Pontil, 10 3/4 In. 280.00
Dyottville Glass Works, Phila, Black Glass, Yellow Amber, Double Collar, IP, 11 1/8 In. . . 246.00
E. Herbert, Black Glass, Green, Pontil Kick-Up, Mallet Form, England, 1721, 6 1/2 In. . . 9100.00
E. Herbert 1721, Black Glass, Mallet, Olive Green, Applied Lip, Pontil, 6 1/2 In. 3620.00
E.G. 1762, Heart Frame, Black Glass, Olive Green, Applied Lip, Pontil, 8 1/2 In. 1190.00
Elixir De Guillie G, Black Glass, Olive Amber, String Lip, Kick-Up, Pontil, 6 3/4 In. 390.00
Eman Coll., Black Glass, Olive Green, Kick-Up, Pontil, 11 1/2 In. 130.00
Eman Coll., Olive Green, 60 Oz. 48.00
F.A. Parker, Black Glass, Glassworks, Bristol, Amber, Pontil, 3-Piece Mold, 8 7/8 In. 460.00
Flask, Ambrosial BM & EAW & Co., Amber, Chestnut, Applied Handle, Open Pontil 225.00
Fortuna Sequatur, Black Glass, Olive Yellow, Sterling Neck, Stopper, 10 3/4 In. 625.00
G 1800, Black Glass, Deep Olive Amber, Double Collar, 10 In. 728.00
Greyhound Head Beneath Coronet, Black Glass, Olive Amber, String Lip, Pontil, 6 5/8 In. 3020.00
Griffin, Black Glass, Yellow Green, Applied String Lip, Pontil, England, c.1780, 8 3/4 In. . . 420.00
H. Ricketts & Co., Black Glass Bristol, Olive Amber, Double Collar, 10 7/8 In. 258.00
H. Ricketts & Co., Black Glass Bristol, Olive Yellow, Double Collar, 8 3/4 In. 420.00
H. Ricketts & Co., Black Glass, Olive Amber, Sloping Collar, Pontil, 10 1/2 In. 448.00
H.C., Human Hand, Black Glass, Olive Amber, Double Collar, Pontil, England, 11 In. 392.00
H.C. Hand, Black Glass, Olive Amber, Applied Lip, Pontil, 10 7/8 In. 475.00
H.E. Jefferys, 1827, Black Glass, Olive Amber, 3-Piece Mold, Double Collar, 9 3/4 In. . . . 476.00
Honi Soit Qui Mal Y Pense, Black Glass, Mallet, Olive Yellow, Pontil, 7 7/8 In. 2850.00
Horse & AGG, Olive Green, Pontil, England, 10 3/4 In. 330.00
I Watson Esqr Bilton Park, Black Glass, Olive Green, String Lip, Pontil, 8 3/8 In. 1010.00
I. Smith, Black Glass, Olive Amber, String Lip, Pontil, Onion, England, 1706, 6 3/4 In. . . 9100.00
I. Smith 1706, Black Glass, Onion, Olive Amber, Applied String Lip, Pontil, 6 3/4 In. . . . 9100.00
I.B.B., Black Glass, Olive Amber, Sloping Double Collar, Clover Leaf Pontil, 9 1/4 In. . . . 784.00
I.H.M., Black Glass, Olive Amber, Applied String Lip, Pontil, 9 1/2 In. 560.00
ICC, Black Glass, Olive Yellow Amber, Applied String Lip, Open Pontil, Dutch, 10 In. . . . 420.00
ICC, Black Glass, Olive Yellow, Amber Tone, String Lip, Pontil, 10 In. 235.00
Inner Temple, Black Glass, Deep Olive Green, Amber Tone, Applied Mouth, 10 In. 75.00
J.M. & Co., New York, Amber, Applied Double Collar & Handle, Pontil, 10 In. 1232.00
J.W.C., Deep Olive Green, Sloping Double Collar, 3-Piece Mold, England, 11 In. 269.00
Jas. Oakes Bury, Black Glass, Olive Amber, Applied Lip, Pontil, 10 1/4 In. 336.00

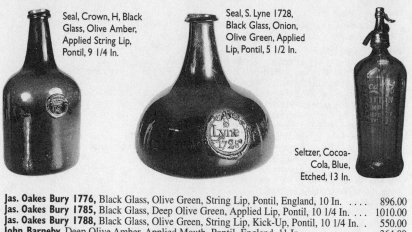

Seal, Crown, H, Black Glass, Olive Amber, Applied String Lip, Pontil, 9 1/4 In.

Seal, S. Lyne 1728, Black Glass, Onion, Olive Green, Applied Lip, Pontil, 5 1/2 In.

Seltzer, Cocoa-Cola, Blue, Etched, 13 In.

Jas. Oakes Bury 1776, Black Glass, Olive Green, String Lip, Pontil, England, 10 In. 896.00
Jas. Oakes Bury 1785, Black Glass, Deep Olive Green, Applied Lip, Pontil, 10 1/4 In. ... 1010.00
Jas. Oakes Bury 1788, Black Glass, Olive Green, String Lip, Kick-Up, Pontil, 10 1/4 In. . 550.00
John Barneby, Deep Olive Amber, Applied Mouth, Pontil, England, 11 In. 364.00
John Winn Jr., Black Glass, Olive Amber, Sloping Double Collar, Pontil, 9 In. 134.00
John Winn Jr., H. Ricketts & Co., Black Glass Bristol, Olive Amber, Double Collar, 9 In. 336.00
Lupton, Black Glass, Olive Amber, Sloping Double Collar, 10 3/4 In. 224.00
Madera, Black Glass, Olive Green, Amber, Sloping Double Collar, Pontil, 12 1/4 In. 213.00
Manufacture De Tabac De Natchitoches, Black Glass, Sloping Double Collar, 9 1/8 In. .. 420.00
PE Herring, Ribbon, Amber, Pontil, Double Collar, Dip Mold Blown, Denmark, 1820, 8 In. 168.00
Picton Castle, 1827, Black Glass, Olive Amber, 3-Piece Mold, Sloping Double Collar, 11 In. 448.00
R. Baker 1729, Black Glass, Mallet, Olive Green, String Lip, 4-Lobed Pontil, 7 3/8 In. ... 3460.00
R.H.C., Griffin, Black Glass, Olive Amber, Double Collar, Pontil, England, 11 In. 476.00
R.H.C. 1815, Black Glass, Deep Olive Amber, Double Collar, Pontil, England, 10 3/4 In. . 504.00
R.H.C. 1815, Black Glass, Olive Amber, Applied Lip, Pontil, 11 1/8 In. 475.00
Rampant Lion, Black Glass, Olive Green, Applied Lip, Pontil, 10 1/4 In. 375.00
Refined Salad Oil, Baldwin & Cie, New York, Olive Yellow Green, Pontil, 12 1/4 In. 448.00
Rev. J.B. Burrington, Black Glass, Deep Olive Amber, Sloping Double Collar, 10 1/2 In. . 476.00
Revd J.P. Melhursh, H. Ricketts & Co., Olive Green, Amber, Double Collar, 11 In. 420.00
Rousdon Jubilee 1887, Black Glass, Olive Amber, Sloping Double Collar, 11 3/4 In. 224.00
S. Lyne 1728, Black Glass, Onion, Olive Green, Applied Lip, Pontil, 5 1/2 In. ......*Illus* 3620.00
S. Twelves, Mobile, Black Glass, Olive Amber, Sloping Double Collar, 11 1/4 In. 448.00
Sans Gratuite, Cat, Black Glass, Olive Amber, 3-Part Mold, Applied Lip, 12 7/8 In. 360.00
Sargent, 1830, Reversed 3, Amber, 2-Piece Mold, Double Collar, Squat, Pontil, 9 x 4 In. . 375.00
Sargent, In Embossed Seal, Deep Root Beer Amber, England, c.1880, 8 1/4 In. 78.00
Sir Wm Strickland Br. 1809, Black Glass, Olive Green, Kick-Up, Pontil, 10 3/8 In. ... 1075.00
T. Grove Esq Fernhouse 1805, Black Glass, Tobacco Amber, Pontil, 10 3/8 In. 1350.00
T. Iones Esq 1775, Black Glass, Olive Amber, Applied String, 4-Lobed Pontil, 10 7/8 In. . 1400.00
T.H. Hunt 1816, Black Glass, Olive Amber, Double Collar, Pontil, England, 10 7/8 In. ... 840.00
Tabac De A. Delpit, Nouvelle Orleans, Black Glass, Olive Amber, String Lip, 10 3/8 In. .. 728.00
TC, CR, Black Glass, Dark Olive Amber, 3-Piece Mold, Double Collar, 11 1/4 In. 112.00
Vieille Cure De Cenon, Black Glass, Olive Green, Applied Lip, Labels, 10 In. 110.00
W Baftaro 1753, Olive Green, Applied String Lip, Kick-Up, 4-Lobed Pontil, 10 1/8 In. .. 3680.00
W. Cooke, Black Glass, Olive Amber, Pontil, Applied Lip, 9 7/8 In. 1344.00
W. Williams Surgeon Llandover, Patent, Black Glass, Olive, Bristol, 3-Piece Mold, 10 3/4 In. 1070.00
W.A., Black Glass, Olive Amber, Double Collar, Pontil, England, 11 In. 336.00
Wine, P.C. Brooks, 1820, Black Glass, Double Collar, Pontil, England, 9 7/8 In. 3360.00
Zara, Aqua, 8 3/4 In. 60.00

SELTZER

The word *seltzer* was first used for mineral water with medicinal properties at Selters, Germany. Seltzer was thought to be good for intestinal disorders. The word soon was used for any of the artificially carbonated waters that became popular in the nineteenth century. Seltzer bottles were advertised in Philadelphia by 1816. *Soda* and *seltzer* mean the same thing. Some collectors want the bottles that say *seltzer* and the special pump bottles that dispensed it. These pump bottles were usually covered with a metal mesh to keep glass from flying in case of an explosion. The top of the bottle was a spigot and carbonation was added to the water when the spigot was pressed. Related bottles may be found in the Coca-Cola, Mineral Water, Pepsi-Cola, and Soda categories.

Belfast, San Francisco, Green ACL, Qt.	30.00 to 35.00
Berlin Bottling, M. Singer & Son, N.J., Green, 11 In.	19.00
C. Proust, Eaude Seltz & Limonades Argentevil, Wreath, Flowers, Ribs, Canary, 12 In.	79.00
Cascade Sparkling Seltzer, Ashtabula, Ohio, 12 In.	176.00
Coca-Cola, Blue, Etched, 13 In. *Illus*	448.00
Greenock Apothecaries, Pink, Acid Etched, Metal Tap, 6 3/4 In.	409.00
Havant, Pure High Class Aerated Waters, L Dubuis Wine, Spirit Merchant, Bear, Blue, 12 In.	418.00
Heath Mineral Waters, Acid Etched, Plastic Tap, 11 3/4 In.	58.00
Jacobson Bros., Dispenser, Green, Lakewood, N.J., 26 Oz., 12 1/4 In.	50.00
Magners Table Waters, Bright Green, Acid Etched, Chrome Metal Tap, 12 In.	84.00
Mid Blue Glass, Faceted, Birds Head Spout, Pewter Tap, 12 In.	17.00
Red Dragon, New York, Green, Cylindrical, 12 3/4 In.	30.00
Reno Brewing Co., Full Glass Stem, c.1915, 12 x 3 3/4 In.	207.00
Royal Palm, Terre Haute, Indiana, 12 In.	220.00
San Francisco Seltzer Water, Etched, 12 In.	35.00
Scarborough & Whitby Breweries, Pale Green, Sloped, Fluted, Pewter Tap, 7 In.	500.00
SF Seltzer, Grizzly Bear, Etched Label, Qt.	30.00
Somarex Casablanca, Embossed, Pewter Metal Tap, Green, England, 12 In.	23.00
Wieland Bottling Works, Washoe, Nevada, c.1912	109.00

─────────────────────── **SKI COUNTRY** ───────────────────────

Ski Country bottles are issued by The Foss Company of Golden, Colorado. These decanters are sold empty and filled by various distillers. The first bottles were made in 1973. By 1975 the company was making about 24 different decanter designs in each size each year, plus one decanter in the gallon size. They made 3 designs in 1995. The firm has marketed many series of decanters.

Animal, Badger, 1981, Miniature	8.00
Animal, Bear, Brown, 1974	3.80
Animal, Bear, Polar, 1984	25.00
Animal, Bobcat, 1981, Miniature	14.00
Animal, Buffalo, Stampede, 1982, Miniature	10.50
Animal, Bull, Charolais, 1974	15.00
Animal, Cow, Holstein, 1973	9.50 to 20.00
Animal, Coyote, Family, 1978, Miniature	12.00
Animal, Dog, Labrador With Mallard, 1978, Miniature	6.50
Animal, Elk, American, 1980, Miniature	21.00
Animal, Ferret, Blackfooted, 1976, Miniature	10.00
Animal, Fox, Family, 1979, Miniature	10.00
Animal, Fox, On Log, 1974, Miniature	18.00 to 38.00
Animal, Fox, With Butterfly, 1983	18.00
Animal, Fox, With Butterfly, 1983, Miniature	10.00
Animal, Goat, Mountain, 1975	25.00
Animal, Goat, Mountain, 1975, Miniature	9.50
Animal, Jaguar, 1983, Miniature	40.00
Animal, Kangaroo, 1974	5.00
Animal, Kangaroo, 1974, Miniature	12.00
Animal, Leopard, Snow, 1979	25.00
Animal, Lion, Mountain, 1973	20.00 to 40.00
Animal, Lions, African, Safari, 1987 *Illus*	20.00
Animal, Lions, African, Safari, 1987, Miniature	10.00
Animal, Otter, River, 1979, Miniature	9.00 to 13.50
Animal, Raccoon, 1975	16.00 to 30.00
Animal, Rhinoceros, White, 3 In.	40.00
Animal, Sheep, Desert, Grand Slam, 1980, Miniature	15.00
Animal, Sheep, Rocky Mountain, 1981	70.00
Animal, Sheep, Rocky Mountain, 1981, Miniature	7.00
Animal, Skunk, Family, 1978	25.00
Animal, Squirrels, 1983, Club Decanter	38.00
Animal, Squirrels, 1983, Club Decanter, Miniature	40.00
Animal, Walrus, Alaskan, 1985, Miniature	10.00

Bird, Blackbird, Red Wing, 1977 . . . . 25.00
Bird, Blackbird, Red Wing, 1977, Miniature 12.00
Bird, Cardinal, 1977, Miniature . . . . .5.50 to 15.00
Bird, Cardinal, Holiday, Box, 1991 . . . . 20.00
Bird, Condor, California, 1973 . . . . .8.00 to 10.00
Bird, Condor, California, 1973, Miniature . . . . .5.00 to 10.00
Bird, Dove, Peace, 1973 . . . . .8.00 to 10.00
Bird, Dove, Peace, 1973, Miniature . . . . .7.00 to 12.00
Bird, Duck, Blue Wing Teal, 1976, Miniature 22.00
Bird, Duck, Canvasback, 1981 . . . . 20.00
Bird, Duck, Green Wing Teal, 1983, Miniature . . . . *Illus* 20.00
Bird, Duck, King Eider, 1977 . . . . 20.00
Bird, Duck, King Eider, 1977, Miniature 15.50
Bird, Duck, Merganser, Female Hooded, 1981, Miniature 18.00
Bird, Duck, Old Squaw, 1992 . . . . 20.00
Bird, Duck, Pintail, 1978, Miniature 15.00
Bird, Duck, Red Head, Box, 1974 . . . . 9.50
Bird, Duck, Wood, 1974, Miniature 18.50
Bird, Eagle, Bald, On Water, 1981, 750 Milliliters 38.00
Bird, Eagle, Birth Of Freedom, 1976, Miniature 23.00
Bird, Eagle, Easter Seals, 1980, Miniature 10.00
Bird, Eagle, Harpy, 1973 . . . . 30.00
Bird, Eagle, Majestic, 1971, Miniature 31.00
Bird, Eagle, Majestic, 1973, Gal. . . . . .280.00 to 464.00
Bird, Eagle, Mountain, 1973, Miniature 29.00
Bird, Eagle, On Drum, 1976, Miniature . . . . .11.00 to 25.00
Bird, Falcon, Gyrfalcon, 1983, Miniature 13.00
Bird, Falcon, Peregrine, 1979, 750 Milliliters 25.00
Bird, Falcon, Peregrine, 1979, Miniature . . . . .9.50 to 20.00
Bird, Falcon, Prairie, 1981, Miniature . . . . .12.50 to 15.00
Bird, Falcon, White, 1977, Miniature 13.00
Bird, Flycatcher, 1979 . . . . 25.00
Bird, Gamecock, Survivor, 1983, Miniature 26.00
Bird, Goose, Snow, 1988, Miniature 15.00
Bird, Grouse, Ruffed, 1981, Miniature . . . . .10.00 to 34.00
Bird, Grouse, Sage, 1974 . . . . 25.00
Bird, Grouse, Sage, 1974, Miniature . . . . .30.00 to 31.00
Bird, Hawk Eagle, 1974, 4/5 Qt. . . . . .43.00 to 50.00
Bird, Hawk, Red-Tailed, 1977 . . . . 25.00
Bird, Kestrel, Plaque, 1986 . . . . 22.00
Bird, Kestrel, Plaque, 1986, Miniature . . . . .9.00 to 17.50
Bird, Mallard, Banded, 1980, Miniature 22.00
Bird, Mallard, Family, 1977, Miniature 25.00
Bird, Meadowlark, 1980, Miniature 10.00
Bird, Oriole, Baltimore, 1977, Miniature . . . . .10.00 to 13.00
Bird, Owl, Barn, 1979 . . . . 29.00
Bird, Owl, Barn, 1979, Miniature . . . . .9.00 to 12.50
Bird, Owl, Great Horned, 1974 . . . . 25.00
Bird, Owl, Great Horned, 1974, Miniature 6.00
Bird, Owl, Northern Snowy, 1972 . . . . 10.00
Bird, Owl, Northern Snowy, 1972, Miniature 20.00
Bird, Owl, Saw Whet, 1977, Miniature . . . . .8.00 to 20.00
Bird, Owl, Screech, Family, 1977, Miniature 25.00
Bird, Owl, Snow, Baby, 1976, Miniature . . . . .13.00 to 19.00
Bird, Owl, Spectacled, 1976, Miniature 20.00
Bird, Partridge, Chukar, 1979, Miniature 8.00
Bird, Peacock, 1973, Miniature . . . . .10.50 to 13.00
Bird, Pelican, Brown, 1976 . . . . 25.00
Bird, Pelican, Brown, 1976, Miniature 10.00
Bird, Penguin, Family, 1978, Miniature 19.00
Bird, Pheasant, Golden, 1984, Miniature 15.00
Bird, Pheasant, In Corn, 1982, Miniature 21.00
Bird, Prairie Chicken, 1976, Miniature 10.00

Ski Country, Animal, Lions,
African, Safari, 1987

Ski Country, Bird, Duck, Green
Wing Teal, 1983, Miniature

Ski Country, Indian,
Lookout, 1977

Bird, Seagull, Plaque, 1985	14.50
Bird, Swallows, Barn, 1977, Miniature	10.00
Bird, Swan, Black, 1974, Miniature	7.50 to 25.00
Bird, Turkey, 1976	27.00 to 51.00
Bird, Woodpecker, Gila, 1972	7.00 to 10.00
Bird, Woodpecker, Gila, 1972, Miniature	7.00
Bird, Woodpecker, Ivory Billed, 1976	18.00 to 37.00
C.S.M. Burro, Customer Specialty, 100th Anniversary, 1973, Miniature	13.00
Christmas, Bob Cratchit & Tiny Tim, 1977, Miniature	10.00
Christmas, Scrooge, Box, 1979	30.00
Christmas, Scrooge, Box, 1979, Miniature	10.00
Circus, Clown, 1974	5.50
Circus, Horse, Lippizaner, 1976	21.00
Circus, Horse, Lippizaner, 1976, Miniature	13.25
Circus, Horse, Palomino, 1976	52.00
Circus, Jenny Lind, Blue, 1976	6.00 to 22.00
Circus, Jenny Lind, Yellow, 1976	37.00
Circus, Lion, 1976	1.00
Circus, P.T. Barnum, 1976	1.25
Circus, Ringmaster, 1974	6.00
Circus, Tiger, 1975	12.25
Circus, Tom Thumb, 1974	.95
Fish, Muskellunge, 1977	25.00
Fish, Muskellunge, 1977, Miniature	12.00
Fish, Salmon, 1977	25.00
Fish, Salmon, 1977, Miniature	10.00 to 13.00
Fish, Trout, Rainbow, 1976	20.00 to 25.00
Indian, Ceremonial Dancer, Buffalo, 1980	10.00
Indian, Ceremonial Dancer, Eagle, 1979, Miniature	8.00 to 10.00
Indian, Ceremonial Dancer, Wolf, No. 4, 1981, Miniature	17.00 to 21.00
Indian, Cigar Store, 1974	14.00
Indian, Cigar Store, 1974, Miniature	13.00
Indian, Great Spirit, 1976, Miniature	11.00
Indian, Lookout, 1977	*Illus* 28.00
Indian, Lookout, 1977, Miniature	15.50
Indian, North American Tribes, Arapaho, 1977	27.00
Indian, Talavia Kachina, 1992, Miniature	15.00
Indian, Warrior, Hatchet, Chief, No. 1, 1975	23.00 to 28.00
Indian, Warrior, Hatchet, Chief, No. 1, 1975, Miniature	7.00 to 11.00
Indian, Warrior, Lance, Chief, No. 2, 1975	77.00
Indian, Warrior, Lance, Chief, No. 2, 1975, Miniature	8.00 to 10.00
Lady Of Leadville, Brown, Customer Specialty, 1973, Miniature	5.00
Mill River Country Club, Customer Specialty, 1974	10.00
Phoenix Bird, Customer Specialty, Box, 1981	10.00

Political, Donkey, Customer Specialty, 1976 .... 35.00
Political, Donkey, Customer Specialty, 1976, Miniature 16.00
Political, Elephant, Customer Specialty, 1976, Miniature 16.00
Rodeo, Barrel Rider, Box, 1982, Miniature 20.00
Rodeo, Bull Rider, 1980 .... 43.00
Rodeo, Wyoming Bronco, 1979, Miniature 8.50
Skier, Olympic, Customer Specialty, Box, 1980, Miniature 7.00
Submarine, Customer Specialty, 1976, Miniature 20.00
Submarine, Customer Specialty, Box, 1976 .... 21.00

SNUFF

Snuff has been used in European countries since the fifteenth century, when the first tobacco was brought back from America by Christopher Columbus. The powdered tobacco was inhaled through long tubes. The French ambassador to Portugal, Jean Nicot, unknowingly made his name a household word when he sent some of the powdered tobacco to his queen, Catherine de Medici. The stuff became known as *nicotine*. Tobacco was at first considered a remedy and was used in many types of medicines. In the sixteenth and seventeenth centuries, royalty enjoyed snuff and kept it in elaborate gold and silver snuffboxes. Snuff was enjoyed by both royalty and laboring classes by the eighteenth century. The nineteenth-century gentleman no longer used snuff by the 1850s, although poor Southern women used snuff by dipping, not sniffing, and putting it in the mouth, not the nose. Snuff bottles have been made since the eighteenth century. Glass, metal, ceramic, ivory, and precious stones were all used to make plain or fancy snuff holders. Commercial bottles for snuff are made of dark glass, usually shaped more like a box or a jar than a bottle. Snuff was also packaged in stoneware crocks. Most oriental snuff bottles have a small stick with a spoon end as part of the closure. The International Chinese Snuff Bottle Society, 2601 North Charles Street, Baltimore, MD 21218, has a colorful, informative publication.

Agate, Brown, Beige, Tan, Macaroni, Mask, Ring Handles, Coral Stopper, 2 In. 460.00
Agate, Cameo, Dragon, Lion, Oval, Floater, Agate Stopper, 2 In. 575.00
Agate, Cameo, Rats, Oval, Agate Stopper, 2 1/4 In. 207.00
Agate, Caramel Color, Leaves, Double Gourd, Chinese, 1800s, 2 In. 147.00
Agate, Carnelain, Beans, Vines, Flowers, Melon Shape, Stopper, 2 3/4 In. 288.00
Agate, Chalcedony, Tan Body, Coral Stopper, 2 3/4 In. 150.00
Agate, Chalcedony, White Horse, Gray Body, Oval, Stone Stopper, 2 1/2 In. 748.00
Agate, Flower Scrolls, Vasiform, Early 1900s, 3 1/2 In. 118.00
Agate, Gray, Black Marking, Round, 1800s, 2 1/4 In. 235.00
Agate, High Relief Dragon, Flask Shape, Chinese, 2 1/2 In. 259.00
Agate, Honey, Chinese Coins, Pilgrim Flask, Jadeite Stopper, 2 In. 230.00
Agate, Honey, Flattened Oval, Green Glass Stopper, 2 In. 127.00
Agate, Honey, Mask, Mock Ring Handles, Oval, Green Glass Stopper, 3 In. 345.00
Agate, Honey, Sage, Deer Under Peach Tree, Rectangular, Jadeite Stopper, 2 1/4 In. 259.00
Agate, Man Watering Tree, Relief, Oval, Coral Stopper, 2 In. 920.00
Agate, Pear Shape, 123 Label, 1800s, 3 In. 323.00
Amber, Hollowed, 258 Label, 1700s, 2 In. 588.00
Amber, Mask, Mock Ring Handles, Landscape, Oval, Rose Quartz Stopper, 2 3/4 In. 374.00
Amber, Sages, Figures, Landscape, Mock Ring Handles, Tourmaline Stopper, 2 1/4 In. ... 1725.00
Bamboo, Buddha's Hand, Fruit, Leaves, Blossoms, c.1800, 2 1/2 In. 1150.00
Carnelian, Goldfish Shape, Chinese, 1800s, 2 1/4 In. 264.00
Cinnabar, Carved, Bone Spoon, Asia, 2 5/8 x 1 7/8 In. 95.00
Cloisonne, Trigrams, Cloud Border, Chinese, 1800s, 3 In. 1116.00
Coconut Shell, Calligraphy, Oval, Coral Stopper, 2 1/2 In. 920.00
Coral, Bird, Peony, Relief, Temple Jar, Mother-Of-Pearl Stopper, 2 1/2 In. 920.00
Coral, Birds, Trees, Animals, Chinese, 1800s, 2 1/4 In. 3055.00
Coral, Pink, Phoenix, Dragon, Temple Jar, Stopper, 2 1/2 In. 3450.00
Enamel, Crane & Pine Tree, Metal Spoon, Chinese, 1800s, 2 3/4 In. 250.00
Glass, Amber, Applied Lip, Pontil, 4 1/2 In. 385.00
Glass, Amber, Sheared Top, Open Pontil, Square, 4 1/4 In. 121.00
Glass, Amber, Square, Tooled Mouth, Open Pontil, 1850-60, 4 In. 200.00
Glass, Amber, Yellow, Rectangular, Beveled Corners, Flared, Tubular Pontil, 5 In. 504.00
Glass, Bamboo Carved, Late 1800s, 4 In. 118.00
Glass, Blue Green, Sheared Mouth, Neck Ring, Tubular Pontil, 1770-1800, 11 In. 784.00
Glass, Blue Green, Square, Tooled, Flared Lip, 4 1/2 In. 224.00

Glass, Chinese Elder & Child, Reverse Painted, 2 x 1 3/4 x 1 1/4 In. 33.00
Glass, Cobalt Blue, Cased, Cut To Clear, Lip Neck, Polished Pontil, 2 1/4 x 1 3/4 In. 175.00
Glass, Cobalt Blue, Square, Tooled Mouth, 1880-1900, 4 1/8 In. 310.00
Glass, E. Roome, Troy, N.Y., Blue Green, Tooled Mouth, Pontil, 4 1/4 In. . . . . *Illus* 2200.00
Glass, E. Roome, Troy, N.Y., Olive Yellow, Tooled Mouth, Pontil, 4 1/4 In. . . . . *Illus* 392.00
Glass, Emerald Green, Square, Arched Sides, Sheared Mouth, Pontil, 4 1/2 In. 615.00
Glass, Forest Green, Chamfered Sides, Battledore, Rectangular, 7 x 3 In. 86.00
Glass, Forest Green, Free-Blown, Battledore, Label, Contents, 4 1/2 x 3 In. 460.00
Glass, Forest Green, Sheared Mouth, Rectangular, Pontil Scar, 1800-30, 5 1/8 In. 896.00
Glass, Leonard Appleby Railroad Mills, Golden Amber, 1840-60, 4 1/2 In. 3080.00
Glass, Medium Green, Square, Pontil, Short Shoulder, Flanged Mouth, c.1800, 5 In. 2530.00
Glass, Medium Olive Green, 8-Sided, Tooled Lip, Pontil, 3 1/4 In. 675.00
Glass, Medium Yellow Green, Square, Tooled Flared Lip, Open Pontil, 4 1/8 In. 200.00
Glass, Olive Amber, Rectangular, Beveled Panels, Pontil, Applied Mouth, 5 3/4 In. 364.00
Glass, Olive Amber, Rectangular, Wide Corner Panels, Applied String Lip, Pontil, 6 In. . . 560.00
Glass, Olive Green, Chamfers, Open Pontil, Sheared Top, 4 x 2 In. 489.00
Glass, Olive Green, Flared Lip, Bubbles, Pontil, 4 In. 600.00
Glass, Olive Green, Rectangular, Beveled Corner Panels, Applied Mouth, Pontil, 6 In. . . . 235.00
Glass, Olive Green, Sheared & Tooled Mouth, 3-Piece Mold, 9 3/8 In. 220.00
Glass, Olive Green, Square, 4 1/2 In. 116.00
Glass, Olive Yellow Green, Tooled Mouth, 9 5/8 In. 168.00
Glass, Olive Yellow, 8-Sided, Tooled Lip, Pontil, 4 1/8 In. 840.00
Glass, Olive Yellow, Chamfered Corners, Rectangular, 1860-80, 9 3/4 In. . . . . *Illus* 308.00
Glass, Olive Yellow, Free-Blown, Square, Sheared Mouth, New Eng., c.1820, 6 3/8 In. . . . 504.00
Glass, Olive Yellow, Green, Tooled Mouth, Pontil, Rectangular, 4 1/8 In. 202.00
Glass, Olive Yellow, Rectangular, Beveled Corners, 1860-70, 9 1/2 In. 672.00
Glass, Olive Yellow, Rectangular, Beveled Corners, Applied Mouth, Pontil, 5 5/8 In. 448.00
Glass, Olive Yellow, Rectangular, Beveled Corners, Sheared, Tooled Mouth, 4 3/4 In. 1120.00
Glass, Olive Yellow, Square, Beveled Corners, Tooled Mouth, Pontil, Free-Blown, 4 5/8 In. 179.00
Glass, Olive Yellow, Square, Sheared Flared Mouth, Pontil, 4 3/4 x 2 3/8 In. 375.00
Glass, Olive Yellow, Square, Sheared Mouth, Pontil, 6 1/4 In. 560.00
Glass, Overlay, Dark Red Overlay, Leaping Carp, Plants, Chinese, 2 1/2 In. 201.00
Glass, Overlay, Dragon Medallions, Handles, Opalescent Ground, Glass Stopper, 2 1/2 In. 1265.00
Glass, Overlay, Figures, Landscape, Opalescent, Oval, Carnelian Stopper, 2 1/4 In. 400.00
Glass, Overlay, Figures, Landscape, Opalescent, Pear Shape, Jasper Stopper, 2 1/2 In. 920.00
Glass, Overlay, Grasshopper, Snowflake Ground, Green Glass Stopper, 2 1/2 In. 575.00
Glass, Overlay, Green Frog, Lotus, Opalescent Ground, Green Glass Stopper, 2 3/4 In. . . . 1725.00
Glass, Overlay, Green, Red Fruit, Peach Blossom Ground, Agate Stopper, 2 In. 1495.00
Glass, Overlay, Herd Boy, Water Buffalo, Bat Handles, Malachite Stopper, 2 1/4 In. 316.00
Glass, Overlay, Huang Chenyan Riding Donkey, Attendant, Jade Stopper, 2 1/2 In. 430.00
Glass, Overlay, Lotus Designs, Polychrome On White, 3 1/2 In. 1528.00
Glass, Overlay, Multicolored Flowers, Crab, Mock Handles, Yanchow School, 3 In. 403.00
Glass, Overlay, Multicolored, Carp, Lotus, Pear Shape, Coral Stopper, 2 1/2 In. 2185.00

Snuff, Glass, E. Roome,
Troy, N.Y., Blue Green, Tooled
Flared Mouth, Pontil, 4 1/4 In.

Snuff, Glass, E. Roome, Troy,
N.Y., Olive Yellow, Tooled
Mouth, Pontil, 4 1/4 In.

Snuff, Glass, Olive Yellow,
Chamfered Corners,
Rectangular, 1860-80, 9 3/4 In.

Glass, Overlay, Red Carp, Snowflake Ground, Tiger's-Eye Stopper, 2 1/2 In. 1150.00
Glass, Overlay, Red Dragon, Opalescent Ground, Rose Quartz Stopper, 3 1/4 In. 173.00
Glass, Overlay, Red Fish Dragon, Snowflake Ground, Rose Quartz Stopper, 2 3/4 In. 230.00
Glass, Overlay, Ruby Cut To Clear, Pear Shape, 154 Label, 1800s, 3 In. 470.00
Glass, Overlay, Ruby, Flowers, Snowflake Ground, Jade Stopper, 156 Label, 2 1/2 In. 499.00
Glass, Overlay, Vases, Fruit, Flowers, Fish, White Ground, Jade Stopper, 2 1/2 In. 374.00
Glass, Overlay, White, Green, Children In Garden, Chinese, 3 1/4 In. 259.00
Glass, Overlay, Zodiac Animals, Snowflake Ground, Green Glass Stopper, 2 1/4 In. 316.00
Glass, Pink, 10 Characters, Pink Glass Stopper, 2 1/2 In. 1265.00
Glass, Pink, Blue, White, Splash, Spade Shape, Stained Red Stopper, 2 1/2 In. 575.00
Glass, Red Ribbons, Flattened Oval, Stained Stopper, 2 1/2 In. 316.00
Glass, Ruby, Faceted, Spade Shape, Jadeite Stopper, 2 In. 3105.00
Glass, Sapphire Blue, Gourds, Vines, Coral Stopper, 2 1/4 In. 403.00
Glass, Square Beveled Corners, Sheared Flared Mouth, Pontil, 4 3/4 x 3 In. 350.00
Glass, Taddy & Compy, Wholesale Mfrs. Tobacco, White, Black Transfer, Square, 2 3/4 In. 284.00
Glass, White, Man, On Horse, Attendant, Palace, Silver Top, Chinese, 1800s, 2 1/2 In. . . . 1116.00
Glass, White, Red Enamel, Bat, Cloud, 4 Characters, Rose Quartz Stopper, 2 3/8 In. 374.00
Glass, Yellow Amber, Olive Tone, 12-Sided, Round Neck, Rolled Lip, OP, 4 7/8 In. 3360.00
Glass, Yellow Amber, Paddles, Rectangular, Sheared Mouth, Pontil, 4 3/16 In. 476.00
Glass, Yellow Amber, Square, Tooled, Flared Lip, Open Pontil, 4 3/8 In. 235.00
Glass, Yellow Green, Square, Tooled Flared Lip, Open Pontil, c.1800-30, 4 1/8 In. 199.00
Glass, Yellow Tobacco Amber, Tooled Lip, OP, c.1820, 4 3/8 In. . . . . 72.00 to 80.00
Glass, Yellow, Green, Olive Tone, Flared Mouth, Pontil, 3 3/4 In. 504.00
Hornbill, Banded, Screw Top, 1800s, 1 3/4 x 3/4 In. 78.00
Hornbill, Phoenix, Red Dragon Handles, Green Stone Stopper, Spade Shape, 2 1/2 In. . . . 1150.00
Ivory, Bean Shape, Late 1800s, 3 1/2 In. 295.00
Ivory, Boy Holding Double Gourd, Vines, Stopper, 3 3/8 In. 1150.00
Ivory, Chinese Figure, Inlaid, Carved, Japan, 1920s, 2 3/4 x 1 1/2 In. 650.00
Ivory, Flowers, Carved, High Relief, Rectangular, Chinese, 1800s, 2 3/4 In. 118.00
Ivory, People, Bird, Branch, Scrimshaw, Baluster Vase Shape, Chinese, Late 1800s, 3 In. . . 200.00
Ivory, Polychrome, Ladybug, 2 Ears Of Corn, Stopper, 2 1/2 In. 1610.00
Ivory, Polychrome, Woman, Japan, Early 1900s, 4 1/2 In. . . . . 294.00 to 353.00
Ivory, Texts, Flowers, Lacquer Inlay, Chinese, 1800s, 3 In. 2820.00
Jade, Brown, Oval, Green Glass Stopper, 2 1/4 In. 207.00
Jade, Foo Dog Masks, White, Vasiform, 1800s, 2 In. 1410.00
Jade, Gray White, Leaves, Green Markings, Gourd, Chinese, 1800s, 2 In. 118.00
Jade, Gray Yellow, Peach Shape, Chloromelanite Top, 220 Label, 1800s, 2 In. 705.00
Jade, Green, Melon Shape, 109 Label, 1800s, 2 1/2 In. 470.00
Jade, Hand Carved, Spoon, Jade Lid, 2 1/2 In. 35.00
Jade, Hollowed, Heart Shape, c.1800, 2 1/2 In. 353.00
Jade, Red, Goldfish On Lily Pad, Green Markings, Chinese, 1800s, 2 1/2 In. 5581.00
Jade, Turtle Shape, c.1800, 2 1/2 In. 588.00
Jade, White, Brocade Ribbon, Flattened Oval, Jadeite Stopper, 2 1/2 In. 546.00
Jade, White, Carp, Flattened Oval, Glass Stopper, 3 In. 805.00
Jade, White, Chih-Lung, Dragons, Jadeite Stopper, 2 1/2 In. 2070.00
Jade, White, Enameled Silver Mounts, Chinese, 1800s, 2 1/2 In. 353.00
Jade, White, Mask, Mock Ring Handles, Raised Panels, Rectangular, Coral Stopper, 2 In. . . 748.00
Jade, Yellow, Medallion, Keyfret Border, Round, Coral Stopper, Stand, 2 1/4 In. 9775.00
Jadeite, Green, Lavender, Spade Shape, Rose Quartz Stopper, 2 In. 575.00
Jadeite, Green, White, Purse Shape, Green Glass Stopper, 1 3/4 In. 403.00
Jar, Olive Green, Square, Beveled Edges, Sheared Mouth, Pontil, 1800-30, 4 In. 765.00
Jar, Olive Yellow, Blown, Cylindrical, Collared Mouth, 1800-30, 7 5/8 x 4 5/8 In. 616.00
Jasper, Red, Tan, Brown, Oval, Green Jadeite Stopper, 2 1/4 In. 403.00
Lac Burgaute, Chinese, 1800s, 2 3/4 In. 176.00
Lapis Lazuli, Gourds, Vines, Gourd Shape, Stopper, c.1910, 2 In. 81.00
Peking Glass, Emerald Green, Early 1900s, Chinese, 2 3/4 In. 29.95
Peking Glass, Green Overlay, Green Stopper, Chinese, 2 3/4 x 1 3/4 In. 47.00
Peking Glass, White, Imperial Yellow, Chinese, 2 1/2 In. 225.00
Porcelain, Bird, Flower, 4 Characters, Spade Shape, Glass Stopper, 2 In. 160.00
Porcelain, Dragons, Phoenix, Exotic Animals, 4 Characters, Jade Stopper, 2 3/4 In. 575.00
Porcelain, Figure, Camel Outside Gate, 6 Characters, Underglaze, Agate Stopper, 2 1/2 In. 58.00
Porcelain, Foo Dogs, Lizard, Silver Alloy Wrap, Agate Stopper, Spoon, Chinese, 3 x 2 In. 55.00
Porcelain, Grasshopper, Cafe-Au-Lait Ground, Cylindrical, Coral Stopper, 2 3/4 In. 195.00

Porcelain, Green Glaze, Goose, Lotus, Cylindrical, Green Stone Stopper, 3 In. 184.00
Porcelain, Mythological Figures, Calligraphy, Double Gourd, Glass Stopper, 2 1/4 In. . . . 1150.00
Porcelain, Passion Flower, Gold Ground, 4 Characters, Double Gourd, 2 3/4 In. 633.00
Porcelain, Pink, Green Lotus, Relief, Blue Ground, Spade Shape, Glass Stopper, 2 In. . . .   127.00
Porcelain, Polychrome, Figures, Landscape, Oval, Stone Stopper, 2 1/2 In. 207.00
Porcelain, Royal Copenhagen, Daisies, Silver Lid, 5 3/8 In. 2530.00
Porcelain, Rust, Red, Roosters, White Ground, Teardrop, Green Stone Stopper, 3 In. 173.00
Porcelain, Yellow Glaze, Ear Of Corn, Rose Quartz Stopper, 2 3/4 In. 115.00
Porcelain, Zisha Clay, Waterscapes, Slip Decoration, Flask Shape, Chinese, 2 3/4 In. 230.00
Puddingstone, Teardrop, Incised Silver Ring, Coral Stopper, 2 1/4 In. 2415.00
Shadow Agate, Agate Eye Inclusion, Flattened Oval, Jade Stopper, Chinese, 2 7/8 In. 518.00
Shadow Agate, Birds, Flowering Tree, Turquoise Inlaid Base, Chinese, 1800s, 2 1/2 In. . .   353.00
Shadow Agate, Songbirds, Flowering Tree, Flat Egg Shape, Stopper, 1800s, 2 1/2 In. 144.00
Silver, Enamel, Flowers, Ring Handles, Pear Shape, Chinese, 1800s, 2 3/4 In. 235.00
Soapstone, Tan, Operatic Scenes, Pink & Black Marks, Chinese, 1800s, 3 1/4 In. 382.00
Wood, Silver Mount, Turquoise, Coral, Lapis, Mongol Type, Chinese, 1800s, 3 1/2 In. 118.00

––––––––––––––––––––––––– SODA –––––––––––––––––––––––––

All forms of carbonated drink-naturally carbonated mineral water, artificially carbonated and flavored pops, and seltzer-are forms of soda. The words are often interchanged. Soda bottles held some form of soda pop or carbonated drink. The early soda bottle had a characteristic thick blob top and heavy glass sides to avoid breakage from the pressure of the carbonation. Tops were cleverly secured; the Hutchinson stopper and Coddball stopper were used on many early bottles. The crown cap was not developed and used until 1891. The cork liner inside the crown cap was outlawed in 1969. Some bottles have embossed lettering made with a slug plate, an extra piece inserted into the mold. The first soda was artificially carbonated in the 1830s by John Matthews. He used marble chips and acid for carbonation. It is said he took all the scrap marble from St. Patrick's Cathedral in New York City to use at his plant, which made, so they say, 25 million gallons of soda water. In 1839 a Philadelphia perfume dealer, Eugene Roussel, had the clever idea of adding flavor to the soda. Soon colors were added and the soft drink industry had begun. The late 1800s saw the beginning of Coca-Cola (1886), Pepsi-Cola (1898), Moxie (1876), Dr Pepper (1885), and others. The English brand Schweppes was already established, but they added artificially carbonated sodas as well. Collectors search for the heavy blob top bottles and the newer crown top sodas with embossed lettering or silk-screened labels. Collectors refer to *painted label bottles* as *ACL* or *Applied Color Label.* Recent commemorative bottles are also in demand. In this book, the soda bottle listing includes modern carbonated beverage bottles as well as the older blob tops, Hutchinsons, and other collectible soda bottles. Coca-Cola, Pepsi-Cola, mineral water, sarsaparilla, and seltzer bottles are listed in their own sections. Collector clubs with newsletters include Painted Soda Bottle Collectors Association, Dr Pepper 10-2-4-Collectors Club, Coca-Cola Collectors Club, and Pepsi-Cola Collectors Club and are listed in the front of this book. Related bottles may be found in the Coca-Cola, Mineral Water, Pepsi-Cola, Sarsaparilla, and Seltzer categories.

7Up, 50th Anniversary, St. Louis, Mo., Edward L. Taylor, 1928–1978, 16 Oz. 1.00
7Up, Amber, Embossed, Knoxville, Tenn., 6 1/2 In. 40.00
7Up, Bicentennial, Liberty Bell, First Rung July 8, 1776, Beverage Management, 1975 . . .   1.00
7Up, Cleveland Browns, Contents, Unopened, 1974 . . . .   5.00
7Up, Contents, 3 In. . . . . .10.00 to 11.00
7Up, Dotted Letters, Money Back, 1 Liter, 33.8 Oz. 5.00
7Up, Portland, Oregon, 1952, 7 Oz., 8 In. 5.00
7Up, Return For Deposit, Contents, Early 1970s, 10 Oz. 2.00
7Up, Salt Lake City, Utah, 1940s 7.50
7Up, Salutes Indiana Hurryin' Hoosiers, 1976 NCAA Champs, Red Label, 16 Oz. 5.00
7Up, Salutes Joliet Catholic High School, Football Champs, 4 Years, Ill., c.1978, 16 Oz. . .   2.00
7Up, Silk-Screened Logo, Contents, 1960s, 7 Oz., 8 In. 1.00
7Up, Swimsuit Bubble Girl, Green Glass, White Print, C. Leary & Co., Mass., 1940s, 8 In.   10.50
7Up, Syrup, Norwich, Ct., Gal. 5.00
7Up, UCLA Bruins, Coach John Wooden, NCAA Championships, 16 Oz. 6.00
7Up, Woman, Bathing Suit, Bubbles Over Head, Painted Label, Green, 7 Oz. . . . . .1.00 to 2.25
7Up Lithiated Lemon Soda, Cap, Brown 347.00
A Craven Hulme, Manchester, 4 Rylands, Aqua, Narrow Neck, Codd, 10 Oz. 25.00
A&W Root Beer, Sugar Free, ACL, 16 Oz. . . . .*Illus*   8.50

A&W Root Beer, Sugar Free, Foam Label, No Deposit, No Return, Throw-Away, 16 Oz. .   11.00
A. Richards, Reading, Slug Plate, Union Glass Works, Philada., Emerald Green, 7 In. 1680.00
A. Smith, Charleston, S.C., Sloping Collar, Pontil, Cylindrical, Bubbles, Blue, 1/2 Pt. 896.00
Albert Fischer, Atlantic City., N.J., Amber, Tooled Lip, 7 In. 78.00
Albert Vonharten, Savannah, Ga., Ginger Ale, Teal Blue, Blob Top, 7 1/8 In. 312.00
Allegheny Bottling Co., 48 Taggart St. N.S. Pittsburg, Bottle Not To Be Sold, Pa., Aqua . .   25.00
Antelope Beverages, Antelope, Blue & White ACL 18.00
Aspinock, Indian, Red & White ACL, Putnam, Conn., 1942, 12 Oz. 21.00
August, Full Flavored Beverages, Red & White ACL, Green Glass, Mahanoy City, 7 Oz. .   10.00
B. Carter, West Chester, Blue Green, Applied Mouth, Iron Pontil, 7 In. 560.00
B. Stockton, Blue Aqua, Applied Top, Stopper 88.00
B.R. Lippincott & Co., Stockton, 10-Sided, Cobalt Blue, Iron Pontil 1540.00
B.S. & M.W. Wks., Buffalo, N.Y., Aqua, Hutchinson 20.00
B.W. & Co., New York, Cobalt Blue, Applied Blob Mouth, Iron Pontil, c.1850, 7 1/4 In. . .   240.00
Babb & Co., San Francisco, Cal., Green, Iron Pontil 165.00
Backbar, Hires Root Beer Syrup, Hires Kid Holding Foamy Mug, Drink Hires Root Beer . 15588.00
Bailey Boys Pop, Marshalltown, Iowa, 1912-52, 8 Oz. 45.00
Bartlett Water, White, Blue, Brown ACL, Lake County, Ca., 1951, 7 Oz. 5.50
Bay City Soda Water, S.F., Embossed Star, Teal Blue 132.00
Bay City Soda Water, S.F., Star, Cobalt Blue, Blob Top, 7 In. . . . . .140.00 to 220.00
Bay City Soda Water, S.F., Star, Medium Sapphire Blue, Blob Top, c.1870, 7 3/8 In. 179.00
Bear Beverages, White ACL, San Antonio, Texas, 12 Oz. 90.00
Beehive Beverages, White ACL, Brigham City, Utah, 1969, Qt. 5.00
Ben's Bubbling Beverages, White ACL, Oberlin, Ks., 1947, 7 Oz. 23.00
Berkeley Club Sparkling, Mountains, Red & White ACL, Berkely Springs, c.1945, 7 Oz. .   6.00
Bibbey & Ferguson, This Bottle Not To Be Sold, Yellow, Amber, Blob Top, 9 In. 448.00
Biederharn Candy Co., Vicksburg, Miss., Aqua, Hutchinson, c.1895, 7 1/4 In. 364.00
Big Chief, Indian, Embossed, Green, Rogers, Ark., 1925, 8 In. 42.00
Big Chief Beverages, White & Red ACL, Colorado, Utah, 7 Oz. 9.00
Big Chief Soda, Indian On Horse, Clear, Red & White ACL 59.00
Big Hit, Baseball Player, Embossed, Brunswick, Ga., 8 Oz. 83.00
Bigelow & Co., Green, Applied Collar, Brass Collar, Cast Iron Stopper, 1/2 Pt. 420.00
Bingo, Hy's Beverages, It's A Hit, Red ACL, Oakland, Ca., 7 Oz.   12.00
Birkenhead, Siphon, Metal Tap, Acid Etched, Porcelain Lined, 12 3/4 In. 13.00
Birt, Palm Trees, Mountains, Blue & White ACL, Muncie, Ind., 10 0z. 10.00
Blatz Waukesha Ginger Ale, Indian Girl In Red Triangle, Green, Cap, c.1924 . . . .   24.00
Blue Green, Flattened Tenpin, Sloping Collar, Pontil, 8 1/2 In. 616.00
Boyd Balt., Torpedo, Teardrop Shape, Single Collar, Aqua, 1860, 9 In. 300.00
Bremenkampf & Regli, Eureka, Nev., Aqua, Applied Top 154.00
Bridgeton Glass Works, N.J., Blue Green, Squat, Double Collar 69.00
Brooklyn, Siphon, Fluted, Waisted, Acid Etched, Emerald Green, 12 1/4 In. 51.00
Brown Stout, Teal Blue, Cylindrical, Applied Collar, Iron Pontil, 1/2 Pt. 179.00
Bubble Up, Kiss Of Lemon, Kiss Of Lime, Red & White ACL, Green Glass, 1/2 Qt., 10 In. .   3.00
Bud's Beverages, Flowers, Property Coca-Cola Pennsboro, Orange & Green ACL 77.00
Buffalo Ginger Ale, Columbia, S.C., Straight-Sided, Aqua, 1930s, 6 1/2 Oz., 8 5/8 In. 8.00
Buffum, Pittsburgh, Cobalt Blue, Sloping Collar, Pontil, 7 1/2 In.   672.00
Buffum & Co. Pittsburgh, Blue Aqua, Inverted Mouth, Iron Pontil, c.1850, 7 1/4 In. 78.00
Busch Extra Dry Ginger Ale, Anheuser Busch, St. Louis, Prohibition Era, Paper Label . . .   25.00
Bush Bros B., Syracuse, N.Y., Cornflower Blue, Hutchinson 79.00
C & K Eagle Works, Sac. City., Blue 154.00
C. Matchin Danville, Cobalt Blue, Squat, Pontil, Tapered Top, c.1850, 6 7/8 In. 4950.00
C.B. Casseoy Warren, O., Aqua, Hutchinson 25.00
C.B. Owen, Root Beer, Cincinnati, 12-Sided, Cobalt Blue, Applied Collar, IP, 8 7/8 In. 1456.00
C.W. Rider, Hutchinson Style, Embossed Tombstone, Green Blue, 6 1/2 In. 3025.00
Camwal Table Waters, Etched, Pewter Tap, Siphon, England, 26 1/2 In. 1606.00
Canada Dry Ginger Ale, Green, 1966 . . . .   1.00
Cantrell & Cochrane's Ginger Ale, 1925 . . . .   5.00
Carbonated BW, Denver Colo, Hutchinson 10.00
Carl H. Schultz, C-P-M-S Pat. May 1868, New York, Aqua, Tenpin 39.00
Carter's Natural Lemon Phosphate, Dice, Red & White ACL, Green Glass, Middletown, O.   21.00
Cascade Ginger Ale, 6-Pack, Box, 8 x 10 x 5 1/2 In. 17.00
Cawley, Dover, N.J., Aqua, Hutchinson 10.00
Chadsey & Bro, New York, Cobalt Blue, Iron Pontil, c.1850, 7 3/8 In. 123.00

Champlainette Brand, Lake Champlain Bottle Works, Port Henry, Green, 1910, 8 In. . . .   12.00
Chautauqua Root Beer, Paper Label, Crown Top, Southerntier Brewing, N.Y., 12 Oz., 9 In.   10.00
Cheer Up Coca-Cola, White & Red ACL, Green Glass, Salina, Ks., Pre 1951, 7 Oz. 18.00
Chero, A Perfect Cola, Nehi Bottling Co., Texarkana, Texas, 6 Oz. 5.00
Chero-Cola Bott. Co., Frankfort, Ind., Light Green 25.00
Cherry Smash, Hot Soda, Metal Cap, 12 In. 187.00
Chuk-Ker, The Sporting Thing To Drink, ACL 30.00
Circle A Brand Orange, Blue & White Label, Contents, Sacramento 10.00
Circle A Sparkling Beverages, Dr Pepper, Green & White ACL, Topeka, Ks., 1948, 9 Oz. .   4.00
Citro, Thirst Quencher, Brookland Wood Spring, Co., Balto., Cobalt Blue, Teardrop, 7 In.   59.00
City Bottling Co., Albany, Ore., Hutchinson 50.00
City Bottling Works, Toledo, Ohio, Applied Lip, Sapphire Blue, 6 3/8 In. 448.00
City Of Parks, Stanges Park, White ACL, Prairie River, Merrill, Wisc., 7 Oz. 5.00
Classen & Co., San Francisco, Pacific Soda Works, Green, Blob Top 55.00
Cleo Cola, Red & White ACL, 1938, 12 Oz. 239.00
Clicquot Club Ginger Ale, Paper Label, Cap, c.1920 . . . .   6.50
Clow & Co., New Castle, Blue Aqua, Sloping Collar, Iron Pontil, c.1850, 7 1/2 In. 202.00
Cod Liver Oil Soda Water, Hyatt & Co., Patent Jan 1869, Golden Amber, c.1865, 6 In. . .   616.00
Collins & Latham Barton, Rylands & Codd, Aqua, c.1880, 10 Oz. 25.00
Comstock Gove & Co., Teal, Blob Top, 7 1/4 In. 504.00
Cottle Post & Co, Eagle, Portland, Ore., Phoenix Bird, Blue Green, c.1880, 7 In. 295.00
Cream Soda Taylor & Wilson, Aqua, Blob Top, 6 In. 79.00
Cresswell & Co., Reliance Patent, Rylands, Barnsley, Aqua, Cobalt Blue Lip, Codd, 9 In. .   294.00
Crystal Palace, Union Glass Works, Philada., Blue Green, Applied Blob Top, IP, 7 1/8 In.   896.00
Crystal Soda Water Co., Patented Nov. 12, 1872, Aqua, Blob Top, Pedestal Base, 7 In. . .   130.00
D.J. Whelan, Cobalt Blue, Stopper, Hutchinson Style, 1880, 6 5/8 In. 3850.00
D.T. Sweeny, Key West, Fla, Yellow Amber, Applied Mouth, Not To Be Sold, 8 1/4 In. . . .   925.00
Dad's Old Fashioned Root Beer, Mama Size, Contents, Buffalo, N.Y., Qt. 15.00
Dad's Root Beer, Diet, Yellow & Blue ACL, 16 Oz. 9.00
Dad's Root Beer, Papa Size, Cap, Chicago, Ill., 1/2 Gal., 11 1/2 In. 6.00
Dan Rylands, Barnsley, Amber, Codd, 7 3/4 In. 430.00
Dana Beverages, Diamonds, White & Red ACL, Clear, Cleveland, Oh., 1956, 8 Oz. 7.25
Darling & Ireland, Deep Blue Green, Torpedo, Applied Square Collar, c.1860, 8 In. 1232.00
Davis Bottling Works, Embossed, Sun Purple, Davis, W.Va., c.1895, 8 Oz., 8 3/4 In. 10.50
De Gruchy & Mayo, Hamilton, Aqua Glass, Embossed, 8 In. 205.00
Defender Bottling Works, Schooner, Moonstone, Tooled Mouth, 9 3/8 In. 364.00
Devizes, Siphon, Green, Acid Etched, 12 In. 72.00
Dillon Beverages, Bronco, Orange & White ACL, Dillon, Montana, 1940, 12 Oz. 10.50
Dillon Beverages, Cowboy, Bronco, Red & White ACL, Crown Top, 8 In. 35.00
Donald Duck Root Beer Fountain Syrup, Gal. 30.00
Dr Pepper, 10 2 4, Bottle Cap Shaped Labels, Red, White, 1955 . . . .   62.00
Dr Pepper, 10 2 4, Brownsville, Texas, 6 Oz 10.00
Dr Pepper, 10 2 4, Debossed, Tyler, Texas, 1953, 6 Oz. 11.50
Dr Pepper, 10 2 4, Good For Life, Clock, Greenwood, Miss., Debossed, c.1935 . . . .   7.45
Dr Pepper, 10 2 4, Green, Red & White Painted Label, 10 Oz., 9 1/2 In. 6.00
Dr Pepper, 10 2 4, Opp. Alabama, Debossed, Clock, 6 Oz. 8.00
Dr Pepper, 10 2 4, Red & White Enameled Paint, 1950s, 8 1/4 In. 5.00
Dr Pepper, Boaz, Ala., Milk Bottle Shape, 1/2 Pt., 7 In. 26.00
Dr Pepper, Commemorative, Texas Vs. Oklahoma Football Game, 1973, 16 Oz. 16.00
Dr Pepper, Dallas Stars, American Airlines Center Inaugural Game, 200l, 12 Oz. 2.50
Dr Pepper, Diet, Applied Label, Green, White Diamonds, Chevron Logo, 12 Oz., 9 3/4 In.   11.00
Dr Pepper, Diet, Chevron Emblem, 12 Oz. 5.50
Dr Pepper, Good For Life, Clock, Impressed, Raised Letters, Auburn Nebraska, 6 1/2 In. .   8.00
Dr Pepper, Lake Crystal, Minn., Farmfest, Bicentennial, Agriculture, Green, 1976, 16 Oz.   5.00
Dr Pepper, Okalahoma Sooners, Nebraska Cornhuskers, 1912-1975 Scores, 16 Oz. 6.00
Dr Pepper, Poplar Bluff, Mo., Milk Bottle Style, 1/2 Pt. 15.00
Dr Pepper Btg. Co., Hattiesburg, Miss., Clear, Crown Top, Embossed, 9 In. 3.50
Drink Paul's Drinks, Paul G. Miller, Every Swallow Pure, Muskegon, 6 1/2 Oz., 8 In. . . .   10.00
Durham's Hi-Tide, Ship, Red, White & Blue ACL, 1955, 8 Oz. 3.95
E. Centsch Buffalo, N.Y., Hutchinson, Aqua 25.00
E. Roussel, Philada, Dyottville, This Bottle Is Never Sold, Cobalt Blue, Pontil, 7 1/2 In. . .   168.00
E.A. Post, Portland, Oregon, Aqua 66.00

Soda, A & W Root
Beer, Sugar Free,
ACL, 16 oz.

Soda, Empire Soda Works,
Frank S. Waldo, San
Francisco, Blue Aqua

Soda, Frostie Root
Beer, Baltimore 28 Md.,
12 Oz., 8 In.

Soda, J.W. Harris, New
Haven, Conn., Sapphire Blue,
8-Sided, Blob Top, IP, 7 1/2 In.

E.S. & H. Hart, Superior Soda Water, Union Glass Works, Blue, Blob Top, IP, c.1850, 7 In.   360.00
Eastern Cider Co., Medium Orange Amber, Blob Top, c.1870, 7 1/4 In. 134.00
Eberle Beverage Co., Embossed Light Aqua Blue, Jackson, Mich., 7 1/2 In. 4.00
Edward Moyle, Savannah, Ga., Ginger Ale, Amber, Applied Mouth, c.1885, 7 1/2 In. 212.00
Elko Bottling Works, Elko, Nev., Blue Aqua 825.00
Empire Soda Works, Frank S. Waldo, San Francisco, Blue Aqua . . . . *Illus*   77.00
Enyart Bottling Works, Logansport, Ind., Clear 10.00
Esquire, ACL, Horse & Rider, Atlanta, Ga., 1947, 7 Oz. 4.95
Estell & Vanderburg, Roseland, Ill., Aqua 25.00
Excelsior, 8-Sided, Green, Iron Pontil 413.00
Excelsior, Ginger Ale, Amber, Blob Top, 7 1/4 In. 280.00
Exors Of M Pomfret Albion Works Bury, Aqua, Codd, Pre 1877, 6 Oz. 25.00
F. & L. Schaum Baltimore Glassworks, Olive Yellow, Tapered Top, Pontil, 7 1/8 In. 1430.00
F. Engle, Lancaster, Pa., Blue Aqua, Blob Top, Gravitating Stopper, c.1875, 7 In. 40.00
F. Gleason, Rochester, N.Y., Cobalt Blue, Sloping Collar, Pontil, 7 5/8 In. 616.00
F. Schmidt, Leadville, Colo., Aqua, Tombstone Slug Plate 70.00
F. Seitz, Easton Pa., Blue Green, Sloping Double Collar, Pontil, 7 In. 134.00
F.L. Schaum, Baltimore Glass Works, Forest Green, Applied Top, Iron Pontil, 7 1/4 In. 2640.00
Fowler's, Quality Beverages, Quality Flavors, Blue, White Label, Charlotte, N.C., 10 Oz. . . .   9.00
Fowler's Cherry Smash, 5 Cents, Label Under Glass, Red, Gold, Brown, ABM, 12 In. . . .   476.00
Francis Dusch, This Bottle Is Never Sold, Cobalt Blue, Blob Top, 7 1/2 In. 179.00
Frank T. Kolbek Boundbrook, N.J., Aqua, Blob Top, 9 In. 9.00
Frostie Root Beer, ACL, 1973, 16 Oz. 3.00
Frostie Root Beer, Baltimore 28 Md., 12 Oz., 8 In. . . . . *Illus*   9.00
Frostie Root Beer, By 7Up, Contents, Cap, Jasper, Alabama, 1950s, 10 Oz. 10.00
Frostie Root Beer, Old Fashion Root Beer Baltimore, 12 Oz., 8 x 2 1/2 In. 9.00
G. Ebberwein, Savannah Geo., Ginger Ale, Yellow Amber, 7 1/2 In. 103.00
G. Lauter, Reading, Pa., Emerald Green, Blob Top, 6 5/8 In. 179.00
G. Schmuck, Cleveland, O., Hutchinson, Aqua, Bubbles 20.00
G. Snider, Cold Spring, N.Y., Golden Amber, c.1875, 8 In. 56.00
G.P. Morrill, Blue Teal, c.1865 . . . .   523.00
G.P. Morrill, Green, Applied Blob Top, c.1868 . . . .   385.00
Gem City Bottling Works, Frankfort, Ind., Clear 25.00
Golden Spray Dry Ginger Ale, Decal, Green, Soo Falls Brewing, Ont., c.1929, 30 Oz. . . .   4.00
Goldenmoon Buckeye Root Beer, Jug, Cleveland Fruit Juice Co., Cleveland, Ohio, Gal. .   6.00
Grapette, B.T. Fooks Mfg. Co., Camden, Ark., Rice's Bottling, Roanoke, Va., 1939, 6 Oz.   4.00
Grapette, Rome, Ga., Camden, Arkansas, c.1946, 6 Oz. 2.00
Grapette Bottling Co., G-B Quality Beverages, Asheville, N.C., 10 Oz. 2.00
Grapette Family Beverage Syrup, Cat, Bank, Lid, Camden, Ark., 6 3/4 x 3 In. . . . . .21.00 to 27.00
Grapette Family Beverage Syrup, Clown, Bank, Lid, Camden, Ark., 7 1/4 x 3 In. 10.00
Grapette Family Beverage Syrup, Elephant, Bank, Lid, Camden, Ark., 7 x 3 In. . . . .12.00 to 18.00
Grapette Imitation Grape Soda, ACL, Clear, Contents, 1960s, 6 Oz. 5.00

Grapette Products, Camden, Arkansas, Elephant, Bank, Carnival Glass, 1950s, 7 1/2 In. .   242.00
Grimsby, Siphon, Blue, Fluted, Acid Etched, 12 1/2 In. 82.00
Groves & Whitnall Ltd. Salford, Amber, Embossed Down Side, Codd, 10 Oz. . . . . . .30.00 to 40.00
Groves & Whitnall Ltd. Salford, Amber, Hand Tooled Crown Cap, Small 25.00
Groves & Whitnall Ltd. Salford, Globe, Sunburst, Amber, Codd, 9 In. 58.00
Groves & Whitnall Ltd. Salford, Honey Amber, Globe, Codd, 10 Oz. 40.00
Gruchy & Mayo's Celebrated Soda Water, Hamilton, Olive Green, 8 1/4 In. 69.00
H. Nash, Root Beer, Cincinnati, 12-Sided, Cobalt Blue, Iron Pontil, c.1850, 8 5/8 In. 1120.00
H.A. Elliott, Idaho Springs, Colo., Aqua, Round, Slug Plate 165.00
Haas Bros., Natural, Napa Soda, Blue 165.00
Haddock & Sons, Olive Yellow, Rolled Lip, Pontil, 1825-35, 6 1/2 In. 1680.00
Haddock & Sons, Olive Yellow, Tenpin, Applied Lip, Pontil, 7 In., 12 Pt. 1792.00
Hall Of Waters, White & Green ACL, Excelsior Springs, Mo., 1948, 7 Oz. 5.50
Harvey's Lake Bot. Works, Alderson, Pa., Aqua, 8 Oz. 6.00
Heep Good, ACL, Indian, Wenatchee Bottling Works, Wenatchee, Wash., 1939, 12 Oz. . .   41.00
Henry Busch, Minnemucca, Nev., Blue, Applied Top 468.00
Henry Roll, Trade Mark, S.F. Reg., Blue Island Ill., SCA, Hutchinson 50.00
Henry Wenzel Soda Water, Covington, Ky., Sea Green, Applied Collar, c.1870, 7 1/4 In. .   44.00
Henry Winkle, Sac. City, Green, Blob Top, Iron Pontil 88.00
Hill Billy Brew, Green 12.95
Hipple & Brickson, Telluride, Colo. 1200.00
Hippo, Embossed Writing, Nov. 2, 1926 Patent, 13 Oz., 9 1/2 In. 12.59
Hires, Amber, Embossed, BIMAL, Pushed Up Bottom, 3 In. 35.00
Hires, Household Extract, Charles E. Hires Co., Philadelphia, Pa., 4 1/2 x 1 1/2 In. 10.00
Hires Old Root Beer Home Recipe Extract, Box, 3 Oz., 4 1/2 In. 10.00
Hires RJ Root Beer, ACL, Soda Bottle, 1948, 12 Oz. 4.00
Hires Root Beer, Amber, Stopper, 7 1/2 In. 28.00
Hires Root Beer, Oldtime Flavor Made By Hires Since 1876, 1958, 12 Oz. 10.00
Hires Root Beer, Since 1876, Contents, 16 Oz. 10.00
Hires Root Beer, Syrup, Reverse Glass Label, Metal Cover, 12 In. 220.00
Hodgson's Soda Water, Bedford Street, Covent Garden, Hamilton, Aqua, 8 1/2 In. 20.00
Hollister Soda Works, A. Mans, Blue Aqua 440.00
Holly Beverages, Christmas Wreath, Clear, Mt. Holly, N.J., Embossed, 8 In. 6.00
Hollywood, Stars, Red & White ACL, Albuquerque, N.M., 1951, 10 Oz. 3.95
Howell & Smith, Buffalo, Yellow Green, Applied Collar, Iron Pontil, 1/2 Pt. 1792.00
Howell & Smith, Buffalo, Yellow Green, Tapered, Cylindrical, c.1850 . . . .   1792.00
Hudson Hot Rod Root Beer, ACL, Brown, Contents, 1947, 7 Oz. 15.00
Huested Beverages, Red & White ACL, Lamar, Co., c.1855, 9 Oz. 2.00
I.T. Fosler Richmond, Ind., Hutchinson 30.00
Ind Coope & Co. Ld., Gloucester, Aqua, Hamilton, 7 1/2 In. 48.00
Indian Rock, Ginger Ale, Richmond, Pepsi, Tenpin Form, c.1911, 7 Fl Oz., 7 5/8 In. 605.00
Isaac Houghland, Leadville, Colo., Aqua, 1889 . . . .   250.00
It's Julep Time, ACL, Glenn's Beverage Co., Champaign-Urbana, Ill., 1950, 10 Oz. 10.50
J. & A . Dearborn, Teal Blue, Heavy Collared Mouth, Pontil, 1/2 Pt. 336.00
J. & A. Soda, City, Bottling Works, Dearborn, N.Y., Teal, Sloping Collar, Pontil, 6 3/4 In. .   308.00
J. Boardman, N.Y., Olive Yellow Green, Sloping Collar, Pontil, 7 1/4 In. 476.00
J. Cairns & Co., St. Louis, Aqua, Iron Pontil, 7 1/4 In. 50.00
J. Eckersley Bolton, Patent Safe Groove, Aqua, Cobalt Blue Lip, Rylands, Codd, 7 1/4 In.   130.00
J. Kennedy, JK, Pittsburg, Ice Blue, Squat, Iron Pontil 139.00
J. Kennedy, Pittsburg, Yellow Lime Green, Applied Mouth, Iron Pontil, 7 3/8 In. 1344.00
J. Popp, Hamburg, Pa., Slub Plate, Blue Green, Applied Double Collar, 7 In. 504.00
J. Reynolds & Co. Bottlers, Philadelphia, Blue Green, Double Collar, Iron Pontil 89.00
J. Schweinhart, Pittsburgh, Pa., Cobalt Blue, Blob Top, 7 In. 90.00
J. Voelker & Bro., Cleveland, O., Cobalt Blue, Applied Mouth, 10 In. 224.00
J.A. Seitz, Easton, Pa., Green, Metal Harness 30.00
J.D. Ludwick, Pottstown, Pa., Green, Hutchinson, Crown, c.1889 . . . .   69.00
J.E. Deegan, Pottsville, Pa., K. Hutter New York, Yellow Amber, Hutchinson 350.00
J.F. Deegan, Yellow Amber, Embossed, Tombstone Shape, Hutchinson, 6 3/8 In. 1045.00
J.G. Parker & Son, New York, Sapphire Blue, Squat, Blob Top, 7 1/4 In. . . . . .139.00 to 149.00
J.H. Fett & Son, Reading, Pa., Apple Green, Blob Top, 9 In. 79.00
J.H. Magee, 118 Vine St., Philada., Cobalt Blue, Applied Top, Iron Pontil 468.00
J.T. Brown, Chemist, Boston, Blue Green, Torpedo, Sloping Collar, c.1860, 8 1/8 In. 532.00
J.T. Brown Chemist, Boston, Emerald Green, Torpedo, Embossed 450.00

J.T. Brown Chemist, Torpedo, Blue Green, Blob Top, 8 3/4 In. 280.00
J.W. Dickey, Youngstown O, Aqua, 1874 .... 35.00
J.W. Dickey, Youngstown, Aqua, Squat, 1824 .... 25.00
J.W. Harris, N.H., Sapphire Blue, Applied Collar, Pontil, 1/2 Pt. 672.00
J.W. Harris, New Haven, 8-Sided, Blue Blob Top, Graphite Pontil, 7 1/2 In. 173.00
J.W. Harris, New Haven, Conn., Sapphire Blue, 8-Sided, Blob Top, IP, 7 1/2 In. ..... *Illus* 364.00
J.W. Keys, Frankfort, Ind., Clear 30.00
JA Lomax, 14 & 16, Charles Place, Chicago, Medium Cobalt Blue, Applied Mouth, 7 1/8 In. 67.00
James Dewar, Elko, Nev., Hutchinson, Aqua 660.00
James Lingard, S Lingard, Salford, Narrow Neck, Aqua, Codd, c.1880, 6 Oz. 25.00
James Lingard & Co, Codds Patent 6, London, Aqua, Narrow Neck, 10 Oz. 25.00
James Wise, Allentown, Pa., c.1860, 7 3/8 x 2 1/2 In. 150.00
Jesse C. Stewart Root Beer, Mother's Brand, Condensed, Box, Cork, 4 1/2 In. 24.00
Jewsbury & Brown, Siphon, Pewter Tap, Pink, England, 12 In. 215.00
Jno. Wyeth & Bro., Phill, Liq Ext. Malt, Amber 10.00
Job Wragg, Birmingham & Shirley, Etched, Siphon, Green, England, 11 3/4 In. 33.00
John Beck, Camden, N.Y., Green, Squat, Blob Top 159.00
John D. Taylor & Co., Pioneer Soda Water Works, Oakland, Cal., Glass Stopper 80.00
John Dahlstrom, Ishpeming, Mich., Green Aqua, Blob Top, Hutchinson, c.1900, 9 1/4 In. 50.00
John Deitrich, Pottstown, Pa., Blue Green, Applied Double Collar, Slug Plate, 7 1/8 In. .. 134.00
John Else, Purity, Cromford, Aqua, BIMAL, Blob Top, Codd, 7 1/4 In. 39.00
John Howell Buffalo, N.Y., Aqua, Hutchinson 20.00
John Mynders, Eagle, Clear, Hutchinson, Schenectady, N.Y. 11.00
John Ryan, 1852, Excelsior, Ginger Ale, Savannah, Geo, Amber, Applied Mouth, 7 3/8 In. 137.00
John Ryan, 1852, Excelsior, Ginger Ale, Savannah, Geo, Green, Applied Mouth, 7 3/8 In. 515.00
John Ryan, 1852, Excelsior, Ginger Ale, Savannah, Geo, Yellow, Applied Mouth, 7 3/8 In. 489.00
John Ryan, 1866, Excelsior Soda Works, Savannah, Geo, Cobalt, Applied Mouth, 7 1/4 In. 120.00
John Ryan, Savannah & Augusta, Ga., Ginger Ale, Aquamarine, Applied Mouth, 9 1/8 In. 250.00
John Ryan, Savannah, Ga., 1859, Cobalt, Blob Top, 7 3/8 In. 210.00
John Ryan, Savannah, Ga., 1859, XX Philadelphia Porter, Cobalt, Iron Pontil, 6 3/8 In. .. 255.00
Johnson & Mason, Etched, Siphon, Plated Metal Tap, Blue, Coventry, England, 13 In. ... 43.00
K.O. Denver, Aqua, Applied Top, Hutchinson 200.00
Keach, Balt., Yellow Green, Torpedo, Applied Collar, c.1860, 8 3/4 In. 952.00
Kelly's Cream Top Root Beer, Brown, Kelly's Beverage Co., Mishawaka, Indiana, 10 Oz. 13.00
Kenton Beverages, Hunter, Gun, Blue & White ACL, Kenton, Ohio, 10 Oz., 9 1/2 In. ... 6.00
Kickapoo Joy Juice, Green, White & Red Label 3.25
Kist, Palmyra, Pa., Red & White ACL 10.00
Koca-Nola, Aqua Green, Blob Top, Hutchinson 575.00
L & V, Dark Emerald Green, Blob Top 176.00
L. House & Sons, Syracuse, N.Y., Amber, Blob Top, Squat, 7 3/4 In. 29.00
L. Werbach, Milwaukee, Aqua, 6-Sided Base, Hutchinson 8.00
L.E. Rousse, Philada., Emerald Green, Iron Pontil, 7 1/8 In. 75.00
Lancaster Glass Works, Cobalt Blue, Sloping Collar, Pontil, 7 1/8 In. 190.00
Lazy-B Beverages, Hi, Pardner!, Red & White ACL, Clear, 1951, 10 Oz. 10.00
Leigh & Co., Salford, Globe, Amber, Codd, 6 Oz. 25.00
Leigh & Co., Salford, Globe, Amber, Codd, 10 Oz. 25.00
Leigh & Co., Salford, Globe, Amber, Cylindrical, Blob Top, Large 20.00
Leigh & Co., Salford, Globe, Amber, Wooden Bullet Stopper, Small 35.00
Lemon Crush, Contents, 1960s, 10 Oz. 6.50
Leonard Sonora Cal., Green Aqua, Tooled Top 88.00
Liberty Soda Works, Eagle, Blue Aqua, Tooled Top 88.00
Lithia Mineral Spring Co., Gloversville, Aqua, Pt., 7 3/4 In. 392.00
Little John's Root Beer, Green 3.00
Loerrbach Milwaukee, 8-Sided, Aqua, Hutchinson 10.00
Love Beverages, Heart Logo, Love Bottling Co., Muskogee, Okla., 10 Oz. 3.75
Lynde & Putnam, San Francisco, Cal., Teal Green, Applied Top, Graphite Pontil 242.00
Lynde & Putnam San Francisco, Dark Teal, Iron Pontil 300.00
Lyons Root Beer, Red, White Ink Label, Be Happy Inside, Honolulu, Hawaii, 1948, 7 Oz. 11.00
M. & J. Duffy, Phila., Brown Stout, Teal Blue Green, Double Collar, Squat 69.00
M.R., Sacramento, Dark Cobalt Blue, Blob Top, 7 1/2 In. 935.00
M.R., Sacrimento, Union Glassworks, Philada., Teal, Sloppy Top, Error 2200.00
Mac Fuddy, Scotsman, White, Green & Red ACL, Mich., 1941, 10 Oz. 12.00
Maicks & Phillipson, Reading, Pa., M & P, Deep Blue Green, Sloping Double Collar, 7 In. 100.00

Mason's Diet Beverages, Orange, White & Blue ACL, Clear, 1964, 10 Oz. 4.95
Mason's Old Fashioned Root Beer, Quality Beverage, Amber, Red, Yellow ACL, 7 Oz. . .   6.00
Mason's Root Beer, Brown, Painted Label, 10 Oz., 8 1/2 In. 3.00
Mason's Root Beer, Yellow & Red ACL, Grand Rapids, Mich., 1949, 10 Oz. 4.00
McBride Earl & Pollard, Detroit, Mich., Aqua, Hutchinson . . . . .9.00 to 10.00
McKay & Clark, Balto., Emerald Green, Blob Top, Iron Pontil, 1840-60 . . . .   532.00
McKeon, Washington, D.C., Yellow Green, Torpedo, Sloping Collar, 8 1/2 In. 728.00
Meikle Bros., 3-Piece Mold, Hutchinson, Vancouver, B.C. 35.00
Merritt & Co., Helena, Montana 55.00
Mission Orange Bottling Company, Blue & White ACL, Idaho Falls & Pocatello, Idaho .   6.50
Mohawk Beverages, Indian, Red & White ACL, Pittsfield, Mass., 7 Oz. 64.00
Monroe Bottling Works, Monroe, LA., Aqua, Hutchinson 10.00
Monterey Soda Works Cal., Tooled Top, Hutchinson 99.00
Mountain Dew, ACL, Hillbilly, Pig, Shooting At A Man, It'll Tickle Your Innards . . . . .4.00 to 7.50
Mountain Dew, Full Screening, Embossed, No Neck, Squat, Cap, Contents, 1965, 10 Oz. . .   20.00
Mountain Dew, J & M, It'll Tickle Your Innards, 10 Oz. 46.00
Mountain Dew, Paper Label, Screw Top, 69 Cents, 1 1/2 Liter 12.00
Moxie, Lehighton, Pennsylvania, 7 Oz., 8 In. 6.50
Moxie, Orange & White ACL, Authority Of Moxie, Boston, Mass., 1954, 7 Oz. 6.88
Mr Cola Jr., ACL, Grapette Co., Camden, Ark., 10 Oz. 1.50
Myopia Club Beverages, Indian, White & Blue ACL, Islington, Mass., 8 Oz. 153.00
Mystic Valley Bottling Co., Indian, Headdress, South Medford, Mass., Aqua, Qt. 20.00
N.C. Peterson, Laramie City, Wyo., Aqua 175.00
N.M.I. & P. Co., Delicia Beverages, Gallup, New Mexico, Aqua, Crown Top 10.00
Nehi, Billings, Montana, Clear, 9 Oz., 9 1/4 In. 3.50
Nehi, Bottle On Top Of A World Globe, Top Of The World, Columbus Georgia, 4 1/2 In. .   118.00
Nehi, Clear, Money Back Bottle, Red Letters, White Ground, 7 Oz., 8 In. 5.00
Nehi, Columbus, Ga., Clear, 1925 . . . .   2.00
Nehi, Thick Glass, Royal Crown Bottling Co., 9 Oz., 9 In. 20.00
Nehi Beverage, Lansing, Mi., Yellow & Red Label, 1956, 7 Oz. 8.00
Nehi Beverage, Portland & Salem Oregon, Red & White Label, 1956, 9 Oz. 7.50
Nehi Beverages, Clear, Paper Label, Yellow Ground, 1925, 10 Oz. 3.00
Nehi Beverages, Columbus, Ga., 9 Oz., 9 1/4 In. 1.00
Nehi Pale Dry Ginger Ale, Labels, Green, Nehi-R.C. Bottling, Greenville, S.C., 12 Oz. . .   10.50
Nehi Strawberry, Red Label, Contents, 7 Oz. 9.50
Nesbitt's, Embossed Logo, Qt., 9 3/4 In. 12.00
Nesbitt's, White Label, Los Angeles, Ca., 10 Oz. 2.25
Nesbitt's Of California, Embossed Shoulder, Black ACL, 1950, 26 Oz., 11 1/2 In. 6.00
Nevada City Bottling Works, Nevada City, Calif., Crown Top, 9 1/2 In. 20.00
New Holland Bottling Works, New Holland, Pa., Teal Blue Green, Blob Top 89.00
Neyhard & Jacoby Bloo. Pa., Teal Blue Green, Double Collar, Sloping Shoulder, Squat . .   200.00
Neyman & Drake, Mok Hill, Philada., Teal, Embossed 1650.00
Neyman & Drake, Union Glass Works, Philada., Blue Green, Blob Top, IP, 7 1/2 In. 1456.00
Nezinscot Beverages, White, Red ACL, Clear, Nezinscot Bottling Co., Turner, Maine, 8 Oz.   8.00
Night Club, Embossed, Fluted Sides, Frosted Top, Trinidad, Colorado, 1920s, 7 1/2 Oz. . .   30.00
Nome, Brewing & Bottle Co., 4-Piece Mold, Aqua, c.1900, 7 13/16 In. 1265.00
Northrop & Sturgis Company, Portland, Oregon, Hutchinson 30.00
Northwestern Bottling Co., Butte, Mt., Tooled Top 55.00
Northwestern Bottling Co., Kremming Colo., Purple, Hutchinson 25.00
NuGrape, Yellow Label, Contents, Salisbury, N.C., 8 Oz. 9.00
O-So Beverages, Recognized For Quality, Red & White Painted Label, 1979, 10 Fl. Oz. . .   10.00
Oceanview Bottling Works, Mendocino, Ca., Aqua 33.00
Ogdens Porter, Slug Plate, Deep Blue Aqua, Iron Pontil, c.1850, 7 In. 246.00
Old Colonial Root Beer, Stoneware, World War I Era, 7 3/4 x 2 1/2 In. 123.00
Old Colony Grape, Leaksville, N.C., Contents, Orange Crush Bottling Co. 23.00
Old Home Made Rootbeer, Hires Extract, Pottery, Brown Top, Cream Bottom, 7 3/8 In. .   132.00
Ole Timer, Coca-Cola Bottling Co., Anderson, Muncie, Ind., Clear, ACL, 8 Oz. 8.00
Orange Crush, Amber, Embossed, South River, N.J., 1929, 1 Pt. 12 Oz., 11 1/2 In. 26.00
Orange Crush, Brown, Orange Diamond Label, Contents, 1974, 7 Oz. 2.00
Orange Crush, Clear, Meridian, Miss., Pat'd July-20-1920, 6 Oz. 3.00
Orange Crush, Clear, Ribs, 1920s, 7 Oz. 7.00
Orange Crush, Clear, Ribs, Crushie, 3 Rivers, Texas, 1920 . . . .   10.00
Orange Crush, Clear, Ribs, Embossed, Pat'd July 20, 1920, 6 Oz. 5.00

Orange Crush, Contents, Miniature, 3 In. 6.00
Orange Crush, Embossed, Horizontal Ribs, Emerald Green, 1920, 7 Oz., 8 3/4 In. 74.00
Orange Crush, Great Falls, Lewiston, Mont., Oval, Diamonds, Pat'd 1929, 7 Oz., 8 3/4 In. 10.00
Orange Crush Bottling & Maple Products Corp., St. Johnsbury, Vt., Green, c.1900, 8 Oz. 8.25
Oregon Trail Beverages, Man, Coonskin Hat, Green, White ACL, Sidney, Nebraska, 8 Oz. 18.50
Owen Casey, Eagle Soda Works, Sac City, Blue 110.00
P.H. Reasbeck Braddock, Pa., Hutchinson, Aqua, P.R. On Base 25.00
Pablo & Co., 334 & 336 Royal St., N.O., Yellow Green, Blob Top, c.1855, 7 1/2 In. 1008.00
Pacific & Puget Sound, Seattle, Wash., Hutchinson 46.00
Pacific Glassworks, W.S. Wright, Teal Blue 468.00
Paradise Club, Green & White ACL, Clear, Tacoma, Wash., 1961, 7 Oz. 3.00
Patio Diet Cola Beverage, ACL, Contents, Lid, 1964, 8 Oz. 5.00
Pearson Bros Placerville, Crown Top, Wide Mouth, Marble & Rubber Stopper, c.1890 .. 120.00
Peerless Mineral, Sweeny & Cherry, New York, Cobalt Blue, Squat 79.00
Peter Frumpf, Spokane, Wash., Tombstone Slug Plate 175.00
Pheasant Beverages, Red & White ACL, Aberdeen, S.D., 7 Oz. 65.00
Pioneer Soda Works, Hutchinson, Anchor Mark 25.00
Pleasant City Beverages, Woman, Green, White ACL, Williams Bottling, Oh., 1948, 7 Oz. 13.00
Portland Soda Works, Blue, Embossed Bird, Applied Top 66.00
Portland Soda Works, Northrop & Sturgis, Blue, Tooled Top, Seed Bubbles, Hutchinson . 99.00
Potsdam, N.Y., T.M. Lennan, Aqua, Embossed, Hutchinson 30.00
Poudre Valley, Ft. Collins, Colo., Hutchinson 190.00
Pringle Bottling Co., Burley, Idaho, Clear, 8 Oz. 6.50
Purple Cane Road Root Beer, Cobalt Blue, Iowa, 12 In. 5.00
Quality Brand Soda Water, Property Of Coca-Cola Bottling Co., Asheville, N.C., 10 Oz. 2.00
Quiky, Yellow ACL, Green Glass, Ribbed Middle, 1956, 7 Oz. 23.00
Quinan & Studer, Savannah, Ga., 1888, Cobalt Blue, Tooled Lip, 7 7/8 In. 213.00
R.C. & T., New York, Teal Green, Iron Pontil, 7 3/8 In. 95.00
R.C. & T., Soda Water, N.Y., Emerald, Applied Sloping Collar, IP, c.1860, 1/2 Pt., 7 In. ... 385.00
R.D. Rawlings, Light Green, Torpedo Bottle, No Closure 33.00
R.W. & S.L. White, Green, Embossed, Screw Stopper, London, Early 1900s, 9 1/8 In. 35.00
Rancho, Cowboy, Black & White ACL, Needles, Calif., 1948, 10 Oz. 6.00
Range Bottling Co., Virginia, Minnesota, Painted Label, 9 In. 29.00
RC Cola, AG/Farming Expo, Salutes, Contents, 1980s 6.50
RC Cola, Royal Crown, Contents, 1950s 7.50
RC Cola, Royal Crown, Painted Label, Pyramid, Brawley, Calif., Nehi, c.1936, 12 Oz. ... 34.00
RC Cola, Santa, White Cap 1.00
Red Arrow, 9 In. 8.00
Red Bird Beverages, Red & White ACL, Hays, Kan., 1949, 8 Oz. 6.50
Red River Lumber Co., Mercantile Dept., Embossed, Crown Top, ABM, c.1920, 7 5/8 In. 55.00
Red Rock Cola, Crown Top, Albany, N.Y. 15.00
Red Rock Cola, Red & White ACL, Vancouver, Wash., 1948, 10 Oz. 2.25
Rich Maid Punch, Non-Carbonated, White ACL, Clear, Phoenix, Ariz., 1950s, 7 Oz. 4.00
Richardson's Birch Beer, Mansfield O., Aqua, Blob Top, Qt. 66.00
Riverside Bottling Works, Allentown, Pa., Anchor, Hutchinson 35.00
Robert Chultz, Sherboycan, Wis., Aqua, Hutchinson 9.00
Robinson Wilson & Legallee, Boston, Emerald Green, Double Collar, Squat 109.00
Root Beer, William Ford 65 Willoughby Street, Cor Lawrence, Brooklyn, N.Y., Aqua, Qt. 45.00
Rose, Family Beverage, Red, White ACL, Green Glass, Providence, R.I., 1964, 7 Oz., 8 In. 5.00
Ross's Belfast, Light Green, Round Bottom 6.50
Royal Crown Cola, Albany, Georgia, ACL, Nehi Bottling, c.1936 .... 4.00
Royal Crown Cola, Paper Label, Return For The Deposit, Screw Cap, c.1974, 32 Oz. 2.50
Royal Crown Cola, West Jefferson N.C., Contents, 354 Milliliters, 12 Oz. 3.25
Royal German Spa, Lime Green, Blob Top, 6 1/2 In. 40.00
Rummy Grapefruit Drink, Husky Beverage, Marysville, Wash., Green Bottle, ACL, 8 In. 10.00
Rushton & Aspinwall, New York, Green Aqua, Rolled Lip, c.1835, 7 1/2 In. 1904.00
Rylands & Codd Makers, Stairfoot, Barnsley, Amber, Codd, 7 1/2 In. ....254.00 to 548.00
S. Crumman, 1870 Norwalk Conn., Aqua 35.00
S. Lingard & Co, Salford, London, Aqua, Narrow Neck, Codd, Pre 1877, 10 Oz. 25.00
S.S. Knickerbocker, 12-Sided, Blue, Applied Top, Graphite Pontil 330.00
San Francisco Glassworks, Aqua 77.00
San Jose Soda Works, Cal., Green, Applied Top 220.00
San Luis Obispo Soda Water Works, S. Ceribelli, Green Aqua 300.00

Scarboro & Whitby Breweries, 2 Dolphins, Emerald Green, Embossed, Codd, 10 Oz. ... 150.00
Scarborough Brewery Company, Emerald Green, Embossed, Codd, 9 In. 98.00
Schweppes, Porcelain Lined, Plated Metal Tap, Siphon, Amber, England, 11 3/4 In. 39.00
Schweppes, Siphon, Golden Amber, Metal Tap, Acid Etched, Coat Of Arms, 12 In. 52.00
Scot Mixer, Scottie Dog, Red & White ACL, Green Glass, Sturgeon, Pa., 1964, 7 Oz. 5.00
Seitz Bros., Easton, Pa., Aqua, Squat 15.00
Seitz Bros., Easton, Pa., Teal Blue Green 35.00
Seitz Bros., Easton, Pa., Teal Blue, Blob Top, 6 3/4 In. 78.00
Seltzogene, Siphon, Ruby Glass, Pewter Tap, Double Globe, 17 In. 327.00
Silver State, Crown Top, Miner, Mule, Scallop Design, ABM, Reno 65.00
Simba, Lion, Green, White Label, Coca-Cola Company, 10 Oz. 2.00
Sky High Old Style Root Beer, Milwaukee, Barrel Shape, 1/2 Gal., 11 1/4 In. 10.00
Smile, Happy Face, Orange & White ACL, Columbus, Mississippi, 10 Oz. 10.00
Snow White Beverages, White & Green ACL, Saxton, Pa., Qt. 7.00
Snowdrop Lyon & Co., Manchester, Fluted Base, 2 Lip Rings, Aqua, 6 Oz. 20.00
Sour Puss, Sour Face, Red & Yellow ACL, Green Glass, Pittsburgh, 1945, 7 Oz. 22.00
Southside A.M., Schademan Bottling House, Aqua, Hutchinson 20.00
Southway Beverage, Southern Belle, Gentleman, Steamboat, ACL, 8 Oz. 10.00
Sparkeeta Club Soda, 3 Horsemen, Black & Red ACL, 35 Oz., 12 x 4 In. 98.00
Spokane Soda Bottling Works, Spokane, Wash., Mug Base, Hutchinson 35.00
Spraul's Beverages, Roman Man, Red & White ACL, Troy, Ohio, 1950, 10 Oz. 10.00
Sprite, Sugar Free, Rocky Mountain Nat'L Park, Yellow ACL, 1979, 10 Oz. 8.50
Squeeze, Boy & Girl, Black & White ACL, Fairmont, W. Va., 1948, 8 Oz. 10.00
Squeeze, Boy & Girl, Red & White ACL, Green Glass, 1960, 7 Oz. 11.50
Squeeze, Boy & Girl, Red & White ACL, Okla City, Okla., 1959, 7 Oz. 12.00
Squeeze, Boy & Girl, Red & Yellow ACL, 1950, 7 1/2 Oz. 20.00
Squeeze, Boy & Girl, Red & Yellow ACL, Idabel, Okla., 1941, 12 Oz. 25.00
Squirt, Red & Yellow ACL, Green, W.Va., 1947, 7 Oz., 8 In. 3.25
Squirt, Squirt Boy, Red & Yellow ACL, Green Glass, 1950, 7 Oz., 8 In. 2.00
Squirt, Yellow ACL, Green Glass, Contents, Mexico, 12 Oz. 1.00
Staley & Zweifel, Wallace, Id., Aqua 450.00
Standard Bottling Co., Denver, Colo. 25.00
Standard Bottling Works, Olive Green, Fluted Panels, Hutchinson, 6 5/8 In. 1045.00
Steinke & Kornahrens, Charleston, S.C., Cobalt Blue, 8-Sided, Pontil, 8 1/4 In. 448.00
Stephens & Jose, Virginia City, Nev., Blue Aqua, Applied Top 660.00
Sun Crest, Idaho Dr. Pepper Bottling Co., Nampa, Idaho, Blue & White ACL, 10 Oz. 6.00
Sun Rise, Buy With Confidence, Drink With Pleasure, Havre, Mont., 1959, 10 Oz. 3.00
Sun Rise Beverage, Sun-Rise Inc., 10 Oz. 2.00
Sun Rise Cola, Buy With Confidence, Drink With Pleasure, 1968, 7 Oz. 10.00
Sun Spot, 1954, 12 Oz. 7.50
Sun Valley Orange, Sunrise, Blue & Orange ACL, Lima, Ohio, Semi-Squat, 1939, 12 Oz. . 14.50
Sun-Drop, Basketweave Label, Contents, 9 Oz. 8.50
Sun-Drop, Dale Earnhart, Rookie Of Year, NASCAR Series No. 1, Contents, 1979, 12 Oz. 5.50
Sun-Drop, Foam Wrap Label, Contents, 28 Oz. 15.00
Sun-Drop Diet Soda, Golden-Cola, Amber, Contents, 12 Oz. 13.50
Sunny Side, Green & White ACL, Clear, Oklahoma City, 1968, 10 Oz. 7.50
Superior Soda Water, Charleston Eagle, Yellow Green, Pontil, c.1855, 7 1/2 In. 1760.00
Syrup, Grape-Julep, Paper Under Glass Label, 13 In. 440.00
Syrup, Strawberry-Julep, Paper Under Glass Label, 13 In. 440.00
Syrup, Stromeyers Grape Punch, Paper Under Glass Label, Cap, 13 In. 210.00
T & R Morton, Newark, N.J., Green, Double Collar, Squat, Iron Pontil ....89.00 to 99.00
T B. Jones & Co., Cobalt Blue, Tapered Top, Iron Pontil, c.1845, 7 In. 1870.00
T. Howarth, Pittston, Pa., Olive Amber, Squat, Embossed, c.1850, 9 In. 3575.00
T.A. Evans, Hutchinson, Cobalt Blue, Embossed In Tombstone Shape, 7 In. 1430.00
T.P. Bowman, Phoenixville, Green Aqua, Blob Top, Squat 200.00
T.W. Gillett, 8-Sided, Sapphire Blue, Applied Collar, Iron Pontil, 1/2 Pt. 728.00
Tab, White ACL, By Coca-Cola, 1964, 7 Oz. 4.00
Tab, Yellow Label, Contents, 16 Oz. 11.50
Tarrytown Bottling Works, D. Cohn Tallytown, N.Y., Clear, Blob Top, 9 In. 9.00
Tassie & Co., 8-Sided, Blue, Green, Applied Collar, Iron Pontil, Pt. 1456.00
Ted Williams, Ted's Delicious Creamy Root Beer, Moxie Bottling, Boston, 1950s, 7 Oz. . 17.00
Ted Williams Root Beer, Contents, Moxie Bottling Co., 7 Oz. 46.00
Thrill, Blue & White Label, 1940s, 9 Oz., 9 1/4 In. 14.50

Tip, Marion, Va., Tip Bottling Co., Tuscaloosa, Ala., White Letters, Red Ground, 10 Oz. . . . 11.00
Tom Moore, Leprechaun, Black & White ACL, Minneapolis, 1955, 7 Oz. 7.50
Trimmerman & Co., Superior Soda Water, St. Louis, Aqua, Iron Pontil, 7 1/4 In. 44.00
Triple AAA Root Beer, Contents, 1946, 12 Oz. 10.50
Triple AAA Root Beer, You Will Like Root Beer, White Label, 6 1/2 Oz., 8 In. 12.00
Twitchell Philada., T In Center, Teal Green, Smooth Base, 1860s, 7 1/2 In. 39.00
Union Glass Works, Phila., Blue Green, Blob Top, Iron Pontil, c.1850, 7 1/4 In. 135.00
Union Glass Works, Phila., Dark Teal, Embossed, Blank Slugs, Iron Pontil 150.00
Union Glass Works, Phila., Peacock Blue Green, Blob Top, Squat, Iron Pontil 59.00
Union Glass Works, Teal Blue, Green, Blob Top, Squat, Iron Pontil 89.00
Upper, Dunsmuir Cal., Aqua, Tooled Crown Top, c.1900, 8 In. 60.00
Upper 10, Green, Yellow Ground, Red Letters, Nehi Soda Co., 12 Oz. 4.25
Upper 10, Yellow & Red ACL, Green, Jasper, Ala., 1952, 9 Oz 5.00
Utica Club Prohibition Era, West End Br'g Co., Utica, N.Y., Embossed, 6 1/2 Oz. 8.00
Vance's, Cowboy, White & Green ACL, Logan, West Virginia, 1966, 16 Oz. 18.00
VanHorn & Sawtell, New York, 4-Sided, W. T. Co. 2 U. S. A., c.1870, 9 1/2 In. 125.00
Venango Bottling Co., Oil City, Pa., Aqua, Blob Top 15.00
Vernor's, Gnome, Yellow & Green ACL, Detroit, Mich., 1957, 8 Oz. 4.00
Vernor's Ginger Ale, Rochester, New York, Yellow Label, 8 Oz. 5.00
Vess Bubble Up Beverage Company Inc., Indianapolis, Indiana, 8 Oz. 36.00
Vess Cola, Martins Ferry, Ohio, ACL, Contents, Lid, 1955, 10 Oz. 5.00
Vess Cola, Whistle Bottling Co., Peru, Ill., Red Letters, White Ground, 10 Oz. 2.00
Vess Dry, Round, Embossed, Crown Top, Green, 32-Sided, Morgantown, W.Va., 6 1/2 Oz. 7.50
Vincent Hathaway, Boston, Forest Green, Round Bottom 145.00
Vincent's Sparkling Ginger Ale, Deer, White & Red ACL, Green Glass, 1948, 28 Oz. 20.00
W.C. Shuler, Blue Green, Sloping Collar, Iron Pontil, c.1850, 7 1/4 In. 100.00
W.H. Burt, SF, Medium Dark Green, Iron Pontil 200.00
W.H. Causley, DBW, Dover, N.J., Aqua, Hutchinson 11.00
W.H. Cawley Co., D.B.W., Dover, N.J., Aqua, Blob Top, 9 In. 9.00
Walker & Homfray Limited, Salford, Shaws Patent, Aqua, 6 Oz. 20.00
Walter & Brother, Reading, Pa., W.&B., Emerald Blue Green, Blob Top, Squat 79.00
Walters Napa County Soda Hutchins & Reynolds, Aqua, Hutchinson 140.00
Waring Webster & Co., Cobalt Blue, 8-Sided, Blob Top, Iron Pontil, 7 3/8 In. 336.00
Washing Liquor Co., Spokane, Wash., Aqua 160.00
Washington Beverages, Man, Feathered Cap, ACL, Washington, Pa., 7 Oz. 154.00
Washington Liquor Co., Spokane, Wash., Aqua 165.00
Weinsteins & Kaplan, Albany, N.Y., Light Purple, Hutchinson 12.00
Western Soda Works, Stag, Facing Right, 3-Part Mold, Hutchinson, 123 On Bottom 40.00
Whistle, Bethlehem, Pa., Raised Diamond Pattern, 1926, 6 1/2 Oz., 8 3/4 In. 3.00
Whistle, J.C. Ranft Bott. Co., Granite City, Ill., 12 Oz. 2.50
Whistle, Keene, N.H., Waisted, 1920s, 6 1/2 Oz. 3.00
Whistle, Thirsty?, Just Whistle, ACL, Stanley Beverage, Bangor, Me., 1962, 12 Oz. 10.50
Whistle, Thirsty?, Just Whistle, Clear, Blue & White Printing, 1949, 10 Oz. 5.00
Whistle, Thirsty?, Just Whistle, Huntington, W. Va., Unused, 7 Oz. 5.50
White Rock Ginger Ale, Green, White & Red Label, Contents 10.00
White Rock Ginger Ale Fountain Syrup, Handle, Cap, Gal. 30.00
White Rock Orange, Paper Label, Contents, Cap, 7 Oz., 7 In. 19.00
Wm. A. Kearney, Soda Water, Shamokin, Pa., Amber, Hutchinson, c.1890, Qt., 8 7/8 In. . . 413.00
Wm. H. Stall, Phoenixville, Pa., Clear, Paneled Base, Hutchinson 17.00
Wm. Padden, Pittsburgh, Aqua, Paneled, Hutchinson 30.00
Yuncker Bottling Co., Tacoma, Wash., Mug Base, Hutchinson, 362 On Bottom 30.00
SPIRIT, see Flask; Gin; Seal

STIEGEL TYPE

Henry William Stiegel, an immigrant to the colonies, started his first factory in Pennsylvania in 1763. He remained in business until 1774. Glassware was made in a style popular in Europe at that time and was similar to the glass of many other makers. It was made of clear or colored glass that was decorated with enamel colors, mold blown designs, or etchings. He produced window glass, bottles, and useful wares. It is almost impossible to be sure a piece is a genuine Stiegel, so the knowing collector now refers to this glass as Stiegel type. Almost all of the enamel-decorated bottles of this type that are found today were made in Europe.

Amethyst, Diamond, Vertical Ribs, Sheared Mouth, Open Pontil, c.1785, 8 In. 4950.00

> If you have an alarm system, set it each time you leave the house, not just at night. Most home burglaries take place during the day or early evening.

Stiegel Type, Blue, Rectangular,
Colored Flowers, Sheared Mouth,
Pewter Collar, 5 3/8 In.

Blue, Rectangular, Colored Flowers, Sheared Mouth, Pewter Collar, 5 3/8 In. . . . . . . *Illus* 476.00
Blue, Rectangular, Conical Neck, Sheared Mouth, Polychrome, 1764, 6 5/8 In. 3190.00
Bowl, Cobalt Blue, Tapered Sides, Molded, Ribbed Sides, Base, 3 3/8 x 2 3/4 In. 165.00
Clear, Rectangular, Multicolored Flowers, Sheared Mouth, Collar, Cap, Pontil, 6 In. 168.00
Enameled, Milk Glass, Flowers, Rectangular, Pewter Collar, 1750-1850, 5 5/8 In. 157.00
Etched Devils Dancing Around Fire, Stopper, Pontil, 8 1/2 In. 165.00
Flowers, Pewter Collar, Pontil Scar, Continental, 1750-1850, 4 7/8 In. 157.00
Grape Amethyst, Diamond Daisy, Tooled Lip, Pontil, 1770-1774, 5 1/8 In. 6720.00
Opalescent Milk Glass, Multicolored Flowers, Pewter Collar, 3 7/8 In. 336.00
Purple Amethyst, 18 Ribs, Swirled To Right, Pontil, Tooled Lip, 5 3/4 In. 179.00
Purple Amethyst, Diamond Daisy, Open Pontil, c.1772, 5 In. 7700.00
Rabbit & Dog, Flower Panels, Screw Top, Clear, 6 x 3 1/4 x 2 1/4 In. 55.00
Spirits, Enameled, Woman Carrying Pails, Pewter Collar, Pontil, 1750-1850, 5 3/4 In. . . . 230.00

STONEWARE

Stoneware is a type of pottery, not as soft as earthenware and not translucent like porcelain. It is fired at such a high temperature it is impervious to liquid and so makes an excellent bottle. Although glazes are not needed, they were often added to stoneware to enhance its appearance. Most stoneware bottles also have the name of a store or brand name as part of their decoration.

Batter Jug, Cobalt Blue Leaves, Swing Handle, Cowden, Wilcox, 1869-87, 1 1/2 Gal. . . . 1265.00
Flagon, Hull, Grey, Green Glaze, Round Shoulder, Slab Seal, 12 In. 74.00
Flagon, K.C. Cyder, Screw Stopper, Brown, White Glaze, Black Transfer, 16 1/2 In. 32.00
Flagon, Maps, Screw Stopper, Double Transfer, Girl Drinking From Glass, 16 1/2 In. 93.00
Flagon, Probyn, Brown Salt Glaze, Sloping Shoulders, Impressed, 12 1/2 In. 33.00
Flagon, Waterford, Brown Salt Glaze, Round Shoulder, Handle, Impressed, 15 In. 82.00
Flask, 2 Men Drinking, Grape Vines, Brown Glaze, Bennington, 6 In. 672.00
Flask, A. Mayes Wine & Spirit, Hip, Shouldered, Brown Salt Glaze, 5 1/2 In. 157.00
Flask, Book, Bennington, Flint Enamel, 7 1/2 In. 330.00
Flask, Embossed Man Smoking Pipe, Woman Not Smoking, Brown, Tan, Pt. 180.00
Jar, A.B. Wheeler & Co., 69 Broad Street, Boston, Mass., Small 33.00
Jar, Bird On Leaf, Incised, Blue, Oval, 3 Gal. 358.00
Jar, Bird On Stump, Blue, Reused Label, 2 Gal. 275.00
Jar, Blue Bird On Floral Branch, Whites Utica, 2 Gal. 408.00
Jar, Brown Slip Flowers, Lyman & Clark, Gardiner, Me., c.1840, 12 1/2 In. 1320.00
Jar, Canning Wax Seal, Manley & Cartwright, East Liverpool, Ohio, Yellow, 5 1/2 In. 90.00
Jar, Cobalt Blue Flower, Lug Handles, Herrmann Family, Wisc., c.1850, 13 3/4 In. 129.00
Jar, Cobalt Blue Flower, Norton & Fenton, Bennington, Vt., Oval, 4 Gal. 297.00
Jar, Cobalt Blue Leaves, 6 3/4 In. 209.00
Jar, Floral Leaf Design, Oval, Pa., 4 Gal. 165.00
Jar, Flower, Cobalt Blue, Hasting & Belding, Ashfield, Mass., 2 Gal. 440.00
Jar, Flower, Leaves, Cobalt Blue, Gal. 110.00
Jar, Fruit, Hamilton & Jones, Greensboro, Pa., Gal. 275.00
Jar, Lid, Partridge, Incised, Cobalt Blue Highlights, Oval, I. Seymour Troy, Gal. 3585.00
Jar, Spitting Tulip, Oval, 3 Gal. 82.00
Jar, Storage, Jas. Hamilton, Salt Glaze, Cobalt Design, Greensboro, Pa., 1860-80, Gal. . . . 198.00
Jar, Tulip, 2 Handles, Cobalt Blue Stencil, T.F. Reppert, Greensboro, Pa., 15 3/4 In. 460.00

Jug, 4 Flowers, 2 Gal. 65.00
Jug, August Warnke, Chicago, 2-Tone, Gal. 100.00
Jug, Ballard & Bros. Burlington, Vt., Double Flower, 1 1/2 Gal. 215.00
Jug, Bellarmine Type, Salt Glaze, Applied Handle, Brown, England, 12 In. 88.00
Jug, Bellarmine, Brown Salt Glaze, Bulbous, Face, Cartouches, Coat Of Arms, 11 In. 245.00
Jug, Bellarmine, Brown, Pottery, Bearded Face, Applied Handle, 15 1/4 In. 532.00
Jug, Bellarmine, Brown, Pottery, Impressed Face, Medallion Cartouche, Handle, 11 1/8 In. 448.00
Jug, Bellarmine, Orange Brown, Pottery, Impressed Face, Serpent Cartouche, 8 3/4 In. . . . 616.00
Jug, Bidwell & Co. Woodbridge, Egg Shape, Salt Glaze, Blue Slip, c.1810, 12 3/4 In. 550.00
Jug, Bird, On Mound, Flowers, Blue Slip, Salt Glaze, W.H. Farrar, c.1855, 2 Gal., 14 In. . 6000.00
Jug, Bisi & Caprini, Fine Wines, Liquors, Cordials & Fancy Groceries, Pittsburg, Gal. . . . 139.00
Jug, Blue Bird, West Troy Pottery, 2 Gal. 368.00
Jug, Boston Highland Yeast, Dark Gray, Impressed, Handle, 7 3/4 In. 134.00
Jug, Charlestown, Eagle & Cannon, Oval, 2 Gal. 385.00
Jug, Cobalt Blue Brush Design, Oval, Gal. 226.00
Jug, Cobalt Blue Dot & Leafy Stem, West Troy Pottery, 5 Gal. 460.00
Jug, Cobalt Blue Flower & Scroll Design, F.B. Norton, Mass., 12 In. 460.00
Jug, Cobalt Blue Flowers, Oval, L. Seymour Troy Factory, 2 Gal. 247.00
Jug, Cobalt Blue Highlights, F.B. Norton & Co., Worc., Mass., Gal. 11.00
Jug, Cobalt Blue Highlights, Glaze Run Front, Potstone, Oval, Gal. 55.00
Jug, Cobalt Blue Slip Flower Scroll, West Troy, N.Y., 12 1/2 In. 460.00
Jug, Cobalt Blue Slip, Butterfly, Double Incised 5, C. Hart & Son, Sherburne, N.Y., 5 Gal. 460.00
Jug, Cobalt Blue Swag, E. Norton & Co., Benn., Vt., 2 Gal. 110.00
Jug, Cobalt Blue Swag, Highlights, Handles, Pa., 4 Gal. 127.00
Jug, Cobalt Blue Swag, Large Potstone Back, 2 Gal. 237.00
Jug, Cobalt Blue Swags & Tassels, Incised, Oval, 3 Gal. 413.00
Jug, Cobalt Blue Tulip, Oval, 3 Gal. 165.00
Jug, Cobalt Blue, Flower, White's Utica, Gal. 66.00
Jug, Cruiskeen Lawn, Mitchell's Old Irish Whisky, Belfast, Handle, 2-Tone, 7 1/4 In. 54.00
Jug, Double Tulip, Riedenger & Caire, Poughkeepsie, N.Y., 2 Gal. 247.00
Jug, Egg Shape, Applied Handle, Molded Face, Bearded Man, Bellarmine, 11 1/8 In. 575.00
Jug, Face, Gray Olive Green, Squat, Handle, Lanier Meaders, 1967-85, 9 1/4 In. 1300.00
Jug, Face, Porcelain Teeth, Brown Pottery Stamp, Carolina, c.1900, 10 In. 1100.00
Jug, Flamingo, Blue, White's Utica, 2 Gal. 275.00
Jug, Floral Spray, Haxstun, Ottman & Co., Fort Edward, 3 Gal. 220.00
Jug, Floral Spray, Potstone Back, Gal. 33.00
Jug, Floral Tornado Decoration, Haxtun, Ottman & Co., Fort Edward, N.Y., 3 Gal. 170.00
Jug, Flowers, Highlights On Handle, Allover Alligator Glaze, Oval, 7 1/2 In. 715.00
Jug, Fulton Whiskey, Capacity Exceeds 3 Gallons, Blue Stencil, 1890-1910, 3 Gal. 132.00
Jug, Goodwin & Webster, Blue, Oval, 2 Gal. 154.00
Jug, Hayes & Co. Liquor Dealers, Manchester, N.H., Cobalt Blue Decoration, Gal. 99.00
Jug, Henry W. Hultgrewe No 1 State St. Corn Whitehall St., Brown, Tan, Handle, Pt. 129.00
Jug, Hochstadter's Eachter Alter Nordhauser Kornbranntwein, c.1900, Qt. 59.00
Jug, Hounds & Horseman, Stag, Windmill, Silver Rim, Cherubs, Salt Glaze, c.1775, 5 3/4 In. 695.00
Jug, Ivanhoe Old Scotch Whisky, Men At Table, Drinking, White, Black Transfer, 7 3/4 In. 134.00
Jug, J. & E. Norton & Co., Benn., Vt., Flowers, 2 Gal. 330.00
Jug, J. & E. Norton, Benn., Vt., Spitting Tulip, 3 Gal. 385.00
Jug, J. & E. Norton, Bennington, Vt., Double Flower, 3 Gal. 358.00
Jug, J. & E. Norton, Bennington, Vt., Blue Bird, Gal. 303.00
Jug, J. Bligh, 29, 31 & 33 Orange Street, Providence, R.I., Cobalt Blue Leaves, 3 Gal. . . . 116.00
Jug, J. Potts & Son Grocers, Handle, Alkaline Glaze, 1890-1910, 7 7/8 In. 146.00
Jug, John Keller & Co., Fashion Saloon, Jerome, Ariz., 1/2 Pt. 2200.00
Jug, Kishere Pottery Mortlake Surrys, Salt Glaze, Grapes, Vines, 2-Tone, 7 1/4 In. 58.00
Jug, L.L. Smith, Atlanta, Ga., Gray Salt Glaze, Handle, 14 In. 95.00
Jug, Large Blue Bird, New York Stoneware Co., Fort Edward, N.Y., 5 Gal. 469.00
Jug, Leaf, Cobalt Blue, J. & E. Norton, Bennington, 3 Gal. 138.00
Jug, Little Brown Jug, 1876, 3 In. 83.00
Jug, Louis Zapp & Co, Louisville, Ky., Brown Glaze, 1870-90, 9 3/4 In., 1/2 Gal. 187.00
Jug, M. Crafts, 3 Flowers, Whately, 2 Gal. 440.00
Jug, Microbe Killer, Embossed, 4 Banners, 12 x 7 In. 330.00
Jug, Mills & Co., Dealers In Stoneware, Cobalt Blue Stencil, Pittsburgh, Pa., 12 In. 230.00
Jug, Moore & Hubbard, Syracuse, N.Y., 2 Gal. 450.00

Jug, Ottman Bros. & Co., Fort Edward, N.Y., Spout, 2 Gal. 247.00
Jug, Parrot On Branch, F. B. Norton & Co., Worc., Mass., 3 Gal. 550.00
Jug, Property Of Herman Freed Wholesale Liquors, Schenectady, 1/2 Gal. 69.00
Jug, R.L. Fenton & Co., East Dorset, Vt., Cobalt Blue Moth, Oval, 2 Gal. 495.00
Jug, Sargent Bros., Thomaston, 5 1/2 In. 209.00
Jug, Swan & States Stonington, Blue, Gal. 275.00
Jug, Swan & States Stonington, Incised Leaf, Oval, 2 Gal. 605.00
Jug, Thomas D. Chollar Homer, Cobalt Blue Spitting Tulip, Oval, 2 Gal. 275.00
Jug, Welcome To Home, Honest Abe, Oatmeal, Brown Top, 1885-1900, 3 1/4 In. 385.00
Jug, Wetts Bros Akron O, Handle, Dark Brown Glaze, 1890-1910, 8 In. 45.00
Mackworth Pure Jersey Cream, Tan, Black Transfer, Metal Lid, 1890-1910, 1/2 Pt. 157.00
Mug, Blue Band, Impressed, Rochester Brew Co., No. 20, 5 1/4 In. 77.00
Pitcher, Cobalt Blue Leaf, Gal. 186.00
Pitcher, Large Drooping Flower, Cobalt Blue Highlights, Oval, 3 Gal. 247.00
Pomroy & Hall, 6 3/4 In. 25.00
Tankard, Hinged Pewter Lid, Blue Bands, 4 1/2 In. 275.00
Tankard, Pewter Lid, Incised Bird & Butterfly, Cobalt Highlights, 8 In. 440.00
Water Cooler, Blue Bands, 4 Gal. 33.00
Water Cooler, Cobalt Blue Flowers, Bands, Edmunds & Co., 4 Gal. 110.00

TARGET BALL

Target balls were first used in England in the early 1830s. Trapshooting was a popular sport. Live birds were released from a trap and then shot as they tried to fly away. The target balls, thrown into the air, replaced the live birds. The first American use was by Charles Portlock of Boston, Massachusetts, about 1850. A mechanical thrower was invented by Captain Adam Bogardus and with this improvement, trap shooting spread to all parts of the country. Early balls were round globes but by the 1860s they were made with ornamental patterns in the glass. Light green, aqua, dark green, cobalt blue, amber, amethyst, and other colors were used. Target balls went out of fashion by 1880 when the *clay pigeon* was invented.

Allover Diamond, Sapphire Blue, Sheared Mouth, 2 1/2 In. 364.00
Amber, 3-Piece Mold, Cork, Feathers, 3 x 3 In. 193.00
Amber, 3-Piece Mold, Hand Blown, 2 1/2 In. 83.00
Amber, Diamond, Rough Sheared Mouth, Germany, 2 5/8 In. 415.00
Amethyst, Man Standing With Gun, Crosshatch Ground, Sheared Lip, 2 7/8 In. 187.00
Aqua, Sheared Lip, 2 1/4 In. 67.00
Black Amethyst, Diamond, Sheared & Ground Lip, Germany, 2 5/8 In. 395.00
Black Resin, 2 1/4 In. 56.00
Blue, 3-Piece Mold, 3-Dot Pattern Near Lip 116.00
Bogardus, Pat'd Apr 10 1877, Diamond, Emerald Green, Puce, Sheared Lip, 2 5/8 In. ... 1232.00
Bogardus, Pat'd Apr 10 1877, Diamond, Yellow Amber, Sheared Lip, 2 5/8 In. 616.00
Bogardus, Pat'd Apr 10 1877, Diamonds, Tobacco Amber, Sheared, 2 5/8 In. 504.00
Bogardus, Pat'd Apr 10 1877, Golden Amber, Sheared Mouth, 2 3/4 In. 392.00
Bogardus, Pat'd Apr 10 1877, Hobnail, Medium Amber, 2 3/4 In. 3000.00

Target Ball, Charlottenburg Glashutten, Dr. A. Frank, Diamond, Olive Yellow, 2 5/8 In.

Target Ball, Cobalt Blue, Squares, Rough Sheared Lip, Australia, 2 5/8 In.

Target Ball, Diamond, Amethyst, Sheared & Ground Lip, Czechoslovakia, 2 1/2 In.

Bogardus, Pat'd Apr 10 1877, Yellow Amber, Sheared Mouth, 2 3/4 In. 952.00
Bogardus, Pat'd Aprl 10 1877, Basket Weave, Yellow ....575.00 to 633.00
Charlottenburg Glashutten, Dr. A. Frank, Diamond, Olive Yellow, 2 5/8 In. ....*Illus* 210.00
Cobalt Blue, 3-Piece Mold, Sheared Mouth, 1880-1900, 2 5/8 In. 195.00
Cobalt Blue, Squares, Rough Sheared Lip, Australia, 2 5/8 In. ....*Illus* 2330.00
Cobalt Blue, Van Gutsem A St Quentin, Raised Rib Fishnet, Center Band 133.00
Diamond, Amethyst, Rough Sheared Mouth, Czechoslovakia, 2 3/4 In. 375.00
Diamond, Amethyst, Sheared & Ground Lip, Czechoslovakia, 2 1/2 In. ....*Illus* 452.00
Diamond, Prussian Blue, Sheared Mouth, Czechoslovakia, 1880-1920, 2 3/4 In. 375.00
Diamond, Yellow Green, Sheared Lip, Czechoslovakia, 2 1/2 In. 128.00
Diamond, Yellow Green, Sheared Mouth, Czechoslovakia, 2 3/4 In. 170.00
F.W. Otte, Diamond, Olive Yellow, Sheared Lip, Germany, 2 5/8 In. 504.00
FBH, Diamond, Cobalt Blue, Circular Panels, Sheared Lip, Australia, 2 5/8 In. 532.00
For Hockey's Patent Trap, Aqua, Olive, Black, Sheared Mouth, England, 2 1/2 In. 750.00
For Hockey's Patent Trap, Olive Green, Sheared Lip, England, c.1880-1900, 2 1/2 In. ... 460.00
Golden Yellow Amber, Diamond, Sheared, Ground Lip, 2 5/8 In. 213.00
Grafl Zu Solms, Diamond, Clear, Sheared Lip, Germany, 2 3/4 In. 672.00
Grass Green, Square Pattern, Center Band, Sheared Mouth, France, c.1880-1900, 2 5/8 In. 250.00
Grass Green, Square, Sheared Lip, France, 2 5/8 In. 616.00
Green, Crisscross Embossing, Sheared Lip, 2 3/4 In. 614.00
Ira Paine's, Filled Ball, Medium Yellow Amber, Sheared Mouth, 2 5/8 In. 2010.00
Ira Paine's, Pat. Oct. 28, 1877, Golden Yellow, Sheared Mouth, 2 5/8 In. 336.00
J. Plamer O'Neil & Co., Pittsburgh, Chocolate Amber, Sheared Mouth, 2 3/4 In. 5500.00
Man, Shooting, Diamond, Pink Amethyst, Sheared Lip, 2 3/4 In. 616.00
Man, Shooting, Diamond, Purple Amethyst, England, 2 5/8 In. 672.00
N.B. Glass Works, Perth, Basket Weave, Light Green 575.00
N.B. Glass Works, Perth, Diamond, Aqua, Medial Band, Sheared Lip, 2 3/4 In. 99.00
N.B. Glass Works, Perth, Diamond, Blue Aqua, Sheared Mouth, 2 5/8 In. 179.00
N.B. Glass Works, Perth, Diamond, Center Band, Sapphire Blue, 2 5/8 In. 136.00
N.B. Glass Works, Perth, Embossed, Crisscross, Cobalt Blue, 3 In. 53.00
Rutherford & Co., Diamond, Golden Yellow Amber, Canada, 2 5/8 In. 2016.00
Sapphire Blue, Embossed Star, Sheared Lip, 2 1/8 In. 123.00
Sophienhutte In Ilmenau, Diamond, Blue Aqua, Sheared Lip, Germany, 2 5/8 In. 1344.00
Sophienhutte In Ilmenau, Diamond, Red Amber, Sheared Lip, Germany, 2 5/8 In. 476.00
Stacey & Co., Square, Sapphire Blue, Sheared Lip, Embossed Neck, England, 2 1/4 In. .. 616.00
Van Gutsem, A St Quentin, Embossed, Crisscross, Cobalt Blue, 3 1/4 In. 42.00
W.W. Greener St. Mary's Works, Diamond, Purple Amethyst, England, 2 5/8 In. 672.00
W.W. Greener St. Mary's Works, Diamond, Smoky Olive Green, 2 5/8 In. 2240.00
W.W. Greener St. Mary's Works, Diamond, Yellow Amber, England, 2 5/8 In. 1232.00
W.W. Greener St. Mary's Works, London, Crisscross, Embossed, Amethyst, 3 In. 635.00
Yellow Amber, 6 Raised Beads On Shoulder, Sheared Lip, c.1880-1900, 2 3/4 In. 190.00
TOILET WATER, see Cologne

--------------------------------- TONIC ---------------------------------

Tonic is a word with several meanings. Listed here are medicine bottles that have the word *tonic* either on a paper label or embossed on the glass. In this book *hair tonic* is listed with cosmetics or cure. There may be related bottles listed in the Cure and Medicine categories.

Aikin's Syrup, Aqua, 8-Sided, Rolled Lip, Open Pontil, 4 1/4 In. 448.00
Aikin's Tonic Syrup, Apple Green, 8-Sided, Inward Rolled Lip, Open Pontil, 4 1/4 In. 330.00
CCC Tonic, Boericke Runyon & Ernesty, New York, Clear, Rectangular, Pt., 8 In. 25.00
Clemen's Indian, Geo. W. House, Indian Holding Herbs, Aqua, OP, c.1850, 5 1/2 In. 895.00
Clemen's Indian, Indian, Blue Aqua, Rolled Lip, Open Pontil, 5 1/2 In. 616.00
Clemen's Indian, Indian, Blue Aqua, Tooled Mouth, Pontil, 5 5/8 In. 840.00
Clemen's Indian, Prepared By Geo. W. House, Aqua, Folded Lip, OP, Label, 5 5/8 In. ... 715.00
Clements, Orange Amber, Tooled Lip, Rectangular, Camphor Corners, 6 3/4 In. 40.00
Clements, Orange Amber, Tooled Lip, Rectangular, Camphor Corners, 7 3/4 In. 50.00
Daltons Ears & Nerve Tonic, Aqua, Rectangular 23.00
Dr. D. Jayne's Vermifuge, Aqua, Open Pontil, 5 In. ....55.00 to 132.00
Dr. E. Blecker's Mixture For Chills & Fever, Blue Aqua, Pontil, 6 7/8 In. 1232.00
Dr. Harrison's, Chalybeate, Emerald Green, Applied Mouth, 1865-75, 9 In. 952.00
Dr. Harter's Iron, Amber, Label, Contents, Box, 9 1/4 In. 495.00
Dr. Harter's Iron, Regulating Kidneys, Liver, Nervousness, Amber, 9 1/4 In. 143.00

Dr. Hess Stock Tonic, Scientific Compound, Free Sample, Box, 5 1/4 x 3 7/8 In. 187.00
Dr. Jones Red Clover, Golden Amber, c.1885, 8 1/4 In. 135.00
Dr. Miles', Aqua, Contents, Label, Box, Sample Envelope, 8 1/4 In. 440.00
Dr. Miles', Aqua, Label, Contents, Box, 8 1/4 In. 105.00
Dr. Shoop's Restorative, Racine, Wis., Aqua, Contents, Labels, 6 3/4 In. 83.00
Dr. Smith's Columbo, Sunken Panel, Amber, Tooled Collar, 1885-95, 9 In. 75.00
Dr. Thompson's Eye Water, New London, Connt., Aqua, Cylindrical, Open Pontil, 4 In. . . . 45.00
Dr. Townsend's, Aromatic, Square, Red Amber, Sloping Collar Mouth, 9 In. 179.00
Dr. Warren's Tonic Cordial, Aqua, Square, Contents, 9 In. 220.00
H. Clay Glover, New York, For Pigs Or Horses, Amber, Contents, Label, 5 In. 61.00
H.H. Warner & Co., Tippecanoe, Stomach, Amber, Mushroom Top, Round, 9 In. 1870.00
Harter's Iron, Contents, Label, Box, Amber, April 1, 1895, 9 In. 209.00
Herba Blood Purifier & Stomach, Yellow Amber, c.1895, 9 1/2 In. 165.00
Hi-Vita Tonic, Hi-Vita Pharmaceutical Products Co., Miami, Florida, 8 1/2 In. 5.42
Hop, Semi-Cabin, Amber, Tooled Mouth, 1880-90, 9 7/8 In. 112.00
Johnson's Chill & Fever, A.B. Girardeau, Savh., Ga., Aqua, Square, 6 In. 48.00
Kodol Nerve, Clear, Embossed, Contents, Wrap Label, Round, Sample, 3 1/2 In. 83.00
Lash's, Natural Tonic Laxative, Paper Label, Amber, Contents, Square, 4 3/4 In. 440.00
Lash's, Natural Tonic Laxative, Paper Label, Amber, Square, May, 1913, 9 1/2 In. 132.00
Mara Nova, Boston, Mass., Green Aqua, Double Collar, 1890-1900, 8 1/2 In. 25.00
Mascare Tonique For Hair, Martha Matilda Harper, Rochester, Amethyst, Cylindrical 45.00
Mexican, Embossed, Amber, 8-Sided, Tapered Collar, 1890-1900, 11 In. 75.00
Orange Tonica Risley & Co., N.Y., Yellow, Drum Body, Lady's Leg Neck, c.1875, 10 In. . . 65.00
Primley's Iron & Wahoo, Jones & Primley Co., Elkhart, Ind., Amber, 1880-90, 9 1/2 In. . . . 90.00
Reed's Gilt 1878, Golden Amber, Applied Tapered Collar, Partial Labels, 1880-85, 9 In. . . 125.00
Rohrer's Expectoral Wild Cherry, Lancaster, Pa., Amber, Double Collar, IP, 10 3/4 In. . . . 392.00
Rohrer's Expectoral Wild Cherry, Lancaster, Pa., Amber, Roped Corners, 10 3/8 In. 504.00
Rohrer's Expectoral Wild Cherry, Lancaster, Pa., Amber, Roped Corners, 10 5/8 In. 202.00
Rohrer's Expectoral Wild Cherry, Lancaster, Pa., Medium Amber, Double Collar, 11 In. . . 1430.00
Rohrer's Expectoral Wild Cherry, Red Amber, Double Collar, Iron Pontil, 10 5/8 In. 550.00
Ross's Aromatic, J.R.R. & Co., Amber, Applied Tapered Collar, 8 3/4 In. 95.00
Schenck's Seaweed, Aqua, Square, Box, 8 1/2 In. 154.00
Vernal Female Tonic For Women, Label, Contents, Pamphlet, Box, 9 In. 66.00
Vin Vitalia, Green, Triangular, Tooled Double Ring Lip, 1890-1910, 9 1/2 In. 75.00
Warner's Safe, Amber, 1/2 Pt. 550.00
Warner's Safe, Amber, Embossed, Slug Plate, Contents, Label, 9 1/2 In. 2200.00
Warner's Safe, Rochester, Slug Plate, 1/2 Pt. 850.00

--------------------------------- VINEGAR ---------------------------------
Vinegar was and is sold in glass bottles. Most vinegar packers prefer a large jug-shaped bottle with a small handle, the shape used today even for modern plastic vinegar bottles. The collector wants any bottle with the name *vinegar* on a paper label or embossed on the glass. The most famous vinegar bottles were made by National Fruit Product Company for their White House Brand vinegar. Bottles with the embossed brand name and a picture of a house, the trademark, were made in the early 1900s. Jugs in three or four sizes, apple-shaped jars, canning jars, fancy decanters, cruets, a New York World's Fair bottle, rolling pins, vases, a refrigerator water jar, and other fanciful reusable shapes were used until the 1940s. The company is still in business.

D.L. Gregory Vinegar Co., Elko County, Pure Apple Juice, Jug, Handle, Brown Top, 3 In. . 55.00
Jones Bros. & Co., Manufacturers Of Cider & Vinegar, Louisville, Ky., Handle, 3 1/2 In. . . 55.00
Jug, O.L. Gregory Vinegar Co., Elko County, Pure Apple Juice Vinegar, 3 1/4 x 2 In. 85.00
Maple Sap & Boiled Cider, Cobalt Blue, East Rindge, N.H., 11 1/2 In. 633.00
Maple Sap & Boiled Cider, Cobalt Blue, Tooled Mouth, 11 3/8 In. . . . .*Illus* 560.00
Maple Sugar & Boiled Cider, C.I. Co., East Rindge, N.H., Cobalt Blue, 11 3/8 In. 616.00
Triple Strength White Wine Vinegar, Guaranteed To Keep Pickles, Stoneware, Jug, 3 In. . 110.00
Wallace & Gregory Bros., Elko County, Apple Juice Vinegar, Paducah, Ky., Jug, Mini . . . 85.00
White House, 2 Handles, Crackled Cabbage Rose Pattern, Cork, 9 1/2 In. 30.00
White House, Ballerina, Green, Glass Stopper, Filigree Decoration, Qt. 300.00
White House, Clear, Double Handle, Flowers, Embossed Base 15.00
White House, Embossed, Jug, Pour Spout, 10 In. 18.00
White House, Handle, Spout, 7 1/2 In. 49.00
W.A. LACEY, see Lacey
WATER, MINERAL, see Mineral Water

Vinegar, Maple Sap & Boiled Cider, Cobalt Blue, Tooled Mouth, 11 3/8 In.

─── ✍ ───

When you go away on a driving trip, be sure to cover the window in your garage door, so the missing car won't be noticed. New garage doors usually have no window at all, for security reasons.

─── ✍ ───

─── **WHEATON** ───

Wheaton Glass Co. produced machine-made reproductions of old American bottles and commemorative bottles from 1967 to 1975 and sold them through their Nuline division. From 1975 to 1982 some Wheaton commemorative limited editions bottles were made on semiautomatic bottling machines. In 1982 the rights to make the bottles were sold to Millville Art Glass Co. The company is now out of business. Reproductions of Wheaton bottles have been made by Viking Glass Co. and others.

Ball & Claw Bitters, Amethyst, 9 1/2 In.	51.00
Ball & Claw Bitters, Amethyst, Cork, 1971, 5 1/2 In.	5.00
Ball & Claw Bitters, Ruby Red, 5 1/2 In.	10.00
Berring's Apple, Phila., Berring's Bitters, Apples, Cobalt Blue, 9 1/2 In.	10.00
Berring's Apple, Phila., Berring's Bitters, Purple, 9 1/4 In.	8.00
Berring's Bitters, Apple, Purple, Cork, 9 3/4 In.	2.00
Cape May Bitters, Amber, c.1971, 3 In.	3.00
Cape May Bitters, Blue, c.1971, 3 In.	3.00
Chester A. Arthur, Pink, Box, Millville Art Glass, 1983, 7 1/2 In.	16.00
Church Ink, Red, 1 1/2 x 3 In.	5.50
Doctor Fisch's Bitters, Fish Shape, Brown, Cork, Millville, 1970s, 8 In.	2.00
Doctor Fisch's Bitters, Fish Shape, Pink, 7 3/4 x 3 In.	6.50
Dr. Chandler's Jamaica Ginger Root Bitters, Keg Shape, Milk Glass, Gold Top, 9 In.	5.00
E.G. Booz's Old Cabin Whiskey, Log Cabin, Etched Door, 3 Windows, 8 1/4 In.	12.00
Final Apollo Flight To Moon, Schmitt, Cernan, Evans, Purple Carnival Glass, 1972, 8 In.	2.25
Fisch's Bitters, Red, Cork	5.25
Frank's Safe Kidney Liver Cure, Since 1892, Blue, c.1971, 3 In.	3.00
Franklin Pierce, Evergreen, Box, 7 1/2 In.	16.00
George Washington, Cobalt Blue, 8 1/2 In.	10.00
Horseshoe, Amber, Cork, 3 1/2 In.	2.00
Horseshoe, Horse, 5 Stars, Blue, 3 1/4 In.	3.00
Humphrey, Muskie, Democratic Campaign, Green, Box, 1968	10.00
James Polk, Amber, Box, 7 1/2 In.	20.00
Jenny Lind, Swedish Nightingale, Purple, 5 1/2 In.	5.50
John Quincy Adams, Dark Amber, Box, 7 1/2 In.	20.00
John Tyler, Dark Amber, Box, 7 1/2 In.	26.00
Liberty Bell, Green, Cork, 3 In.	2.00
Martin Luther King Jr., 1929-68, Marigold Carnival Glass, 1968, 8 1/4 In.	2.25
Martin Luther King Jr., Amber, Crinkle, 8 1/2 In.	5.50
Martin Van Buren, Colonial Blue, Box, 7 1/2 In.	29.00
McGiver's American Army Bitters, Pink, 7 3/4 x 3 1/4 In.	6.00
Octagon, Starburst Panels, Green, 10 In.	7.00
Paul Revere, Riding His Horse, Eagle, Blue, Clear Glass Stopper, 10 In.	2.00
Poison, Green, 5 1/4 In.	91.00
R.I.P., Coffin, Skull & Crossbones, Use With Care, Yellow, 3 In.	23.00
Root Bitters, Barrel Shape, Red, 3 In.	3.00
Rutherford Hayes, Pink, Box, Millville Art Glass, 1983, 7 1/2 In.	16.00
Sen. Robert Francis Kennedy, 1925-68, Green Carnival Glass, 1968, 8 1/4 In.	2.25
Straubmuller's Elixir, Tree Of Life Since 1880, Blue, 3 1/2 In.	3.00
Theodore Roosevelt, Blue Carnival Glass, 1st Edition	5.00

Theodore Roosevelt, Purple, Blue Green Carnival Glass 6.00
Thomas Jefferson, Ruby Red, First Edition, Box, 1970 .... 10.00

WHISKEY

Whiskey bottles came in assorted sizes and shapes through the years. Any container for whiskey is included in this category. Although purists spell the word *whisky* for Scotch and Canadian and whiskey for bourbon and other types, we have found it simpler in this book to use only the spelling *whiskey*. There is also blended whiskey, which includes blended bourbon, Scotch, Irish, or Canadian. Although blends were made in Scotland and Ireland for many years, it was not a process popular in the United States until 1933. One way to spot very new whiskey bottles is by the size. The 1 3/4-liter bottle is slightly less than a half gallon, the 1-liter bottle slightly more than a quart, and the 3/4-liter bottle almost the same size as a fifth. These bottles were introduced in 1976. Several years ago there was a contest to find the oldest bourbon bottle made in America. It was thought to be one dated 1882. The contest turned up an even older bottle, a Bininger made in 1848. Bourbon was first made in 1789 in Kentucky. Rum was made in America by the mid-seventeenth century; whiskey made of corn, rye, or barley by the early 1700s. It was the tax on this whiskey that caused the so-called Whiskey Rebellion of 1794. See also modern manufacturers categories by brand name, and the Figural category.

26 Ribs, Golden Orange Amber, Midwestern, Open Pontil, Cone Shape, 1820-35, 10 In. ... 359.00
A Margulis Wholesale Liquor Dealer, Philadelphia, Jug, Pottery, Brown, Tan, Gal. 40.00
A. Frohmann & Co., Philadelphia, Olive Green, 1860-70, Qt., 11 In. 175.00
A.B. Gardner, 16 & 20 Front St., Salem, Mass., Clear 15.00
AAA Old Valley, Red Amber, Embossed Cross, Roll Collar, Flask 935.00
Adler Co., Red Amber, Ball Shape, Flattened Sides, Qt., 7 1/2 In. 79.00
Albion Maryland Whiskey, Lamdin Thompson, Green, Rectangular, Baltimore, 1/2 Pt. ... 59.00
Ambrosial, B.M. & E.A.W. & Co., Golden Amber, Flattened Chestnut, c.1850, 8 7/8 In. ... 275.00
Andrew Forbes & Co., 6 & 8 North 11th, Phila., Amber, Cylindrical, Qt., 11 1/2 In. 19.00
Anthracite Brand California Brandy, L.L. Weith & Sons, Wilkes-Barre, Pa., ABM, Qt. .. 39.00
Applied Collar, Yellow Lime-Citron, Squat, Kick-Up Base, 1855-65, Qt., 9 1/2 In. 79.00
Auld Lang Syne Pure Old Barley Malt, Weideman Co., Jug, Brown, 7 3/4 In. ......*Illus* 179.00
B.M. & E.A Whitlock & Co., Barrel, Blue Aqua, Open Pontil, Applied Lip, 8 1/8 In. 1232.00
Backbar, Amber, Oval Label Panel, Patent 1862 & 1867, Qt., 12 In. 29.00
Backbar, Angelo Myers Philadelphia Rye, Clear, Cut Glass Neck, Enameled Letters, 11 1/8 In. 275.00
Backbar, Chicken Cock Bourbon, Amethystine Tint, Enamel, Tooled Lip, 7 In. 2200.00
Backbar, Elks Milk, 10 Panels, Cylindrical, Clear, Pewter Stopper, 12 In. ....*Illus* 1064.00
Backbar, Fay-Mus, 6-Sided, Enameled Flowers, Pressed Glass Stopper, c.1890, 9 In. 440.00
Backbar, Glass Label, Color Label, Amber, Tapered Cylindrical, 12 In. 159.00
Backbar, Hawthorne, Ribs Swirled Right, Enamel, Tooled Lip, Pour Stopper, c.1900, 11 In. 180.00
Backbar, Iroquois Club Rye, Indian Torso, Flutes, Tooled Lip, Polished Pontil, 8 7/8 In. 1540.00
Backbar, Kellerstass Belle Of Missouri Rye, Enameled Flowers, Glass Stopper, 1900, 9 In. 1045.00
Backbar, Maryland Club, White Enamel Letters, Green Shamrock, Stopper, c.1900, 8 In. .. 300.00
Backbar, Michelson's Brandy, Cork, 15 Cents, 14 In. 121.00
Backbar, Old Rosebud, Clear, Jockey On Horse, Enameled Letters, Whiskey Stopper, 9 In. . 1320.00
Backbar, Old Underwood Baltimore Pure Rye, Clear, Enameled Letters, 11 1/4 In. 125.00
Backbar, Robert Johnston Distiller, Rye, Wheat, Malt, Label Under Glass, 10 Cents, 11 3/8 In. 475.00
Backbar, Rum, White Enamel Decoration, Clear, Cylindrical, 11 In. 59.00
Backbar, Sandwich Style, Thumbprint Design, Applied Lip, Pontil, 1848-70, 12 In. 44.00
Backbar, Sunny Brook, Inspector Holding Bottle, Enamel Decoration, Stopper, 11 In. 550.00
Backbar, West Point, Amber, White Enamel Letters, Copper Cocks Head Stopper, 11 In. ... 190.00
Baldwin's Celebrated Wines & Brandies, Clear, Tooled Top, Fifth 230.00
Barley Bree, Jug, 3 Men, At Table, Rear Handle, William Gillies, Glasgow, 7 1/4 In. 313.00
Bass & Co., Jug, Pub, White, Red, Black Label, 6 3/4 In. 655.00
Belle Of Anderson, Handmade Sour Mash, Milk Glass, 6-Point Star, c.1900, 6 3/4 In. ... 75.00
Beveridge Bros., Jug, Tan Neck, White Glaze, Handle, Black Transfer, Stag, Thistles, 8 In. 3193.00
Billie Taylor, Embossed, Paper Label, Box, c.1910, 1/2 Pt. 115.00
Bininger, see the Bininger category
Bob Taylor, Shoulder Seal, Lion & Arrows, Jos. A Magnus, Red Amber, Squat, 9 1/2 In. .. 49.00
Borgfeldt Propfe Co., Embossed, Flask, c.1905, 1/2 Pt. 230.00
Bouquet, Pure Rye, Flowers, Reverse Under Glass, Ground Stopper, Late 1800s, 10 In. ... 1760.00
Bouvier Buchu Gin, For Kidneys & Bladder, Labels, Square, ABM, c.1906, Pt., 12 In. ... 69.00
Boyle & McGlinn, Amber, Squat, Qt., 9 1/2 In. 29.00

Boyle & McGlinn, Philada., Red Amber, Squat, Qt., 9 1/2 In. 45.00
Brassy & Cos, Sunny Brook, Blend, Label, Amethyst Tint, Pt. 15.00
Braunschweiger Inc., Rye, Amber, Tooled Top, 1871 .... 770.00
Brookfield Rye, Jug, Handle, 1867, 5 In. 55.00
Brooklyn Glass Bottle Works, Golden Amber, 1865-75, Fifth, 11 1/4 In. 303.00
Bulbous, Griffith Hyatt & Co., Baltimore, Yellow Amber, 7 In. 952.00
Bulloch Lade, Jug, Pub, Mottled Blue Glaze, White, Black, Red Print, 5 In. 327.00
Burke's Schiedam Schnapps, Aqua, Square, 4 In. 75.00
C.A. Essman's, Elk Club, Flask, Shoofly, Fish Shaped Label, I Am Dry, c.1890, 5 In. 154.00
California Port Brassy & Co., San Jose, Cal., Label Only, Qt. 220.00
Cartan, McCarthy & Co., San Francisco, Cal., Amber, Applied Top, Monogram, Fifth ... 300.00
Casper Co., Mail Order House, Blue Stencil, Cream, Stoneware, Jug, 1890-1910, Gal. ... 143.00
Casper's, Made By Honest North Carolina People, Clear, Tooled Mouth, 1890, 12 In. 392.00
Casper's, Made By Honest North Carolina People, Cobalt Blue, Cylindrical, 12 1/4 In. 500.00
Casper's, Made By Honest North Carolina People, Cobalt Blue, Tooled Mouth, 12 In. ... 680.00
Chapin & Gore Sour Mash, Jug, Pottery, Gold Letters, 1879, Qt. 100.00
Chapin & Gore's Bourbon, Jug, Tan, Blue & Gold Gilt Transfer, 8 5/8 In. 100.00
Chenery Souther, Amber, Applied Top, Qt. 80.00
Chestnut Grove, C. Wharton, Amber, Applied Ring, Handle, Pontil, 8 In. 120.00
Chestnut Grove, C.W. In Seal, Amber, Applied Handle & Band, Open Pontil, 8 In. 198.00
Chestnut Grove, C.W., Seal, Amber, Flattened Chestnut, Handle, Double Collar, 8 In. ... 392.00
Chestnut Grove, Chestnut Shape, Light Amber, Handle, Open Pontil, 8 In. 88.00
Chestnut Grove, G.W., Chestnut, Amber, Applied Seal, Mouth, Handle, OP, 8 7/8 In. 175.00
Chevalier's Ginger Brandy, Amber, Applied Lip, 1884-88, Fifth 209.00
Chum's, S.D.C., Triangle, Embossed, Cylindrical, Yellow Amber, Qt., 12 In. 69.00
Claymore Scotch, Jug, Pub, Blue Top, Cream, Black Transfer, Crossed Swords, 5 In. 593.00
Commodore's Royal Old Bourbon & Rye, E.C. Jorgensen, Screw Thread, 11 3/4 In. ... 495.00
Constitution, Olive Yellow, Cylindrical, Sloping Collared Mouth, Ring, Pontil, Qt. 560.00
Cordial, see the Cordial category
Coronation, King George V & Queen Mary, Jug, A. Usher, Edinburgh, 1911, 10 In. 117.00
Cream Of Irish Whiskey, Shamrock, Black Transfer, Stoneware, 8 3/4 In. 60.00
Crown Distilleries, Monogram, Amber, Screw Cap, c.1900, Fifth 330.00
Crown Distilleries Company, Amber, Slug Plate, Internal Threads, Miniature 35.00
Cutter OK Whisky, J.H. Cutter Old Bourbon, Orange Amber, Tool Top, 12 In. 75.00
D.J. O'Connell Fine Liquors, Clear, Qt., 11 1/2 In. 29.00
Dagger, Black Base, Screw Top, Tin Lid, Nipper, 9 1/2 In. 28.00
Dickson & White, Kenton, O, Aqua, Flask, Applied Lip, c.1875, Qt. 99.00
Drink Schneiders, Trade 905 Mark, Jug, Pottery, Tan, Brown, Gal. 100.00
Duffy Malt Whiskey, Amber, Short Neck, Patd Aug 24, 1886, 1/5 Gal., 10 1/4 In. 15.00
Duffy Malt Whiskey, Rochester, N.Y., Cylindrical, ABM, Labels, c.1885, 10 1/4 In. 29.00
Duffy Malt Whiskey, Rochester, N.Y., Pat'd Aug. 24, c.1886, 10 In. 25.00
Durkin Mill & Sprague, Spokane, Wash., Paper Label, Pt., 8 3/4 In. 35.00
Dyottville Glass Works, Phila, Salt River, Olive Yellow, Label, 1855-70, 11 1/8 In., Fifth . 358.00
Dyottville Glassworks, Blue Aqua, Cylindrical, 3-Piece Mold, Applied Mouth, 11 3/8 In. . 225.00
Dyottville Glassworks, Cherry Puce, Cylindrical, 3-Piece Mold, Applied Mouth, 11 3/8 In. 425.00
Dyottville Glassworks, Patent, Yellow Amber, Cylindrical, 3-Piece Mold, 11 3/8 In. 115.00

Whiskey, Auld Lang
Syne Pure Old Barley
Malt, Weideman Co.,
Jug, Brown, 7 3/4 In.

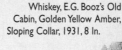

Whiskey, E.G. Booz's Old
Cabin, Golden Yellow Amber,
Sloping Collar, 1931, 8 In.

Whiskey, Backbar,
Elks Milk, 10 Panels,
Cylindrical, Clear,
Pewter Stopper,
12 In.

Dyottville Glassworks, Patent, Yellow Green, Cylindrical, 3-Piece Mold, IP, 11 3/8 In. 125.00
Dyottville Glassworks, Patent, Yellow Olive Amber, Cylindrical, 3-Piece Mold, 11 3/8 In. . 95.00
E. Bloch & Co., Blue Star Monogram, Cleveland, O., Jug, Cream, Brown Glaze, 7 3/8 In. . 157.00
E. Evans, No. 211 Main St., St. Louis, Olive Amber, Applied Top, 9 1/2 In. 523.00
E. Martin & Co., Old Bourbon, Olive Amber, Blob Top, Flask, 7 1/4 In. 350.00
E.D. Brown & Co., Orange Amber, Applied Double Tapered Top, 9 3/4 In. 99.00
E.G. Booz's Old Cabin, 120 Walnut St, Philadelphia, Cottage, Amber, 7 3/4 In. 800.00
E.G. Booz's Old Cabin, Amber, Applied Lip, Green Flag, Eagle, 8 In. 60.00
E.G. Booz's Old Cabin, Amber, Applied Sloping Collar, 8 In. 4760.00
E.G. Booz's Old Cabin, Golden Yellow Amber, Sloping Collar, 1931, 8 In. . . . .*Illus* 190.00
E.G. Booz's Old Cabin, Philadelphia, Cabin, Amber, Collar, 1865, 7 3/4 In. . . . . .4950.00 to 5190.00
E.G. Booz's Old Cabin, Philadelphia, Cabin, Amber, Applied Mouth, 7 3/4 In. 2700.00
E.H. Taylor Jr. & Sons, Cream, Blue Transfer, Jug, 10 1/2 In. 112.00
E.H. Taylor Jr. & Sons, Frankfort, Ky., Cream, Black Transfer, Jug, 9 1/2 In. 56.00
E.O. Middleton & Bros., Pure Rye, Orange, Amber, Squat, Applied Seal, Qt., 9 1/2 In. . . . 159.00
E.P. Middleton Wheat Whiskey, Golden Amber, Squat, Applied Seal, Qt., 9 1/2 In. 149.00
E.P. Middleton Wheat Whiskey, Red, Gasoline Puce, Squat, Applied Seal, Qt., 9 In. 249.00
Elephant, Flask, Gold Amber, Flattened Chestnut, Handle, c.1850, Pt. 1792.00
Elk's Pride, On Square, Jno. S. Low, Sole Owner, Carlisle, Pa., 2-Tone, Square, Jug, Mini 250.00
Emerald Brand, Steinhardt Bros., & Co., Jug, Cream, Brown Glaze, 7 3/8 In. 123.00
Emerald Green, Cylindrical, Base Kick-Up, 1860-70, Qt., 11 In. 69.00
Evans & Ragland, Lagrange, Ga., Amber, Tooled Mouth, 1870-80, 10 1/4 In. 112.00
F. Chevalier & Co., Old Bourbon Castle, Amber, Tooled Top 165.00
F. Chevalier & Co., Old Castle, Amber, Cork, 11 1/2 In. 40.00
Father Marquette, F.P. Gluck Co., 2-Tone, Jug, 1866 Pure Rye, Miniature 140.00
Figural, Shields, Scottish Man, Japan, 12 In. 55.00
Flask, see the Flask category
Fletcher & Coy, Cincinnati, O., Jug, Cream, Brown Glaze, Black Transfer, 8 1/4 In. 200.00
Forest Lawn, J.V.H., Bulbous, Olive Yellow Amber, Sloping Collar, 1845-65, 7 1/4 In. . . . 550.00
Forest Lawn, J.V.H., Olive Amber, Pontil, Sloping Collar, 1855-1975, 7 1/4 In. 336.00
Forty Second, Jug, White Glaze, Tan Neck, Black Transfer, 8 In. 1315.00
Freiberg Bros., Cream, Brown Glaze, Black Transfer, Jug, 1879, 10 3/4 In. 67.00
G.H. Clark's, Bourbon Co., Ky., Samuel More & Co., Amber, 1880-95, Fifth 1100.00
G.O. Blake's, Bourbon Co., Ky., More, Reynold's & Co., Amber, 1875-90, Fifth 1980.00
G.O. Blake's, Bourbon Co., Ky., More, Reynold's & Co., Yellow Amber, Fifth, 11 3/4 In. . 1650.00
G.O. Blake's Rye & Bourbon Whiskey, Adams Taylor & Co., Clear, Qt., 12 1/2 In. 29.00
G.W. Middleton Philada., 1843 Bourbon, Tobacco Amber, Double Collar, Qt., 9 1/2 In. . . 169.00
Gagen's 1885 Hand Made Cedar Grove, Lafayette, Ind., Tan, Brown, Jug, 10 7/8 In. 420.00
Gavin & L'Abbe Leadville & Cripple Creek, Colo., Screw Threads, Ground Top, Flask, Pt. 600.00
George's Beers & Wylds Scotch, Jug, Pub, Red, Black Handle, Harnessed Horse, 4 1/4 In. 900.00
Getty & Co., Old Premium Pure Rye, Jug, White China, Green Transfer, 7 1/2 In. 532.00
Gilmour Thomson's Royal Stag Whisky, White, Brown Glaze, Pottery, Scotland, 8 1/4 In. 44.00
Gin, see the Gin category
Glen Garry, Old Highland Whisky, Jug, Rear Handle, Port Dundas, 8 1/4 In. 39.00
Glen Garry, Very Old Scotch Whisky, Jug, Port Dundas, Stamp 29.00
Glenco Brand Scotch Whiskey, Jug, Thistle Transfer 129.00
Golden Dome, Amber, Qt. 55.00
Gordon's London Gin, Jug, Pub, Black Transfer, White, 6 3/4 In. 655.00
Gottschalk Co., Pointed Maryland Rye, Cream, Black Transfer, Jug, 7 1/4 In. 100.00
Gow's Grand Liqueur, Jug, Pub, Blue, Gray Glaze, Black Transfer, 4 1/2 In. 450.00
Grandpa's, Cylindrical, Ribbed Shoulders & Neck, 12 In. 29.00
Greybeard, Heather Dew Whisky, Jug, Mitchell Bros., Port Dundas, Glasgow, 7 In. 49.00
Greybeard, Heatherdrew Whisky, Jug 39.00
Griffith Hyatt & Co., Baltimore, Yellow Amber, Jug, Bulbous, Handle, c.1850, 7 In. 1008.00
Griffith Hyatt & Co., Yellow Amber, Olive, Applied Square Collar, Pontil, Bulbous, 7 In. . 952.00
Groff & Collins Wines & Liquors, Denver & Salida, Colo., Coffin, Qt. 550.00
Grommes Ulrich, Chicago, Slug Plate, Clear, Qt. 15.00
Gross' Cereal Extract Of Oats & Barley, Red Amber, Oval, Flattened Sides, Qt, 10 1/2 In. 69.00
H. & Co. Philada., Orange Apricot Amber, Applied Glass Shoulder Seal, Qt., 9 1/2 In. 79.00
H.F. & B., N.Y., Strawberry Puce, 6-Sided, Sloping Double Collar, 1870, 11 In. 1232.00
Haig & Haig, Jug, Pub, Blue Top, Salt Glaze, Lion & Crown, 5 1/2 In. 450.00
Happy Days Famous Old Rye Whiskey, Jug, Cream, Brown, Black Transfer, 7 3/4 In. . . . 78.00
Hayner Distilling Co., Dayton, Ohio & St. Louis, Mo., Nov 30, 1897, Qt. 5.50

Whiskey, Kinahan's Old Scotch, For Auld Lang Syne, Brown, 7 3/8 In.

Whiskey, Old Continental, Yellow Amber, Sloping Collar, 1865-75, 9 3/8 In.

Whiskey, Meredith's Diamond Club Pure Rye, Jug, White China, Teal Transfer, 5 3/4 In.

Hayner Whiskey Distillery, Troy, Ohio, Amber, 1897, Qt.	10.00
HB Special Private Stock Hafbrau House, Jug, Pottery, Maroon Top, Qt.	325.00
Hollywood, Amber, Cylindrical, Kick-Up, Glob Top, c.1880, 11 1/2 In.	40.00
Hollywood, Amber, Qt., 11 1/2 In.	19.00
Hollywood, Cylindrical, Red Amber, Qt.	29.00
Humphrey & Martin, Philadelphia, Orange Amber, Squat, Qt., 9 1/2 In.	39.00
Humphrey & Martin Philada. Pa., Golden Amber, Rectangular, Kick-Up, Qt., 10 In.	48.00
Hunter Whiskey, Back Bar, Stopper, Polished Pontil, Enamel, BIMAL, 10 1/2 In.	125.00
I Got My Fill At Jakes, Clear, Pumpkinseed, Tooled Mouth, Flask, 1890-1910, 6 5/8 In.	258.00
I. Trager Co., Cincinnati, O., Lady's Leg, Amber, Qt., 11 1/2 In.	19.00
I.W. Harper, 29th National Encampment, G.A.R., Label Under Glass, 1895, Louisville, 6 In.	560.00
I.W. Harper, Bottled At Distillery, Quality Unsurpassed, Jug, Pottery, Blue Transfer, Qt.	100.00
Iron Front, Neff & Duff, Austin, Texas, Steer's Head, Cobwebs, Clear, Amethyst, 6 5/8 In.	5310.00
Ivanhoe Old Scotch Whiskey, Cream, Brown, Handle, Jug, 6 3/4 In.	308.00
J. Kellengberger Wholesale Wines & Liquors, Durango, Co., Amethyst, Slug Plate	325.00
J. Moore Old Bourbon, E. Chielovich & Co., Red Orange Amber, Embossed Antlers, Fifth	2420.00
J. Moore Old Bourbon, E. Chielovich & Co., Yellow Amber, Embossed Antlers, Fifth	3960.00
J.A. Stovell & Co. Phila. Pa., Red Amber, Cylindrical, 10 1/2 In.	45.00
J.F. & Co., Established 1821, Philada., Golden Orange Amber, Squat, Kick-Up, Qt.	149.00
J.F. Cutter Extra Old Bourbon, Trade Mark, Medium Amber, Embossed Shield, 11 7/8 In.	660.00
J.F. Tobias & Co., Amber, Applied Handle, Melon Shaped, Vertical Ribbing, 7 In.	978.00
J.F.T. & Co., 26-Ribs, Embossed, Yellow Amber, Jug, Double Collar, Handle, 7 In.	2016.00
J.F.T. & Co., Orange, Amber, Squat, Applied Seal, Qt., 9 1/2 In.	139.00
J.F.T. & Co., Red, Amber, Black, Squat, Applied Seal, Qt., 9 1/2 In.	149.00
J.F.T. & Co., Yellow, Amber, Squat, Applied Seal, Qt., 9 1/2 In.	159.00
J.H. Cutter Old Bourbon, A.P. Hotaling & Co., Amber, Olive, Applied Top, 11 7/8 In.	523.00
J.H. Cutter Old Bourbon, A.P. Hotaling & Co., S.F., Amber, Coffin, 1875, 7 1/2 In.	495.00
J.H. Cutter Old Bourbon, A.P. Hotaling & Co. Sole Agents, Dark Amber, 1869-71	1210.00
J.T. & Co., 341 Walnut St. Philada., Amber, Squat, Glass Shoulder Seal, Qt., 9 1/2 In.	99.00
J.T. Bickford & Bartlett, Boston, Chestnut, Amber, Applied Seal, Handle, OP, 8 3/4 In.	330.00
Jameson's Old Irish, Dragons, Shamrocks, Jug, Stencil, Dublin Trademark, Qt.	159.00
Jeroboam, Royal Blend, Jug, Stag, Port Dundas, Glasgow, 7 3/4 In.	157.00
Jesse Moore Old Bourbon, Trade Mark, Antlers, Red Amber, 1876-85, Fifth	660.00
Jesse Moore Old Bourbon, Trade Mark, Antlers, Yellow Amber, Fifth	358.00
John C. Stalfort, Baltimore, Md., U.S.A., Clear, Cylindrical, 9 In.	29.00
John H. Walsh & Co., Haymarket Sq., Boston, Clear	20.00
John McGlinn Distilling, Fat Lady's Leg, Golden Orange Amber, Seed Bubbles, Qt., 11 In.	39.00
John McPherson & Sons, Newcastle, Man Chipping Letters In Cliff, England	462.00
Johnnie Walker, Jug, Pub, White, Green Handle, Rim, Figure Pouring Drink, 6 1/4 In.	1064.00
Jos Leopold, Belleville, Ill., Fine Kentucky Whiskies, Jug, Brown, Blue Transfer, Gal.	100.00
Jos. Melczer & Co., Clear, Applied Top	110.00
Jug, Alice In Wonderland, Amber, Painted Gold, Black, Red, Flat Chestnut, 8 In., Pair	504.00
Jug, Stoneware, Square, Sloping Shoulders, Impressed, Irish Whiskey, 7 In.	32.00
Jug, Strawberry Puce, Globular, Applied Handle, Pontil, 5 7/8 In.	448.00
Jurgen Peters, Olive Yellow, Applied Sloping Collar, 8 3/4 In.	78.00
Kellogg's Nelson County Extra Kentucky Bourbon, Red Amber, Fifth	825.00

Kellogg's Nelson County Extra Kentucky Bourbon, W.L. Co., Red 875.00
Kentucky Belle Sour Mash, Distillery Anderson Co., Ky., Jug, Cream, Brown, 8 3/8 In. ... 420.00
Kentucky Club Old Bourbon, W.M. Watson & Co., Oakland, Cal., Fifth 120.00
Keystone Malt Whiskey, Orange, Amber, Oval, Qt., 10 1/2 In. 69.00
Kinahan's Old Scotch, For Auld Lang Syne, Brown, 7 3/8 In. ....*Illus* 1064.00
Labor's Choice, Union Made, Cylindrical, Red Amber, Qt., 11 1/2 In. 29.00
Laughlan Ross & Co, Aqua, Embossed, Thistles, Barley, 10 1/4 In. 159.00
Life Preserver, Stoneware, Tan Glaze, Nipper, 1880-1910, 7 1/2 x 6 3/4 In. 77.00
Lilienfeld's Washington Club, Cream, Brown Glaze, Gold Letters, Flowers, Jug, 7 1/4 In. 123.00
Lilienthal & Co., Cognac, Yellow, Olive Tone, 8 1/2 In. 2500.00
Lilienthal & Co., S.F., Gold, Red, Amber, Double Collar, Embossed, Flask, 8 1/2 In. 130.00
Liqueur De Merise, Olive Green, Handle, Metal Overlay, Late 1800s, 6 In. 45.00
Louis Taussig & Co., San Francisco, Amethyst, Embossed Slug Plate, 11 1/2 In. 45.00
Lowenstein & Co., Old Harvest Corn, Statesville, N.C., Clear, 1/2 Pt. 95.00
Lowenstein & Co., Old Harvest Corn, Statesville, N.C., Embossed, 1/2 Pt. 90.00
Macy & Jenkins, Jug, Applied Handle, Cylindrical, Amber, Qt., 9 1/2 In. 39.00
Martindale & Johnston, Minnehaha, Cream, Brown Transfer, Jug, 7 1/4 In. 728.00
McCormick Distilling Co., 100 Proof Straight Corn Whiskey, Stoneware, Jug, 1/2 Pt. 10.00
McKenna & Magills, Old Irish Whisky, Ireland, 8 In. 150.00
Meredith's Diamond Club Pure Rye, East Liverpool, O., White, Blue Transfer, 7 3/8 In. . . 168.00
Meredith's Diamond Club Pure Rye, East Liverpool, Oh., Jug, White China, 5 3/4 In. . . 56.00
Meredith's Diamond Club Pure Rye, Jug, Green Transfer, 7 3/4 In. ....179.00 to 246.00
Meredith's Diamond Club Pure Rye, Jug, White China, Teal Transfer, 5 3/4 In. .....*Illus* 179.00
Michael B. Wolfe, Aromatic Schnapps, Schiedam, Olive, Square, Embossed, 9 3/4 In. 275.00
Middleton & Gross Phila., Orange Amber, Squat, Qt., 9 1/2 In. 39.00
Miller's Extra, E. Martin & Co., Old Bourbon, Amber, Roll Top, Pt. 770.00
Miller's Extra, E. Martin, Old Bourbon, Orange, Rolled Collar, 1875, Pt. 1100.00
Miniature, see the Miniature category
Minnehaha, Martindale & Johnston, Philadelphia, Jug, Cream, Dark Brown Transfer, 7 In. 532.00
Mist Of The Morning, S.M. Barnett & Company, Amber, Barrel, 1865-75, 10 In. . .269.00 to 504.00
Mohawk, Indian Queen, Golden Amber, Inward Rolled Lip, Gold Paint, Feb. 11, 1968, 12 In. 4200.00
Monopole Rye, Black Bar, Cut Glass, Zipper Neck, Gilt, 3 3/4 x 9 1/2 In. 110.00
Mt. Vernon Rye Whiskey, Amber, Double Collar, Embossed, Display, 22 3/4 In. 448.00
Mulford's Natural Fruit Juices, Philadelphia, Orange Amber, Cylindrical, Qt., 12 1/2 In. . . 39.00
Mullins & Crigler Distillers Office Covington, Ky., Clear, 10 1/2 In. 14.00
Myers & Company Dist's Fulton, Covington, Ky., Aqua, Mold Blown, Gal. 90.00
N. Van Bergen & Co., Gold Dust Kentucky Bourbon, Horse, Aqua, Applied Top, Fifth ... 1320.00
Nabob, Green, Glob Top, Green, Cylindrical, Kick-Up, 4-Piece Mold, 1870-80, 8 In. 395.00
Nathans Bros., 1863 Phila., Yellow Amber, 8-Sided, Double Collar, Qt., 9 1/2 In. 189.00
Nathans Bros., Philad., Golden Amber, Crescent, Applied Wafer Seal, Mouth, 7 1/2 In. .. 364.00
Neal's Ambrosia, Cobalt Blue, Applied Mouth, Ring, Cylindrical, Seal, 9 1/4 In. 3080.00
Netter Bros., Clear, Amethyst, Man In Moon, Indian Queen, Qt., 10 In. 49.00
Netter Bros., Golden Amber, Man In Moon, Indian Queen, Qt., 10 In. 79.00
O'Donnel's Old Irish Whisky Belfast, Green Transfer, Stoneware, 7 5/8 In. 75.00
O.B.L. Scotch, Jug, Pub, White, Red, Black Letters, 5 3/4 In. 409.00
O.K. Bourbon Castle, F. Chevalier & Co. Sole Agents, Golden Amber, 1875, 12 In. 1045.00
O.K. Old Bourbon Castle, F. Chevalier & Co., Amber, 12 In. 264.00
O.K. Old Bourbon Castle, F. Chevalier & Co., Light Amber, 1875-80, Fifth 770.00
Old Bourbon, Honey Amber, Hog Shape, 1875-90, 6 5/8 In. 413.00
Old Bourbon, Wilson Fairbank & Co., Aquamarine, 1870-90, 10 In. 143.00
Old Bourbon, Wilson Fairbank & Co., Sole Agents, Blue Aqua, Applied Mouth, 10 In. 175.00
Old Bourbon Castle, F. Chevalier Sole Agents, Light Amber, Applied Lip, Fifth 1210.00
Old Cold Spring Sour Mash, Dreuffus & Well, Paducah, Ky., Jug, Cream, 7 1/4 In. 168.00
Old Continental, Yellow Amber, Sloping Collar, 1865-75, 9 3/8 In. ....*Illus* 4760.00
Old Dominick Bourbon, D. Canale & Co., Memphis, Tenn., Clear, Squat, Qt., 11 In. 29.00
Old Drum You Can't Beat It Whiskey, Maryland Dist., Screw Cap, Label, Clear 12.00
Old Governor 1879 Sour Mash, A. Graf & Co., Jug, Cream, Brown Glaze, 7 1/2 In. 78.00
Old Hettermann Sour Mash, Bourbon Whiskey, Gray Tan, Brown Glaze, Jug, 10 1/4 In. . 168.00
Old Maryland 1881 Pure Rye, G. Reismeyer, St. Louis, Mo., Jug, White, 7 1/2 In. 560.00
Old Monongahela Pure Rye, Sam Thompason, Amber, West Brownsville, Pa., 9 1/2 In. .. 12.00
Old Monongahela Rye, Paul Jones, Louisville, Ky., Red Amber, Tapered Cylinder, 9 1/2 In. 59.00
Old Prentice Whisky, Inside Fluted Panels, Ground Pontil, 3 1/2 x 11 In. 209.00
Old Quaker Brand, Bust, Sheaf Of Wheat, Screw Cap, 7 1/2 x 4 1/4 In. 10.00

Old Quaker Rye Whiskey, Lawrenceburg, Indiana, Embossed, Colorful Labels, 1/2 Pt. 10.00
Old Quaker Rye Whiskey, Lawrenceburg, Indiana, Embossed, Colorful Labels, Pt. 10.00
Old Rye Whiskey, Monongahela, Olive Green, BIMAL, Wheat, 1860 . . . . 300.00
Old Sherman House Bourbon, Chicago, Flask, Leather Cover, 1/2 Pt. 90.00
Olive Green, Shoulder Seal, Squat, Qt., 10 1/2 In. 69.00
Optimus Kentucky Whiskies Very Fine, Jug, Stoneware, Brown, Cream, 1885, Qt. 119.00
Oregon Importing Co., Chocolate Amber, Fluted Shoulder, Cylindrical, 1904-15, Qt. 50.00
Parker Rye, Embossed, BIMAL, 3 1/4 In. 35.00
Pascal Caron Salmon Falls, N.H., Clear, Tooled, Double Collar Top, Qt. 50.00
Patent, Black Glass, 3-Piece Mold, Kick-Up, Applied Top, 1855-65, 4/5 Qt., 11 In. 29.00
Perfection Old Valley, Jug, Tan, Brown Glaze, Blue Transfer, 7 1/2 In. 134.00
Perrine's Ginger, Apple, Phila., Cabin, Amber, Roped Corners, 1880-90, 10 In. 190.00
Perrine's Pure Barley Malt, Philadelphia, Pa., Orange Amber, Cylindrical, 10 1/2 In. 39.00
Petts Bald Eagle, Tooled Top, Flask, 1/2 Pt. 55.00
Pfeiffer Bros., Awarded Gold Medal, Louisiana Purchase Expo, Swirled, 1904, Fifth 55.00
Phil. G. Kelly, Richmond Va., Cream, Black Transfer, Jug, 6 5/8 In. 168.00
Phoenix Old Bourbon, San Francisco, Yellow, c.1896, 1/2 Pt. 495.00
Pickaway Liquor Co., Circleville, O., Jug, White, Blue Transfer, 1890-1915, 7 1/4 In. 560.00
Pig, Embossed, C.F. Knapp, Philada, BIMAL, 3 3/4 In. 50.00
Pink, Double Collar, Flask, 1860-80, Pt. 1008.00
Pointer Maryland Rye, Baltimore, Md., Jug, Pottery, Cream, Maroon Transfer, 7 1/4 In. . . 616.00
R. Stumpf, Baltimore, Aqua, Cylindrical, Applied Lip Ring, c.1860, Pt., 11 1/2 In. 48.00
R.B. Cutter, Louisville, Medium Amber, Applied Top & Handle, Open Pontil, 8 3/4 In. . . . 468.00
R.B. Cutter, Pure Bourbon, Apricot, Handle, Pear Shape, Pontil, c.1850, 8 1/8 In. 1680.00
R.B. Cutter, Pure Bourbon, Cherry Puce, Pontil, Handle, c.1860, 8 1/2 In. 728.00
Reed's Old Lexington Club, Golden Amber, Applied Sloping Double Collar, 11 In. 728.00
Reiger, Embossed, J. Reiger & Co., Kansas City, Mo., BIMAL, 4 5/8 In. 30.00
Roberts Steel, Philadelphia, Black, Cylindrical, Embossed, 12 In. 39.00
Roche Brand Irish, Jug, Cream, Brown Glaze, Black Transfer, 7 3/8 In. . . . .*Illus* 213.00
Roches Maguseleum, Balt'o, Md., Clear, Cylindrical, Pt., 11 1/2 In. 29.00
Rochester Distilling Co., Est'd 1842, Honey Amber, Bulbous, Applied Top, Qt., 10 In. . . . 79.00
Rosedale O.K., Siebe Bros & Plagemann, Amber, Glob Top, 11 1/2 In. 1250.00
Rosskam Gerstley & Co. Philada., Fine Old Whiskey, Clear, Squat, Qt., 10 In. 59.00
Rothschild Bros., Yellow, Amber, Squat, Applied Seal, 1868, Qt., 9 1/2 In. 169.00
Roxbury Rye, Geo. T. Gambrill, Baltimore, Md., Clear, Square, Qt., 10 1/2 In. 19.00
Royal Halburton, Town Crier, Green Coat, Red Scarf, c.1976, 13 3/4 x 5 In. 35.00
S. Rosenthal & Co., Wines & Liquors, Amber, Square, Qt., 12 In. 29.00
S.A. Wertz Phila Superior Old Rye, Red Amber, Tapered Cylindrical, 10 In. 89.00
S.A. Wertz Superior Old Rye, Amber, Tapered Shoulder, Squat, Qt., 10 In. 89.00
S.A. Wertz Superior Old Rye, Red, Amber, Squat, Applied Seal, 9 1/2 In. 139.00
S.B. Wetherhold Pottstown, Pa., Aqua, Square, 12 In. 29.00
S.F. Twomey & Miholovich, Yellowstone, White, Brown Glaze, Jug, 6 3/4 In. 213.00
S.W. Smith Philadelphia, Orange Amber, Squat, Applied Top, Qt., 9 1/4 In. 59.00
Sanderson's, Liqueur Special, Pure Malt, Jug, Side Handle, Portobello, 8 In. 108.00
Sandersons Mountain Dew Scotch, Leith, Brown & White, Black Transfer, Stoneware, 7 In. 150.00
Seltzer & Miller, 1017 Market St., Phila, Reddish Amber, Squat, Qt., 10 In. 169.00

Whiskey, Roche
Brand Irish, Jug,
Cream, Brown
Glaze, Black
Transfer,
7 3/8 In.

Whiskey, Udolpho
Wolfe's Aromatic
Schnapps, Schiedam,
Olive Amber, IP,
9 1/2 In

Whiskey, Star,
New York, W.B.
Crowell Jr.,
Amber, Applied
Spout, Handle,
Pontil, 8 In.

Selzer & Miller, Orange, Amber, Squat, Applied Seal, 9 1/2 In. 99.00
Shaw's Quality Store, Monogram, Robert Shaw Company, Haverhill, Slug Plate, Qt. 40.00
Sheedan's Canada Malt, Cylindrical, Clear, Qt., 10 1/2 In. 29.00
Silas F Miller & Co., Louisville, Amber, Double Collar, Flask, 1875-85, 6 1/4 In. 1008.00
Simmond's Nabob, Kentucky Bourbon, Nabob Smoking Hookah, Red Amber 990.00
Sir Edward Lee's, Jug, Pub, Brown Top, Tan Salt Glaze, Coat Of Arms, Thistles, 6 1/2 In. 1023.00
Slater's Premium Bourbon, Light Yellow Amber, Cylindrical, Tooled Top, 11 3/4 In. 50.00
Snow & Co, Jug, Tan Neck, White Glaze, Black Transfer, 7 1/4 In. 737.00
South Carolina Dispensary, Palmetto Tree, Clear, 1900-07, 9 1/8 In., Qt. 385.00
South Carolina Dispensary, Strap Sides, Aquamarine, 1893-1907, 1/2 Pt., 6 1/4 In. 176.00
Spring Lake Handmade Sour Mash Bourbon, Jug, White China, 7 1/2 In. 90.00
Spring Lake Sour Mash, Klein Bros., & Hyman, Cincinnati, O., Jug, White, 7 1/2 In. 123.00
Spruance Stanley & Co., Horseshoe, San Francisco, Cal., Amber, Glop Top, 11 5/8 In. ... 207.00
Spruance Stanley & Co., San Francisco, Cal., Amber, Star, Fifth, 10 3/4 In. 143.00
Star, Amber, Applied Lip, Pouring Spout, Applied Handle, Open Pontil, 8 In. 748.00
Star, New York, Golden Yellow Amber, Rib, Petticoat, Pontil, Double Collar, 8 1/8 In. 1064.00
Star, New York, W.B. Crowell Jr., Amber, Applied Spout, Handle, Pontil, 8 In. .....*Illus* 605.00
Steinhart Bros., & Co., Mountain Dew, Jug, Tan, Brown Glaze, Black Transfer, 7 1/4 In. . 235.00
Stoddard Glasshouse, Reddish Amber, Applied Square Collared Mouth, 10 In. 784.00
Stoneware, Cream, Brown Glaze, Black Transfer, 10 3/4 In. 112.00
Telegram Rye, David Netter & Co., Clear, Qt., 11 In. 19.00
The Torton, Denver, Amethyst, Metal Screw Cap, 1/2 Pt. 90.00
Theodore Netter, Uncle Sam Toasting Miss Liberty, Clear, Square, Qt., 11 In. 45.00
Theodore Netter, Uncle Sam, Miss Liberty, Clear, Amethyst Tint, Square, Qt., 10 1/2 In. . 39.00
Thos. H. Gill's Son Fine Liquors, Philada., Lady's Leg Neck, Honey Amber, Qt., 11 In. . 19.00
Thos. Taylor & Co., Old Bourbon, Louisville, Ky., Amber, 1880-86, Fifth 330.00
Tiffany Club, Fluted Neck, c.1945 .... 45.00
Truet Jones & Arrington, Golden Amber, Cylindrical, Applied Mouth, c.1865, 10 1/8 In. . 1650.00
Tucker, Suspects His Master, Bulldog, Enamel Decoration, 1880-1900, 11 In. 660.00
Turner Brothers, Barrel, Amber, Applied Mouth, 10 In. ....728.00 to 896.00
Turner Brothers, Barrel, Amber, Applied Sloping Collar, 9 3/4 In. 336.00
Tyrconnell Whisky, Donegal Castle, White Glaze, Black Transfer, Stoneware, Jug, 9 In. ... 50.00
UAM-VAR, Jug, Pub, White, Red, Black, Blue Transfer, Medals, 5 1/2 In. 777.00
Udolpho Wolfe, Amber, Iron Pontil, Qt. 25.00
Udolpho Wolfe, Olive, Iron Pontil, Qt. 95.00
Udolpho Wolfe's Aromatic Schnapps, Amber, Applied Top, Graphite Base, 10 In. 220.00
Udolpho Wolfe's Aromatic Schnapps, Aqua, Double Taper Top, Pontil, 8 In. 303.00
Udolpho Wolfe's Aromatic Schnapps, Olive Amber, Iron Pontil, Sloping Collar, 9 7/8 In. . 101.00
Udolpho Wolfe's Aromatic Schnapps, Olive, Sloping Collar, Square, Iron Pontil, 10 In. ... 130.00
Udolpho Wolfe's Aromatic Schnapps, Pink Copper Puce, Sloping Collar, 8 3/8 In. 123.00
Udolpho Wolfe's Aromatic Schnapps, Schiedam, Green Aqua, Double Collar, 8 In. 179.00
Udolpho Wolfe's Aromatic Schnapps, Schiedam, Green, Applied Top, 8 In. 66.00
Udolpho Wolfe's Aromatic Schnapps, Schiedam, Olive Amber, IP, 9 1/2 In. ....*Illus* 139.00
Udolpho Wolfe's Aromatic Schnapps, Schiedam, Yellow Olive Green, c.1865, 8 1/4 In. ... 67.00
Union Club Rye, Geo. B. Woodman, Amber, Label, 3-Piece Mold, 1860s, 11 1/2 In. 69.00
Van Schuyver, Portland, Monogram, Amber, 1887-91, Fifth 275.00
Vic Trolio, Whiskeys, Canton, Miss., Brown, Tan, Stoneware, Jug, Cobalt Letters, Gal. ... 130.00
Voldner's Aromatic Schnapps, Schiedam, Light To Medium Green, Applied Top, 9 7/8 In. 120.00
Voldner's Aromatic Schnapps, Schiedam, Olive Amber, Square, 9 3/4 In. 145.00
W.B. Crowell, Star, 26 Ribs, Amber, Pontil, Applied Mouth, Handle, 8 In. 420.00
Watson's, Jug, Pub, Blue Luster Glaze, White, Blue Letters, 5 1/4 In. 655.00
Watson's Dundee Whisky, Cream, Dark Brown Glaze, Scotland, c.1890-1915, 8 5/8 In. ... 120.00
Watson's Dundee Whisky, Stoneware, Jug, Handle, Pour Lip, 2-Tone, 8 1/2 In. 50.00
Weeks & Gilson, S. Stoddard, N.H., Olive Amber, 1860-70, 12 x 3 1/2 In. 1008.00
Wharton's, 1850, Chestnut Grove, Amber, Applied Spout & Handle, 10 1/2 In. 230.00
Wharton's, 1850, Chestnut Grove, Amber, Flask, Teardrop, Pocket, 5 1/2 In. 357.00
Wharton's, 1850, Chestnut Grove, Gold Amber, Bubbles, Flask, Pocket, 5 1/4 In. 229.00
Wharton's, 1850, Chestnut Grove, Urn, Yellow Amber, Handle, Pour Spout, 10 1/8 In. 784.00
Wharton's, 1850, Sapphire Blue, Oval, Double Collar, Flask, Pocket, 5 1/4 In. 616.00
Wharton's, Chestnut Grove, Cobalt Blue, Pumpkinseed, Glass Stopper, Flask, 5 In. 280.00
Wharton's, Yellow Amber, Handle, Whitney Glass, c.1865, 10 1/8 In. 784.00
White Lily Pure Rye, S.B. & Co., Jug, White China, Olive Green Transfer, 7 3/8 In. 134.00
White Sulphur Springs, West Virginia, Jug, Cream, Blue Top, Handle, Spout, 7 In. 224.00

Wichman Lutgen & Co., Old Gilt Edge, O.K. Bourbon, Tooled Lip, Flask, 1/2 Pt. 132.00
William Jameson & Co., Cream, Brown, Black Transfer, Jug, 7 3/8 In. 235.00
William Jameson & Co., Whiskey Distillers Dublin, Jug, Kennedy Stamp 139.00
Wm., Edwards & Co., Cleveland, Ohio, Tan, Black Transfer, Stopper, Jug, 10 3/4 In. 123.00
Wolff Distillery, Stoneware, Jug, Brown Shoulders, Oatmeal Body, 1880-1900, 1/2 Gal. .. 110.00
Woman In Corset, Amethyst Tint, Screw Top, Sampler, 1890-1910, 6 1/2 In. 22.00
Yellow Lime Citron, Squat, Kick-Up Base, Applied Double Collar, 9 3/4 In. 59.00
Yellow Lime Green, Citron, Squat, Double Collar, Bubble, Qt., 9 1/2 In. 59.00

WILD TURKEY

Wild Turkey is a brand of bourbon made by Austin Nichols Distillery. The company says the bourbon was originally made as a gift for some hunting companions and so was named for their favorite gamebird. A crystal bottle with an etched flying turkey design was made in 1951. The company made turkey-shaped ceramic bottles from 1971 to 1989. The first bottle, filled with bourbon, sold for $20. In 1981 the company added miniature bottles. For a short time during the 1980s, the company marketed a line of *go-withs* such as plates and plaques. After 1989, Wild Turkey sold two limited-edition bottles: a Rare Breed Whiskey bottle in a teardrop shape, which is still made, and a Kentucky Legend decanter shaped like a violin, which is no longer in production. Since mid-1994, under the Rare Breed label, Austin Nichols & Co. Distillery has issued a Kentucky Spirit, single barrel bourbon in a distinctive bottle with a pewter-style top, available year-round in a gift box. Wild Turkey figural decanters are no longer being made.

Charleston, Centennial, 1974, 10 1/2 In. 76.00
Decanter, Baccarat, Crystal, 1979 .... 374.00
Mack Truck 75th Anniversary, Bull Dog, 1975, 10 3/4 In. .... 5.00 to 10.00
Series 1, No. 1, Standing, Male, 1971 .... 46.00 to 65.00
Series 1, No. 1, Standing, Male, 1971, Miniature .... 5.00 to 10.00
Series 1, No. 2, On Log, Female, 1972 .... 89.00 to 100.00
Series 1, No. 2, On Log, Female, 1981, Miniature .... 4.00 to 8.50
Series 1, No. 3, On Wing, 1973 .... 10.50 to 26.00
Series 1, No. 3, On Wing, 1982, Miniature .... 18.00 to 22.00
Series 1, No. 4, With Poult, 1974 .... 6.50 to 8.00
Series 1, No. 4, With Poult, 1982, Miniature 17.50
Series 1, No. 5, With Flags, 1975 .... 3.75 to 10.50
Series 1, No. 6, Striding, 1976 .... 5.00 to 10.00
Series 1, No. 7, Taking Off, 1977 .... 5.00 to 15.50
Series 1, No. 7, Taking Off, 1983, Miniature 8.00
Series 1, No. 8, Strutting, 1978 .... 9.00 to 26.00
Series 2, No. 1, Lore, 1979 .... 10.00 to 20.00
Series 2, No. 2, Lore, 1980 .... 5.00 to 20.00
Series 2, No. 3, Lore, 1981 .... 18.50
Series 2, No. 4, Lore, 1982 .... 19.00 to 27.00
Series 3, No. 1, In Flight, Box, 1983 .... 26.00 to 100.00
Series 3, No. 2, With Bobcat, 1985, Miniature 78.00

Wild Turkey, Series 3, No. 3,
Turkeys Fighting, Box, 1983

Wild Turkey, Series 3, No. 7,
With Fox, 1985

Wild Turkey, Series 3, No. 8,
With Owl, 1985

Series 3, No. 3, Turkeys Fighting, Box, 1983 . . . . *Illus*   100.00
Series 3, No. 4, With Eagle, 1984 . . . . .35.00 to 38.00
Series 3, No. 5, With Raccoon, Box, 1984 . . . . .43.00 to 100.00
Series 3, No. 6, With Poult, 1984, Miniature 21.00
Series 3, No. 6, With Poult, Box, 1984 . . . . .80.00 to 100.00
Series 3, No. 7, With Fox, 1984, Miniature 50.00
Series 3, No. 7, With Fox, 1985 . . . . *Illus*   58.00
Series 3, No. 8, With Owl, 1985 . . . . *Illus*   61.00
Series 3, No. 8, With Owl, 1985, Miniature 77.00
Series 3, No. 8, With Owl, Box, 1985 . . . .   51.00
Series 3, No. 10, With Coyote, 1986 . . . .   90.00
Series 3, No. 10, With Coyote, 1986, Miniature 45.00
Series 3, No. 11, With Falcon, 1986 . . . .   60.00
Series 3, No. 11, With Falcon, 1986, Miniature 51.00
Series 3, No. 12, With Skunk, 1986, Miniature 78.00
Series 3, No. 12, With Skunk, Box, 1986 . . . .   71.00

WINE

Wine has been bottled since the days of the ancient Greeks. Wine bottles have been made in a variety of sizes and shapes. Seal bottles were used from the second century and are listed in their own section in this book. Most wines found today are in the standard shapes that have been used for the past 125 years. The Bordeaux shape has square shoulders and straight sides while the Burgundy shape is broader with sloping shoulders. The German or Rhine wine flute bottle is tall and thin. Other wines, such as champagne, are bottled in slightly different bottles. A *dumpy* holds 500 ml of wine.

Aqua, Flat Bladder, 3 1/2 In. 164.00
Bell Brothers Wine Merchants, New Castle, Olive Amber, Double Collar Lip, 8 In. 60.00
Black Glass, Dip Mold, Olive Amber, Open Pontil, Applied String, Dutch, 1760-80, 12 In.   202.00
Black Glass, Magnum, Olive Amber, Applied String Lip, Pontil, 10 1/8 In. 1344.00
Black Glass, Olive Amber, Applied Mouth, Pontil, 8 7/8 In. 308.00
Black Glass, Pancake Onion, Opalescent Olive Amber, Pontil, 5 1/2 x 6 In. 2352.00
Boar, Coronet, Olive Green, Pontil Base, Applied Double Collar Lip, Seal, 11 1/4 In. 400.00
Chocolate Amber, Applied String Lip, Pontil, 9 x 3 1/2 In. 134.00
Cylindrical, Mid Olive Green, Short Neck, Flared Lip, Kick-Up Base, Dumpy, 18 1/4 In. .   286.00
Cylindrical, Olive Green, Applied Collar, 3-Piece Mold, 10 1/4 In. 552.00
Cylindrical, Olive Green, Applied Collar, Kick-Up Base, Pontil, Dumpy 17 3/4 In. 35.00
Cylindrical, Olive Green, Applied Collar, Pontil, c.1790, 8 1/4 In. 25.00
Cylindrical, Olive Green, Applied Collar, Seal, 10 1/2 In. 185.00
Cylindrical, Olive Green, Applied Collar, Seal, 11 1/2 In. 575.00
Cylindrical, Olive Green, Seal, Squat, 9 3/4 In. 1841.00
Durkin Wholesale & Retail Wines & Liquors, Megaphone Shape, 1907-15, 13 In. 468.00
Dutch Onion, Olive Green, Pontil, Kick-Up Base, Applied Rim, 7 In. 266.00
Garrett & Co., Virginia Dare, Tooled Top, N.Y., 1/2 Gal. 100.00
Genuine Vernal Saw Palmetto Berry Wine, Buffalo, N.Y., Clear 18.00
Globular, Applied Neck, Olive Green, White Flecks, Horse, Nailsea Form, 1830, 9 1/2 In. 6012.00
H. Ricketts Glass Works Bristol, Olive Amber, Double Collar, Pontil, 8 5/8 x 3 1/2 In. . .   123.00
Henry Brand Wine Co., Toledo, Oh., Amber, Applied Crown Top 45.00
Lupton, Olive Green, Applied Double Collar Lip, Seal, 11 In. 418.00
Mallet, Olive Amber, Applied String Lip, Pontil, 6 1/2 x 3 3/4 In. 784.00
Mallet, Olive Amber, Applied String Lip, Pontil, 7 x 4 5/8 In. 308.00
Mallet, Olive Amber, Applied String Lip, Pontil, 8 x 4 3/4 In. 224.00
Mallet, Olive Amber, Applied String Lip, Pontil, 9 1/8 x 3 1/2 In. 179.00
Mallet, Olive Amber, Applied String Lip, Pontil, Matte, 7 1/2 x 4 1/2 In. 308.00
Mallet, Olive Green, Applied Collar, Pontil, Iridescent, Dumpy, 8 3/4 In. 205.00
Mallet, Olive Green, Applied String Lip, Pontil, 6 1/4 x 3 3/4 In.   336.00
Mallet, Olive Green, Applied String Lip, Pontil, 6 In. 560.00
Mallet, Olive Green, Applied String Rim, Pontil, 6 1/4 In. 369.00
Mallet, Olive Green, Applied String Rim, Pontil, 8 1/2 In. 70.00
Mallet, Olive Green, Applied String Rim, Pontil, Patinated, England, c.1760, 8 1/4 In. . . .   75.00
Miniature, see the Miniature category
Napoleon, Cronstadt, Paris, Toulon, Marine Blue, Enameled, Crests, Leaves, 8 x 3 5/8 In.   200.00
Olive Amber, Applied String Lip, Pontil, 9 x 3 3/4 In. 134.00
Olive Amber, Bladder, Applied String, Pontil, 5 5/8 x 3 5/8 x 3 1/4 In. 504.00

Olive Amber, Opalescent Blue, Applied Lip, Pontil, Matte, 5 3/8 x 5 In. 308.00
Olive Green, Champagne Shoulder, Applied Collar, String Rim, Seal, 1789, 10 1/4 In. . . . 1841.00
Olive Green, Shaft & Globe, Applied String Lip, Pontil, 8 1/2 x 3 1/8 In. 2688.00
Olive Green, Tapered Neck, Applied Collar, Graphite Pontil, Dumpy, 13 3/4 In. 184.00
Onion, Nichs Hallam 1712, Olive Green, Applied String Rim, Pontil, 6 3/4 In. 5177.00
Onion, Olive Amber, Applied Lip, Pontil, 5 1/2 x 5 In. 336.00
Onion, Olive Amber, Applied Lip, Pontil, Matte, 5 x 5 5/8 In. 336.00
Onion, Olive Amber, Applied String Lip, Pontil, 6 3/4 x 4 1/2 In. 336.00
Onion, Olive Amber, Applied String Lip, Pontil, Matte, 5 1/2 x 3 3/4 In. 336.00
Onion, Olive Green, Applied Double Collar, Engraved Crown, Thistle, 10 1/4 In. 552.00
Onion, Olive Green, Seal, 1720, 7 3/4 In. 2046.00
Onion, Olive Green, Stipple Engraved, Long Neck, Collar Lip, Pontil, 8 1/4 In. 617.00
Onion, Olive Green, Tapered, String Rim, Pontil, England, c.1700, 5 3/4 In. 284.00
Onion, Olive Yellow, Applied String Lip, Pontil, 5 3/8 x 3 5/7 In. 560.00
Onion Mallet, Olive Green, Applied String Lip, 5 3/4 In. 1146.00
P.C. Brooks, Cylindrical, Olive Amber, Applied Lip, Ring, Pontil, c.1820, 9 1/2 In. 1792.00
Pancake Onion, Olive Amber, Applied Lip, Pontil, 5 3/4 x 5 3/8 In. 560.00
Pouronne, Light Amethyst, Applied Lip, Pontil, 5 3/4 In. 275.00
T. Reynolds, Black, Olive Amber, Applied Seal, Applied String Lip, 9 3/4 x 4 3/8 In. 2576.00
Tobacco Amber, Olive Tone, Applied String Lip, Pontil, 8 3/4 x 3 1/2 In. 146.00
W.M. Watson & CO, Wine Growers, Oakland, Cal., Pumpkinseed Flask, Pt. 225.00
Welch's, Milk Glass, White, Spatter Paint Look, 1955, 11 In. 39.00

ZANESVILLE

The Zanesville Manufacturing Company started making glass in Zanesville, Ohio, in
1815. This glassworks closed in 1838 but reopened from 1842 to 1851. The company
made many types of blown and mold blown pieces. At least one other glassworks operated in Zanesville from 1816 to the 1840s. The products of all the Zanesville factories
are sometimes identified as *Midwestern* glass and are grouped with pieces made in
Mantua, Kent, Ravenna, and other Ohio towns. The blown glass pieces include diamond patterned and ribbed pieces in clear, blue, amethyst, aquamarine, and amber colored glass. Collectors prize the Zanesville swirl pieces and identify them as *right* or *left*
swirl.

24 Ribs, Swirled To Right, Blue Aqua, Globular, Outward Rolled Lip, Pontil, 7 3/4 In. . . .   336.00
24 Ribs, Swirled To Right, Yellow Amber, Globular, Rolled Lip, Pontil, 7 3/4 In. 616.00
24 Ribs, Swirled To Right, Yellow Amber, Globular, Rolled Lip, Pontil, 9 3/8 In. 2464.00
24 Vertical Ribs, Globular, Blue Aqua, Applied Mouth, Pontil, 7 3/8 In. 146.00

GO-WITHS

There are many items that interest the bottle collector even though they are not bottles:
all types of advertising that picture bottles or endorse bottled products like whiskey or
beer, many small items like bottle openers or bottle caps, and related products by well-
known companies like trays and plaques. Collectors call all of these *go-withs.* A variety of the items are listed here. Many others can be found under company names in
other price lists such as *Kovels' Antiques & Collectibles Price List.* Clubs and publications that will help collectors are listed in the bibliography and club list in this book.

Advertisement, Dr. M. McHenry Stomach Bitters, Liniment, Frame, 11 x 14 In. 48.00
Almanac, Swamp-Root, Factory, Black & White, 1919, 16 Pages, 8 1/2 x 6 In. 187.00
Ashtray, Coca-Cola Bottle Under Lamp Shade Top, Match Pull, Bakelite, c.1930, 7 1/2 In.   850.00
Ashtray, Coca-Cola, Cup Holders, During Game Enjoy, Metal, 8 1/2 x 8 1/2 In. 149.00
Ashtray, Crown Of Crowns, German Wines, Porcelain 51.00
Ashtray, Great Falls Select Fine Beer, Red ACL Glaze, Milk Glass, Round, 5 1/4 In. 12.00
Ashtray, Kuntz's Old German Lager, Enamel, Yellow, Rectangle 30.00
Ashtray, Suntory Whisky, 1 1/4 x 4 In. 20.00
Bank, Milk Bottle, 1/2 Pt. Coin Bank, Small Boy, Big Coin, Padlock, Key, 4 1/2 In. 39.00
Bank, Snow Crest Bottle, Bear Shape, Glass, Tin Lid, Salem, Mass. 29.00
Bank, Squirt, Boy, 7 1/4 In. . . . .*Illus*   175.00
Banner, Dr. Daniel's Medicines For Your Stock, Cloth, 10 3/4 x 23 1/2 In. 1760.00
Baseball Scorekeeper, Coca-Cola, Red, White, Green, c.1910-20 . . . .   77.00
Beer Knife, Kiewel, White Seal Beer, Crookston, Minn. 381.00
Blotter, A.V. Whiteman, N.Y., Milk Bottle Shape, Die Cut, Rivet, 3 Pages, 1898 . . . .   154.00
Blotter, Coca-Cola Gum, Chew This, 3 3/4 x 6 In. 2320.00
Blotter, Dr. Kilmer's Swamp-Root, Dr. F.S. Gray, Druggist, 4 x 9 In. 137.00

Go-Withs, Bank,
Squirt,Boy,
7 1/4 In.

Don't open a collectible beer can from the top. Leave the pull tab intact and open the can from the bottom using a standard punch-type opener.

Book, Coca-Cola, Bottler, Mar.-Sept. 1946	28.00
Booklet, Coca-Cola, Bottler, January, 1960	39.00
Booklet, Dr. Kilmer's Swamp-Root Makes Friends, Girls, Boat, 1904, 8 3/4 x 6 In.	121.00
Booklet, Dr. Kilmer's Swamp-Root, Like A Thief In The Night, 1900, 8 3/4 x 6 In.	99.00
Booklet, What People Want To Know, S. Andral Kilmer M.D., 1890, 11 x 8 1/2 In.	154.00
Bookmark, Coca-Cola, Drink Coca-Cola, Girl, Heart Shape, Celluloid, 1898, 2 1/4 x 2 In.	440.00
Bookmark, Coca-Cola, Drink Coca-Cola, Girl, Heart Shape, Celluloid, 1900, 2 1/4 x 2 In.	468.00
Bookmark, Coca-Cola, Girl, At Soda Fountains, 5 Cents, Frame, 1905, 6 x 2 In.	550.00
Bookmark, Coca-Cola, Woman, Mug Of Coca-Cola, Frame, 1904, 6 x 2 In.	253.00
Bottle Cap, 7Up, Superman Sweepstake, Crown, Canada, 1978	10.00
Bottle Cap, Clown Root Beer, Cork Lined, 1940s	5.00
Bottle Cap, Coca-Cola, Chicago, Ill., Cork Lined, 1930s, 6 Oz.	23.00
Bottle Cap, Coca-Cola, Los Angeles, Cork Lined, 1930s, 6 Oz.	6.25
Bottle Cap, Coca-Cola, Salem Depot, N.H., Cork Lined, c.1920, 6 Oz.	7.25
Bottle Cap, Coca-Cola, Test, Aluminum, Rip Cap, For 6 Oz. Bottle	9.25
Bottle Cap, Dutch Hendricks, Skiatook, Okla., Red & Blue On White	118.00
Bottle Cap, Evervess, Sparkling Water, Cork Caps, 4 Piece	8.50
Bottle Cap, Lemon-Lime Crush, Cork Lined, 1940s	1.75
Bottle Cap, Nehi Cola, Cork Lined, Red, Yellow, Louisville, Ky., 1930s	5.00
Bottle Cap, Nehi Ginger Ale, Cork Lined, Unused, 1930s	7.00
Bottle Cap, Nesbitt's Lemon Soda, Cork, Yellow Ground, Green Letters	3.50
Bottle Cap, Old Monterey Bock, Ram's Head	92.00
Bottle Cap, Pepsi-Cola, Green Ground, White Letters, Unused, c.1910, 1 In.	31.00
Bottle Cap, Pepsi-Cola, Red Letters, Border, Yellow Ground, Unused, 1930s	10.00
Bottle Cap, Pepsi-Cola, World's Largest, Tin, 65th Anniversary, 1958, Fresno, Ca., 3 In.	10.00
Bottle Cap, Pepsi-Cola, Yellow Ground, Red Letters, Cork Lined, Double Dash	4.00
Bottle Cap, RC Cola, Worth 1 Cent, Save-A-Seal, Cork Lined	2.00
Bottle Cap, Simba Carbonated Beverage, Cork Lined, Coca-Cola Bottling, Seattle, Wash.	6.50
Bottle Cap, White Rock Quinine Water Q-9, Cork Lined, Unused, Los Angeles, Cal.	24.00
Bottle Opener, 7Up Likes You, You'll Like It, 3 3/4 In.	8.50
Bottle Opener, Anchor Beer, 3 1/2 In.	3.00
Bottle Opener, Ashtray, Bourbon St., Cast Iron, 5 In.	40.00
Bottle Opener, Beverwyck Beer, Wire Type	6.00
Bottle Opener, Coca-Cola, Consolidated Cork Corp., Brooklyn, 3 1/2 In.	12.50
Bottle Opener, Coca-Cola, Juo Coca-Cola Jaakylmana, Olympics, Finland, 1952, 3 In.	25.00
Bottle Opener, Coca-Cola, Starr X, Brown Co., N. News Va., 1925 Patent	5.00 to 22.00
Bottle Opener, Drink Coca-Cola, Consolidated Cork Corp., Brooklyn, N.Y., 3 3/8 x 1 In.	7.00
Bottle Opener, Drink Coca-Cola, Starr X, Brown Co., N. News, Va., 1925	15.50
Bottle Opener, Drink Pepsi-Cola, Wire Type, Long Handle, Ekco, 4 3/4 x 1 1/2 In.	3.00
Bottle Opener, Enjoy Grapette, Thirsty Or Not, 3 3/4 In.	5.00
Bottle Opener, Evervess Sparkling Water, Pepsi-Cola Co., Reseal Cap, 3 5/8 x 1 1/8 In.	12.25
Bottle Opener, Extra 6 Beer, Made Famous By Public Favor, 1901 Patent, Style B-21	35.00
Bottle Opener, Famous Narraganset Ale, Style B-24	18.00
Bottle Opener, Fresh Up With 7Up, Consolidated Cork Corp., Brooklyn, N.Y., 3 3/8 In.	7.50
Bottle Opener, Genesee Beer & 12 Horse Ale, Rochester, N.Y., 5 In.	5.00
Bottle Opener, Gopher Club Brew, Engesser Brewing Co., St. Peter, Minn.	80.00
Bottle Opener, Gunther Premium Dry Beer, Copper, 3 In.	10.00

Bottle Opener, Have A Coke, Drink Coca-Cola, It's The Real Thing, Enjoy Coca-Cola .. 2.75
Bottle Opener, Krueger Beer, Krueger's Finest, Ambassador, Wire Type, Newark, N.J. .. 5.00
Bottle Opener, Lobster, Red 9.00
Bottle Opener, Mermaid, Compliments Lebanon Bottling Works 18.00
Bottle Opener, Nehi, Wall Mount, Starr X, New Port News, Va., 1925 .... 47.00
Bottle Opener, Old German Beer, 3 In. 14.95
Bottle Opener, Orange Crush, Bottle 20.00
Bottle Opener, Orange Crush, Starr X, Wall Mount, Metal, 3 1/4 x 2 3/4 In. 36.00
Bottle Opener, Pabst Blue Ribbon, Flat Type 5.00
Bottle Opener, Pearl Beer, Folding, Bead Chain, Vaughn 18.00
Bottle Opener, Pepsi-Cola, Double Dash, Wall Mount, Star, c.1940 .... 31.00
Bottle Opener, Pepsi-Cola, Starr X, Brown Co., Wall Mount 8.00
Bottle Opener, RC Royal Crown Cola, Go Fresher, Wire, 3 1/2 x 1 1/2 In. 1.00
Bottle Opener, Royal Crown Cola, Best By Taste-Test, C.M.I., Vaughan, 3 x 1/2 In. 3.75
Bottle Opener, Ruppert Beer, Metal, 1940s Style, 3 1/4 In. 15.00
Bottle Opener, S. Grabfelder & Co. Distillers, Louisville, Ky., Rose Valley, Wood 8.00
Bottle Opener, Schlitz Export Beer, Wood, Bottle Shape, c.1939 .... 60.00
Bottle Opener, Shea's Select, Shea's Stock Ale, Made In USA, Style B-4 .... 18.00
Bottle Opener, Sunshine Extra Light, Premium, Wire Type 6.00
Bottle Opener, Toast To The Host, International Toasts, Can Opener, Aluminum, Italy ... 13.00
Bottle Opener, Warsteiner Beer, Crown, Metal, Gold Finish, German Text 5.00
Bottle Opener, White Rock Sparkling Beverages, Vaughan, Chicago .... 2.00 to 3.75
Bottle Opener & Cap Catcher, Fresh Up With 7Up, Wall Mount, Box, '40s, 6 x 2 1/2 In. .. 77.00
Bottle Opener & Knife, Drink Nehi, 5 Cents, Leg Shape, High Heel Shoe, Brass, 3 1/4 In. 11.00
Bottle Opener & Knife, Drink Nehi, Lady's Boot, 5 Cent, Brass Color, 3 3/8 In. 26.00
Bottle Opener-Corkscrew, Sommelier Bartender, Figural, Metal, Signed, 8 x 3 In. 60.00
Bottle Protector, Pepsi-Cola, No Drip, Red Letters, Waxed Paper, 1932 Patent, 7 x 4 In. .. 22.00
Bottle Stopper, Clown, Movable Hat, Bisque, Germany, 3 3/4 In. 25.00
Bottle Stopper, Glass, Hexagonal, Plastic End Piece, 2 1/2 x 1 1/2 In. 2.00
Bottle Stopper, Hires Root Beer, Cast Iron, Metal, Embossed 10.00
Bottle Stopper-Pourer, Carstairs, Seal, Balancing Red Ball On Nose, Plastic, 3 3/4 In. .. 25.00
Bottle Stopper-Pourer, Man With Cigar, Wood, Tin Cigar, Cork Neck, 2 1/2 In. 60.00
Bottle Topper, 7Up, Fresh Up, Boy, In Beanie, Cardboard, 1949, 8 x 5 In. 12.50
Bottle Topper, Coca-Cola, We Let You See The Bottle, Plastic, Metal, 1950s 1365.00
Bottle Topper, Enjoy A 7Up Float, Green Arrow 26.00
Bottle Topper, Seagram's 7, Plastic, Cork Stopper, Pour Spout, 3 1/4 In. 10.00
Box, Apothecary, Owl Drug Co., 6th Ave., Metal, Black, Gold, Red Stripe, Tray, 4 x 9 3/8 In. .. 220.00
Box, Bola-A Tonic, For The Nerves & Blood, Wooden, 12 x 17 In. 50.00
Box, Box, E.R. Durkee & Co. Spices, Wood, Dovetailed, Leather Hinges, 4 x 14 x 8 In. .. 476.00
Box, Cuticura Resolvent, New Blood Purifier, Potter Drug, Wooden, 11 x 8 x 8 1/2 In. ... 79.00
Box, Dick Bros. Beer, Hinged Lid, Wood, Metal Corners, Quincy, Ill., 11 1/2 x 20 1/2 In. . 49.00
Box, Dr. Harter's Wild Cherry Bitters, Wood, 21 x 9 x 12 In. 61.00
Box, Frank Miller's Peerless Blacking, Uncle Sam Shaving, Wood, 3 x 12 x 9 In. 235.00
Box, Heilman Brewing Co., Hinged Lid, Wood, Metal, LaCrosse, Wis., 11 x 21 In. 24.00
Box, Scotts Emulsions, 1 Doz. Bottles, Cardboard, Unopened, 8 x 8 x 7 In. 132.00
Box, Watkin's Remedies, J.R. Watkin's Med. Co., Wooden, 15 x 25 x 10 In. 59.00
Button, Miller High Life, Woman On Moon, Celluloid, Hanger Of Woman, 7/8 In. Button 87.00
Button, Try Tourist Rye, Thomas McNulty, Baltimore, Man, Woman, Celluloid, 1 1/4 In. .. 146.00
Cabinet, DeLaval, Cream Separator, World's Standard, Wood, Tin Lithograph, 17 x 23 In. 990.00
Calendar, Clicquot Club, 1951, Eskimo Boy, Woman, In Swimsuit, 14 x 22 1/2 In. 72.00
Calendar, Clicquot Club, 1953, Ginger Ale, Eskimo Boy, Holding Bottle, 12 x 23 In. 72.00
Calendar, Coca-Cola, 1902, Drink Coca-Cola, 5 Cents, Frame 11000.00
Calendar, Coca-Cola, 1919, Girl, Pink Dress, Hat, Frame, 21 x 40 In. 1540.00
Calendar, Coca-Cola, 1920, Girl, Holding Bottle, 12 x 27 1/2 In. 3400.00
Calendar, Coca-Cola, 1924, Pad, Frame, 24 x 11 3/4 In. 990.00
Calendar, Coca-Cola, 1926, Girl, Sitting, Holding Bottle, 10 x 18 1/2 In. .... 901.00 to 1013.00
Calendar, Coca-Cola, 1936, Girl, Boat, Fisherman Holding Bottle, Frame, 10 x 18 1/2 In. .. 625.00
Calendar, DeLaval, 1916, Cream Separators, Boy, Girl On Counter, Frame, 16 x 28 In. 374.00
Calendar, H. Levinson Wines, Liquors & Cigars, 1908, Black Boy & Goose, 13 x 10 In. .. 24.00
Calendar, Hood's, 1907, Sarsaparilla, Frame, 14 x 21 In. 88.00
Calendar, Nehi Soda, Chero-Cola, 1927, 20 x 6 In. 220.00
Calendar, Pabst, 1914, Extract, Victorian Lady, Orange Dress, 10 x 37 In. 220.00
Calendar, Pabst, 1917, Pabst Extra, Woman, Yellow Dress, Black Stole, Frame, 13 x 40 In. 253.00

Go-Withs, Clock, Dr. Pepper,
Reverse On Glass, Light-Up

Go-Withs, Clock,
Squirt, Light-up,
Square, 15 3/4 In.

Calendar, Pepsi-Cola, 1921, 5 Cents, Cops, Double Dash, Full Pad, 18 3/4 x 9 In.	32.00
Calendar, Sharp Bros. Milk, 1929, Lady, Red Roses, Frame, 22 x 48 In.	330.00
Calendar, Steffens Dairy Products, 1962, Pointing The Way, Boy Scouts, 23 x 11 In.	44.00
Carrier, Coca-Cola, 6 For 25 Cents, Holds 6 Bottles, Aluminum, Late 1940s	242.00
Carrier, Coca-Cola, Aluminum, 6-Pack, Handle, 5 x 8 In.	26.00
Carrier, Coca-Cola, Bottle & Wings On Sides, Handle, Wood, 1940s	220.00
Carrier, Coca-Cola, Handy To Carry Home, Christmas Bottles On Ends, Wood, 1940s . . .	275.00
Carrier, Coca-Cola, Seasons Greetings, Red, White, Green, Cardboard, Wood, 1930s	440.00
Carrier, Drink Coca-Cola In Bottles, Red Letters, Metal Corners, Chattanooga, 1962	8.00
Carrier, Drink Coca-Cola, Aluminum, Red Wood Handle, Acton Mfg., 1950	76.00
Carrier, Drink Coca-Cola, Enjoy Coke, Aluminum, 1950s, 8 x 7 1/2 x 5 In.	51.00
Carrier, Drink Pepsi-Cola, Double Dash, Tin, Steel, Extending Handle, 3 3/4 x 5 x 8 In. . .	10.00
Carrier, Pepsi-Cola, Bigger, Better, Double Dash, Metal	20.00
Carrier, Pepsi-Cola, Double Dash, Metal, Embossed, Red Paint, 4 x 8 1/4 x 5 1/2 In.	30.00
Carrier, Royal Crown Cola, 6-Pack, Embossed, Aluminum, c.1940	77.00
Carrier Carton, Nehi Soda, 6-Pack, Cardboard, Bottle Master, Atlanta Paper Co., 1949 . .	10.50
Carton, Root Beer, Cardboard, 6 Bottle Holes, Mead Packaging, Bottle Master, Unused . .	6.00
Chalkboard, Coca-Cola, Fishtail, Tin, 1959, 28 x 20 In.	154.00
Charm, 7Up Bottle, 1 In.	9.50
Charm, Borden, Elsie The Cow, Molded Loop, Yellow, Plastic, 3/4 In.	18.00
Cigarette Case, Coca-Cola, Frosted Glass, Embossed, 2 Piece, 1936	425.00
Clock, A&W Root Beer, Bubble, Light-Up, c.1940-50	1210.00
Clock, Borden's, Ice Cream, Elsie The Cow, Light-Up, Glass, Metal, 15 In.	220.00
Clock, Coca-Cola, Bottle, Sun Highlight, Electric, Round, 1940-50	1045.00
Clock, Coca-Cola, Drink Coca-Cola In Bottles, Red, White, Duralite, 15 In. Diam.	1200.00
Clock, Coca-Cola, Drink Coca-Cola, Metal, Glass, Electric, 15 1/4 x 15 1/4 In.	154.00
Clock, Coca-Cola, Silhouette Girl, Neon, c.1941, 18 In.	2090.00
Clock, Dr Pepper, Light-Up, 15 x 9 In.	110.00
Clock, Dr. Pepper, Reverse On Glass, Light-Up . . . . *Illus*	3360.00
Clock, Milkmaid Milk, Now's The Time To Buy It, Metal Over Wood, 18 In. Diam.	770.00
Clock, Old Mr. Boston Fine Liquor, Wood, Flask Form, 11 x 6 In.	236.00
Clock, Old Mr. Boston, Fine Liquors, White, Blue, Bottle Form, Metal, c.1920, 22 In.	385.00
Clock, Old Mr. Boston, Gilbert, Bottle Shape, 21 1/2 In.	179.00
Clock, Orange Crush, Telechron, Light-Up, Round, 1940s	413.00
Clock, Pepsi-Cola, Neon, Silver, Bottle Cap 15 In.	43.00
Clock, Pepsi-Cola, Telechron, Light-Up, Round, 1940s	468.00
Clock, Squirt, Light-Up, Square, 15 3/4 In. . . . . *Illus*	224.00
Coaster, Have You Made The Budweiser Test, Scalloped Edge	8.00
Coaster, It's The Age Of Acme, Fine Beer Since 1860, San Francisco, 1936-43	15.00
Compact, Dr. Miles, Anti-Pain Pills, Tin Slider, Mirror, 2 1/4 In. Diam.	303.00
Container, Warner's Log Cabin Liver Pills, Paper, 2 1/4 In.	65.00
Cooler, Coca-Cola, Airline, Stainless Steel, 1950s, 10 x 15 x 6 In.	1210.00
Cooler, Coca-Cola, Junior, 34 x 25 x 18 In.	550.00
Cooler, Coca-Cola, Picnic, 6-Pack, Stainless Steel, Acton, 1950s	275.00
Cooler, Coca-Cola, Salesman's Sample, c.1939, 10 x 12 In.	2200.00
Cooler, Coca-Cola, Tray, Opener, Red, Vinyl, 17 x 14 x 11 1/2 In.	248.00
Cooler, Coca-Cola, Wood, Metal Liner, Yellow Paint, Red Stenciling, c.1939, 10 x 12 In. . .	384.00

Cooler, Pepsi, Stand-Up, Metal, Pepsi Bottle Opener, 1970s, 18 x 36 x 36 In. 31.00
Cooler, Squirt, Merry-Go-Round, Swing Handle, 14 In. 28.00
Counter Display, Bust, Paul Jones Whiskey, Cast White, Metal 165.00
Counter Display, S. Andral Kilmer, M.D., Swamp-Root, Cardboard, 9 1/2 x 6 x 3 3/4 In. . 132.00
Coupon, Coca-Cola, Free Drink, Cardboard, Opera Star, Hilda Clark, 1 5/8 x 3 3/8 In. ... 523.00
Crate, Allen's Sarsaparilla, 128 Doses, 50 Cts., Wooden, Hinged Lid, 11 1/4 x 13 1/2 In. . 45.00
Crate, Babylon Milk & Cream, Lindenhurst, Long Island, Wooden 59.00
Crate, Dr. J. Hostetter's Celebrated Stomach Bitters, 1 Doz., Wood, Leather, 10 x 14 In. ... 180.00
Crate, Drink Coca-Cola In Bottles, Painted, Yellow, Red, 18 1/2 x 11 3/4 In. 8.75
Crate, Enjoy Coca-Cola, Wood, 24-Bottle Capacity, Red, 1971 .... 13.00
Crate, Falstaff Beer, Cardboard, Staples, 12-Bottle Capacity, 10 x 12 x 16 In. 13.00
Crate, Fresh Up With 7Up, Santa Fe, Mexico, White, Red, Temple Mfg., 4 x 19 x 12 In. . 14.00
Crate, Golden Rule Dairy, Cumberland Case Co., Wooden Slat, Metal, 12 x 16 In. 75.00
Crate, Nesbitt California Orange Soda, Wood, Metal Corner Strips, For 24 Bottles, 1966 . 61.00
Crate, Pepsi-Cola, Chattanooga, Tenn., For 32 Oz. Bottles, Yellow, Wood, 1973 .... 2.00
Crate, Pepsi-Cola, Wood, 24 Slots, Goldsboro, N.C., Yellow, Metal Corners, 1976 .... 10.00
Crate, Sanford's Inks, No. 32 Royal Black Ink, Chicago, New York, 14 In. .... *Illus* 56.00
Cup, Coca-Cola, Diamonds, Red, White, 10 Oz., Sweetheart, Box, 100 Piece, 1960s 61.00
Cup, Coca-Cola, Things Go Better, 10 Oz., Sweetheart, Box, 100 Piece, 1963 .... 39.00
Dish, Coca-Cola, Pretzel, 3 Bottles, Around Bowl 248.00
Dispenser, Buckeye Root Beer, 5 Cent, Satyrs Around Bottom 1650.00
Dispenser, Buckeye Root Beer, Black Body, Cleveland Fruit Juice Co. Mfg., c.1918 ..... 743.00
Dispenser, Buckeye Root Beer, Black, White Letters, Horseshoe Pump, Knob, c.1918 ... 440.00
Dispenser, Buckeye Root Beer, Tree Stump Shape, Horseshoe Ball Pump, c.1920 .... 495.00
Dispenser, Cherry Smash, Always Drink, Your Nation's Beverage, Ceramic, 14 x 9 In. ... 2700.00
Dispenser, Cherryallen-Allen's Red Tame Syrup, White Globe 1760.00
Dispenser, Coca-Cola, Frosted Glass Body, Porcelain Base, c.1930, 17 In. 6500.00
Dispenser, Dr. Miles' Anti-Pain Pills, For Headache, Blue, Red, Tin, Hanging, 17 x 3 In. . 300.00
Dispenser, Green River, Glass Center, Metal Base, Original Jug, c.1910, 17 In. 286.00
Dispenser, Julep, Crock Base, Spigot, Nesbitt Gallon Jug, c.1900-10, 18 In. .... 88.00 to 120.00
Dispenser, Lash's Dixie Dew, Glass, Pedestal Base, Spigot, c.1900, 16 In. 743.00
Dispenser, Mission Grapefruit, Black Base, Lid, Spigot, c.1900, 14 In. 330.00
Dispenser, Mission Orange, Yellow, Black, c.1920-30, 28 In. 330.00
Dispenser, Orange Crush, Black Glass Base, Frosted Globe, Metal Lid, c.1910, 17 In. ... 495.00
Dispenser, Syrup, Buckeye Root Beer, Black, 15 In. 1650.00
Dispenser, Syrup, Buckeye Root Beer, Buckeyes, Cleve Fruit Juice, 1970s, 15 In. 3080.00
Dispenser, Syrup, Getz Blend Root Beer, Red, White, Blue, Gold, C.F.G. Co., 1920, 13 In. 4290.00
Display, Blatz, Dancing Can & Bottles, Light-Up, 17 In. .... *Illus* 150.00
Display, Coca-Cola, Christmas, Light Green, Cap, 1923, 20 In. 308.00
Display, Dr. Daniels, Horse & Dog Remedies, 2-Sided, Die Cut, Hanging, 1906, 7 x 31 In. 6270.00
Display, Pepsi-Cola, Die Cut, Fold-Out, Bottle Holder, 13 1/2 x 6 5/8 In. 165.00
Display Card, Ramona Perfume, Indian Maiden, Contents, Nipola Co., 15 x 10 In. 303.00
Display Case, 7Up, 4 Shelves, Wood, Glass, 7Up Decal, 24 x 18 In. 209.00
Display Case, Diamond Inks, Wood, 4 Glass Panels, Shelves, Decals, 16 x 16 x 16 In. ... 532.00
Display Case, Palmer Perfumes, Metal, Glass, Early 1900s, 7 1/2 x 9 1/4 In. 33.00
Display Case, Waterman's Ideal Fountain Pen, Wood, Black, Gold Lettering, 5 3/4 x 18 In. 460.00
Door Plate, Coca-Cola, Delicious, Refreshing, Metal, c.1939, 3 1/2 x 33 In. 633.00

Go-Withs, Crate, Sanford's Ink, No. 32 Royal
Black Ink, Chicago, New York, 14 In.

Go-Withs, Display,
Blatz, Dancing Can &
Bottles, Light-Up, 17 In.

Door Pull, Coca-Cola, Refresh Yourself, Green, Red, White, Porcelain, 1940-50 .... 880.00
Door Push, Birely's Soda, Bottle, Embossed, Tin Lithograph, 12 x 3 In. 187.00
Door Push, Clicquot Club, Eskimo Boy, Bottle, Yellow, Black, Embossed, Tin, 3 x 9 In. . 105.00
Door Push, Coca-Cola, Drink Coca-Cola, Blue, White, Aluminum, c.1905, 3 x 8 In. 1013.00
Door Push, Dr Pepper, Drink A Bite To Eat, Metal, c.1940, 4 x 8 In. 325.00
Door Push, Dr Pepper, Emergency Notification Insert, Metal, c.1940, 4 x 8 In. 366.00
Door Push, Dr. King's Cure For Consumption, Porcelain, 7 x 3 1/2 In. 1100.00
Door Push, Grain Belt, From Perfect Brewing Water, Adjustable, 30 In. 125.00
Door Push, Orange-Ade, Bottle, Embossed, Tin Lithograph, 10 x 3 1/2 In. 132.00
Door Push, Pabst, Blended Splendid, Embossed, Tin Lithograph, 4 x 9 In. 66.00
Door Push, Pepsi-Cola, Have A Pepsi, Yellow, Red, White, Blue, Porcelain 165.00
Door Push, Pepsi-Cola, Worth Twice Its Price, Yellow, Tin, c.1930, 3 1/2 x 13 1/2 In. 825.00
Door Push, Ridgways Coffee, Yellow, Red, Metal, 3 1/4 x 9 In. 44.00
Door Push, Texas Punch, Hello, You'll Love It, Tin, 1940s, 9 1/2 In. 160.00
Dose Glass, Compliments Of J.H. Mercer Druggist, Bloomsburg, Pa. 16.00
Dose Glass, Dr. Harter's Bitters, Clear, Embossed, Footed, 3 In. 50.00
Dose Glass, Electric Medical Co., Richmond, Va., Pouring Spout 20.00
Dose Glass, Smith's Green Mountain Renovator 15.00
Fan, RC Cola, Shirley Temple, Flat River, Missouri 35.00
Fan, Sorin Cognac, Green Cloaked Figure In White, Holding Glass, 7 1/2 In. 25.00
Figure, Big Bill Best Bitters, Portly Man, Multicolored Paint, Plaster, 15 In. 1650.00
Figure, Frankenmuth Beer, Ale, Dachshund Dog, Plaster, c.1930s, 4 x 7 x 6 In. 50.00
Figure, Kessler Whiskey, Man In Top Hat, Bowling Ball, Chalkware, 14 In. 132.00
Figure, Lowenbrau Beer, Lion, Holding Bottle Of Beer, Gold, Composition, 17 In. 55.00
Figure, Schmidts Beer, Waiter, Holding Mugs Of Beer, Cast Spelter, Painted, 13 In. 118.00
Glass, A&W, Bear, Arms Outstretched, 5 3/4 In. 6.00
Holder, Enjoy Coca-Cola While You Shop, Metal, For Shopping Cart, 2 1/2 x 6 In. 39.00
Ice Bowl, Coca-Cola, Green, Vernon Ware, 1930s, 4 x 10 In. 468.00
Jar Rings, Flite Rubber, Crunden Martin Mfg. Co., St. Louis, Blue Box, 12 Rings 6.00
Keg, Schutz & Hilgers Jordan Brewery, Jordan, Minn., Wood 309.00
Kickplate, Coca-Cola, Drink Coca-Cola, Embossed Tin, 1933, 11 x 34 In. ...... .625.00 to 647.00
Kickplate, Coca-Cola, Drink Coca-Cola, Fountain Service, Porcelain, c.1950, 12 x 28 In. . 550.00
Kickplate, Coca-Cola, Fountain Service, Porcelain, c.1950s, 12 x 28 In. 563.00
Kickplate, Coca-Cola, Girl & Bottle, Tin, 1940 .... 605.00
Knife, Coors, Cream, Red Script, 2 Blades, Riveted To Sides, Folding, Plastic, 3 1/2 In. .. 15.00
Label, Alt Heidelberg Beer, Jumbo Full Quart, Burnished Gold, 1933-50, 4 x 5 In. 10.00
Label, Columbia Beer, Burnished Gold, Unused, 1933-50, 11 Oz., 3 x 3 5/8 In. 7.00
Label, Columbia Pale Ale, Burnished Gold & Green, Unused, 1933-50, 3 x 4 In. 8.00
Label, Foodland Evaporated Milk, Holstein Cow, Blue, Yellow, Red, 1973, 10 x 3 1/2 In. . 5.00
Label, Townsend Lager Beer, Port Townsend Brewing, Wash., c.1906-16 .... 4.00
Lamp, Borden, Elsie The Cow, Head, Daisy Necklace, Figural, c.1960, 9 x 8 In. 395.00
Lamp, Coca-Cola, Frosted Globe, Metal Tassel, Chain, c.1930 .... 3600.00
Letter Opener, Glyco, Heroin, Compliments Of Martin H. Sith Co., 1880-1900 .... 79.00
Letterhead, Dr. Kilmer & Co., Manufacturing Chemists, Building, c.1910, 8 x 5 1/4 In. ... 300.00
Lighter, Coca-Cola, Bottle Shape, Plastic, 1950s, 2 1/2 In. 28.00
Lighter, Coca-Cola, Bottle Shape, Plastic, Metal Cap, c.1960, 2 1/2 In. 11.25
Lighter, Pepsi-Cola, Bottle Shape, The Light Refreshment, KEM, 1950s, 2 3/4 In. 40.00
Match Holder, Bruces Juniper Salve, For Family Use, No Equal, Shield Form, 4 7/8 x 3 In. 88.00
Match Holder, Coca-Cola, Drink, Strike Matches Here, Porcelain, Canada, 1939, 4 1/2 In. 770.00
Match Holder, Coca-Cola, Tin, 20 Matchbooks, 1950-60 .... 440.00
Match Holder, DeLaval, Silver Highlights, Dual Compartments, Die Cut, 6 1/2 In. 66.00
Match Holder, Old Judson Whiskey, J.C. Stevens, Tin Lithograph, c.1910 .... 143.00
Match Safe, Anheuser-Busch, Eagle, 2-Sided, Silver Plate, 3 x 1 1/2 In. 303.00
Match Safe, Compliments Buffalo Brewing Co., Sacramento, Cal., Metal, Horse, Buffalo . 225.00
Matchbook, Ask For Richbrau Beer, Richmond, Va., c.1939 .... 3.00
Matchbook, Budweiser, St. Louis, Mo., Compliments Club Bar, Cordova, Alaska, c.1939 . 2.00
Matchbook, Kessler Brewing Co., Moose Club, Deer Lodge, Mont., c.1939 .... 3.00
Matchbook, Owl Drug Co. 4.00
Matchbook, Regal Pale, San Francisco, c.1939 .... 2.00
Matchbook, Schlitz, World's Fair, New York, 1939 .... 2.00
Milk Bottle Cap, Abraham Lincoln Assassination, Ford's Theater, 1865, 1 7/16 In. 4.00
Milk Bottle Cap, Alta Crest Farm Products, Quality Goes In, Before Name Goes On, Cow 1.75
Milk Bottle Cap, Arethusa Farm, Guernsey Light Cream, Litchfield, Conn. 4.25

Go-Withs, Paperweight,
High Rock Springs
Mineral Water, Paper
Under Glass, 4 1/2 In.

Go-Withs, Plate,
Coca-Cola,
Ceramic,
7 3/4 In.

Milk Bottle Cap, Belfry Farms, RD 2, Norristown, Pa., 1 3/4 In.	.25
Milk Bottle Cap, Black's Dairy, Raw Chocolate Milk, Millerstown, Pa.	41.00
Milk Bottle Cap, Buffalo Rock Ginger Ale, Cork Lined	31.00
Milk Bottle Cap, Buffalo Valley Dairy, Pasteurized Cream, Milton, Pa., 1 3/4 In.	.25
Milk Bottle Cap, Cleary Dairy, Grade A, Pasteurized, Whole Milk, Green Edge, Salem, Ore.	35.00
Milk Bottle Cap, Cream Valley Dairy, Woodstown, N.J., Aluminum	.25
Milk Bottle Cap, DeLaval Christmas, Wreath, Tree, Red Bow, 1 13/16 In.	5.00
Milk Bottle Cap, Dell Dale Farm Inc., Black Letters, Aluminum	.20
Milk Bottle Cap, Edwin Schultz Dairy, Pure Milk, Montello, Wis.	13.00
Milk Bottle Cap, Eggnog, Holly Wreath, 1 11/16 In.	4.00
Milk Bottle Cap, Eggnog, Sealright Sanitary Service, Ribbon, Holly, 1 3/4 In.	4.00
Milk Bottle Cap, Elwell's Pinebrook Farm, Bridgeton, N.J., 1 3/4 In.	.25
Milk Bottle Cap, Fenn Dairy, Whipping Cream, Kent, O.	3.25
Milk Bottle Cap, Florence Cairy, Florence, N.J., 2-Color, 1 3/4 In.	.25
Milk Bottle Cap, Grant's Dairy, Elmer, N.J., 2-Color, 1 3/4 In.	.50
Milk Bottle Cap, H.F. Morrill, Milk & Cream, Concord, N.H., 2-Color, 1 3/4 In.	.25
Milk Bottle Cap, Japan Attacks US Fleet At Pearl Harbor, 1941, 1 1/4 In.	.75
Milk Bottle Cap, Jersey Raw Cream, Gardnerville, Nevada	33.00
Milk Bottle Cap, Joyeux Noel Et Bonne Et Heureuse Annee, Star, 1 5/8 In.	4.00
Milk Bottle Cap, Korean War Begins, 1950, 1 1/4 In.	.75
Milk Bottle Cap, Lamring's Dairy, River Road, Fairlawn, N.J., 1 3/4 In.	.25
Milk Bottle Cap, Lone Pine Farms, Hanover, N.J., Sunrise, 2-Color, 1 3/4 In.	.25
Milk Bottle Cap, M. Burns Dairy Products, Six Lakes, Mich.	26.00
Milk Bottle Cap, Maplewood Dairy, Hudson Falls & Franville, N.Y., 1 3/4 In.	.25
Milk Bottle Cap, McCloud Dairy, McCloud, Ca., Mountain, Yellow, Brown	12.55
Milk Bottle Cap, Med-O Bloom, Homogenized, Pasteurized Milk, Kokomo, Ind.	41.00
Milk Bottle Cap, Mettowee Farms, Skim Milk, Upper Saddle River, N.J., 1 3/4 In.	.25
Milk Bottle Cap, Morrill's Dairy, Lemon & Lime, 1 3/4 In.	.25
Milk Bottle Cap, N.Y. Mattson, Swedesboro, N.J., 1 3/4 In.	.25
Milk Bottle Cap, National Dairy, Sour Cream, Whiting, Ind.	1.85
Milk Bottle Cap, Norman's Dairy, Jewett City, Conn., Approved Milk, 1 1/4 In.	.50
Milk Bottle Cap, Peters Dairy, Oriskany Falls, N.Y., Red Letters, White Ground, 2 Piece	2.25
Milk Bottle Cap, Pioneer Farms, Heavy Cream, Warwick, N.Y., 1 1/4 In.	.50
Milk Bottle Cap, Plains Dairy Cream, Cheyenne, Wyo.	61.00
Milk Bottle Cap, Pure Guernsey Milk, Bottled On Farm, Metal Ring	2.50
Milk Bottle Cap, Puritan Dairy, Perth Amboy, N.J., 2-Color, 1 3/4 In.	.50
Milk Bottle Cap, S.W. Higbee, 3 Percent B.F. Whole Milk, T.B. Tested, Jeffersonville, O.	11.50
Milk Bottle Cap, Shimko's Good Rich Milk, Strong, Pa., Orange, White	1.50
Milk Bottle Cap, Walker's Folly Dairy, Melfa, Va., Buttermilk, Green Letters, 1 3/4 In.	.25
Milk Bottle Cap, Walker's Folly Dairy, Melfa, Va., Skim Milk, Red Letters, 1 3/4 In.	.25
Mirror, Family Liquor Store, Los Angeles, 8 3/4 x 10 3/4 In.	35.00
Mirror, Mathie Red Ribbon Beer, Purity, Quality, Oval, 2 3/4 x 1 3/4 In.	98.00
Mixer, Hires, Malt, Porcelained Cast Iron, Hand Crank, c.1897	770.00
Mug, Coors, Porcelain, 1933-41, Miniature, 1 In.	5.00
Mug, Hires Root Beer, Boy With Bib, Holding Mug, Porcelain, 4 x 4 In.	143.00
Mug, On Base, Have A Heidelberg, Columbia Breweries, Tacoma, Wash., 8 1/2 In.	35.00
Napkin Dispenser, Coca-Cola, Cooler Shape, Tome Coca-Cola, Bien Fria, c.1940	1100.00

Paperweight, High Rock Springs Mineral Water, Paper Under Glass, 4 1/2 In. . . . . . .*Illus* 130.00
Paperweight, Lamb Club Whiskey, Gold Leaf Border, 7/8 x 3 7/8 x 2 1/2 x In. 110.00
Patch, Carling Black Label Beer, Red Ground, Tilted Label Design, Square, 4 x 3 In. 2.00
Patch, Olympia Beer, Yellow Letters, Border, Rectangular, 4 x 2 In. 2.00
Patch, Ranier Light, Red Letters, Border, Round 1.00
Patent Model, Beer Cooler, No. 9243, A. Hammer, Tin, Mahogany Box, 1852, 9 1/2 In. . . 323.00
Picture, Coca-Cola, Airplane, Cardboard, 1943, 15 x 13 In. 44.00
Picture, Coca-Cola, Helicopter, Dropping Coke Bottle, 1943, 15 x 13 In. 55.00
Plaque, Coca-Cola, Dalton CC Bottling Co., 1946 & 1956, 18 x 7 1/2 In. 220.00
Plate, Coca-Cola, Bottle & Glass, c.1930, 8 1/4 In. 1650.00
Plate, Coca-Cola, Bottle, Glass Of Coke, Knowles China, 1931, 7 1/4 In. . . . . .500.00 to 534.00
Plate, Coca-Cola, Ceramic, 7 3/4 In. . . . .*Illus* 252.00
Plate, Coca-Cola, Good With Food, Scalloped Edge, Wellsville China, 1940s, 7 1/4 In. . . 1430.00
Pole Topper, Hamm's Bear, Plastic, St. Paul, Minn., 29 In. 787.00
Postcard, Borden, Home Scene, Elsie, Elmer, Beauregard 6.00
Postcard, Coca-Cola, Motor Girl, 1911 . . . . 578.00
Postcard, Coca-Cola, Soda Fountain, Welch's Grape Juice Bottles, 3 1/2 x 5 1/2 In. 275.00
Postcard, Dawes Black Horse Beer, Canada 15.00
Postcard, Falstaff, Calendar, Wm. J. Lemp Brewing, St. Louis, 1911-31 . . . . 130.00
Postcard, Hood's Sarsaparilla Factory, Lowell, Mass. 15.00
Poster, Anheuser-Busch, Budweiser Girl, Red Dress, Bottle, Frame, 1907, 39 x 23 In. . . . 1650.00
Poster, Arrow Beer, Matchless Body, Earl Moran, Frame, c.1940, 28 x 17 1/2 In. 175.00
Poster, Bock Beer, Indianapolis Brewing Co., Lady With Goats, 29 x 10 1/2 In. 495.00
Poster, Cer-Ola, A Non-Intoxicating Cereal Beverage, Bay City, Mich., 11 x 17 1/2 In. . . . 50.00
Poster, Coca-Cola, Canadian Girl, Delicious & Refreshing, 1948 . . . . 330.00
Poster, Coca-Cola, Clown, Ice Skater, Pause, Frame, 1950, 16 x 27 In. 1650.00
Poster, Coca-Cola, Drink For Busy People, Scenes, Cardboard, Die Cut, 1930s, 43 x 22 In. 660.00
Poster, Coca-Cola, Face Your Job Refreshed, Canada, 1943, 27 x 56 In. 1870.00
Poster, Coca-Cola, Girl Holding Glass, Bottle, Pause That Refreshes, 1939, 30 x 50 In. . . 358.00
Poster, Coca-Cola, Girl In Bikini, Sitting, Yes, Cardboard, Frame, 1946, 20 x 36 In. 770.00
Poster, Coca-Cola, Girl, Soda Fountain, Pause & Refresh, 1948, 23 1/2 x 41 In. 770.00
Poster, Coca-Cola, Have A Coke Now, Bottle, Cardboard, 2-Sided, 1951, 16 x 27 In. 375.00
Poster, Coca-Cola, Home Hospitality, 3 People Singing, 1951, 30 x 50 In. 700.00
Poster, Coca-Cola, Home Refreshment, Take Some Home, 2-Sided, 1950, 16 x 27 In. 950.00
Poster, Coca-Cola, Lady, Groceries, Cardboard, 2-Sided, 1950, 16 x 27 In. 950.00
Poster, Coca-Cola, Sprite Boy, Coca-Cola Cap, Die Cut, Frame, c.1975, 38 x 30 In. 110.00
Poster, Dr Pepper, Fireside Fun, Cardboard, 1940s, 15 x 25 In. 187.00
Poster, Dr Pepper, Fireside Fun, Lady Popping Popcorn, Frame, c.1940-50, 33 x 52 In. . . 261.00
Poster, Hires, Lady, Holding Glass, Hires R-J Root Beer, c.1940-50, 34 x 58 In. 250.00
Potlid, Anne Hathaway's House, Multicolored, Pearl, Dot Border, Wood Frame, 4 In. 61.00
Potlid, Anthracoline, Pink Ground, Black, 3 1/4 In. 143.00
Potlid, Areca Nut Cherry, Bristol Toothpaste, False Teeth, 3 1/2 In. 2046.00
Potlid, Barnstaple Toothpaste, Coat Of Arms, 3 1/4 In. 655.00
Potlid, Base, Grand International Building, 1851, Multicolored, 5 In. 226.00
Potlid, Blanchflower, Great Yarmouth, Farmyard, Cows, Sheep, Pigs, Hens, 3 3/4 In. . . . 655.00
Potlid, Burgoyne Burbidges & Co., Girl With Long Hair, Smiling, 2 3/4 In. 4910.00
Potlid, Crown Perfumery Co., Cherry Toothpaste, 2 3/4 In. 61.00
Potlid, Dr. Dosteels, Cherry Toothpaste, Queen Victoria, 3 1/4 In. 2660.00
Potlid, Erasmic Shaving Cream, Woman, Brown Transfer, 3 1/2 In. 1228.00
Potlid, Hamlet, Father's Ghost, Multicolored, 4 In. 134.00
Potlid, J.J. Matthias Unrivalled Cherry Toothpaste, Prince Of Wales, 3 In. 1228.00
Potlid, John Gosnell & Co., Cherry Toothpaste, Yellow, Bronze Ground, 3 1/4 In. 35.00
Potlid, Oriental Toothpaste, Pyramids, Camels, Pink Marble Flange, Base, 3 1/4 In. 102.00
Potlid, Osox Toothpaste, Black Transfer, Square, 2 1/2 In. 328.00
Potlid, Pansalia Shaving Cream, Lilac Ground, 3 In. 266.00
Potlid, Patrician Tooth Powder, Woman In Dress, Headdress, Oval, 3 3/4 In. 704.00
Potlid, Seven Ages Of Man, Multicolored, Wood Frame, 4 In. 134.00
Potlid, Shakespeare's House, Henley Street, Stratford On Avon, Multicolored, 4 In. 65.00
Potlid, Thompson Millard & Cos, Cherry Toothpaste, 2 3/4 In. 266.00
Potlid, Thorntons Anthracoline, Pink Ground, Black Print, 3 1/2 In. 246.00
Puzzle, Hood's Balloon, Hood's Sarsaparilla, Cardboard, 1891, 10 1/2 x 15 1/2 In. 195.00
Rack, Pepsi-Cola, Bag, Drink Pepsi-Cola, Bigger, Better, 2-Sided, c.1940, 19 x 24 x 6 In. . 1870.00
Radio, Coca-Cola, Bottle, 1930s, 24 In. 4620.00

Go-Withs, Scooter,
Coca-Cola, 1960s

*To hang an old Coca-Cola tray, use a
wire plate holder. The bent parts of the
holder that touch the tray should be
covered with plastic tubing. Thin plastic
tubing is sold for use in fish aquariums.*

Radio, Coca-Cola, Cooler Form, c.1950, 9 1/2 x 12 In. 944.00
Radio, Heinz Ketchup Bottle, Transistor, AM, Box, 1980s 75.00
Radio, Old Parr Scotch Whiskey, Bottle Shape 42.00
Radio, Pepsi-Cola Bottle Shape, AM, Box 10.50
Radio, Pepsi-Cola Bottle, Tube, Bakelite, 1947, 23 1/4 In. 850.00
Ruler, Coca-Cola, Compliments The Coca-Cola Bottling Co., Wooden, 12 In. 12.00
Salt & Pepper, Ball Perfect Mason, 1988 . . . . 15.00
Salt & Pepper, Budweiser Beer Bottle, Muth Buffalo, 4 In. 59.00
Salt & Pepper, Coca-Cola, Bottle Shape, Ceramic, 5 In. 4.00
Salt & Pepper, Heinz Ketchup Bottle Shape, Tray 15.00
Salt & Pepper, Old Koppitz Beer, Glass, Amber, Metal Tops, Muth, Buffalo, 3 1/2 In. . . . 45.00
Salt & Pepper, Olympia Beer, Stein Shape 18.00
Salt & Pepper, Pepsi-Cola, Swirl Bottle Shape, Glass, Plastic Cap, Box, 1958, 4 1/2 In. . . 10.00
Salt & Pepper, Warminster Farm Dairies Hatboro, Pa., Muth, Buffalo, 1930s, 3 1/2 In. . . . 55.00
Saltshaker, Acme Beer, Aluminum Cap, Decal Label, Non-Fattening, c.1940, 3 In. . .18.00 to 25.00
Saltshaker, Acme Beer, Aluminum Cap, Decal, Does Not Contain Beer, c.1950, 3 In. 12.00
Saltshaker, Blatz Pilsner Beer, Paper Label, Does Not Contain Beer, c.1944, 4 1/4 In. . . . 5.00
Saltshaker, Budweiser Lager Beer, Decal Label, c.1948, 4 In. 5.00
Saltshaker, De Luxe Old Shay Beer, Fort Pitt Brewing Co., Decal Label, c.1952, 3 In. . . . 8.00
Scooter, Coca-Cola, 1960s . . . . *Illus* 392.00
Screwdriver & Bottle Opener, Mac's Elec., Balko, Oklahoma, 6 1/2 In. 10.00
Service Emblem, Coca-Cola, Booker Design, 3 Green Stones, 15 Year 44.00
Shoe, Heineken Holland Beer, Wooden, 3 3/4 x 9 x 4 In. 16.00
Shot Glass, Botanic Pharmacy, L. Freedman, Ph. G., White Letters, 2 1/8 In. 5.00
Shot Glass, Buck & Rayner, Established 1858, Embossed, 1 7/8 In. 30.00
Shot Glass, Carlisle Whiskey, Sheaves Of Wheat & Lions, White Letters, 2 3/8 In. 30.00
Shot Glass, Compliments Of Harry Stein Wholesale & Retail, Passaic, N.J., 2 3/4 In. 30.00
Shot Glass, Compliments Of Thomas Burke, 196 Water St., Fitchburg, Mass., 2 3/4 In. . . 24.00
Shot Glass, Compliments Of Wm. Kirchgessner, 897 Joseph Ave., Rochester, N.Y., 2 In. . 30.00
Shot Glass, Davis & Drake, Boston, Every Time We Drink Things Look Different, 2 In. . . . 35.00
Shot Glass, Dr. M.T. Reeder, Druggist, Millersville, Pa., Embossed, 1 7/8 In. 30.00
Shot Glass, Eagle Supply House, Rochester, N.Y., Don't Drink Water, 3 1/2 In. 75.00
Shot Glass, Fine Chemicals, Mallinckrodt, Since 1867, Gold Trim, Box, 2 1/4 In. 40.00
Shot Glass, Fulton, Myers & Company Distillers, Covington, Ky., 2 5/16 In. 30.00
Shot Glass, Great American Herb Co., Washington D.C., Embossed, 2 3/8 In. 24.00
Shot Glass, Higgins' XXXX Monongahela, White Letters, 2 1/2 In. 30.00
Shot Glass, Old Kimberly, Pennsylvania Pure Rye Whiskey, Johnstown, Pa., 2 1/4 In. . . . 40.00
Shot Glass, Old Thompson, D G Co, White Letters, 2 1/4 In. 18.00
Shot Glass, Our Native Herbs, Alonzoo Bliss Co, Washington D.C., Embossed, 2 3/8 In. . 16.00
Shot Glass, Perkins Herb Co., National Herb Co, Washington, D.C., Embossed, 2 3/8 In. . 20.00
Shot Glass, Reade's California Gold Paint, 638 Washington, Phila., Embossed, 1 3/4 In. . . 40.00
Shot Glass, Reifert & Kimmey, Syracuse, N.Y., Embossed, 1 7/8 In. 24.00
Shot Glass, Silk Rye, Maplewood Distilling Co., Rochester, N.Y., White Letters, 2 3/8 In. . 32.00
Shot Glass, Smith's Green Mountain Renovator, Embossed, 1 7/8 In. 35.00
Shot Glass, Swiss Pharmacy, 3001 E. Monument Street, We Deliver, White Letters, 3 In. . 16.00
Shot Glass, Tamblyn Saves You Money, 157 St. Paul St. E. 163, White Letters, 2 15/16 In. 12.00
Sign, 2 For 1 Orange Drink, Ace Of Fruit Drinks, Red, Yellow, Tin, Embossed, 27 x 11 In. 220.00
Sign, 66 Lithiated Lemon Soda, Double Eagle Bottling Co., Tin, Embossed, 11 1/2 x 29 In. 259.00
Sign, 7Up Your Thirst Away, Tin, Embossed, c.1960, 19 x 13 In. 70.00

Sign, 7Up, Bottle Cap, White Ground, Green, Red, 1970s, 8 1/2 In. 7.50
Sign, 7Up, Man & Bottle, Die Cut, Easel Back, 1940-50, 18 x 12 In. 66.00
Sign, 7Up, The Best Stop Sign On The Road, Cardboard, Wood Frame, 13 x 22 In. 110.00
Sign, 7Up, Your Fresh Up, Red, Green, Bather On Bottle, Tin, 1947, 27 x 19 1/2 In. 165.00
Sign, Alt Heidelberg, Columbia Brewing, Tacoma, Cardboard, Frame, 16 3/4 x 13 In. 25.00
Sign, Anheuser-Busch, Budweiser Girl, Victorian Lady, Red Dress, Frame, 24 x 38 In. . . . 1430.00
Sign, Ayer's Cherry Pectoral, Santa Claus, Best Gift To Friend, Cardboard, 13 x 7 In. 413.00
Sign, Ayer's Sarsaparilla, Old Folks At Home, Cardboard, Die Cut, Easel Back, 13 x 7 In. . 176.00
Sign, Ayer's Sarsaparilla, The Deacon, Cardboard, Die Cut, Easel Back, 13 x 7 In. 330.00
Sign, B-1 Lemon Lime Soda, Metal, 2-Sided, Bracket, 1940-50, 20 x 28 In. 550.00
Sign, Bieres Fines Excelsior, Bottle, Orange, Gold, Green Ground, c.1930, 13 In. 45.00
Sign, Big Boy Pale Dry, 5 Cents, In Green Bottles Only, Tin, 19 x 9 In. 330.00
Sign, Big Giant Cola, 16 Oz., Bigger, Better, Red, Tin, Embossed, 29 1/2 x 11 1/2 In. 253.00
Sign, Bireley's, Grape, So Drink Up Smile, Motion Spinner, Light-Up, c.1950, 12 x 24 In. 440.00
Sign, Blue Ribbon Bourbon, Farm Scene, Oil On Canvas, Frame, 29 x 39 In. 275.00
Sign, Borden, Borden's Ice Cream, Elsie, Tin, 15 x 24 In. 800.00
Sign, Borden, Eagle Brand Condensed Milk, Girl, Cardboard, 13 1/2 x 10 In. 275.00
Sign, Borden, Eagle Brand, Partners Since 1857, 11 x 21 In. 39.00
Sign, Borden, Elsie The Cow, Tin, 18 x 18 In. 330.00
Sign, Borden, Ice Cream, Elsie The Cow, Yellow, Red, Blue, Tin, c.1954, 28 x 54 In. 150.00
Sign, Botl'o Grape, Call For Botl'o Grape, And Other Flavors, Black, Green, Tin, 7 x 20 In. 44.00
Sign, Braems, Bottle, Embossed Rope Edging, Tin Lithograph, c.1907, 13 1/2 x 7 In. 143.00
Sign, Budweiser, Lady, Pink Dress, Tin Lithograph, Self-Framed, 22 1/2 x 28 1/2 In. . . . 3850.00
Sign, Budweiser, We Feature, Bottle, Pilsner Glass . . . . *Illus* 100.00
Sign, Buffalo Brewing Co., Tin, Self-Framed, 22 x 28 In. 523.00
Sign, Canada Dry, Green, White, Red, Yellow, Porcelain, Oval, 19 x 16 In. 88.00
Sign, Canoe Club Beverage, Once You Try It, You'll Always Buy It, 14 x 30 In. 248.00
Sign, Centlivres Beer, Black Porter Serving Couple On Train, Nickel Plate, 24 x 20 In. . . . 605.00
Sign, Cherry Blossoms Drink, In Bottles Only, 2 Men, Cardboard, Die Cut, 7 1/2 x 16 In. . 220.00
Sign, Cherry Smash Soda, Tin Over Cardboard, Chain Hung, 2 Piece, 18 x 8 3/4 In. 770.00
Sign, Clicquot Club, Eskimo Boy, Red, White, Tin Litho, Embossed, c.1950, 9 x 20 In. . . . 187.00
Sign, Cloverdale Pale Dry Ginger Ale, 4-Leaf Clover, Metal, 12 1/2 x 9 3/4 In. 38.00
Sign, Coca-Cola, 2 Bottles, Button, Sprite Boys, Fluted, 2 Panels, c.1950, 16 x 30 1/2 In. . 330.00
Sign, Coca-Cola, 6-Bottle Carton, 27 Cents, 18 x 32 In. 33.00
Sign, Coca-Cola, 6-Pack, Big King Size, 1961, 20 x 28 In. 2813.00
Sign, Coca-Cola, 6-Pack, King Size, Tin, Die Cut, Embossed, 1960, 38 x 31 In. 1980.00
Sign, Coca-Cola, 6-Pack, Red, 6 For 25 Cents, Tin, Die Cut, September 1950, 11 x 14 In. . 1375.00
Sign, Coca-Cola, 6-Pack, Red, Cardboard, Die Cut, 1951, 11 x 14 In. 1045.00
Sign, Coca-Cola, 6-Pack, Take Home Carton, Red, Tin, Embossed, c.1940, 54 x 18 In. . . . 495.00
Sign, Coca-Cola, Arrow, Tin Lithograph, Self-Framed, c.1950, 18 x 54 In. 385.00
Sign, Coca-Cola, Betty, Tin Lithograph, Self-Framed, 1914, 41 x 31 In. 2860.00
Sign, Coca-Cola, Black & White, Script, Porcelain, Die Cut, 5 1/2 x 18 In. 633.00
Sign, Coca-Cola, Bottle Cap, Banner, Tin Lithograph, 36 In. 220.00
Sign, Coca-Cola, Bottle Cap, Bottle, Flange, Tin Lithograph, c.1950, 22 1/2 x 18 1/4 In. . . 440.00
Sign, Coca-Cola, Bottle Cap, Bottle, Red, White, Brown, Porcelain, 1950s, 24 In. 468.00
Sign, Coca-Cola, Bottle Cap, Bottle, Red, White, Brown, Tin, Painted, 1955, 24 In. 523.00
Sign, Coca-Cola, Bottle Cap, Celluloid Over Cardboard, Easel Stand, c.1950, 9 In. 232.00
Sign, Coca-Cola, Bottle Cap, Coca-Cola, Red, Aluminum, 12 In. 138.00
Sign, Coca-Cola, Bottle Cap, Drink Coca-Cola In Bottles, Red, Tin, Jan. 1957, 12 In. 385.00
Sign, Coca-Cola, Bottle Cap, Drink Coca-Cola, Ice Cold, Blue, Porcelain, 14 In. 523.00
Sign, Coca-Cola, Bottle Cap, Drink Coca-Cola, Red, White, Metal, 12 In. 248.00
Sign, Coca-Cola, Bottle Cap, Drink Coca-Cola, Red, White, Porcelain, 36 In. 330.00
Sign, Coca-Cola, Bottle Cap, Red, Aluminum, 12 In. 138.00
Sign, Coca-Cola, Bottle In Sun, Die Cut Filigree, 2-Sided, 1940, 24 x 20 1/2 In. 527.00
Sign, Coca-Cola, Bottle, 1948, 36 x 18 In. 165.00
Sign, Coca-Cola, Bottle, Big King Size, Ice Cold, 1950s, 28 x 20 In. 440.00
Sign, Coca-Cola, Bottle, Die Cut, Relief, 71 1/2 x 20 In. 40.00
Sign, Coca-Cola, Bottle, Ice Cold, 2-Sided, Tin, Die Cut, Flange, 1951, 18 x 22 In. 619.00
Sign, Coca-Cola, Bottle, Metal, Die Cut, 1953, 9 In. 990.00
Sign, Coca-Cola, Bottle, Porcelain, Die Cut, 16 1/2 x 5 In. 369.00
Sign, Coca-Cola, Bottle, Porcelain, Die Cut, c.1940-50, 16 1/2 x 5 In. 366.00
Sign, Coca-Cola, Bottle, Tin, Silver Wood Frame, 1947, 36 x 18 In. 248.00
Sign, Coca-Cola, Coca-Cola, Red, White, Porcelain, 16 x 44 In. 230.00

| Go-Withs, Sign, Budweiser, We Feature, Bottle, Pilsner Glass | Go-Withs, Sign, Cocoa-Cola, Crossing Guard, Iron Base, 1950s, 63 In. | Go-Withs, sign, Dickinson's Witch Hazel, Easel-Back, Cardboard, 21 In. |

Sign, Coca-Cola, Coke Adds Life To Everything Nice, Metal, 18 x 36 In. 110.00
Sign, Coca-Cola, Coke Time, Join Friendly Circle, Cardboard, Frame, c.1954, 36 x 20 In. . 468.00
Sign, Coca-Cola, Coke, Bottle, Porcelain, Die Cut, c.1940-50, 16 1/2 x 5 In. 328.00
Sign, Coca-Cola, Crossing Guard, Metal, Iron Base, 1959, 63 In. . . . . *Illus* 3850.00
Sign, Coca-Cola, Delicious & Refreshing, Man, Woman, Tin, 20 x 28 In. 220.00
Sign, Coca-Cola, Drink Coca-Cola Here, Porcelain, Die Cut, Canada, 1940, 20 x 17 In. . . 688.00
Sign, Coca-Cola, Drink Coca-Cola In Bottles, 5 Cents, Tin, 1908, 11 3/4 x 35 1/2 In. . . . 550.00
Sign, Coca-Cola, Drink Coca-Cola, Bottle In Sun, 2-Sided, Die Cut, 1940, 24 x 20 In. . . . 528.00
Sign, Coca-Cola, Drink Coca-Cola, Good Taste, Lollipop, Porcelain, Base, 1950s, 63 In. . . 990.00
Sign, Coca-Cola, Drink Coca-Cola, Porcelain, Die Cut, 60 x 38 In. 300.00
Sign, Coca-Cola, Drink Coca-Cola, Shield, Die Cut, Flange, 1934, 13 x 20 In. 688.00
Sign, Coca-Cola, Drink Coca-Cola, Waitress, Car, Red, Black, Porcelain, 36 x 54 In. 2420.00
Sign, Coca-Cola, Drink Coca-Cola, Wood, Aluminum Bottle, c.1939, 17 In. Diam. 358.00
Sign, Coca-Cola, Edgar Bergen, Charlie McCarthy, CBS Sunday, Paper, 1949, 11 x 24 In. . 248.00
Sign, Coca-Cola, Enjoy Refreshing New Feeling, 2-Sided, Flange, Oct., 1961, 15 x 18 In. . 422.00
Sign, Coca-Cola, Flange, Bottle In Sun, Die Cut Filigree, 2-Sided, 24 x 20 1/2 In. 193.00
Sign, Coca-Cola, Fountain Dispenser, Porcelain, 2-Sided, c.1950, 28 x 28 In. 2145.00
Sign, Coca-Cola, Fountain Service, Shield, Red, Green, Die Cut, 2-Sided, 1936, 23 x 25 In. 2320.00
Sign, Coca-Cola, Fountain, 2 Glasses Of Coke, Wood, c.1930s, 11 x 9 In. 523.00
Sign, Coca-Cola, French-Canadian, Buvez, Tin, Self-Framed, c.1930, 17 1/4 x 53 In. 165.00
Sign, Coca-Cola, Gas To-Day, Tin, 1932, 54 x 18 In. 2600.00
Sign, Coca-Cola, Girl, Slow School Zone, Steel, Die Cut, 2-Sided, c.1940, 53 x 16 In. . . . 4950.00
Sign, Coca-Cola, Good Company, Frame, 1927, 11 x 21 In. 2860.00
Sign, Coca-Cola, Good With Food, Paper, 1951, 11 x 24 1/2 In. 440.00
Sign, Coca-Cola, Have A Coke Now, Cardboard, 2-Sided, 1951, 16 x 27 In. 374.00
Sign, Coca-Cola, Hilda Clark, Tin, 1903, 16 x 19 In. 7150.00
Sign, Coca-Cola, Home Refreshment, Cardboard, 2-Sided, 1950, 16 x 27 In. 1013.00
Sign, Coca-Cola, Ice Cold Coca-Cola Sold Here, Tin, Embossed, 1933, 19 1/2 In. .650.00 to 675.00
Sign, Coca-Cola, Ice Cold, Coke Bottle, Die Cut, 2-Sided, Flange, 1951, 18 x 22 In. 600.00
Sign, Coca-Cola, Lady Drinking Bottle Of Coke, Cardboard, Die Cut, 22 In. 220.00
Sign, Coca-Cola, Lady Lighting Candle, Hospitality Coca-Cola, c.1950, 27 x 56 In. 660.00
Sign, Coca-Cola, Lady, Groceries, Cardboard, 1946, 16 x 27 In. 1463.00
Sign, Coca-Cola, Lunch & Soda, Porcelain, c.1950, 18 x 30 In. 1267.00
Sign, Coca-Cola, Please Pay The Cashier, Reverse Glass, Backbar Mirror, Round, 1920s . 385.00
Sign, Coca-Cola, Refreshing New Feeling, Tin, 2-Sided, Flange, October 1961, 15 x 18 In. 423.00
Sign, Coca-Cola, Sidewalk, Take Home A Carton, Big King Size, Frame, 1961, 20 x 28 In. 2813.00
Sign, Coca-Cola, Sign Of Good Taste, Tin, 2-Sided, Flange, February, 1959, 15 x 18 In. . . 422.00
Sign, Coca-Cola, Sold Here, Refresh Yourself, Porcelain, Die Cut, 1930s, 20 x 17 In. 935.00
Sign, Coca-Cola, Take Home A Carton, Big King Size, Frame, 1961, 20 x 28 In. 2700.00
Sign, Coca-Cola, Tin, Die Cut, Triangle, 2-Sided, Bracket, 1936, 28 x 36 In. . . . .1365.00 to 1412.00
Sign, Creagans Drug Store, Lilly Pharmaceuticals, Reverse On Glass, 15 x 22 1/2 In. 154.00
Sign, Cremo Quality Ale & Lager, Tin Over Cardboard, New Britain, Conn., 6 x 9 In. 329.00
Sign, Crystal Rock Beverages Ginger Ale, Bottle, Tin Lithograph, 23 x 8 1/4 In. 33.00

Sign, Dad's Root Beer, Drink Genuine Old Fashioned Draft Root Beer, Tin, 11 x 14 In. . .   358.00
Sign, DeLaval, Cream Separators, Yellow, Black, White, Tin, Flange, 18 x 26 In. 880.00
Sign, DeLaval, Local Agency, Porcelain, 2-Sided, 18 x 27 In. 1980.00
Sign, DeLaval, Sooner Or Later You Will Buy A DeLaval, A.M. Kimball, 41 x 29 In. 1650.00
Sign, DeLaval, Woman, Separator, Child, Cow, Pasture, Tin, Self-Framed, 1905, 26 In. . . .   2200.00
Sign, Diamond Wedding Whiskey, Woman, Tin Lithograph, Self-Framed, Round, 12 In. . .   1650.00
Sign, Dickinson's Witch Hazel, Easel-Back, Cardboard, 21 In. . . . .*Illus*   336.00
Sign, Diet-Rite Cola, Sugar Free, Tin, Embossed, 32 x 12 In. 66.00
Sign, Domaine Rolet Winery, Cotes Du Jura, France, c.1940, 38 x 26 In. 1035.00
Sign, Double Cola, Enjoy, Green, White, Red, Tin, 31 3/4 x 11 3/4 In. 77.00
Sign, Double Cola, Tin, Die Cut, Flange, 1947, 15 x 18 In. 550.00
Sign, Double Cola, Woman, Holding Bottle, Frame, 27 x 22 In.   275.00
Sign, Dr Pepper, Corral Scene, Dr Pepper Picks Your Energy Up, Cardboard, 30 x 49 In. .   2000.00
Sign, Dr Pepper, Drink A Bite To Eat, Paper Lithograph, Easel, c.1940, 9 x 11 1/2 In. 281.00
Sign, Dr Pepper, Drink Dr Pepper, Porcelain, Raised Logo, c.1940, 10 1/2 x 26 1/2 In. . . .   383.00
Sign, Dr Pepper, Good For Life, Raised Logo, Porcelain, c.1940, 10 1/2 x 26 1/2 In. 365.00
Sign, Dr Pepper, Thank You, Call Again, Paper, Lithograph, c.1940, 8 3/4 x 11 1/2 In. . . .   281.00
Sign, Dr. Caldwell Originator Of Syrup Pepsin, Man, Box, Easel Back, 15 x 6 In. 715.00
Sign, Dr. D. Jayne's Family Medicines, Glass, Reverse Painted, Gold Frame, 26 x 14 In. . .   1568.00
Sign, Dr. Daniels, Horse & Dog Medicines, Home Treatment, Tin, Embossed, 17 x 28 In. .   413.00
Sign, Dr. Fulton's Wild Cherry Cough Elixir, Girl, Well, Bucket, Die Cut, 13 x 11 In. 1045.00
Sign, Dr. Harter's The Only True Iron Tonic, Man, Woman, Paper, 14 x 10 1/2 In. 220.00
Sign, Dr. Harter's Wild Cherry Bitters, Bottle, Testimonials, Paper, c.1886, 17 x 14 In. . . .   209.00
Sign, Dr. Jayne's Expectorant, Woman, Reverse On Glass, Frame, 14 1/2 x 12 1/2 In. 165.00
Sign, Dr. Morse's Indian Root Pills, Indian, Landscape, Pills, Trifold, 27 x 42 In. 385.00
Sign, Dr. Ricord Celebrated Remedies For Sexual Diseases, Jorgensen, Paper, 10 x 7 In. . .   198.00
Sign, Dr. Rochester, Black, Gold Ground, Beveled, Reverse On Glass, 5 1/8 x 19 In. 385.00
Sign, Dr. Swett's Original Root Beer, Boy Holding Glass, Lithograph, 21 x 14 In. 100.00
Sign, Dr. Walker's California Vinegar Bitters, Blood Purifier, Glass, 3-Sided, 10 x 12 In. .   495.00
Sign, Drewerys Ale & Beer, Thrill Of Lifetime, Men, Canoe, Tin Lithograph, 23 x 17 In. .   146.00
Sign, Drink Big Boy Beverages, Tin, Embossed, 34 x 18 In. 83.00
Sign, Drink Grape Smash, You Will Like It, 5 Cents, Diamond Form, 12 x 8 1/2 In. 55.00
Sign, Drink JC Cola, Its Delightful, Reverse Glass, Dura-Products, c.1940, 9 x 12 In. 844.00
Sign, Drink Mt. Cabin, Washes Thirst Away, Bellhop, Tin, Embossed, 18 x 12 In. 270.00
Sign, Drink Orange Crush, Feel Fresh, Crushie, Metal, Embossed, 16 3/4 x 46 1/2 In. 291.00
Sign, Drink Pepsi-Cola Ice Cold, Bottle Cap, Metal, Double Dash, Red, Blue, 31 In. 510.00
Sign, Drink Pop Cola, America's Finest Cola, Mirror, Frame, c.1940, 9 x 13 In. 74.00
Sign, Drink Royal Crown Cola, White, Red, Blue, Tin, Embossed, 12 x 32 In. 110.00
Sign, Drink Squirt, Bottle, Green, Yellow, Blue Ground, Metal, Embossed, 17 x 40 In. . . .   243.00
Sign, Dub-L-Valu Soda, 5 Cents, Bottle, Tin, Embossed, Die Cut, 30 x 7 1/2 In. 219.00
Sign, Eberhardt & Ober Brewing Co., Buildings, Print, Frame, 36 x 50 In. 1155.00
Sign, Emersons, Ginger-Mint Julep, Gives Pep, Quenches Thirst, Paper, c.1920, 4 x 20 In.   22.00
Sign, Excelsior Beer, Bottle, Celluloid Over Cardboard, 13 x 9 1/2 In. 72.00
Sign, Falstaff, Irishman, Holding Up Beer, Print, Frame, 29 x 41 In. 193.00
Sign, Father John's Medicine, Girl, Bottle, Cardboard Lithograph, c.1930, 35 In. 78.00
Sign, Fields Champion Whiskey, Tin, Frame, c.1890, 26 x 35 In.   1980.00
Sign, Fuller's Beer, Independent Family Brewers, Porcelain, England, 21 x 25 In. 165.00
Sign, Gail Borden Eagle Brand Condensed Milk, Paper Lithograph, 13 x 17 In. 168.00
Sign, Garrigues' Vegetable Worm Confections, For Sale Here, Cardboard, 6 5/8 x 4 5/8 In.   45.00
Sign, Golden Grain Whiskey, Buffalo Distilling Co., Celluloid, Concave, 24 x 27 In. 10080.00
Sign, Golden Guernsey Milk, 11 3/4 x 17 1/4 In. 80.00
Sign, Goldyrock Birch Beer, Clifton Bottling Works, Metal, Embossed, Frame, 12 x 23 In.   230.00
Sign, Good Grape Soda, Tin Lithograph, Embossed, 5 1/2 x 19 1/2 In. 110.00
Sign, Grapette, Woman In Swimming Pool, Cardboard, 1940-50, 19 x 30 In. 132.00
Sign, Green Mountain Boys, Balm Of Gilead & Cedar Plaster, Black, White, 20 x 15 In. . .   77.00
Sign, Green River Whiskey, Black Man, Mule, Paper, Frame, c.1930, 6 1/2 x 8 1/2 In. . . .   165.00
Sign, Heinz, Indian Relish, 1 Of The 57 Varieties, Cardboard, Frame, 14 x 23 In. 330.00
Sign, Hill, Evans & Co. Pure Malt Vinegar, Yellow, Red, Tin, Embossed, c.1890, 12 x 9 In.   118.00
Sign, Hills Bros. Coffee, Flavoring Extracts, Arab Drinking Coffee, Cardboard, 11 x 14 In.   66.00
Sign, Hills Bros. Coffee, Red Can, Flavor Determines Value, Cardboard, c.1930, 19 x 10 In.   176.00
Sign, Hires Root Beer, Kid & Mug, Oval, Self-Framed, 1907, 20 x 24 In. 935.00
Sign, Hires Root Beer, Take Home A Carton, Lady, Holding Glass, Cardboard, 9 x 11 In. .   33.00
Sign, Hires Root Beer, Triple AAA Root Beer 5 Cents, Frame, 11 x 17 In. 17.00

Sign, Hires Root Beer, With Real Root Juice, Tin, Embossed, 12 In. Diam. 187.00
Sign, Husemans Soda, Clear & Sparkling, Red Bud, Tin, Ill., 20 x 13 In. 55.00
Sign, I.W. Harper Whiskey, Dog, Animal Skins, Guns, Vitrolite, 1906, 25 x 18 In. 1100.00
Sign, Indians On Raft With Keg, Father Of Waters, Anheuser-Busch, St. Louis, 22 x 14 In. 308.00
Sign, Ironbrew, In Bottles, Ice Cold, Gloglas, Chrome Frame, c.1940, 9 x 12 In. 844.00
Sign, Japps Hair Rejuvenator, Hair Color Samples, Tin, 13 1/4 x 9 1/4 In. 209.00
Sign, JC Soda, Dura-Products, Reverse On Glass, c.1940, 9 x 12 In. 800.00
Sign, L. Hoster Brewery, Monk, Man, On Keg, Tin Lithograph, 1880-1900, 20 x 17 In. . . . 88.00
Sign, Lime Cola, Double Size, 5 Cents, White, Red, Parker Metal Co., 3 x 20 In. 44.00
Sign, Lipton's Instant Cocoa, Lady Holding Cup, Tin Over Cardboard, 1920-30, 13 x 9 In. 578.00
Sign, Liquer Hanappier, Lady, With Glass, Tin, Die Cut, Embossed, 19 1/4 x 19 1/2 In. . . . 460.00
Sign, Lithiated Lemon Soda, Embossed, 11 1/2 x 29 1/2 In. 198.00
Sign, Lotta Cola, Serves 3, 16 Oz. Soft Drink, Tin, Embossed, 1959, 11 3/4 x 21 1/2 In. . . 193.00
Sign, Ma's Root Beer, Lady, White Hair, Metal, Embossed, c.1950, 19 1/2 x 27 1/2 In. . . . 197.00
Sign, Mi-Grape, The Taste Lingers, Tin, Embossed, 23 1/2 x 12 In. 110.00
Sign, Moehn Brewing Company, Maltodextrine Tonic, Tin, Round, 15 In. 495.00
Sign, Mountain Dew, Do The Dew, Neon, 22 x 24 In. 127.00
Sign, Mountain Dew, It'll Tickle Yore Innards, Tin, Embossed, 1965, 17 x 35 In. 468.00
Sign, Moxie, Red, Yellow, White, Black, Tin, 2-Sided, Flange, 9 x 18 In. 242.00
Sign, Moxie, Yes!, We Sell, Very Healthful, Convex, Tin, 19 1/2 x 27 In. 880.00
Sign, Mumms Extra Dry Whiskey, Victorian Lady, Black Dress, Hat, Frame, 24 x 29 In. . . 578.00
Sign, Natural Chilean Soda, Yassuh, Uncle Natchel, 2-Sided, Flange, 1950s, 2 In. 440.00
Sign, Navy Scotch Snuff, Blue, White, Tin, Embossed, 18 x 12 In. 83.00
Sign, Nehi, Enjoy Nehi Orange, Cup, Light-Up, 14 x 18 x 5 In. 500.00
Sign, Nehi, Red, Yellow, Tin, Die Cut, Flange, c.1940, 13 x 18 In. 413.00
Sign, Nelsons Dairies, 5 Cent, Chocolate Flavored Milk, Red, Black, Tin, 23 3/4 x 12 In. . . 300.00
Sign, Nichol Kola, 5 Cent Twice As Good, Tin, Embossed, Parker Metal, 12 x 35 1/2 In. . . 138.00
Sign, Nichol Kola, A Long Drink, America's Taste Sensation, Tin, 12 x 36 In. 110.00
Sign, Nichol Kola, America's Taste Sensation, 5 Cents, Black, Red, White, Tin, 11 x 27 In. . 39.00
Sign, Nichol Kola, Toy Soldier, Bottle, Yellow, Red, White, Tin, 29 x 11 3/4 In. 72.00
Sign, Norka Orange, Tastes Better, Red, White, Black, Tin, 24 x 12 1/4 In. 138.00
Sign, Nu-Grape, Tin Lithograph, Embossed, 13 3/4 x 5 In. 523.00
Sign, Old Virginia Cheroots, Girl, Red Vest, Tam, Cardboard, c.1890s, 10 1/2 x 6 1/4 In. . . 66.00
Sign, Old Virginia Cheroots, Girl, Rose In Hand, Cardboard, c.1890s, 10 1/2 x 6 1/4 In. . . . 143.00
Sign, Old Virginia Cheroots, Girl, White Boa, Cardboard, c.1890s, 10 1/2 x 6 1/4 In. 180.00
Sign, Old Virginia Cheroots, Mildest & Best, Paper, Metal Strips, Frame, 21 In. 763.00
Sign, Pabst Extract, Lady, Yellow Dress, 1917, 7 x 35 In. 314.00
Sign, Part T Pak Beverages, 10 Cents, Full Quart, Serves 6, 33 x 12 In. 110.00
Sign, Pearl Foam, Michigan's Favorite, Mt. Clemens Brewing, Tin, Cardboard, 9 x 13 In. . . 367.00
Sign, Pepsi-Cola, Big Shot, Boy & Girl, Cardboard, 11 x 28 In. 35.00
Sign, Pepsi-Cola, Bigger & Better Reputation, 5 Cents, Paper, Frame, c.1925, 12 x 30 In. . . 66.00
Sign, Pepsi-Cola, Bottle Cap, Metal, July, 1968, 19 In. 89.00
Sign, Pepsi-Cola, Bottle, 5 Cents, A Sparkling Beverage, Tin, Die Cut, c.1940, 5 x 45 In. . . 575.00
Sign, Pepsi-Cola, Bottle, 5 Cents, Tin, Die Cut, 45 x 1 2 In. 500.00
Sign, Pepsi-Cola, Mirror, Light-Up, Shadowbox, 1950s, 12 x 12 x 5 In. 660.00
Sign, Pepsi-Cola, More Bounce To The Ounce, Tin, 17 1/2 x 47 In. 275.00
Sign, Pepsi-Cola, Pepsi & Pete, A Nickel Drink Worth A Dime, Frame, c.1940, 10 x 20 In. 990.00
Sign, Pepsi-Cola, Say Pepsi Please, Bottle, Tin, Embossed, Self-Framed, 46 x 17 In. 385.00
Sign, Pepsi-Cola, Say Pepsi Please, Tin, Embossed, Frame, 1969, 47 x 17 In. 330.00
Sign, Pepsi-Cola, Why Take Less When Pepsi's Best, 6-Pack, 1940s, 11 x 25 In. 770.00
Sign, Peter Schoenhofen Brewing, Chicago, Paper Lithograph, Frame, c.1890, 20 x 25 In. 413.00
Sign, Postal Telegraph, International System Here, Blue, White, Porcelain, 16 x 30 In. . . . 160.00
Sign, Red Seal Beverages, Red, Beige, Tin, 23 1/2 x 12 In. 110.00
Sign, Reymonds Butter Crust Bread, Quality-Service, Yellow, Tin, 1939, 20 x 14 1/4 In. . . 33.00
Sign, Rite-Way Milker, It Milks The Right Way, Red, Black, Tin, 9 3/4 x 13 3/4 In. 37.00
Sign, Rochester Root Beer, Always Cold, Reverse On Glass, Frame, 10 1/2 x 12 1/2 In. . . . 187.00
Sign, Royal Crown Cola, Best By Taste Test, Tin, Die Cut, 2-Sided, 1940, 16 x 24 In. 255.00
Sign, Royal Crown Cola, Diet-Rite Cola, Sugar Free, Tin, 18 x 54 In. 143.00
Sign, Royal Crown Cola, Drink RC Cola, Tin, 18 x 54 In. 303.00
Sign, Royal Crown Cola, Pop Bottle, Tin, Self-Framed, 16 x 36 In. 100.00
Sign, Royal Crown Cola, RC Tastes Best Says June Haver, Paper, 39 x 26 In. 134.00
Sign, Russells' Ales, Men Unloading Kegs, Tin, Self-Framed, 21 x 29 In. 413.00
Sign, Say Burgie, Truly Fine Pale Beer, Burgermeister, Light-Up, 1940s, 13 x 19 In. 150.00

Sign, Schoenling Lager Beer, Pours Bottle To Glasses, Glass, Aluminum, 25 x 12 x 4 In. . . 468.00
Sign, Slenderize, Nonfat Milk, Overeating?, Tin, 2-Sided, 24 x 40 In. 165.00
Sign, Snider's Tomato Catsup, Tin, 6-Sided, 16 x 11 In. 450.00
Sign, Sparkeeta Up, California's Favorite, Woman, Bottle, Easel Back, 30 x 24 In. 232.00
Sign, Stabler's Cherry Expectorant, Embossed, Gold Leaf, Frame, Md., 10 x 13 In. 193.00
Sign, Stoekers Old Fashioned Lemon Soda, It's Got Pep, Tin, c.1920, 13 x 19 In. 118.00
Sign, Sunshine Beer, 3 Triple Crown Winners, Paper, Frame, 27 x 34 In. 275.00
Sign, Switch To Squirt, Never An After Thirst, Red, Metal, Embossed, 9 x 27 In. 207.00
Sign, Take Thorns Genuine Sarsaparilla, White Dog, Blue Bow, Die Cut, 10 x 7 In. 440.00
Sign, Thirsty Or Not! Enjoy Grapette, Smiling Woman, Cardboard, 31 x 20 In. 104.00
Sign, Tippecanoe, Fine As Silk, Try It, Reverse On Glass, 3 7/8 x 16 In. 358.00
Sign, Tippecanoe, The Best For Dyspepsia, Paper, Frame, 12 x 24 5/8 In. 275.00
Sign, Tippecanoe, The Best For Loss Of Energy & Appetite, Paper, Frame, 12 x 24 5/8 In. 330.00
Sign, Tippecanoe, The Best For Mal-Assimilation Of Food, Paper, Frame, 12 x 24 5/8 In. . 198.00
Sign, Tongaline, Medicine Man, Indian Chief, Cardboard, 2-Sided, c.1903, 11 3/4 x 8 In. . 132.00
Sign, Triple 16 Cola, Red, White, Tin, 11 1/2 x 31 1/2 In. 275.00
Sign, True Fruit Soda, Victorian Statue, Fruit, Glass, Tin, Self-Framed, 24 x 38 In. 302.00
Sign, Use Celery Tonic & Bitters, Celery Medicine, Kalamazoo, Mich., Couples, 7 x 4 In. 224.00
Sign, Van Houten's Cocoa, Best & Goes Farthest, Woman With Tea Set, Paper, 24 x 36 In. 168.00
Sign, Vitalized Ginger Ale, Woman Surfer, Picks You Up, Tin Over Cardboard, 6 x 9 In. . . 204.00
Sign, Warner's, Safe Rheumatic Cure, Reverse On Glass, 3 7/8 x 16 In. 220.00
Sign, West End Brewery Co., 2 Children, On Bench, Lithograph, 17 1/2 x 13 3/4 In. 300.00
Sign, West End Utica Beer, Reverse Glass, Crimped Metal Frame, 18 x 4 1/2 In. 1660.00
Sign, Whistle Soda, Bottle, Thirsty?, Just Whistle, Cardboard, Frame, 60 x 20 3/4 In. 198.00
Sign, Whistle Soda, Thirsty?, Just Whistle, Tin Lithograph, Embossed, 14 x 19 1/2 In. . . . 495.00
Sign, White Crow Whiskey, Elmira, N.Y., John M. Connelly, Reverse Painted, 37 x 26 In. 2576.00
Sign, White House Tea, Lady Pouring Tea, Paperboard, 2-Sided, 15 x 10 In. 275.00
Sign, Wiedmann's Beer, Man Reading Paper, Children, Tin, Die Cut, 13 3/4 x 9 3/4 In. . . . 605.00
Sign, Wieland's Pale Lager, Indian Maiden, Lithograph, Self-Framed, 1901, 17 1/4 In. Diam. 4840.00
Sign, Wilson Whiskey, People, Carriage, Tin Lithograph, Frame, c.1890, 38 x 50 In. 990.00
Sign, Zulichs Vet Medicine, Blood, Alternative & Tonic Powder, Cardboard, 14 x 11 In. . . 59.00
Stein, Budweiser, Budman, Figural, Ceramarte, 1989, 8 x 4 1/4 In. 55.00
Straws, Coca-Cola, Box, 500 Straws, 1930s, 8 1/2 In. 193.00
Tap Knob, Krueger Extra Light Dry Beer, c.1950 . . . . 65.00
Tap Knob, Princeton Pale, Wisc. 685.00
Tap Knob, Schlitz, Enamel Insert, Chrome 50.00
Thermometer, Coca-Cola, Bottle Cap, Red, Drink Coca-Cola In Bottles 385.00
Thermometer, Coca-Cola, Bottle, 1950s, 16 3/4 x 5 1/4 In. 70.00
Thermometer, Coca-Cola, Bottle, c.1936, 16 In. . . . . .193.00 to 215.00
Thermometer, Coca-Cola, Bottle, c.1950, 17 In. 88.00
Thermometer, Coca-Cola, Christmas Bottle, 1923, 16 In. . . . . .193.00 to 215.00
Thermometer, Coca-Cola, Double Bottle, Tin, Embossed, 1941, 16 In. 275.00
Thermometer, Coca-Cola, Drink Coca-Cola In Bottles, Dial, Red, 1950s, 12 In. 143.00
Thermometer, Coca-Cola, Drink Coca-Cola, Sign Of Good Taste, Red, c.1950, 8 x 30 In. 575.00
Thermometer, Coca-Cola, Girl Silhouette, Tin, Embossed, 1940 . . . . 358.00
Thermometer, Coca-Cola, Gold Bottle, Metal, 1923 . . . . 110.00
Thermometer, Coca-Cola, Robertson, Tin, 1950s-60s, 17 x 5 In. 17.50
Thermometer, Coca-Cola, Sign Of Good Taste, Red, White, Tin, c.1950, 8 x 30 In. 591.00
Thermometer, Diet Rite Cola, Sugar Free, Blue, Glass Cover, 12 In. Diam. 138.00
Thermometer, Dr Pepper, Hot Or Cold, Tin Lithograph, 12 x 7 1/2 In. 55.00
Thermometer, Hires Root Beer, Bottle, 28 In. 116.00
Thermometer, Hires Root Beer, Bottle, Drink Hires, Metal, c.1950, 27 x 8 In. 187.00
Thermometer, Moxie, Drink Moxie, Frank Archer, Tin, Die Cut, Wood Crate, 38 x 12 In. 1898.00
Thermometer, Moxie, Frank Archer, Girl With Bottle, Glass, 9 1/2 x 12 In. 1430.00
Thermometer, NuGrape, Double Bottle, Green, Yellow, Red, c.1940, 17 x 6 In. 495.00
Thermometer, Pepsi-Cola, Bigger, Better, Double Dash, c.1940, 16 x 6 1/2 In. 83.00
Thermometer, Pepsi-Cola, Double Dash, Tin, Lithograph, 27 In. 25.00
Thermometer, Remember To Buy Grapette, Thirsty Or Not, 1950s, 14 x 6 In. 52.00
Thermometer, Royal Crown Cola, Red, Yellow Arrow, 1957, 26 x 10 In. 232.00
Tin, Colman's Mustard, 5 Scenic Panels, To The Queen, 7 x 10 In. 118.00
Tin, Log Cabin Syrup, Cabin Shape, c.1950, 2 Lb., 4 1/2 x 5 x 2 3/4 In. 55.00
Tin, Paramount Root Beer Syrup, San Francisco, 5 Gal., 14 In. 560.00
Tip Tray, Coca-Cola, 1907, Relieves Fatigue, Oval, 6 x 4 1/4 In. . . . . .330.00 to 1100.00

Tip Tray, Coca-Cola, 1914, Betty, Oval, 6 x 4 1/4 In. . . . . .85.00 to 176.00
Tip Tray, Coca-Cola, 1916, Elaine, Oval, 6 1/8 x 4 3/8 In. 83.00
Tip Tray, Coca-Cola, 1920, Golfer Girl, Yellow Dress, 6 1/4 x 4 1/2 In. 431.00
Tip Tray, Doniphan Vineyards, Bottle, 4 1/4 In. Diam. 61.00
Tip Tray, John Imbecheid & Co. Wholesale Liquors, Stag's Head, Tin Lithograph, 4 In. . . 123.00
Tip Tray, John Imbecheid & Co., Liquors, Woman, Flowing Hair, Tin Lithograph, 4 1/4 In. 146.00
Tip Tray, Liberty Beer, Indian Maiden, Tin Lithograph, 4 1/2 In. 256.00
Tip Tray, Liebers Gold Medal Beer, Indianapolis Brewing Co., 5 In. 94.00
Tip Tray, Modox Soda, Indian Chief, Tin Lithograph, 4 3/4 x 4 3/4 In. 1073.00
Tip Tray, Olympia Beer, It's The Water, Gentleman, Holding Bottle, c.1920, 4 In. 45.00
Tip Tray, Pepsi-Cola, Soda Fountain, Tin Lithograph, 6 x 4 3/8 In. 743.00
Tip Tray, Quandts Famous Beer & Ales, Mercury Figure Atop Globe, c.1900, 4 1/8 In. . . . 80.00
Toy, Car, Coca-Cola, Refresh With Zest, Red, White, 10 1/2 In. 94.00
Toy, Dominoes, Warner's Safe Remedies, Dovetailed Box, 25 Piece 200.00
Toy, Elsie, Pull, Wood, Cow Jumped Over Moon, Wood Commodities Corp., 10 x 7 In. . . 320.00
Toy, Horse & Wagon, Borden's Milk, Wood, 13 1/2 x 28 1/2 In. 250.00
Toy, Milk Carrier, Sealtest, 8 Wooden Bottles 52.00
Toy, Soda Dispenser, Coca-Cola, Drink Coca-Cola, Red, 4 Glasses, Box, 9 x 12 1/2 In. . . . 120.00
Toy, Truck, Coca-Cola, Decals, Bottles, Metalcraft 1200.00
Toy, Truck, Coca-Cola, Route, Yellow, Battery Operated, Sanyo, Box, c.1950, 12 1/2 In. . . 478.00
Trade Card, Burdock Blood, Invalid Ladies, Boy Carrying Books, 4 1/4 x 3 3/8 In. 19.00
Trade Card, Dr. Kilmer & Co., Standard Herbal Remedies, Man In Bottle, 5 x 3 In. 121.00
Trade Card, Hires Root Beer, Die Cut, Lithograph, 5 x 3 1/2 In. 83.00
Trade Card, Warner's Safe Cure & Safe Yeast & Safe Pills, c.1887, 5 x 3 1/2 In. 35.00
Tray, Alabama Brewing Co., The 2 Ideals, Lady, Beer Bottle, Lithograph, 13 In. Diam. . . . 495.00
Tray, American Brewing Co., 20th Century Bottled Beer, Kids, Puppy, Kitten, 13 x 13 In. 413.00
Tray, Bartlett Spring Mineral Water, San Francisco, Ca., Lady, Bottle, 13 In. Diam. 1430.00
Tray, Budweiser, Pub Scene, Fox Hunters Enjoying Brew, 10 1/2 x 13 1/4 In. 61.00
Tray, C.A. Lammer's, Ph. Zang Bottling Co., Denver Co., Round, 13 In. 346.00
Tray, Carlsburg, Old Man, Holding Stein, Round, 13 In. 12.00
Tray, Cherry Sparkle Bottling Co., So. Milwaukee, 13 x 10 In. 175.00
Tray, Coca-Cola, 1900, Hilda Clark, At Table, Coke Glass, Round, 9 1/4 In. 7000.00
Tray, Coca-Cola, 1903, Hilda Clark, Round, 9 3/4 In. 2320.00
Tray, Coca-Cola, 1909, Relieves Fatigue, 13 1/4 x 10 In. . . . .*Illus* 350.00
Tray, Coca-Cola, 1913, Hamilton King Girl, Oval, 15 1/4 x 12 1/4 In. 1100.00
Tray, Coca-Cola, 1914, Betty, Oval, 16 x 13 In. 468.00
Tray, Coca-Cola, 1916, Elaine, Yellow Dress, 19 x 8 1/2 In. 220.00
Tray, Coca-Cola, 1923, Flapper Girl, 13 1/4 x 10 1/2 In. 248.00
Tray, Coca-Cola, 1925, Party Girl, 13 1/4 x 10 1/2 In. 121.00
Tray, Coca-Cola, 1930, Bather Girl, 13 1/2 x 10 1/2 In. 220.00
Tray, Coca-Cola, 1930, Telephone Girl, 13 1/4 x 10 1/2 In. 198.00
Tray, Coca-Cola, 1933, Frances Dee, 13 1/4 x 10 1/2 In. 138.00
Tray, Coca-Cola, 1936, Hostess, 13 1/4 x 10 1/2 In. 220.00
Tray, Coca-Cola, 1937, Running Girl, On Beach, 13 1/4 x 10 1/2 In. . . . . .132.00 to 237.00
Tray, Coca-Cola, 1938, Girl In Yellow Hat, 13 1/4 x 10 1/2 In. 198.00
Tray, Coca-Cola, 1939, Springboard Girl, Sitting On Diving Board, 13 1/2 x 10 1/2 In. . . . 165.00
Tray, Coca-Cola, 1940, Sailor Girl, 13 x 10 1/2 In. . . . . .253.00 to 338.00

Go-Withs, Tray,
Coca-Cola, 1909,
Relieves Fatigue,
13 1/4 x 10 In.

Go-Withs, Tray,
Independent Home
Brewing Co., Couple At
Picnic, 13 1/4 In.

Go-Withs, Tray,
Pabst Blue Ribbon,
Green Background,
13 1/2 x 10 1/2 In.

Go-Withs, Tray, St.
Louis ABC Beers, Red
Center, Gold Trim,
Embossed Metal, 10 1/2 In.

Tray, Coca-Cola, 1941, Skater Girl, 13 1/2 x 10 1/2 In. . . . . .149.00 to 237.00
Tray, Coca-Cola, 1942, 2 Girls At Car, Roadster, 13 1/4 x 10 1/2 In. . . . . .165.00 to 209.00
Tray, Coca-Cola, 1953, Menu Girl, 13 1/2 x 10 1/2 In. 83.00
Tray, Coors, Snow Covered Mountains, Round, 13 In. 10.00
Tray, Crutch Rye, Chrysanthemum Girl, c.1910, 13 1/4 x 10 1/2 In. 132.00
Tray, Duesseldorfer, Grand Prize, St. Louis, 1904, Baby Holding Beer, Tin, 12 In. 392.00
Tray, Edelweiss Beer, Girl, Short Red Hair, Tin Lithograph, 1913, 13 In. 176.00
Tray, Eichler's Beer, New York, N.Y., Round, 1936, 12 In. 25.00
Tray, Fehr's Famous F.F.X.L. Beers, Man & Woman Embracing, 1910, 13 In. 532.00
Tray, Harvard Brewery, Lady, Calendar On Rim, 1907, 10 In. Diam. 220.00
Tray, Hayfield Whiskey, Tin Lithograph, Man Drinking, Smoking, 10 1/8 In. 230.00
Tray, Hires Root Beer, Things Is Getting Higher, Josh Slinger, 1915, 13 In. Diam. 1430.00
Tray, Independent Home Brewing Co., Couple At Picnic, 13 1/4 In. . . . .*Illus* 425.00
Tray, Kist, Orange Border, Bottle, Pinup Girl, Sailboat, 13 1/4 x 10 1/2 In. 179.00
Tray, Miller High Life, Woman On Moon, Round, 12 In. 60.00
Tray, New Yorker Beer & Ale, Innkeeper, 4 Men At Table, Round, 1936, 12 In. 45.00
Tray, Old Crutch Rye, Monk Bottling Whisky, Oval, 16 1/2 x 13 1/2 In. 132.00
Tray, Olympia Beer, Horseshoe, Water Fall, Black Ground, Round, 13 In. . . . . .20.00 to 23.00
Tray, Olympia Bottling Co., Golden Brew, Chrysanthemum Girl, 1910, 13 x 10 1/2 In. 468.00
Tray, Olympia Brg. Co., Tum Water, Green Ground, Pre-Prohibition, 12 1/4 In. Diam. . . . 95.00
Tray, Orange Crush, Crushy In Center, Oranges, Tin Lithograph, 13 x 10 1/2 In. 210.00
Tray, Orange Julep, Lady Holding Drink, 13 1/4 x 10 1/2 In. 165.00
Tray, Pabst Blue Ribbon, Bartender, 3 Glasses On Arm, Nutron Plastic, 13 1/2 In. 12.00
Tray, Pabst Blue Ribbon, Green Background, 13 1/2 x 10 1/2 In. . . . .*Illus* 50.00
Tray, Polar Ginger Ale, Polar Bear, Green, Yellow, Round, 13 In. 61.00
Tray, Rainier Beer, Chrome, Oval, Pre-Prohibition, 12 x 16 In. 60.00
Tray, Rainier Beer, Cowgirl On Horse, 13 In. Diam. 1660.00
Tray, Rainier Beer, Woman, Bonnet, Round, Seattle, Wash., 13 In. 202.00
Tray, Rainier Pale Beer, Woman, Holding Glass, Pre-Prohibition, 13 1/4 x 10 1/2 In. 95.00
Tray, Red Ribbon Beer, Old Dutch Lager, Mathie Brewing, Girl, Ukulele, 13 In. Diam. . . . 660.00
Tray, Rheingold Extra Dry, Brooklyn, N.Y., Round, 13 1/4 In. 20.00
Tray, Sanborn's Kidney & Liver Vegetable Bitters, Tin Lithograph, 12 In. 1595.00
Tray, Schlitz, The Beer That Made Milwaukee Famous, 1954, 12 In. Diam. 36.00
Tray, St. Louis ABC Beers, Red Center, Gold Trim, Embossed Metal, 10 1/2 In. . . . . .*Illus* 600.00
Tray, Steigmaier's Quality Beers, Wilkes-Barre, Pa., Round, 13 1/2 In. 30.00
Tray, Taka-Kola, Take No Other, Lady, Roman Numerals, 13 In. Diam. 330.00
Tray, Tuborg Gold Label, Copenhagen, Denmark, Round, 11 3/4 In. 15.00
Tray, Utica Club, West End Brewing Co., Round, 12 In. 35.00
Tray, Valley Forge Beer & Rams Head Ale, Adam Scheidt, Round, 11 1/2 In. 30.00
Tray, Walter Brewing Co., Brewery, Eau Claire, WI, 10 x 14 3/4 In. 330.00
Tray, Yuenling's Fine Beer, Ale, Porter, Woman, Drinking From Glass, Round, 12 In. 25.00
Tray, Zipp's, Cherri-O, Bird, Drinking From Glass, c.1920, 12 In. . . . . .625.00 to 647.00
Tumbler, A&W, Bear, Outstretched Arms Around, 5 3/4 In. 6.00
Tumbler, Big Top Peanut Butter, Pressed Glass, Tin Lid, Premium 14.00
Tumbler, Dubuque Star Brewing Co., Etched, Dubuque, Iowa 345.00
Tumbler, Pepsi-Cola, 1940s, 5 1/8 x 2 1/2 In. 25.00

Vending Machine, Coca-Cola, 10 Cent, Model No. 23, 38 x 24 In. 1430.00
Vending Machine, Coca-Cola, Vendo, 60 x 27 In. 2310.00
Vending Machine, Pepsi-Cola, Block Letters, Bottles, 6 To 12 Oz., Free To $1, 53 In. 300.00
Vending Machine, Pepsi-Cola, Blue, Round Top, 60 In. 1760.00
Vending Machine, Pepsi-Cola, Old Logo, Blue, 25 Cents, La Crosse Cooler, 60 In. 449.00
Watch Fob, Clarke's Pure Rye, Man, Glass, Bottle, Sterling, 1930s, 1 1/2 x 1 3/4 In. 38.00
Watch Fob, Dr Pepper, Good Luck Billiken, Giggling, Holding Paper, 1930-40 .... 48.00
Watch Fob, Pepsi-Cola, Eagle, Perched On Crossed Arrows, Pepsi Bottles, Silver 48.00
Whiskey, Monopole Rye, Black Bar, Cut Glass, Zipper Neck, Gilt, 3 3/4 x 9 1/2 In. 110.00
Window Decal, Coca-Cola, This Is The Genuine Coca-Cola, 7 x 12 In. 495.00

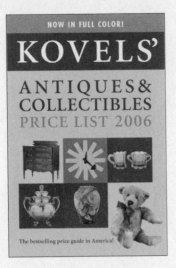

KOVELS' DEPRESSION GLASS & DINNERWARE

PRICE LIST · 8TH EDITION

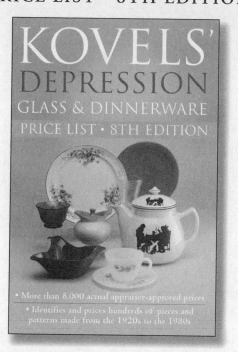

LEARN FROM AMERICA'S ANTIQUES EXPERTS!

- *More than 8,000 actual appraiser-approved prices*

- *More than 250 Depression glass patterns,*
  with photos and line drawings

- *Ceramic dinnerware patterns from the 1920s to the 1980s—*
  the patterns seen most often at shops and flea markets

- *Prices and histories of collectible plastic dinnerware*

- *Sixteen-page full-color report featuring "Decades of Design"*

- *Factory histories, makers, dates, and marks*

272 PAGES • PAPERBACK • $16.00 • ISBN: 1-4000-4663-7

KOVELS'
AMERICAN ANTIQUES
1750-1900

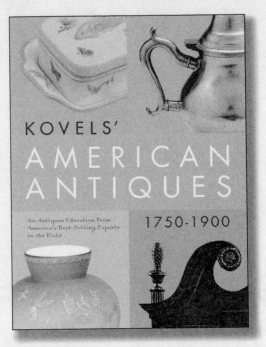

THE ULTIMATE GUIDE TO OUR
AMERICAN TREASURES!

A full-color reference complete with basic facts, fresh information, helpful historical details, and hundreds of photographs, all designed to make you a smarter, more discerning collector

- Furniture, pottery and porcelain, jewelry, silver, glass, and more
- Over 400 color photographs, plus hundreds of identifying marks
- Extensive lists of designers and manufacturers, with locations, dates, and marks

400 PAGES • PAPERBACK • $24.95 • ISBN: 0-609-80892-3

KOVELS' LIBRARY

Kovels' Advertising Collectibles
Price List
0-375-72080-4 • $16.95

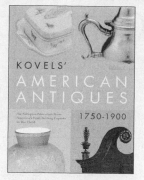

Kovels' American Antiques,
1750-1900
0-609-80892-3 • $24.95

Kovels' Antiques & Collectibles
Price List, 2006
0-375-72099-5 • $19.95

Kovels' Bottles Price
List, 13th ed.
1-4000-4730-7 • $16.95

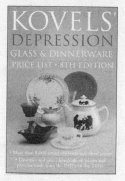

Kovels' Depression Glass &
Dinnerware Price List, 8th ed.
1-4000-4663-7 • $16.00

Kovels' Know Your
Collectibles
0-517-58840-4 • $17.00

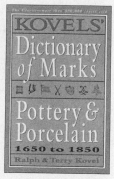

Kovels' Dictionary of
Marks: Pottery & Porcelain
0-517-70137-5 • $17.00

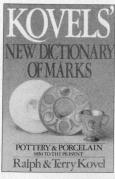

Kovels' New
Dictionary of Marks
0-517-55914-5 • $19.00

Kovels' Yellow Pages,
2nd ed.
0-609-80624-6 • $19.95

K O V E L S'

Send orders and inquiries to:
RANDOM HOUSE, INC.
400 Hahn Road, Westminster, MD 21157
Web site: www.randomhouse.com

Toll-free ordering and
customer service
1-800-733-3000
Fax: 1-800-659-2436

Name: _____

Address: _____

City & State: _____ Zip: _____

Please send me the following books:

Item No.	Qty.	Title	Price	Total
0-375-72080-4	___	Kovels' Advertising Collectibles Price List	$16.95	___
0-609-80892-3	___	Kovels' American Antiques	$24.95	___
0-375-72099-5	___	Kovels' Antiques & Collectibles Price List	$19.95	___
0-517-70137-5	___	Dictionary of Marks: Pottery and Porcelain	$17.00	___
1-4000-4730-7	___	Kovels' Bottles Price List	$16.95	___
1-4000-4663-7	___	Kovels' Depression Glass & Dinnerware Price List	$16.00	___
0-517-58840-4	___	Kovels' Know Your Collectibles	$17.00	___
	___	**TOTAL ITEMS** **TOTAL RETAIL VALUE:**		___

- -

ENCLOSE CHECK OR MONEY ORDER PAYABLE TO **RANDOM HOUSE, INC.**
OR CALL 1-800-733-3000

CHARGE: ❏ Master Card   ❏ Visa ❏ American Express
Account number (include all digits) Expires MO ____ YR ____

Signature _____

POSTAGE & HANDLING			
CARRIER	**ADD**	Total Books	_____
USPS	$5.50	Total Dollars	$_____
UPS	$7.50	Sales Tax*	$_____

Total Books   _____
Total Dollars $_____
Sales Tax* $_____
Postage & Handling $_____
Total Enclosed $_____

*Please calculate according to your state sales tax rate.